2003 Edition

Children's Book Market

The Writer's Sourcebook

Published by
Institute of Children's Literature

Acknowledgments

The editors of this directory appreciate the generous cooperation of our instructor and student contributors and the children's book editors who made clear their policies and practices.

MARNI MCNIFF, Editor

SUSAN TIERNEY, Articles Editor

BARBARA COLE, Associate Editor

MAUREEN GARRY, Assistant Editor

GERRI MORRELL, Research Assistant

Contributing Writers: Barbara Cole, Vicki Hambleton, Caroline LaFleur, Pam Purrone

Cover Design: Joanna Horvath

Contents

Step-by-Step Through the Submissions Process

5

This section offers step-by-step instructions for compiling a submissions package.

Ready, Aim . . . Research and Prepare to Sell 6
Step-by-Step Through Query Letters & Proposals 20
Query Letter Checklist 24
Sample Query Letter–Nonfiction 28
Sample Cover Letter–Nonfiction 29
Sample Cover Letter–Fiction 30
Sample Query Letter–Fiction 31
Sample Synopsis–Fiction 32
Sample Synopsis–Nonfiction 33
Sample Outline–Nonfiction 34
Sample Proposal–Nonfiction 35
Sample Bibliography 36
Sample Résumé 37
Sample Manuscript Pages 38
Manuscript Preparation 39
Picture Book Dummy 40
Picture Book Submissions 41
Step-by-Step Through the Business of Publishing 42
Postage Information 47
Frequently Asked Questions 48
Publishing Terms 51

Gateway to the Markets

55

An Experiment in Science Books, *by Joanne Mattern* 56

Editor Profiles
  Beth Townsend, Enslow Publishers 183
  Lori Shein, Lucent Books/KidHaven Press 274
  Aimee Jackson, NorthWord Books 310
  Sue Thies, Perfection Learning 333

Contents (Cont.)

Selling a Mystery, *by Patricia Curtis Pfitsch*   **63**

Editor Profiles
Lauri Hornik, Dial Books   **159**
Michael Steere, Down East   **168**
Peg Ross, Pleasant Company   **345**
Kathy Tucker, Albert Whitman & Company   **424**

The Picture Book Biz, *by Sue Bradford Edwards*   **69**

Editor Profiles
Stephanie Owens Lurie, Dutton Books   **171**
Deborah Halverson, Harcourt, Inc.   **221**
Lisa Banim, Peachtree   **327**
Simon Boughton, Roaring Brook Press   **362**

Listings   75

How to Use the Listings   **76**
This year's directory offers 540 updated listings
including 45 completely new listings

Listings of Book Publishers   **78**

Additional Listings   **438**

Selected Contests and Awards   521

Provides basic guidelines for 28 book writing contests,
awards, and grants.

Indexes   537

2003 Market News   **538**
Identifies new listings and publishers not listed.

Category Index   **540**
Lists publishers under selected categories according to
the type of material they are interested in acquiring.

Publisher and Contest Index   **577**
Provides page references for publishers and contests.

Step-by-Step Through the Submissions Process

Ready, Aim . . . Research and Prepare to Sell

Writers are like archers. Our target is to compose the best possible work and find it a home, a market, a bull's-eye. To be a good archer, we first have to have a strong interest, a passion, for the sport. We acquire the best possible equipment, a high-quality of bow and arrows, and maintain them well. We practice our aim and technique, and train with a coach if needed. The better these requirements are followed, the more frequently we hit the bull's-eye. Now substitute the following steps and see if the simile holds for your favorite "sport"—writing.

1 - Target the subject. Is it of personal interest and a subject you feel passionate about? An editor isn't going to be enthusiastic about a book if you're not. What type of research will make it interesting and successful? Children's editors today require first-rate, primary research.

2 - Target the quality. Have you done your best writing? Practiced your skills, gone to writers' conferences, taken courses, joined critique groups, or in some way worked at your craft and gained the right "equipment"?

3 - Target the audience. Can you see it clearly? What is the age? Reading level? Interests? Voice?

4 - Target the competition. Are there other books on comparable subjects? If you're writing in one genre, what else is out there? Do you have a truly different slant to offer?

5 - Target the market generally. Is your book to be trade, mass-market, religious, crossover, educational?

6 - Target the individual publisher and editor. What is this particular company and editor most interested in, most successful with?

We will take you step-by-step through the process of hitting some of these targets. Only you can work on the quality, but we will coach you through subject, audience, competition, and market objectives and how to reach them. You'll come nearer and nearer to a bull's-eye with every arrow—every manuscript sent flying.

Target the Subject

Whether you're finding new ideas, developing a defined project, or searching for markets for your completed manuscript, you can improve the submission process by taking time to do fundamental research. The first step is to select an idea that interests you, that you believe will appeal to readers as much as it does to you, and collect information about it.

This idea and research development step is an important first measure toward selling your book. While most editors and successful writers will tell beginners to focus on writing a good book, not on worrying about what's fashionable in the market and what's not—and they're correct—a good book requires authenticity if it's fiction, and accuracy if it's nonfiction. Subject research is essential in composing the best possible manuscript, whether it's historical background for a novel or a text, geographical information on a region or city, updated data for a scientific principle, or even searches for good character names on a census or genealogical site. Finding and refining your idea with research will strengthen your work, and poise it to sell.

Research resources. Writers have a surfeit of research resources today in the Internet quiver. The Web gives writers access to libraries, research studies, museums, associations, businesses, and a seemingly endless supply of miscellaneous sites available through myriad search engines. You can do this research at your local library if you're not set up at home. Look at:

- encyclopedia sites that might provide links to more detailed pages on other sites.
- university libraries online.

7

- government resources like the Library of Congress, the Smithsonian, NASA.
- museum sites, such as the Metropolitan Museum of Art in New York, the British Museum, and many other world-class museums.
- the sites of smaller, more focused museums, historical sites, even corporations (for that article on sneakers, for example).
- organizations that range from the social to the arts to sports, from the local to the universal.
- journalism and other sites that lead to "experts" for interviews.

Some sites help you to find the existence of material, but you'll need to get it physically from the library or another source. Some sites, however, provide actual content—text, photos, data—online.

Accuracy and annotations. Websites have links to other sites. Follow the trail, the links, and keep clear notes on where you go and what you learn, so you don't lose important resources or unintentionally plagiarize. Narrow your sights in on your topic, and be sure to check and recheck your information against other sources. Take every care with accuracy, since children's editors today want to see primary research sources and they want precision. Keep a running bibliography; you may need it for your submission package and even if you don't, it's a good idea for back-up and additional research, if it's needed. Be sure to check the *Children's Book Market* listings for indications of the kind of bibliographical or other research annotations targeted editors require. (See, for example, the bibliography on page 36.)

Fiction and research. Perhaps you're writing fiction and don't believe you need to do research. You might not, but you very well may. Is your story set in a seaside town you recall from childhood? What's the weather like there when your story is set? Are you sure? Do you need inspiration for character names for a contemporary or historical story? Check local newspapers for stories about children of a particular age and time. Remember that

Internet Research Resources

A list of possible Internet research sites that purports to be comprehensive would take up many pages, but here are broad categories and site examples to start the subject research process.

● **Search engines:** www.google.com and www.dogpile.com are effective search engines because they provide specificity and variety when searching a subject. For a different kind of search, try www.about.com, which offers expert guides to help you navigate through a subject.

● **Government sites:** The U.S. government's sites are a great place to begin research: Look for books, historical archives, photos, and much more at the Library of Congress (www.loc.gov). At NASA (www.nasa.gov), try the Strategic Enterprises sites for space, technology, exploration, earth and physical sciences, and biology. The Smithsonian site (www.smithsonian.org) is divided into Art & Design, History & Culture, Science & Technology. Go to the Government Printing Office (www.access.gpo. gov) and FirstGov (www.firstgov.gov), for everything from government operations to health to mining to special education.

● **Reference sites:** The *Encyclopedia Britannica* (www. britannica.com) site gives brief information on myriad topics, and provides helpful links; a subscriber service allows access to longer articles and more information. The Learning Network's www.infoplease.com is an almanac site with facts on topics from world events to art, architecture, biographies, holiday calendars, weather, health, weights and measures, and much more.

● **Museums:** Large and small museums across the country, and the world, can be indispensable to the writer. Through a search engine, see if local historical societies, for example, have websites. Or try the Metropolitan Museum of Art (www.metmuseum.org), British Museum (www.thebritishmuseum.ac.uk), or try the Virtual Library museums pages (www.icom.org/vlmp) to find museums around the world.

"local" has new meaning on the Internet. You can look up *The Columbus Dispatch* (Ohio) or *The Waterbury Republican* (Connecticut) or *The Mercury News* (San Jose, California). Check a genealogy site for names, or for story ideas, or for nonfiction research. Use all your resources, and of course, turn to print, too. Through your local library you have access to networks of other libraries that will help you borrow virtually any book you need.

Target the Audience

Developing ideas means not only thought and research about your topic or story, but information about the readers. Audience is the meeting place of idea and market research. Who will read this story? Who is this ultimate market (assuming the editor takes the role of the intermediate, not the ultimate market)? What grabs them?

Experts. You know "experts" who can help you find out which books kids are reading at which ages, or what parents or educators are reading, if they're your projected audience. Talk to children's librarians and teachers about the kinds of stories and topics currently, or universally, appealing to young readers. Ask them about curriculum needs, especially for nonfiction. Go to bookstores and speak to managers who specialize in children's books. Online, go to library and reading sites, like those for the American Library Association (ALA) and the International Reading Association (IRA).

Developmental stages. Find out what's happening developmentally at a given age, what's being studied at school, what interests spark your audience. Talk to scout leaders, coaches, music teachers. Observe and talk to the children themselves, especially about books if you can. Go to children's websites to see the topics they cover, and watch television programming and read young people's magazines to learn more about contemporary youth culture. Go to parenting websites to see what problems and joys arise. But remember, you'll need to find your own slants on these subjects—your own way of holding your bow and releasing your arrow.

Age ranges. Use *Children's Book Market*: Browse through

Age-Targeting Resources

- **American Library Association (ALA)** and **International Reading Association (IRA):** The lists of books for children compiled by these two organizations will help direct you to age-appropriate writing. (www.ala.org and www.reading.org). The ALA also lists "Great Sites!" for children, which helps writers focus in on kids' interests.
- **American Academy of Pediatrics:** Try the AAP's (www.aap.org) You and Your Family page, or the publications page.
- **Bright Futures:** Available on this organization's website (www.brightfutures.org) are downloads of tip sheets on developmental stages, and a variety of resources on juvenile and adolescent health and behavioral development.
- **National Network for Child Care (NNCC):** The website (www.nncc.org/child development) page on child development is divided into infant, toddler, preschooler, school age, brain development, as well as topics such as intellectual, language, emotional/social, and an Ages and Stages series.
- **Search Institute:** This nonprofit's organization (www.search-institute.org) and website highlight 40 developmental assets for children from grades 6 to 12.

Finding Child and Teen Sites
- **Berit's Best Sites for Children:** A list of 1,000 sites for children, (www.beritsbest.com).
- **KidsClick!:** A librarian-generated list of more than 600 sites for children (http://sunsite.berkeley.edu/KidsClick!). Categories include facts & reference, weird & mysterious, religion & mythology, machines & transportation, and more.
- **The Kids on the Web:** A list of sites compiled since 1994 by the author of *Children and the Internet: A Zen Guide for Parents and Educators;* ALA-recommended site.
- **Surfing the Net with Kids:** A newspaper columnist's recommendations (www.surfnetkids.com), with current topics, a calendar of interesting events, many topics.

the listings to look at the ages covered and review the sample titles. Or start with the Category Index (page 540) and look under "preK" or "middle-grade" or "young adult," and review the publishers listed. Request their catalogues or visit their websites. Catalogues are generally free upon request with a stamped, self-addressed, 9x12 envelope. Examining the catalogues, in print or online, is a very helpful practice even at this stage of research, though it will be essential once you focus in on publishers where you'll target your specific work. See how many titles are published in what genres, for what age ranges, and give you a sense of their subjects and style. What feel do you get for the picture book illustrations, for example, if that is what you want to write, and how is the text likely to reflect that? Is this a wide-ranging publisher, or does it fill a niche?

You might need or want to buy a book to advance your research into what a segment of the children's audience is reading. Amazon.com or Barnesandnoble. com, along with other sites that help you buy books or locate out-of-print titles, have become one of a writer's best friends. Not only do they help you locate children's books you know you want, they give you information on readership ages. Reverse the process and begin your search at one of these sites with a designated age range and see what titles come up. Lots of humor? Nonfiction, but not the fiction you expected? Does this help you in thinking about what you want to write?

Target the Competition & General Markets

When you're doing your audience or subject research, you might find that two or three large publishers specialize in books for a particular age or field, but the titles they list are old. That's a beginning for your competition research— looking into titles already in the marketplace similar to your idea and finding the publishers that match.

Competitive titles. When you get to the stage of pulling together your submissions package, adding this competition information in a paragraph to your query or proposal, or in a separate one-page summary, will give you a

Competition Research Form

Title	Author	Publisher	Pub. Date	Description/Differences from My Book

definite advantage. It will show editors your professionalism, skills at research, and dedication to your work. If you use the research well, it will also indicate to the editor that you know what that particular company publishes and why your book will fit its list. Doing your competition research, the questions you'll need to ask are:

- What books are in print that are similar to my idea?
- Who are the publishers, and what kinds of companies are they?
- When were they published?
- How are they different in slant, format, audience, etc., from mine?
- If one or more are not different, how will I reslant my idea to make my title more distinct?

This is where you'll need to strike a balance between selecting a subject or a story that is of such significant interest to the audience you're targeting that other authors have addressed it, and the challenge of giving it a new twist. The same subjects will come up over and over again, and there's a reason—a large segment of four-year-olds are always interested in trucks and always will be, for example. But how do you write another picture book on trucks and make sure it's distinct? How do you know that your book on a kindergartener's school tribulations will attract an editor's attention?

Perhaps those kindergarteners are ready for a new book on the subject, because it's been more than five years since the last one was published by one publisher, or any publisher. To find that out, once again you might go to:

- bookstores, to review the selection, put your hands on the books, and peruse them
- *Children's Book Market*, for an overview of companies publishing possibly competitive books
- online booksellers, with subject and age searches
- libraries, whether the catalogues, or *Subject Guide to Children's Books in Print*
- publisher websites and publisher catalogues

At bookstores, ask for a list of all the books on a given subject. They should be able to print one out for you from their computer system. At the library, use the computer database to do a comparable search, or look at the *Subject Guide to Children's Books in Print.*

Market types. Use *Children's Book Market*'s Category Index to generate a list of companies that publish in the category of your book and to start you thinking about the marketplace in general. You might want to use a form like that on page 13. Are the companies with competitive titles generally educational, trade, religious, special interest? Or are they all over the map? Do they have a strong backlist of older titles that they continue to support, or are titles allowed to go out of print?

The individual publisher listings in *Children's Book Market* also give you information on how many books a company publishes each year and how many it accepts from new authors. You're another step closer to selecting the publishers to whom you'll send your submission.

Target the Publisher & Editor

It's time to look more closely at the individual listings in *Children's Book Market* to find out what a company has published and what its editors are currently seeking. *Children's Book Market* can be wonderfully well used to create comparative lists of competitive titles, as above, and even better used to align your work with a publisher who is looking for it.

If you've followed the process here, you've focused in on an idea, determined your readership, and learned what books on that subject and readership are available. But editors' needs change. How do you know who wants what now? The listings in *Children's Book Market* are updated annually, with an emphasis on finding exactly what the editor needs now.

Turn again to the Category Index on page 540, or leaf through the listings themselves, and write down those publishers with interests similar to your own, especially those you didn't find in your earlier research. You've done this in researching the field and competition as a whole, but now you need to focus on the publishers you will pursue for your book. Here's how the listings break down and how to use them best.

- ◆ **Publisher's Interests:** Does the publisher you have in mind produce hardbacks, paperbacks, or both? Is it an imprint of a larger company? Does it publish fiction and/or nonfiction? Does it have a specialization, such as history, regional subjects, educational? Is your book compatible with the publisher's profile?

  Don't stretch to make a match—make it a close one—but if you believe you can slant your book solidly toward a publisher's needs, work toward that in pulling together your proposal. If you've written fiction that just can't be reshaped, be honest, and don't consider a given publisher's needs a good target.

- ◆ **Freelance Potential:** How many books did the publisher produce last year? Of the books published, how many came from unpublished writers? (For an idea of your odds, compare the number of submissions the publisher received last year to the number of titles it published.) What age range does it focus on? Are there particular topics or types of books it specializes in? What genres did the company publish, in fiction or nonfiction?

- ◆ **Editor's Comments:** This section reveals a publisher's current needs, and the types of manuscripts it *doesn't* want to see. It may also give you insight into preferred style or other editor preferences. This information will be one of your best tools in deciding where to submit your work.

You can also keep up with current needs through trade publications like *Children's Writer* newsletter (www.childrenswriter.com or 1-800-443-6078) and *Publishers Weekly* (http://publishersweekly.reviewsnews.com/), which has improved its regular coverage of children's publishing in recent years. *PW* also offers special feature

About Agents

Writers of books at some point face the question of whether or not to look for an agent. Some successful writers never work with an agent, while others much prefer to find a strong representative for their work to deal with the business side. Some publishers, a limited number and usually very large companies, will not accept unsolicited materials except through an agent. But a good manuscript or book proposal will find its home with or without an agent, if you are committed to finding the right publisher to match your work.

How to find an agent: Look at listings in *Literary Marketplace (LMP)*, or the *Writer's Digest Guide to Literary Agents,* or contact the Association of Authors' Representatives or go to their website (http://209.67.253.214/aar) for their members list. Identify agents who work with writers for children. Check in your agent guide or go online if the agent has a website for specific contact requirements. If not, send a well-written, professional cover letter describing your work and background, accompanied by an outline or synopsis and sample chapter.

What an agent does: An agent will review your work editorially before deciding to represent you, but the primary work of an agent is to contact publishers, market your material, negotiate for rights and licenses, and review financial statements. In a good working relationship, an agent will offer solid editorial advice on the direction your proposals and stories might take.

Fees: Be careful about agent fees. Increasingly, some will charge for readings and critiques, even without taking you on as a client. Compare the fees, and the commission if you do enter into a contract. A typical rate is 15 percent for domestic sales, 20 percent for foreign.

issues on children's publishing every spring and fall. A *PW* subscription is expensive, but many libraries carry the publication.

Narrow your choices to 6 to 12 publishers, and if you have not yet requested their catalogues, do so, along with their writers' guidelines. Ask a final set of questions—those in the sidebar on page 19.

You're about to pull together your submissions package. First, review the writers' guidelines, if a company has them. Whether or not they do, read the *Children's Book Market* listing closely for specifications, and follow them exactly. Suppose you have completed a biography of Georgia O'Keeffe you'd like to propose to Lerner Publishing. It's ready to go, but it happens to be August. If you check the Lerner listing, and their guidelines, you'll see that the company only accepts submissions in March or October. Don't send your work anyway, assuming they'll hold it until October. They won't. Do exactly what the publisher directs.

Now you're ready to fire your arrow: Submit.

Take Close Aim

When you've narrowed your targeted publishers to a short list, review the individual publishers' catalogues closely or go to their online sites (indicated in the listings) to find out about their overall list and specific titles—dates of publication, slant, format. With even greater focus now as you sight your target, ask:

- Is this a large house, a smaller publisher, or an independent press with 10 or fewer books published yearly?
- How many books are on its backlist?
- What audience does the publisher target?
- Are most books single titles, or does the publisher focus on series books?
- Does it aim for one or two age groups, or does it feature books for all age groups?
- Does the publisher use the same authors repeatedly, or are many different authors featured?
- Are newer authors also represented?
- Is there a mix of fiction and nonfiction books, or is there more of one than the other?
- Is there a range of subject matter? Does my book fit in their range?
- Does the publisher specialize in one or more types of books, such as picture books or easy-to-reads? Is my book one of these, or not?
- Are there books similar to yours? Too similar and too recent, so the publisher might not want duplication?
- Would your book fit in with others this house has published?
- What are the specific requirements of the writers' guidelines and how will I meet them?

Step-by-Step Through Query Letters & Proposals

One publisher may prefer to receive a submission consisting of a query letter and nothing else. Another wants an extended proposal packaged in a very specific format: a cover letter, outline, résumé, samples, bibliography, competition research. A query or a cover letter is always required, but many writers find them challenging. How are query letters and cover letters different? How much information should they include? What information? What tone should they take?

Query Letters

The query letter is perhaps the most important component of a book proposal package. It should capture the editor's interest and give a sense of your treatment of the topic. It should also convince an editor that you are the person to write this book. The best advice:

- Be succinct, positive, enthusiastic, and interesting.
- Briefly describe your book proposal.
- Identify the publisher's needs by indicating your familiarity with titles on their list.
- Outline your qualifications to write the book.

Review the query letter samples on pages 28 and 31. Note each of the following elements:

Opener: A direct, brief lead that:
- captures and holds the editor's interest (it could be the first paragraph of your book);
- tells what the subject is and conveys your particular angle or slant;
- reflects your writing style, but is at all times professional; you need not be overly formal, but do not take a casual tone.

Subject: A brief description of your proposed manuscript and its potential interest to the publisher.

Specifications: If applicable, include the following:
- your manuscript's word length;
- number and type of illustrations;
- a brief indication of the research and interviews to be done; if this is extensive, include it on a separate page with a reference to it in your query;
- market information and intended audience; again, if you've done more extensive competition research, attach it separately.

Reader Appeal: A brief description of why your target audience will want to read your proposed book.

Credits: If you have publishing credits, list them briefly, including magazine credits. Don't tell the editor you've read your book to your child's class, or that several teachers have encouraged you to send it in, or that you've taken a writing course. If you have particular qualifications that helped you write the book (e.g., you run obedience classes and have written a book on dog training), say so. Many publishers request résumés. If you're attaching one in your submissions package, your query should mention relevant credits, and then refer to the résumé.

Closing: Let the publisher know if this is an exclusive or simultaneous submission.

Queries are very common for nonfiction submissions, but in the past were very uncommon in fiction. Most editors preferred to see complete manuscripts or several chapters and a synopsis for novels and early fiction. That has changed somewhat in recent years; some editors want a query for fiction before they'll read anything more. Here are some of the distinctions in the queries and packages for nonfiction and fiction:

Nonfiction Query Letter
A nonfiction package may include:

- a query or cover letter (see page 23 for which to use);

- a synopsis (see page 33);
- a detailed outline (topical or chapter) that describes each chapter's contents (see page 34);
- alternatively, a proposal that incorporates the synopsis, outline, and other information, such as the audience targeted (see page 35);
- representative chapters;
- a bibliography, consisting of the books, periodicals, and other sources you have already used to research the project, and those that you will use, including expert sources and interviews (see page 36);
- a résumé (see page 37).

Fiction Query Letters
A fiction query package may also contain any or all of the following:

- one- to two-page synopsis that briefly states the book's theme and the main character's conflict, then describes the plot, major characters, and ending;
- chapter-by-chapter synopsis consisting of one to two paragraphs (maximum) per chapter, describing the major scene or plot development of each chapter. Keep the synopsis as brief as possible. You may either single space or double space a synopsis (see page 32);
- the first three chapters (no more than 50 pages). But check the *Children's Book Market* listing and publisher's writers' guidelines carefully, as some editors prefer to see only the first chapter.

Essentials
Editors need to know from the start that you write well and that you are careful in your work. Many submissions are rejected because queries are poorly written, contain grammatical errors, or show carelessness. Since form as well as content counts, make sure your package:

- is free of spelling, typographical, and grammatical errors;

Query Letter v. Cover Letter

When to use a query letter:

❏ Always when a query is the specific requirement in the publisher's writers' guidelines.

❏ When you are including no other, attached information; the query should be specific, but not exceed a single page.

❏ When you are attaching some additional materials, such as a synopsis or sample chapter.

When to use a cover letter:

❏ When an editor has requested that you send a specific manuscript and it is attached. The cover letter is a polite, professional reminder.

❏ When you have had previous interactions with an editor, who will know who you are. Perhaps you've written something for the editor before, or you had a conversation at a conference when the editor clearly suggested you send your work.

❏ When your proposal package is comprehensive, and explains your book completely enough that a cover letter is all that is needed to reiterate, very briefly, the nature of the proposal.

♦ is cleanly presented and readable, whether typewritten or computer-printed;

♦ includes an SASE—a self-addressed stamped envelope with correct postage, or International Reply Coupons for foreign publishers;

♦ is photocopied for your records.

Query Letter Checklist

Use this checklist to evaluate your query letter before you send it with the rest of your book proposal.

Basics:
- ❏ Address the letter to the current editor, or as directed in writers' guidelines or market listings (for example, Submissions Editor or Acquisitions Editor).
- ❏ Spell the editor's name correctly.
- ❏ Proofread the address, especially the numbers.

Opening:
- ❏ Create a hook—quote a passage from your manuscript, give an unusual fact or statistic, ask a question.

Body:
- ❏ Give a brief overview of what your book proposal is about, but do not duplicate the detailed information you give in the outline or synopsis.
- ❏ List your special qualifications or experience, publishing credits/organization memberships, and research sources.
- ❏ State whether you can or cannot supply artwork.
- ❏ Note if this is a simultaneous submission.

Closing:
- ❏ Provide a brief summation.

Last steps:
- ❏ Proofread for spelling and punctuation errors, including typos.
- ❏ Sign the letter.

Cover Letters

A cover letter accompanies a submitted manuscript and provides an overview of your fiction or nonfiction submission, but it does not go into the same level of detail as a query letter. A cover letter is a professional introduction to the materials attached. It's just the facts. If you are attaching a large package of materials in your submission—a synopsis, outline, competition research, résumé, for example— you don't need a full-blown query, but a cover letter.

Cover letters range from a very brief business format, stating, *"Enclosed is a copy of my manuscript, [Insert Title] for your review"* to something more. In a somewhat longer form, the letter may include information about your personal experience with the topic; your publication credits; if you have them, special sources for artwork; and, if relevant, the fact that someone the editor knows and respects suggested you submit the manuscript.

A cover letter is always included when a manuscript is sent at the request of the editor or when it has been reworked following the editor's suggestions. The cover letter should remind the editor that he or she asked to see this manuscript. This can be accomplished with a simple phrase along the lines of "Thank you for requesting a copy of my manuscript, [Insert Title]." If you are going to be away or if it is easier to reach you at certain times or at certain phone numbers, include that information as well. Do not refer to your work as a book; it is a manuscript until it is published.

Proposals

A proposal is a collection of information with thorough details on a book idea. Arguably, a query alone is a proposal, but here we'll consider the various other components that may go into a proposal package. Always consult—and follow to the letter—writers' guidelines to see what a publisher requires.

Query or cover letter. The descriptions on pages 20–25 should help you construct your query or cover letter.

Synopsis. A brief, clear description of the fiction or nonfiction project proposed, conveying the essence of the entire idea. A synopsis may be one or several paragraphs on the entire book, or it may be written in chapter-by-chapter format. Synopses should also convey a sense of your writing style, without getting wordy. See the samples on pages 32 and 33.

Outline. A formally structured listing of the topics to be covered in a manuscript or book. Outlines may consist of brief phrases, or they may be annotated with one or two-sentence descriptions of each element. See the sample on page 34.

Note that synopses are more common for fiction than outlines. Both outlines and synopses are used to describe nonfiction, but not necessarily both in the same proposal package.

Competition/market research. The importance of researching other titles in the marketplace that might be competitive to yours was discussed earlier (pages 12–15). The presentation of this information to the editor might be in synopsis form or presented as an annotated bibliography.

Bibliography. Bibliographies are important in nonfiction submissions, considerably less so with fiction, except possibly when writing in a genre such as historical fiction. A well-wrought bibliography can go a long way toward convincing an editor of the substance behind your proposal. Include primary sources, which are more and more important in children's nonfiction; book and periodical sources; Internet sources, (but be particularly careful these are well-established); expert sources you've interviewed or plan to interview. For format, use a style reference such as *Chicago Manual of Style, Modern Language Association (MLA) Handbook,* or one of the major journalist references by organizations such as the *New York Times* or Associated Press. See the sample on page 36.

Résumé/publishing credits. Many publishers request a list of publishing credits or a résumé with submissions. The résumé introduces you to an editor by indicating your background and qualifications. An editor can judge from a résumé if a prospective writer has the necessary experience to research and write material for that publishing house. The résumé that you submit to a publisher is different from one you would submit when applying for a job, because it emphasizes writing experience, memberships in writing associations, and education. Include only those credentials that demonstrate experience related to the publisher's editorial requirements, not all of your work experience or every membership. In the case of educational or special interest publishers, be sure to include pertinent work experience.

No one style is preferable, but make sure your name, address, telephone number, and e-mail address (if you have one) appear at the top of the page. Keep your résumé short and concise—it should not be more than a page long. If you have been published, those credits may be included on the one page, or listed on a separate sheet. See the sample on page 37.

Sample chapters or clips. As well-written as a query or even a synopsis might be, nothing can give an editor as clear a sense of your style, slant, and depth of the work you are proposing, or can do, than sample chapters or clips of published work. One of the obvious dilemmas of new writers is that they may not have clips, or they may be few and not suitable to a given proposal. But sample chapters, almost always the first and perhaps one or two others that are representative, help an editor make a judgment on your abilities and the project, or determine how to guide you in another direction—and toward a sale.

Sample Query Letter – Nonfiction

Street Address
City, State ZIP
Telephone Number
E-mail Address
Date

Ms.Sue Thies
Perfection Learning Corporation
1000 North Second Avenue
Logan, IA 51546

Dear Ms. Thies,

Opener/ Hook

Look, to your left, off the port side of our four-man dinghy. Just below the surface, a giant, black shadow tracks us. Our boat seems tiny, indeed. Salty sea spray stings your eyes. But the V-shaped dorsal fin skimming the water is easy to identify. A lump jumps up your throat. You've heard tales about orcas. Are they ferocious killer whales, all teeth and no brain? Or are they something more? You came on an orca watch to find out. Here you are. But who's watching whom?

Subject/ Reader Appeal

Did you know that orcas are giant dolphins that "see" like Superman? Or that some eat only fish and never stray from their native waters, while others roam, following the small marine mammals that make up their diet? Find out more in *Orca Watch*, a real life high seas adventure for children 8-12.

Orca Watch also explores this question: Could we really "free Willy"? Would he find his family, and would they accept him as their long lost relative? With the move of Keiko, the orca who played Willy in the movie, to his native Icelandic waters, young readers will be especially interested as the world awaits his ultimate release into the wild.

Credits/ Special Experience

I am a freelance writer well published in the children's market, with clips available. Having also written on an adult level for Dr. Randall Eaton, who has studied wild orcas since 1979, I am knowledgeable on the subject and have a number of beautiful photographs. Please let me know if you would like to see an outline, sample chapters, and the photographs for *Orca Watch*.

Closing

Thank you very much for your time and consideration.

Sincerely,

Ellen Hopkins

Sample Cover Letter – Nonfiction

Street Address
City, State ZIP
Telephone Number
E-mail Address
Date

Jean Reynolds, Vice President and Editorial Director
The Millbrook Press
2 Old New Milford Road
Brookfield, CT 06804

Dear Ms. Reynolds:

Opener/Subject

I am pleased to submit my manuscript with the working title of *Apple Cider-Making Days*. It is based on the workings of the Meckley orchard and cider mill near Jackson, Michigan. The participation of the extended family, including the very youngest members, is critical to the continuity of the operation. Ray Meckley, age 73, believes most of the family-owned cider mills in the U.S. will disappear in the coming years.

Competition

I wrote this manuscript to fill a gap among children's books. There are books available about apples, such as *The Seasons of Arnold's Apple Tree*, by Gail Gibbons, and *How to Make an Apple Pie and Travel Around the World*, by Marjorie Priceman. But I could not find any books in print that give children the experience of being on a working farm and making cider.

Market/Appeal

Through my experience in elementary school classrooms, I know that teachers and librarians look every fall for books related to apples. This is especially true as fewer classes take field trips to real orchards. Teachers want a book such as *Apple Cider-Making Days* to read aloud to classes before seasonal lessons and activities. I see this picture book as a readaloud book for kindergarten and first- and second-grades, and as a book for independent readers in grades three, four, and five. The book will give me many opportunities for school visits.

Specifications

While I have indicated page breaks on the attached manuscript, there are a variety of ways the sections could be handled. I would be happy to write to the specifications of the editor and needs of the illustrator.

Submission status/closing

It would please me very much to have The Millbrook Press publish *Apple Cider-Making Days*. I have submitted the manuscript to other editors, but sincerely hope that you will find the book is a good fit for your list. I look forward to hearing from you.

Sincerely,

Ann Purmell
encl: publishing and professional credentials

Sample Cover Letter – Fiction

Street Address
City, State ZIP
Telephone Number
E-mail Address
Date

Liz Flanagan, Managing Editor
Pavilion Children's Books
64 Brewery Road
London, England N7 9NT

Dear Ms. Flanagan,

Opener/ Subject

Making friends can be difficult, especially when peers judge one to be "different." From a young age, children struggle with the issues involved in finding, making, and keeping friends.

Ms Enclosed/ Synopsis

Please find enclosed a manuscript for a picture storybook, titled *Poetry and Potatoes*. Sonnet returns home after an eventful world tour (racing on camels, outsmarting ostriches, riding in dug-out canoes and on yaks). This feisty and unconventional heroine wants a friend with whom to share her poems and memories of the world. After many attempts to find one, Sonnet concludes that the parochial townspeople are just not ready to broaden their horizons. It seems that loneliness will be Sonnet's fate — yet, if only she knew it, the perfect friend is very near.

Specifications/ Appeal

Set in the Edwardian era, this story uses gentle humor to contrast Sonnet's adventurous spirit with society's judgmental views. My story is 1250 words in length, and targeted toward readers age 7 to 9 years.

Credits

I am the author of 11 books for children and teens. Please see my attached publishing credits. Historical fiction is one of my interests.

Closing

Thank you for your time and consideration.

Best wishes

Troon Harrison

Enclosed: Manuscript, *Poetry and Potatoes*
          Publishing credits
          SAE with IRC

Sample Query Letter – Fiction

Street Address
City, State ZIP
Telephone Number
E-mail Address
Date

Guy King, Director of Publishing Operations
Sword of the Lord
P.O. Box 1099
Murfreesboro, TN 37133-1099

Dear Mr. King:

Opener/ Subject

I have written a Western adventure that I believe will appeal to readers from 8 to 12, and have enclosed a synopsis and samples for your review. The story is the tale of 12-year-old Artemus Anderson and his mother, who leave Ohio and head west to take over a ranch after the death of Arty's father. *Arty Goes West* is the first of a projected series of six books.

Slant/ Competition

From the time Arty and his mother step into the stagecoach, they experience the adventures of everyday life and perils. Without an overlay of preachiness, these adventures allow young readers to witness the benefits, even the practicality, of living the Bible on a daily basis. I hope to make the books similar to the Moody Press's Sugar Creek Gang series, by Paul Hutchens. My books will differ in setting, time period, and voice, but the Biblical values will be the same.

Experience

I have been a junior high and high school English teacher for 15 years. During that time, my wide reading among books for young people and for adults has led me to the realization that the fictional characters who most influence young readers are those rich and developed enough to appear in more than one book. I have completed the second book and am working on the third in the Arty series.

Specifications/ Attached

Please find attached a simple chapter-by-chapter outline of the first book, a brief synopsis, a list of characters, synopses for three more projected books in the series, and my résumé.

Publisher Needs/ Closing

Thank you for taking time to consider my proposal for The Adventures of Artemus Anderson, which I am also submitting to other publishers. I know that Sword of the Lord already publishes fine books for young readers, and I would be honored to add my work to your list. I believe you will find it to be in harmony with the Sword's doctrinal positions.

Sincerely,
Mark L. Redmond
encl: synopsis and outline for book one, character list, series synopses, résumé

Sample Synopsis – Fiction

<u>Synopsis: The Artemus Anderson Series</u>

Set primarily in the small Texas town of White Rock and the surrounding area, this series covers events in the life of Artemus Anderson at ages 12 and 13. The time is the mid-1870s. Arty and his mother travel from Ohio to take possession of a cattle ranch that Mr. Anderson purchased shortly before his death in a fire. Arty and his mother struggle to overcome the heartache that accompanies their loss. Arty has a personal battle with anger and bitterness toward God. Meanwhile, he faces numerous daily struggles as he finds that life in the West rapidly pushes a boy toward manhood.

As he makes friends, Arty learns about responsibility, sorrow, love, relationship to God, joy. As readers follow Arty through the series, they will learn what life was like in the "Wild West," how kids were much the same as they are today, and that Biblical living, then and now, is rewarding both practically in the world and spiritually.

<u>Chapter Synopses: The Adventures of Artemus Anderson, Book 1</u>

Chapter 1: Arty and his mother, Mrs. Anderson, are on their way by stagecoach to claim their Texas ranch. They are confronted by two villains, whom they manage to defeat by using their wits.
Chapter 2: Arty and Mrs. Anderson arrive in White Rock, Texas, the town closest to their ranch. They have a misunderstanding with the marshal.
Chapter 3: They spend the night in town. The following morning, Arty and his mother go to the ranch, escorted by the marshal and ranch foreman, who has ridden into town to meet them.
Chapter 4: Before they leave town, they are again confronted by the two villains from the stagecoach, but the marshal and foreman intervene and the villains land in jail. At the ranch, the Andersons meet several cowboys, and the old cook, who is the focal point of a funny incident.
Chapter 5: Two months have passed. Arty witnesses to the cook, who is bitter toward God because of past events. Although the cook doesn't share Arty's beliefs, he likes the boy. The cowboys present Arty with a pony, and more humor follows, mixed with a spiritual lesson.

. . .

[The outline continues through Chapter 12. A synopsis for each additional book in the series is included in the proposal package.]

Sample Synopsis – Nonfiction

Name   Address, Telephone, E-mail

DANGER ON ICE: THE SHACKLETON ADVENTURE

Sir Ernest plans to return to the South Pole with the goal of traveling across the continent of Antarctica. He must prepare for the voyage by finding the right crew—men of courage and adventure—finding a ship, and gathering supplies. On August 8, 1914, five days after World War I is declared, the *Endurance* leaves England. A stowaway is discovered on board, hiding in a locker with his cat. After stopping to replenish fuel, the *Endurance* leaves South Georgia Island, headed for the Antarctic Circle.

By December 19, the ship reaches the Antarctic ice pack. The heavy wooden ship plows through, but soon must sail through paths in the maze of ice. The ice eventually becomes so thick the men must walk alongside the ship, breaking up the ice around and ahead of it. On January 18, 1915, the ice is too thick to move forward. Shackleton decides to wait for a path to open. During the night, frigid winds tighten the ice around the ship, freezing it in place.

The expedition members live on the ship, moving the dog kennels from the deck to the ice. The scientists study currents, climate, and the changing ice formations that lift and tilt their vessel. In August, blizzards add to the extreme conditions. By October 27, ice pressure begins crushing the ship. They abandon ship and set up Ocean Camp. The daytime sun causes ice melt, soaking their tents, bed rolls, and clothing. Nighttime temperatures freeze every-thing. When the ice is thin enough for them to feel seasick with the movement below, they march inland to safer ice. On December 29, they set up Patience Camp, their home until April 8, 1916.

Supplies are now running low. They need to change plans once again, and leave the ice pack for land. They push lifeboats to the edge of the ice pack, then sail the short distance to Elephant Island. They prepare the largest lifeboat, the *James Caird*, for Shackleton and five others to sail for help. They'll make an 800-mile journey in a 22-foot boat across some of the most dangerous waters of the south polar region.

The six leave Elephant Island on April 24. The open boat is surrounded by whales during the two-week journey through the
. . .

Sample Outline – Nonfiction

Outline of <u>Off-the-Wall Soccer for Kids</u>

I.   Introduction
II.   History and size of competitive youth indoor
        soccer
III.   How indoor soccer differs from outdoor soccer
           A. size of playing surface
           B. number of players
           C. out of bounds
           D. substitutions
           E. uninterrupted play
           F. using the boards as another teammate
           G. quick transitions between offense and
              defense
           H. speed of play
IV.   Basic skills for offense
V.   Using the boards on offense
VI.   Basic skills for defense
VII.   Using the boards on defense
VIII.   Drills for offense
IX.   Drills for defense
X.   Situation strategies for offense
XI.   Situation strategies for defense
XII.   Handling parents and pressure
XIII.   Conditioning requirements for a faster, more
        exhausting game
XIV.   Appendix: Official Rules of Indoor Soccer

Sample Proposal – Nonfiction

Date
Mr. Rob Taylor, Editor
McGraw-Hill/Contemporary Books
1 Prudential Plaza
130 E. Randolph St., Suite 900
Chicago, IL 60601

Dear Mr. Taylor:

I am enclosing my proposal for the book *Off the Wall Soccer Kids*. It is presented in conformance with the McGraw-Hill submission guidelines.

A. Rationales

1. There is no book on coaching youth indoor soccer.
2. Three million boys and girls play the game—the same number who were playing Little League baseball when I wrote my first book on that sport. That book was the first on the subject, and now 8 publishers offer 11 Little League books.
3. Youth indoor soccer is a burgeoning sport, organized as a youth winter sport in 1995, yet it had its first national championship tournaments in 1997.

B. Subject

It is called indoor *arena* soccer to differentiate it from *futsal*, an international version of indoor soccer. The U.S. version is a hybrid of outdoor soccer and indoor hockey, i.e., hockey played with a ball, with sidebards, no out-of-bounds, on-the-fly substitutions, and no time-outs. It is fast-paced and high scoring. The United States Indoor Soccer Association reports more than 500 private indoor facilities, each housing from two to six indoor soccer arenas. In addition, . . . *[continues]*

C. The Market

1. Three thousand youngsters play youth soccer, supported by their parents, coaches, officials, and administrators.
2. There are more than 300,000 websites on the subject of *indoor soccer*, and 30,000 for *youth indoor soccer*.
3. There are 9 national soccer organizations, four of which have *youth* in the title.
4. There are four national soccer magazines . . .

D. Book Competition

No books have been published on coaching youth indoor soccer. A brief review of 17 books on soccer and coaching outdoor youth soccer is attached.

E. Book Size and Completion

I anticipate 170 to 200 pages, color cover, 30 black-and-white photos and 200 diagrams inside. I anticipate six months to complete the writing. . . .

Sample Bibliography

SOURCES FOR <u>DANGER ON ICE: THE SHACKLETON ADVENTURE</u>

Alexander, Caroline. "Endurance." *Natural History.* vol. 108, no. 3 (April 1999): 98-100.

——————————. *The Endurance: Shackleton's Legendary Antarctic Expedition.* New York: Alfred A. Knopf, 1998.

Armstrong, Jennifer. *Shipwreck at the Bottom of the World: Shackleton's Amazing Voyage.* New York: Crown Publishers, 1998.

——————————. *Spirit of Endurance.* New York: Crown Publishers, 2000.

Explorers and Discoverers of the World. Edited by Daniel B. Baker. Detroit: Gale Research, 1993.

Briley, Harold. "Sail of the Century." *Geographical*, vol. 71, no. 4 (April 1999): 48-53.

"The Furthest South." *Geographical*, vol. 68 (February 1996): 30-35.

Hammel, Sara. "The Call of the Sea: It Was a Matter of Endurance." *U.S. News & World Report.* (May 31, 1999: 67)

Kimmel, Elizabeth Cody. *Ice Story: Shackleton's Lost Expedition.* New York: Clarion Books, 1999.

Lane, Anthony. "Breaking the Waves." *The New Yorker* (April 12, 1999): 96-101.

Rogers, Patrick. "Beyond Endurance." *People Weekly,* vol. 51, no. 9 (March 8, 1999): 151-153.

"A Salute to Survival." *USA Today*, vol. 129, no. 2667 (December 2000): 8-9.

Shipwrecks. Edited by David Ritchie. New York: Facts on File, 1996): 74, 117.

Shackleton, Sir Ernest. *South: A Memoir of the* Endurance *Voyage.* (New York: Carroll & Graff, 1999 reissue of 1918 edition).

Shackleton, Sir Ernest. *Shackleton: His Antarctic Writings.* (London: British Broadcasting Corp., 1983).

"Shackleton Expedition." American Museum of Natural History website. www.amnh.org/exhibitions/shackleton

Sample Résumé

Ann Purmell
Address, Telephone Number, E-mail

Experience
- Writer of inspirational and children's literature.
- Freelance journalist and feature writer for *Jackson Citizen Patriot* (Michigan), a Booth Communications daily. Affiliate newspapers throughout Michigan carry my articles.
- Freelance writer for *Jackson Magazine,* a monthly business publication.
- Guest lecturer for Children's Literature and Creative Writing classes at Spring Arbor College, Spring Arbor, Michigan.
- Performs school presentations for all grade levels.

Publications/Articles
Published numerous articles, including:
- "Prayers to the Dead," *In Other Words: An American Poetry Anthology* (Western Reading Services, 1998).
- "Promises Never Die," *Guideposts for Teens* (June/July 1999). Ghost-written, first-person, true story.
- "Teaching Kids the Financial Facts of Life," *Jackson Citizen Patriot* (July 20, 1999). An interview with Jayne A. Pearl, author of *Kids and Money.*
- "New Rules for Cider? Small Presses Might Be Put Out of Business," *Jackson Citizen Patriot* (December 12, 1999).
- "Jackson Public Schools Prepare for Change: Technology, Ideas Shaping Education," *Jackson Magazine* (December 1999). An interview with Dan Evans, Superintendent of Jackson Public Schools.

Education
- B.S., Nursing, Eastern Michigan University.
- Post-B.A. work, elementary education, Spring Arbor College.
- *Highlights for Children* Chautauqua Conference, summer 1999.

Sample Manuscript Pages

Title Page

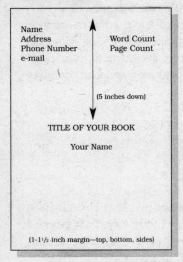

New Chapter

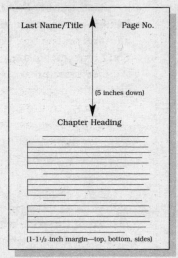

Following Pages

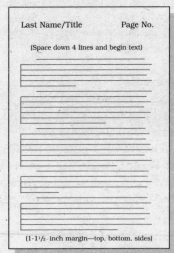

Manuscript Preparation

Prepare and mail your manuscript according to the following guidelines:

- Use high-quality 8½x11 white bond paper.
- Double-space manuscript text; leave 1- to 1½-inch margins on the top, bottom, and sides. (See page 38.)
- Send typewritten pages, letter-quality computer print-outs, or clear photocopies. You may send a computer disk if the publisher requests one.
- *Title Page.* In the upper left corner, type your name, address, phone number, and e-mail address.

  In the upper right corner, type your word count, rounded to the nearest 10 to 25 words. For anything longer than a picture book, you may also type the number of pages. (Don't count the title page.) Center and type your title (using capital letters) about 5 inches from the top of the page with your byline two lines below it.

  Start your text on the next page. (Note: if this is a picture book or board book, see page 41.)
- *Following Pages.* Type your last name and one or two key words of your title in the upper left corner, and the page number in the upper right. Begin new chapters halfway down the page.
- *Cover Letter.* Include a brief cover letter following the guidelines on page 25.

Mailing Requirements

- Assemble pages unstapled. Place cover letter on top of title page. Mail in a 9x12 or 10x13 manila envelope. Include a same-sized SASE marked "First Class." If submitting to a publisher outside the US, enclose an International Reply Coupon (IRC) for return postage.
- To ensure that your manuscript arrives safely, include a self-addressed, stamped postcard the editor can return upon receipt.
- Mail your submissions First Class or Priority. Do not use certified or registered mail.

Picture Book Dummy

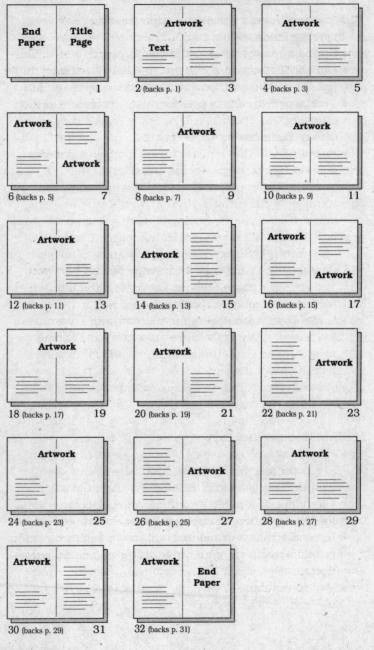

40

Picture Book Submissions

Most editors will accept a complete manuscript for a picture book without an initial query. Because a picture book text may contain as few as 20 words and seldom exceeds 1,500 words, it is difficult to judge if not seen in its entirety. Do not submit your own artwork unless you are a professional artist; editors prefer to use illustrators of their own choosing.

Prepare the manuscript following the guidelines for the title page on pages 38–39. Drop down four lines from the byline, indent, and begin your manuscript on the title page. Type it straight through as if it were a short story. Do not indicate page breaks.

Before submitting your picture book, make certain that your words lend themselves to visual representation and work well in the picture book format. Preparing a dummy or mock-up similar to the sample on page 40 can help you.

The average picture book is 32 pages, although it may be as short as 16 pages or as long as 64 pages, depending on the age of the intended audience. To make a dummy for a 32-page book, take eight sheets of paper, fold them in half, and number them as the sample indicates; this will not include the end papers. (Each sheet makes up four pages of your book.) Lay out your text and rough sketches or a brief description of the accompanying illustrations. Move these around and adjust your concept of the artwork until you are satisfied that words and pictures fit together as they should.

Do not submit your dummy unless the editor asks for it. Simply submit your text on separate sheets of paper, typed double-spaced, following the format guidelines given on page 38. If you do choose to submit artwork as well, be sure to send copies only; editors will *rarely* take responsibility for original artwork. Be sure to include a self-addressed, stamped envelope (SASE) large enough for the return of your entire package.

Step-by-Step Through the Business of Publishing

Book Contracts

Once a publisher is interested in buying your work, he or she will send a book contract for your review and signature. While book contracts vary in length and precise language from publisher to publisher, the basic provisions of these contracts are more similar than different. All writers should understand publishing contract standards, know enough to acknowledge an offer as appropriate, and recognize when there may be room to negotiate. Remember, the agreement isn't complete until the contract is signed.

In Plain English

The best advice for your first contract reading is not to let the legal terminology distract you. A book contract is a complex legal document that is designed to protect you. It defines the rights, responsibilities, and financial terms of the author, publisher, and artist (when necessary).

Because some publishers issue standard contracts and rarely change wording or payment rates for new writers, you may not need an agent or a lawyer with book-publishing experience to represent you in the negotiation of the contract. But if you choose to negotiate the contract yourself, it is advisable that you read several reference books about book contracts and have a lawyer, preferably with book-contract experience, look it over prior to signing the agreement.

In either case, you should be familiar enough with the basic premises of the contract to communicate what items you would like to change in the document. For your protection, reread the contract at every stage of negotiation.

On the following pages you'll find a primer on the basic provisions of a book contract. If a statement in your contract is not covered or remains unclear to you, ask the editor or an attorney to "translate" the clauses into plain English.

Rights and Responsibilities

A standard book contract specifies what an author and a publisher each agree to do to produce the book and place it in the marketplace. It explicitly states copyright ownership, royalty, advance, delivery date, territorial and subsidiary rights, and other related provisions.

Grant of Rights

A clause early in the contract says that on signing, the author agrees to "grant and assign" or "convey and transfer" to the publisher certain rights to a book. You thus authorize, or license, the publisher to publish your work.

Subsidiary rights are negotiated in a contract. These rights include where a book is distributed, in what language it is printed, and in what format it is published. While most publishers want world English-language rights, some publishers will consent to retaining rights only to the United States, the Philippines, Canada, and US dependencies. With the United Kingdom now part of the European Community, more and more publishers want British publication rights, in English, so they can sell books to other members of the European Community.

Other subsidiary rights often included in contracts are:

- *Reprint Rights:* These consist of publishing the work in magazines (also known as serial rights), book club editions, and hardcover or paperback versions.
- *Mechanical Rights:* These cover audio and video cassettes, photocopying, filmstrips, and other mechanical production media.
- *Electronic or Computer Rights:* More and more contracts include rights to cover potential use on software programs, multimedia packages, online services, etc.
- *Dramatic Rights:* These include versions of the work for film, television, etc.
- *Translation Rights:* These allow a work to be printed in languages other than English.

If you don't have an agent, you may want to assign a publisher broad rights since you may not have the necessary connections or experience to sell them on your own.

If possible, seek a time limit that a publisher has to use subsidiary rights. That way certain rights will revert to you if the publisher has not sold them within a specific period.

Copyright Ownership

According to the Copyright Act of 1976 (which became effective January 1, 1978), you own all rights to your work for your lifetime plus 50 years, until you choose to sell all or part of the copyright in very specific ways. According to this law, your idea is not copyrighted; it is your unique combination of words—how you wrote something—that this law protects and considers copyrighted. A separate clause in a book contract states that you retain the copyright in your name.

Once you complete your manuscript, your work is protected. You don't need to register your work, published or unpublished, with the United States Copyright Office. In most contract agreements, a publisher is responsible for registering the published version of your work. However, registration does offer proof of ownership and a clear legal basis in case of infringement. If you decide to register, send a completed application (obtained from the Copyright Office), a $30 filing fee, and one copy of your unpublished manuscript to the Register of Copyrights, Copyright Office, Library of Congress, Washington, DC 20559.

You should realize that writers who provide a copyright notice on their submitted manuscript may be viewed as amateurs by many editors. If you have registered your unpublished manuscript with the Library of Congress, notify your publisher of that fact once your book is accepted for publication.

Manuscript Delivery

A book-publishing contract sets a due date by which you must complete and deliver an acceptable manuscript of a certain length. This clause allows a publisher to request editorial changes, permits editing of the manuscript with your review and approval, establishes editorial schedules, and indicates how many author's alterations (also known as editorial changes) you may make without cost after the book has been typeset.

Warranty and Indemnification

You will be asked to ensure that the manuscript is your original work; that it contains nothing libelous, obscene, or private; and that you own it. The clause also stipulates that the author must pay the publisher's court costs and damages should it be sued over the book. Publishers do not alter this provision readily, but the author who has written in good faith should not be concerned. Discuss a ceiling on the amount of the author's liability, just in case.

Obligation to Publish

The publisher agrees to produce and distribute the book in a timely manner, generally between one and two years. The contract should specify the time frame and indicate that if the publisher fails to publish the book within that period, the rights return to you (reversion of rights) and you keep any money already received.

Option

The option clause requires the author to offer the publisher the first chance at his or her next book. To avoid a prolonged decision-making process, try to negotiate a set period for the publisher's review of a second book, perhaps 60 or 90 days from submission of the second manuscript.

Payment

Calculations for the amount of money an author receives as an advance or in royalties are fairly standardized.

- ◆ *Advance:* An advance is money the writer receives in a lump sum or installments when a manuscript is accepted or delivered. It is paid "against" royalties coming from anticipated profits.
- ◆ *Royalty:* A royalty is a percentage of sales paid to the author. It is based either on a book's retail price or on net receipts, and it may be fixed or arranged on a sliding scale. Standard royalty is 10% of the retail price for the first 5,000 copies, 12.5% for the next 5,000 copies, and 15% thereafter. A new author may be offered only 10% or the scale may slide at a higher number of copies. Depending on the extent of artwork and who

supplied it to the publisher, author and artist may divide royalties or the artist may be paid a flat fee.

♦ *Accounting Statements:* The publisher must provide the author with earning statements for the book. Most companies provide statements and checks semi-annually, three or more months after each accounting period ends. Be sure to determine exactly when that is. For example, if the accounting periods end June 30 and December 31, you should receive statements by October 1 and April 1.

Before You Sign . . .

The explanations presented here include suggestions for a reasonable and (we hope) profitable approach to your book contract. Every situation presents distinct alternatives, however. Your agreements with a publisher must be undertaken in good faith on both sides and you should feel comfortable with the deal you strike.

You can find additional information about copyrights and publishing law in *The Copyright Handbook: How to Protect and Use Written Words* (fifth ed) by Stephen Fishman (Nolo Press, 2000) and *Every Writer's Guide to Copyright and Publishing Law* by Ellen Kozak (Henry Holt, 1997).

A Note About Self, Subsidy, and Co-op Publishing Options

When you self-publish your book, you assume the cost of and responsibility for printing and distributing your book. By contrast, subsidy presses handle—for a fee—the production and, to some degree, the marketing and distribution of a writer's book. Co-op or joint-venture publishers assume responsibility for marketing and distribution of a book, while the author pays some or all of the production costs. Based on your own needs and expectations, you may choose to try one of these approaches. If you do, exercise caution. Be sure you understand the terms of any contract, including exactly how much you will be required to pay, the marketing and distributing services the publisher is promising, and the rights you are retaining. It is advisable to consult a lawyer before entering into any arrangement.

Postage Information

When you send a manuscript to a publisher, always enclose a return SASE with sufficient postage; this way, if the editor does not want to use your manuscript, it can be returned to you. To help you calculate the proper amount of postage for your SASE, here are the US postal rates for first-class mailings in the US and from the US to Canada based on the June 2002 increase.

Ounces	8½x11 Pages (approx pgs)	US 1st-Class Postage Rate	US to Canada
5	21–25	$1.26	$1.60
6	26–30	1.49	1.85
7	31–35	1.72	2.10
8	36–40	1.95	2.35
9	41–45	2.18	3.10
10	46–50	2.41	3.10
11	51–55	2.64	3.10
12	56+	2.87	3.10

How to Obtain Stamps

People living in the US, Canada, or overseas can acquire US stamps through the mail from the Stamp Fulfillment Service Center: call 800-STAMP-24 (800-782-6724) to request a catalogue or place an order. For overseas, the telephone number is 816-545-1100. You pay the cost of the stamps plus a postage and handling fee based on the value of the stamps ordered, and the stamps are shipped to you. Credit card information (MasterCard, Visa, and Discover cards only) is required for fax orders. The fax number is 816-545-1212. If you order through the catalogue, you can pay with a US check or an American money order. Allow 3–4 weeks for delivery.

Frequently Asked Questions

How do I request a publisher's catalogue and writers' guidelines?

Write a brief note to the publishing company: *"Please send me a recent catalogue and writers' guidelines. If there is any charge please enclose an invoice and I will pay upon receipt."* The publisher's website, if it has one, offers a faster and less expensive alternative. Many companies put their catalogues, or at least their latest releases and their writers' guidelines on the Internet.

Do I need an agent?

There is no correct answer to this question. Some writers are very successful marketing their own work, while others feel more comfortable having an agent handle that end of the business. It's a personal decision, but if you decide to work through an agent, be an "informed consumer." Get a list of member agents from the Association of Authors' Representatives, 3rd Floor, 10 Astor Place, New York, NY 10003 (available for $7.00 and SAE with $.60 postage).

I need to include a bibliography with my book proposal. How do I set one up?

The reference section of your local library can provide several sources that will help you set up a bibliography. A style manual such as the *Chicago Manual of Style* will show you the proper format for citing all your sources, including unpublished material, interviews, and Internet material.

What do I put in a cover letter if I have no publishing credits or relevant personal experience?

In this case you may want to forego a formal cover letter and send your manuscript with a brief letter stating, *"Enclosed is my manuscript, [Insert Title], for your review."* For more information on cover letters see page 25.

I don't need my manuscript returned. How do I indicate that to an editor?

With the capability to store manuscripts electronically and print out additional copies easily, some writers keep postage costs down by enclosing a self-addressed stamped postcard (SASP) saying, "*No need to return my manuscript. Please use this postcard to advise me of the status of my manuscript. Thank you.*"

Do I need to register or copyright my manuscript?

Once completed, your work is automatically protected by copyright. When your manuscript is accepted for publication, the publisher will register it for you.

Should I submit my manuscript on disk?

Do not send your manuscript on disk unless the publisher's submission guidelines note that this is an acceptable format.

When a publisher says "query with sample chapters," how do I know which chapters to send? Should they be chapters in sequence or does that matter? And how many should I send?

If the publisher does not specify which chapters it wishes to see, then it's your decision. Usually it's a good idea to send the first chapter, but if another chapter gives a flavor of your book or describes a key action in the plot, include that one. You may also want to send the final chapter of the book. For nonfiction, if one chapter is more fully representative of the material your book will cover, include that. Send two to three but if the guidelines state "sample chapter" (singular), just send one.

How long should I wait before contacting an editor after I have submitted my manuscript?

The response time given in the listings can vary, and it's a good idea to wait at least a few weeks after the allocated response time before you send a brief note to the editor asking about the status of your manuscript. If you do not get a satisfactory response or you want to send your manuscript elsewhere, send a certified letter to the editor withdrawing your work from consideration and requesting its return. You are then free to submit the work to another publishing house.

A long time ago, in 1989, I was fortunate enough to have a picture book published. If I write a query letter, should I include that information? It seems to me that it may hurt more than it helps, since I have not published anything since that.

By all means include it, though you need not mention the year it was published Any publishing credit is worth noting, particularly if it is a picture book, because it shows you succeeded in a highly competitive field.

How do I address the editor, especially if she is female (e.g., Dear Miss, Dear Ms., Dear Mrs., Dear Editor-in-Chief, or what)?

There is no accepted preference, so the choice is really yours, but in general Ms. is used most frequently. Do use the person's last name, not his or her first. Before you decide which title to use, make sure you know if the person you are addressing is male or female.

If a publisher does not specify that "multiple submissions" are okay, does that imply they are not okay?

If a publisher has a firm policy against multiple submissions, this is usually stated in its guidelines. If not mentioned, the publisher probably does not have a hard and fast rule. If you choose to send a multiple submission, make sure to indicate that on your submission. Then it's up to the publisher to contact you if it prefers not to receive such submissions.

Publishing Terms

Advance: initial payment by publisher to author against future sales

Agent: professional who contacts editors and negotiates book contracts on author's behalf

All rights: an outright sale of your material; author has no further control over it

Anthropomorphization: attributing human form and personality to things not human, for example, animals

Backlist: list of publisher's titles that were not produced this season but are still in print

Beginning readers: children ages 4 to 7 years

Book contract: legal agreement between author and publisher

Book packager/producer: company that handles all elements of producing a book and then sells the final product to a publisher

Book proposal: see **Proposal**

Caldecott Medal: annual award that honors the illustrator of the current year's most distinguished children's book

CD-ROM: (compact-disc read-only memory) non-erasable electronic medium used for digitalized image and document storage

Clean-copy: a manuscript ready for typesetting; it is free of errors and needs no editing

Clip: sample of a writer's published work. See also **Tearsheet**

Concept book: category of picture book for children 2 to 7 years that teaches an idea (i.e., alphabet or counting) or explains a problem

Contract: see **Book contract**

Co-op publishing: author assumes some or all of the production costs and publisher handles all marketing and distribution; also referred to as "joint-venture publishing"

Copyedit: to edit with close attention to style and mechanics

Copyright: legal protection of an author's work

Cover letter: brief introductory letter sent with a manuscript

Disk submission: manuscript that is submitted on a computer disk

Distributor: company that buys and resells books from a publisher

Dummy: a sample arrangement or "mock-up" of pages to be printed, indicating the appearance of the published work

Electronic submission: manuscript transmitted to an editor from one computer to another through a modem

E-mail: (electronic mail) messages sent from one computer to another via a modem or computer network

End matter: material following the text of a book, such as the appendix, bibliography, index

Final draft: the last version of a polished manuscript ready for submission to an editor

First-time author: writer who has not previously been published

Flat fee: one-time payment made to an author for publication of a manuscript

Front matter: material preceding the text of a book, such as title page, acknowledgments, etc.

Galley: a proof of typeset text that is checked before it is made into final pages

Genre: category of fiction characterized by a particular style, form, or content, such as mystery or fantasy

Hard copy: the printed copy of a computer's output

Hi/lo: high-interest/low-reading level

Imprint: name under which a publishing house issues books

International Reply Coupon (IRC): coupon exchangeable in any foreign country for postage on a single-rate, surface-mailed letter

ISBN: International Standard Book Number assigned to books upon publication for purposes of identification

Letter-quality printout: computer printout that resembles typed pages

Manuscript: a typewritten, or computer-generated document (as opposed to a printed version)

Mass-market: books aimed at a wide audience and sold in supermarkets, airports, and chain bookstores.

Middle-grade readers: children ages 8 to 12 years

Modem: an internal or external device used to transmit data between computers via telephone lines

Ms/Mss: manuscript/manuscripts

Newbery Medal: annual award that honors the author of that year's most distinguished children's book

Outline: summary of a book's contents, usually nonfiction, often organized under chapter headings with descriptive sentences under each to show the scope of the book

Packager: see **Book Packager**

Pen name/pseudonym: fictitious name used by an author

Picture book: a type of book that tells a story primarily or entirely through artwork and is aimed at preschool to 8-year-old children

Pre-K: children under 5 years of age; also known as preschool

Proofread: to read and mark errors, usually in typeset text

Proposal: detailed description of a manuscript, usually nonfiction, and its intended market

Query: letter to an editor to promote interest in a manuscript or idea

Reading fee: fee charged by anyone to read a manuscript

Reprint: another printing of a book; often a different format, such as a paperback reprint of a hardcover title

Response time: average length of time for an editor to accept or reject a submission and contact the writer with a decision

Résumé: short account of one's qualifications, including educational and professional background and publishing credits

Revision: reworking of a piece of writing

Royalty: publisher's payment to an author (usually a percentage) for each copy of the author's work sold

SAE: self-addressed envelope

SASE: self-addressed, stamped envelope

Self-publishing: author assumes complete responsibility for publishing and marketing the book, including printing, binding, advertising, and distributing the book

Simultaneous submission: manuscript submitted to more than one publisher at the same time; also known as a multiple submission

Slush pile: term used within the publishing industry to describe unsolicited manuscripts

Small press: an independent publisher that publishes a limited or specialized list

Solicited manuscript: manuscript that an editor has asked for or agreed to consider

Subsidiary rights: book contract rights other than book publishing rights, such as book club, movie rights, etc.

Subsidy publishing: author pays publisher for all or part of a book's publication, promotion, and sale

Synopsis: condensed description of a fiction manuscript

Tearsheet: page from a magazine or newspaper containing your printed story or article

Trade book: book published for retail sale in bookstores

Unsolicited manuscript: any manuscript not specifically requested by an editor; "no unsolicited manuscripts" generally means the editors will only consider queries or manuscripts submitted by agents

Vanity press: see **Subsidy publishing**

Whole language: educational approach integrating literature into classroom curricula

Work-for-hire: work specifically ordered, commissioned, and owned by a publisher for its exclusive use

Writers' guidelines: publisher's editorial objectives or specifications, which usually include word lengths, readership level, and subject matter

Young adult: children ages 12 years and older

Young reader: the general classification of books written for readers between the ages of 5 and 8

Gateway to
the Markets

An Experiment in Science Books

By Joanne Mattern

Researchers use the scientific method to prove or disprove a theory. Let's use the same approach to create, write, and market a science idea to an appropriate publisher.

You might remember the scientific method from your school days. Basically, it is a process that results in proving or disproving an idea. The steps include making observations, creating a hypothesis based on your observations, conducting experiments and gathering data, and then using that information to prove your hypothesis.

Let's Get Specific

If you're interested in science writing, you've probably observed that there are many books about animals. Therefore, your hypothesis could be, "A book about animals would appeal to children and publishers of science books." Now let's set about proving that hypothesis and using it to discover the best way to publish in the science field.

The first thing you'll realize is that *animals* is a pretty broad topic. Instead, most science books focus on a much narrower idea. For example, there are books about specific animals (tigers, snakes, mosquitoes); classes of animals (wild cats, reptiles, insects); and about specific topics related to animals, such as parts of their bodies or where they live. So, the first modification you might make to your hypothesis is to replace "a book about animals" with something more specific.

But how do you find that specific topic? There are several painless ways to come up with great book ideas. The first is to open your senses to the wealth of information in the world. Perhaps you watch a TV special on animals that live in the rain forest. You read a magazine article about orphan elephants, or find a website about rare birds of the world. Several years ago, I read a newspaper article about unusual ways animals survive the cold winter months. I used that idea as the basis for "Frozen Frogs and Sleepy Squirrels," which was published as part of a classroom anthology.

Books, magazines, newspapers, and the Web aren't the only sources of information. Your neighborhood can be full of good ideas too! Take a tour of a local zoo, museum, or park. Read the billboards along the highway or posted on the bus. You might see an advertisement for an exhibit at the local museum, or a new product that sparks your interest. Keep a notebook or PDA handy to jot down ideas as they come to you. Then use them to brainstorm ideas for a book or article.

Another great idea generator is your own curiosity. Ask questions about what you see around you, and you might be surprised at where the answers take you! Say you watch the dogs in your neighborhood. Dogs come in all shapes and sizes, you think. A chihuahua looks very different from a great dane, yet both are still dogs! Why are there so many different kinds of dogs? What led to their different physical characteristics? There—you've just come up with a good idea for a science book!

> ## What the Editors Say About Science
>
> Read what these four editors have to say about the science market and their companies' needs:
>
> ♦ Beth Townsend, Enslow Publishers, page 183.
> ♦ Lori Shein, Lucent Books/KidHaven Press, page 274.
> ♦ Aimee Jackson, NorthWord Books, page 310.
> ♦ Sue Thies, Perfection Learning, page 333.

Focus on the Differences

After making your observations, you are now flooded with ideas and topics. But before you start writing, stop, take a breath, and go back to modifying your hypothesis. You want to choose a topic that is as specific as possible. You also want to make it different from everything else on the market.

For a long time, I had wanted to write about endangered animals. But I soon discovered that libraries and bookstores

What's Hot, What's Not

I asked several editors what they think of the science market today. Their answers provide excellent guidance for what authors should be writing about!

Sue Thies, Editorial Director, Perfection Learning Corporation:

"I think the move has been toward more entertaining-type books to compete with TV, Internet, video games, etc. Topics must be cutting-edge to satisfy curiosity in our rapidly changing world."

Aimee Jackson, Executive Editor, NorthWord Press:

"I think science publishing is becoming more fun! Information is being delivered in more exciting formats. I think publishers are finally recognizing how savvy kids today are, which is reflected in the sophistication of the books, and themes of the books. Publishers also seem to be finding ways to bring science to younger and younger age groups. And as children become more savvy about the world around them (because of technology), I think many of them become more socially conscious and globally aware as well, and I would expect this to influence science book publishing for children."

Helen Moore, Product Planning Editor, Capstone Press

"Educational publishers, especially those producing science-related materials, must take extra care to ensure the accuracy, currency, and relevancy of their products. We need to make sure that we present science information in an engaging format with real-life examples and opportunities for hands-on applications. Books on science topics have become much more colorful and interactive in recent years. There's been much more of an effort to make science education fun."

were already filled with books about rare species, and publishers weren't exactly eager to take on yet another title on this well-covered subject. Then I read about a program to remove all California condors from the wild, breed them in captivity, and release the young birds back into the wild to increase the population. The program was controversial, but it worked! I wondered, "What other animal species have been saved by unusual or unique programs?" I did some research and came up with a list of animals that fit the bill. Now I had a unique angle on the topic of endangered animals, and a look at published titles showed me that there were no books on this precise subject. I called my book *Going, Going, Gone? Saving Endangered Animals*, and it sold quickly to Perfection Learning Corporation.

Look at the market, see what's out there, and then give your idea a twist to make it stand out and fill a gap. As Aimee Jackson, Executive Editor of NorthWord Books for Young Readers, advises, "Research the marketplace. See how other books like yours are selling, or see if there's a hole in the market for one like yours (or a glut, for that matter)."

Going to Market

You have come up with a strong idea that hasn't been done before. Now it's time to find a publisher that is just right for your book. Take a trip to your local library or bookstore, and you'll probably be overwhelmed at the number of publishers who put out science books. Some publishers are huge and well known. Eyewitness Books, for example, practically jump off the shelves because of their unusual design and wealth of information. Just about everyone has heard of publishers such as Random House or HarperCollins. These publishers produce high-quality books and reach a huge audience. But they certainly aren't the only markets out there!

Smaller publishers are also a good fit for science books. NorthWord may not be a household name, for example, but its publishing list is 100 percent animal-oriented.

Other publishers have found their niche by publishing for the educational market. You may not find books from Capstone Press or Rosen Publishing at the bookstore, but odds are your library or school district has many titles from these

Series Publishing

Peruse the books at your library or bookstore, or page through a publisher's catalogue, and you're likely to see many books appearing in series. Series publishing is perfectly suited for the science markets because topics can be grouped together so easily. For example, instead of a single title about parrots, a publisher would be more likely to produce a series on birds of the world. This allows the publisher to cover the market better and also increase sales, because odds are that a school or store that buys one book in a series will buy all the other books as well.

Series books are generally all written in the same style, even if they are written by different authors. They tend to be organized the same way, present information in the same order, and are designed to look the same.

If you have a science idea, take some time to brainstorm and see if you can build a series around it. Your work may pay off in additional sales!

publishers on their shelves. Educational publishers focus on what children are learning in the classroom, and publish specifically in these subject areas. These companies may not be household names, but they reach an audience of millions.

You can test and modify your publishing hypothesis by studying publishers and what they do. Look through books at the library or bookstore. Go online to Amazon.com or Barnesandnoble.com and see who's publishing books on animal topics. Grab this copy of *Children's Book Market* to find publishers and addresses and send away for catalogues and guidelines. The better fit you find for your book, the better your chances of finding a publisher.

Sue Thies, Editorial Director of Perfection Learning, says it best when she advises writers to "Do a little research on the company and make sure what you are proposing fits, and don't try to force the proposal to fit by claiming it's something it isn't." Beth Townsend, Editor at Enslow Publishing, echoes this advice: "Before an author submits any type of work, they should know something about the company, i.e., what types of books they publish."

What to Include

The contents of your submission package should be determined by each publisher's specific guidelines and requirements, but a typical package includes:

- a query letter describing the book and asking the editor if he or she is interested in reviewing it;
- a résumé and/or list of your publishing credits (if applicable);
- a synopsis and/or outline of the book;
- a sample chapter;
- a self-addressed, stamped envelope for the editor's response.

Testing Your Hypothesis in the Market

Once you've chosen a specific and unique topic and found several markets that look like good fits, it's time to put together a submissions package that will make a publisher sit up and take notice!

Your package should start with a strong cover letter. This is the first thing editors read, and it's their introduction to you as an author. Be sure to present yourself as professionally as possible. State your idea and why you think it's unique. Don't try to write the whole book in the cover letter—just sum up your idea in one or two sentences. If you have publishing credits or life experience that make your book more appealing, mention those. For example, "I have published several nature articles in our local newspaper," or "My volunteer work at a local wildlife center has given me firsthand experience with the creatures profiled in my book."

Along with being succinct, your cover letter should look professional. Just as you wouldn't show up for a corporate job interview wearing ripped jeans and a faded T-shirt, don't let your cover letter look sloppy. Beth Townsend of Enslow Publishers says authors can increase their odds of making a sale if they "submit a clear and concisely written cover letter, résumé, and sample chapter. A big pet peeve of mine is misspelled words on any of these."

Should you send the entire manuscript, or just a brief

synopsis or outline? The answer to this lies in the publisher's guidelines. Read them carefully, find out what they want, and follow their directions. Many publishers prefer a synopsis or outline of the book along with one sample chapter, especially if the book is more than a few hundred words. Picture book manuscripts, on the other hand, are so short that publishers usually are willing to read the entire manuscript.

Proving Your Hypothesis

You've observed the market, come up with a topic, and modified your idea to find success. Have you proved that a book on your chosen topic will sell? Only time and the market will tell. But by following the scientific method and applying it to the publishing process, the odds are good that your experiment will be a success!

Selling a Mystery

By Patricia Curtis Pfitsch

What is it about the mystery that is so compelling? The exciting plot? The challenge of figuring it out along with or maybe even before the character? Or maybe there's a more complicated appeal. Nancy Werlin, author of many thrillers, most recently *The Black Mirror* and *Locked Inside,* suggests, "Thrillers and mysteries are one of the more direct forms for attempting to gain control over our understanding of morality and fairness in life and death."

Whatever the reason, the mystery may be one of the most long lasting and universally popular genres in litera-ture. It's one many writers aspire to write. Which of us hasn't at least briefly contemplated writing something like *The Westing Game,* by Ellen Raskin, or *Silent to the Bone,* by E.L. Konigsburg. We may have read stacks from Baby-Sitters Club or Encyclopedia Brown and dreamed of contributing to a well-known series. Perhaps we've entertained the notion of starting a series of our own for fun and profit.

What about these dreams? Is it possible for aspiring mystery writers to succeed in even "belt-tightening" times in the publishing industry? Let's take a look at the evidence and see if there's a chance for a happy—or at least a hope-ful—ending.

Clues to a Happy Outcome

The hard fact is this: Some of the larger publishing houses do not accept unsolicited *manuscripts*. The reasons include economics and the strains on company postal systems in the aftermath of September 11.

This is most apparent in the market for series in general and mystery series in particular, and markedly less true for single titles. Scholastic, the most well known and prolific publisher of mystery series, is typical: "In the rare instance when we need to find a new writer for a series, we usually go to writers we know or have heard about, almost always previously published authors," says Senior Editor David Levithan. "I would not encourage people to send in proposals for existing series—especially if the proposal contains potential plot material. We will not look at it, for legal reasons."

But buried in this news are a few clues to a happier outcome for writers of single-title mysteries, and even writers of mystery series: Even though many houses are not open to unagented submissions, some still accept unsolicited queries and proposals. Smaller houses and regional publishers also accept proposals, and some even look at complete manuscripts.

This is good news for people who want to write single title mysteries. But it also means there's hope for series writers, too. Read Levithan's words again. When a publisher of series fiction is looking for a writer, he goes to someone he already knows—who's already published in the genre. Elementary, my dear Watson. If you want to publish in a mystery series, then it will help to publish a single title or standalone mystery first. It doesn't take Sherlock Holmes to make this deduction—selling a great single title mystery may lead to other standalones or series.

Read Between the Lines

Detectives learn to read between the lines. The key word is *great*. Your novel must be outstanding. But how do you write a great mystery? Is it all about thinking up an exciting plot with lots of action, or is there more to it? Let's interview the pros and use their evidence to build a case.

"For me, writing a novel is a kind of magic," Edgar-Award-winning Werlin has written in a letter to *The Horn Book* (www.hbook.com/horningin_werlin.shtml). "The only thing about it that is not mysterious in some way is the part where I show up, sit down, and stay seated," Werlin continues. Yet, as mysterious as the process is, writers can follow clues to help write, and ultimately sell, mysteries.

"I think good mysteries delve into character, motivation, and theme in the same way any good novel does," Werlin says in an interview with *Children's Book Market*. "In the best mysteries, the personal conflicts and motivations of the characters (the subplot) are related to the mystery and its solution (the main plot)."

Eleanora Tate, author of standalone and series mysteries, adds another clue. "Mystery 101 tells us that a good mystery involves a main character who cares so passionately about something close to her or him that he or she will go to any length to soothe that itch." She points out that the mysteries must be child-centered. "Ophelia in *The Minstrel's Melody* is persuaded by her older sister to enter the Stone Shed (off-limits because of mysterious parental rules), but it's up to her to find and read the old newspaper, to rummage through other folks' personal possessions, ask questions, and keenly observe what's going on to reach her conclusions."

How do you create such a passionate character? "If any ordinary, nice, sympathetic young woman or young man could be dropped into my story and the story would still work," says Werlin, "then I'm afraid it's a story I'm not interested in telling. So one of the things I do is uncover the idiosyncrasies and weirdness and *secrets* of my character. *Those* power the mystery plot."

That's a solid piece of evidence. Many good single-title mysteries, like any good fiction, begin with a passionate character who has secrets and idiosyncrasies and who wants something so strongly that she's willing to do anything to achieve her goal.

What the Editors Say About Mysteries

Read what these four editors have to say about the market for mysteries and what their companies publish:

♦ Lauri Hornik, Dial Books, page 159.
♦ Michael Steere, Down East, page 168.
♦ Peg Ross, Pleasant Company, page 345.
♦ Kathy Tucker, Albert Whitman & Company, page 424.

Perfect Sense

But once that character begins to grow in the mind of the writer, how does the plot develop?

Editor-in-Chief Kathy Tucker of Albert Whitman & Company, publisher of the Boxcar Children mysteries, encourages writers to think through the plot. "The biggest thing to be wary of is making the plot too complicated. The plot may appear complicated in the beginning, but it must be fairly simple in the end."

Vicki Erwin, who has written numerous stand-alone and series mysteries, for Scholastic and other publishers, agrees. "You want readers to have the feeling that when they get to the end it was hard to figure out but that it makes perfect sense." At the end, the reader should think, "Of course. Why didn't I think about that?"

Unlike Werlin and Tate, Erwin usually starts with a germ of a plot idea, or at least a hook for the mystery. A friend told her about a German man abroad, for example, who committed suicide at the outbreak of World War I because he didn't want to go back to a country at war. Erwin thought, "'but what if he didn't kill himself? What if someone killed him?' That's how one mystery started."

After she knows what the mystery is, Erwin focuses on character. "I have to know who the villain is and his motivation—and know the detective or protagonist and what her motivation is." When she's writing for a series, Erwin always outlines her novels because the series editor usually wants to see the outline. "When I'm just writing something on my own I don't tend to outline."

Tate's first mystery, *The Secret of Gumbo Grove*, wasn't carefully outlined. "I didn't know the exact ending until after I got there," Tate says, "but all along I had a vague idea that Raisin would get her answers. I didn't create a chapter-by-chapter outline until my wonderful editor, the late Jean Vestal, insisted. I had so many characters, involved in so many interlocking activities over several hundred years, that she was getting confused and so was I!"

The Minstrel's Melody, written for Pleasant Company's History Mysteries series, "was much more deliberately planned out and took me much less time," says Tate. "After I got my initial idea, I created a chapter-by-chapter outline, which continued to evolve as I wrote it."

Werlin, on the other hand, just steps off into the void. "I

usually know very little about either the story or the characters when I begin; I learn in the process of writing. For *Locked Inside,* I knew that the setting was a boarding school and that my protagonist was a rich girl, and that was all I knew as I began. The computer and the weird teacher and the Elf showed up in the first chapter, and one thing grew from another. I've learned to 'trust the process' to know that if I show up and write, I'll learn what I need to know to go on writing."

Get a Clue

Werlin rarely thinks about clues when she's writing. "I don't think I write 'puzzle-type' mysteries. I'm not even concerned about the reader figuring it out; my focus as I write is entirely on my character and his or her dilemma."

Tate had a similar experience writing *The Secret of Gumbo Grove.* "I didn't know it was a mystery, so I didn't knowingly drop clues. I tried to write the story as Raisin went along and I discovered the clues as she did."

With *The Minstrel's Melody,* however, clues were more important. "I got a lot of help from the editors who were attuned to formulating my clues," she says.

"In a way," explains Tate, "clues are like foreshadowing, and each *plant* is supposed to make the reader eagerly read on for more. It's easy to miss clues, but even the simplest ones can be the most important to the unraveling of the plot."

Kathleen Ernst, who's written several mysteries for the History Mysteries series, believes that the clues are an essential element of a mystery. It's important to "let the readers be the sleuth right along with the main character. You want the clues to be there so that in the end the reader says, 'Oh I should have seen that.' But if the reader figures it out before the end, then it's a disaster. So you have to try to strike that very fine line of putting the clues there, but making them subtle enough that the reader doesn't figure it out in advance."

For Ernst, that means burying the clue, presenting it in such a way that it seems like the information is being presented either to reveal something about character or to progress another kind of action. So the information is there, but because of the way it's presented "it doesn't stick out like the gun over the mantle."

Ernst finds that combining historical fiction and mystery makes things easier. "There has to be a reason why the mystery takes place in this point in time. If it could take place in another time, then there's no point in it being historical. So that helps narrow down ideas."

Whistler in the Dark takes place in a newspaper office in Colorado. "I read a lot about what the newspaper business was like on the frontier," says Ernst. "The reality of history gave me a lot of ideas for mysteries because it was a dangerous business. There was a lot of competition and editors trying to drive each other out of business. There was a lot there to work with."

Ernst finds that her historical research not only adds to the richness of the story, it also helps with clues. "To write an effective historical mystery you have to follow the rules of historical fiction in general—you must create a whole world. The historical fabric makes the story seem more real and it means your clues won't stick out."

Genre-Merger

For some, like Ernst, working with the historical fabric and the mystery makes the process more fun. But Tucker warns writers that combining a mystery with another genre, like history or fantasy, might make the writing more difficult. "The setting is not just the world you're familiar with, it's some other world that has to be set up. It's another layer to tackle."

"The genre-merge happens best when it's subtle," says Levithan. "If you're trying to sell a mystery, I don't think having another angle either helps or hurts. Utlimately, we're looking beyond the label to the book itself."

Not so elementary, dear Watson, but true. The key to publishing a mystery is to use all the fiction techniques in your arsenal to create the best literature you can write. Think less about genre and more about good fiction. The result will be a book that sells, both to the editors and the eventual audience—your young readers.

The Picture Book Biz

By Sue Bradford Edwards

Authors long to find and work with an editor. They soon discover the key is not only finding the right editor but also presenting themselves as writers who know the market in which their work must compete. Nowhere is this more true than for picture books, a diverse and rewarding market.

Distinguishing Qualities

A survey of existing picture books reveals an overwhelming variety from board books on shapes to picture storybooks set in every culture and time imaginable. This variety may suggest that anything goes, but nothing could be less true.

Editors want manuscripts with characteristics that will repeatedly draw in readers, because children like reading the same books over and over and because, at prices that range from around five dollars to nearly twenty, adults tend to purchase picture books that invite those multiple readings. The books are great readalouds, humorous, emotionally satisfying, and have outstanding characters.

Whether their audience is preliterate or early readers, picture books are meant to be read aloud. Great readalouds draw children in again and again. This happens because, even before children know the vocabulary of a picture book, they get drawn into the patter, pattern, and rhythm of language. Two outstanding readaloud tools are rhythm and rhyme—when the verse is modern and unique. Check out Lloyd Moss's *Zin, Zin, Zin.* An important readaloud tool is onomatopoeia. Children love sound words, the crazier the better, and quickly repeat the *Moo Baa La La La,* of Sandra Boynton.

Another great way to snare readers is with humor. This humor is often wackily excessive but should respect the audience. Children should be in on the joke, not the brunt of it, and the jokes shouldn't be sly or mean. Younger children especially love being in the know, laughing at stories that contradict how things work. Readers love the turkey that puts his clothes on wrong in Sandra Boynton's *Blue Hat, Green Hat*, for example. Humor for older readers is more sophisticated, thanks in large measure to Jon Scieszka and Lane Smith, who broke new ground with the recently re-issued *The Stinky Cheese Man and Other Fairly Stupid Tales*. Other humorous picture books by this innovative team include *Baloney, Henry P.*; *The Frog Prince, Continued*; and *The Math Curse*.

Readers are also drawn repeatedly into emotionally satisfying stories that incorporate universal themes. In *Daisy Comes Home*, Jan Brett tells the story of a hen who learns to stand up against bullies. This story resonates with small children, who often feel powerless and return eager to re-experience Daisy's victory.

When readers discover universal themes, they also discover characters they identify with and will want to visit again and again. Not all of these characters are children, but they do experience things familiar to their audience. In John Agee's *Milo's Hat Trick*, Milo is a magician who fails at magic to the dismay of the theater manager. Children who fear disappointing the adults in their lives identify with Milo and cheer him on as he searches for a solution.

Through the Ages

Appealing language, humor, themes that touch all readers, and sympathetic characters will produce manuscripts with the power to attract an audience repeatedly, but, first, marketing writers must know the different types of picture books and the age spans they target.

Board books, for ages six months to two years, tell a brief story or focus on basic ideas such as colors or sizes, trucks or flowers. These paperboard books are often created by author/illustrators. In addition to Boynton, successful board book creators include photographer Margaret Miller who has a series of Look Baby! Books. Many board books are adaptations of picture book texts, especially classics by authors such as Margaret Wise Brown, Eric Carle, or Maurice Sendak, or best-sellers. Be aware that this is a very hard market to crack. Many of the books are produced by packagers—companies that work for publishers to put together the art and text.

Concept books, for ages two to five, explore a basic concept such as telling time or the alphabet. Concept books may be board books, or they may be paperbacks or even hardcovers. Some authors combine a simple story with the concept, as does Christyan Fox in *Count to Ten Piggy Wiggy*. With so many concept books in existence, authors must be certain the way that they slant their idea is original.

Also for ages two to five is the **novelty book**. This book tells a story through gimmicks, such as pop-ups, lift-the-flaps, or die-cuts. The most famous, classic version is *Pat the Bunny*. A recent title, Mark Birchall's *Hen Goes Shopping*, incorporates both lift-the-flaps and pull-tabs.

What the Editors Say About Picture Books

Read what these four picture book editors have to say about the market for this perennially favorite genre:

◆ Stephanie Owens Lurie, Dutton Books, page 171.
◆ Deborah Halverson, Harcourt, Inc., page 221.
◆ Lisa Banim, Peachtree, page 327.
◆ Simon Boughton, Roaring Brook, The Millbrook Press, page 362.

The **true picture book** is also for ages two to five. Normally 32 pages long, the illustrations take up much of the page. Although excellent text is essential, the manuscript itself is generally limited to two to three pages in length. These books include:

♦ *Realistic Stories:* Explore everyday situations in a unique way, as in Phyllis Limbacher-Tildes's *Billy's Big-Boy Bed.* A wide variety of actions and scenes fuel illustrations.
♦ *Animal fantasies:* Substitute animals for children dealing with difficult situations in a believable manner. See

Rosemary Wells's Edward books. Be careful with animals in fiction, however. Some editors, especially at certain conservative religious publishers, don't want animals to be anthropomorphized. Other editors are tired of animal fiction. So be sure to do your market research if you have an animal story.

◆ *Mood pieces:* Portray the essence of an experience, transcending the ordinary to the truly poetic. These plotless manuscripts have a hard time holding reader interest. Difficult to sell, they must compete with classics like Jane Yolen's *Owl Moon.*

◆ *Retold tales:* These can be fairy tales, multicultural legends, animal fantasies. Avoid retellings of classics like *The Three Bears* unless you have an extremely unique slant (like *The Stinky Cheese Man*). Seek out previously overlooked tales.

More complex in characterization and plot are **picture storybooks** for ages five to eight, and sometimes older. They deal with more mature themes and interests and may be up to 48 pages in length, or four to eight manuscript pages. They also include:

◆ *Realistic Stories:* A wide range of stories with more depth and breadth than for younger readers, but still touching on universal themes.

◆ *Concept books:* Expanded to include nonfiction subjects that intrigue older children, such as Sylvia James's *Dolphins* or Ruth Heller's *Behind the Mask: A Book about Prepositions.*

◆ *Retold tales:* Concentrate on human, not animal, stories. See Lisa Campbell Ernst's *The Three Spinning Fairies.*

◆ *Original folktales:* Mimic traditional tales' form and language. Newcomers must compete against the well-established, like Jane Yolen's *Greyling.*

Once authors know what type of manuscript they have, they must find a home for it, choosing between large and small publishers.

Supersize It

Before choosing, authors should understand the differences between larger and smaller publishers. Most obvious is the number of imprints. Larger houses publish numerous imprints; Penguin Putnam alone has 11 juvenile imprints. Some imprints, such as Dutton Books, were once independent publishers and were acquired or merged with another company. Others, such as Phyllis Fogelman Books, were always imprints that originated within a company.

To avoid competition, each imprint seeks a different type of book. Of Penguin Putnam's imprints, six publish original picture books: Phyllis Fogelman, Dial, Dutton, G.P. Putnam's Sons, Philomel, and Viking. To understand the differences between Dutton's entertaining titles, Viking's innovative books, and the offerings of other imprints, authors must study the books themselves.

A smaller publisher may have only one or two imprints, and their specialties are usually easier to determine. Authors studying The Millbrook Press list can see that Roaring Brook concentrates on trade titles while the imprint called Millbrook is curriculum-oriented.

Acquisitions procedures also differ between larger and smaller publishers. While all publishers are profit-driven or they wouldn't be in business, larger publishers are often more so, and give individual editors less autonomy in acquisitions. These editors' choices are often taken "to committee," where marketing personnel decide if a manuscript is saleable. Emphasis on profit also means editors have less time to nurture new authors; manuscripts must arrive near-perfect to make the cut. Smaller publishers may put less emphasis on rapid profit, freeing editors to comment on a promising, but not yet publishable manuscript. New talent can be cultivated.

Payments and marketing budgets also differ. Larger advances are more likely from larger publishers, but they mean a book must earn more before paying for itself. Although the advertising budget of a big house is also larger, most of the budget is committed to a few choice books and others receive only catalogue listings. This can make it difficult to get a book to potential buyers and if the book doesn't quickly earn back its advance, it may be taken out of print. At smaller publishers, advances and advertising budgets are smaller, but books receive more individual attention. With a commitment to sell each title, there is more time for the book to earn back its advance.

These are not absolutes, but general truths. Some larger publishers have a small publisher's autonomy in acquisitions. Publishers also change over time, adding imprints or selling off divisions. And all publishers must profit from successful books.

Position That Book

All the genre and market study should work in the cover or query letter to position the manuscript to the editor the author wants to work with. *Positioning* may sound intimidating, but it is nothing more than showing the editor where a manuscript fits in among children's books today, and specifically, where it fits that publisher's catalogue.

Positioning a manuscript in the general market, the author shows the editor there is a market for the manuscript—that no similar titles are in print or existing titles do not compete because they are out-of-print or dated; aim at another age level; or are for a trade audience versus an educational audience.

Finally, authors should tell editors why they chose to submit to their companies. Perhaps the manuscript has something in common with titles already on their list—a theme, wry humor, or multicultural elements. This shows familiarity with this publisher's work.

Authors who shirk from placing this information in a few short lines in their cover letter or query are missing a critical chance to impress the editor. Editors, especially at larger publishers, must present this kind of information to the sales or marketing departments. Authors who help them do this and make the effort to be more professional, have already begun a working relationship with the editors they want to work with.

Listings

How to Use the Listings

On the following pages are over 500 profiles of publishers involved in the wide range of children's publishing. Over 40 publishers are new to the directory. These publishing houses produce a variety of material from parenting guides, textbooks, and classroom resources to picture books, photo essays, middle-grade novels, and biographies.

Each year we update every listing through mailed surveys and telephone interviews. While we verify everything in the listing before we go to press, it is not uncommon for information such as contact names, addresses, and editorial needs to change suddenly. Therefore, we suggest that you always read the publisher's most recent writers' guidelines before submitting a query letter or manuscript.

If you are unable to find a particular publisher, check the Publishers' Index beginning on page 577 to see if it is cited elsewhere in the book. We do not list presses that publish over 50% of their material by requiring writers to pay all or part of the cost of publishing. While we cannot endorse or vouch for the quality of every press we list, we do try to screen out publishers of questionable quality.

To help you judge a publisher's receptivity to unsolicited submissions, we include a Freelance Potential section in each listing. This is where we identify the number of titles published in 2002 that were written by unpublished writers, authors new to the publishing house, and agented authors. We also provide the total number of query letters and unsolicited manuscripts a publisher receives each year. When possible, we list the number of books published in 2002 by category (e.g. picture books, young adult novels).

Use this information and the other information included in the listing to locate publishers that are looking for the type of material you have written or plan to write. Become familiar with the style and content of the house by studying its catalogue and a few recent titles.

Legacy Press

☆ New Listing

P.O. Box 261129
San Diego, CA 92196

Editorial Director: Christy Scannell

Publisher's Interests
Launched in 1997, Legacy Press offers non-denominational, evangelical Christian books that are marketed primarily through Christian bookstores. Its catalogue features fiction and nonfiction for children between the ages of two and twelve, and all of its titles include activity ideas.
Website: www.rainbowpublishers.com

Freelance Potential
Published 7 titles in 2002: all were developed from unsolicited submissions. Of the 7 titles, 1 was by an author who was new to the publishing house. Receives 240 unsolicited mss each year.

- **Fiction:** Publishes books in series, 8–12 years. All titles include activities and devotionals.
- **Nonfiction:** Publishes middle-grade books, 8–12 years. Features activity books and how-to books, 8–12 years. Topics include crafts, hobbies, and religion.
- **Representative Titles:** *The Official Christian Babysitting Guide* (8–12 years) is a handbook for Christian pre-teens that offers ideas for keeping kids busy with Bible-based crafts, games, snacks, and songs and includes a free flashlight key chain. *The Un-Halloween Book* (parents and educators) is a reproducible book that features everything churches need to organize and direct an inspirational fall festival.

Submissions and Payment
Guidelines available with 9x12 SASE (2 first-class stamps). Send complete ms with table of contents and 3 sample chapters. Accepts photocopies. SASE. Responds in 3 months. Publication in 6–36 months. Royalty, 8%+; advance, $500.

Editor's Comments
At this time, we're primarily interested in nonfiction for children up to the age of 12. Books dealing with topics of interest to pre-teens, especially pre-teen girls, are needed. Remember that all of our titles include activities or additional components. Don't send anything on death, divorce, or abortion.

Who to Contact
Website Address
Categories of Current Titles
How to Submit

Profile of Publisher & Readership
Number of Unsolicited Submissions Published & Received
Recent Titles to Study
Editor's Current Needs & Tips for Writers

Icon Key

☆ New Listing   🖰 E-Publisher

⊗ Not currently accepting submissions

Abdo Publishing Company

Suite 622
4940 Viking Drive
Edina, MN 55435

Editor-in-Chief: Paul Abdo

Publisher's Interests
Abdo Publishing Company provides high-interest/low-reading-level books that range from early picture books through middle-grade titles. Its newest imprint, Buddy Books, publishes books for children in grades one through three. Abdo publishes nonfiction titles only, most of which appear as part of a series.
Website: www.abdopub.com

Freelance Potential
Published 225 titles in 2002: 1 was developed from an unsolicited submission. Of the 225 titles, 1 was by an unpublished writer and 3 were by authors who were new to the publishing house. Receives 120 queries yearly.
- **Nonfiction:** Published 50 early picture books, 0–4 years; 50 easy-to-read books, 4–7 years; 50 story picture books, 4–10 years; 50 chapter books, 5–10 years; and 25 middle-grade books, 8–12 years. Topics include travel, geography, animals, nature, science, social studies, sports, history, leisure, and multicultural and ethnic subjects. Also publishes reference books and biographies.
- **Representative Titles:** *Amelia Earhart* (grade 4) details the events in the life of this famous aviator; part of the Breaking Barriers series. *Heroes of the Day* (grade 5) looks at the September 11, 2001 terrorist attacks, focusing on the police, firefighters, and passengers aboard Flight 93; part of the War on Terrorism series.

Submissions and Payment
Query with résumé. No unsolicited mss. Accepts photocopies, computer printouts, and simultaneous submissions if identified. SASE. Responds in 2–4 months. Publication on October 1 of each year. Flat fee.

Editor's Comments
Send us your ideas for books we can add to our history, sports, or science series. These are the areas in which we have a particular interest for the coming year.

Absey and Company

23011 Northcrest Drive
Spring, TX 77389

Publisher: Edward E. Wilson

Publisher's Interests
Fictional picture books, story picture books, chapter books, and young adult novels can all be found in Absey and Company's catalogue. It also publishes educational nonfiction and language arts resource materials for educators.
Website: www.absey.com

Freelance Potential
Published 10 titles in 2002: all were developed from unsolicited submissions. Receives 1,000 queries yearly.
- **Fiction:** Published 1 early picture book, 0–4 years; 2 story picture books, 4–10 years; 2 chapter books, 5–10 years; and 2 young adult books, 12–18 years.
- **Nonfiction:** Publishes educational titles, 0–18 years. Features biographies and books about religion and history. Also offers educational activity books and poetry collections, as well as language arts resource titles for educators.
- **Representative Titles:** *Just People & Paper/Pen/Poem* by Kathi Appelt is a collection of poetry specifically selected for use with middle-grade and upper-aged readers, and includes suggestions by the author for young writers. *Where I'm From* by George Ella Lyon is a book about how to write poetry by an author of poetry collections and picture books.

Submissions and Payment
Guidelines available. Query with résumé, outline, and sample chapters. Accepts photocopies. No simultaneous submissions. SASE. Responds in 6–9 months. Publication in 1 year. Payment policy varies.

Editor's Comments
You do not need an agent to submit your proposal to us. In fact, we do not accept submissions from agents. Query us directly, and include a chapter-by-chapter outline, two or three sample chapters, and an information sheet that outlines your relevant qualifications and previous publishing experience. Our needs this year include young adult fiction and fiction for readers in the middle grades.

Advocacy Press

P.O. Box 236
Santa Barbara, CA 93102

Curriculum Specialist: Roxanne Brecek

Publisher's Interests
Established as the publishing arm of Girls Incorporated of
Greater Santa Barbara in 1983, Advocacy Press is dedicated
to promoting learning environments that help children and
young adults develop life skills and encourage realistic life
and career planning.
Website: www.advocacypress.com

Freelance Potential
Published 2 titles in 2002: both were assigned. Receives 500
unsolicited mss yearly.
- **Fiction:** Published 1 story picture book, 4–10 years; and 1
  young adult title, 12–18 years. Topics include family values,
  self-reliance, assertiveness, leadership, personal growth, sibling
  rivalry, competition, career planning, and emotions.
- **Nonfiction:** Publishes resource books, workbooks, programs,
  and videos for parents and educators. Topics include cultural
  diversity, adolescent development, personal relations, career
  planning, and parenting.
- **Representative Titles:** *Shadow and the Ready Time* by Patty
  Sheehan (4–12 years) uses wolf behavior to teach important
  lessons about family responsibilities. *Berta Benz and the Motor-
  wagen* by Mindy Bingham (5–12 years) is the inspiring and historically accurate story of a German housewife who made auto-
  mobile history in 1888 by driving the world's first long-distance
  road trip.

Submissions and Payment
Guidelines available with SASE or at website. Send complete
ms. Accepts photocopies. SASE. Responds in 1 month. Publication in 1 year. Royalty.

Editor's Comments
We seek material that provides children and young adults
with the skills they need to achieve success. We like to see
books that build character and self-esteem, emphasize positive values, stimulate personal growth, and encourage personal responsibility.

Africa World Press

Suite D
11 Princess Road
Lawrenceville, NJ 08648-2319

President & Publisher: Kassahun Checole

Publisher's Interests
Now in its twentieth year, Africa World Press features books
about African, African-American, Caribbean, and Latin-American issues. For children, it offers folktales, picture books,
and books that address social and cultural issues; for adults
it publishes non-mainstream academic texts, African literature and poetry, and literary criticism.
Website: www.africaworld.com

Freelance Potential
Published 120 titles in 2002: 1 was by an agented author.
Receives 500 queries yearly.
- **Fiction:** Publishes young adult novels, 12+ years. Features
  folktales.
- **Nonfiction:** Publishes books about African, Caribbean, and
  Latin American history, culture, and social issues. Also publishes educational and parenting titles.
- **Representative Titles:** *The Song of the Mandela: The Freedom
  to Be* by Jon Gadsby (3–8 years) is a picture book that tells
  how Nelson Mandela's memories of the freedom and enjoyment
  he experienced as a child sustained him during his long
  imprisonment. *The Confused Zebra* by Di Hood et al. (3–8
  years) features a little brown gnu who has a confusing conversation with a zebra.

Submissions and Payment
Query with outline/synopsis and sample chapter. No unsolicited mss. Accepts photocopies, computer printouts, and
simultaneous submissions if identified. SASE. Responds in 2
weeks. Publication in 6–12 months. Royalty; advance.

Editor's Comments
Please note that we do not accept complete manuscripts; if you
think your book is suitable for our publishing program, send
us a proposal that includes an outline or synopsis and a sample chapter. Children's books that focus on African, African-
American, Caribbean, and Latin-American themes will be welcome. We like to publish a number of new books each year.

Aladdin Paperbacks

Simon & Schuster Children's Publishing Division
4th Floor
1230 Avenue of the Americas
New York, NY 10020

Submissions Editor

Publisher's Interests
Aladdin is the paperback imprint of the Simon & Schuster
Children's Publishing Division. It features reprints of successful hardcover books from the Simon & Schuster
imprints, and from selective outside sources. Its list includes
young reader nonfiction, beginning readers, and middle-grade
and young adult series titles.
Website: www.simonsayskids.com

Freelance Potential
Published 150 titles in 2002: 15 were developed from unso-
licited submissions and 75 were by agented authors.
- **Fiction:** Publishes story picture books, 4–10 years; middle-
  grade novels, 8–12 years; and young adult novels, 12–18 years.
  Genres include historical and contemporary fiction, mystery,
  suspense, and adventure.
- **Nonfiction:** Publishes biographies and books about nature,
  science, and history.
- **Representative Titles:** *Alice in April* by Phyllis Reynolds
  Naylor (9–13 years) addresses the concerns of young readers
  as it humorously describes a girl who is about to become a
  teenager, with predictable and hilarious results. *Woodsong* by
  Gary Paulsen (10–14 years) is the inspiring autobiography of
  Iditarod racer Gary Paulsen.

Submissions and Payment
Guidelines available. Query with biography, outline/synopsis,
and writing sample. No unsolicited mss. SASE. Response
time, publication period, and payment policy vary.

Editor's Comments
If you decide to send us a query, be sure to include a brief
introduction of yourself, a plot summary or outline, and a
sample of your best writing. Because most of our titles are
reprints of our other hardcover books, we are not interested
in picture books. Send us your ideas for early chapter books,
mysteries for middle-grade readers, and series books for
young adults.

ALA Editions

American Library Association
50 East Huron Street
Chicago, IL 60611

Editorial Director: Patrick Hogan

Publisher's Interests

As the publishing division of the American Library Association, ALA Editions publishes books of interest to researchers and library professionals. In addition to programming books, bibliographic resources, and children's programming materials, it publishes science texts and reference books. ALA Editions produces approximately 40 new titles each year.
Website: www.ala.org/editions

Freelance Potential

Published 35 titles in 2002: 3 were developed from unsolicited submissions. Of the 25 titles, 12 were by authors who were new to the publishing house. Receives 50 queries yearly.
- **Nonfiction:** Publishes textbooks, resource materials, and reference books for librarians and educators. Also offers children's library programming materials.
- **Representative Titles:** *Teens.library* by Linda W. Braun (librarians) helps young adult specialists, youth services librarians, and school library media specialists get teens to think of the library as *the* place to be. *Teaching Banned Books: 12 Guides for Young Readers* by Pat R. Scales provides an overview of 12 books that are frequently challenged and kept out of many school libraries and tells how to teach them while respecting all views.

Submissions and Payment

Guidelines available at website. Query with outline/synopsis. SASE. Responds in 2–8 weeks. Publication in 7–9 months from completion of manuscript. Royalty.

Editor's Comments

We suggest that writers who are interested in submitting their work to us review the guidelines and catalogue that are available at our website. Most of our books are developed from proposals by professionals in the library and information services field. We're always interested in original ideas and new approaches to the challenges faced by today's librarians—send us something distinctive.

Alef Design Group

4423 Fruitland Avenue
Los Angeles, CA 90058

Submissions Editor: Jane Golub

Publisher's Interests

Parenting books, books on education, and books about religion—all as they relate to Judaism and the Jewish faith—are found on this publisher's list. Most of its children's books target middle-grade and young adult readers.
Website: www.torahaura.com

Freelance Potential

Plans to resume publishing (1 or more titles) in 2003. Receives 36 queries, 36 unsolicited mss yearly.

- **Fiction:** Publishes story picture books, 4–10 years; and chapter books, 5–10 years. Features religious fiction with Jewish themes.
- **Nonfiction:** Publishes chapter books, 8–10 years; middle-grade books, 8–12 years; and young adult books, 12–18 years. Topics include religious issues and parenting as related to Judaism and Jewish life.
- **Representative Titles:** *The Swastika on the Synagogue Door* by J. Leonard Romm (10–14 years) follows a group of contemporary teens who learn from a vandal's attack on their synagogue. *Teens & Trust* by Rabbi Steven Bayar & Fran Hirschman (parents) is based on practical experience and seeks to help anyone who works with teens.

Submissions and Payment

Prefers query with sample chapters. Accepts complete ms. Accepts photocopies and computer printouts. SASE. Responds to queries in 1–2 weeks, to mss in 3–6 months. Publication in 1–2 years. Royalty, 5–10%.

Editor's Comments

Everything we publish deals with issues examined from a Jewish perspective. We welcome submissions of both fiction and nonfiction for middle-grade and young adult readers. Books that relate to education and parenting are also of interest to us, if written by qualified individuals. We strongly urge prospective authors to carefully review our guidelines and catalogue before submitting.

All About Kids Publishing

Suite C
6280 San Ignacio Avenue
San Jose, CA 95119

Editor: Linda L. Guevara

Publisher's Interests
Each year, All About Kids Publishing develops a number of picture books for children between the ages of two and ten. It also offers toddler books, chapter books, and middle-grade books. It accepts both fiction and nonfiction.
Website: www.aakp.com

Freelance Potential
Published 13 titles (9 juvenile) in 2002: all were developed from unsolicited submissions. Of the 13 titles, all were by authors who were new to the publishing house. Receives 7,500 unsolicited mss yearly.
- **Fiction:** Published 9 story picture books, 4–10 years. Also publishes toddler books, 0–4 years; and chapter books, 5–10 years. Genres include multicultural and inspirational fiction; adventure; fantasy; humor; animal books; and alphabet books.
- **Nonfiction:** Publishes story picture books, 2–10 years. Topics include animals, crafts, history, nature, the environment, mathematics, and science. Also publishes cookbooks.
- **Representative Titles:** *The Moon Smiles Down* by Tony Waters (2–8 years) depicts the moon as it watches over creatures big and small while they prepare for the evening. *My Name Is Andrew* by Mary May Burke (4–10 years) is an alphabet book that takes readers on a crazy caper with 26 boys and girls, one for each letter of the alphabet.

Submissions and Payment
Guidelines available with SASE or at website. Send complete ms with résumé. No queries. Requests digital file with acceptance. SASE. Responds in 2–3 months. Publication in 30 months. Royalty, 3–5%; advance, varies.

Editor's Comments
We're looking for fiction that will uplift the reader, whatever the genre. For nonfiction, we're primarily interested in how-to books, educational books, and cookbooks. We don't accept queries; you must send the full manuscript along with information on your personal or professional background.

Amsco School Publications

315 Hudson Street
New York, NY 10013-1085

President: Henry Brun

Publisher's Interests
Amsco School Publications has been providing high-quality,
inexpensive textbooks and supplementary educational materials to high schools for more than 65 years. Its titles cover
the major curriculum areas, such as language arts, social
studies, foreign languages, mathematics, and science. Many
of its titles are written by educators.
Website: www.amscopub.com

Freelance Potential
Published 10–15 titles in 2002: 1 was developed from an
unsolicited submission. Receives 60 queries yearly.
- **Nonfiction:** Publishes educational textbooks, workbooks, and
  teachers' guides. Topics include mathematics, chemistry, earth
  science, economics, history, geography, reading, composition,
  literature, health, and psychology.
- **Representative Titles:** *Civics for Today: Participation and Citizenship* by Steven C. Wolfson (grades 9–12) is designed to help
  students understand how government works at the national,
  state, and local levels and emphasizes the importance of participation in civic life. *A Quick Reference to Grammar* by Sharon
  Sorenson (grades 9–12) is an easy-to-use reference book that
  provides students with the tools they need to put grammar into
  practice in academic and practical settings.

Submissions and Payment
Guidelines available. Query with résumé, outline, prospectus,
and sample chapters with activities. Accepts photocopies,
computer printouts, and simultaneous submissions if identified. Availability of artwork improves chance of acceptance.
SASE. Responds in 1 month. Publication in 18–24 months.
Royalty.

Editor's Comments
Please keep in mind that many of the titles we publish are by
experienced teachers. If you have an innovative idea for a sec-
ondary-school classroom text, contact us. We especially need
foreign language texts.

Anchorage Press Plays, Inc.

P.O. Box 2901
Louisville, KY 40201

Publisher: Marilee Miller

Publisher's Interests
Anchorage Press publishes dramatic, musical, and humorous plays for children and youth in preschool through high school. Its catalogue also features books on theater education and production.
Website: www.applays.com

Freelance Potential
Published 6–8 titles in 2002: 2 were by unpublished writers and 3 were by authors who were new to the publishing house. Receives 800+ unsolicited mss yearly.
- **Fiction:** Publishes plays and musicals for grades K–12. Genres include fantasy, fable, history, and adventure. Also features plays with journey and self-discovery themes.
- **Nonfiction:** Publishes books for educators. Topics include theater production, dramatic literature, theater history, costume, stage props, and make-up,
- **Representative Titles:** *Paper Lanterns, Paper Cranes* by Brian Kral is a powerful drama about the impact of war and nuclear fallout on the children of Japan. *The Invisible People* by William Lavender is a musical adventure into the world of General Grumpdump and his weasly sidekick, Wince.

Submissions and Payment
Guidelines available at website. Send complete ms with proof of production in three different locations. Query with outline for nonfiction. Accepts photocopies. SASE. Responds in 3–6 months. Publication period varies. Royalty, 50–75% for plays.

Editor's Comments
We are looking for material that is appropriate in subject, theme, and language for juvenile and young adult audiences. Send us your plays about contemporary youth issues, newfound maturity skills, or teenage self-discovery. All submissions must include proof of production. Please remember that adaptations of favorite books require proof of authorization to create a dramatic adaptation and permission to submit for publication.

Annick Press

15 Patricia Avenue
Toronto, Ontario M2M 1H9
Canada

The Editors

Publisher's Interests
This Canadian publisher offers both fiction and nonfiction for middle-grade and young adult readers. While picture books do appear in its catalogue, it is no longer accepting picture book manuscripts.
Website: www.annickpress.com

Freelance Potential
Published 10 titles in 2002.
- **Fiction:** Publishes middle-grade books, 8–11 years; and young adult books, 12–18 years. Genres include contemporary fiction and humor.
- **Nonfiction:** Publishes middle-grade books, 8–11 years; and young adult books, 12–18 years.
- **Representative Titles:** *The Mess* by Jennifer Wolfe (5–8 years) is a novelty book where readers help write the story of a family that is too messy. *The Witch in the Lake* by Anna Fienberg (10–14 years) is a story about challenging one's fears that is set in a sixteenth-century Italian village with many secrets, including a town witch.

Submissions and Payment
Guidelines available. Query with synopsis and sample chapter. Accepts photocopies and computer printouts. SAE/IRC. Response time, publication period, and payment policy vary.

Editor's Comments
Please note that we are not accepting picture book submissions at this time. What we are interested in are books for teens and middle-grade readers. We look for teen novels that possess a high degree of originality and capture strong, contemporary voices. The reader must be able to see the real teen experience reflected through the story line. For middle-grade readers, we want to see manuscripts that will engage the reader's interest with vivid settings and characters that really come to life. Humor is always a plus. We will review submissions that include a synopsis and sample chapter. Please don't send completed manuscripts.

Arnold Publishing

11016 127th Street
Edmonton, Alberta T5M 0T2
Canada

President: Phyllis A. Arnold

Publisher's Interests
Since 1967, this educational publisher has provided students
and teachers in grades three through twelve with curriculum-
based textbooks and educational resources. 10% self-,
subsidy-, co-venture, or co-op published material.
Website: www.arnold.ca

Freelance Potential
Published 12 titles (10 juvenile) in 2002: 4 were by unpublished writers and 2 were by authors who were new to the
publishing house. Receives 20 queries yearly.
- **Nonfiction:** Publishes middle-grade books, 8–12 years; and
  young adult books, 12–18 years. Topics include Canadian and
  international history, social studies, and geography. Also publishes resource materials and textbooks for teachers.
- **Representative Titles:** *Canada Revisited* by Phyllis A. Arnold
  (grade 6) highlights the historical context of current Canadian
  issues and applies history concepts through a variety of disci-
  plines. *A Geography of Canada and the United States* by Tony
  Burley & Jim Latimer helps students understand the relationship of geography to patterns of life in Canada and the US.

Submissions and Payment
Guidelines available at website. Query with outline and market information. No unsolicited mss. Accepts photocopies and
computer printouts. SAE/IRC. Responds in 8 weeks. Publication period varies. Royalty, 10%.

Editor's Comments
This year, we continue to seek submissions of social studies
textbooks that incorporate relevant personal planning and
organizational strategies within a historical context. New writers are encouraged to submit material for sixth-grade classroom use. We prefer highly visual presentations that appeal
to students. Chapter overviews and summaries should be
included to provide useful direction for reading and study, as
well as maps, charts, photos, and diagrams to promote
inquiry-based active learning.

Atheneum Books for Young Readers

1230 Avenue of the Americas
New York, NY 10020

Executive Editor: Caitlyn Dlouhy

Publisher's Interests
Toddlers through teenagers read the fiction and nonfiction published by this division of Simon & Schuster. It offers hardcover picture books, chapter books, and biographies.
Website: www.simonsayskids.com

Freelance Potential
Published 80 titles in 2002: 5 were developed from unsolicited submissions, 19 were by agented authors, and 8 were reprint/licensed properties. Of the 80 titles, 4 were by unpublished writers and 10 were by authors who were new to the publishing house. Receives 20,000 queries yearly.

- **Fiction:** Publishes concept books and early picture books, 0–4 years; story picture books, 4–10 years; middle-grade novels, 8–12 years; and young adult novels, 12–18 years. Genres include historical and science fiction; mystery; fantasy; and adventure. Also publishes poetry.
- **Nonfiction:** Publishes story picture books, 4–10 years; chapter books, 5–10 years; middle-grade books, 8–12 years; and young adult books, 12–18 years. Topics include science, nature, the environment, history, sports, and multicultural issues. Also publishes biographies.
- **Representative Titles:** *Wenny Has Wings* by Janet Lee Carey (8–12 years) is a novel about a boy whose sister is killed in a car accident. *The Secret of the Great Houdini* by Robert Burleigh (7–10 years) is an illustrated book about the life of the great magician.

Submissions and Payment
Guidelines available. Query for nonfiction. Send 3 sample chapters with summary for fiction. Accepts photocopies and computer printouts. SASE. Responds in 3 months. Publication period varies. Royalty.

Editor's Comments
Our editors are more interested in well-crafted books than in books that have a gimmick or follow a trend or fad. We'll consider books of all styles and on almost any subject.

Augsburg Books

Augsburg Fortress Publishers
P.O. Box 1209
Minneapolis, MN 55440

Editorial Assistant, Augsburg Books

Publisher's Interests
Fiction and nonfiction children's books that reflect Christian faith and traditions are available from Augsburg Books. The official publisher of the Evangelical Lutheran Church in America, it also offers books for adults about spiritual life, healing, and grief.
Website: www.augsburgfortress.org

Freelance Potential
Published 40 titles in 2002: 1 was developed from an unsolicited submission and 5 were by agented authors. Receives 2,500 queries yearly.
- **Fiction:** Publishes early picture books, 0–4 years; easy-to-read books, 4–7 years; story picture books, 4–10 years; and middle-grade books, 8–12 years. Genres include religious and inspirational fiction.
- **Nonfiction:** Publishes concept books and toddler books, 0–4 years; and story picture books, 4–10 years. Also publishes activity books, devotionals, and educational materials. Topics include Lutheranism, family life, spirituality, prayer, parenting, and Christian education.
- **Representative Titles:** *Tess's Touchstone* by Gina Linko (grades 6–8) is a novel about a girl who faces the possibility of the death of her grandmother; part of The Seekers series. *Christopher Bear's First Christmas* by Stephanie Jeffs (3–5 years) revolves around a preschool Christmas pageant.

Submissions and Payment
Catalogue and guidelines available at website. Query with résumé, outline, and synopsis. Accepts photocopies, computer printouts, and simultaneous submissions if identified. SASE. Responds in 1–3 months. Publication in 2–3 years. Royalty, 5–10% of gross.

Editor's Comments
Well-written story collections, interactive picture books, and activity books that celebrate the human experience will always get a second look from our editors.

A/V Concepts Corporation

30 Montauk Boulevard
Oakdale, NY 11769

Editor-in-Chief: Laura Solimene

Publisher's Interests
A/V Concepts Corporation is part of the EDCON Publishing
Group. It specializes in educational software designed to help
students improve their vocabulary and reading skills. Its catalogue features original stories along with classic novels
designed to meet the needs of hi/lo students.
Website: www.edconpublishing.com

Freelance Potential
Published 12 titles in 2002. Of the 12 titles, 6 were by
unpublished writers and 3 were by authors who were new to
the publishing house. Receives 300 queries, 200 unsolicited
mss yearly.
- **Fiction:** Publishes middle-grade books, 8–12 years; and young
  adult books, 12–18 years. Genres include fantasy, adventure,
  science fiction, and horror. Also publishes biographies and stories about nature.
- **Representative Titles:** *Hound of the Baskervilles* (grade 5
  reading level) is an easy-reading adaptation for struggling readers. *The Call of the Wild* (grade 2 reading level) is a 10-chapter
  hi/lo adaptation of this classic story.

Submissions and Payment
Guidelines and catalogue available with 9x12 SASE ($.37
postage). All work is assigned. Submissions are not returned.
Responds in 3–6 weeks. Flat fee.

Editor's Comments
Most of our writers have a background in education and are
familiar with the needs of hi/lo students of all ages. We welcome both original stories as well as retellings of famous
classics. Keep in mind that all of our books are written on
assignment. We do not accept unsolicited manuscripts. Send
us a résumé that demonstrates your ability to meet our publishing needs, along with some writing samples or published
clips. If we have a project that we feel is right for you, we will
contact you. We will make every effort to get back to you within
six weeks.

Avisson Press

3007 Taliaferro Road
Greensboro, NC 27408

Editor: M. L. Hester

Publisher's Interests
This small publishing house features a nonfiction list of
books for young adults. Its titles deal with multicultural
and historical issues. Biographies are also a large part of
its publishing program.

Freelance Potential
Published 6 titles (5 juvenile) in 2002. Receives 500 queries
each year.
- **Nonfiction:** Publishes young adult books, 12–18 years. Topics
  include history and multicultural and ethnic subjects. Also
  publishes biographies.
- **Representative Titles:** *Go, Girl!* by Jacqueline Robb (YA) exam-
  ines the lives of young women superstars of popular music.
  Elusive Glory by John Robert Bruning, Jr. (YA) looks at the
  African-American heroes of World War II.

Submissions and Payment
Query with outline, author biography, and writing samples.
Accepts photocopies, computer printouts, and simultaneous
submissions if identified. SASE. Responds in 2 weeks. Publication in 12 months. Royalty, 8–10%.

Editor's Comments
We are always interested in hearing from writers who are
familiar with our books. Our primary need continues to be
books that will fit into our young adult biography series. If you
are not familiar with these books, it's a good idea to review a
recent catalogue so you know what we have covered and where
our interests lie. In general, we welcome queries on notable
individuals from all walks of life. Specifically, we would like to
see more in the way of ideas for biographies of African Americans. Your book should be suitable for readers between the
ages of twelve and eighteen years of age, and be between
12,000 and 14,000 words in length. Send us a fresh idea:
someone who has made significant achievements in his or her
field and who will spark the interest of young readers.

Avon Books

HarperCollins Paperbacks
1350 Avenue of the Americas
New York, NY 10019

Submissions Editor

Publisher's Interests
A division of HarperCollins Paperbacks, Avon publishes fiction and nonfiction titles for middle-grade and young adult readers. It specializes in contemporary topics of interest to children and teens.
Website: www.harperchildrens.com

Freelance Potential
Published 300 titles in 2002: most were by agented authors and many were reprint/licensed properties. Receives 1,500 queries yearly.
- **Fiction:** Publishes chapter books, 7–10 years; middle-grade novels, 8–12 years; and young adult novels, 12–18 years. Genres include historical fiction, adventure, fantasy, and mystery. Also publishes stories about social issues, sports, romance, and family relationships.
- **Nonfiction:** Publishes middle-grade books, 8–12 years; and young adult books, 12–18 years. Topics include history, sports, education, peer pressure, social issues, computers, and popular culture.
- **Representative Titles:** *Going for the Gold: Sarah Hughes* by R. S. Ashby follows the dreams of a Long Island teenager to win the Olympic gold medal. *Initiation* by Isobel Bird follows three teenage witches as they celebrate their Wiccan initiation and face unexpected choices; part of the Circle of Three series.

Submissions and Payment
Guidelines available. Query with résumé, outline/synopsis, and sample chapters. Accepts photocopies, computer printouts, and simultaneous submissions if identified. SASE. Responds in 2–4 months. Publication in 3 years. Royalty; advance. Flat fee.

Editor's Comments
We offer popular fiction to an audience of young teen readers. Although many of the titles submitted to us come from agents, we will consider unagented submissions as well. We like to see fresh material by new authors.

Baker's Plays

P.O. Box 699222
Quincy, MA 02269-9222

Managing Director: Kurt Gombar

Publisher's Interests
Baker's Plays caters to high school, university, community, family, regional, and children's theaters with its full-length and one-act plays, musicals, and drama-related texts. Its catalogue also includes sound-effect and dialect tapes, anthologies, and audition materials.
Website: www.bakersplays.com

Freelance Potential
Published 30 titles (12 juvenile) in 2002: 2 were by agented authors and 5 were reprint/licensed properties. Of the 30 titles, 10 were by unpublished writers and 12 were by authors who were new to the publishing house. Receives 50–75 queries, 300+ unsolicited mss yearly.
- **Fiction:** Publishes plays for family, high school, and children's theater groups. Genres include comedy, mystery, folktales, fairy tales. Also offers holiday plays, classics, and musicals. Religious plays are produced under a separate division.
- **Nonfiction:** Publishes theater texts.
- **Representative Titles:** *Adventures of Ben Boy, Ben Dog, and Ben Cat* by Ray Hamby (5–9 years) is a collection of 10 short, whimsical plays that follow the adventures of a boy named Ben. *The Everyday Adventures of Harriet Handelman (Super Genius)* by Greg Atkins is a play about a girl who is called upon to "save the world" when a mysterious figure steals her classmate's science project.

Submissions and Payment
Guidelines available. Query with script history, reviews, and sample pages or synopsis; or send ms. Accepts photocopies, laser-quality printouts, and simultaneous submissions if identified. SASE. Responds to queries in 1 month, to mss in 3–4 months. Publication period and payment policy vary.

Editor's Comments
We continue to look for plays for young adults that deal with contemporary issues. We prefer to review plays that have had a staged reading, workshop reading, or full production.

Bantam Doubleday Dell

1540 Broadway
New York, NY 10036

Editor

Publisher's Interests

This well-known publisher features fiction and nonfiction for readers of all ages, from preschool to young adult. It accepts queries from agented authors only, but two annual contests that it sponsors are open to all writers. The Marguerite de Angeli Prize is awarded for a middle-grade book, and the Delacorte Press Prize goes to a young adult novel.
Website: www.randomhouse.com

Freelance Potential

Published 300 titles in 2002: 270 were by agented authors and 90 were reprint/licensed properties. Of the 300 titles, some were by unpublished writers. Receives 2,000 queries each year.

- **Fiction:** Publishes early picture books, 0–4 years; easy-to-read books, 4–7 years; story picture books, 4–10 years; chapter books, 5–10 years; middle-grade books, 8–12 years; and young adult books, 12–18 years.
- **Nonfiction:** Publishes young adult books, 12–18 years.
- **Representative Titles:** *The Making of a Writer* by Joan Lowery Nixon (10+ years) shares the author's advice along with memoirs of her writing career. *It Was You, Blue Kangaroo!* by Emma Chichester Clark (2–5 years) is the story of Lily and her kangaroo and how they get into trouble with Lily's mother.

Submissions and Payment

Submit queries through agents only. New writers may submit middle-grade novels for the Marguerite de Angeli Prize, and young adult novels for the Delacorte Press Prize. See the Contests and Awards section of this directory. No simultaneous submissions. SASE. Response time varies. Publication in 2 years. Royalty; advance.

Editor's Comments

Keep in mind that we only review queries from authors with agents, and submissions made to one of our contests. At this time, we are not reviewing picture books for the First Choice Chapter series.

Beach Holme Publishing

226-2040 West 12th Avenue
Vancouver, British Columbia V6J 2G2
Canada

Publisher: Michael Carroll

Publisher's Interests
This Canadian publisher recently celebrated its 30th anniversary. Beach Holme Publishing and its imprints, Porcepic Books, Sandcastle Books, and Prospect Books, offer historical novels, poetry, and fiction for readers ages six and up. Many of its titles focus on Canadian themes and are written by Canadian authors.
Website: www.beachholme.bc.ca

Freelance Potential
Published 5 titles in 2002: 1 was developed from an unsolicited submission. Of the 5 titles, 2 were by authors who were new to the publishing house. Receives 400 queries each year.
- **Fiction:** Published 5 middle-grade books, 8–13 years. Also publishes young adult novels, 12–18 years. Genres include historical, contemporary, and multicultural fiction and mysteries—many with Canadian themes.
- **Representative Titles:** *Ghosts of James Bay* by John Wilson (8–13 years) describes a young boy's trip through time to the seventeenth century when explorer Henry Hudson was cast adrift by his mutinous crew. *Tiger in Trouble* by Eric Walters (8–13 years) tells of a brother's and sister's adventures with exotic animals.

Submissions and Payment
Guidelines available. Query with 3 sample chapters, market analysis, and description of intended audience. Accepts photocopies and computer printouts. SAE/IRC. Responds in 4–6 months. Publication in 1 year. Royalty; advance.

Editor's Comments
We select books for publication based on originality, plot development, dialogue and narrative, genre technique, and thematic cohesion. Most of the manuscripts we accept have some historical or regional significance and are set in Canada. Historical fiction for middle-grade readers is especially welcome. Include teachers' guides and resources if possible.

Behrman House

11 Edison Place
Springfield, NJ 07081

Acquisitions Editor

Publisher's Interests
Jewish children in elementary schools and secondary schools use the educational materials from Behrman House. Its titles cover Jewish faith, history, ethics, and holidays, and include Jewish textbooks, teaching guides, teacher resources, and books with family education components.
Website: www.behrmanhouse.com

Freelance Potential
Published 7 titles in 2002: all were developed from unsolicited submissions. Receives 250 queries, 250 unsolicited mss each year.
- **Nonfiction:** Published 5 chapter books, 5–10 years; and 2 middle-grade titles, 8–12 years. Also publishes young adult books, 12–18 years. Topics include Judaism, religion, theology, prayer, holidays, the Bible, the Holocaust, history, liturgy, Hebrew, and ethics. Also offers educational resource materials and religious instructional materials for adults.
- **Representative Titles:** *Making a Difference* by Bradley Shavit Artson & Gila Gevirtz (grades 7–9) discusses both ethical and ritual mitzvot along with practical and creative suggestions on how to observe them. *The Book of Jewish Holidays* by Ruth Lurie Kozodoy (grades 4–5) covers the feasts, fasts, and festivals that mark the Jewish year and presents information on modern customs.

Submissions and Payment
Prefers query with table of contents and sample chapter. Will accept complete ms with résumé and author biography. Accepts photocopies, computer printouts, and simultaneous submissions if identified. SASE. Responds in 2 months. Publication in 18 months. Royalty, 5–10%; advance, $1,500. Flat fee, to $5,000.

Editor's Comments
We're looking for books that will inspire children and welcome them into our tradition; we want them to appreciate its magnificence and majesty and seize it as their own.

Benchmark Books

Marshall Cavendish
99 White Plains Road
Tarrytown, NY 10591

Editorial Director: Kate Nunn

Publisher's Interests

Benchmark Books is dedicated to publishing curriculum-related nonfiction titles for students in kindergarten through twelfth grade. An imprint of Marshall Cavendish, it publishes all of its books in series that cover subjects such as math, science, social studies, and world cultures. It does not accept fiction submissions.

Website: www.marshallcavendish.com

Freelance Potential

Published 140 titles in 2002.

- **Nonfiction:** Publishes chapter books, 5–10 years; and middle-grade books, 8–12 years. Topics include mathematics, science, animals, social studies, history, and world cultures.
- **Representative Titles:** *Women in 19th Century America* (grades 3 and up) explores the role of women in this historical era, includes a biography section about women who sought to change the accepted ways of society, and includes a time chart of women's campaigns; part of The Other Half of History series. *Paranormal Powers* by Gary Blackwood (grades 5 and up) brings the world of the paranormal to young readers; part of the Secrets of the Unexplained series.

Submissions and Payment

Query with 1–3 chapters and table of contents. Accepts photocopies and computer printouts. SASE. Responds in 6–8 weeks. Publication in 9–18 months. Payment policy varies.

Editor's Comments

We are not accepting children's fiction at this time. We are only interested in nonfiction books that relate to the kindergarten through twelfth-grade curricula. Virtually all our books are published as parts of series, so proposals that target our existing series are more likely to be accepted. Review our catalogue and you'll get a feel for the type of material we need. If you have a unique idea for a new nonfiction series, we suggest that you contact Judith Whipple at our sister imprint, Cavendish Children's Books.

The Benefactory

P.O. Box 128
Cohasset, MA 02025

Creative Director: Cynthia Germain

Publisher's Interests
The Benefactory publishes children's books with companion audiotapes, toys, and video cassettes for children ages seven to nine. It holds licenses with a number of non-profit animal protection groups, and each book is based on the true story of a real animal.
Website: www.readplay.com

Freelance Potential
Published 12 titles in 2002: Of the 12 titles, 6 were by unpublished writers. Receives 200 queries yearly.
- **Nonfiction:** Publishes story picture books, 4–10 years. Topics include nature, wildlife, the environment, farm life, and animals. Also publishes teacher resources and educational activity books.
- **Representative Titles:** *Condor Magic* by Lyn Littlefield Hoopes (6-10 years) is a lyrical rhyming tale that tells the true story of the near-extinction of the California condor. *Bentley and Blueberry* by Randy Houk (5–8 years) teaches children how to train a new pet with patience and kindness.

Submissions and Payment
Guidelines available. Most work is assigned. Query only. No unsolicited mss. SASE. Responds in 6–8 weeks. Publication in 2 years. Royalty; advance on royalty, 5%.

Editor's Comments
Our mission is to produce and distribute top-quality products that entertain and educate while meeting our objectives—to foster animal protection and environmental preservation, to teach literacy and motivate reading, to encourage children to become creative proactive individuals, to teach core values and augment a child's sense of self-esteem, and to encourage community linkages. To further our purpose, we give a percentage of all book proceeds to non-profit groups with aligned missions. Query us with your true stories about real, living animals that will appeal to children, parents, and teachers.

The Bess Press

3565 Harding Avenue
Honolulu, HI 96816

Editor: Revé Shapard

Publisher's Interests
The Bess Press publishes books about Hawaii and the Pacific Islands. Its list includes elementary, intermediate, and high school textbooks. It also publishes coloring, activity, and board books that focus solely on Hawaii.
Website: www.besspress.com

Freelance Potential
Published 5 titles in 2002: 4 were developed from unsolicited submissions. Of the 5 titles, 2 were by unpublished writers and 2 were by authors who were new to the publishing house. Receives 100 unsolicited mss yearly.
- **Fiction:** Publishes early picture books, 0–4 years; and story picture books, 4–10 years.
- **Nonfiction:** Published 1 story picture book, 4–10 years; 1 middle-grade book, 8–12 years; and 1 young adult book, 12–18 years. Also publishes coloring books, board books, and activity books. Topics include Pacific studies, language, geography, nature, wildlife, and literature.
- **Representative Titles:** *From the Mountains to the Sea: Early Hawaiian Life* by Julie Stewart Williams describes the life, activities, and natural environment of the Hawaiian Islands before Western contact. *The Surfrider: A Midwestern Odyssey* by Thomas Paul Rogo is the story of a young farm boy from Illinois who sets out to fulfill his dream to learn how to surf.

Submissions and Payment
Guidelines available. Send complete ms. Accepts photocopies, computer printouts, and simultaneous submissions if identified. SASE. Responds in 4–6 weeks. Publication in 6–12 months. Royalty, 5–10%.

Editor's Comments
This year, we're particularly interested in developing a new emergent reader series that has a Hawaiian focus. We are also interested in revisions of existing textbooks. Please remember that we only consider fiction, board books, and coloring books that have a distinct Hawaiian theme.

Bethany House Publishers

11400 Hampshire Avenue South
Minneapolis, MN 55438

Submissions Editor

Publisher's Interests
Established more than 40 years ago, this evangelical Christian publishing company offers fiction and nonfiction books for children and adults.
Website: www.bethanyhouse.com

Freelance Potential
Published 52 titles (51 juvenile) in 2002: 42 were by agented authors. Receives 50–75 queries yearly.
- **Fiction:** Published 6 easy-to-read books, 4–7 years; 1 story picture book, 4–10 years; 4 chapter books, 5–10 years; 19 middle-grade novels, 8–12 years; and 11 young adult novels, 12–18 years. Genres include contemporary, inspirational, and historical fiction; mystery; and suspense. Also publishes adventure stories.
- **Nonfiction:** Published 1 concept book and 1 early picture book, 0–4 years; 2 middle-grade books, 8–12 years; and 3 young adult books, 12–18 years. Topics include contemporary issues, spirituality, theology, family, and social issues. Also publishes devotionals, curriculum guides, and educational resources.
- **Representative Titles:** *The Super-Duper Blooper* by Robert Elmer (7–11 years) is the story of a futuristic kid who learns that compromising friends often leads to disaster; part of the AstroKids series. *Get Smart* by Kevin Johnson (11–14 years) includes Bible studies to help answer basic questions with upbeat information that early teens can relate to.

Submissions and Payment
Guidelines available at website. Query appropriate editor by sending fax to 952-996-1304. Not currently accepting unsolicited submissions. Responds in 4–6 weeks. Publication period varies. Royalty; advance.

Editor's Comments
We are not actively seeking juvenile or young adult fiction. Nonfiction for all ages is a priority at this time. We would like to see material that sends a biblical message to readers, and helps them apply Christian principles to their lives.

Beyond Words Publishing

Suite 500
20827 NW Cornell Road
Hillsboro, OR 97124-9808

Managing Editor: Barbara Mann

Publisher's Interests

Inspirational books for very young children through young adults appear on the list of Beyond Words Publishing. Its goal is to help young readers achieve their dreams. It specializes in picture books and nonfiction. Books by young authors are also accepted.

Website: www.beyondword.com

Freelance Potential

Published 7 titles in 2002: 3 were developed from unsolicited submissions and 3 were by agented authors. Of the 7 titles, all were by authors who were new to the publishing house. Receives 3,000 unsolicited mss yearly.

- **Fiction:** Published 1 early picture book, 0–4 years. Also publishes story picture books, 4–10 years. Genres include fairy tales, folktales, stories about nature, and multicultural fiction.
- **Nonfiction:** Published 1 story picture book, 4–10 years; and 2 young adult books, 12–18 years. Also publishes middle-grade titles, 8–15 years, as well as middle-grade books written by young authors.
- **Representative Titles:** *Coyote Stories for Children* by Susan Strauss (6–10 years) offers a series of four stories that show the creative and foolish nature of this popular animal trickster. *The Book of Fairies* by Rose Williams (all ages) is an anthology of tales about fairies from around the world.

Submissions and Payment

Guidelines available. Send complete ms with description of market and competition. Accepts photocopies, computer printouts, and simultaneous submissions if identified. SASE. Responds in 4–6 months. Publication in 1 year. Royalty, 5–10%; advance.

Editor's Comments

We are actively seeking interesting nonfiction for readers between the ages of 8 and 18. Picture books for children ages four-and-up, historical fiction, and multicultural folklore are also welcome.

Blackbirch Press

10911 Technology Place
San Diego, CA 92127

Editorial Director: Beverly Larson

Publisher's Interests

Blackbirch Press publishes educational, nonfiction books for elementary and middle school students. It primarily offers books in series, illustrated with four-color photographs. Blackbirch Press was recently acquired by the Gale Group, a leading publisher of library reference products.
Website: www.blackbirch.com

Freelance Potential

Published 50+ titles in 2002. Receives 1,000 queries yearly.

- **Nonfiction:** Publishes story picture books, 4–10 years; chapter books, 5–10 years; middle-grade books, 8–12 years; and young adult books, 12–18 years. Topics include science, nature, the environment, ecology, American history, women's history, geography, business, architecture, sports, and multicultural issues. Also publishes workbooks.
- **Representative Titles:** *The Blackbirch Kid's Visual Reference of the World* is a kid-friendly, full-color reference that covers countries of the world; includes maps, flags, charts, and graphs, and information on climate, land use, and daily life. *Bosnia* by John Isaac is a photoessay that connects readers to the struggles and triumphs of children and families from one of the world's most troubled regions; part of the Children in Crisis series.

Submissions and Payment

Guidelines available. Query with résumé. No unsolicited mss. Accepts photocopies and simultaneous submissions if identified. SASE. Responds in 4 months. Publication in 1 year. Royalty; advance.

Editor's Comments

As an imprint of Gale, we will now be able to accelerate our expansion. We plan to offer more titles on a greater variety of subjects, focusing on the innovation, creativity, and high editorial and production standards that have been a part of our company's success. We welcome résumés from writers or freelance editors with prior experience in book publishing.

Blue Marlin Publications

823 Aberdeen Road
West Bay Shore, NY 11706

Publisher: Francine Poppo Rich

Publisher's Interests
This small house offers two books a year for middle-grade children and young adults. Its catalogue includes both fiction and nonfiction titles, and it welcomes work by both new and established writers.
Website: www.bluemarlinpubs.com

Freelance Potential
Published 2 titles in 2002: 1 was developed from an unsolicited submission. Of the 2 titles, 1 was by an unpublished writer and 1 was by an author who was new to the publishing house. Receives 1–2 unsolicited mss yearly.
- **Fiction:** Publishes early picture books, 0–4 years; and story picture books, 4–10 years. Genres include humor, folklore, folktales, and historical fiction.
- **Nonfiction:** Publishes early picture books, 0–4 years; story picture books, 4–10 years; and middle-grade books, 8–12 years. Topics include humor and biography. Also features titles on gifted education for parents and teachers.
- **Representative Titles:** *Why Can't I Spray?* by Francine Poppo Rich is a picture book about a skunk who learns that he can only use his sprayer when he is in danger. *A Police Officer . . . That's What I'll Be!* by Ron Pinkston is a story designed to assure children that the police are their friends.

Submissions and Payment
Guidelines available on website. Send complete ms. Accepts photocopies and simultaneous submissions if identified. Artwork may improve chance of acceptance. SASE. Responds in 6 weeks. Publication in 12–18 months. Royalty; advance.

Editor's Comments
While we do encourage unsolicited manuscripts, we remind you that since we publish so few books each year, we are very selective. We only accept completed manuscripts, no queries. If you are new to us, take a look at some of the books that we have published in recent years and you will have a better understanding of the kinds of stories that appeal to us.

Blue Sky Press

Scholastic Inc.
557 Broadway
New York, NY 10012-2223

Acquisitions Editor: Bonnie Verburg

Publisher's Interests
An imprint of the Scholastic company, Blue Sky Press offers
fiction and nonfiction for readers of all ages. Only authors
who have been previously published will be considered.
Website: www.scholastic.com

Freelance Potential
Published 17 titles in 2002: 1 was by an agented author.
Receives 5,000 queries yearly.
- **Fiction:** Publishes toddler and early picture books, 0–4 years;
  easy-to-read books, 4–7 years; story picture books, 4–10 years;
  chapter books, 5–10 years; middle-grade novels, 8–12 years;
  and young adult novels, 12–18 years. Genres include historical
  and multicultural fiction, folklore, fairy tales, fantasy, humor,
  and adventure.
- **Nonfiction:** Publishes middle-grade books, 8–12 years. Topics
  include nature, the environment, and history.
- **Representative Titles:** *The Christmas Adventures of Space Elf
  Sam* by Audrey Woods is the story of a young elf's first mission
  for Santa. *Duck on a Bike* by David Shannon (3+ years) is a
  picture book about a duck who decides to learn how to ride a
  bike and how he influences his friends.

Submissions and Payment
Accepts queries from previously published authors only. No
unsolicited mss. Accepts photocopies. SASE. Responds in 6
months. Publication in 2–5 years. Royalty; advance.

Editor's Comments
Because our list is small, we only consider submissions from
previously published authors. We look for stories or topics that
offer a fresh or unique perspective. We are very particular
about what we choose to publish. If you are new to us, we
strongly urge you to review some of our titles. Then, if you
think your book is right for us, and you are a published
author, send us a query. We will not read unsolicited manuscripts. Descriptions of our titles can be found by searching
the Scholastic website.

Borealis Press Ltd.

110 Bloomingdale Street
Ottawa, Ontario K2C 4A4
Canada

Senior Editor: Glenn Clever

Publisher's Interests
This Canadian publisher offers a list of both fiction and non-fiction for children. Its list features approximately four new juvenile titles each year.
Website: www.borealispress.com

Freelance Potential
Published 20 titles (4 juvenile) in 2002: 18 were developed from unsolicited submissions. Of the 20 titles, 2 were by unpublished writers and 8 were by authors who were new to the publishing house. Receives 50 queries yearly.
- **Fiction:** Publishes story picture books, 4–10 years; and young adult books, 12–18 years. Genres include ethnic and multicultural fiction and fantasy.
- **Nonfiction:** Publishes reference titles about Canadian history. Also offers drama, poetry, and books with multicultural themes.
- **Representative Titles:** *Angelina and Giorgio* by Gabrielle Kirschbaum is the story of a friendship between a young girl and a squirrel. *Letters from Tom* by Janet Read is the story of a teenage girl who discovers letters between a brother and sister written during World War I.

Submissions and Payment
Guidelines available. Query with outline/synopsis and sample chapter. No unsolicited mss. Accepts photocopies and disk submissions. No simultaneous submissions. SAE/IRC. Responds in 3–4 months. Publication in 1–2 years. Royalty, 10% of net.

Editor's Comments
We publish most genres but specialize in Canadian authored or oriented material. We look for material that seriously involves the human condition. In fiction, action should be driven by character. We are not in the market for material that is agenda-driven. In work for children we prefer humor and a sense of fun, or, in a serious work, engagement with the wonder and beauty of life, as well as the anger and anguish.

BOW Books

Suite 109
803 Forest Ridge Drive
Beford, TX 76022

Editor: Jennifer Noland

Publisher's Interests

BOW Books publishes picture books, chapter books, audio books, and ancillary products for 3- to 12-year-old children that encourage correct behavior in daily life and demonstrate Christian values.
Website: www.bowbooks.com

Freelance Potential

Published 6 titles in 2002: 1 was developed from an unsolicited submission. Of the 6 titles, 1 was by an unpublished writer and 1 was by an author new to the publishing house.

- **Fiction:** Publishes easy-to-read books, 4–7 years; story picture books, 4–10 years; and chapter books, 5–10 years. Also publishes books in series, 5–8 years. Genres include adventure and inspirational fiction.
- **Representative Titles:** *Chris Mouse and the Christmas House* by Deanna Luke is the story of a small mouse who lives in a Christmas store, and the important lesson he learns when he stows away in a shopping bag. *Marky & the Seagull* by Deanna Luke follows the adventures of a young boy and his seaside friend; part of the Marky series.

Submissions and Payment

Guidelines and catalogue available with 6x9 SASE ($.60 postage). Query with information on intended audience, length, and author biography. SASE. Responds 3 months. Publication in 18 months. Royalty. Flat fee.

Editor's Comments

We are seeking manuscripts that offer values and principles in a fun and entertaining way. We recommend that you visit our website and become familiar with the types of books we publish. As a publishing company guided by Christian values, we consider works that maintain biblical truth. Submissions will be tested using the Bible as the barometer, as well as the opinions of our submissions team. We focus on the positive aspects of life, so do not send us stories that deal with dark or heavy subjects.

Boyds Mills Press

815 Church Street
Honesdale, PA 18431

Manuscript Coordinator: Kathryn Yerkes

Publisher's Interests
For more than a decade, Boyds Mills Press has been providing fiction and nonfiction books that enlighten and entertain children of all ages.
Website: www.boydsmillspress.com

Freelance Potential
Published 50 titles in 2002: 10 were developed from unsolicited submissions, 10 were by agented authors, and 6 were reprint/licensed properties. Of the 50 titles, 3 were by unpublished writers and 8 were by authors who were new to the publishing house. Receives 8,000 queries, 8,000 unsolicited mss yearly.

- **Fiction:** Publishes concept books and early picture books, 0–4 years; easy-to-read books, 4–7 years; middle-grade novels, 8–12 years; and young adult novels, 12–18 years. Genres include adventure and ethnic and multicultural fiction. Also publishes poetry books.
- **Nonfiction:** Publishes concept books, 0–4 years; easy-to-read books, 4–7 years; and middle-grade books, 8–12 years. Topics include science, nature, history, and geography.
- **Representative Titles:** *My Brother Loved Snowflakes* by Mary Bahr (5–8 years) tells the remarkable story of the childhood of Wilson A. Bentley, the man who first photographed a snowflake. *The Promised Land* by Neil Waldman (10+ years) recounts the story of the Jewish people from their arrival in Canaan to the Exodus from Egypt.

Submissions and Payment
Guidelines available. Query with outline and 3 sample chapters; or send complete ms. Accepts photocopies and computer printouts. SASE. Responds in 1 month. Publication period and payment policy vary.

Editor's Comments
We aim to publish good stories with lasting value. We are particularly interested in board books, picture books, middle-grade novels, and nonfiction and poetry for all ages.

Boynton/Cook Publishers

Heinemann
361 Hanover Street
Portsmouth, NH 03801-3912

Editorial Assistant: Eric Chalek

Publisher's Interests
The educational materials published by Boynton/Cook are
used in high school and college classrooms. It specializes in
texts about English literature, language arts, writing, composition, and drama. It also develops professional resources
and textbooks for educators.
Website: www.heinemann.com

Freelance Potential
Published 70 titles in 2002: 1 was developed from an unsolicited submission and 10–15 were by agented authors.
Receives 1,000+ queries yearly.
- **Nonfiction:** Publishes textbooks, grades 9 and up. Also publishes professional resource materials for educators. Topics
  include language arts, literature, rhetoric, communication,
  composition, writing, style, and drama.
- **Representative Titles:** *Writing, Teaching, Learning: A Sourcebook* by Richard L. Graves, ed. (teachers) includes 32 essays
  about the writing-teaching process. *Lifers: Learning from At-
  Risk Adolescent Readers* by Pamela N. Mueller (grades 6–12)
  examines the lives of 22 high school students who have been
  in remedial programs throughout their educational careers and
  discusses three reading workshops implemented by the author
  and her colleagues.

Submissions and Payment
Catalogue and guidelines available at website. Query with
cover letter, project description, table of contents, sample
illustrations if applicable, chapter summaries, and 3 sample
chapters. Accepts photocopies, computer printouts, and
simultaneous submissions if identified. SASE. Responds in
6–8 weeks. Publication in 10–12 months. Royalty.

Editor's Comments
We are constantly on the lookout for new voices and visions,
and we welcome proposals from published authors as well as
previously unpublished writers. Log on to our website to review
our guidelines and to see if your work is appropriate for us.

Branden Books

P.O. Box 812094
Wellesley, MA 02482

Editor: Adolph Caso

Publisher's Interests
Branden Books is a small publisher that features a list of
nonfiction and some fiction titles for young people up to the
age of fourteen. Its books target the trade market.
Website: www.branden.com

Freelance Potential
Published 2 titles in 2002. Receives 500 queries yearly.
- **Fiction:** Publishes story picture books, 4–10 years; and
  middle-grade novels, 8–12 years. Genres include mystery and
  historical fiction. Also publishes stories about friendship and
  stories with problem-solving themes.
- **Nonfiction:** Publishes young adult books, 12–18 years. Topics
  include health, sports, and legal, ethnic, social, and multicultural subjects. Features reference books and biographies.
- **Representative Titles:** *Fighting Men* by John Zubritsky chronicles the lives of three black soldiers during the Civil War.
  Hiroshima by Katharine Johnson & John Rasche recounts the
  days before and after the dropping of the first atomic bomb in
  1945 during World War II.

Submissions and Payment
Query with 2-paragraph synopsis. No unsolicited mss.
Accepts photocopies and computer printouts. SASE.
Responds in 1 week. Publication in 6–10 months. Royalty,
5–10%.

Editor's Comments
We focus primarily on biographies and reference titles for
middle-grade readers. We strive to produce a list that is
diverse, and we continue to be committed to literary excellence.
We're always open to submissions from new writers who can
tackle a subject of interest to us with style and focus backed
up by solid research. If you are new to us, we suggest you
review our catalogue (available on our website) and then review
some of our books. If you think we are right for each other,
send a targeted, well-written query no more than two paragraphs long. We will not review unsolicited manuscripts.

Breakwater Books

P.O. Box 2188
St. John's, Newfoundland A1C 6E6
Canada

General Manager: Wade Foote

Publisher's Interests
Established in 1973, Breakwater Books publishes resource
materials and educational books for all ages that preserve the
unique culture of Newfoundland, Labrador, and the Maritime
provinces.
Website: www.breakwater.nf.net

Freelance Potential
Published 10 titles (2 juvenile) in 2002: 6 were developed
from unsolicited submissions. Of the 10 titles, 5 were by
unpublished writers and 5 were by authors who were new to
the publishing house. Receives 600+ queries yearly.
- **Fiction:** Publishes early picture books, 0–4 years; and young
  adult novels, 12–18 years. Genres include adventure, historical
  fiction, and humor.
- **Nonfiction:** Publishes chapter books, 5–10 years; middle-grade
  books, 8–12 years; and young adult books, 12–18 years. Topics
  include history, current events, religion, and social and multicultural issues. Also publishes anthologies of Canadian history.
- **Representative Titles:** *Captured by the Vikings* by Torill
  Thorstad Hauger is the tale of a brother and sister, slaves in
  tenth-century Norway, who seek to escape their harsh lives.
  Seawolves from the North by Michael Mullen is a story of a
  young Viking who must lead his band on a sea chase full of
  suspense and excitement.

Submissions and Payment
Catalogue available at website. Query with résumé and clips.
No unsolicited mss. Availability of artwork improves chance
of acceptance. SAE/IRC. Responds in 8 months. Publication
in 1 year. Royalty, 10%.

Editor's Comments
We publish curriculum resources that maintain the rich cultural heritage of Atlantic Canada. We work with teachers, educators, academics, curriculum consultants, and students to
develop textbooks to match classroom needs. Send us material that helps students appreciate their Canadian history.

Broadman & Holman Publishers

127 Ninth Avenue North
MSN 198
Nashville, TN 37234-0198

Children's Team

Publisher's Interests
Broadman & Holman Publishers offers books that introduce people of all ages to Jesus Christ. Its children's list includes board books, picture books, Bible story books, and books that explain traditions of the faith for children up to age ten. It does not publish chapter books or young adult titles. This publisher accepts agented submissions only.
Website: www.broadmanholman.com

Freelance Potential
Published 22 titles in 2002: 8 were developed from unsolicited submissions and 4 were by agented authors. Of the 22 titles, 2 were by authors who were new to the publishing house. Receives 300 unsolicited mss yearly.
- **Fiction:** Published 8 story picture books, 4–10 years. Genres include historical and contemporary fiction with biblical themes.
- **Nonfiction:** Published 4 toddler books, 0–4 years; and 4 story picture books, 4–10 years. Also publishes concept books, 0–4 years; and easy-to-read books, 4–7 years. Topics include contemporary issues, traditional and retold Bible stories, and Christianity.
- **Representative Titles:** *Don't Worry About Tomorrow* by Melody Carlson (4–10 years) deals with feelings of dread that come from worrying about things beyond our control; part of the Just Like Jesus Said series. *Baby's First Book of Blessings* by Stephen Elkins (0–3 years) is a board book of simple blessings.

Submissions and Payment
Guidelines available. Send complete ms for educational resources. Accepts agented submissions only for children's books. Accepts photocopies, computer printouts, and simultaneous submissions. SASE. Responds in 3 months. Publication in 12–18 months. Royalty; advance.

Editor's Comments
We'd like to see proposals for books homeschoolers could use to teach the Bible. Our other needs include modern day parables, and picture books that focus on character building.

The Brookfield Reader

137 Peyton Road
Sterling, VA 20165

Submissions Editor: Dawn Manausa

Publisher's Interests
This publisher offers books for toddlers through young adult readers. Its list includes fiction and nonfiction for middle-grade children and young adults, picture books, and illustrated chapter books.
Website: www.brookfieldreader.com

Freelance Potential
Published 6 titles in 2002: 5 were developed from unsolicited submissions and 1 was by an agented author. Of the 6 titles, 1 was by an unpublished writer and 4 were by authors new to the publishing house. Receives 600 queries yearly.

- **Fiction:** Published 2 easy-to-read books, 4–7 years; 2 story picture books, 4–10 years; and 2 young adult books, 12–18 years. Genres include folklore, mystery, suspense, adventure, contemporary and historical fiction, and stories about sports.
- **Representative Titles:** *Blessed Be the Light of Day* by Anita McAndrews (grades 3–5) is a story based on Columbus's diaries of an abused boy who joined the crew of the *Santa Maria*. *Welby the Worm Who Lost His Wiggle* by Lee Hargus Hunter (3–5 years) describes the adventures of a worm with a special ability. *Blood Runs Deep* by R. Scott Mackey (YA) is a story of suspense focusing on a young man bound for college and his mother's apparent murder.

Submissions and Payment
Guidelines available at website. Query. SASE. Responds in 1–2 months. Publication in 18 months. Royalty, 5–10%; advance, $1,000–$2,000.

Editor's Comments
We have no requirements regarding subject matter or manuscript length; we are interested in fresh, imaginative ideas. We seek manuscripts that inspire imagination and creative play, invite communications between child and adult, celebrate our American heritage, explore our world, and promote traditional family values. Check our website for periodic updates of our current topic requests.

The Bureau for At-Risk Youth

Guidance Channel Company
135 Dupont Street
P.O. Box 760
Plainview, NY 11803-0760

Editor-in-Chief: Sally Germain

Publisher's Interests

Now in its tenth year of publishing, The Bureau for At-Risk Youth specializes in materials on social issues. Its target audience includes educators, parents, counselors, and other professionals who work with young people from kindergarten through grade twelve. Topics covered include life skills, mentoring, character education, self-esteem, decision making, violence prevention, drug abuse prevention, sexuality, and general guidance issues. Its catalogue includes a wide variety of resources, including pamphlets, booklets, videos, activity-based curricula, and multi-media products.
Website: www.at-risk.com

Freelance Potential

Published 12 titles in 2002. Receives 300 queries, 150 unsolicited mss yearly.
- **Nonfiction:** Publishes curriculum and classroom materials, activity books, workbooks, and reference titles, grades K–12. Topics include health and social issues, special education, and multicultural and ethnic subjects.
- **Representative Titles:** *The Emotional Resource Recovery Kit* is a guide for parents, educators, and counselors working with children recovering from traumatic events. *Kelly Bear C.A.R.E.S.* (teachers) is a multi-media curriculum that teaches character and resiliency skills.

Submissions and Payment

Query or send complete ms. SASE. Responds to queries in 1–3 months, to mss in 2–6 months. Publication in 6 months. Payment policy varies.

Editor's Comments

Children's health issues and drug and alcohol prevention continue to be among our top needs when it comes to new materials. Keep in mind that most of our products are used by professionals working with young people. Our writers are individuals with very specific skills in the areas our materials cover. We prefer submissions that work as series.

Butte Publications

P.O. Box 1328
Hillsboro, OR 97123-1328

Acquisitions Editor

Publisher's Interests

With several new titles appearing each year, Butte Publications offers a catalogue of titles relating to hearing loss and deafness. Topics covered include skill building, language, and recreation. It also publishes parenting titles and professional resource materials for those working with the deaf or hearing impaired.
Website: www.buttepublications.com

Freelance Potential

Published 8 titles in 2002: all were developed from unsolicited submissions. Receives 30 queries yearly.

- **Nonfiction:** Publishes resource and educational books on signing; interpreting; vocabulary; reading, writing, and language skills; and speech reading. Also publishes parenting titles.
- **Representative Titles:** *Raising and Educating a Deaf Child* by Marc Marschark (parents) answers questions parents have about bringing up a child with hearing issues, including education, language, and employment. *The Silent Garden* by Paul W. Ogden (parents) features case studies and interviews with parents of deaf children in an effort to bring parents as much information as possible about raising a deaf child.

Submissions and Payment

Guidelines available. Query with table of contents, market analysis, and sample chapters. Accepts computer printouts. Availability of artwork improves chance of acceptance. SASE. Responds in 3–6 months. Publication in 1 year. Royalty.

Editor's Comments

Our needs are very specific—we only deal with topics related to deafness. Given that, we include books for a varied community on this subject matter. We are interested in titles directed at children, parents, and educators, as well as materials that can be used by professionals in the field. Most of our books originate as unsolicited queries, so we encourage you to review our catalogue, then send a query that outlines your idea and explains what sets your book apart from others.

Carolrhoda Books

Lerner Publishing Group
241 First Avenue North
Minneapolis, MN 55401

Submissions Editor: Rebecca Poole

Publisher's Interests

Established in 1969, Carolrhoda Books features critically acclaimed and award-winning picture books, nonfiction, and fiction titles for children in kindergarten through grade six. **Website:** www.lernerbooks.com

Freelance Potential

Published 46 titles in 2002: 1 was developed from an unsolicited submission, 5 were by agented authors, and 28 were reprint/licensed properties. Receives 500 queries, 2,000 unsolicited mss yearly.

- **Fiction:** Published 11 story picture books, 4–10 years; 5 middle-grade novels, 8–12 years; and 4 young adult novels, 12–18 years. Genres include contemporary, historical, and multicultural fiction and mystery.
- **Nonfiction:** Published 12 easy-to-read books, 4–7 years; and 12 chapter books, 5–10 years. Topics include social issues, life science, geography, history, the environment, and sports.
- **Representative Titles:** *Annie Quinn in America* by Mical Schneider (grades 4–7) follows a twelve-year-old girl as she leaves her family in Ireland to begin a new life in nineteenth-century New York City. *A Book Takes Root* by Michael Kehoe takes readers on a step-by-step journey through the making of a book, from manuscript through bound and printed book.

Submissions and Payment

Guidelines available. Accepts submissions in March and October only. Query with outline and sample chapters; or send complete ms. Accepts photocopies and computer printouts. SASE. Responds 2–6 months. Royalty; advance. Flat fee.

Editor's Comments

We look for nonfiction that is interesting and entertaining, as well as informative. Send us biographies, photo essays, and nature and science books. For fiction, we are looking for unique, honest stories with original plots for middle-grade and young adult readers.

Carson-Dellosa Publishing Co.

P.O. Box 35665
Greensboro, NC 27425-5665

Senior Editor, Acquisitions: Wolfgang D. Hoelscher

Publisher's Interests

Teachers working in preschools, elementary schools, and middle schools use the supplementary educational materials offered by Carson-Dellosa. It publishes resource and activity books, student workbooks, bulletin board sets, charts, and decorative classroom items.
Website: www.carson-dellosa.com

Freelance Potential

Published 100 titles in 2002: 25 were developed from unsolicited submissions. Receives 150–200 queries and many unsolicited mss yearly.

- **Nonfiction:** Publishes supplementary educational materials, pre-K–grade 8. Topics include science, mathematics, language arts, arts and crafts, and multicultural subjects.
- **Representative Titles:** *Tongue Twisters to Teach Phonemic Awareness: Beginning Consonants and Vowels* (grades K–2) is a resource supplement to the Four-Blocks™ Literacy Model and includes teacher instructions, tongue twisters, a parent letter, and an observation and assessment guide. *Systematic Sequential Phonics They Use* by Patricia Cunningham helps beginning readers of any age learn phonics through Word Wall and Making Words activities.

Submissions and Payment

Guidelines available. Query with outline and representative pages. Accepts photocopies, computer printouts, and simultaneous submissions if identified. SASE. Responds in 6–8 weeks. Publication in 1–2 years. Flat fee.

Editor's Comments

We welcome book proposals and product ideas from teachers and writers. We encourage you to send us ideas that will help us provide teachers, parents, and students around the world with high-quality educational resources. In your query, tell how your book will stand out from the competition and how it compares to other books on the market. Works of fiction, including children's storybooks, are generally not accepted.

Cartwheel Books

Scholastic Inc.
557 Broadway
New York, NY 10012-3999

Executive Editor: Grace Maccarone

Publisher's Interests
A division of Scholastic Inc., Cartwheel Books accepts submissions from agented or previously published authors only. It publishes concept books and early picture books, as well as storybooks with concept or holiday themes.
Website: www.scholastic.com

Freelance Potential
Published 100 titles in 2002: 13 were by agented authors and 35 were reprint/licensed properties. Of the 100 titles, 2 were by unpublished writers and 6 were by authors who were new to the publishing house. Receives 2,500 queries, 2,500 unsolicited mss yearly.
- **Fiction:** Published 11 concept books, 20 toddler books, and 15 early picture books, 0–4 years; 14 easy-to-read books, 4–7 years; and 3 story picture books, 4–10 years. Genres include humor and stories about families, friendship, holidays, and animals. Also publishes puzzle books.
- **Nonfiction:** Published 12 concept books, 9 toddler books, and 1 early picture book, 0–4 years; 12 easy-to-read books, 4–7 years; and 2 story picture books, 4–10 years. Topics include mathematics and science.
- **Representative Titles:** *Wake Up, Big Barn!* by Suzanne Tanner Chitwood (3–7 years) is a picture book that features cut-paper illustrations of a rowdy, rollicking farm. *Hugs and Hearts* by Toni Trent Parker (0–4 years) is a holiday picture book that stars African American children.

Submissions and Payment
Accepts submissions from agents and previously published authors only. Accepts photocopies and computer printouts. SASE. Responds in 3–6 months. Publication period varies. Payment policy varies.

Editor's Comments
Easy-to-read fiction for children between the ages of four and eight remains a top editorial priority here. We also welcome ideas for novelty books for toddlers.

Charlesbridge

85 Main Street
Watertown, MA 02472

Submissions Editor

Publisher's Interests
Charlesbridge and its imprints, Whispering Coyote and
Talewinds, offer picture books for children ages one through
ten. Charlesbridge focuses exclusively on nonfiction titles;
Talewinds specializes in plot-driven books; and Whispering
Coyote features stories told in whimsical verse or prose.
Website: www.charlesbridge.com

Freelance Potential
Published 26 titles in 2002: 2 were developed from unsolicited submissions, 1 was by an agented author, and 5 were
reprint/licensed properties. Of the 26 titles, 3 were by
authors who were new to the publishing house. Receives
2,500 unsolicited mss yearly.
- **Fiction:** Published 9 story picture books, 4–10 years. Genres
  include fairy tales and animal stories. Also publishes concept
  books and early picture books.
- **Nonfiction:** Published 4 concept books and 1 toddler book, 0–4
  years; and 11 story picture books, 4–10 years. Topics include
  art, ecology, history, social studies, math, multicultural issues,
  nature, and social issues. Also publishes biographies and poetry.
- **Representative Titles:** *Did You Hear That?* by Caroline Arnold
  (5–10 years) explores the world of animals that create and hear
  sounds human ears can't hear. *The Orangutan* by Christine
  Sourd (7–10 years) introduces readers to the only ape that lives
  outside of Africa.

Submissions and Payment
Guidelines available. Send complete ms. Accepts photocopies
and computer printouts. No simultaneous submissions.
SASE. Responds in 2–6 months. Publication in 2–5 years.
Royalty. Flat fee.

Editor's Comments
We will consider only manuscripts that are submitted exclusively to us. "Exclusive Submission" must appear on your
envelope as well as on your cover letter. Please do not submit
chapter books, coloring or activity books, or board books.

Charles River Media

Suite 3
20 Downer Avenue
Hingham, MA 02043

President: Dave Pallai

Publisher's Interests
This specialty publisher focuses on books and CD-ROMS about the Internet. Topics covered by titles on its list include computer graphics, animation, networking, and game programming. Its CyberRookies™ series is written for readers ages 12 to 18.
Website: www.charlesriver.com

Freelance Potential
Published 50 titles (10 juvenile) in 2002: 3 were developed from unsolicited submissions and 6 were by agented authors. Receives 100 queries yearly.
• **Nonfiction:** Publishes how-to and informational books and CD-ROMS about computer graphics, animation, game programming, the Internet, and networking.
• **Representative Titles:** *Programming Dynamic Character Animation* by David Paull focuses on the programming that is needed to create and animate 3D models. *Animation: Master 2002* by David Rogers teaches the skills and fundamentals needed to create quality models, textures, and animation.

Submissions and Payment
Guidelines and catalogue available at website or with #10 SASE (3 first-class stamps). Query. Accepts photocopies. Availability of artwork improves chance of acceptance. SASE. Responds in 1 month. Publication in 4 months. Royalty, 5–15% of net; advance, $1,000–$7,500.

Editor's Comments
Most of our topics are geared toward individuals with some level of experience in computers and electronics. They'll purchase your book for the useful, accurate information it will provide. All our material is aimed at readers age 11 and older. For the coming year, we continue to need titles focusing on the areas of graphics, animation, game programming, and networking. If your expertise matches our needs, send us a query. You can review our guidelines as well as a catalogue at our website. We suggest you do so before sending a submission.

Chelsea House Publishers

Suite 400
1974 Sproul Road
Broomall, PA 19008-0914

Editorial Assistant

Publisher's Interests

Chelsea House is an educational publisher that develops nonfiction books for middle-grade and young adult readers. Most of its titles are published in series and cover topics such as social studies, health, and multicultural studies. It also publishes biography series.

Website: www.chelseahouse.com

Freelance Potential

Published 369 titles in 2002: 75 were reprint/licensed properties. Of the 369 titles, 73 were by unpublished writers and 110 were by authors who were new to the publishing house. Receives 300 queries, 50 unsolicited mss yearly.

- **Nonfiction:** Publishes middle-grade books, 8–12 years; and young adult books, 12–18 years. Topics include American history, world history, African-American studies, the classics, criminal justice, popular culture, sports, science, travel, drug education, and Christian studies. Also publishes books about parenting, literary criticism, and reference titles for adults.
- **Representative Titles:** *Langston Hughes* by Harold Bloom examines Hughes's poetry, including his use of simplicity and humanistic techniques. *Stevie Wonder, Entertainer* by Tenley Williams talks about this musician's innovative style and the daily struggles he faces as a blind man.

Submissions and Payment

Guidelines available. All books are assigned. Send résumé with clips or writing samples. No queries or unsolicited mss. SASE. Publication period varies. Advance. Flat fee.

Editor's Comments

We develop most of the titles for our series in-house and then assign those titles to writers with whom we have worked in the past. We will, however, consider ideas that are accompanied by your credentials and some samples of your writing. We're looking for authors who have some experience writing for readers between the ages of 13 and 15. We particularly need writers who can address multicultural and ethnic issues.

Chicago Review Press

814 North Franklin Street
Chicago, IL 60610

Editorial Director: Cynthia Sherry

Publisher's Interests
Founded in 1973, this mid-sized publisher offers approximately 35 titles a year under three imprints. The Chicago Review Press imprint features general nonfiction for all ages, including regional titles, parenting books, children's activity books, how-to books, and biographies. It does not publish fiction or poetry.
Website: www.ipgbook.com

Freelance Potential
Published 35 titles (4 juvenile) in 2002: 5 were developed from unsolicited submissions, 10 were by agented authors, and 5 were reprint/licensed properties. Of the 35 titles, 7 were by unpublished writers and 16 were by authors who were new to the publishing house. Receives 520 queries, 400 unsolicited mss yearly.

- **Nonfiction:** Published 4 middle-grade books, 8–12 years. Also publishes toddler books, 0–4 years; primary books, 6–9 years; and young adult titles, 12–18 years. Topics include science, mathematics, literature, history, social issues, photography, arts and crafts, gardening, cooking, and camping.
- **Representative Titles:** *Monet and the Impressionists for Kids* by Carol Sabbeth (9+ years) teaches young readers about the impressionist painters and their paintings; includes more than 20 activities. *How the Earth Works* by Michelle O'Brien-Palmer (6–9 years) brings earth science alive for kids with activities that explore earthquakes, fossils, and volcanoes.

Submissions and Payment
Guidelines available. Query with 1–2 short chapters and/or projects; or send complete ms with résumé. Accepts photocopies, computer printouts, and simultaneous submissions if identified. SASE. Responds in 8–10 weeks. Publication in 1–20 months. Royalty, 7–10%; advance, $1,500.

Editor's Comments
We continue to look for activity books as well as books on nonfiction topics, particularly for readers ages six through nine.

Children's Book Press

2211 Mission Street
San Francisco, CA 94110

Editorial Submissions

Publisher's Interests
Established in 1975, Children's Book Press is a nonprofit
publisher of multicultural and bilingual children's picture
books that give readers a sense of their culture, history,
and importance.
Website: www.cbookpress.org

Freelance Potential
Published 4 titles in 2002: 1 was developed from an unsolicited submission. Receives 1,200 unsolicited mss yearly.
- **Fiction:** Published 2 story picture books, 4–10 years. Genres
  include ethnic, multicultural, and social fiction.
- **Nonfiction:** Published 2 story picture books, 4–10 years. Topics include multicultural, ethnic, and social issues.
- **Representative Titles:** *The Barber's Cutting Edge* by Gwendolyn Battle-Lavert (6+ years) tells about the town barber who
  mentors a young boy on the joy of learning new words. *Leaving
  for America* by Rosyln Bresnick-Perry (6+ years) portrays life in
  a Russian Jewish community in the 1920s, as a family pre-
  pares to start a new life in America.

Submissions and Payment
Guidelines available. Send complete ms. Accepts photocopies,
computer printouts, and simultaneous submissions if identified. SASE. Responds in 2+ months. Publication in 12–18
months. Royalty; advance.

Editor's Comments
Many of our authors and artists have a strong commitment
to and connection with their communities, and many are
activists committed to affecting social change. We like to
think our efforts are part of a larger movement to create literature that serves as a model for young children. To that end,
we are looking for material about children in Latino/Chicano,
African American, Asian American, Muslim American, and
Native American communities. Authentic stories about contemporary issues are at the top of our list. New writers
should visit our website to check out our editorial guidelines.

Children's Press

Scholastic Inc.
90 Sherman Turnpike
Danbury, CT 06816

Editor-in-Chief: Kate Nunn

Publisher's Interests
This division of Scholastic specializes in nonfiction books for the school and library markets. Its audience includes both middle-grade and high school students. A wide variety of nonfiction topics are covered by its titles. Most books appear as a part of a series.
Website: www.scholastic.com

Freelance Potential
Published 400 titles in 2002: 50 were by agented authors. Of the 400 titles, 15 were by authors who were new to the publishing house. Receives 2,000 queries yearly.

- **Nonfiction:** Publishes concept books, 0–4 years; easy-to-read books, 4–7 years; story picture books, 4–10 years; chapter books, 5–10 years; and middle-grade books, 8–12 years. Topics include science, geography, sports, social studies, and career guidance. Also publishes biographies, books written in Spanish, and hi/lo titles. All titles support elementary and middle school curricula.
- **Representative Titles:** *The Thirteen Colonies* by Gail Sakurai (9–11 years) covers our nation's early history. *Personal Computer* by Tom Kazunas (8–10 years) discusses the history, components, software, and uses of personal computers.

Submissions and Payment
Query with outline/synopsis and sample chapters. No unsolicited mss. SASE. Responds in 2–6 months. Publication in 1–2 years. Royalty. Flat fee.

Editor's Comments
Our audience is comprised of teachers, parents, and librarians. Our goal is to bring them books they can use with students in kindergarten through the middle grades that will broaden their horizons about the world around them and its rich history. All of our books are curriculum-based and most appear in series. We welcome ideas for new series as well as biographies of notable individuals of the past and present. Keep in mind that your book should entertain and educate.

Children's Story Scripts

2219 West Olive Avenue
PMB 130
Burbank, CA 91506

Editor: Deedra Bébout

Publisher's Interests

Children's Story Scripts offers theater-style scripts for children; that is, the telling of a story that is divided among a number of children who read aloud from the scripts.

Freelance Potential

Published 4 titles in 2002: all were developed from unsolicited submissions. Of the 4 titles, 3 were by unpublished writers and 2 were by authors who were new to the publishing house. Receives 500 unsolicited mss yearly.

- **Fiction:** Publishes story scripts, grades K–8.
- **Representative Titles:** *Dave's Unhappy Teeth* by Helen Ksypka (grades K–2) offers basic dental information through the story of a boy who loses all his teeth because he doesn't take care of them. *The Song of the Tree Frogs* by Mary MacDonald (grades 3–6) is a retelling of an aboriginal legend that explains why tree frogs sing through the night.

Submissions and Payment

Guidelines available. Send complete ms. Accepts computer printouts and simultaneous submissions if identified. SASE. Responds in 2–4 weeks. Publication period varies. Royalty, 10–15%.

Editor's Comments

If you decide to send us a script, keep in mind that you are essentially writing a prose story that gets divided into parts. These are not plays, they are stories that contain descriptive narration (written in the past tense) and character dialogue (written in the present tense). Your story must have thrust and an objective to it. Ask yourself what the purpose is. A story does not have to be perfect to be accepted, but it does have to correlate with the classroom curriculum. You can send us the best story in the world, but if it doesn't relate to a school subject, we won't be able to use it. We are always interested in hearing from writers of all cultural and ethnic backgrounds. Take a look at some of our materials before you consider sending us your submission.

Childswork/Childsplay

Guidance Channel Company
135 Dupont Street
P.O. Box 760
Plainview, NY 11803-0760

Editor: Karen Schader

Publisher's Interests
Childswork/Childsplay is a specialty publisher focusing on
the social and emotional needs of children and adolescents.
Its target audience includes teachers, therapists, and parents. Books, games, audio and video tapes, and software
programs are found in its catalogue.
Website: www.childswork.com

Freelance Potential
Published 6 titles in 2002. Receives 360 queries, 100 unsolicited mss yearly.
- **Nonfiction:** Publishes informational titles and activity books,
  6–12 years.
- **Representative Titles:** *Anger Management for Children* by Dr.
  Adolph Moser (parents, teachers) explains the causes of anger
  and offers methods that help children reduce the amount of
  anger they feel. *Kid Power Tactics for Dealing with Depression*
  by Nicholas & Susan E. Dubuque (8+ years) provides information on coping with the problem of childhood depression.

Submissions and Payment
Guidelines available. Query with clips and writing samples.
Accepts photocopies and computer printouts. No simultaneous submissions. SASE. Responds in 1 month. Publication in
6 months. Flat fee.

Editor's Comments
Our primary target audience is therapists and teachers, but
some of our products are suitable for parents as well. Because
children are the ultimate users of most of our products, they
must be fun to read, play with, listen to, or view. We strongly
urge you to familiarize yourself with our materials before you
consider sending a submission. If, after reviewing our catalogue, you feel your idea would meet our needs, send us a
query with a cover letter that specifies the market you envision
for your product and describes how your submission is similar
to and different from other products we produce. We will consider previously published and out-of-print books.

Child Welfare League of America

3rd Floor
440 First Street NW
Washington, DC 20001

Acquisitions Editor

Publisher's Interests
Both child welfare professionals and the children they serve read the books from this publisher. Its Child & Family Press imprint offers children's books and parenting titles that appeal to the general public, while the CWLA Press imprint presents books and training materials for professionals who work with children and families.
Website: www.cwla.org/pubs

Freelance Potential
Published 40 titles (6 juvenile) in 2002: few were developed from unsolicited submissions and 1 was a reprint/licensed property. Receives 200 queries yearly.
- **Fiction:** Publishes story picture books, 4–10 years; and middle-grade novels, 8–12 years.
- **Nonfiction:** Publishes titles for parents, professionals, and volunteers in the fields of social work, human services, child welfare, and child care. Topics include adoption, foster care, child abuse and neglect, and teen pregnancy.
- **Representative Titles:** *Benni & Victoria: Friends Through Time* by Patricia H. Aust is the story of boy who is sent to a foster home in the country and a girl ghost who haunts a run-down chapel on the grounds of an old school. *The Coffee Can Kid* by Jan Czech is an illustrated book about a girl who makes connections to her past and her origins by going through the contents of an old coffee can with her adoptive father.

Submissions and Payment
Query with sample chapters. Accepts photocopies, computer printouts, and e-mail submissions to eklein@cwla.org. SASE. Responds in 3–6 months. Publication in 1 year. Royalty.

Editor's Comments
The children's books that interest us usually provide resources that help young readers deal with the challenging life situations they face. They should also be entertaining, original, imaginative, and engaging. Titles for professionals should reflect current developments and research.

Christian Ed. Publishers

P.O. Box 26639
San Diego, CA 92196

Senior Editor: Dr. Lon Ackelson

Publisher's Interests
This small publishing house specializes in Christian curriculum-based books for children and youth. It is committed to publishing materials that introduce children and teens to a personal faith in Jesus Christ.
Website: www.christianedwarehouse.com

Freelance Potential
Published 80 titles in 2002: 6 were by unpublished writers and 10 were by authors who were new to the publishing house. Receives 300 queries yearly.
- **Fiction:** Publishes religious fiction, pre-K–grade 12.
- **Nonfiction:** Publishes Christian educational titles, Bible-based curriculum, and Bible club materials, grades K–12.
- **Representative Titles:** *The Big Book of Kindergarten Puzzles* features Bible puzzles that reinforce Bible stories and biblical truths. *Color, Cut & Paste God's Creatures* (2–5 years) includes activities related to 44 Bible lessons.

Submissions and Payment
Catalogue and guidelines available with 9x12 SASE (4 first-class stamps). All work by assignment only. Publication in 12–18 months. Flat fee, $.03 per word.

Editor's Comments
We're looking for writers who have the following qualities: those who love the Lord and are active members of a Bible-believing church; those who have hands-on experience with children or youth; and those who write well and can meet deadlines. We welcome both new and established writers. We ask that interested writers contact us for an application. Return this with a copy of a résumé of your Christian experience, the age group you wish to write for, and your writing background. Include clips if available. We will then send you a sample assignment. If we accept your assignment, we will put you on our list of active writers and contact you when an appropriate project comes along. Please do not send queries or manuscripts. All work is done on assignment only.

Christian Publications

3825 Hartzdale Drive
Camp Hill, PA 17011

Managing Editor: David E. Fessenden

Publisher's Interests
Christian Publications is the official publishing house of The
Christian and Missionary Alliance Church, and its books
adhere to the same evangelical doctrinal position as this
denomination. Its catalogue includes books about theology,
the church, the Christian home, and Christian living. It does
not publish fiction or children's books.
Website: www.christianpublications.com

Freelance Potential
Published 25 titles in 2002. Receives 200–300 queries yearly.
- **Nonfiction:** Publishes young adult books, 12–18 years. Fea-
  tures books for young adults, parents, and families about
  devotional studies, Bible studies, theology, the Christian home,
  Christian living, spirituality, and a deeper life.
- **Representative Titles:** *Smashed Tomatoes, Bottle Rockets . . .
  and Other Outdoor Devotionals You Can Do With Your Kids* by
  Tom Shoemaker (8–15 years) is a collection of 24 outdoor devotionals designed especially for fathers to do with their children.
  All Mothers Are Working Mothers by Laura Sabin Riley features
  devotional readings that address issues faced by both working
  and stay-at-home moms.

Submissions and Payment
Guidelines available. Query with 2 sample chapters (including
chapter 1), overview/synopsis, and résumé or biography.
SASE. Responds in 1–2 months. Publication in 1 year. Royalty.
Flat fee.

Editor's Comments
Among evangelical publishing houses, we occupy a unique,
middle-of-the-road theological position between congregation-
al/baptistic and pentecostal/charismatic theology. All manuscripts must be compatible with our doctrinal position. Before
submitting, log on to our website and review our writers' guidelines; we want to see a complete proposal with information on
competitive titles and marketing possibilities. Please *do not*
send children's books, works of fiction, or poetry.

Christopher-Gordon Publishers

Suite 12
1502 Providence Highway
Norwood, MA 02062

Vice President: Susanne F. Canavan

Publisher's Interests

In-service educators working with kindergarten through twelfth-grade students are the target audience for the titles offered by Christopher-Gordon Publishers. In addition to books on assessment and instruction, it also offers titles that address professional self-development.
Website: www.christopher-gordon.com

Freelance Potential

Published 10 titles in 2002: 3 were developed from unsolicited submissions. Receives 100 queries, 50 unsolicited mss each year.

- **Nonfiction:** Publishes in-service development materials for educators at all grade levels. Topics include assessment and instruction, children's literature, teaching literature, supervision and school improvement, professional self-development, technology, math, and education law.
- **Representative Titles:** *Writing for Publication: A Practical Guide for Educators* by Mary Renck Jalongo (teachers) offers advice on how to publish works on such topics as classroom experience, conference presentation, and research projects. *Creating Literacy Communities in the Middle School* by Leigh Van Horn (teachers) offers insights into how middle school students understand literature.

Submissions and Payment

Guidelines and catalogue available with #10 SASE (2 first-class stamps). Query with table of contents, sample chapters, and market analysis; or send complete ms. Accepts photocopies. SASE. Response time varies. Publication in 18 months. Royalty, varies; advance, varies.

Editor's Comments

If you have a particular perspective or philosophical orientation, be sure to state it up front when you send us your submission. Tell us what you hope to accomplish by writing your book, and explain how it will benefit readers. View your book as a learning tool that must provide practical information.

Chronicle Books

6th Floor
85 Second Street
San Francisco, CA 94105

Submissions Editor

Publisher's Interests

Founded in 1966, Chronicle Books offers a children's catalogue that includes picture books for children up to the age
of eight and nonfiction for middle-grade readers. For adults,
it publishes fine art titles about design, art, architecture,
and photography.
Website: www.chroniclekids.com

Freelance Potential

Published 45 titles in 2002: 12 were developed from unsolicited submissions, 8 were by agented authors, and 18 were
reprint/licensed properties. Receives 2,500 queries, 20,000
unsolicited mss yearly.

- **Fiction:** Publishes concept books, toddler books, and early picture books, 0–4 years; easy-to-read books, 4–7 years; and story
  picture books, 4–10 years. Genres include folktales and contemporary, multicultural, and ethnic fiction.
- **Nonfiction:** Publishes chapter books, 5–10 years; and middle-
  grade books, 8–12 years. Topics include nature, science, history, and social issues.
- **Representative Titles:** *Who Am I? Wild Animals* by Alain
  Crozon is an interactive lift-the-flap book that uses simple
  guessing games to reveal the identity of favorite wild animals.
  The Fairy Tale Catalog by Sally Gardner allows readers to
  create and customize their very own fairy tales, attend a fairy
  wedding, and raise a magical garden.

Submissions and Payment

Guidelines available. Send complete ms for picture books.
Query with outline/synopsis and 3 sample chapters for
longer works. Accepts photocopies and simultaneous submissions if identified. SASE. Responds in 4–6 months. Publication in 1–4 years. Royalty; advance. Flat fee.

Editor's Comments

Our objective is to create and distribute exceptional publishing
that's instantly recognizable for its spirit, creativity, and value.
We specialize in high-quality, reasonably priced books.

Clarion Books

Houghton Mifflin Company
215 Park Avenue South
New York, NY 10003

Editorial Director: Dinah Stevenson

Publisher's Interests
Picture books, fiction, and nonfiction titles for children and young adults are found on the list of this well-known publisher, which is an imprint of Houghton Mifflin Company.
Website: www.hmco.com

Freelance Potential
Published 60 titles in 2002: 6 were developed from unsolicited submissions, 15 were by agented authors, and 6 were reprint/licensed properties. Receives 100+ queries, 1,000+ unsolicited mss yearly.

- **Fiction:** Publishes picture books, 3–6 years; story picture books, 2–6 years; chapter books, 7–10 years; middle-grade novels, 8–12 years; and young adult novels, 12–18 years. Genres include adventure, folktales, fairy tales, and historical and science fiction.
- **Nonfiction:** Publishes picture books, 3–6 years; and middle-grade books, 8–12 years. Topics include nature, ecology, history, holidays, and multicultural and ethnic issues.
- **Representative Titles:** *When My Name Was Keoko* by Linda Sue Park (10–14 years) follows the lives of two Korean children living under Japanese occupation during the years before World War II. *Martin and the Giant Lions* by Caron Lee Cohen (2–6 years) is the story of a young boy whose dream is to climb to the top of the jungle ladder and roar.

Submissions and Payment
Guidelines available. Query for chapter books and novels; send complete ms for picture books. Accepts photocopies and computer printouts. SASE. Responds in 4 months. Publication in 2 years. Royalty.

Editor's Comments
Chapter books for readers ages six to ten, as well as picture books and nonfiction for all ages, are of interest to us for the coming year. Please be aware that we will not review submissions sent on computer disk, nor will we read those that arrive via fax or e-mail.

I. E. Clark Publications

P.O. Box 246
Schulenburg, TX 78956-0246

General Manager: Donna Cozzaglio

Publisher's Interests

I. E. Clark Publications features plays that can be performed and enjoyed by people of all ages. Its catalogue includes plays for children's theater and school classrooms, young adult plays, and musicals—all with both classical and contemporary themes.
Website: www.ieclark.com

Freelance Potential

Published 5 titles in 2002: 1 was developed from an unsolicited submission and 2 were by agented authors. Of the 5 titles, 2 were by unpublished writers and 1 was by an author who was new to the publishing house. Receives 500+ unsolicited mss yearly.

- **Fiction:** Publishes middle-grade plays, 8–12 years; and young adult plays, 12–18 years. Features drama classics, musicals, religious and holiday plays, and plays with bilingual and multicultural themes.
- **Representative Titles:** *Holiday Dream* by Allan Kuester is an interactive play for children's theater that allows the audience to help a young boy build his self-esteem by rescuing famous fairy tale characters. *Splits* by Jerome McDonough (YA) is a one-act play that uses an ensemble technique to address the issues faced by children of divorce.

Submissions and Payment

Guidelines available. Send complete ms with reviews, programs, or other proof of production. Accepts photocopies, computer printouts, and simultaneous submissions if identified. SASE. Responds in 6+ months. Publication in 6–12 months. Royalty.

Editor's Comments

We continue to seek one-act plays appropriate for young adults, as well as dramatizations of classic stories. We seldom publish a play that hasn't been produced; so if your play has not been on stage, we suggest that you make every effort to get it produced by a skilled director.

Clear Light Publishers

823 Don Diego
Santa Fe, NM 87501

Publisher: Houghton Harmon

Publisher's Interests
Clear Light Publishers specializes in books on Native American culture, Hispanic culture, the Southwest, nature, and the environment. Its catalogue offers fiction and nonfiction for children, including picture books and easy-to-read titles.
Website: www.clearlightbooks.com

Freelance Potential
Published 25 titles (5 juvenile) in 2002: 5 were developed from unsolicited submissions and 5 were by agented authors. Of the 25 titles, 3 were by unpublished writers and 3 were by authors who were new to the publishing house. Receives 250+ unsolicited mss yearly.
- **Fiction:** Publishes story picture books, 4–10 years; and young adult novels, 12–18 years. Genres include historical, regional, multicultural, and inspirational fiction.
- **Nonfiction:** Publishes middle-grade books, 8–12 years; and young adult books, 12–18 years. Topics include nature, religion, history, multicultural and ethnic subjects, social issues, health, and fitness. Also publishes biographies.
- **Representative Titles:** *The Man Who Set the Town Dancing* by Candice Stanford is based on the true story of José Tena, a maestro of dance who popularized folk dances in Mexico; told in both English and Spanish. *When Animals Were People* by Bonnie Larson is a bilingual story that retells a myth from the Huichol Indian folklore.

Submissions and Payment
Send complete ms. Accepts photocopies, computer printouts, and simultaneous submissions if identified. Availability of artwork improves chance of acceptance. SASE. Responds in 3 months. Publication in 1 year. Royalty.

Editor's Comments
Our goal is to enrich young readers' lives with stories from Native American and Hispanic cultures that will broaden their horizons. We are particularly interested in seeing more stories that can appear in a bilingual format.

Concordia Publishing House

3558 South Jefferson Avenue
St. Louis, MO 63118-3968

Acquisitions Editor: Jane Wilke

Publisher's Interests
Concordia Publishing House is the publishing division of the
Lutheran Church-Missouri Synod. Its list offers nonfiction
materials for children and adults that relate to some aspect
of the Christian faith. It is no longer accepting any freelance
submissions. All work is now being done by assignment only.
Website: www.cphmall.com

Freelance Potential
Published 40 titles (16 juvenile) in 2002: 4 were developed
from unsolicited submissions, 1 was by an agented author,
and 10 were reprint/licensed properties. Of the 40 titles, 4
were by authors who were new to the publishing house.
- **Nonfiction:** Published 4 early picture books, 0–4 years; 4 easy-
  to-read titles, 4–7 years; and 2 story picture books, 4–10. Topics include religious issues.
- **Representative Titles:** *Alphabet Adventures* by Karen Miller
  (4–7 years) is a reproducible activity book that shares the
  Gospel and teaches Bible stories through the use of the alphabet. *Running the Race of Faith* by Pam Ausenhus (YA) is an
  eight-week devotional guide for teens designed to offer practical
  applications they can use in real life.

Submissions and Payment
No longer accepting unsolicited submissions. All work is now
done by assignment only. Query or send résumé.

Editor's Comments
Please note that as of 2003 we will be dropping down the
number of books we publish annually to approximately fifteen.
All unsolicited submissions are being returned now, as we are
only working with authors on assignment. If you are interested
in working with us, you may send us a résumé listing your
qualifications, but be aware that the chances are slim here, as
we are cutting back and do have a number of authors with
whom we have worked in the past. Keep in mind that we only
publish nonfiction and that our books target church and lay
personnel.

Contemporary Drama Service

Meriwether Publishing Ltd.
885 Elkton Drive
Colorado Springs, CO 80907

Associate Editor: Theodore Zapel

Publisher's Interests

Plays, skits, musicals, and speech resource materials are
available from Contemporary Drama Service. It markets its
materials to community theater groups, middle and high
schools, and churches.
Website: www.contemporarydrama.com

Freelance Potential

Published 70 titles in 2002: 60 were developed from unsolicited submissions and 5 were by agented authors. Of the 70
titles, 35 were by unpublished writers and 35 were by
authors who were new to the publishing house. Receives
1,600 queries, 1,500 unsolicited mss yearly.

- **Fiction:** Publishes middle-grade plays, 8–12 years; and young
  adult plays, 12–18 years. Genres include musicals, folktales,
  and fantasy. Also offers skits, adaptations, novelty plays,
  parodies, and social commentary.
- **Nonfiction:** Publishes young adult books, 12–18 years. Features books about improvisations, theater games, speech, acting techniques, and theater arts.
- **Representative Titles:** *Thirty Pieces of Silver* by Gary Shank
  (all ages) is a small-cast Easter play about the miraculous
  events of the Resurrection of Christ. *Murder at the Grammies*
  by Mimi Bodel (12–18 years) is a classroom play that teaches
  the parts of speech and punctuation.

Submissions and Payment

Guidelines available. Query with outline/synopsis. Accepts
photocopies, computer printouts, and simultaneous submissions if identified. SASE. Responds in 6 weeks. Publication in
6 months. Royalty. Flat fee. Special projects, negotiable.

Editor's Comments

If you are submitting a play for publication, please include a
cast list, prop list (if required), costume information, and set
specifications. Define the market and potential audience, and
tell us why your work deserves to be published. Inspirational
middle-grade plays remain a top priority.

Cook Communications Ministries

4050 Lee Vance View
Colorado Springs, CO 80918-7100

Editorial Assistant

Publisher's Interests
A Christian publisher, Cook Communications Ministries offers books for children up to the age of 12. It also offers Bible-based study guides and reference books for adults.
Website: www.faithkids.com

Freelance Potential
Published 75 titles (33 juvenile) in 2002: 1 was developed from an unsolicited submission and 49 were by agented authors. Of the 75 titles, 1 was by an unpublished writer and 5 were by authors who were new to the publishing house. Receives 1,500 queries yearly.

- **Fiction:** Published 5 concept books, 5 toddler books, and 4 early picture books, 0–4 years; 2 easy-to-read books, 4–7 years; 6 chapter books, 5–10 years; and 2 middle-grade books, 8–12 years. Also publishes books in series, 8–12 years. Genres include inspirational and religious fiction.
- **Nonfiction:** Published 1 concept book and 2 early picture books, 0–4 years; 1 story picture book, 4–10 years; and 1 middle-grade book, 8–12 years. Topics include religion and social issues. Also publishes self-help titles and reference books for adults.
- **Representative Titles:** *A School of Her Own* (8+ years) explores the spiritual and emotional challenges of growing up; part of the Grandma's Attic series. *The Mockingbird Mystery* (7–10 years) is an adventure set in Thomas Jefferson's White House; part of the White House Adventure series.

Submissions and Payment
Guidelines available. Query with clips. Accepts photocopies and simultaneous submissions if identified. SASE. Responds in 2 weeks. Publication in 2 years. Payment policy varies.

Editor's Comments
New writers have a good chance at publication with the submission of a children's board book or a picture book based on Bible stories. We'd like to see stories on Christian topics with a clearly stated moral, and chapter books for middle-grade kids.

Coteau Books

401-2206 Dewdney Avenue
Regina, Saskatchewan S4R 1H3
Canada

Managing Editor: Nik L. Burton

Publisher's Interests

A literary publisher, Coteau Books features chapter books for middle-grade and young adult readers. It accepts submissions from Canadian authors only.
Website: www.coteaubooks.com

Freelance Potential

Published 21 titles (12 juvenile) in 2002: 20 were developed from unsolicited submissions, 3 were by agented authors, and 1 was a reprint/licensed property. Of the 21 titles, 14 were by unpublished writers and 16 were by authors who were new to the publishing house. Receives 250 queries, 250 unsolicited mss yearly.

- **Fiction:** Published 10 middle-grade books, 8–12 years; and 2 young adult novels, 12–18 years. Also publishes chapter books, 5–10 years. Genres include regional, contemporary, and historical fiction; adventure; mystery; suspense; and humor. Also publishes stories about nature and the environment.
- **Representative Titles:** *Captain Jenny and the Sea of Wonders* by Duncan Thornton (9+ years) is a story of a girl's quest to find a city that has slipped beneath the waves. *Tunnels of Terror* by Mary Harelkin Bishop (10+ years) features a brother and sister who journey through a tunnel to the past.

Submissions and Payment

Canadian authors only. Guidelines available with 9x12 SASE ($.90 Canadian postage). Query with summary, writing samples, and curriculum vitae; or send complete ms. Accepts photocopies and computer printouts. No simultaneous submissions. SASE. Responds in 3–6 months. Publication in 1–2 years. Royalty; 10%.

Editor's Comments

Fiction for middle-grade or young adult readers is needed at this time. We do not want to see submissions of picture books for young children, nor will we consider horror. We are a literary publisher, and our books have won many awards. The work you submit to us must be of the highest quality.

Covenant Communications

Box 416
American Fork, UT 84003-0416

Acquisitions Editor: Tyler Moulton

Publisher's Interests
All of the material published by Covenant Communications
supports the doctrine and values of The Church of Jesus
Christ of Latter-day Saints, although it has no direct affilia-
tion with the church. Its catalogue includes a wide range of
materials including books, videos, CD-ROMs, and audio cassettes for readers of all ages.
Website: www.covenant-lds.com

Freelance Potential
Published 12 titles in 2002: 4 were developed from unsolicited submissions. Receives 50 queries, 50 mss yearly.
- **Fiction:** Publishes early picture books, 0–4 years; story picture
  books, 4–10 years; and young adult books, 12–18 years. Genres include adventure, humor, suspense, romance, science fiction, and inspirational and historical fiction.
- **Nonfiction:** Publishes concept books and early picture books,
  0–4 years; and story picture books, 4–10 years. Also publishes
  biographies, activity books, novelty and board books, photo
  essays, reference titles, and books in series. Topics include history, religion, and regional subjects.
- **Representative Titles:** *Follow the Prophet* by Val Chadwick
  Bagley is a lift-the-flap book featuring stories from Adam to the
  modern prophets. *Popcorn Popping on the Apricot Tree* by
  Michael Muir is a board book that features illustrations to
  accompany this popular children's song.

Submissions and Payment
Guidelines available at website. Query or send complete ms
with summary. Accepts e-mail queries to tylerm@
covenant-lds.com, photocopies, computer printouts, and disk
submissions. SASE. Responds in 3 months. Publication in
6–12 months. Payment policy varies.

Editor's Comments
If you are familiar with our materials and feel your idea is right
for us, by all means, send it on. We prefer to see a complete
manuscript for fiction submissions.

Creative Bound

P.O. Box 424
151 Tansley Drive
Carp, Ontario K0A 1L0
Canada

President: Gail Baird

Publisher's Interests
Founded in 1985 as a general trade book publishing house, Creative Bound now focuses on publishing nonfiction works for personal growth and enhanced performance. Its list includes parenting titles, self-help titles, and books about body, mind, and spirit. It will not be accepting children's books until 2004.
Website: www.creativebound.com

Freelance Potential
Published 4 titles in 2002: 3 were developed from unsolicited submissions. Of the 4 titles, 2 were by unpublished writers and 2 were by authors who were new to the publishing house. Receives 120 queries yearly.
- **Nonfiction:** Publishes informational and self-help books. Topics include parenting, personal growth, health, fitness, spirituality, recovery, healing, business, motivation, and teaching.
- **Representative Titles:** *Laughter, Love & Limits: Parenting for Life* by Dr. Maggie Mamen (parents) explores the various myths associated with parenting and creates a general parenting philosophy. *Nice on My Feelings: Nurturing the Best in Children and Parents* by Dr. Terry Orlick provides information that helps parents not only become better parents, but better people.

Submissions and Payment
Catalogue available with 6x9 SAE/IRC. Query. Accepts photocopies and IBM disk submissions. SAE/IRC. Responds in 1 month. Publication in 6–12 months. Royalty.

Editor's Comments
Please note that we will not be reviewing manuscripts for children until 2004. We are interested in seeing innovative ideas for books about parenting, as well as titles that explore personal growth and issues of body, mind, and spirit. Healing and recovery titles are also welcome. Tremendous satisfaction is derived for our authors, and our company personnel, from writing and publishing in these areas. We find it inspiring to help individuals throughout North America and worldwide.

Creative Editions

123 South Broad Street
Mankato, MN 56001

Managing Editor: Aron Frisch

Publisher's Interests
Fiction, nonfiction, poetry, and picture books are all part of
the catalogue of Creative Editions, an imprint of the The Creative Company. Its list includes books for all ages.

Freelance Potential
Published 5 titles in 2002: 3 were by agented authors.
Receives 50 queries yearly.
- **Fiction:** Publishes story picture books, 4–10 years; and young
  adult books, 12–18 years. Genres include fairy tales and folktales. Also publishes poetry.
- **Nonfiction:** Publishes young adult books, 12–18 years. Topics
  include nature, the environment, animals, and sports. Also features biographies.
- **Representative Titles:** *Life in the Sea* (9+ years) examines the
  many creatures who live underwater; part of the LifeViews
  series. *Tigers* (9+ years) features color photographs and illustrations that detail the tiger's development and habitat; part of
  the Zoobooks series.

Submissions and Payment
Query with 500-word sample from manuscript. Accepts photocopies and computer printouts. No simultaneous submissions. SASE. Responds in 4–6 months. Publication in 4
years. Royalty; advance.

Editor's Comments
With more than 70 years in the publishing business, we are
proud to bring our readers the very highest quality books.
While we are always on the lookout for new talent, we are
highly selective and publish only a limited number of new
books each year. We suggest that prospective writers review
our current catalogue as well as some of the titles on our list
before sending a submission. We look for books that are
unique and that we feel will be recognized for their excellent
writing, design, and illustration. Send us a 500-word sample of
a book you feel will touch readers in a way that will make it
special for them for years to come.

Creative Education

123 South Broad Street
Mankato, MN 56001

Managing Editor: Aron Frisch

Publisher's Interests

Creative Education is an imprint of the Creative Company.
Catering to the library and school markets, it specializes in
books for readers between the ages of eight and eighteen.
Most of its titles are used as resource materials in the classroom. Topics covered include animals, nature, culture, the
arts, literature, history, and science. Many of its titles are
published as part of a series.

Freelance Potential

Published 130 titles in 2002: 10–20 were developed from
unsolicited submissions and 5 were by agented authors.
Receives 75 queries yearly.

- **Fiction:** Publishes story picture books, 4–10 years.
- **Nonfiction:** Publishes story picture books, 4–10 years; middle-
  grade books, 8–12 years; and young adult books, 12–18 years.
  Topics include nature, science, geology, endangered species,
  Native Americans, astronomy, the arts, humanities, literature,
  world history, and explorers. Also publishes biographies.
- **Representative Titles:** *India* (9+ years) introduces readers to
  fascinating facts about the culture, history, and economics of
  India; part of the Let's Investigate series. *World Agriculture* (10+
  years) looks at the wonders of agriculture around the world
  and is accompanied by quizzes, games, and ideas for activities;
  part of the Creative Discoveries series.

Submissions and Payment

Guidelines available. Query with manuscript sample. Accepts
photocopies and computer printouts. No simultaneous submissions. SASE. Responds in 4–6 months. Publication in 4
years. Payment policy varies.

Editor's Comments

Most of what we publish is in the nonfiction arena and qualified writers are always welcome to send us a query. Keep in
mind that we target the school and library markets, and make
sure your idea is compatible with the current curriculum
needs of your book's target age range.

Creative Learning Press

1733 Storrs Road
Holiday Mall
Storrs, CT 06268

Editor: Kris Morgan

Publisher's Interests
Educational materials, textbooks, activity books, and how-to titles for children in elementary school through high school are available from Creative Learning Press. It also offers a number of resource titles for parents and teachers of gifted students. This publisher has been in business for more than 25 years.
Website: www.creativelearningpress.com

Freelance Potential
Published 5 titles in 2002. Receives 40 queries, 40 unsolicited mss yearly.
- **Nonfiction:** Publishes textbooks, educational materials, how-to titles, teaching resources, and audio cassettes, grades K–12. Topics include science, mathematics, language arts, geography, history, research skills, business, fine arts, and leadership.
- **Representative Titles:** *Frank Lloyd Wright for Kids* by Kathleen Thorne-Thomsen (grades 3–8) offers a narrative of the architect's life combined with photographs of his designs and the nature that inspired him. *How to Tape Instant Oral Biographies* by William Zimmerman (grades 4–8) explains how to create a library filled with spoken histories from various family members and friends.

Submissions and Payment
Query with sample pages; or send complete ms with résumé and artwork. Accepts photocopies, computer printouts, and e-mail to raknox@creativelearningpress.com. SASE. Responds in 1 month. Publication period varies. Royalty.

Editor's Comments
Creative how-to books for children are always of interest here. Possible subjects include drawing, writing, photography, gardening, and the Internet. We would also like to see more manuals and activity books for teachers working with gifted children. Proposals must be detailed and include concrete examples that illustrate your ideas. Use concise, direct writing and tell us about the book's intended audience.

Creative Teaching Press

P.O. Box 2723
Huntington Beach, CA 92647

Director of Product Development: Carolea Williams

Publisher's Interests

This publisher's educational resource materials are used in preschool through eighth-grade classrooms. Many of its titles are written by teachers themselves. Creative Teaching Press's product line also includes bulletin board sets, puzzles, borders, and charts.
Website: www.creativeteaching.com

Freelance Potential

Published 75 titles n 2002: 18–20 were developed from unsolicited submissions. Of the 75 titles, 48 were by unpublished writers. Receives 500 queries yearly.
- **Fiction:** Publishes easy-to-read books, 4–7 years. Genres include ethnic and multicultural fiction, fantasy, and folktales.
- **Nonfiction:** Publishes easy-to-read titles, 4–7 years. Topics include history, social issues, arts and crafts, and mathematics. Also features special education and multicultural titles.
- **Representative Titles:** *I'm Through! What Can I Do?* (teachers, grades 3–6) helps teachers occupy kids who finish class assignments ahead of others and includes word puzzles, logic problems, and creative-thinking tasks. *Responding to Literature* (teachers, grades 1–6) includes a number of activities that help students strengthen reading comprehension.

Submissions and Payment

Guidelines available. Query with outline and sample pages. Accepts photocopies, computer printouts, and simultaneous submissions if identified. SASE. Responds in 1–2 months. Publication period and payment policy vary.

Editor's Comments

We offer a diverse array of products designed to make life easier for teachers and parents of elementary and middle-school children. Our products are constantly growing and changing—just like the kids. We're interested in reviewing fresh, new teaching ideas that have been successfully tested in the classroom. Send us an outline of your idea and some sample pages of your manuscript.

Creative With Words Publications

P.O. Box 223226
Carmel, CA 93922

Editor and Publisher: Brigitta Geltrich

Publisher's Interests
Creative With Words Publications is a small press that develops thematic anthologies for readers of all ages. Its anthologies include folkloristic matter, as well as poetry, prose, and computer art by children. The books cover topics such as animals, nature, school, travel, family, friends, and values.
Website: http://members.tripod.com/CreativeWithWords

Freelance Potential
Published 12 titles in 2002. Receives 800–1,000 queries and unsolicited mss yearly.
- **Fiction:** Publishes anthologies for all ages. Genres include fairy tales, folktales, romance, and humor, as well as stories about nature, the environment, animals, sports, holidays, and school issues.
- **Nonfiction:** Publishes educational anthologies for all ages. Topics includes animals, pets, nature, sports, and humor.
- **Representative Titles:** *We Are Writers, Too!* (all ages) presents creative writing and artwork by children. *Nature!* (all ages) features a variety of poems and short stories by child and adult authors that focus on nature.

Submissions and Payment
Guidelines available. Query or send complete ms. Accepts photocopies and computer printouts. No simultaneous submissions. SASE. Responds to queries in 1–4 weeks, to mss 1 month after anthology deadline. Publication in 1 month. No payment; 20% discount on copies purchased. "Best of Month" entry wins one copy of the issue.

Editor's Comments
Our motto is: Look at the world from a different perspective, research your topic thoroughly, be creative, apply brevity, tell the story from a viewpoint, tighten dialogue, be less descriptive, proofread before submitting, and be patient. We suggest that you check our website for guidelines and monthly themes before you submit your work. Work by unpublished writers is always welcome!

Cricket Books

Suite 1100
332 South Michigan Avenue
Chicago, IL 60604

Submissions Editor

Publisher's Interests
This imprint of the well-known Cricket Magazine Group features chapter books, middle-grade fiction, and young adult novels. It also considers high-quality nonfiction for readers of all ages.
Website: www.cricketbooks.net

Freelance Potential
Published 18 titles in 2002: 3 were by agented authors. Of the 18 titles, 3 were by unpublished writers and 10 were by authors who were new to the publishing house. Receives 500 queries, 1,500 unsolicited mss yearly.
- **Fiction:** Publishes chapter books, 5–10 years; middle-grade novels, 8–12 years; and young adult books, 12–18 years. Genres include fantasy and contemporary, historical, and multicultural fiction. Also publishes poetry books, bilingual books, picture books, and humor.
- **Nonfiction:** Publishes books about history, mathematics, science, technology, social issues, and sports.
- **Representative Titles:** *Robert and the Great Pepperoni* by Barbara Seuling (6–9 years) is the story of a boy who opens a pet-sitting service and experiences all kinds of adventures with birds, cats, and a stray dog. *Scorpio's Child* by Kezi Matthews (YA) is a novel set in a small Southern town in the 1940s about healing family wounds.

Submissions and Payment
Guidelines and catalogue available at website. For nonfiction, query with clips, table of contents, sample chapters, and description of competition. Send complete ms for fiction. Accepts photocopies. SASE. Responds to queries in 3 months, to mss in 4 months. Publication in 18 months. Royalty, up to 10%; advance, $2,000.

Editor's Comments
At this time, we are most interested in reviewing chapter books and titles for middle-grade readers and young adults; however, we will consider picture books.

Critical Thinking Books & Software

P.O. Box 448
Pacific Grove, CA 93950

Publisher: Michael O. Baker

Publisher's Interests
For more than 25 years, this publisher has been a leader in teaching thinking skills to students in kindergarten through college. It provides easy-to-use products that improve learning in all areas of the curriculum. 20% self-, subsidy, co-venture, or co-op published material.
Website: www.criticalthinking.com

Freelance Potential
Published 15 titles in 2002: 2 were developed from unsolicited submissions. Of the 15 titles, 2 were by unpublished writers and 1 was by an author new to the publishing house. Receives 10 unsolicited mss yearly.

- **Fiction:** Publishes easy-to-read books, 4–7 years. Genres include mysteries related to classroom subjects.
- **Nonfiction:** Publishes easy-to-read books, 4–7 years; chapter books, 5–10 years; middle-grade books, 8–12 years; and young adult books, 12–18 years. Topics include language arts, mathematics, science, social studies, and general thinking skills.
- **Representative Titles:** *Critical Thinking* by Anita Harnadek (grades 7–12) teaches students the fundamentals of logic, argumentation, and critical reading they will need to succeed in the future. *Think Analogies* (grades 3–5) includes analogies based on synonyms and antonyms to analyze the structure of relationships between word pairs.

Submissions and Payment
Guidelines available. Send complete ms. Accepts photocopies, computer printouts, and Macintosh and DOS disk submissions. SASE. Responds in 1–9 months. Publication in 1–2 years. Royalty, 10%.

Editor's Comments
Our products use higher-order thinking to teach standards-based content. We do not want material that teaches through drill and memorization. Our goal is to provide resources that empower the mind to improve test scores and solve problems. We need activities appropriate for gifted and remedial students.

Crocodile Books, USA

Interlink Publishing Group, USA
46 Crosby Street
Northhampton, MA 01060

Editor: Ruth Moushabeck

Publisher's Interests

Crocodile Books, USA offers a line of story picture books for children up to the age of 12. An imprint of Interlink Publishing Group, it features nonfiction titles on a variety of subjects, including animals, nature, and the environment. Fiction genres include adventure, fantasy, and folktales.
Website: www.interlinkbooks.com

Freelance Potential

Published 8 titles in 2002: 1 was developed from an unsolicited submission, 4 were by agented authors, and 4 were reprint/licensed properties. Receives 500 unsolicited mss each year.

- **Fiction:** Publishes story picture books, 3–12 years. Genres include ethnic and multicultural fiction, adventure, fantasy, and folktales.
- **Nonfiction:** Publishes story picture books, 3–12 years. Topics include animals, pets, nature, and the environment.
- **Representative Titles:** *The Jade Necklace* by Paul Yee (3–8 years) is a story about a girl living at the turn of the nineteenth century in South China whose fisherman father vanishes in a ferocious storm. *Elvis the Camel* by Barbara Devine (3–12 years) depicts the true story of a young camel whose life is shattered when he is hit by a truck late at night.

Submissions and Payment

Query with up to 10 ms pages, illustration sample, synopsis, and author biography. Accepts photocopies and computer printouts. SASE. Responds in 1–2 months. Publication in 18 months. Royalty; 6–7%.

Editor's Comments

If you want us to consider your story, samples of illustrations that would appear in your published book must accompany your manuscript. We do not match writers with artists. If you review our catalogue, you'll see that we publish a variety of stories from all over the world; many of our titles have international themes.

Crossquarter Publishing Group

P.O. Box 8756
Sante Fe, NM 87504

Submissions Editor: Tony Ravenscroft

Publisher's Interests
This electronic publisher offers books with ideas to balance
the body, mind, heart, and spirit. Its imprints feature science
fiction titles for young adults, as well as biographies and
autobiographies.
Website: www.crossquarter.com

Freelance Potential
Published 6 titles (1 juvenile) in 2002: each was developed
from unsolicited submissions. Of the 6 titles, 5 were by
unpublished writers and all were by authors who were new
to the publishing house. Receives 150+ queries yearly.
- **Fiction:** Published 1 young adult novel, 12–18 years. Features
  science fiction titles. Also publishes science fiction titles for
  adult readers.
- **Nonfiction:** Published 1 young adult book, 12–18 years. Topics
  include health, fitness, metaphysics, healing techniques, the
  environment, and cultural issues. Also publishes New Age
  titles for adults.
- **Representative Titles:** *Gods & Goddesses of the Zodiac* by
  Anne Marie Garrison is a coloring book that features a collection of gods and goddesses from around the world. *Beyond
  One's Own* by Gabriel Constans features interviews with 15
  people who have transformed personal grief into social and
  political reform following the death of a family member.

Submissions and Payment
Guidelines available at website. Query. Accepts photocopies
and simultaneous submissions if identified. SASE. Responds
in 2–3 months. Publication in 9 months. Royalty, 8–10%.

Editor's Comments
We seek e-books that promote personal sovereignty, foster
cross-cultural understanding, and increase environmental
awareness. Send us young adult fiction for our CrossTIME
imprint, metaphysics and magic titles for our Fenris Brothers
imprint, and essays, autobiographies, and visionary fiction
for our Xemplar imprint.

Crossway Books

Good News Publishers
1300 Crescent Street
Wheaton, IL 60187

Editorial Administrator: Jill Carter

Publisher's Interests

This publisher's juvenile list includes middle-grade novels and Bible stories. For adults, it offers parenting titles and books about Christian living and homeschooling. Everything published by Crossway Books is written from an evangelical Christian perspective.
Website: www.crosswaybooks.org

Freelance Potential

Published 70 titles (9 juvenile) in 2002: 4 were developed from unsolicited submissions, 6 were by agented authors, and 4 were reprint/licensed properties. Of the 70 titles, 3 were by unpublished writers and 7 were by authors who were new to the publishing house. Receives 2,500 queries yearly.

- **Fiction:** Published 3 toddler books, 0–4 years; 3 story picture books, 4–10 years; and 3 middle-grade novels, 8–12 years. Genres include historical and contemporary fiction and adventure, all with Christian themes.
- **Nonfiction:** Publishes adult parenting and educational books on home and family life, Christian living, homeschooling, health, the Bible, and church issues.
- **Representative Titles:** *Yes or No, Who Will Go?* by Melody Carlson uses rhyming verse to retell several of Jesus' parables. *Retta Barre's Oregon Trail* by Stephen Bly (8–12 years) is a historical novel about a 12-year-old girl who encounters prairie pirates and stubborn buffaloes on the Oregon Trail.

Submissions and Payment

Guidelines available. Query with outline/synopsis and 2 sample chapters. No e-mail queries or unsolicited mss. Accepts photocopies and simultaneous submissions if identified. SASE. Responds in 6–8 weeks. Publication in 12–18 months. Payment policy varies.

Editor's Comments

Your book must be written from an evangelical Christian perspective to be considered for our list. While we're interested in juvenile fiction, we aren't accepting picture books at this time.

Crown Books for Young Readers

Random House
1540 Broadway
New York, NY 10036

Submissions Editor

Publisher's Interests
A division of Random House Children's Books, Crown Books for Young Readers offers a list that includes titles for readers from birth through the young adult years. It offers nonfiction titles only.
Website: www.randomhouse.com/kids

Freelance Potential
Published 25 titles in 2002: 1 was developed from an unsolicited submission, 11 were by agented authors, and 4 were reprint/licensed properties. Receives 500 queries, 1,000 unsolicited mss yearly.
- **Nonfiction:** Publishes concept books and toddler books, 0–4 years; story picture books, 4–10 years; chapter books, 5–10 years; middle-grade titles, 8–12 years; and young adult titles, 12–18 years. Topics include social issues, history, sports, science, and nature.
- **Representative Titles:** *Grow! Babies!* by Penny Gentieu (0–4 years) follows a year in the lives of 20 babies and brings readers photos and text about each developmental stage. *Model T* by David Weitzman (8+ years) tells the story of the legendary car built by Henry Ford.

Submissions and Payment
Guidelines available. Query or send complete ms. Accepts photocopies, computer printouts, and simultaneous submissions if identified. Availability of artwork improves chance of acceptance. SASE. Responds in 3 months. Publication period varies. Royalty; advance.

Editor's Comments
As a major publisher of children's titles, we receive hundreds of queries and unsolicited manuscripts each year, many of which are rejected because they simply do not fit our requirements. If you are interested in submitting your work, please review our guidelines as well as some of the titles in our current catalogue before you send your work. Books that include artwork are encouraged.

CSS Publishing Company

P.O. Box 4503
517 South Main Street
Lima, OH 45802-4503

Submissions Editor: Stan Purdum

Publisher's Interests
This publishing company is an ecumenical resource center for religious leaders and educators who are interested in promoting an active Christian lifestyle.
Website: www.csspub.com

Freelance Potential
Published 180 titles in 2002: 100 were developed from unsolicited submissions, 2 were by agented authors, and 10 were reprint/licensed properties. Of the 180 titles, 25 were by unpublished writers and 80 were by authors who were new to the publishing house. Receives 1,000 unsolicited mss yearly.
- **Nonfiction:** Publishes story picture books, 4–10 years; and young adult books, 12–18 years. Topics include religious education, prayer, worship, and family life. Also publishes resource materials, program planners, newsletters, and church supplies for Christian educators.
- **Representative Titles:** *Old Testament Stories* by Mark Lawrence presents favorite stories of the Bible in rhyming verse to help readers learn God's word. *My Guardian Angel in My Mourning* by Regina Ann Shay (pre-K–grade 8) uses allegories and analogies to introduce the concept of death and dying as the beginning of a new spiritual dimension.

Submissions and Payment
Guidelines and catalogue available at website. Send complete ms with résumé. Accepts photocopies, computer printouts, and simultaneous submissions if identified. SASE. Responds in 6 months. Publication in 6 months. Royalty. Flat fee.

Editor's Comments
Among others, our audience includes Lutheran, United Methodist, and Episcopal congregations. We want material that meets a real need in those congregations. Our resources are practical—we like children's object lessons and other resources for youth; parish-tested materials for education, youth ministry, and stewardship; and resources for worship, preaching, and study with children.

Dandy Lion Publications

Suite L
3563 Sueldo
San Luis Obispo, CA 93401-7331

Editor: Dianne Draze

Publisher's Interests
In operation for more than 20 years, this publisher provides educational teaching materials for use in kindergarten through eighth-grade classrooms. It targets teachers working in regular classrooms as well as in special and gifted education programs.
Website: www.dandylionbooks.com

Freelance Potential
Published 10 titles in 2002: 3 were developed from unsolicited submissions and 7 were by agented authors. Of the 10 titles, 3 were by authors who were new to the publishing house. Receives 30–40 queries yearly.
- **Nonfiction:** Publishes educational teaching materials, grades K–8. Features books that include educational activities, exercises, games, or instructional procedures. Topics include literature, language, research, mathematics, science, and critical and creative thinking.
- **Representative Titles:** *Jury Trials in the Classroom* by Betty M. See (grades 5–8) includes six trial simulations that teach students about criminal and civil law. *Marine Science 1* by Lisa Wood (grades K–2) features information, experiments, and activities that focus on the tide pool ecosystem.

Submissions and Payment
Guidelines available. Accepts queries from practicing teachers only. Query with sample chapters. No unsolicited mss. Accepts photocopies, computer printouts, and simultaneous submissions if identified. SASE. Responds in 2–4 weeks. Publication in 6–9 months. Royalty; advance.

Editor's Comments
We are a leading publisher of educational teaching materials that stress the development of creative and critical thinking in students. We're primarily interested in materials that can be used with above-average, creative students. In your query, tell us how the material will be used in the classroom and where it will fit in the curriculum.

May Davenport, Publishers

26313 Purissima Road
Los Altos Hills, CA 94022

Publisher & Editor: May Davenport

Publisher's Interests
Fiction for children in kindergarten through high school is
the specialty of this small, family-owned publishing house. It
also features fiction material to supplement high school literature curricula.
Website: www.maydavenportpublishers.com

Freelance Potential
Published 5 titles in 2002: all were developed from unsolicited
submissions and 2 were by agented authors. Of the 5 titles, 3
were by unpublished writers and 3 were by authors who were
new to the publishing house. Receives 1,000+ queries yearly.
- **Fiction:** Published 5 young adult novels, 12–15 years. Genres
  include adventure, humor, mystery, and historical fiction. Also
  publishes read-and-color books, 6–8 years; story picture books,
  4–10 years; and middle-grade novels, 8–12.
- **Representative Titles:** *Surviving Sarah* by Dinah Leigh (YA) is
  the story of a single-parent mother raising her three children in
  New York during the 1940s. *Newman Assignment* by Kurt Har-
  berl (YA) compares the different lifestyles between a boy who
  finishes a special writing assignment to boost his grade and
  the handicapped school janitor, who also completes the assignment to finally earn his first A.

Submissions and Payment
Guidelines available. Query. SASE. Responds in 1–2 weeks.
Publication in 1–2 years. Royalty, 15%. Flat fee.

Editor's Comments
We are always interested in books that serve as supplementary
novels to high school English and creative writing courses.
Material that motivates reluctant readers will always be considered. We also like to see humorous fiction for 15- to 18-
year-old readers, as well as historical fiction. A hint for writers who want to submit to us—use your literary tools pur-
posefully so your audience can read silently and imagine
what is happening in your story.

Jonathan David Publishers

68-22 Eliot Avenue
Middle Village, NY 11379

Editor-in-Chief: Alfred J. Kolatch

Publisher's Interests
Jewish life and culture are the subjects of the juvenile and
adult titles from Jonathan David Publishers. Founded more
than 50 years ago, it offers both hardcover and paperback
titles in its catalogue.
Website: www.jdbooks.com

Freelance Potential
Published 22 titles (2 juvenile) in 2002. Receives 1,200
queries yearly.
- **Fiction:** Publishes easy-to-read books, 4–7 years; and story
  picture books, 4–10 years. Genres include Jewish culture and
  folktales.
- **Nonfiction:** Publishes easy-to-read books, 4–7 years; and middle-grade titles, 8–12 years. Topics include religion, Judaica,
  history, culture, and multicultural issues.
- **Representative Titles:** *A Child's First Book of Jewish Holidays*
  by Alfred J. Kolatch & Harry Araten (3–6 years) uses bright
  and colorful illustrations to introduce young children to the
  major Jewish holidays. *Classic Bible Stories for Jewish Children*
  by Alfred J. Kolatch & Harry Araten tells the story of the biblical figures who have become a familiar and important part of
  Jewish heritage, including Cain, Noah, Moses, David, Jonah,
  Daniel, and Queen Esther.

Submissions and Payment
Guidelines available. Query with résumé, table of contents,
synopsis, and sample chapter. No unsolicited mss. Accepts
photocopies and computer printouts. No simultaneous submissions. SASE. Responds in 1–2 months. Publication in 18
months. Royalty; advance. Flat fee.

Editor's Comments
Although we're interested in all kinds of books dealing with
Jewish life, for children we're especially interested in books
focusing on Bible stories, culture, heroes and heroines, and
Jewish sports personalities. Please note that we do not accept
submissions that have been sent to more than one publisher.

DAW Books

375 Hudson Street
New York, NY 10014

Associate Editor: Peter Stampfel

Publisher's Interests
Science fiction and fantasy novels for young adults and
adults are the specialty of this publishing house. Many of
its titles appear as part of a series. It does not publish short
stories or nonfiction.
Website: www.dawbooks.com

Freelance Potential
Published 48 titles in 2002: 20 were by agented authors. Of
the 48 titles, 1 was by an unpublished writer and 1 was by
an author who was new to the publishing house. Receives
1,000+ unsolicited mss yearly.
- **Fiction:** Publishes science fiction, thriller, and fantasy novels
  for young adults and adults.
- **Representative Titles:** *Heritage and Exile* by Marion Zimmer
  Bradley (YA–Adult) follows the adventures of Regis Hastur,
  monarch of Darkover. *The Gates of Sleep* by Mercedes Lackey
  is set in rural Cornwall and follows the adventures of Marina
  Rosewood.

Submissions and Payment
Guidelines available. Send complete ms. Accepts photocopies
and computer printouts. No simultaneous submissions.
SASE. Responds in 3 months. Publication in 8–12 months.
Royalty, 6%; advance.

Editor's Comments
In business for more than 25 years, we were the first publishing company ever devoted exclusively to science fiction and
fantasy. Over the years, we have earned a reputation for discovering some of the hottest talents in these genres publishing
today. We are still committed to developing new talent, and we
are known to publish first novels of superior quality. Most of
our books run about 80,000 words in length—never shorter.
We are not interested in novellas, poetry, short stories, or
short story collections. Review some of our titles, then send
us your best work. If you are a unique new voice, you will get
our attention.

Dawn Publications

P.O. Box 2010
Nevada City, CA 95959

Editor: Glenn Hovemann

Publisher's Interests

Dawn Publications describes itself as "an inspiration and nature awareness publisher for adults and children." Its purpose is to teach children about the wonders of nature through high-quality picture books, including trade books that are suitable for classroom use.
Website: www.dawnpub.com

Freelance Potential

Published 8 titles (6 juvenile) in 2002: 1 was developed from an unsolicited submission. Of the 8 titles, 2 were by unpublished writers and 3 were by authors who were new to the publishing house. Receives 300 queries, 2,500 unsolicited mss yearly.

- **Nonfiction:** Publishes story picture books, 4–12 years. Topics include the environment, conservation, ecology, family relationships, personal awareness, and multicultural and ethnic issues. Also offers teacher guides.
- **Representative Titles:** *Born With a Bang: The Universe Tells Our Cosmic Story* by Jennifer Morgan (7+ years) tells how time after time the universe nearly perishes, then bravely triumphs and turns itself into new forms. *Under One Rock* by Anthony D. Fredericks (4–10 years) is a rhyming picture book that teaches children about the communities of insects that live under rocks.

Submissions and Payment

Guidelines available at website. Query or send complete ms. Accepts photocopies, computer printouts, and simultaneous submissions if identified. SASE. Responds in 2–3 months. Publication in 18–24 months. Royalty; advance.

Editor's Comments

We feel that nature affirms in young people their natural inclination toward beauty, truth, and a sense of unity and harmony with all life. While many of our titles are by first-time authors, we accept only a few of the thousands of submissions we receive each year, so please follow our guidelines carefully.

Lauri Hornik, Dial Books
Emotional Growth of Protagonists

Dial Books for Young Readers publishes books for children of all ages. "We publish standalone hardcover mysteries, and we'd love it if a book was popular enough to warrant growing a series from it," says Associate Publisher and Editorial Director Lauri Hornik. By *series* she does not mean the standard mass-market variety, but rather several novels featuring the same characters. She points to the John Bellairs series about Johnny Dixon and Lewis Barnavelt. "Our few current series have evolved after a first standalone book was published successfully."

In mysteries, Hornik looks for "uniqueness and fascination—the characters, plot points and narrative style need to be compelling, believable and fresh, and the ending needs to be surprising and satisfying." "In my mind," Hornik says, "truly successful mysteries don't differ at all from other novels in their characters, settings, and plots. That's the intense challenge of writing a mystery—making sure that the mystery elements are included without being overly noticed: providing constant wonder in the reader while also—in the very best mysteries—providing a deeper core of the protagonist's emotional development. I absolutely prefer mysteries that also include emotional growth for the protagonist."

Hornik sees clues as an important mystery element for two reasons: "so that the ending is natural and believable, as well as being surprising, and so that the reader can go back and enjoy the clue-spotting as a second enriching experience."

When submitting to Dial, send a summary and up to 10 pages. Hornik would prefer not to be told the solution but instead receive a summary of the basic story, characters, setting, and theme. "I prefer that the sample be the first chapter of the book," says Hornik. "What I look for most when reviewing a book proposal is compelling sample writing."

(Listing for Dial Books on following page)

Dial Books for Young Readers

Penguin Putnam Inc.
345 Hudson Street
New York, NY 10014

Submissions Editor

Publisher's Interests
This imprint of Penguin Putnam offers a variety of fiction and nonfiction titles for young readers, from toddlers through teens. Its catalogue includes picture books, chapter books, and easy-to-read titles.
Website: www.penguinputnam.com

Freelance Potential
Published 41 titles (40 juvenile) in 2002: 25 were developed from unsolicited submissions, 16 were by agented authors, and 3 were reprint/licensed properties. Receives 2,000+ queries, 1,000+ unsolicited mss yearly.
- **Fiction:** Published 1 concept book, 1 toddler book, and 2 early picture books, 0–4 years; 4 easy-to-read books, 4–7 years; 20 story picture books, 4–10 years; 1 chapter book, 5–10 years; 6 middle-grade titles, 8–12 years; and 5 young adult books, 12–18 years.
- **Nonfiction:** Published 1 easy-to-read book, 4–7 years. Also publishes concept and early picture books, 0–4 years; story picture books, 4–10 years; middle-grade books, 8–12 years; and young adult books, 12–18 years.
- **Representative Titles:** *The Mysterious Tadpole* by Steven Kellogg (4–8 years) is a humorous picture book that deals with typical kid concerns. *The Girls* by Amy Goldman Koss (10+ years) is a contemporary young adult novel that addresses issues of concern to junior high girls.

Submissions and Payment
Guidelines and catalogue available with SASE. Query with up to 10 pages; send complete ms for picture books. SASE. Response time, publication period, and payment policy vary.

Editor's Comments
We accept unsolicited picture book manuscripts and query letters for longer works. Your query letter should briefly describe your manuscript's plot, genre, the intended age group, and your publishing credits. Cue your writing to a child's emotional stepping stones.

Didax

395 Main Street
Rowley, MA 01969

Vice President: Martin Kennedy

Publisher's Interests

Activity books, manipulatives, software, and other teacher resources are found in the Didax catalogue. Its list targets preschool through high school students and covers all areas of learning.
Website: www.didaxinc.com

Freelance Potential

Published 50 titles in 2002: 3–5 were developed from unsolicited submissions and most were reprint/licensed properties. Of the 50 titles, 1 was by an unpublished writer and 2 were by authors who were new to the publishing house. Receives 30–40 queries yearly.

- **Nonfiction:** Publishes reproducible activity books and teacher resources, grades K–12. Topics include counting, measurement, money, geometry, algebra, phonics, spelling, grammar, and language comprehension.
- **Representative Titles:** *Comprehension Lifters: Animals* (grades 2–12) are theme-based reproducibles designed to improve reading skills. *Mathematics Today* (grades 2–7) is a multibook series covering a wide range of math topics.

Submissions and Payment

Guidelines available. Query with résumé and outline; or send complete ms. Accepts photocopies, computer printouts, disk submissions (Microsoft Word), e-mail submissions to development@didaxinc.com, and simultaneous submissions if identified. SASE. Responds to queries in 2 weeks, to mss in 1 month. Publication in 1 year. Royalty; advance.

Editor's Comments

We are always interested in queries or manuscripts for teacher resource books with solid pedagogy and activities. Ideas should be easy for teachers to implement in the classroom and should have been classroom-tested. All curriculum areas are of interest, and we accept material for students in all grades through high school. If you are new to us, please review several of our titles in your area of expertise before submitting.

Discovery Enterprises

31 Laurelwood Drive
Carlisle, MA 01741

President: JoAnne Weisman-Deitch

Publisher's Interests

This specialty publisher offers a catalogue of reproducible plays on topics related to American history, as well as books on history based on primary source material. The plays are geared toward students in grades four through ten and are based on letters, diaries, journals, letters, and government documents. 5% self-, subsidy-, co-venture, or co-op published material.

Website: www.ushistorydocs.com

Freelance Potential

Published 12 titles in 2002: 1–2 were developed from unsolicited submissions. Of the 12 titles, 1 was by an unpublished writer and 2 were by authors who were new to the publishing house. Receives 50–60 queries yearly.

- **Fiction:** Publishes plays, grades 4–10. Also publishes middle-grade novels, 8–12 years; and young adult books, 12–18 years. Genres include historical fiction.
- **Nonfiction:** Published 1 easy-to-read book, 4–7 years; 1 chapter book, 5–10 years; and 6 middle-grade books, 8–12 years. Topics include history. Also publishes education titles.
- **Representative Titles:** *Families at Home—World War II* by Phyllis Raybin Emert deals with the political, social, and economic impact of World War II on American society. *Placing Out: A Play About the Orphan Trains* by Susan Bassler Pickford (grades 4–7) looks at the practice in the US between 1850 and 1930 of sending needy children to families in the West.

Submissions and Payment

Guidelines available. Query with résumé, outline, and nonfiction clips. No unsolicited mss. Accepts photocopies and simultaneous submissions. SASE. Responds in 3 months. Publication in 2–8 months. Royalty.

Editor's Comments

At this time, we're only interested in plays based on American history. Plays should be about 40 minutes in length and must be based on original source material.

DiskUs Publishing

P.O. Box 43
Albany, IN 47320

Chief Executive Officer: Marilyn Nesbitt

Publisher's Interests

DiskUs is an electronic publisher offering fiction and nonfiction for readers of all ages. Its list includes concept and toddler books, easy-to-read titles, and novels for middle-grade readers and young adults. Readers may purchase books through the mail, or may download the titles. The company was established in 1997.

Website: www.diskuspublishing.com

Freelance Potential

Published 60–70 titles (10 juvenile) in 2002: 10 were developed from unsolicited submissions. Receives 12,000 queries each year.

- **Fiction:** Publishes concept and toddler books, 0–4 years; easy-to-read books, 4–7 years; middle-grade novels, 8–12 years; and young adult books, 12–18 years. Features all genres.
- **Nonfiction:** Publishes concept and toddler books, 0–4 years. Topics include religion and self-help issues. Also publishes puzzle books.
- **Representative Titles:** *Baby for Sale 10 Cents* by Betty Jo Schuler is a humorous story about a young girl who tries to sell her new baby brother. *The Lollipop Tree* by Jeanne K. Grieser is about two friends who work at a factory that makes lollipops, and the adventure they find.

Submissions and Payment

Guidelines available at website. Query with résumé, word length, synopsis, and first 3 chapters. Accepts e-mail queries to DiskUsSubs@aol.com. SASE. Responds in 3–6 months. Publication in 5 months. Royalty.

Editor's Comments

We have changed our guidelines. If you send us a query by e-mail, you must include a subject head that reads "DiskUs," followed by your subject. If that subject line is not used, your e-mail will be deleted unopened. Your query should briefly describe your story or subject and include the first three chapters as an attachment.

Displays for Schools

1825 NW 22nd Terrace
Gainesville, FL 32605

Manager: Sherry DuPree

Publisher's Interests
Established in 1976, Displays for Schools features tested
books and materials for classroom use that represent a range
of student interests.
Website: www.displaysforschools.com

Freelance Potential
Published 4 titles in 2002: 1 was developed from an unsolicited submission. Of the 4 titles, all were by unpublished
writers. Receives 500 queries yearly.
- **Nonfiction:** Publishes educational and religious resource material, grades K–12. Topics include history, religion, writing,
  reading, African-American religious history, special education,
  and character-building. Also features reference books, flashcards, CDs, rhyming books, and posters.
- **Representative Titles:** *Busy Bookworm: Good Conduct Book* by
  Herbert C. DuPree shows young readers that good conduct
  builds good character. *Rhymes and Times of Cleo-cat-tra* by
  Lucy T. Geringer (3–7 years) helps children learn to enjoy language and stimulates their language development by showing
  them that rhyming words are fun.

Submissions and Payment
Guidelines available. Query with outline/synopsis and
sample chapters. Accepts disk submissions. SASE. Responds
in 8 weeks. Publication in 4–24 months. Royalty, 10%.

Editor's Comments
New writers are invited to visit our website to review our published material. We seek educational material that can be
used in primary and secondary schools, churches, libraries,
museums, and community centers. Our goal is to supply
educators with useful and instructive materials that will promote learning for students of all ages. This year we are interested in how-to books and flash cards for primary-grade
classrooms, as well as nonfiction resource books for high
school and adult education classes. Send us your ideas for
practical, tested activities or learning projects.

Domhan Books

Suite 514
9511 Shore Road
Brooklyn, NY 11209

Young Adult Editor

Publisher's Interests
This publisher's list includes middle-grade and young adult fiction titles in a variety of genres, as well as nonfiction books. Domhan Books produces many titles that have strong multicultural and ethnic themes, with an emphasis on African-American and Irish themes.
Website: www.domhanbooks,com

Freelance Potential
Published 50 titles (20 juvenile) in 2002: 48 were developed from unsolicited submissions and 12 were by agented authors. Of the 50 titles, 25 were by unpublished writers and 25 were by authors who were new to the publishing house. Receives 500+ queries, 1,500+ unsolicited mss yearly.
- **Fiction:** Published 5 middle-grade novels, 8–12 years. Also publishes young adult books, 12–18 years. Genres include adventure, fantasy, folktales, mystery, suspense, romance, Westerns, and contemporary, historical, inspirational, multi-cultural, religious, and science fiction.
- **Nonfiction:** Published 15 young adult books, 12–18 years. Publishes how-to and informational titles.
- **Representative Titles:** *God's Children* by Clarence Guenter (10–12 years) is the story of a boy growing up in a Mennonite Community in Canada in the 1940s and 1950s. *Obstacles of Love* by Tonya Taylor Ramagos (YA) is a romance about a teenage girl who develops feelings for the student she tutors.

Submissions and Payment
Guidelines and catalogue available at website or with 9x12 SASE ($.60 postage). Query with clips for nonfiction; send complete ms for fiction. Accepts disk submissions (RTF or ASCII). SASE. Responds to queries in 1–2 weeks, to mss in 4–6 weeks. Publication in 6 months. Royalty, 30–50% net.

Editor's Comments
This year we're looking for fantasies, folktales, and romances for readers over twelve. We're also interested in nonfiction focusing on health and literature for this same age group.

Dorling Kindersley

375 Hudson Street
New York, NY 10014

Submissions: Beth Sutinis

Publisher's Interests
This international company specializes in illustrated informational books, interactive software, and CD-ROMs for children of all ages, as well as adults.
Website: www.dk.com

Freelance Potential
Published 250 titles in 2002: 3 were by agented authors and 50 were reprint/licensed properties. Receives 1,000 queries each year.
- **Fiction:** Publishes concept books, toddler books, and early picture books, 0–4 years; easy-to-read books, 4–7 years; story picture books, 4–10 years; chapter books, 5–10 years; middle-grade novels, 8–12 years; and young adult novels, 12–18 years. Genres include contemporary and historical fiction, science fiction, fairy tales, folktales, folklore, humor, mystery, stories about nature, and romance.
- **Nonfiction:** Publishes concept books and toddler books, 0–4 years; easy-to-read books, 4–7 years; middle-grade books, 8–12 years; and young adult books, 12–18 years. Topics include animals, computers, crafts, current events, geography, health and fitness, history, religion, science, social issues, and sports. Also publishes bilingual titles and activity books.
- **Representative Titles:** *American Revolution* (8+ years) offers an eyewitness account of the American war for independence. *My First Farm Touch and Feel* (1–4 years) focuses on the animals, foods, and machines found on a farm.

Submissions and Payment
Guidelines available. No unsolicited mss. Agented queries only. SASE. Responds 6 months. Publication in 2 years. Royalty, 10%; advance, varies.

Editor's Comments
Our titles cover a range of subject areas for all age groups. We like to see books with a combination of educational value and strong visual style that appeal to both parents and children. We work with our authors to ensure our material is the most authoritative, helpful, and engaging available.

Dover Publications

31 East 2nd Street
Mineola, NY 11501-3582

Editor-in-Chief: Paul Negri

Publisher's Interests

Established in 1941, Dover Publications features fiction
reprints for children; juvenile titles on math, science, and
music; and coloring books, activity books, and sticker books
for all ages.
Website: www.doverpublications.com

Freelance Potential

Published 500 titles (120 juvenile) in 2002. Receives 400
queries, 400 unsolicited mss yearly.
- **Fiction:** Publishes reprints of children's classics and story
  books. Genres include folktales, fantasy, and fairy tales. Also
  publishes animal stories.
- **Nonfiction:** Publishes educational titles, anthologies, and
  biographies. Also publishes activity, craft, and coloring books.
  Topics include Native Americans, ancient history, animals,
  dinosaurs, science, mythology, Americana, American history,
  needlework, fashion, languages, literature, hobbies, adventure,
  and fine art.
- **Representative Titles:** *My Family Tree Workbook* by Rosemary
  Chorzempa is an easy-to-use introduction to genealogy
  designed for children. *Plains Indian TeePee Village* by A. G.
  Smith is an accurate representation of Native American life to
  build from paper.

Submissions and Payment

Catalogue available at website. Query or send complete
ms. SASE. Response time varies. Publication period varies.
Flat fee.

Editor's Comments

We encourage you to visit our website to see the variety of
titles we publish. High-quality, historically accurate, original
books for adults and children are our specialty. Young readers like our sticker books, tattoos, and craft titles that
explain life in different times and different places. Projects
children can do with parents and adults are of interest. We
do not accept original fiction or poetry.

Michael Steere, Down East
Mysteries in Maine & New England

Down East Books, based in Camden, Maine, is a small, regional publisher of books for adults and children that includes picture books, chapter books, and novels on its list. "The one criterion that we require in all our books is a strong Maine/New England connection," says Associate Editor Michael Steere.

Down East has published two mysteries for children. "Though we don't intentionally seek out series, two of the adult and both YA mysteries form two unrelated two-book series." The company is not looking specifically for mysteries, but, says Steere, "if a mystery manuscript comes in that we like, then we'll publish it."

Steere looks for mysteries with "interesting, provocative and believable plotting, as well as convincing and plausible characters. No matter what type of book we're considering, the characters have to be convincing. Their voices, actions, mannerisms, all have to make the reader think the character is a real person. Setting, too, must be realistic in regard to the plot." And he stresses that the regional connection is paramount.

Steere points out that tension and suspense are important in a good mystery plot. "Plot should not necessarily have more emphasis than characters. A strong plot shouldn't be an excuse for poor characterization or vice versa."

As for clues, Steere believes that a good mystery should be a puzzle for the reader. "They should be given a chance to solve the mystery along with the character. If I was reading a book and knew I wouldn't be able to solve the mystery, I'd simply skip to the end to find out the answers."

In submitting to Down East, Steere directs writers to send a few sample chapters and an outline for the remainder of the book. "Though it's not necessary to give away the final solution, we'd be very reluctant to sign a book if we weren't absolutely certain of the writer's ability to create a convincing, realistic ending."

Down East Books

P.O. Box 679
Camden, ME 04843

Associate Editor: Michael Steere

Publisher's Interests
This regional publisher specializes in books with strong
Maine or New England themes. For its children's list, Down
East Books prefers titles for very young children over those
written for young adults. 2% self-, subsidy-, co-venture, or
co-op published material.
Website: www.downeastbooks.com

Freelance Potential
Published 26 titles (5 juvenile) in 2002: 3 were developed
from unsolicited submissions, 2 were by agented authors,
and 4 were reprint/licensed properties. Of the 26 titles, 4
were by unpublished writers and 18 were by authors new to
the publishing house. Receives 1,000+ queries each year.
- **Fiction:** Published 3 early picture books, 0–4 years; and 1
  young adult novel, 12–18 years. Also publishes story picture
  books, 4–10 years; easy-to-read books, 4–7 years; chapter
  books, 5–10 years; and middle-grade novels, 8–12 years.
  Genres include adventure, mystery, humor, and contemporary
  fiction—all with New England settings.
- **Nonfiction:** Published 1 early picture book, 0–4 years. Also
  publishes story picture books, 4–10 years. Topics include life
  and nature in Maine and New England.
- **Representative Titles:** *Miss Renée's Mice* by Elizabeth Stokes
  Hoffman (4–8 years) is about a family of mice that takes up
  residence in a dollhouse. *The Orphan Seal* by Fran Hodgkins is
  the true story of the rescue and rehabilitation of a seal pup.

Submissions and Payment
Guidelines available. Query with clips or writing samples.
Accepts photocopies, computer printouts, and simultaneous
submissions if identified. SASE. Responds in 2–8 weeks. Publication in 1 year. Royalty, 9–12%; advance, $300–$600.

Editor's Comments
We welcome submissions of children's books with New England settings, but please do not send us fantasy stories or
stories with Christmas, Halloween, or other holiday themes.

Dramatic Publishing

311 Washington Street
Woodstock, IL 60098

Acquisitions Editor: Linda Habjan

Publisher's Interests

Professional, stock, community, school, and children's theater groups use the dramatic arts materials offered by this publisher. In addition to one-act and full-length plays and musicals, it publishes resource materials and reference texts about the theater arts.
Website: www.dramaticpublishing.com

Freelance Potential

Published 50 titles in 2002. Receives 250 queries, 600 unsolicited mss yearly.

- **Fiction:** Publishes full-length and one-act plays, musicals, and anthologies.
- **Nonfiction:** Publishes books about the theater arts and production guides. Topics include stagecraft, audition techniques, and directing.
- **Representative Titles:** *The Dream Thief* by Robert Schenkkan is a play about two preteens who become convinced that someone has stolen their father's dreams after he becomes mysteriously ill. *Still Life with Iris* by Steven Dietz is a fantastical adventure that focuses on a little girl's search for home.

Submissions and Payment

Guidelines available. Send complete ms with résumé, synopsis, production history, reviews, cast list, set and technical requirements; include audiocassette for musicals. Accepts photocopies and computer printouts. SASE. Responds in 10–12 weeks. Publication in 18 months. Royalty.

Editor's Comments

We continue to look for original plays that appeal to families, as well as one-act plays for large casts. Productions that explain human behavior in new and insightful ways are welcome as well. Always send a properly bound script. Do not send loose pages or pages held together with an elastic band or paper clip. A hard cover keeps the script intact as it is passed around. If you're submitting a musical or a play with music, include a cassette and sheet music if available.

Stephanie Owens Lurie, Dutton Books
Picture Books Go Where Passion & Imagination Lead

As President and Publisher of Dutton Books, Stephanie Owens Lurie personally edits 18 to 22 books a year, most of them picture books. "We are actively seeking imaginative, well-written stories whose primary purpose is to entertain, not instruct, children," Lurie says. "We look for a command of language, wit, characters, and situations that young children can relate to."

Authors are encouraged to go where passion and imagination lead them. "The most successful books spring from the author's imagination, not from any *requirements* on our end. In the case of *The Three Spinning Fairies*, Lisa Campbell Ernst was inspired to interpret this little-known Brothers Grimm tale after reading it to her daughter. She wanted the chance to put her own unique spin on this story about not judging people by their appearances. We felt it was fresh and funny enough to sell despite the fact that we keep hearing there isn't much consumer demand for fairy tales and folktales."

Lurie recommends that authors interested in Dutton review these titles: *Blabbermouse*, by True Kelly; *Little Red Hen Makes a Pizza*, by Philemon Sturges; *School Picture Day*, by Lynn Plourde; *The Old Woman Who Swallowed a Pie*, by Alison Lester; and *Pepito the Brave*, by Scott Beck.

In terms of artwork, a text must offer "plenty of opportunity for active and varied illustrations," Lurie says. Dutton editors favor texts that don't tell the entire story, but allow the artwork to play off the text.

When she receives a query, the following items—in this order—entice Lurie to request the manuscript: "First, the author's ability to communicate; second, the concept; third, a demonstrated wit or cleverness; and fourth, market savvy."

(Listing for Dutton Books on following page)

Dutton Children's Books

Penguin Putnam Books for Young Readers
14th Floor
345 Hudson Street
New York, NY 10014

Queries Editor

Publisher's Interests
Dutton Children's Books is a division of Penguin Putnam Books for Young Readers. Its catalogue offers fiction and non-fiction picture books, early reader books, middle-grade titles, and books for young adults.
Website: www.penguinputnam.com

Freelance Potential
Published 109 titles in 2002: 11 were developed from unsolicited submissions, 53 were by agented authors, and 45 were reprint/licensed properties. Of the 109 titles, 8 were by unpublished writers and 18 were by authors who were new to the publishing house. Receives 2,500 queries yearly.
* **Fiction:** Published 2 concept books, 3 toddler books, and 9 early picture books, 0–4 years; 6 easy-to-read books, (4–7 years); 26 story picture books, 4–10 years; 21 middle-grade books, 8–12 years; and 11 young adult books, 12–18 years. Genres include adventure, mystery, suspense, fantasy, and humor.
* **Nonfiction:** Published 4 story picture books, 4–10 years; 6 middle-grade books, 8–12 years; and 2 young adult books, 12–18 years. Topics include history and nature. Also publishes biographies and interactive nonfiction.
* **Representative Titles:** *The Day My Runny Nose Ran Away* by Jason Eaton (5–9 years) is the story of a boy with a cold whose nose feels it is being mistreated and runs away. *The President and Mom's Apple Pie* by Michael Garland (3–8 years) is about a young boy's meeting with President William Howard Taft.

Submissions and Payment
Guidelines available. Query with brief synopsis, sample pages (up to 10 for novels, up to 5 for picture books), and publishing credits. No unsolicited mss. SASE. Responds in 2–3 months. Publication in 1+ years. Royalty; advance.

Editor's Comments
Two years ago, we changed our submission policy to query letters only. Our aim is to respond to query letters within one month of receipt.

Eager Minds Press

1501 County Hospital Road
Nashville, TN 37218

Assistant Publisher: Dayne E. Kellon

Publisher's Interests

Formerly known as Ideals Children's Books, this small publisher features a list of both fiction and nonfiction books for readers between the ages of three and eight. It accepts submissions from agented authors, members of the Society of Children's Book Writers and Illustrators (SCBWI), and previously published authors only.

Freelance Potential

Published 12 titles in 2002: 6 were developed from unsolicited submissions and 6 were reprint/licensed properties. Of the 12 titles, 6 were by unpublished writers and 6 were by authors who were new to the publishing house. Receives 125 queries, 500–600 unsolicited mss yearly.

- **Fiction:** Published 12 story picture books, 3–8 years. Also publishes easy-to-read books, 3–8 years. Genres include inspirational, multicultural, religious, contemporary, and historical fiction, fairy tales, folktales, and adventure stories.
- **Nonfiction:** Publishes easy-to-read and story picture books, 3–8 years. Topics include religion and history.
- **Representative Titles:** *See the Ocean* by Estelle Condra (5–8 years) is the story of a young girl's love for the sea. *Do I Belong with You?* by Patricia Reeder Eubank (3–7 years) is the story of a baby rhino looking for his home.

Submissions and Payment

Guidelines available. Agented authors, SCBWI members, and previously published book authors only (submit with a list of writing credits). Accepts photocopies, computer printouts, and simultaneous submissions if identified. SASE. Responds in 3–6 months. Publication in 2 years. Payment policy varies.

Editor's Comments

We are interested in seeing picture books for children between the ages of three and eight, both fiction and nonfiction. Our books are either 24 or 32 pages, and between 600 and 1,600 words in length. We look for strong, character-driven stories that also instill a moral or teach a lesson.

Eakin Press

Sunbelt Media, Inc.
P.O. Drawer 90159
Austin, TX 78709-0159

President: Edwin Eakin

Publisher's Interests
Texas and the American Southwest are the focus of the books from Eakin Press. Its titles deal with the history, geography, and culture of the region. It offers both fiction and nonfiction for preschoolers through teens.
Website: www.eakinpress.com

Freelance Potential
Published 70 titles (30 juvenile) in 2002: 30 were developed from unsolicited submissions. Receives 1,200 queries yearly.
- **Fiction:** Publishes early picture books, 0–4 years; easy-to-read books, 4–7 years; chapter books, 5–10 years; and middle-grade novels, 8–12 years. Genres include historical and multicultural fiction, folklore, and stories about animals.
- **Nonfiction:** Publishes easy-to-read titles, 4–7 years; story picture books, 4–10 years; chapter books, 5–10 years; and middle-grade books, 8–12 years. Features books on regional history and biographies.
- **Representative Titles:** *What Did I Do to Deserve a Sister Like You?* by Angela Shelf Medearis is an easy-to-read chapter book about a girl who has to deal with her bossy but beautiful older sibling. *Oklahoma and Its Heroes* by James M. Smallwood focuses on the men and women of diverse cultures and races who helped create Oklahoma's heritage.

Submissions and Payment
Guidelines available. Query with résumé, sample chapter, and clips or writing samples. Accepts photocopies, computer printouts, and simultaneous submissions if identified. SASE. Responds in 1–3 months. Publication in 2–18 months. Royalty.

Editor's Comments
We publish only about 70 of the more than 1,000 manuscripts we receive each year. To make it out of the slush pile, you must be familiar with our publishing objectives. Don't submit a query until you send for a copy of our most recent catalogue. Picture books and chapter books for children in preschool through third grade remain a top priority.

ebooksonthe.net

Write Words, Inc.
2934 Old Route 50
Cambridge, MD 21613

Publisher: Constance Foster

Publisher's Interests
Now under new ownership, this e-publisher plans to produce
a minimum of 15 new titles a year, with approximately one-
third directed at children. It offers both fiction and nonfiction
books for people of all ages.
Website: www.ebooksonthe.net

Freelance Potential
Published 18 titles (5 juvenile) in 2002: 8 were developed
from unsolicited submissions. Receives 1,200 queries, 1,500
unsolicited mss yearly.
- **Fiction:** Publishes fiction for all ages. Genres include mainstream, experimental, historical, Western, and science fiction;
  adventure, horror, and mystery.
- **Nonfiction:** Publishes nonfiction for all ages. Topics include
  psychology, money, business, and self-help issues. Also publishes inspirational titles, and books of international interest
  and subject matter.
- **Representative Titles:** *Time Quake* by Patricia Uletilovic
  (10–14 years) is a science fiction tale about two children's
  travels through time, thanks to an invention by their father.
  The Ghost Who Lived on Jefferson Street by Rebecca J. Zarrin-
  negar features a young hero who never believed in ghosts . . .
  until he met one.

Submissions and Payment
Guidelines available. Query or send complete ms. Accepts
disk submissions and e-mail submissions to publisher@
ebooksonthe.net. SASE. Responds to queries in 1 day, to mss
in 3 months. Publication in 3 months. Royalty, 40%.

Editor's Comments
While we do include books for children, parents, and teachers
on our list, most of our titles are for all ages. For the coming
year, we are interested in seeing craft and how-to books for all
ages, as well as biographies and self-help titles. We are always
interested in reviewing work by new writers and encourage
them to submit their work.

Educational Ministries

165 Plaza Drive
Prescott, AZ 86303-5549

Submissions Editor: Linda Davidson

Publisher's Interests

Educational Ministries has been publishing Christian education resources for mainline Protestant churches for more than 20 years. Its catalogue is filled with educational fiction with Christian themes, activity books, parenting titles, and videos for use in religious education classes. Its products are used by Christian educators and worship leaders.
Website: www.educationalministries.com

Freelance Potential

Published 5 titles (1 juvenile) in 2002: 1 was developed from an unsolicited submission. Receives 200 queries, 190 unsolicited mss yearly.

- **Fiction:** Publishes toddler books, 0–4 years. Also publishes educational fiction with Christian themes and adult fiction.
- **Nonfiction:** Publishes educational resource books.
- **Representative Titles:** *Ash Wednesday Through Easter: Devotions for Children* by Elaine M. Ward is a devotional book that can be used at home that encourages youngsters to "walk and talk" with Jesus during Lent. *Life and Bible Times* by Anne Gilbert is a complete unit of Bible studies, activity sheets, creative arts, music, recreation, worship, and field trips for three age groups.

Submissions and Payment

Guidelines available. Send complete ms. Accepts photocopies, computer printouts, and simultaneous submissions if identified. SASE. Responds in 6–8 weeks. Publication in 1–4 months. Flat fee.

Editor's Comments

If you have ideas for innovative and creative approaches to Christian education, we want to hear from you. We continue to look for titles that focus on the importance of parental role modeling, as well as books that tell how to keep senior citizens involved in church life. We also use ideas for vacation church school and summer programming. Writers should be familiar with the types of material we publish prior to submitting.

Educators Publishing Service

31 Smith Place
Cambridge, MA 02138-1089

Vice President, Publishing: Charlie Heinle

Publisher's Interests

Books and workbooks for use in kindergarten through high school classrooms fill the pages of Educators Publishing Service's catalogue. It publishes materials designed to teach reading, spelling, vocabulary, English, handwriting, typing, and elementary mathematics.
Website: www.epsbooks.com

Freelance Potential

Published 30 titles in 2002: 10 were developed from unsolicited submissions. Of the 30 titles, 5 were by unpublished writers and 5 were by authors who were new to the publishing house. Receives 200 unsolicited mss yearly.

- **Fiction:** Publishes easy-to-read books, 4–7 years; chapter books, 5–10 years; and middle-grade novels, 8–12 years. Genres include multicultural and ethnic fiction.
- **Nonfiction:** Publishes reading, writing, vocabulary, grammar, comprehension, and elementary math workbooks, grades K–12. Also publishes educational materials for students with learning disabilities.
- **Representative Titles:** *Just Write: An Elementary Writing Sourcebook* (grades 2–3) encourages students to use brainstorming and other techniques to get their ideas on paper. *Writing Skills 3* by Diana Hanbury Kind (grades 9–12) helps students generate ideas, argue points, and understand the process of expository writing.

Submissions and Payment

Send complete ms with résumé. Accepts photocopies, computer printouts, and simultaneous submissions if identified. SASE. Responds in 2 months. Publication in 1 year. Royalty.

Editor's Comments

If you have developed curriculum or created lessons that have met with success and that you believe have wider applications, we encourage you to contact us. We're also interested in ideas for book or workbook series for kindergarten through twelfth-grade classrooms.

Edupress

208 Fabricante, #200
San Clemente, CA 92675

Submissions Editor: Amanda Meinke

Publisher's Interests

Classroom resources, activity books, and educational materials are all a part of the publishing program of Edupress. Its titles target students and teachers of grades two to six, as well as homeschoolers.
Website: www.edupress.com

Freelance Potential

Published 45 titles (18 juvenile) in 2002: 1 was developed from an unsolicited submission. Of the 45 titles, 4 were by authors who were new to the publishing house. Receives 72 queries yearly.

- **Fiction:** Published 18 easy-to-read books, 4–7 years.
- **Nonfiction:** Publishes books for educators, grades 2–6. Topics include social studies, science, language arts, math, art, early childhood skills, and curriculum development.
- **Representative Titles:** *If Dogs Ruled the World* (grades 1–3 and up) is a picture book with two reading levels on alternating pages; part of the Two Can Read series. *Biographies That Build Character* (grades 4–6) helps students develop language arts skills while reading about good character traits; part of the Character Links series.

Submissions and Payment

Guidelines available. Query with outline and sample pages. Accepts photocopies and computer printouts. SASE. Responds in 4–5 months. Publication in 1 year. Flat fee.

Editor's Comments

Here at Edupress, we strive to raise the creative bar when it comes to products for the classroom. We are constantly looking for ideas that will help teachers meet assessment standards while still making learning fun for children. Education with imagination is our motto. For the coming year, we would like to expand our offerings in the areas of grammar, phonics, math, and reading for use in grades one through six. Most of our authors have extensive classroom experience and a firm grasp of the essentials of early education.

Eerdmans Books for Young Readers

255 Jefferson Avenue, SE
Grand Rapids, MI 49503

Children's Books Publisher: Judy Zylstra

Publisher's Interests

This inspirational publisher features picture books as well as middle-grade and young adult fiction and nonfiction titles designed to foster faith in God and in God's world.
Website: www.eerdmans.com

Freelance Potential

Published 15 titles in 2002: 5 were developed from unsolicited submissions, 6 were by agented authors, and 4 were reprint/licensed properties. Of the 15 titles, 1 was by an unpublished writer and 3 were by authors who were new to the publishing house. Receives 5 unsolicited mss yearly.

- **Fiction:** Publishes easy-to-read books, 4–7 years; story picture books, 4–10 years; middle-grade novels, 8–12 years; and young adult novels, 12–18 years. Genres include inspirational and religious fiction. Also publishes retellings of classic tales.
- **Nonfiction:** Publishes early picture books, 0–4 years; and middle-grade books, 8–12 years. Topics include Christian living, the Bible, and prayer. Also publishes educational titles and biographies.
- **Representative Titles:** *The Angel and Other Stories* by Sue Stauffacher (8+ years) includes ten folktales with spiritual themes about faith, kindness, and the power of God's grace. *Auntee Edna* by Ethel Footman Smothers (5–12 years) is a warm story of kinship and family heritage that teaches readers an appreciation for an old-fashioned way of life.

Submissions and Payment

Guidelines available. Send complete ms for picture books. Query with 3–4 sample chapters for longer works. Accepts photocopies, computer printouts, and simultaneous submissions if identified. SASE. Responds in 3–4 months. Publication period varies. Royalty.

Editor's Comments

We seek manuscripts that help children and young people understand and explore life in God's world—its wonder and joy, and challenges.

Eldridge Publishing Company

P.O. Box 1595
Venice, FL 34284

Editor: Susan Shore

Publisher's Interests
Established in 1906, Eldridge Publishing Company offers a
variety of plays suitable for performance in junior and senior
high schools and community theaters.
Website: www.histage.com

Freelance Potential
Published 70 titles in 2002: 2 were by agented authors.
Receives 500+ unsolicited mss yearly.
- **Fiction:** Publishes full-length and one-act plays, skits, and
  musicals, grades 6–12. Genres include humor, contemporary
  issues, holidays, humor, folktales, melodrama, Westerns, Bible
  stories, and classical drama. Also publishes adult drama for
  community theaters.
- **Representative Titles:** *Aesop's Hop* by Wade Bradford combines characters from Aesop's fables with a contemporary
  birthday party for an unusual celebration. *Rainbow Review* by
  Christy Long offers a new perspective on the Bible story about
  Noah and the Ark.

Submissions and Payment
Send complete ms stating play length and age ranges for
actors and audience. Include cassette and sample score with
musical submissions. Accepts photocopies, computer printouts, and simultaneous submissions if identified. SASE.
Responds in 2 months. Publication in 6–12 months. Royalty,
varies. Flat fee for religious plays.

Editor's Comments
We are always looking for comedies, mysteries, serious plays,
children's theater plays, and musicals for actors in junior
high school and up. Plays with flexible casting are appreciat-
ed. We're open to new ideas and welcome submissions at any
time, but we prefer that your work be performed prior to submission. Take a look at the new titles featured every month
at our website and in our catalogues to get an idea of what
we publish. We continue to need holiday plays, and children's
plays with religious themes.

E. M. Press

P.O. Box 336
Warrenton, VA 20188

Publisher: Beth A. Miller

Publisher's Interests

A small publishing company established in 1991, E. M. Press
primarily offers children's books, with an emphasis on books
for readers between the ages of five and twelve. It also publishes adult regional titles and books by authors living in
Maryland, Virginia, and Washington, D.C.
Website: www.empressinc.com

Freelance Potential

Published 2 titles in 2002: both were developed from unsolicited submissions. Both were by unpublished writers who
were new to the publishing house. Receives 1,000 queries,
1,000 unsolicited mss yearly.

- **Fiction:** Publishes chapter books, 5–10 years; and middle-
  grade books, 8–12 years. Genres include adventure; suspense;
  mystery; historical and contemporary fiction; and stories about
  animals and holidays.
- **Nonfiction:** Publishes regional and how-to titles, autobiographies, and books with religious themes for all ages.
- **Representative Titles:** *Looking for Pa* by Geraldine Lee Susi is
  a historical novel about a brother and sister whose mother dies
  of pneumonia after their father has joined the Confederate
  forces. *Sassparilla's New Shoes* by Wing and Wah Chen is an
  illustrated book that features a young Asian girl who is given
  her sister's hand-me-down shoes.

Submissions and Payment

Query with 1–2 sample chapters for novels; or send complete
ms for children's titles. Accepts photocopies, computer printouts, and simultaneous submissions if identified. SASE.
Responds in 8 weeks. Publication in 18 months. Royalty;
6–9%.

Editor's Comments

We're always interested in reviewing submissions by first-
time and under-represented authors. Take the time to log on
to our website before contacting us; you'll see that we publish
a variety of fiction for children.

Encore Performance Publishing

P.O. Box 692
Orem, UT 84059

President: Michael Perry

Publisher's Interests
This publisher of dramatic arts materials caters to school and community theater groups that perform for adults, families, and children. Encore Performance Publishing offers full-length and one-act plays, skits, musicals, and monologues, as well as books about the theater arts and stage makeup.
Website: www.encoreplay.com

Freelance Potential
Published 10 titles (5 juvenile) in 2002: 1 was by an agented author. Of the 10 titles, 1 was by an unpublished writer and 7 were by authors who were new to the publishing house. Receives 100 queries yearly.
- **Fiction:** Publishes plays and dramatic series, 5–18 years. Features dramas with multicultural, religious, and ethnic themes, as well as educational, bilingual, and humorous plays.
- **Nonfiction:** Publishes books about theater arts, all ages. Topics include acting, auditions, improvisation, stage management, set design, lighting, and makeup.
- **Representative Titles:** *The Boy Who Knew No Fear* by G. Riley Mills is a musical based on a Brothers Grimm story about a boy who goes on a series of frightening adventures. *Where Is Jill?* by Shirlee H. Shields is a musical about Jack's worldwide search for Jill, who turns out to be on the moon.

Submissions and Payment
Guidelines available. Query with résumé, synopsis, and production history. Accepts photocopies and computer printouts. SASE. Responds in 2 weeks. Publication in 2 months. Royalty, 50% performance, 10% book.

Editor's Comments
We love challenging plays that will encourage actors and audiences, both young and old, to become involved in the process of theater as participants and/or spectators. We like plays about topical issues, especially for young people. Plays that deal with moral issues are also encouraged. We're looking for the type of theater that will uplift and edify families.

Beth Townsend, Enslow Publishers
Space, Biology, and Open Authors

Enslow Publishers has been in business since 1976, and publishes nonfiction only, for grades 1 to 12. The company's primary markets are school and public libraries. Its books cover many topics, including experiments, science fair projects, space, technology, and famous scientists. Over the years, Enslow Publishers' books have been recognized by organizations such as the American Library Association and the NAACP.

Editor Beth Townsend says, "We look for ideas and topics related to school science standards and the curriculum. These ideas can be related to science biographies, science fair ideas, and science topics that are interesting and exciting to kids." She welcomes queries and sample chapters: "That gives us an idea of how the author writes, and we can always contact him or her for more." Townsend advises writers to be open to possibilities. "Any idea is welcome, but the author should also be open to writing about anything. If we see potential in an author, we might want him or her to write about a different topic than what they submitted."

Of current interest to Enslow Publishers is "more on human and animal biology, and less on dinosaurs. 'How things work' is another great idea," says Townsend. She also projects that space and technology will be very popular subjects.

Like other publishers of children's nonfiction, research is more and more important to Enslow Publishers. "We pride ourselves on producing quality nonfiction," Townsend says. "We ask all our authors to do their research from scholarly sources. Although more authors are using the Internet for research, not everything on the Internet is accurate. Finding a good book is still preferred!"

(Listing for Enslow Publishers on following page)

Enslow Publishers

Box 398
40 Industrial Road
Berkeley Heights, NJ 07922-0398

Editor: Brian Enslow

Publisher's Interests

Students in grades two through twelve are the target audience of this educational publisher. Established in 1976, Enslow Publishers specializes in nonfiction in the areas of history, science, biography, and social issues. Some of its titles are high interest/low vocabulary, and nearly all are published as part of a series.
Website: www.enslow.com

Freelance Potential

Published 200 titles in 2002: 7 were developed from unsolicited submissions. Of the 200 titles, 45 were by authors who were new to the publishing house. Receives 1,000 queries yearly.

- **Nonfiction:** Publishes middle-grade books, 8–12 years; and young adult books, 12–18 years. Topics include social issues, health, history, the environment, science, and multicultural issues. Also publishes biographies.
- **Representative Titles:** *Abigail Adams* by Pat McCarthy (grades 6 and up) describes the life of this First Lady who is often referred to as America's first feminist; part of the Historical American Biographies series. *The 1910s: From World War I to Ragtime Music* by Stephen Feinstein (grades 5 and up) traces some of the events and people that made this an era of great wealth and great turmoil; part of the Decades of the 20th Century series.

Submissions and Payment

Guidelines available. Query with outline and market analysis. Accepts photocopies and computer printouts. SASE. Responds in 1–6 months. Publication in 1 year. Royalty; advance. Flat fee.

Editor's Comments

We are always extending our current series and considering new ones. We welcome queries from authors who can bring us a book that is exciting as well as informational. Tell us what makes your idea special and why we should publish it.

ETC Publications

700 East Vereda del Sur
Palm Springs, CA 92262

Senior Editor: Richard W. Hostrop

Publisher's Interests
The list for this publisher includes academic reference books for teachers and administrators at all levels, educational titles, and chapter books and nonfiction titles for middle-grade and young adult readers.

Freelance Potential
Published 6 titles (2 juvenile) in 2002: 1 was developed from an unsolicited submission. Of the 6 titles, 1 was by an unpublished writer and 1 was by an author who was new to the publishing house. Receives 100+ queries, 50+ unsolicited mss yearly.

- **Nonfiction:** Published 1 middle-grade book, 8–12 years; and 1 young adult book, 12–18 years. Topics include history, education, curriculum development, homeschooling, reference, and careers.
- **Representative Titles:** *The ABC's of the Open Classroom* (teachers) by Leslie Gingell explains how to open up a self-contained classroom. *The Effective High School Principal* by Gene E. Megiveron (administrators) provides practical skills and tools to use as a guide throughout the school year.

Submissions and Payment
Query with 2 sample chapters. No unsolicited mss. Accepts photocopies, computer printouts, and simultaneous submissions if identified. Availability of artwork improves chance of acceptance. SASE. Responds in 1 month. Publication in 9 months. Royalty, 5–15%.

Editor's Comments
Our audience consists of elementary, secondary, and high school teachers and administrators. This year, we are again interested in receiving proposals for state histories for elementary school classrooms, homeschooling titles with a Christian focus, and reference books for educators at all grade levels. We ask that you review our list of published titles before submitting your work, as we may have already covered your topic.

Evan-Moor Educational Publishers

18 Lower Ragsdale Drive
Monterey, CA 93940

Senior Editor: Marilyn Evans

Publisher's Interests
Evan-Moor Educational Publishers specializes in titles for most
curriculum areas in preschool though grade six classrooms. It
features materials for interdisciplinary and cross-cultural
units, materials that emphasize critical thinking and problem-
solving skills, and homeschooling programs for parents.
Website: www.evan-moor.com

Freelance Potential
Published 45 titles in 2002: 1 was by an unpublished writer
and 8 were by authors who were new to the publishing
house. Receives 150 queries, 100 unsolicited mss yearly.
- **Nonfiction:** Publishes classroom and homeschooling resources,
  teaching materials, and activity books, pre-K–grade 6. Topics
  include social studies, mathematics, science, technology, reading, writing, language arts, early learning, arts and crafts, and
  thematic units.
- **Representative Titles:** *Grammar & Punctuation* (teachers,
  grades 1–6) is part of a six-book series on writing correctly.
  Take It to Your Seat Math Centers (teachers, grades 1–6) features full-color patterns and task cards for creating learning
  centers in the classroom.

Submissions and Payment
Guidelines available at website. Query with outline and sample pages; or send complete ms. Accepts photocopies and
computer printouts. SASE. Responds in 3 months. Publication in 1–2 years. Flat fee.

Editor's Comments
We suggest you spend time researching your market before
you submit to us. Does your idea fit what we publish in
terms of grade level, page length, and curriculum areas?
You'll notice that we focus more on language arts than on
other areas, and that we have more materials for primary
grades than for intermediate. We like titles that work as part
of a group or series. Please note that we do not publish fiction or nonfiction children's literature.

Exclamation! Publishers

P.O. Box 664
Phoenixville, PA 19460

Editors: Denise E. Heap & Joyce Light

Publisher's Interests
Now in its second year of operation, Exclamation! Publishers develops historical fiction titles, as well as well-researched straight nonfiction and creative nonfiction. Its list also features poetry and cookbooks.
Website: www.deheap.com

Freelance Potential
Published 5 titles (2 juvenile) in 2002: 1 was developed from an unsolicited submission.
- **Fiction:** Publishes historical fiction and poetry, all ages.
- **Nonfiction:** Publishes straight nonfiction and creative nonfiction, all ages.
- **Representative Titles:** *Changing Seasons* by Ruth Sachs is a book of poetry that takes readers through the seasons, from spring to winter. *Jotter's Blotter: Twelve Exercises to Better Writing* by Ruth Sachs presents creative writing exercises in a workbook format.

Submissions and Payment
Guidelines available at website. Query with author biography or résumé. No unsolicited mss. E-mail queries to dheap@deheap.com (no attachments). SASE. Responds in 4–6 weeks. Publication period varies. Royalty, 15% of gross profits.

Editor's Comments
We publish materials for students, young adults, and adults. Unfortunately, because we are a new publisher, we cannot take on all the projects that we deem worthwhile. Our primary interests are in the areas of historical fiction, creative nonfiction, straight nonfiction, poetry, and cookbooks. We are especially interested in projects that can stand alone and that can be easily transformed into textbooks. We are also interested in writers for our newsletter, *History Project*, which covers history, civics, and international politics for middle-school and high school students. If you'd like to write for the newsletter, log on to the website or e-mail a query with your credentials.

Facts On File

17th Floor
132 West 31st Street
New York, NY 10001

Editorial Director: Laurie Likoff
Senior Editor, Young Adult: Nicole Bowen

Publisher's Interests

Facts On File has been producing school and library reference titles for more than 60 years. Its catalogue includes curriculum-related books, published in series, for children ages five-and-up on topics such as history, literature, social studies, and science.
Website: www.factsonfile.com

Freelance Potential

Published 175 titles in 2002: 10 were developed from unsolicited submissions, 65 were by agented authors, and 6 were reprint/licensed properties. Of the 175 titles, 5 were by authors who were new to the publishing house. Receives 200 queries yearly.

- **Nonfiction:** Published 5 chapter books, 5–10 years; 30 middle-grade books, 8–12 years; and 30 young adult books, 12–18 years. Also published 5 illustrated reference titles. Topics include social issues, history, current affairs, politics, multicultural issues, mathematics, science, and the environment.
- **Representative Titles:** *Winning Soccer for Girls* by Deborah Crisfeld (YA) provides young women interested in soccer with a guide to the detailed mechanics of this sport, including shooting, passing, and ball handling. *Career Ideas for Kids Who Like Music and Dance* by Gayle Bryan profiles careers such as arts administrator, booking agent, choir director, composer, costume designer, and dance instructor.

Submissions and Payment

Query with outline, sample chapter, description of audience, competitive titles, and marketing ideas. Accepts photocopies, computer printouts, and simultaneous submissions if identified. SASE. Responds in 2 months. Publication in 1 year. Royalty; advance.

Editor's Comments

We draw our authors from a wide array of freelance writers, researchers, professors, and teachers. You must have expertise in the field you are writing about.

Faith Kids

4050 Lee Vance View
Colorado Springs, CO 80918

Editorial Assistant

Publisher's Interests
Faith Kids, an imprint of Cook Communications ministries, offers a list of fiction and nonfiction for children between the ages of six and twelve. It also publishes some parenting titles. All the books that appear on its list are written from a Christian perspective. Faith Kids also produces games, toys, and other media.
Website: www.faithkids.com

Freelance Potential
Published 27 titles in 2002. Receives 1,000+ queries, 1,000 unsolicited mss yearly.
- **Fiction:** Publishes easy-to-read books, 4–7 years; chapter books, 5–10 years; and middle-grade books, 8–12 years. Genres include religious and inspirational fiction.
- **Nonfiction:** Publishes easy-to-read books, 4–7 years; chapter books, 5–10 years; and middle-grade books, 8–12 years.
- **Representative Titles:** *The Baby Bible Storybook* by Robin Currie is a board book filled with favorite Bible stories for young children; part of the Baby Bible series. *French Fry Forgiveness* by Nancy Lavene Simpson (7–10 years) is a story about how to make friends and the importance of friendship; part of the Alex series.

Submissions and Payment
Query or send complete ms; include writing credits and market analysis of comparative products. Accepts photocopies and computer printouts. SASE. Response time and publication period vary. Payment policy varies.

Editor's Comments
We have no primary focus for our books other than that they should present a Christian viewpoint. Our goal is to create the very best books and other products that will help promote spiritual growth in children. If, after reviewing our current catalogue and some of our titles, you feel your book is right for us, we ask that you send us a completed manuscript as well as an analysis of the competition in the marketplace.

Falcon Publishing

246 Goose Lane
P.O. Box 480
Guilford, CT 06437

Acquisitions Editor

Publisher's Interests
Falcon Publishing is now a division of Globe-Pequot Press. It specializes in photographic books about regional natural history, as well as guides to the outdoors and books on environmental themes. It does not publish fiction or picture books for children.
Website: www.globe-pequot.com

Freelance Potential
Published 150 titles (10–15 juvenile) in 2002: 3 were developed from unsolicited submissions, 90 were by agented authors, and 6 were reprint/licensed properties. Of the 150 titles, 60 were by unpublished writers and 60 were by authors who were new to the publishing house. Receives 100 queries each year.
- **Nonfiction:** Publishes chapter books, 5–10 years; middle-grade books, 8–12 years; and 2 young adult books, 12–18 years. Topics include nature, animals, the environment, history, and regional subjects.
- **Representative Titles:** *Astronomy for All Ages* by Philip Harrington & Edward Pascuzzi features more than fifty activities to help readers of all ages understand astronomy. *Climbing with Children* by Gary Joyce (parents) offers tips for getting children ready for rock-climbing; includes stretching techniques, pre-climbing exercises, and a climbing selection.

Submissions and Payment
Guidelines available. Query with synopsis, table of contents, and sample chapter. Accepts photocopies and computer printouts. SASE. Responds in 3 months. Publication in 1 year. Royalty.

Editor's Comments
Our list focuses on outdoor recreation, both how-to and where-to, with hiking, biking, climbing, and other specialized lines, including regional history. We welcome appropriate submissions. Be sure to include a definition of your book's targeted audience as well as an analysis of competing titles.

Family Learning Association & ERIC/REC Press

Suite 101, 3925 Hagan Street
Bloomington, IN 47401

Director: Carl B. Smith

Publisher's Interests
The target audience of this educational publisher includes teachers and parents of kindergarten through middle-grade students. Most of its titles deal with the subjects of English, reading, and communications.
Website: www.kidscanlearn.com

Freelance Potential
Published 20–25 titles in 2002: 1–2 were developed from unsolicited submissions and 5–10 were reprint/licensed properties. Of the 20–25 titles, 1–5 were by unpublished writers and 1–5 were by authors who were new to the publishing house. Receives 100 queries yearly.

- **Fiction:** Published 5 easy-to-read books, 4–7 years.
- **Nonfiction:** Published 5 easy-to-read books, 4–7 years; 5 story picture books, 4–10 years; 2 chapter books, 5–10 years; and 2 middle-grade books, 8–12 years. Also publishes professional development resources, research materials, and reference titles for educators. Features parent meeting leader guides, parent handouts, and Spanish and bilingual materials. Topics include reading, writing, English, communications, and family and intergenerational literacy. Also offers interactive books with audio cassettes and turnkey packages for family involvement workshops and family resource centers.
- **Representative Titles:** *Character Development Through Literature* by Evelyn Holt Otten (educators) offers resources for character education programs. *Teach a Child to Read with Children's Books* (parents) offers an integrated approach to help parents help their children learn to enjoy reading.

Submissions and Payment
Query with table of contents, sample chapter, and market analysis. Accepts photocopies and computer printouts. SASE. Responds in 1 month. Publication in 1–2 years. Royalty, 6–10%. Flat fee, $250–$1,000.

Editor's Comments
We continue to need books for parents and educators related specifically to communicating, reading, or English.

Farrar, Straus & Giroux

19 Union Square West
New York, NY 10003

Children's Editorial Department

Publisher's Interests
Original hardcover titles and paperback reprints can be
found in Farrar, Straus & Giroux's catalogue. It publishes
fiction and nonfiction for preschoolers through teens.
Website: www.fsgbooks.com

Freelance Potential
Published 80 titles in 2002: 3 were developed from unsolicited
submissions, 35 were by agented authors, and 5 were reprint/
licensed properties. Of the 80 titles, 2 were by unpublished
writers. Receives 1,000 queries, 6,000 unsolicited mss yearly.
- **Fiction:** Publishes toddler books, 0–4 years; easy-to-read
  books 4–7 years; story picture books, 4–10 years; chapter
  books, 5–10 years; middle-grade books, 8–12 years; and young
  adult books, 12–18 years. Genres include contemporary fiction,
  fantasy, and humor.
- **Nonfiction:** Publishes middle-grade books, 8–12 years; and
  young adult books, 12–18 years. Topics include social issues,
  science, and nature.
- **Representative Titles:** *She Did It!* by Jennifer A. Ericsson
  (4–8 years) is a picture book about the spirited antics of four
  sisters. *Flood* by James Heneghan (12+ years) is a novel about
  a boy who searches for a true home after he survives a flood,
  but loses his mother and stepfather, and must go to live with
  his aunt on the opposite side of the country.

Submissions and Payment
Guidelines available. Query for mss longer than 10 pages;
send complete ms for shorter works. Accepts photocopies,
computer printouts, and simultaneous submissions if identified. SASE. Responds in 1–3 months. Publication in 18
months. Royalty, 3–10% of list price, $3,000–$15,000.

Editor's Comments
The length of the story depends on the age of the reader for
whom it is intended; there are no fixed lengths. Please don't
expect an editor to offer specific comments on your work—we
receive far too many submissions for that to happen.

Frederick Fell Publishers

Suite 305
2131 Hollywood Boulevard
Hollywood, FL 33020

Senior Editor: Barbara Newman

Publisher's Interests
Self-help and how-to titles for young adults and adults can be found in Frederick Fell Publishers' catalogue. It also offers religious and inspirational fiction that appeals to teens. This independent publisher has been in business for more than 60 years.
Website: www.fellpub.com

Freelance Potential
Published 30 titles in 2002: 17 were developed from unsolicited submissions and 15 were by agented authors. Of the 30 titles, 17 were by unpublished writers and 17 were by authors who were new to the publishing house. Receives 4,000 queries yearly.
- **Fiction:** Publishes young adult books, 12–18 years. Genres include inspirational and religious fiction.
- **Nonfiction:** Features how-to and self-help titles, 12–18 years. Topics include health and spirituality. Also publishes biographies and titles about parenting, child care, business, science, and entertainment.
- **Representative Titles:** *How to Develop a Super Power Memory: More Money, Higher Grades, More Friends* by Harry Lorayne (YA) provides a unique system of memory builders that helps readers learn to accurately recall important facts. *The Know-It-All's Guide to Palm Reading* by Raymond Gibson discusses the important lines that indicate life, destiny, fortune, and family.

Submissions and Payment
Guidelines available. Query with résumé and marketing plan. Availability of artwork improves chance of acceptance. Accepts photocopies and simultaneous submissions if identified. SASE. Responds in 1 month. Publication in 9–12 months. Royalty.

Editor's Comments
Send proposals for books that are full of information of interest to young adult readers. Titles that deal with spiritual issues and self-help books are needed.

The Feminist Press

The Graduate Center
365 Fifth Avenue
New York, NY 10016

Publisher: Jean Casella

Publisher's Interests
Part of the City University of New York, The Feminist Press is
a not-for-profit publisher dedicated to preserving the legacy
of women's history and women's experiences. Its juvenile list
includes chapter books with strong female protagonists and
multicultural settings, as well as biographies of female role
models. It has been publishing since 1970.
Website: www.feministpress.org

Freelance Potential
Published 15 titles (4 juvenile) in 2002: 2 were by agented
authors and 2 were reprint/licensed properties. Receives 800
queries yearly.
- **Fiction:** Publishes chapter books, 10+ years; and middle-grade
  novels, 8–12 years. Genres include multicultural and ethnic
  fiction with strong female characters.
- **Nonfiction:** Publishes middle-grade books, 8–12 years. Features biographies and books about multicultural subjects.
- **Representative Titles:** *A Clear Spring* by Barbara Wilson is a
  novel for young readers about a girl who spends a summer in
  Seattle with her Aunt Ceci and her partner, Janie, and who
  learns about the value of family from her diverse, confident,
  and eccentric relatives. *Red Sand, Blue Sky* by Cathy Applegate
  is a mystery and adventure story set in the Australian outback.

Submissions and Payment
Guidelines available at website. Query via e-mail (200 words
or less) with "submissions" in subject line to jcasella@
gc.cuny.edu. Responds in 3–4 months. Publication period
varies. Royalty; advance.

Editor's Comments
Currently we are considering manuscripts only for readers
ages nine and up for our two series, Girls First! and Women
Changing the World. Review the series descriptions and current titles in these series before you submit. We're looking for
books that feature important and challenging themes, humor,
charm, and excellent writing.

Ferguson Publishing Company

7th Floor
200 West Jackson Boulevard
Chicago, IL 60606-6941

Managing Editor, Career Publications: Andrew Morkes

Publisher's Interests

Books found on this educational publisher's list include career and vocational guides. Its books are used by high school and college guidance counselors as well as career counselors. Its catalogue also includes titles on occupational forecasts and financial aid.

Website: www.fergpubco.com

Freelance Potential

Published 25 titles in 2002: 1–2 were developed from unsolicited submissions. Of the 25 titles, 3 were by authors new to the publishing house. Receives 20–30 queries yearly.

- **Nonfiction:** Published 5 chapter books, 5–10 years; 5 middle-grade books, 8–12 years; and 10 young adult books, 12–18 years. Topics include college planning, career awareness, and job training. Also publishes professional development titles and general reference books.
- **Representative Titles:** *Tim Berners-Lee: Inventor of the World Wide Web* (grades 5 and up) follows the career of this remarkable individual; part of the Career Biography series. *How to Get a Job and Keep It* by Sue Morem (YA) helps students understand the realities of the working world.

Submissions and Payment

Guidelines available at website. Query with table of contents; or send complete ms with proposal. Accepts photocopies, computer printouts, e-mail submissions to editors@ fergpubco.com, and simultaneous submissions if identified. SASE. Responds in 3–6 months. Publication period varies. Work for hire and some royalty assignments.

Editor's Comments

Career biographies top the list of our current needs. We are interested in individuals who have made a difference in their field and can offer students inspiration about career choices. Our guidelines are available on our website, and we urge you to review them carefully before you consider sending us a query or a manuscript.

Focus on the Family
Book Development

8675 Explorer Drive
Colorado Springs, CO 80920

Submissions Editor: Mark Maddox

Publisher's Interests
Focus on the Family Book Development is a nonprofit, Christian, pro-family publisher with a list that includes both fiction and nonfiction titles for children and adults. Its books are designed to help individuals lead Christian lives. Many of its titles are produced on a work-for-hire basis.
Website: www.family.org

Freelance Potential
Published 10 titles in 2002: 5 were reprint/licensed properties.
- **Fiction:** Publishes young adult books, 12–18 years. Genres include adventure and historical, inspirational, and religious fiction.
- **Nonfiction:** Publishes young adult books, 12–18 years. Topics include crafts, hobbies, current events, entertainment, religion, self-help, and social issues.
- **Representative Titles:** *Protecting Your Child in an X-Rated World* (parents) looks at how we can keep our children focused on healthy values. *A Child Is a Precious Gift* (parents) reflects on the joys of parenthood.

Submissions and Payment
Guidelines available. Query with outline/synopsis, résumé, and market analysis. Accepts photocopies, disk submissions (Microsoft Word/RTF), and e-mail submissions to maddoxmh@fotf.org. SASE. Responds in 1 month. Publication in 12–14 months. Payment policy varies.

Editor's Comments
We are not currently accepting proposals in the area of fiction for any age, or nonfiction in the area of family values. We are seeking queries in the area of family advice. This includes topics such as marriage and parenting, teen issues, encouragement for women, and senior issues. We have an on-going need for writers who will work with us on various projects as needs or opportunities arise. These projects can be either fiction or nonfiction. We are not interested in materials that do not have a strong Christian content.

Forest House Publishing Company

P.O. Box 738
Lake Forest, IL 60045

President: Dianne Spahr

Publisher's Interests
Forest House Publishing features high-quality books for the school and library markets. Its list features titles for children and young adult readers, including fiction, nonfiction, and bilingual Spanish titles.
Website: www.forest-house.com

Freelance Potential
Published 40 titles in 2002. Of the 40 titles, 24 were by unpublished writers and 16 were by authors who were new to the publishing house. Receives 100 unsolicited mss yearly.

- **Fiction:** Publishes concept books, toddler books, and early picture books, 0–4 years; easy-to-read books, 4–7 years; story picture books, 4–10 years; chapter books, 5–10 years; and middle-grade novels, 8–12 years. Genres include animal stories, contemporary and multicultural fiction, fairy tales, and adventure.
- **Nonfiction:** Publishes easy-to-read books, 4–7 years; and chapter books, 5–10 years. Topics include history, the environment, sign language, special education, multicultural and ethnic issues, arts and crafts, nature, and animals. Also publishes activity books, bilingual books, how-to titles, and teacher resource materials.
- **Representative Titles:** *Captain Jim and the Killer Whales* (grades 1–8) teaches kids that killer whales are not dangerous to people, only to the seals and penguins they hunt for food. *Find Nat* (pre-K–grade 2) helps readers learn the *at* sound while meeting a gnat, a rat, and a bat.

Submissions and Payment
Send complete ms. Accepts photocopies and computer printouts. SASE. Responds 6 months. Publication in 1 year. Royalty; advance. Flat fee.

Editor's Comments
This year, we need books on American history for grades one through six, mysteries for grades four through six, and story books for preschool through grade two. Stories on the Old West continue to be popular.

Formac Publishing Company Ltd.

5502 Atlantic Street
Halifax, Nova Scotia B3H 1G4
Canada

Senior Editor: Elizabeth Eve

Publisher's Interests
Formac Publishing offers fiction and nonfiction for middle-grade readers, novels for young adults, chapter books, and easy-to-read titles. In operation for more than a quarter of a century, it distributes its own titles, as well as titles from other publishers.
Website: www.formac.ca

Freelance Potential
Published 20 titles (10 juvenile) in 2002: 1 was developed from an unsolicited submission, 3 were by agented authors, and 4 were reprint/licensed properties. Receives 80 queries each year.
- **Fiction:** Published 9 chapter books, 5–10 years; and 1 young adult book, 12–18 years. Also publishes easy-to-read books, 4–7 years; and middle-grade novels, 8–12 years. Genres include mystery, suspense, fantasy, adventure, humor, stories about sports, and historical fiction.
- **Nonfiction:** Publishes middle-grade books, 8–12 years. Topics include sports, nature, the environment, and regional, multi-cultural, and ethnic subjects.
- **Representative Titles:** *Rink Rivals* by Jacqueline Guest (8–13 years) is a book about twin, pre-teen boys who sign up for the same hockey team; part of the Lorimer's Sports Stories series. *Heartbreak High* by Nazneen Sadiq (YA) is a novel about a high school couple who find themselves at war with their parents over issues they don't understand.

Submissions and Payment
Send résumé or query with outline and sample chapters. No unsolicited mss. Accepts photocopies, computer printouts, and simultaneous submissions if identified. SAE/IRC. Responds in 1–12 months. Publication in 1–2 years. Royalty.

Editor's Comments
If you have an idea for a book that you think will interest us, send a résumé or an outline with sample chapters. We still need chapter books for readers ages six to nine.

Forward Movement Publications

412 Sycamore Street
Cincinnati, OH 45202

Submissions Editor: Edward S. Gleason

Publisher's Interests
Forward Movement Publications produces books and pamphlets related to the lives and concerns of members of the Episcopal Church. Its children's list includes titles for middle-grade readers and young adults.
Website: www.forwardmovement.org

Freelance Potential
Published 32 titles (6 juvenile) in 2002: most were developed from unsolicited submissions. Of the 32 titles, 16 were by unpublished writers and 16 were by authors who were new to the publishing house. Receives 375 queries yearly.
- **Fiction:** Published 1 middle-grade book, 8–12 years. Features contemporary fiction with Christian themes.
- **Nonfiction:** Published 1 middle-grade book, 8–12 years. Also publishes young adult titles, 12–18 years. Topics include meditation, spirituality, church history, and contemporary issues such as drugs and AIDS.
- **Representative Titles:** *Take Some Time to Talk* by Sister Mary Rose McGeady (parents) is a pamphlet that looks at the darker side of rap music. *How To Evangelize a Gen X-er [Not]* by Beth Maynard is a pamphlet written by a Generation X priest that discusses this growing edge of the Episcopal Church—a group hungry for authentic faith.

Submissions and Payment
Guidelines, catalogue, and sample pamphlet available ($1.72 postage; no SASE). Query with sample chapters. Accepts photocopies and computer printouts. SASE. Responds in 1 month. Publication period varies. Flat fee.

Editor's Comments
Most of the titles we produce each year are four- to sixteen-page pamphlets on spiritual topics and issues of concern to the church. We have a special need for pamphlets between four and eight pages long, roughly 500 to 1,000 words. Consult our catalogue for an overview of the types of books, booklets, and pamphlets we publish, or send for a sample copy.

Frances Foster Books

Farrar, Straus & Giroux
19 Union Square West
New York, NY 10003

Editor: Frances Foster
Assistant Editor: Janine O'Malley

Publisher's Interests

This well-known imprint of Farrar, Straus & Giroux features hardcover books for children from birth through the young adult years. Its list is made up primarily of fiction, but it will consider nonfiction submissions, particularly those related to historical subjects.

Freelance Potential

Published 20 titles in 2002: 10 were by agented authors. Receives 100 queries, 12,000 unsolicited mss yearly.

- **Fiction:** Published 1 early picture book, 0–4 years; 9 story picture books, 4–10 years; 2 chapter books, 5–10 years; 4 middle-grade novels, 8–12 years; and 4 young adult books, 12–18 years. Genres include contemporary, historical, and ethnic fiction; fantasy; adventure; and drama.
- **Nonfiction:** Publishes a few titles on historical subjects.
- **Representative Titles:** *The Turtle and the Hippopotamus* by Kate Banks (3+ years) is a rebus about a turtle who is afraid to swim across the river. *Straydog* by Kathe Koja (12+ years) is the story of a girl whose relationship with a dog helps her discover her own emotional needs.

Submissions and Payment

Guidelines available. Query with 3 sample chapters and synopsis for novels. Send complete ms for picture books. Do not send original art. Accepts photocopies, computer printouts, and simultaneous submissions if identified. SASE. Responds in 3+ months. Publication in 2+ years. Royalty; advance.

Editor's Comments

We receive many unsolicited submissions and select very few for publication. We look for memorable characters and stories that will grab a child's attention. Our books are all of the highest quality, and we only consider stories that we feel will stand the test of time and become literary classics in their own way. We will consider completed manuscripts for picture books only. If you are proposing a longer book, please send us a cover letter and three sample chapters.

Free Spirit Publishing

Suite 200
217 Fifth Avenue North
Minneapolis, MN 55401-1299

Acquisitions Assistant: Douglas J. Fehlen

Publisher's Interests
Self-help books for children and teens on topics such as
character building, bullying, relationships, and learning disabilities are available from Free Spirit Publishing. It also
offers titles for parents, educators, and youth workers.
Website: www.freespirit.com

Freelance Potential
Published 18 titles (11 juvenile) in 2002: 10 were developed
from unsolicited submissions and 3 were by agented authors.
Receives 1,650 queries yearly.
- **Nonfiction:** Published 1 early picture book, 0–4 years; 1 easy-
  to-read book, 4–7 years; 5 middle-grade books, 8–12 years;
  and 4 young adult books, 12–18 years. Topics include family
  and social issues, character building, relationships, stress
  management, creativity, self-awareness, and self-esteem. Also
  publishes titles for parents, teachers, youth workers, and
  child-care professionals on learning disorders, psychology, and
  gifted and talented education.
- **Representative Titles:** *The Kid's Guide to Service Projects* by
  Barbara A. Lewis (10+ years) features more than 500 ideas for
  service projects, from simple projects to large-scale commit-
  ments. *The Right Moves* by Tina Schwager & Michele Schuerger
  (11+ years) encourages girls to develop a healthy self-image, eat
  right, and exercise.

Submissions and Payment
Guidelines available. Query with résumé, outline, and 2
sample chapters. Accepts photocopies and computer printouts. SASE. Responds in 1–3 months. Publication in 1–3
years. Royalty; advance.

Editor's Comments
Our mission is to provide children and teens with the tools
they need to succeed in life and to make a difference in the
world. Our authors include parents, professionals, and
experts. Please study our catalogue and send for a copy of our
brochure "How to Become an Author" before contacting us.

Samuel French

45 West 25th Street
New York, NY 10010

Editor: Lawrence Harbison

Publisher's Interests
Established in 1830, Samuel French provides scripts for
theatrical groups of all levels of experience, including schools,
communities, and professionals.
Website: www.samuelfrench.com

Freelance Potential
Published 45 titles in 2002: 9 were developed from unsolicited
submissions, 36 were by agented authors, and 2 were
reprint/licensed properties. Of the 45 titles, 10 were by
authors who were new to the publishing house. Receives 240
queries, 1,500 unsolicited mss yearly.

- **Fiction:** Publishes full-length and one-act plays, monologues,
  readings, scenes, and anthologies for theater groups of all ages.
  Genres include musicals and operettas, religious and holiday
  plays, and Shakespearean drama.
- **Nonfiction:** Publishes books and resource materials for theater
  teachers and directors. Topics include acting methods, direction, stage design, lighting, management, auditions, comedy,
  improvisation, and film production.
- **Representative Titles:** *The Magic Pebble* by Nancy Kierspe
  Carlson is a musical about four youths who discover a pirate
  ship from the past and bring it into the present. *An Actor
  Behaves* by Tom Markus guides actors through professional
  etiquette, including auditioning, training, and work patterns.

Submissions and Payment
Guidelines available. Query or send complete ms. Accepts
photocopies. SASE. Responds to queries in 1 week, to ms in
2–3 months. Publication in 1 year. Payment policy varies.

Editor's Comments
We continue to need fresh plays about issues that concern
today's youth. We will consider full-length plays, as well as
monologues, audition material, classroom guides, and classic
works. We are not interested in adaptations of fables or fairy
tales for young audiences, as we have far too many. Plays do
not have to be performed before submission.

Front Street Books

Suite 403
20 Battery Park Avenue
Asheville, NC 28801

Submissions Editor: Joy Neaves

Publisher's Interests

Front Street Books is an independent publisher that offers picture books as well as middle-grade and young adult fiction and nonfiction. Its catalogue includes educational titles, books on family and social issues, historical fiction, poetry, and humor.
Website: www.frontstreetbooks.com

Freelance Potential

Published 17 titles in 2002: 3 were developed from unsolicited submissions and 1 was by an agented author. Of the 17 titles, 2 were by unpublished writers and 2 were by authors who were new to the publishing house. Receives 1,000 queries, 1,000 unsolicited mss yearly.

- **Fiction:** Published 7 early picture books, 0–4 years; 2 middle-grade books, 8–12 years; and 8 young adult books, 12–18 years. Genres include humor, adventure, fantasy; historical, multicultural and science fiction; and stories about animals.
- **Nonfiction:** Publishes young adult books, 12–18 years. Also publishes novelty books, educational books, and poetry.
- **Representative Titles:** *The Comic Book Kid* by Adam Osterweil (8+ years) is a novel about two boys who travel through time, both to the past and to the future. *Carver: A Life in Poems* by Marilyn Nelson (12+ years) is a collection of poems that offer a portrait of the life of George Washington Carver.

Submissions and Payment

Guidelines available. Query with sample chapter for nonfiction. Send complete ms for fiction under 100 pages, or two sample chapters for fiction over 100 pages. Accepts photocopies. SASE. Responds in 3 months. Publication in 12–18 months. Royalty; advance.

Editor's Comments

We believe picture books should reflect the joy, spontaneity, and energy of infants and toddlers. For middle-grade books, we look for depictions of the various settings and activities of school-age children.

Fulcrum Publishing

Suite 300
16100 Table Mountain Parkway
Golden, CO 80403-1672

Submissions Editor: T. J. Baker

Publisher's Interests
Established in 1984, Fulcrum Publishing is an independent, nonfiction, trade book publisher. Its focus is on gardening, travel, history, nature, and Native American culture. Its list offers books for children as well as resources for educators.
Website: www.fulcrum-resources.com

Freelance Potential
Published 7 titles (2 juvenile) in 2002: 2 were by agented authors. Of the 7 titles, 2 were by authors who were new to the publishing house. Receives 250 queries, 1,500 unsolicited mss yearly.

- **Fiction:** Publishes story picture books and folktale collections, 4–10 years. Genres include folklore and multicultural fiction.
- **Nonfiction:** Publishes story picture books, 4–10 years; chapter books, 5–10 years; and middle-grade titles, 8–12 years. Also publishes educational activity books and books for parents and educators. Topics include science, nature, animals, geography, and multicultural subjects.
- **Representative Titles:** *In Search of the Perfect Pumpkin* by Gloria Evangelista (pre-K–grade 4) follows a family's hilarious adventure as they search for the perfect pumpkin. *Power and Place* by Vine Deloria, Jr. & Daniel R. Wildcat (educators) takes a critical look at the education of Native American students in the US.

Submissions and Payment
Guidelines available. Query or send complete ms with résumé and competition analysis. Accepts photocopies, computer printouts, and simultaneous submissions if identified. SASE. Responds to queries in 1 month, to unsolicited mss in 2–3 months. Publication in 18–24 months. Royalty; advance.

Editor's Comments
We are always interested in hearing from good writers who are working in our areas of interest. If you are interested in sending us a submission for consideration, please take the time to carefully review some of the titles on our backlist first.

Gibbs Smith, Publisher

P.O. Box 667
Layton, UT 84040

Children's Book Editor: Suzanne Taylor

Publisher's Interests
The children's division of this publisher, Gibbs Smith Junior,
specializes in picture books for young readers under the age
of 10. Many of its books have Western themes. It also offers
activity books that focus on the outdoors.
Website: www.gibbs-smith.com

Freelance Potential
Published 53 titles (7 juvenile) in 2002. Of the 53 titles, 6
were by unpublished writers and 16 were by authors who
were new to the publishing house. Receives 1,200 unsolicited
mss yearly.
- **Fiction:** Publishes story picture books, 4–10 years. Genres
  include Westerns, adventure, humor, fantasy, folktales, and
  stories about animals, nature, and the environment.
- **Nonfiction:** Publishes activity books, 4–10 years. Features
  books about the outdoors.
- **Representative Titles:** *Ordinary Mary's Extraordinary Deed* by
  Emily Pearson (4–8 years) tells about a girl who does a good
  deed for her neighbor that causes a chain reaction of good
  deeds around the town. *Make Something Ugly . . . for a Change*
  by Dan Reeder (7+ years) is a guide for creating papier and
  cloth mâché projects.

Submissions and Payment
Guidelines available. Send complete ms for picture books.
Query with outline and writing samples for nonfiction.
Accepts photocopies, computer printouts, and simultaneous
submissions if identified. SASE. Responds in 10–12 weeks.
Publication in 1–2 years. Royalty; advance.

Editor's Comments
Please note that we are not accepting fiction manuscripts of
any kind, including chapter books and young adult novels. We
are mainly interested in children's picture books, especially
those that have cowboy or ranch lifestyle themes or backdrops;
these should remain under 1,000 words. Activity books should
focus on the outdoors and have fewer than 15,000 words.

Gifted Education Press

10201 Yuma Court
Manassas, VA 20108

Publisher: Maurice D. Fisher

Publisher's Interests
This publisher specializes in teaching guides and textbooks that can be used to educate gifted students. It markets its titles to teachers, homeschoolers, parents, educational administrators, and librarians. Gifted Education Press also publishes a quarterly newsletter that addresses issues relating to this field.
Website: www.giftededpress.com

Freelance Potential
Published 5 titles in 2002. Receives 100 queries, 20 unsolicited mss yearly.
- **Nonfiction:** Publishes concept books, 0–4 years. Also publishes educational resources for teachers and parents working with gifted students and school administrators of gifted education programs.
- **Representative Titles:** *Technology Resource Guide: Transporting Gifted and Advanced Learners to the 21st Century* by Adrienne O'Neill & Mary Ann Coe contains descriptions of websites and software products that deal with critical thinking, problem solving, research skills, and writing skills. *Helping Gifted Children Succeed at Home and School: A Comprehensive Resource for Parents and Teachers* by James Carroll addresses the education and social development of the gifted, from preschool through college.

Submissions and Payment
Submit 1-page query only. No unsolicited mss. SASE. Responds in 3 months. Publication in 3 months. Royalty, 10%.

Editor's Comments
We welcome queries from writers who are experts in the field of gifted education they propose to address. Please review and familiarize yourself with our current list before contacting us. We only consider queries that are one-page long. Do not submit a complete manuscript. We continue to look for titles on gifted education advocacy.

Girl Press

1512 Las Palmas Avenue
Los Angeles, CA 90028

Editor: Pam Nelson

Publisher's Interests
Girl Press is dedicated to creating books for girls that teach self-reliance and personal strength, and prepare them for life's adventures in today's world. It donates a portion of its profits to nonprofit organizations that help girls.
Website: www.girlpress.com

Freelance Potential
Published 4 titles in 2002: 1 was a reprint/licensed property. Receives 100 queries yearly.
- **Fiction:** Publishes young adult titles, 12–18 years. Genres include contemporary fiction. Also publishes short story collections.
- **Nonfiction:** Publishes young adult titles, 12–18 years. Topics include popular culture, entertainment, contemporary and social issues, business skills, careers, travel, and humor.
- **Representative Titles:** *The Real Rules for Girls* by Mindy Morgenstern (YA) is packed with helpful hints to navigate today's girls through life. *Girl Boss* by Gillian Anderson (YA) is full of cool ideas to start a home-based business. *Cool Women* (YA) features biographies of some of the ultimate role models for girls, including Amelia Earhart, Lucille Ball, and Madame Curie.

Submissions and Payment
Guidelines available. Query with synopsis and market analysis. Accepts photocopies. Availability of artwork improves chance of acceptance. SASE. Responds in 1 month. Publication in 1–2 years. Payment policy varies.

Editor's Comments
Our audience is young, smart, and hip. We like to see books that instill self-confidence in our readers. Writers who understand the concerns that affect girls today, and who can help them deal with the issues that trouble them, are welcome to submit queries for consideration. New writers are encouraged to visit our website before submitting—make sure your material suits our editorial policy.

The Globe Pequot Press

246 Goose Lane
Guilford, CT 06437

Submissions Editor: Shelley Wolf

Publisher's Interests
The Globe Pequot Press specializes in travel guides about destinations around the globe and throughout the US. Its Falcon line features how-to and where-to books on outdoor recreation, including hiking, biking, and climbing, while its Fun With Families line offers ideas for family vacations.
Website: www.globe-pequot.com

Freelance Potential
Published 350 titles in 2002: 30 were developed from unsolicited submissions and 15 were by agented authors. Receives 1,000 queries yearly.
- **Nonfiction:** Publishes regional titles and travel guides, all ages. Also publishes nature books, cookbooks, and home-based business books. Topics include travel, recreation, and regional history.
- **Representative Titles:** *Pony Bob's Daring Ride: A Pony Express Adventure* by Joe Benson & John Potter tells the story of a brave young man who made the longest and most daring ride in the history of the Pony Express. *Astronomy for All Ages* by Philip Harrington & Edward Pascuzzi features 51 engaging activities that help children identify, understand, and appreciate the objects in the Milky Way and galaxies beyond.

Submissions and Payment
Catalogue and guidelines available on website. Query with résumé, table of contents, and first chapter. Accepts computer printouts and simultaneous submissions if identified. SASE. Responds in 1–2 months. Publication in 6–12 months. Royalty; advance. Flat fee.

Editor's Comments
We strongly recommend that you peruse our website to see if your book idea is right for our list. Your proposal should include a definition of the book's projected target audience and an analysis of competing titles. Tell us who the book is for and why it is better than what is already on the bookshelves. Also tell us why you are qualified to write the book.

Goodheart-Willcox

18604 West Creek Drive
Tinley Park, IL 60477-6243

Managing Editor: Paul Schreiner

Publisher's Interests
An educational publisher, Goodheart-Willcox features a catalogue that includes textbooks, software, and resource materials. Its products are used in secondary schools all the way to the university level. Resources for industrial training are also found on its list.
Website: www.goodheartwillcox.com

Freelance Potential
Published 50 titles in 2002. Receives 100+ queries yearly.
- **Nonfiction:** Publishes textbooks and how-to titles. Topics include life skills, professional development, child care and development, family living, career, education, clothing and textiles, and personal development.
- **Representative Titles:** *Children: The Early Years* by Celia Anita Decker (educators) examines children's physical, intellectual, and social development. *Working with Young Children* by Judy Herr (educators) focuses on the application of child development principles to the care of children in group settings.

Submissions and Payment
Guidelines available. Query with résumé, outline, sample chapter, and list of illustrations. SASE. Responds in 2 months. Publication in 2 years. Royalty.

Editor's Comments
We are always interested in hearing from writers who are familiar with our titles and feel they can add to our list of resources. We are open to industrial and technical products as well as family and consumer science products. Our goal is to bring our target audience the most innovative and up-to-date materials available. Send us a proposal that details your idea and demonstrates why you are the person to write this book for us. Explain what courses or student populations your book will serve and why your idea is better than the titles in this area that have already found their way to the shelves. Tell us how long you think it will take you to complete the book.

Graphic Arts Center Publishing Co.

P.O. Box 10306
Portland, OR 97296-0306

Submissions Editor: Tricia Brown

Publisher's Interests
The children's titles on this regional publisher's list include
fiction and nonfiction, primarily with Alaskan themes. The
company also publishes titles on the history, nature, cooking,
arts, and crafts of the Pacific Northwest for adults.
Website: www.gacpc.com

Freelance Potential
Published 21 titles (7 juvenile) in 2002: 13 were developed
from unsolicited submissions, 1 was by an agented author,
and 4 were reprint/licensed properties. Of the 21 titles, 4
were by unpublished writers and 8 were by authors who were
new to the publishing house. Receives 250 queries, 100
unsolicited mss yearly.
- **Fiction:** Published 2 story picture books, 4–10 years; and 1
  young adult book, 12–18 years. Also publishes chapter books,
  5–10 years. Genres include historical fiction, folklore, suspense,
  and stories about animals, nature, and the environment.
- **Nonfiction:** Published 1 easy-to-read book, 4–7 years; and 2
  story picture books, 4–10 years. Also publishes middle-grade
  books, 8–12 years, and young adult books, 12–18 years. Topics
  include animals, geography, natural history, and humor.
- **Representative Titles:** *Winter Is* by Ann Dixon (3–6 years) is a
  celebration of the many joys of the winter season. *Runaways
  on the Inside Passage* by Joe Upton is the story of thirteen-
  year-old twins, abandoned by their mother in Seattle, who
  head for Alaska in search of their father.

Submissions and Payment
Guidelines available. Query with clips for fiction; send complete ms for children's books. Accepts photocopies, disk submissions, and simultaneous submissions. SASE. Responds in
2–4 months. Publication in 2 years. Payment policy varies.

Editor's Comments
Our titles focus on Alaska, the Western US, and the Pacific
Northwest. Occasionally we'll consider out-of-region subjects,
but only if you can demonstrate reader interest and market.

Greene Bark Press

P.O. Box 1108
Bridgeport, CT 06601-1108

Associate Publisher: Michele Hofbauer

Publisher's Interests

This small fiction house specializes in early childhood young
reader picture books for children between the ages of three
and nine. It offers between two and six titles annually. Its
catalogue also features story-based CD-ROMs that come with
teacher guides filled with follow-up activities.
Website: www.greenebarkpress.com

Freelance Potential

Published 2 titles in 2002: both were developed from unsolicited submissions. Receives 600 unsolicited mss yearly.
- **Fiction:** Publishes story picture books, 4–10 years. Genres
  include fantasy and mystery. Also offers teachers' guides and
  titles on CD-ROM.
- **Representative Titles:** *To Know the Sea* by Frances Gilbert
  (3–8 years) is a fairy tale about a princess' dream to sail on a
  ship of her own. *A Pumpkin Story* by Mariko Shinju (3–8 years)
  is a story about sharing and living in harmony with nature.

Submissions and Payment

Guidelines available. Send complete ms with illustrations and
story board. Accepts photocopies and simultaneous submissions if identified. SASE. Responds in 2–6 months. Publication
in 12–18 months. Royalty, 10–15%.

Editor's Comments

Please note that we only publish fiction for children between
the ages of three and nine. We look for stories that have a
unique story line and possess lots of color and imagery. Send
us something that is original; we try our best to avoid stories
that have well-worn plots and classic themes. Don't send us an
ugly duckling story or a story about the creature in the bed-
room closet. We are looking for clean, clear, fresh stories that
are well written. We prefer to see one story at a time and ask
that completed manuscripts come with copies of color artwork
(no originals please), but we will not necessarily disqualify a
submission that comes without artwork. Please be patient, we
try to respond to writers within six months.

Greenhaven Press

10911 Technology Place
San Diego, CA 92127

Managing Editor: Scott Barbour

Publisher's Interests
Greenhaven Press offers a number of educational series for
young adults. Its books address topics such as American history, world history, and literary criticism. It also publishes
biographies and titles dealing with contemporary social
issues. In November of 2000, Greenhaven Press was purchased by Gale, a publisher of library reference products.
Website: www.galegroup.com/greenhaven

Freelance Potential
Published 145 titles in 2002: 20 were developed from unsolicited submissions and 2 were by agented authors. Of the
145 titles, 15 were by unpublished writers and 20 were by
authors who were new to the publishing house. Receives 25
queries yearly.
- **Nonfiction:** Publishes young adult books, 12–18 years. Features anthologies and books in series about history, literary
criticism, world authors, and contemporary social issues.
- **Representative Titles:** *Ireland* (YA) recounts the efforts of this
nation, torn by political and religious strife, to take its place
among the community of nations; part of the Nations in Tran-
sition series. *Dating* (YA) strives to promote healthy, responsible
decision-making while respecting the rights of teens to make
their own choices; part of the Teen Decisions series.

Submissions and Payment
Guidelines available. All work done on a work-for-hire basis
by assignment only. Query for guidelines and catalogue.
SASE. Response time varies. Publication in 1 year. Flat fee,
first book, $2,500; subsequent books, $3,000.

Editor's Comments
We will not look at unsolicited manuscripts. If you think you
would like to write for us, we suggest that you familiarize
yourself with some of our current titles. Then, if you feel you
have the appropriate credentials, send us a résumé. We
always need qualified writers and editors who can help us in
developing our book series.

Greenwood Publishing Group

88 Post Road West
P.O. Box 5007
Westport, CT 06881-5007

Managing Editor: Emily Birch

Publisher's Interests
This publisher targets the school and library markets with its curriculum-based titles for use in middle school classrooms. Greenwood Publishing Group offers titles on topics such as world history and culture, health, literature, science, and the arts.
Website: www.greenwood.com

Freelance Potential
Published 12 titles in 2002: 1 was by an unpublished writer and 9 were by authors who were new to the publishing house. Receives 10 queries, 10 unsolicited mss yearly.
- **Nonfiction:** Publishes reference books and high-interest/low-vocabulary titles, 12–15 years. Topics include history, geography, mathematics, science, nature, the environment, sports, social issues, and multicultural and ethnic subjects.
- **Representative Titles:** *Japanese American Internment During World War II* by Wendy Ng (12–15 years) is a reference guide that helps students understand the Japanese American wartime experience through the words of those who were interned. *Student Companion to Ernest Hemingway* by Lisa Tyler (12–15 years) provides information about Hemingway's eventful life and guides students through all of his major literary works.

Submissions and Payment
Guidelines and catalogue available at website. Query with clips; or send complete ms with résumé. Accepts photocopies. Availability of artwork improves chance of acceptance. SASE. Responds in 2–4 weeks. Publication in 9 months. Royalty, varies. Flat fee, varies.

Editor's Comments
We're looking for reference books that correlate directly to the middle-school curriculum in the areas of social studies, science, language arts, and health. Most of the authors we publish teach the topic they are writing about to middle school students or have an advanced degree in the field.

Group Publishing

P.O. Box 481
Loveland, CO 80539

Editorial Assistant: Kerri Loesche

Publisher's Interests
Christian educators are the target audience for this religious publisher. Its list includes nonfiction activity, how-to, and novelty books for all ages. 5% subsidy-published material.
Website: www.grouppublishing.com

Freelance Potential
Published 50 titles in 2002: 2 were developed from unsolicited submissions, 1 was by an agented author, and 2 were reprint/licensed properties. Of the 50 titles, 3 were by unpublished writers and 4 were by authors who were new to the publishing house. Receives 500+ queries yearly.

- **Nonfiction:** Publishes activity, how-to, and novelty books. Also publishes game books for preschool to adult readers. Features Christian educational titles and books on special education, hobbies, crafts, and religion.
- **Representative Titles:** *Lively Bible Lessons* (grades K–3) offers 20 fast-paced lessons. *Jr. High Retreats & Lock-ins* by Karen Dockrey offers suggestions for twelve complete retreats.

Submissions and Payment
Guidelines available. Query with outline, book introduction, and 2–3 sample chapters or activities. Accepts photocopies, computer printouts, and simultaneous submissions if identified. SASE. Responds in 3–6 months. Publication period varies. Royalty, to 10%. Flat fee, varies.

Editor's Comments
Our mission is to encourage Christian growth in children, youth, and adults. We are always looking for good writers who know kids, understand active learning, and have the ability to write lessons that help kids apply the Bible to their daily lives. Our editors have set up a trial assignment that allows potential writers to try their hand at writing curriculum. Check out our various curriculum lines at your local Christian bookstore, then write to request a trial assignment specifying the age level and curriculum line that interests you. Keep in mind that it may take as long as six months for us to respond.

Gryphon House

P.O. Box 207
Beltsville, MD 20704-0207

Editor-in-Chief: Kathy Charner

Publisher's Interests

This publisher specializes in educational resource materials that can be used by parents and teachers working with children under the age of eight. Its catalogue includes books about infancy and toddlerhood, as well as titles about early childhood teaching strategies and program development.
Website: www.gryphonhouse.com

Freelance Potential

Published 14 titles in 2002: 9 were developed from unsolicited submissions. Of the 14 titles, 2 were by unpublished writers and 3 were by authors who were new to the publishing house. Receives 200 queries yearly.

- **Nonfiction:** Publishes titles for parents and teachers working with children under the age of eight. Topics include art, math, science, language development, teaching strategies, conflict resolution, program development, and bilingual education.
- **Representative Titles:** *Help! There's a Toddler in My House!* by Nancy Kelly (parents and caregivers) provides stimulating activities that play to the curiosity and creativity of children in this age group. *The Complete Resource Book* by Pam Schiller & Kay Hastings (educators) is an early childhood curriculum that includes circle time activities, learning center ideas, and music and movement activities.

Submissions and Payment

Guidelines available. Query with table of contents, introductory material, and 20–30 pages of activities. Accepts photocopies and computer printouts. SASE. Responds in 3–4 months. Publication in 1–2 years. Payment policy varies.

Editor's Comments

In your query, tell us why your book is one teachers would want to own and use every day. Books that appeal to another audience in addition to teachers are especially welcome. Please note that we do not publish children's books, and we are not interested in activity books that feature paper-and-pencil activities or cut-and-paste projects.

Guardian Press

Suite 225
10924 Grant Road
Houston, TX 77070

Acquisitions Editor: Richard Eaves

Publisher's Interests
This electronic publisher features the Mightybook imprint
that offers downloadable titles for children and parents. Its
list includes titles for ages two through preteen, as well as
interactive vocabulary games and puzzles. It also offers video
song books. 20% self-, subsidy, co-venture, or co-op published material.
Website: www.mightybook.com

Freelance Potential
Published 25 titles in 2002: 10 were developed from unsolicited submissions, 22 were by agented authors, and 2 were
reprint/licensed properties. Of the 25 titles, 10 were by
authors who were new to the publishing house. Receives 200
unsolicited mss yearly.
- **Fiction:** Published 2 concept books, 5 toddler books, and 5
  early picture books, 0–4 years; 5 easy-to-read books, 4–7
  years; and 8 story picture books, 4–10 years. Genres include
  fairy tales, fantasy, folklore, folktales, humor, multicultural and
  ethnic fiction, and stories about nature and the environment.
- **Representative Titles:** *Barnyard Babies* by Richard Wayne
  (2–4 years). *The Great Royal Race* by Carl Sommer (8–12 years).

Submissions and Payment
Guidelines available at website. Send complete ms. Availability of artwork improves chance of acceptance. Accepts photocopies, disk submissions (Microsoft Word), and e-mail submissions to reaves@houston.rr.com. SASE. Responds in 3–4
weeks. Publication period varies. Royalty, 20%.

Editor's Comments
Stories that are no more than 500 words in length are our top
priority for the coming year. Subject matter is open, but books
should target readers between the ages of two and ten. We do
not publish any young adult material at this time. All our
books are designed to be read aloud and shared by the whole
family. Our mission is to spread the love of books and the joy
of reading.

Gulliver Books

15 East 26th Street
New York, NY 10010

Editorial Director: Elizabeth Van Doren

Publisher's Interests

Fiction and nonfiction for children between the ages of three
and seven, easy reader and chapter books, and select middle-
grade and young adult books are found on the list of Gulliver
Books. An imprint of Harcourt Brace & Company, this publisher will consider submissions from agented, previously
published authors, or writers who are members of the Society
of Children's Book Writers and Illustrators.
Website: www.harcourtbooks.com

Freelance Potential

Published 30 titles in 2002.
- **Fiction:** Publishes early picture books, 3–7 years; middle-grade
  fiction, 8–12 years; and young adult books, 12–18 years. Genres include historical and contemporary fiction and adventure.
  Also publishes animal stories and poetry.
- **Nonfiction:** Publishes early picture books, 3–8 years. Topics
  include sports, history, nature, the environment, and science.
  Also features biographies.
- **Representative Titles:** *My Somebody Special* by Sarah Weeks
  (2–5 years) is the story of a toddler anxiously waiting for his
  mother at the end of the school day. *The Marvelous Mouse Man*
  by Mary Ann Hoberman (5–8 years) relates the adventures of a
  man who comes to town to lead all the mice away, but ends up
  taking more than he bargained for.

Submissions and Payment

Accepts submissions only from agented, previously published
authors, or from members of the Society of Children's Book
Writers and Illustrators (SCBWI). SASE. Responds in 6–8
weeks. Publication in 2–4 years. Royalty; advance.

Editor's Comments

Please note that we only review manuscripts from agented
authors who have already been published, and from writers
who are members of SCBWI. Picture books and fantasy stories
for young readers, as well as rhyming picture books for toddlers, continue to top our list of current interests.

Hachai Publishing

156 Chester Avenue
Brooklyn, NY 11218

Submissions Editor: D. Rosenfeld

Publisher's Interests

High-quality picture books for readers up to the age of 10 that focus on Jewish themes are the specialty of this small publishing house. Books that deal with Jewish history, tzedakah, shabbos, mitzvos, middos, and Torah learning are included in its catalogue.

Website: www.hachai.com

Freelance Potential

Published 5 titles in 2002: 2 were developed from unsolicited submissions. Of the 5 titles, 2 were by unpublished writers and 2 were by authors who were new to the publishing house. Receives 300+ unsolicited mss yearly.

- **Fiction:** Published 1 concept book and 1 early picture book, 0–4 years; 2 story picture books, 4–10 years; and 1 chapter book, 5–10 years. Genres include historical, religious, ethnic, and multicultural fiction; adventure; and folktales.
- **Nonfiction:** Publishes concept books, 0–4 years; and story picture books, 4–10 years. Also publishes biographies.
- **Representative Titles:** *Is It Shabbos Yet?* by Ellen Emerman (2–5 years) helps children understand the holiday of Shabbos. *The Wise Little Judge* by David Sholom Pape, ed. (8–12 years) offers stories relating to Jewish history.

Submissions and Payment

Guidelines available. Send complete ms. Accepts photocopies. SASE. Responds in 2–6 weeks. Publication in 12–18 months. Flat fee.

Editor's Comments

At Hachai, we are dedicated to creating books that may be read aloud by adults and children. We believe that reading aloud not only develops language skills and encourages the imagination, but also creates memories that last a lifetime. All of our books are of the highest quality and all have Jewish content. We continue to look for submissions that convey Jewish traditions of today as well as long ago—books that will impart a love of Judaism to the very youngest children.

Hampton-Brown Books

26385 Carmel Rancho Boulevard
Carmel, CA 93923

Submissions Editor

Publisher's Interests

Educators working in language arts, English-as-a-Second-Language, and dual-language programs turn to Hampton-Brown Books for easy-to-read titles and textbooks. This publisher features a number of high-interest, low-vocabulary books. Its materials are designed for use in preschool through eighth-grade classrooms.
Website: www.hampton-brown.com

Freelance Potential

Published 100 titles (50 juvenile) in 2002: 60 were reprint/licensed properties. Of the 100 titles, 2–3 were by unpublished writers and 4–5 were by authors who were new to the publishing house. Receives 100 queries yearly.

- **Fiction:** Publishes early picture books, 0–4 years; easy-to-read books, 4–7 years; story picture books, 4–10 years; chapter books, 5–10 years; and middle-grade books, 12–18 years. Genres include fairy tales, folklore, drama, and contemporary and multicultural fiction.
- **Nonfiction:** Publishes early picture books, 0–4 years; easy-to-read books, 4–7 years; story picture books, 4–10 years; chapter books, 5–10 years; and middle-grade books, 8–12 years. Also publishes books on phonics, ESL, early literacy, dual-language programs, content-area reading, and homeschooling.
- **Representative Titles:** *Early Intervention Levels* is a collection of leveled books that support educational programs designed to assist students in the early grades who are at risk of failure in reading and writing. *The Basic Bookshelf* includes high-interest, low-level books for building literacy.

Submissions and Payment

Query. No unsolicited mss. SASE. Responds in 3–6 months. Publication period varies. Flat fee.

Editor's Comments

Right now, our top editorial priority is high-interest, low-vocabulary, content-based fiction and nonfiction. If you think you are qualified to write for us, send a query.

Hampton Roads Publishing

1125 Stoney Ridge Road
Charlottesville, VA 22902

Associate Editor: Pat Adler

Publisher's Interests

Hampton Roads publishes books of a metaphysical and inspirational nature, nonfiction as well as visionary fiction. Books for young readers appear under its Young Spirit imprint, and include easy-to-read books, story picture books, and middle-grade and young adult titles.
Website: www.hamptonroadspub.com

Freelance Potential

Published 46 titles (4 juvenile) in 2002. Receives 1,000+ queries yearly.

- **Fiction:** Publishes easy-to-read books, 4–7 years; story picture books, 4–10 years; middle-grade novels, 8–12 years; and young adult books, 12–18 years. Genres include inspirational, visionary, and metaphysical fiction.
- **Nonfiction:** Publishes picture books, 4–10 years; middle-grade books, 8–12 years; and young adult books, 12–18 years. Topics include spirituality, metaphysics, and alternative medicine.
- **Representative Titles:** *Dreamsong of the Eagle* by Ted Andrews is a fairy tale about two children, shunned by their village for being different, who find solace and friendship among the creatures of the woods. *The Boy from Nine Miles* by Cedella Marley & Gerald Hausman chronicles the childhood years of musician Bob Marley.

Submissions and Payment

Guidelines and catalogue available with SASE. Query with synopsis, chapter-by-chapter outline, and 1–2 sample chapters. Send complete ms with artwork for children's books. Accepts computer printouts and simultaneous submissions if identified. SASE. Responds in 6 months. Publication in 18 months. Royalty, 10%–20%; advance, $1,000.

Editor's Comments

We're looking for books for our Young Spirit line that will stimulate children's intellect, teach them valuable lessons in a metaphysical context, and allow their spirits to grow. Do not submit genre fiction, poetry, or short story collections.

Deborah Halverson, Harcourt, Inc.
Eclectic & Sophisticated Picture Books

One of the first qualities writers notice about Harcourt's list of picture books is how eclectic it is. From the standpoint of Assistant Editor Deborah Halverson, this is an extraordinary plus. "It allows me to acquire a wide variety of picture books," she says. "I find myself especially drawn to irreverently funny, witty books as well as manuscripts that exhibit unusual language and rhythmic qualities."

When asked about Harcourt's reputation for publishing highly sophisticated picture books, Halverson explains that they also want books that "appeal to a broader, more commercial audience." Because of this wide scope, they concentrate less on looking for specific subjects and more on looking for "manuscripts that are well written, have a strong sense of story and language, and engaging characters," Halverson says. "Most of the nonfiction we publish is story- and character-driven, and it's often illustrated with artwork rather than photos."

Halverson herself edits about 12 picture books annually and recommends the following books that reflect her personal tastes: *The Moon & Riddles Diner and the Sunnyside Café*, by Nancy Willard; any of the Old Badger and Little Badger books by Eve Bunting; *Whose Shoes?* by Anna Grossnickle Hines; and *If You Find a Rock*, by Peggy Christian

When reading submissions, Halverson spends little time on the query, jumping instead into the manuscript itself, but the query letters that most attract her attention "are those that succinctly state key selling points of the story and indicate a familiarity with the children's book market. Most important, the writing needs to be strong in the query letters since those give me my first impression of the writer's skill with language."

(Listing for Harcourt Children's Books on
following page)

Harcourt Children's Books

Suite 1900
525 B Street
San Diego, CA 92101

Submissions Editor

Publisher's Interests
Harcourt is a well-known publisher that offers an extensive
list of fiction and nonfiction titles for children of all ages. Its
imprints include Gulliver Books, Red Wagon Books, Voyager
Books, and Odyssey. This publisher considers submissions
from agented authors only.
Website: www.harcourtbooks.com

Freelance Potential
Published 165 titles in 2002: 132 were by agented authors.
Receives 2,000 unsolicited mss yearly.
- **Fiction:** Publishes concept books, toddler books, and early
  picture books, 0–4 years; easy-to-read books, 4–7 years; story
  picture books, 4–10 years; chapter books, 5–10 years; middle-
  grade novels, 8–12 years; and young adult novels, 12–18 years.
  Genres include mystery, fantasy, suspense, and contemporary,
  historical, and multicultural fiction. Also publishes stories
  about sports, nature, and the environment, and poetry.
- **Representative Titles:** *The First Thing My Mama Told Me* by
  Susan Marie Swanson (3–7 years) is the joyful story of a child's
  growing sense of identity as she realizes that her name is hers
  alone. *The Big Burn* by Jeanette Ingold (12+ years) is a drama
  about the biggest wildfire of 1910 that paints a portrait of a
  time, a place, and an event that altered the landscapes of
  Idaho and Montana.

Submissions and Payment
Agented authors only. No simultaneous submissions.
Responds to agented submissions in 1 month. Publication
in 2 years. Royalty; advance.

Editor's Comments
High-quality books for children are our specialty, and we
publish only the best examples for our readers. Have your
agent send us your work if you feel it will meet our criteria.
We receive thousands of submissions each year, so do not be
disappointed if we reject your work. You may want to submit
your manuscript to a smaller publishing house.

Harcourt Religion Publishers

1655 Embassy West
Dubuque, IA 52002

Managing Editor: Marge Krawczuk

Publisher's Interests
Catholic catechism programs use the religious educational
materials offered by Harcourt Religion Publishers. It carries
textbooks, classroom programs, and resource materials for
preschool through high school students. Materials for Vacation Bible Schools and sacramental preparation are also
found in its catalogue.
Website: www.harcourtreligion.com

Freelance Potential
Published 20 titles in 2002: 2 were by unpublished writers
and 4 were by authors who were new to the publishing
house. Receives 30–35 queries yearly.
- **Nonfiction:** Publishes easy-to-read books, 4–7 years; chapter
  books, 5–10 years; middle-grade books, 8–12 years; and young
  adult books, 12–18 years. Topics include faith, catechism, education, Christian lifestyles, contemporary issues, prayer, worship, and family life.
- **Representative Titles:** *Celebrating Our Faith* (grades 7–9) is a
  program that helps junior high candidates for Confirmation
  understand the order of the Rite and prepare for the celebration of the sacrament. *Celebrating Our Faith* (grades 2–4) is a
  new series that follows the order of the Mass and the commu-
  nal Rite of Reconciliation.

Submissions and Payment
Query with outline, résumé, and 3 sample chapters. Accepts
photocopies, computer printouts, and simultaneous submissions if identified. SASE. Responds in 2–6 weeks. Publication
in 1 year. Royalty. Flat fee.

Editor's Comments
We're looking for submissions that creatively enhance the catechetical process, promote religious literacy, and celebrate the
Catholic faith. We continue to look for material to add to our
preschool programs. We also need new ideas for our Growing
in Love program, which introduces the seven key catechetical
themes to students in kindergarten through eighth grade.

HarperCollins Children's Books

1350 Avenue of the Americas
New York, NY 10019

Senior Editor: Ruth Katcher

Publisher's Interests
One of the leading publishers of children's books, Harper-Collins offers quality fiction and nonfiction titles for children of all ages.
Website: www.harpercollinschildrens.com

Freelance Potential
Published 500 titles in 2002: 50 were developed from unsolicited submissions, 450 were by agented authors, and 100 were reprint/licensed properties. Of the 500 titles, 5 were by authors who were new to the publishing house. Receives 15,000 unsolicited mss yearly.

- **Fiction:** Publishes concept books, toddler books, and early picture books, 0–4 years; easy-to-read books, 4–7 years; story picture books, 4–10 years; chapter books, 5–10 years; middle-grade novels, 8–12 years; and young adult novels, 12–18 years. Genres include historical, multicultural, and contemporary fiction; mystery; fairy tales; suspense; science fiction; and humor. Also publishes sports and adventure stories.
- **Nonfiction:** Publishes easy-to-read books, 4–7 years; story picture books, 4–10 years; chapter books, 5–10 years; and middle-grade books, 8–12 years. Topics include animals, mathematics, science, history, humor, and entertainment.
- **Representative Titles:** *Biscuit Goes to School* by Alyssa Satin Capucilli (3–5 years) is the story of a cute little puppy who is determined to go to school with his owner. *All-American Girl* by Meg Cabot (12+ years) is a humorous tale of a teenage girl who inadvertently saves the life of the President of the United States.

Submissions and Payment
Accepts submissions from agented authors only. Responds in 1 month. Publication in 1–2 years. Royalty; advance.

Editor's Comments
Our website can give you more information on the type of material we publish. Please note that we consider submissions from agented authors only. Freelance writers are welcome to query our Avon imprint.

HarperTrophy Paperbacks

HarperCollins Children's Books
1350 Avenue of the Americas
New York, NY 10019

Vice President & Editorial Director: Elise Howard

Publisher's Interests
This imprint of HarperCollins Children's Books publishes chapter books, fiction, and nonfiction titles for middle-grade readers and young adults.
Website: www.harperchildrens.com

Freelance Potential
Published 250 titles in 2002: 1 was developed from an unsolicited submission, 110 were by agented authors, and 15 were reprint/licensed properties. Of the 250 titles, 1 was by an unpublished writer. Receives 200 unsolicited mss yearly.

- **Fiction:** Publishes easy-to-read books, 4–7 years; story picture books, 4–10 years; chapter books, 7–10 years; middle-grade novels, 8–12 years; and young adult novels, 12–18 years. Genres include mystery, suspense, humor, and romance.
- **Nonfiction:** Publishes easy-to-read books, 4–7 years; story picture books, 4–10 years; chapter books, 7–10 years; middle-grade books, 8–12 years; and young adult books, 12–18 years. Topics include sports, history, and science. Also publishes biographies.
- **Representative Titles:** *Joey Pigza Loses Control* by Jack Gantos tells the story of a boy who wants to show his dad he's not as "wired" as he used to be. *What Happens to a Hamburger?* by Paul Showers takes readers on a journey through the human digestive tract.

Submissions and Payment
Guidelines available. Prefers complete ms. Accepts query with sample chapters. Accepts photocopies, computer printouts, and simultaneous submissions if identified. SASE. Responds in 3 months. Publication in 18 months. Royalty; advance.

Editor's Comments
We look for ideas that are fresh and imaginative. As always, good writing that involves the reader in a story or subject is essential, and subject matter, length, and vocabulary should be age appropriate. Each manuscript—whether agented or unsolicited—is given careful consideration.

Harvest House Publishers

990 Owen Loop North
Eugene, OR 97402

Manuscript Coordinator

Publisher's Interests
This evangelical publishing house features books about
Christian living, education, family life, and Bible study. Its
juvenile list features both fiction and nonfiction for children
between the ages of two and eighteen.
Website: www.christianpub.com

Freelance Potential
Published 170 titles in 2002: 26 were by agented authors
and 3 were reprint/licensed properties. Of the 170 titles, 5
were by authors who were new to the publishing house.
Receives 1,500 queries yearly.
- **Fiction:** Publishes children's picture books, 2–8 years. Genres
  include religious and inspirational fiction. Features books
  about religious holidays and Bible stories.
- **Nonfiction:** Publishes concept books and toddler books, 0–4
  years; and young adult books, 12–18 years. Topics include
  prayer and Bible studies. Also features books about Christian
  education, Christian living, family issues, church holidays, and
  contemporary issues.
- **Representative Titles:** *Kirby the Disgruntled Tree* by Lori Wick
  (0–8 years) is the tale of a maple tree whose journey from
  unhappiness to contentment teaches children a lesson about
  facing changes and challenges. *Help! My Little Boy's Growing
  Up* by Annette Smith (parents) provides positive advice and
  encouragement to adolescent boys on topics such as puberty,
  peer pressure, dating, and faith in Christ.

Submissions and Payment
Query. No unsolicited mss.

Editor's Comments
Our mission is to glorify God by providing high-quality books
and products that affirm biblical values, help people grow spiritually strong, and proclaim Jesus Christ as the answer to
every human need. Ideas for children's or parenting titles that
are original, relevant, well-written, and grounded in the teach-
ings of Scripture are most likely to catch our attention.

Hayes School Publishing Company

321 Pennwood Avenue
Pittsburgh, PA 15221

President: Mr. Clair N. Hayes III

Publisher's Interests

This publisher specializes in teaching aids that have been designed and tested by educators. Hayes School Publishing offers reproducible masters, classroom posters and charts, and bulletin board materials for use in kindergarten through twelfth-grade classrooms.

Website: www.hayespub.com

Freelance Potential

Published 60 titles in 2002: 5 were developed from unsolicited submissions. Of the 60 titles, 6 were by authors new to the publishing house. Receives 200–300 queries yearly.

- **Nonfiction:** Publishes educational resource materials, grades K–12. Topics include reading, vocabulary, language arts, foreign languages, social studies, math, science, art, music, mythology, and creative thinking.
- **Representative Titles:** *How to Use a Library* (grades 4 and up) includes detailed activity pages that explain the classification and arrangement of books, card catalogues, and dictionary and encyclopedia use. *A Trip to Spain: Beginning Spanish Reader* helps students practice their Spanish reading skills as they take an imaginary trip to Spain.

Submissions and Payment

Guidelines available. Query with résumé, outline, table of contents, and sample pages. Accepts photocopies, computer printouts, and simultaneous submissions if identified. SASE. Responds in 2–3 weeks. Publication period varies. Flat fee.

Editor's Comments

We specialize in motivating, learning-by-doing educational resources. We welcome new materials on all subjects for all grade levels; this year we're particularly interested in reviewing materials that teach foreign languages, social studies, reading, and math. While many of our titles are produced in-house, we accept a sizable number of manuscripts each year from teacher-writers. These often turn out to be among our most popular titles.

Hazelden Foundation

P.O. Box 176
Center City, MN 55012-0176

Manuscript Coordinator

Publisher's Interests

Hazelden Foundation specializes in books and multi-media products that deal with substance abuse treatment, prevention, and recovery. Books on family and youth leadership issues also appear on its list. Its materials are used by educators, counselors, and doctors.
Website: www.hazelden.org

Freelance Potential

Published 100 titles in 2002: 60 were developed from unsolicited submissions and 5 were by agented authors. Receives 300 queries yearly.

- **Nonfiction:** Publishes middle-grade books, 8–12 years; and young adult books, 12–18 years. Also publishes self-help titles and books for parents and educators. Topics include alcohol and substance abuse, health, fitness, and social issues.
- **Representative Titles:** *101 Bullying Support Group Activities for Children Who Bully* by Dave Matthews (grades 6–12) features activities that help students who bully other children recognize and change their destructive behaviors. *Changing Families* by Teresa Schmidt (educators) is a group activities manual for middle and high school students who come from separated, divorced, or single-parent families.

Submissions and Payment

Guidelines available. For catalogue, call toll-free, 1-800-328-0098. Query with outline/synopsis, 3 sample chapters, and clips or writing samples. Accepts photocopies. SASE. Responds in 3 months. Publication in 12–18 months. Royalty. Flat fee.

Editor's Comments

We continue to look for high-quality, research-based curricula materials for children in kindergarten through grade twelve. While most of our titles deal with substance abuse, prevention, treatment, and recovery, we do offer a number of titles on family and social issues that are relevant to today's children and teens.

Heinemann

361 Hanover Street
Portsmouth, NH 03801-3912

Editorial Assistant: Eric Chalek

Publisher's Interests
Educators working with students in kindergarten through
college use the professional resources from Heinemann. Its
catalogue features books and videotapes on teaching math,
science, social studies, and art education. The company was
founded in 1978.
Website: www.heinemann.com

Freelance Potential
Published 70 titles in 2002. Receives 1,000+ queries yearly.
- **Nonfiction:** Publishes educational resource and multi-media
  materials for teachers and school administrators. Topics
  include math, science, social studies, art education, reading,
  writing, ESL, bilingual education, gifted and special education,
  early childhood, school reform, curriculum development, and
  the creative arts. Also publishes professional development and
  assessment materials.
- **Representative Titles:** *Young Mathematicians at Work: Con-
  structing Fractions, Decimals, and Percents* by Catherine Twomey
  Fosnot & Maarten Dolk (teachers, grades 5–8) provides strategies to help teachers turn their classrooms into math workshops. *Math Stories from a Kindergarten Classroom* by Angela
  Andrews & Paul R. Trafton is a collection of stories from the
  authors' classrooms that highlight the problem-solving potential of very young students.

Submissions and Payment
Guidelines available. Query with résumé, proposal, outline,
table of contents, and chapter summaries. Accepts photocopies and computer printouts. SASE. Responds in 6–8
weeks. Publication in 10–12 months. Payment policy varies.

Editor's Comments
We have a passion for publishing works by professionals for
professionals. Most of our authors are exemplary educators
who are eager to support the practice of other teachers. We're
looking for materials that support teachers' efforts to help children become literate, empathetic, and knowledgeable citizens.

Hendrick-Long Publishing Company

P.O. Box 1247
Friendswood, TX 77549

Vice President: Vilma Long

Publisher's Interests
This regional publisher specializes in books related to the history and culture of Texas and the Southwest. Readers from kindergarten through high school will find both fiction and nonfiction books on a wide range of subjects.
Website: www.hendricklongpublishing.com

Freelance Potential
Published 6 titles in 2002: 3 were developed from unsolicited submissions. Of the 6 titles, 3 were by unpublished writers and 3 were by authors who were new to the publishing house. Receives 200+ queries yearly.
- **Fiction:** Published 3 middle-grade books, 8–12 years; and 3 young adult books, 12–18 years. Also publishes story picture books, 4–10 years. Genres include historical and regional fiction.
- **Nonfiction:** Publishes easy-to-read titles, 4–7 years; chapter books, 5–10 years; and young adult books, 12–18 years. Also offers biographies. Topics include geography, animals, nature, and history.
- **Representative Titles:** *Pioneer Children* by Betsy Warren features six stories that illustrate the vital role children played in the settlement of early Texas. *Cowboy Stories from East Texas* by John Lash (6+ years) features stories from life in present-day Texas.

Submissions and Payment
Guidelines available. Query with résumé, table of contents, outline/synopsis, and 1–2 sample chapters. Accepts photocopies, computer printouts, and simultaneous submissions if identified. SASE. Responds in 1–2 months. Publication in 18 months. Royalty; advance.

Editor's Comments
Books about Texas——its history, people, and stories——are our primary area of interest. We feature books for a wide range of ages, and we're interested in new writers who can write about Texas and the Southwest from a solid, informed viewpoint. Subjects of interest include history, geography, and folklore.

Heritage House

#301-3555 Outrigger Road
Nanoose Bay, British Columbia V9P 9K1
Canada

Publisher: Rodger Touchie

Publisher's Interests

Established in 1969, this Canadian publisher features titles of interest to western Canadian readers. Its list includes non-fiction books and activity books on Canadian history and nature for middle-grade children.
Website: www.heritagehouse.com

Freelance Potential

Published 26 titles in 2002: 18 were developed from unsolicited submissions and 2 were reprint/licensed properties. Of the 26 titles, 4 were by unpublished writers and 6 were by authors who were new to the publishing house. Receives 100 queries yearly.

- **Nonfiction:** Publishes middle-grade books, 8–12 years. Topics include the environment, history, nature, and wildlife of western Canada; and the Royal Canadian Mounted Police. Also publishes activity books.
- **Representative Titles:** *The Royal Canadian Mounted Police* by Tom Hunter features word games, puzzles, drawings, and historical information on the RCMP force. *Eagle's Reflection and Other Northwest Coast Stories* by Robert James Challenger shows how the creatures of nature all have something to tell us through special messages.

Submissions and Payment

Guidelines and catalogue available with 9x12 SAE/IRC. Query with sample illustrations. Accepts photocopies, computer printouts, and disk submissions (Microsoft Word or PageMaker). Artwork improves chance of acceptance. SAE/ IRC. Responds in 1 month. Publication in 8–10 months. Royalty.

Editor's Comments

Most of our authors are Canadian citizens, or reside in Canada, but we will consider appropriate material from all writers. We publish material with Canadian themes only, and at this time we are interested in original submissions about western Canadian native myths, totem poles, animals, and nature. Please note that we do not accept fiction works.

Heuer Publishing Company

P.O. Box 248
Cedar Rapids, IA 52406

Editor: C. E. McMullen

Publisher's Interests
Heuer publishes one-act plays, full-length plays, and musicals, monodramas, and monologues in collections, as well as theater-related texts for schools and community theaters.
Website: www.hitplays.com

Freelance Potential
Published 15 titles in 2002: 14 were developed from unsolicited submissions and 1 was by an agented author. Of the 15 titles, most were by unpublished writers and 14 were by authors who were new to the publishing house. Receives 200 queries, 150 unsolicited mss yearly.
- **Fiction:** Publishes middle-grade plays, 8–12 years; and young adult plays, 12–18 years. Genres include comedy, musicals, drama, mystery, suspense, and satires. Also publishes books on theater arts, stage production, auditions, sound effects, and theater resources.
- **Representative Titles:** *Laffin' School* by Keith Jackson is a one-act comedy about a substitute teacher in a daffy school where the students don't want to graduate. *Scenes That Happen* by Mary Krell-Oishi is a book of dramatizations about the bearable and impossible situations of teenage existence.

Submissions and Payment
Guidelines available. Query or send complete ms with synopsis, cast list, running time, and set requirements. Accepts photocopies and computer printouts. SASE. Responds in 2 months. Publication period varies. Royalty. Flat fee.

Editor's Comments
The majority of groups performing our plays have little or no theatrical experience. Drama directors are often burdened with other duties, and are not prepared to present plays with numerous scenes and/or complicated set requirements. With that in mind, send us material with easy-to-find props and costumes and simple stage effects. At this time, we are especially interested in receiving plays, musicals, and specialty books for school and church theater groups.

Holiday House

425 Madison Avenue
New York, NY 10017

Associate Editor: Suzanne Reinoehl

Publisher's Interests

Both fiction and nonfiction for children of all ages are featured in the catalogue of Holiday House. Its books appeal equally to youngsters who are just learning to read and young adults.

Website: www.holidayhouse.com

Freelance Potential

Published 60 titles in 2002: 5 were developed from unsolicited submissions and 55 were by agented authors. Of the 60 titles, 5 were by unpublished writers and 8 were by authors who were new to the publishing house. Receives 8,000 queries yearly.

- **Fiction:** Publishes early picture books, 0–4 years; story picture books, 4–10 years; chapter books, 5–10 years; middle-grade novels, 8–12 years; and young adult books, 12–18 years. Genres include mystery, fantasy, humor, and historical and multicultural fiction.
- **Nonfiction:** Publishes story picture books, 4–10 years; and young adult books, 12–18 books. Topics include history, social issues, and science. Also publishes biographies.
- **Representative Titles:** *Quilt Alphabet* by Lesa Cline-Ransome (2–6 years) is an alphabet poem accompanied by folk-art illustrations. *B. Franklin, Printer* by David A. Adler (9+ years) profiles the amazing career of this statesman who wanted to be remembered simply as a printer.

Submissions and Payment

Guidelines available. Query. Accepts photocopies and computer printouts. SASE. Responds in 2 months. Publication period varies. Royalty; advance.

Editor's Comments

We continue to be interested in queries for literary fiction that will appeal to middle-grade readers. Send us a story that will keep young readers turning pages with interest and delight. We like to see fresh ideas that will encourage a love of reading in children. Please do not send queries for serial titles.

Henry Holt and Company

115 West 18th Street
New York, NY 10011

Submissions: Books for Young Readers

Publisher's Interests
This well-known publisher offers a full spectrum of books
for children of all ages. Its list includes picture books, fiction
in a variety of genres, and nonfiction about topics such as
animals, nature, science, and history.
Website: www.henryholt.com

Freelance Potential
Published 63 titles in 2002: 18 were by agented authors.
Receives 7,000 unsolicited mss yearly.
- **Fiction:** Publishes concept books, toddler books, and early picture books, 0–4 years; story picture books, 4–10 years; chapter
  books, 5–10 years; middle-grade novels, 8–12 years; and 5
  young adult books, 12–18 years. Genres include adventure,
  mystery, suspense, fantasy, folklore, fairy tales, and contemporary and historical fiction. Also publishes poetry.
- **Nonfiction:** Publishes story picture books, 4–10 years; middle-
  grade books, 8–12 years; and young adult books, 12–18 years.
  Topics include multicultural subjects, animals, nature, history,
  mathematics, science, and technology.
- **Representative Titles:** *Visiting Langston* by Willie Perdomo
  (4–8 years) is a rhythmic tale about a young poet who visits the
  home of Langston Hughes. *The Scrambled States of America* by
  Laurie Keller (4–9 years) is a quirky story that stars all 50
  states and includes introductory geographic facts.

Submissions and Payment
Guidelines available with 9x12 SASE ($.60 postage). Send
complete ms. Accepts photocopies. No simultaneous submissions. SASE. Responds in 3–4 months. Publication in 18
months. Royalty, 8–10%; advance, $4,000–$6,000.

Editor's Comments
Our Books for Young Readers department accepts solicited as
well as unsolicited submissions. We continue to look for well-
crafted chapter books and nonfiction picture books for readers
between the ages of six and eleven. We're not interested in textbooks of any type.

Honor Books

Suite 4800
2448 East 81st Street
Tulsa, OK 74037

Product/Brand Manager

Publisher's Interests

This Christian publisher strives to inspire, encourage, and motivate readers to draw nearer to God. Honor Books' juvenile list includes devotionals, Bible stories, children's Bibles, story picture books, board books, and activity books for readers up to the age of 12.
Website: www.honorbooks.com

Freelance Potential

Published 11 titles in 2002: 1 was developed from an unsolicited submission and 3 were by agented authors. Of the 11 titles, 5 were by unpublished writers and all were by authors who were new to the publishing house. Receives 120 unsolicited mss yearly.

- **Nonfiction:** Publishes concept books, toddler books, and early picture books, 0–4 years; easy-to-read books, 4–7 years; story picture books, 4–10 years; and middle-grade books, 8–12 years. Also offers activity, novelty, and board books, and titles in series. Features books about Christianity.
- **Representative Titles:** *My Promise Bible* is a collection of Bible promises for young children that uses simple words to tell about God's love. *God's Little Devotional Book for Kids* combines inspiring quotes and corresponding Scriptures with meditations that provide spiritual encouragement.

Submissions and Payment

Guidelines available. Send complete ms with interior sample spreads. Accepts simultaneous submissions if identified. Availability of artwork improves chance of acceptance. SASE. Responds in 3 months. Publication in 1–2 years. Royalty; advance. Flat fee.

Editor's Comments

While we often publish titles by authors who are new to us, it does help to have an agent. Our primary needs are for nonfiction devotionals, Bible stories, and board books. We will consider fiction, but it must have a religious theme. Don't submit young adult titles or fantasy.

Houghton Mifflin Children's Books

222 Berkeley Street
Boston, MA 02116

Submissions Coordinator: Hannah Rodgers

Publisher's Interests
Fiction and nonfiction titles for young children, beginning readers, and young adults appear on the list of this well-known publisher.
Website: www.houghtonmifflinbooks.com

Freelance Potential
Published 90 titles in 2002: 3 were developed from unsolicited submissions, 25 were by agented authors, and 5 were reprint/licensed properties. Receives 13,000–15,000 unsolicited mss yearly.
- **Fiction:** Publishes concept books, toddler books, and early picture books, 0–4 years; easy-to-read books, 4–7 years; chapter books, 5–10 years; middle-grade novels, 8–12 years; and young adult novels, 12–18 years. Genres include historical and multicultural fiction, adventure, and humor.
- **Nonfiction:** Publishes picture books, 0–4 years; middle-grade books, 8–12 years; and young adult books, 12–18 years. Topics include history and science. Also publishes biographies.
- **Representative Titles:** *Little Pig Is Capable* by Denis Roche (4–8 years) is the tale of a small pig who shows that he is clever and resourceful all on his own. *Black Potatoes: The Story of the Irish Famine, 1845–1850* by Susan Campbell Bartoletti (10–14 years) tells the history of the biggest disaster to strike Ireland in the nineteenth century.

Submissions and Payment
Guidelines available with SASE, at website, or by calling 617-351-5959. Send complete ms for fiction. Query with synopsis and sample chapters for nonfiction. Accepts photocopies and computer printouts. SASE. Responds in 3 months. Publication period varies. Royalty; advance.

Editor's Comments
We pride ourselves on the high-quality books we publish. Although we encourage new writers to submit their books, prospective authors must realize that we receive thousands of manuscripts each year.

Humanics

P.O. Box 7400
Atlanta, GA 30357

Acquisitions Editor

Publisher's Interests
Humanics specializes in teacher resources and activity books
for use with children up to the age of six. Its titles are used
by teachers, child-care specialists, and parents. Only nonfiction books appear on its list.
Website: www.humanicspub.com

Freelance Potential
Published 60 titles (10 juvenile) in 2002: 30 were developed
from unsolicited submissions and 10 were by agented
authors. Of the 60 titles, 6 were by unpublished writers and
6 were by authors who were new to the publishing house.
Receives 500 queries yearly.
- **Nonfiction:** Published 5 concept books and 10 toddler books,
  0–4 years. Topics include crafts and hobbies. Also publishes
  titles for parents and educators.
- **Representative Titles:** *Creative Teaching: Bringing a New Spirit
  to Education* by James Downton, Jr. (teachers) explores creative approaches to teaching. *How to Get Kids to Do What You
  Want: The Power and Promise of Solution-Focused Parenting* by
  Bill Crawford (parents) helps parents establish the type of relationship where their children hear what they are saying and
  look to them for help and guidance.

Submissions and Payment
Guidelines and catalogue available with 9x12 SASE ($.60
postage). Query with résumé, synopsis, and marketing plan.
Accepts photocopies, computer printouts, and disk submissions (Microsoft Word or WordPerfect.). Availability of artwork
improves chance of acceptance. SASE. Responds in 3
months. Publication in 6 months. Royalty, 8%.

Editor's Comments
This year, we continue to seek submissions for activity books.
As always, we welcome new writers who are familiar with our
titles and can add to our list. We look for individuals with
knowledge of current educational needs as well as a sense of
what works in the classroom.

Hunter House Publishers

P.O. Box 2914
Alameda, CA 94501-0914

Acquisitions Editor: Jeanne Brondino

Publisher's Interests
Hunter House Publishers targets therapists, educators, and other professionals who work with children. Its list includes self-help and psychology books as well as many books about trauma and violence prevention. Coloring and activity books for children also appear in its catalogue.
Website: www.hunterhouse.com

Freelance Potential
Published 20 titles (1 juvenile) in 2002: 1 was developed from an unsolicited submission, 3 were by agented authors, and 6 were reprint/licensed properties. Of the 20 titles, 5 were by unpublished writers and 10 were by authors who were new to the publishing house. Receives 1,000 queries yearly.
- **Nonfiction:** Published 2 middle-grade activity books, 8–12 years. Topics include music, dance, and drama. Also publishes titles for counselors and educators. Features self-help and psychology books on relationships, sexuality, health, fitness, violence prevention, and trauma.
- **Representative Titles:** *Keeping Kids Safe: A Child Sexual Abuse Prevention Manual* by Pnina Tobin & Sue Levinson Kessner is a how-to manual that teaches personal safety skills to children. *Making the Peace* by Paul Kivel & Allan Creighton is a 15-step violence prevention program designed to help young people break away from violence, develop self-esteem, and regain a sense of community.

Submissions and Payment
Guidelines available. Query with résumé, overview, chapter-by-chapter outline, competitive analysis, and marketing ideas. Accepts photocopies, computer printouts, and simultaneous submissions. SASE. Responds in 3–4 months. Publication in 1–3 years. Royalty.

Editor's Comments
It is crucial that the authors of educational and professional books have credentials and experience in the areas they address. Please don't send picture books or fiction.

John Hunt Publishing

46a West Street
New Alresford, Hants SO24 9AU
United Kingdom

Editor: John Hunt

Publisher's Interests
Established in 1988, this British publisher features books on
Christianity and related subjects for adults and children, as
well as general religious education titles.
Website: www.johnhunt-publishing.com

Freelance Potential
Published 60 titles (32 juvenile) in 2002: 3 were developed
from unsolicited submissions, 20 were by agented authors,
and 4 were reprint/licensed properties. Of the 60 titles,
5 were by unpublished writers and 15 were by authors
who were new to the publishing house. Receives 600 queries
each year.

- **Nonfiction:** Published 11 toddler books and 8 early picture
  books, 0–4 years; 4 chapter books, 5–10 years; 5 middle-grade
  books, 8–12 years; and 1 young adult book, 12–18 years. Topics include religion, prayer, faith, family issues, and social
  issues. Also publishes Bible stories and educational titles.
- **Representative Titles:** *Hawkeye of Paradise Row* by Veronica
  Heley (8–15 years) is the story of a boy who has found a place
  he wants to keep secret, but one he must tell about to save the
  townspeople. *The Dancing Horse* by Fay Sampson (7–10 years)
  is a tale about how an "Obby Oss" saved a Cornwall town
  during the Hundred Years War.

Submissions and Payment
Query with clips. Accepts photocopies. SASE. Responds in 1
week. Publication in 18 months. Royalty. Flat fee.

Editor's Comments
We still publish mostly in the area of Christian books for children and adults, but we are now doing more straight textbooks and general religion titles. We like books that show us
we can benefit from learning about others. Send us your
ideas for board books and novelty titles that tell about Christian holidays, especially Christmas and Easter. For older
readers, send us material that helps them understand the
traditions, culture, beliefs, and history of other faiths.

Impact Publishers

P.O. Box 6016
Atascadero, CA 93423

Acquisitions Editor: Freeman Porter

Publisher's Interests

This publisher offers psychology and self-improvement books written by psychologists, therapists, or other human service professionals. Its titles address the needs and concerns of adults, children, families, organizations, and communities.
Website: www.impactpublishers.com

Freelance Potential

Published 6 titles in 2002: 1 was developed from an unsolicited submission and 1 was by an agented author. Receives 500 queries yearly.

- **Nonfiction:** Publishes middle-grade books, 8–12 years; and young adult books, 12–18 years. Also publishes adult titles on marriage, parenting, popular psychology, social issues, self-esteem, mental health, creativity, relationships, social and emotional growth, and multicultural and ethnic issues.
- **Representative Titles:** *Creative Therapy 2: Working with Parents* by Kate Ollier & Angela Hobday (therapists) offers resources for working with parents of children with emotional or behavioral problems. *The Divorce Handbook for Kids* by Cynthia MacGregor discusses the issues that trouble many kids when their parents get divorced and offers exercises for dealing with stress.

Submissions and Payment

Guidelines available. Query with résumé and sample chapters. Accepts photocopies, computer printouts, and simultaneous submissions if identified. SASE. Responds in 1–3 months. Publication in 1 year. Royalty; advance.

Editor's Comments

We are not seeking submissions for the coming year. Keep in mind that we only consider manuscripts written by qualified professionals—therapists, psychologists, and others who work in the area of human services. For more than 30 years, our books have offered practical, reader-friendly help on such personal matters as relationships, divorce, parenting, stress, personal growth, and mental health.

Imperial International

30 Montauk Boulevard
Oakdale, NY 11769

Editor-in-Chief: Laura Solimene

Publisher's Interests

This division of EDCON Publishing features educational
materials for students in primary and secondary schools.
Topics covered by its titles include phonics, mathematics,
language arts, science, reading, and writing. In addition to
books, Imperial International also produces CD-ROMs, videos,
and audio cassettes.
Website: www.edconpublishing.com

Freelance Potential

Published 12 titles in 2002. Of the 12 titles, 6 were by
unpublished writers and 3 were by authors who were new to
the publishing house. Receives 100 unsolicited mss yearly.
- **Fiction:** Published 12 chapter books, 5–10 years. Also publishes easy-to-read books, 4–7 years; chapter books, 5–10 years;
  and middle-grade titles, 8–12 years. Genres include multicultural and ethnic fiction, fairy tales, adventure, and science
  fiction. Also publishes hi/lo fiction, 6–18 years; and activity
  books, 6–12 years.
- **Nonfiction:** Publishes chapter books, 5–10 years; and young
  adult books, 12–18 years. Topics include mathematics, science, and technology. Also publishes special education titles.
- **Representative Titles:** *Thoughts into Words* (grades 3–6) helps
  students learn the mechanics of writing by identifying paragraph purposes, using metaphors, and developing character
  traits. *Sports Math* (grades 2–6) helps remedial students grasp
  math concepts through the world of sports.

Submissions and Payment

Guidelines available with 9x12 SASE ($1.49 postage).
Send complete ms. Accepts photocopies and simultaneous
submissions if identified. Submissions are not returned.
Responds in 1–2 weeks. Publication in 6 months. Flat fee,
$300–$1,000.

Editor's Comments

We continue to be interested in books that teach math concepts for different age and skill levels.

Incentive Publications

3835 Cleghorn Avenue
Nashville, TN 37215

Editor: Jean Signor

Publisher's Interests

Research-based educational books covering math, science, social studies, and language arts are the foundation of Incentive Publications' publishing program. It offers material for preschools and elementary and middle schools, as well as for English-as-a-Second-Language programs.
Website: www.incentivepublications.com

Freelance Potential

Published 24 titles in 2002: 5 were developed from unsolicited submissions. Of the 24 titles, 1 was by an unpublished writer and 1 was by an author who was new to the publishing house. Receives 350 queries yearly.

- **Nonfiction:** Published 6 chapter books, 5–10 years; 18 middle-grade books, 8–12 years; and 6 young adult books, 12–18 years. Also publishes early picture books, 0–4 years; and teacher resources. Topics include education and special needs, writing, language arts, mathematics, arts and crafts, social studies, self-awareness, and student achievement.
- **Representative Titles:** *Language Literacy Lessons* by Imogene Forte (grades K–6) is a language arts series designed to help students reach literacy milestones through reinforcement of key language skills. *The BASIC/Not Boring Middle Grades Social Studies Book* by Imogene Forte & Marjorie Frank (grades 4–5) includes creative exercises to practice skills, a skills checklist, and pre- and post-tests to assess achievement.

Submissions and Payment

Guidelines available. Query with table of contents, outline/synopsis, and 1–3 sample chapters. Accepts photocopies and simultaneous submissions if identified. SASE. Responds in 4–6 weeks. Publication period varies. Royalty. Flat fee.

Editor's Comments

This year we're looking for quality, research-based resources for elementary and middle-grade teachers, as well as early learning materials for three- to six-year-old students. Please do not send fiction.

Innovative Kids

18 Ann Street
Norwalk, CT 06854

Publisher's Assistant: Catherine Savitz

Publisher's Interests
This publisher offers a line of interactive, hands-on books for children under the age of 12. Innovative Kids publishes both fiction and nonfiction titles with an educational emphasis. Its list also includes novelty books and books in series.
Website: www.innovativekids.com

Freelance Potential
Published 24 titles in 2002: 12 were by unpublished writers and 12 were by authors who were new to the publishing house. Receives 180 queries, 180 unsolicited mss yearly.
- **Fiction:** Publishes educational books, novelty books, and board books, 1–12 years. Genres include adventure, fairy tales, folklore, folktales, religious fiction, humor, and books about nature, the environment, and sports.
- **Nonfiction:** Published 5 concept books and 2 toddler books, 0–4 years; 9 easy-to-read books, 4–7 years; 6 story picture books, 4–7 years; and 2 middle-grade books. Topics include animals, pets, crafts, hobbies, geography, mathematics, nature, and the environment. Also publishes humor.
- **Representative Titles:** *Animal Patters* by Cynthia Capetta (3–5 years) is a novelty book about animals that's really two books in one. *Where Will We Go Today?* by Mary Thelan (3–6 years) allows children to choose a place to explore by turning the dial and selecting an image on the front cover.

Submissions and Payment
Guidelines available. Query or send complete ms with dummies. Accepts photocopies. SASE. Responds in 4–6 months. Publication period and response time vary. Flat fee.

Editor's Comments
If you think you have an idea for a book that will work in our product line, please send it along. Just remember that we only develop titles that have one or more interactive components that are integrated parts of the books. We're primarily interested in reviewing books that develop early learning skills in children under the age of 12.

Interlink Publishing Group

46 Crosby Street
Northampton, MA 01060

Associate Publisher: Pamela Thompson

Publisher's Interests
Crocodile Books, the juvenile imprint of Interlink Publishing Group, specializes in picture books for young readers. Established in 1987, this publisher also offers travel guides and history titles.
Website: www.interlinkbooks.com

Freelance Potential
Published 86 titles (6 juvenile) in 2002: 6 were developed from unsolicited submissions, 3 were by agented authors, and 48 were reprint/licensed properties. Of the 86 titles, 2 were by authors who were new to the publishing house. Receives 2,500 queries, 1,000 unsolicited mss yearly.
- **Fiction:** Published 4 story picture books, 3–8 years. Genres include international folklore and folktales.
- **Nonfiction:** Publishes story picture books, 3–8 years. Topics include travel and history. Also publishes travel guides, and literature, history, politics, and ethnic cooking titles for adults.
- **Representative Titles:** *Russian Gypsy Tales* by Yefin Druts & Alexei Gessler is a collection of colorful stories narrated by gypsies from various areas, including Leningrad, Moscow, and Gorky. *London for Families* by Larry Lain presents practical information for a family-friendly holiday in England.

Submissions and Payment
Query with synopsis. Accepts photocopies and computer printouts. Availability of artwork improves chance of acceptance for picture book submissions. SASE. Responds in 1 month. Publication in 18 months. Royalty; advance.

Editor's Comments
We like to think our books change the way people think about the world. International writers are invited to submit material for Our Emerging Voices: New International Fiction series, which brings translated fiction from around the world to a North American audience. Our children's books are designed for ages three to eight, and we will not consider picture-book manuscripts that are not illustrated.

International Reading Association

P.O. Box 8139
800 Barksdale Road
Newark, DE 19714-8139

Publications Manager: Beth Doughty

Publisher's Interests
The International Reading Association is a nonprofit, global
network of individuals and institutions committed to literacy.
It supports professionals with a wide range of resources covering such topics as early literacy; adolescent literacy,
assessment, reading research, and reading difficulties.
Website: www.reading.org

Freelance Potential
Published 30 titles in 2002. Receives 100 queries yearly.
- **Nonfiction:** Publishes educational titles, research reports, and
  monographs. Topics include literacy programs, reading
  research and practice, language comprehension at all levels,
  and professional development.
- **Representative Titles:** *To Be a Boy, To Be a Reader* by William
  G. Brozo (educators) offers solutions for engaging preteen and
  teen boys in reading. *Classroom Strategies for Interactive Learning* by Doug Buehl (educators) provides middle school and high
  school educators with literacy development strategies.

Submissions and Payment
Guidelines available. Request a Publication Proposal Form
before sending ms. Accepts photocopies. No simultaneous
submissions. SASE. Responds in 2–3 months. Publication
period varies. Payment policy varies.

Editor's Comments
Our goal is to provide educators with the best professional
resources for reading and literacy training. We respond to
these needs with a list of approximately 20 new books each
year. We welcome individuals who would like to become a part
of the prestigious circle of professionals who write for the International Reading Association. You may add your name to our
author roster by submitting a manuscript for publication, after
you have sent for our Publication Proposal Form. We ask that
applicants have a knowledge or expertise in selected aspects of
reading or literacy education; that they have the ability to communicate effectively; and that they be familiar with our books.

InterVarsity Press

P.O. Box 1400
Downers Grove, IL 60515

Editorial Department

Publisher's Interests
As the publishing arm of the InterVarsity Christian Fellowship,
a university ministry, this publisher offers a catalogue of nonfiction titles that target college students and teachers. Its current list offers books on topics of general interest to Christians
as well as academic, theological, and reference titles.
Website: www.ivpress.com

Freelance Potential
Published 125 titles in 2002: 15 were by agented authors
and 30 were reprint/licensed properties. Receives 1,500
queries yearly.
- **Nonfiction:** Publishes biblically based, religious titles for parents, college students, and educators. Features informational,
  educational, how-to, and reference books.
- **Representative Titles:** *An Incomplete Guide to the Rest of Your
  Life* by Stan D. Gaede is a practical guide to life that points
  readers to God, who offers true happiness and lasting satisfaction. *Singleness* by Ruth Goring addresses the notion of being
  single through a series of Bible studies.

Submissions and Payment
Guidelines and catalogue available at website. Query with
résumé, chapter-by-chapter summary, and 2 sample chapters. SASE. Responds in 6–10 weeks. Publication in 2 years.
Payment policy varies.

Editor's Comments
We publish five types of books: Bible study, academic, reference, theological, and issue-oriented books. All our titles are
nonfiction; we do not publish fiction, prophecies, music, or
poetry. We prefer a query that includes a summary of your
book as well as two sample chapters and a résumé. Please
note that we only review unsolicited manuscripts through
The Writer's Edge, a manuscript service used by Christian
publishers. At this time, we're especially interested in queries
from women and from authors of various ethnic backgrounds,
particularly those whose expertise meet our interests.

iPicturebooks, Inc.

24 West 25th Street
New York, NY 10010

Submissions Editor

Publisher's Interests
ipicturebooks publishes children's e-books on the World Wide Web. In addition to acquiring new content, it licenses rights to out-of-print titles. It is primarily interested in picture books for young readers. Its sister company, ibooks, offers books in print format.
Website: www.ipicturebooks.com

Freelance Potential
Published 4 titles in 2002: 1 was developed from an unsolicited submission and 2 were by agented authors. Of the 4 titles, 2 were by unpublished writers and all were by authors who were new to the publishing house. Receives 600 queries each year.
- **Fiction:** Publishes stories about nature and the environment; humor; historical, multicultural, and ethnic fiction; fantasy; fairy tales; folklore; and folktales.
- **Nonfiction:** Publishes books about nature, the environment, animals, pets, science, technology, and multicultural and ethnic subjects. Also offers biographies.
- **Representative Titles:** *At the Zoo* by Paul Simon is a picture book that follows three children as they set out on a trip to visit their favorite animals. *Crafts for Thanksgiving* by Kathy Ross features 20 simple autumn crafts for very young children.

Submissions and Payment
Guidelines available at website. Query via e-mail, following instructions at website. SASE. Responds in 1–2 weeks. Publication in 1 year. Royalty.

Editor's Comments
Our interests are similar to many book publishers, with a few important differences. We publish many "conventional" books, but we are particularly interested in books that use the electronic form in an interesting and integral way. And while we consider manuscripts on their own, we are most interested in submissions of "packages" of text and illustrations, with illustrations that meet a professional standard.

Jalmar Press/Innerchoice Publishing

Suite 702, 24426 South Main Street
Carson, CA 90745

Submissions Editor: Susanna Palomares

Publisher's Interests
Books that focus on self-awareness, self-esteem, character education, emotional intelligence, and social skills are the speciality of Jalmar Press. It targets educators, counselors, and care givers working with children in kindergarten through high school. 1% subsidy-published material.
Website: www.jalmarpress.com

Freelance Potential
Published 10 titles in 2002: 1 was developed from an unsolicited submission. Of the 10 titles, 1 was by an unpublished writer and 2 were by authors who were new to the publishing house. Receives 450 queries yearly.

- **Nonfiction:** Publishes activity-driven education titles, grades K–12. Topics include self-esteem, emotional intelligence, stress management, social skills, character education, prevention of drug and alcohol abuse, conflict resolution, discipline, and communication.
- **Representative Titles:** *Character Booklets for Kids* by Sally Elliott & Gerry Dunne (grades 2–6) is a series of booklets based on six universal moral values that affirm the worth and dignity of all people. *How to Handle a Bully* by Susanna Palomares & Dianne Schilling (grades 3–9) teaches effective prevention and intervention strategies.

Submissions and Payment
Guidelines available. Query with résumé and outline. SASE. Response time varies. Publication in 18 months. Royalty; advance.

Editor's Comments
This year, we are particularly interested in reviewing ideas for books for use with children in kindergarten through twelfth grade that deal with asset building, social skills, and anger management. Send for our guidelines, then query us with specific information on the development of your manuscript. Tell us the reason for its creation. What need did you see that you felt wasn't addressed elsewhere?

JayJo Books

Guidance Channel Company
135 Dupont Street
P.O. Box 760
Plainview, NY 11803-0760

Editor-in-Chief: Sally Germain

Publisher's Interests
This publisher specializes in books for children between the ages of four and twelve. Its focus is on children's health issues, and it covers such subjects as Down Syndrome, asthma, learning disabilities, and other health-related topics.
Website: www.jayjo.com

Freelance Potential
Published 6 titles in 2002. Receives 120 queries, 50 unsolicited mss yearly.
- **Fiction:** Publishes story picture books, 4–10 years. Features stories about children's health issues and special needs.
- **Nonfiction:** Publishes story picture books, 7–12 years. Topics include children's health habits, learning disabilities, ADHD, OCD, and Down Syndrome.
- **Representative Titles:** *Patrick Learns About Parkinson's Disease* is a story about a young boy and his neighbor who suffers from Parkinson's Disease; part of the Special Family and Friends series. *Taking Dyslexia to School* (5–10 years) discusses dyslexia in a positive and upbeat way; part of the Special Kids in School series.

Submissions and Payment
Guidelines available with #10 SASE ($.37 postage). Query. Accepts photocopies. SASE. Responds in 1 month. Publication in 2 years. Flat fee.

Editor's Comments
We publish books in four separate series: Special Kids in School; Substance Free Kids; Healthy Habits for Kids; and Special Family and Friends. Our Special Kids in School and Special Family and Friends series target elementary-age children, while our Healthy Habits series is for preschool and early elementary schoolchildren. The Substance Free Kids titles are for older elementary and middle-grade students. We look for books written from a child's perspective. Please don't send queries that feature animal characters. Be sure to review our guidelines before submitting, as they are quite specific.

Jewish Lights

P.O. Box 237
Sunset Farm Offices
Route 4
Woodstock, VT 05091

Submissions Editor

Publisher's Interests
This publisher features books that draw on the Jewish tradition to deal with the quest for self and meaning. Its readers include people of all faiths and backgrounds. Its juvenile list includes titles for very young readers through young adults.
Website: www.jewishlights.com

Freelance Potential
Published 30 titles (4 juvenile) in 2002: 12 were developed from unsolicited submissions, 1 was by an agented author, and 10 were reprint/licensed properties. Of the 30 titles, 5 were by unpublished writers and 10 were by authors who were new to the publishing house. Receives 600 queries, 300 unsolicited mss yearly.
- **Nonfiction:** Published 2 toddler books, 0–4 years; 1 easy-to-read book, 4–7 years; and 1 story picture book, 4–10 years. Also publishes young adult titles, 12–18 years, as well as religious and inspirational titles, self-help books, and books about recovery for adults.
- **Representative Titles:** *The Story of the Jews* by Stan Mack (10+ years) uses cartoons to chronicle 4,000 years of Jewish history and celebrates the characters and events that have shaped Jewish culture. *The Jewish Family Fun Book* by Danielle Dardashti & Roni Sarig includes holiday projects, home activities, and travel ideas with Jewish themes.

Submissions and Payment
Guidelines available. Prefers query with résumé, table of contents, and 2 sample chapters. Send complete ms for picture books. Accepts photocopies, computer printouts, and simultaneous submissions if identified. SASE. Responds in 4 months. Publication in 1 year. Payment policy varies.

Editor's Comments
We very rarely publish fiction and we never publish biographies, *haggadoth*, or poetry. Send us nonfiction that deals with the Jewish life cycle, history, or spirituality.

JIST Publishing

8902 Otis Avenue
Indianapolis, IN 46216-1033

Acquisitions Editor

Publisher's Interests
Established in 1981, this publisher specializes in career and job search materials. Its list targets middle and high school students as well as adults.
Website: www.jist.com

Freelance Potential
Published 40 titles in 2002: several were developed from unsolicited submissions. Receives 250 queries yearly.
- **Nonfiction:** Features textbooks, assessment devices, reference materials, workbooks, videos, and software packages. Topics include job searches and career development.
- **Representative Titles:** *Career Ideas for Kids Who Like Art* (grades 4–6) looks at different careers in artistic fields; part of the Career Ideas for Kids series. *College Majors Handbook* by Neeta P. Fogg et al. (grades 9 and up) identifies jobs, earnings, and trends for graduates of 60 college majors.

Submissions and Payment
Guidelines available at website. Query with résumé, outline/synopsis, and audience/market analysis. SASE. Responds in 3–4 months. Publication in 1–2 years months. Royalty, 8–10%.

Editor's Comments
We are primarily a job search training firm and most of our titles are directed at training counselors who teach people to conduct their own job searches. Over the years, our publishing program has grown to include text and trade books, assessment devices, reference materials, curricula, workbooks, videos, and software packages. Our primary audience continues to be largely institutional and includes counselors in schools, colleges, and universities. If, after reviewing some of our books, you feel you have an idea that is right for us, send us your résumé, a market survey, an outline, a detailed table of contents, and a detailed outline of the major topics of your book and how you plan to cover them. If we wish to see a completed manuscript, we will let you know.

Bob Jones University Press

1700 Wade Hampton Boulevard
Greenville, SC 29614-0060

Manuscript Editor: Nancy Lohr

Publisher's Interests
The youth trade division of this Christian publisher features fiction for preschoolers through young adults, biographies, and nonfiction. It is not accepting picture book submissions at this time.
Website: www.bjup.com

Freelance Potential
Published 10 titles in 2002: 3 were developed from unsolicited submissions, 1 was by an agented author, and 3 were reprint/licensed properties. Receives 20+ queries, 500+ unsolicited mss yearly.

- **Fiction:** Published 1 early picture book, 0–4 years; 3 easy-to-read books, 4–7 years; 4 chapter books, 5–10 years; and 2 young adult books, 12–18 years. Genres include contemporary and historical fiction. Also features stories about animals.
- **Nonfiction:** Publishes middle-grade books, 8–12 years; and young adult books, 12–18 years. Publishes biographies of well-known Christians and missionaries.
- **Representative Titles:** *Best of Friends* by Susan Walley (8–12 years) is a novel about a girl who is anxious to be friends with the new girl in town. *The Cranky Blue Crab* by Dawn Watkins tells the story of a bored and unhappy crab who leaves the sea to find a better life on land.

Submissions and Payment
Guidelines available. Query with 5 sample chapters; or send complete ms. Accepts photocopies, computer printouts, and simultaneous submissions if identified. SASE. Responds in 3 months. Publication in 18–24 months. Royalty, negotiable. Flat fee.

Editor's Comments
We're looking for writers to create exciting adventure and mystery stories. Good biographies are also welcome. Please don't send picture books. We would like to see more material for children ages six and up. Writing must reflect Christian thought, feeling, and action.

The Judaica Press

123 Ditmas Avenue
Brooklyn, NY 11218

Editor: Norman Shapiro

Publisher's Interests
Books about Jewish traditions and history for children and
adult readers are found in the catalogue of The Judaica
Press. Its list includes titles on the Talmud and Torah, books
about prayer and holidays, inspirational titles, books on Jewish life, novels, and Hebrew textbooks.
Website: www.judaicapress.com

Freelance Potential
Published 20 titles in 2002: 15 were developed from unsolicited submissions. Of the 20 titles, 2 were by unpublished
writers and 10 were by authors new to the publishing house.
Receives 50 queries, 30 unsolicited mss yearly.
- **Fiction:** Publishes early picture books, 0–4 years; easy-to-read
  books, 4–7 years; story picture books, 4–10 years; and young
  adult books, 12–18 years. Genres include inspirational fiction,
  and religious mystery and suspense.
- **Nonfiction:** Publishes story picture books, 4–10 years. Topics
  include Jewish traditions, self-help issues, Bible stories, crafts,
  and hobbies.
- **Representative Titles:** *Beautiful Brachos* by Chaim Finkelstein
  (3+ years) is a story of friends who learn the value of saying
  brachos with feeling and enthusiasm. *The Twisted Menora* by
  Carol Korb Hubner (8–15 years) features the detective Devora
  Doresh who uses her yeshiva education and knowledge of the
  Torah to help her solve mysteries.

Submissions and Payment
Query with outline; or send complete ms. Accepts photocopies and computer printouts. Availability of artwork
improves chance of acceptance. SASE. Responds in 3
months. Publication in 1–2 years. Royalty.

Editor's Comments
Books for young children about the Jewish holidays are always
welcome, as well as well-written stories for children up to the
age of fifteen. We prefer to see submissions that include
accompanying artwork.

Just Us Books

356 Glenwood Avenue
East Orange, NJ 07017

Submissions Editor: Cheryl Hudson

Publisher's Interests
Black history, culture, and experiences are the focus of Just
Us Books. Its catalogue includes concept books, picture
books, and chapter books, as well as nonfiction and biographies. Launched in 1988, it is a leading publisher of books
for young black people.
Website: www.justusbooks.com

Freelance Potential
Published 4 titles in 2002.
- **Fiction:** Publishes story picture books, 4–10 years; and mid-
  dle-grade novels, 8–12 years. Genres include multicultural,
  historical, and contemporary fiction; mystery; and adventure.
- **Nonfiction:** Publishes middle-grade books, 8–12 years. Fea-
  tures biographies.
- **Representative Titles:** *Courtney's Birthday Party* by Dr. Loretta
  Long (6–9 years) deals with the subject of subtle prejudice and
  illustrates the power of true friendship. *Annie's Gifts* by Angela
  Medearis (7–11 years) is a story about a girl who is determined
  to bring happiness and beauty to her world.

Submissions and Payment
Guidelines available. Query with outline/synopsis. Not
accepting unsolicited mss at this time. SASE. Responds in
3–4 months. Publication period varies. Royalty.

Editor's Comments
We are always interested in hearing from writers who have
authentic stories to tell and who are interested in pursing professional, creative writing and publishing. We use a number of
key factors to evaluate books that deal with Afrocentric themes
for children. We look for: positive images that leave lasting
impressions; accurate factual information that's enjoyable to
read; cultural authenticity and specificity; meaningful stories
that reflect a range of African-American values; material that is
self-affirming; and strong, three-dimensional characters. Nonfiction should be timely and relevant to today's world. All products should be designed to open the young reader's mind.

Kaeden Books

P.O. Box 16190
Rocky River, OH 44116

Submissions Editor: Craig Urmston

Publisher's Interests
The fiction and nonfiction titles from Kaeden Books target readers in first through third grade. Its catalogue features classroom collections for emergent readers as well as trade books for guided reading. Many of its titles are used in Reading Recovery, English-as-a-Second-Language, and Title 1 educational programs.
Website: www.kaeden.com

Freelance Potential
Published 8 titles in 2002: 3 were developed from unsolicited submissions. Of the 8 titles, 4 were by unpublished writers and 3 were by authors who were new to the publishing house. Receives 1,200 queries, 500 unsolicited mss yearly.
- **Fiction:** Published 6 easy-to-read books, 4–8 years.
- **Nonfiction:** Published 2 easy-to-read books, 4–8 years. Topics include mathematics, history, and science.
- **Representative Titles:** *Sammy's Hamburger Caper* by Kathleen & Craig Urmston (grade 3) is a fast-moving adventure story about a dog who can't resist the smell of a hamburger. *Last Night at the Zoo* by Michael Garland (4–8 years) is a rhyming picture book about animals who escape from the zoo for a night on the town.

Submissions and Payment
Send complete ms. Accepts photocopies and computer printouts. SASE. Responds only if interested. Publication period varies. Royalty. Flat fee.

Editor's Comments
We are seeking positive fiction and nonfiction titles for entry into the trade book market. We would also like to review high-interest chapter books for children between the ages of four and eight. Stories for early readers in preschool through third grade should have interesting characters, an element of humor, and surprise endings. Nonfiction titles about social studies and science are also needed for students in first through fourth grade.

Kar-Ben Publishing

241 First Avenue North
Minneapolis, MN 55401

Submissions Editor: Beth Heiss

Publisher's Interests
This publisher was recently acquired by Lerner Publishing
Group. It continues to offer nonfiction and fiction with Jewish
themes for very young children. Its list includes picture
books, concept books, toddler books, and easy-to-read books.
Website: www.karben.com

Freelance Potential
Published 7 titles in 2002: 2 were developed from unsolicited
submissions. Of the 7 titles, 2 were by unpublished writers
and 2 were by authors who were new to the publishing
house. Receives 350+ mss yearly.
- **Fiction:** Published 1 concept book, 1 toddler book, and 1 early
  picture book, 0–4 years; and 1 easy-to-read book, 4–7 years.
  Features Bible stories, holiday stories, life-cycle stories, and
  folklore. Also publishes activity and board books.
- **Nonfiction:** Published 1 concept book, 1 toddler book, and 1
  early picture book, 0–4 years.
- **Representative Titles:** *The Hardest Word* by Jacqueline Jules
  (3–7 years) is a story about Yom Kippur that features the
  adventures of a prehistoric bird. *The Shabbat Box* by Lesley
  Simpson (3–6 years) tells about a preschool boy who loses the
  Shabbat Box when it's his turn to bring it home from school.

Submissions and Payment
Guidelines available. Send complete ms. Accepts photocopies,
computer printouts, and simultaneous submissions if identified. SASE. Responds in 3–5 weeks. Publication in 1 year.
Royalty, 5–8%; advance, $500–$2,000.

Editor's Comments
We're looking for short stories—no more than 3,000 words—
that have interesting, believable characters and action that
holds the listener's attention. We feel that good prose is far
better than tortured verse. Please remember that all of our
books deal with Jewish themes and target children in
preschool and primary school. Do not send games, textbooks,
or books in Hebrew.

Key Curriculum Press

1150 65th Street
Emeryville, CA 94608

President and Editorial Director: Steve Rasmussen

Publisher's Interests
Key Curriculum Press specializes in materials targeted to secondary mathematics educators. Its list includes textbooks, workbooks, software, and videos. All books follow the standards set by the NCTM.
Website: www.keypress.com

Freelance Potential
Published 30 titles in 2002: 2 were developed from unsolicited submissions. Of the 30 titles, 1 was by an unpublished writer and 2 were by authors who were new to the publishing house. Receives 50 queries yearly.
- **Nonfiction:** Publishes middle-grade books, 8–12 years; and young adult books, 12–18 years. Also publishes titles for mathematics educators. Features classroom materials, posters, puzzles, textbooks, workbooks, tools and supplies, and books on professional development.
- **Representative Titles:** *Discovering Algebra* by Jerald Murdock et al. (grades 8–10) offers a fresh approach to high school algebra. *Problem Solving Strategies: Crossing the River with Dogs and Other Mathematical Adventures* by Ken Johnson & Ted Herr (grades 9 and up) teaches mathematical reasoning.

Submissions and Payment
Guidelines available. Query with résumé, prospectus, table of contents, and sample chapters. Accepts photocopies, computer printouts, Macintosh disk submissions, and simultaneous submissions if identified. SASE. Responds in 2 months. Publication period varies. Royalty, 6–10%.

Editor's Comments
For the coming year, we are particularly interested in math textbooks for use in grades nine through twelve. Remember that we only publish textbooks and related material on mathematics—no other subjects. If, after reviewing our catalogue and some of our titles, you feel you have a book for us, send a one-page proposal that defines the significance of your idea and the philosophy behind the proposal.

Key Porter Books

70 The Esplanade
Toronto, Ontario M5E 1R2
Canada

Editorial Assistant: Imoinda Romain

Publisher's Interests
Based in Canada, Key Porter Books specializes in books that
focus on history, nature, animals, and the environment. Its
list includes both fiction and nonfiction titles for children age
four and up, as well as some parenting titles and nonfiction
for older readers.
Website: www.keyporter.com

Freelance Potential
Published 80 titles (12 juvenile) in 2002: 3 were developed
from unsolicited submissions. Receives 100 queries yearly.
- **Fiction:** Publishes story picture books, 4–10 years; middle-
  grade books, 5–10 years; and young adult books, 12–18 years.
  Genres include folklore, fairy tales, and stories about animals,
  nature, and the environment. Also publishes anthologies.
- **Nonfiction:** Publishes story picture books, 4–10 years; middle-
  grade books, 8–12 years; and young adult books, 12–18 years.
  Topics include nature, the environment, natural history, history,
  health, and ethnic and multicultural subjects. Also publishes
  parenting titles.
- **Representative Titles:** *Ancient Adventures for Modern Kids* by
  John Mardon & Vesna Krstanovich features ancient stories
  from around the world. *The Cat and The Wizard* by Dennis Lee
  is the story of a disgruntled wizard, his unwanted bag of tricks,
  and his black cat.

Submissions and Payment
Guidelines available. Query with résumé, proposal, table of
contents, and sample chapter or excerpt of 20 pages. SAE/
IRC. Response time varies. Publication period and payment
policy vary.

Editor's Comments
We are interested in books that bring the world to life for children. Our catalogue brings them books about natural history,
animals, the environment, and the culture of the world as told
in stories and folktales. We are also interested in parenting
titles, and we welcome queries with a fresh angle.

Alfred A. Knopf Books for Young Readers

1540 Broadway
New York, NY 10036-4039

Submissions Editor

Publisher's Interests
This division of Random House Children's Books features fiction titles for the very young through young adults. Alfred A. Knopf Books for Young Readers has a list that includes board books, picture books, chapter books, and novels. It does not publish nonfiction of any kind.
Website: www.randomhouse.com/kids

Freelance Potential
Published 60 titles in 2002: 2 were developed from unsolicited submissions and 12 were by agented authors. Receives 4,000 unsolicited mss yearly.
- **Fiction:** Publishes picture books, 0–8 years; chapter books, 5–10 years; middle-grade novels, 8–12 years; and young adult novels, 12–18 years. Genres include historical, contemporary, and multicultural fiction.
- **Representative Titles:** *Cassie's Word Quilt* by Faith Ringgold (0–4 years) teaches very young readers the words that are associated with the people, places, and things one finds in an urban environment. *Trouble Don't Last* by Shelley Pearsall (9–13 years) is a historical novel set in 1859 about an 11-year-old slave boy who escapes with a friend.

Submissions and Payment
Guidelines available. Accepts agented submissions only. Accepts photocopies, computer printouts, and simultaneous submissions if identified. SASE. Responds in 3 months. Publication in 1–2 years. Royalty; advance.

Editor's Comments
Please note that we are currently accepting submissions through agents only. Visit a local library or bookstore and you'll see that the titles we publish are of exceptional literary quality and are of the highest artistic merit. If you feel your writing is something that will interest us and is of the quality that meets our standards, have a literary agent approach us with your work. While our titles target readers of all ages, we limit ourselves to fiction; don't submit nonfiction.

Lark Books

67 Broadway
Asheville, NC 28801

Acquisitions Editor

Publisher's Interests

Books about crafts and craft kits are available from this publisher. It features illustrated titles about topics such as ceramics, fiber arts, beading, knitting, and crocheting for middle-grade readers, young adults, and adults.
Website: www.larkbooks.com

Freelance Potential

Published 50 titles (6 juvenile) in 2002: 4 were developed from unsolicited submissions and 1 was a reprint/licensed property. Of the 50 titles, 3 were by unpublished writers and 4 were by authors who were new to the publishing house. Receives 200+ queries yearly.

- **Nonfiction:** Publishes middle-grade books, 8–12 years; and young adult books, 12–18 years. Topics include beading, book making, ceramics, doll making, fiber arts, knitting, crocheting, mosaics, nature crafts, paper, quilting, sewing, theater crafts, and weaving.
- **Representative Titles:** *Geography Crafts for Kids* by Joe Rhatigan & Heather Smith (8–12 years) features 50 geography projects and activities that take readers on a trip from their own rooms to the world beyond. *Girls' World* by Joanne O'Sullivan (8–12 years) includes how-to's for making fake-fur covered notebooks, locker organizers, homemade lip gloss, glitter gel, and friendship jewelry.

Submissions and Payment

Guidelines available. Prefers query with résumé, table of contents, introduction, 2–3 sample projects, and a description of artwork and illustrations. SASE. Response time varies. Publication period and payment policy vary.

Editor's Comments

Please note that we are interested in reviewing how-to craft books for 8- to 12-year-old readers only. Send us ideas for books that will inspire young crafters and will tap into their wells of creativity. All of our titles celebrate the joy and satisfaction that come from working creatively.

Learning Horizons

One American Road
Cleveland, OH 44144

Editorial Director: Bob Kaminski

Publisher's Interests
Founded in 1996 as a division of American Greetings, this
publisher offers educational resources for children between
the ages of two and twelve. Activity books, educational workbooks, games, manipulatives, music, and software are all
found in its catalogue.
Website: www.learninghorizons.com

Freelance Potential
Published 20 titles in 2002: all were assigned. Of the 20
titles, 2 were by authors who were new to the publishing
house. Receives 600 queries yearly.
- **Nonfiction:** Publishes toddler books and early picture books,
  0–4 years; and story picture books, 4–10 years. Features educational and informational titles and novelty and board books.
  Topics include animals, pets, mathematics, nature, and the
  environment.
- **Representative Titles:** *Bats!* (4–8 years) tells how bats look,
  where they live, and what they're like as babies; part of the
  Know-It-Alls® series. *Volcanoes and Other Earth Wonders* (6–9
  years) is a science sticker book that explains how volcanoes
  form, what happens during an eruption, and how scientists
  measure their force.

Submissions and Payment
Guidelines available. Query. SASE. Responds in 3–4 months.
Publication in 18 months. Payment policy varies.

Editor's Comments
We always try to pack educational fun and variety into our
books, games, music, and activities, which reach children of all
learning styles and levels. More and more parents are buying
our materials; they know the most important thing they can
give their child is a good education. We look for products that
make it convenient and fun for parents to get involved, and
stay involved, in their child's learning. Materials that teach
math and science are always needed. We also need books
about sports.

Learning Resources

380 North Fairway Drive
Vernon Hills, IL 60061

Submissions Editor

Publisher's Interests
Teachers of students in kindergarten through grade six use
the educational materials published by Learning Resources
to further classroom knowledge. This publisher features
workbooks, manipulatives, and activity books on mathematics, science, and language arts.
Website: www.learningresources.com

Freelance Potential
Published 45–50 titles (25 juvenile) in 2002: 2 were developed
from unsolicited submissions. Receives 10 queries, 5 unsolicited mss yearly.
- **Nonfiction:** Publishes educational materials, manipulatives,
  workbooks, and activity books. Topics include language arts,
  phonics, math, science, geography, and nutrition. Also publishes teacher resources.
- **Representative Titles:** *Geometry & Fractions with Pattern
  Blocks* (grades 3–6) features manipulatives to enrich intermediate math lessons with problem-solving activities for congruent
  and similar shapes, transformational geometry, and fractions.
  Microscopic Investigations (grades 3–6) explains how to collect
  specimens, what to look for under a microscope, and how to
  record observations; includes teaching notes, lab activities,
  journal pages, assessment worksheets, and research projects
  for classroom use.

Submissions and Payment
Catalogue available with 9x12 SASE ($3 postage). Query with
résumé and writing samples; or send complete ms. Accepts
photocopies, computer printouts, and disk submissions.
SASE. Responds in 6–12 weeks. Publication in 1–2 years.
Flat fee.

Editor's Comments
Most of our authors have a strong background in education.
When you send us your material, be sure to include an introduction that provides an overview about the subject, grade-
level appropriateness, and summary of the content.

Lee & Low Books

95 Madison Avenue
New York, NY 10016

Submissions Editor

Publisher's Interests
Lee & Low publishes picture books for children ages two
through ten. Its list includes realistic fiction, historical fiction,
and nonfiction. Specializing in books with multicultural
themes, it does not consider submissions for middle-grade
or young adult readers.
Website: www.leeandlow.com

Freelance Potential
Published 20 titles in 2002: 4 were developed from unsolicited submissions and 3 were by agented authors. Of the 20
titles, 4 were by unpublished writers and 6 were by authors
who were new to the publishing house. Receives 2,000 unsolicited mss yearly.
- **Fiction:** Published 1 toddler book and 1 early picture book,
  0–4 years; and 14 story picture books, 4–10 years. Genres
  include realistic, historical, multicultural, contemporary, and
  ethnic fiction.
- **Nonfiction:** Published 4 story picture books, 4–10 years.
  Topics include multicultural issues.
- **Representative Titles:** *Where on Earth Is My Bagel?* by Frances
  Park & Ginger Park (4+ years) tells the story of a boy in Korea
  who dreams of having a New York bagel. *David's Drawings* by
  Cathryn Falwell (3+ years) explores the issue of shyness through
  the story of a boy in a new school who makes friends by letting
  his classmates add to his drawing of a bare tree.

Submissions and Payment
Guidelines and catalogue available at website or with 9x12
SASE ($1.72 postage). Send complete ms. Accepts photo-
copies, computer printouts, and simultaneous submissions if
identified. SASE. Responds in 2–4 months. Publication in 1–2
years. Royalty; advance.

Editor's Comments
We continue to need submissions of realistic and historical
fiction for the coming year. We're also now looking for multicultural nonfiction submissions, but in picture book format only.

Legacy Press

P.O. Box 261129
San Diego, CA 92196

Editorial Director: Christy Scannell

Publisher's Interests

Launched in 1997, Legacy Press offers non-denominational, evangelical Christian books that are marketed primarily through Christian bookstores. Its catalogue features fiction and nonfiction for children between the ages of two and twelve, and all of its titles include activity ideas.
Website: www.rainbowpublishers.com

Freelance Potential

Published 7 titles in 2002: all were developed from unsolicited submissions. Of the 7 titles, 1 was by an author who was new to the publishing house. Receives 240 unsolicited mss each year.

- **Fiction:** Publishes books in series, 8–12 years. All titles include activities and devotionals.
- **Nonfiction:** Publishes middle-grade books, 8–12 years. Features activity books and how-to books, 8–12 years. Topics include crafts, hobbies, and religion.
- **Representative Titles:** *The Official Christian Babysitting Guide* (8–12 years) is a handbook for Christian pre-teens that offers ideas for keeping kids busy with Bible-based crafts, games, snacks, and songs and includes a free flashlight key chain. *The Un-Halloween Book* (parents and educators) is a reproducible book that features everything churches need to organize and direct an inspirational fall festival.

Submissions and Payment

Guidelines available with 9x12 SASE (2 first-class stamps). Send complete ms with table of contents and 3 sample chapters. Accepts photocopies. SASE. Responds in 3 months. Publication in 6–36 months. Royalty, 8%+; advance, $500.

Editor's Comments

At this time, we're primarily interested in nonfiction for children up to the age of 12. Books dealing with topics of interest to pre-teens, especially pre-teen girls, are needed. Remember that all of our titles include activities or additional components. Don't send anything on death, divorce, or abortion.

Lerner Publications Company

Lerner Publishing Group
241 First Avenue North
Minneapolis, MN 55401

Submissions Editor: grades K–4: Rebecca Poole
Submissions Editor: grades 5–12: Jennifer Zimian

Publisher's Interests
Educational books for readers between the ages of 7 and 18
are the specialty of this publishing company. For more than
40 years, Lerner Publishing has featured titles on social
issues, technology, the environment, and the arts.
Website: www.lernerbooks.com

Freelance Potential
Published 168 titles in 2002: 1 was developed from an unsolicited submission, 5 were by agented authors, and 28 were
reprint/licensed properties. Receives 500 queries, 2,000
unsolicited mss yearly.
- **Nonfiction:** Published 30 easy-to-read books, 4–7 years; 16
  chapter books, 5–10 years; 55 middle-grade books, 8–12 years;
  and 40 young adult books, 12–18 years. Topics include natural
  and physical science, current events, ancient and modern history, world art, special interests, world cultures, and sports.
  Also publishes biographies.
- **Representative Titles:** *Cooking the Italian Way* by Alphonse
  Bisignano (grades 5–12) focuses on the distinctive cooking
  styles and recipes of Italy; part of the Easy Menu Ethnic Cookbooks series. *Fall* by Tanya Thayer (grades K–2) introduces
  beginning readers to this season and shows how animals,
  plants, and people adapt to it; part of the Seasons series.

Submissions and Payment
Guidelines and catalogue available with 9x12 SASE ($3.50
postage). Query with outline and sample chapter; or send
complete ms with résumé. Accepts submissions during
March and October only. Accepts photocopies, computer
printouts, and simultaneous submissions if identified. SASE.
Responds in 2–6 weeks. Publication period varies. Payment
policy varies.

Editor's Comments
We look for quality nonfiction titles for students in elementary
grades through high school. We're particularly interested in the
topics of science, history, social studies, and culture studies.

Arthur A. Levine Books

Scholastic Press
557 Broadway
New York, NY 10012

Editorial Director: Arthur A. Levine

Publisher's Interests
An imprint of Scholastic Press, this publisher offers fiction and nonfiction, including picture books for early readers, middle-grade titles, and young adult books. It welcomes queries from all writers, especially first-time authors and members of the Society of Children's Book Writers and Illustrators (SCBWI).
Website: www.scholastic.com

Freelance Potential
Published 12 titles in 2002: 2 were developed from unsolicited submissions and most were by agented authors. Receives 350 queries yearly.
- **Fiction:** Publishes story picture books, 4–10 years; middle-grade novels, 8–12 years; and young adult novels, 12–18 years. Genres include fantasy and contemporary fiction. Also publishes multicultural stories and poetry.
- **Nonfiction:** Publishes picture books, 4–10 years; middle-grade books, 8–12 years; and young adult titles, 12–18 years. Topics include history, nature, the environment, and multicultural subjects. Also publishes biographies.
- **Representative Titles:** *Frida* by Jonah Winter (4–10 years) illuminates the painful but inspiring life of artist Frida Kahlo. *St. Michael's Scales* by Neil Connelly (YA) deals with the guilt a surviving twin faces over his brother's death.

Submissions and Payment
Guidelines available. Query. Accepts complete ms from agented and previously published authors only. Accepts photocopies. SASE. Responds to queries in 2–4 weeks, to mss in 6–8 months. Publication in 18–24 months. Payment policy varies.

Editor's Comments
We're still interested in seeing queries or submissions of picture books, either fiction or nonfiction. Literary fiction for middle-grade and young adult readers is also needed for the coming year.

Lightwave Publishing, Inc.

26275-98th Avenue
Maple Ridge, British Columbia V2W 1K3
Canada

Assistant Production Coordinator: Mikal Marrs

Publisher's Interests
Established in 1984, Lightwave Publishing is a Canadian
publisher specializing in children's Christian fiction and nonfiction. Its list includes books for readers from birth through
age twelve, as well as resources for parents.
Website: www.lightwavepublishing.com

Freelance Potential
Published 24 titles (20 juvenile) in 2002: all were assigned. Of
the 24 titles, 3 were by authors who were new to the publish-
ing house. Receives 96 queries yearly.
- **Fiction:** Published 3 toddler books, 0–4 years; and 2 story picture books, 4–10 years. Genres include inspirational fiction.
- **Nonfiction:** Published 6 story picture books, 4–10 years; 5
  middle-grade books, 8–12 years; and 4 young adult books,
  12–18 years. Topics include religion.
- **Representative Titles:** *Your Child and the Christian Life* by
  Rick Osborne is a family activity book; part of the Learning for
  Life series. *Money Matters for Kids* by Lauree Burkett (6–10
  years) uses a fun approach to teach kids the basics on issues
  like stewardship, trusting God, tithing and giving, and saving.

Submissions and Payment
Guidelines available. Query with clips. Accepts e-mail sub-
missions to mikal@lightwavepublishing.com. SAE/IRC.
Responds in 1–2 weeks. Publication in 8 months. Flat fee.

Editor's Comments
Our goal is to help children embrace their Christian faith and
to help parents pass their faith on to their children. We welcome both fiction and nonfiction submissions. While everyone
has the same opportunity for getting published here, we do
prefer writers with a biblical background. We only accept
queries and ask that you include a résumé and writing clips
with your query, as well as a brief description of your faith.
Our list is fairly small; we only publish about twenty-five titles
each year, so we ask that you give serious thought to your
query and only send us your very best work.

Lillenas Publishing Company

P.O. Box 419527
Kansas City, MO 64141

Drama Editor: Kimberly R. Messer

Publisher's Interests
This drama publisher provides contemporary, creative, and practical resources for church and school programs. Each "program builder" includes short scripts, program outlines, and verse and recitations.
Website: www.lillenas.com/drama

Freelance Potential
Published 12 titles (4 juvenile) in 2002: 3 were developed from unsolicited submissions. Receives 450 unsolicited mss each year.
- **Fiction:** Publishes full-length and one-act plays, monologues, sketches, skits, recitations, puppet plays, and dramatic exercises, 6–18 years. Also publishes dramatic material on Christmas, Easter, Thanksgiving, Mother's Day, Father's Day, and other holiday themes.
- **Nonfiction:** Publishes theater resource materials. Topics include stage design, scenery, production techniques, and drama ministry.
- **Representative Titles:** *Imagine That* by Jeff Smith features creative and interactive ideas for teaching children about the Bible. *All the Best Programs for Kids* by Debbie Salter Goodwin includes exercises and songs for a year's worth of seasonal programs.

Submissions and Payment
Guidelines available. Send complete ms with cast list, scene description, and prop list. Accepts computer printouts. SASE. Responds in 2–3 months. Publication period varies. Flat fee.

Editor's Comments
We invite you to look at our catalogue, where you will see that our purpose is to supply churches and Christian schools with dramatic resources for ministry—both toward the audience and among the cast and crew. Our publications must reflect a distinctly Christian point of view, but that does not mean sermonizing. Send us material that provides a strong message couched in an entertaining script.

Linnet Books

The Shoe String Press
P.O. Box 657
2 Linsley Street
North Haven, CT 06473

President: Diantha C. Thorpe

Publisher's Interests
Biographies and books about history and society make up the core of Linnet Books' publishing program. It also publishes folktales, storytelling titles, and books about arts education for teachers and librarians.
Website: www.shoestringpress.com

Freelance Potential
Published 12 titles (10 juvenile) in 2002: 6 were developed from unsolicited submissions and 1 was by an agented author. Receives 100 queries yearly.
- **Nonfiction:** Publishes interdisciplinary books, memoirs, biographies, reference books, literary companions, and multicultural children's programming materials. Topics include social studies, natural history, folktales, storytelling, art, archaeology, and anthropology.
- **Representative Titles:** *Four to the Pole! The American Women's Expedition to Antarctica, 1992–93* by Nancy Loewen & Ann Bancroft (grades 6 and up) is the story of the first female expedition to the South Pole. *Chaucer's England* by Diana Childress (grades 9 and up) describes the major events of the fourteenth century and links them to Chaucer's characters.

Submissions and Payment
Query with 2 sample chapters. Accepts photocopies, computer printouts, and simultaneous submissions if identified. SASE. Responds in 4 months. Publication in 1 year. Royalty; advance.

Editor's Comments
Note that we only publish nonfiction—please don't send us fiction submissions! We *are* interested in middle-grade and young adult books about Eastern Europe, Africa, and Asia. Books that focus on the social history of countries other than the United States are of special interest. We would also welcome titles dealing with women's and girls' issues. We're looking for writers who base their books on primary source research and who can come up with something out of the ordinary.

Linworth Publishing

Suite L
480 East Wilson Bridge Road
Worthington, OH 43085

Editorial Director: Carol Simpson

Publisher's Interests
In operation for more than 20 years, Linworth Publishing specializes in books about school libraries, literature, and technology. It also offers professional development titles for media specialists and educators working in kindergarten through high school.
Website: www.linworth.com

Freelance Potential
Published 65 titles in 2002: 5 were developed from unsolicited submissions. Receives 120 queries yearly.
- **Nonfiction:** Publishes books about school libraries, literature, and technology for media specialists and teachers, grades K–12. Also offers professional development books.
- **Representative Titles:** *Catalog It! A Guide to Cataloging School Library Materials* by Alison G. Kaplan & Ann Marlow Riedling is an easy-to-read reference guide that presents the theory and practice for cataloging and classification specific to the school environment. *Collaborating to Meet Standards: Teacher/Librarian Partnerships for K–6* by Toni Buzzeo presents a history and rationale for the delivery of information literacy and gives practical suggestions for implementing the collaborative process.

Submissions and Payment
Catalogue and guidelines available at website. Query or send complete ms with 2 hard copies and IBM disk. Accepts e-mail queries to linworth@linworthpublishing.com. SASE.
Responds in 1 week. Publication in 6 months. Royalty.

Editor's Comments
We're looking for titles that provide practical, professional resources for those who want to learn more about the field of school librarianship. We also want to review materials that will enhance the careers of those who are already practicing school library media specialists. With your proposal, include information about the book's target audience, competitive works, and your experience and background. All manuscripts are reviewed in-house and by experts in the field.

Little, Brown and Company

3 Center Plaza
Boston, MA 02108

Assistant, Children's Books: Leila Little

Publisher's Interests
This popular publisher's catalogue features picture books,
middle-grade titles, and young adult novels. It will consider
submissions from literary agents only.
Website: www.littlebrown.com

Freelance Potential
Published 109 titles in 2002: 28 were by agented authors
and 12 were reprint/licensed properties. Of the 109 titles, 1
was by an author who was new to the publishing house.
Receives 1,000 queries, 1,000 unsolicited mss yearly.
- **Fiction:** Published 6 concept books, 8 toddler books, and 3
  early picture books, 0–4 years; 25 easy-to-read books, 4–7
  years; 20 story picture books, 4–10 years; 10 chapter books,
  5–10 years; 15 middle-grade novels, 8–12 years; and 10 young
  adult novels, 12–18 years. Genres include adventure, humor,
  mystery, suspense, folktales, and multicultural fiction. Also
  publishes poetry.
- **Nonfiction:** Published 1 story picture book, 4–10 years; 5 middle-grade books, 8–12 years; and 1 young adult book, 12–18
  years. Topics include nature, the environment, crafts, and
  social and family issues.
- **Representative Titles:** *No Ordinary Olive* by Roberta Baker
  (4–8 years) introduces a busy little girl who finds it difficult to
  follow the rules. *Gossip Girl* by Cecily von Ziegesar (15+ years)
  is a provocative novel that offers an insider's scoop on some of
  New York's private school students.

Submissions and Payment
Accepts submissions from literary agents only. Send complete ms with author's qualifications and previous publications. Royalty, 5–10%; advance.

Editor's Comments
We continue to seek submissions for quality picture books
and middle-grade and young adult novels, but we will
consider only those manuscripts that have been submitted
through literary agents.

Little Simon

Simon & Schuster Children's Publishing Division
1230 Avenue of the Americas
New York, NY 10020

Editorial Department

Publisher's Interests

Little Simon specializes in novelty books for children from
birth to the age of eight. It publishes mainly fiction. The
books on its list include interactive books, pop-up books,
board books, lift-the-flap books, cloth books, and touch-
and-feel books.
Website: www.simonsayskids.com

Freelance Potential

Published 65 titles in 2002: 20 were by agented authors and
15 were reprint/licensed properties. Receives 200 queries
each year.
- **Fiction:** Publishes concept, toddler, holiday, and board books,
  0–4 years; and pull-tab, lift-the-flap, and pop-up books, 4–8
  years.
- **Representative Titles:** *Valentine's Day at the Zoo* by Nadine
  Bernard Westcott (3–6 years) is a pop-up book featuring
  animals who make a special valentine. *What I Like About
  Passover* by Varda Livney (3–6 years) is a board book that
  recounts each special feature of this holiday. *Bedtime for
  Bunny* by Jane Yolen (2–5 years) is a touch-and-feel book that
  follows a bunny family as they go through their evening ritual
  of getting ready for bed.

Submissions and Payment

Query only. No unsolicited mss. SASE. Responds in 6
months. Publication in 2 years. Royalty; advance. Flat fee.

Editor's Comments

We're interested in queries for books with innovative formats
that would appeal to very young children. Submissions of
standard picture books, chapter books, and middle-grade or
young adult novels are not appropriate for us. Please do not
send your complete project; it will be returned to you unread.
The volume of submissions we receive requires us to request
that you query only. Describe your background and your experience working on novelty projects in your query letter. We will
contact you if we feel your project is right for our list.

Lobster Press

Suites C & D
1620 Sherbrooke Street West
Montreal, Quebec H3H 1C9
Canada

Submissions Editor: Gabriella Mancini

Publisher's Interests
This Canadian publisher specializes in high-quality fiction, nonfiction, and poetry for children, teens, and families. It offers how-to titles and travel guides, and books on careers, health, sports, science, business, and finance.
Website: www.lobsterpress.com

Freelance Potential
Published 10 titles in 2002: all were developed from unsolicited submissions. Of the 10 titles, 9 were by unpublished writers. Receives 2,000 queries, 1,900 unsolicited mss yearly.
- **Fiction:** Published 2 early picture books, 0–4 years; 2 easy-to-read books, 4–7 years; 2 story picture books, 4–10 years; and 2 chapter books, 5–10 years. Also publishes middle-grade fiction, 8–12 years; and young adult books, 12–18 years. Genres include contemporary fiction, adventure, and fantasy. Also publishes humorous stories and poetry.
- **Nonfiction:** Published 2 middle-grade books, 8–12 years. Also publishes chapter books, 5–10 years; and young adult titles, 12–18 years. Topics include science, health, sports, careers, and business. Also publishes family travel guides.
- **Representative Titles:** *Going on a Journey to the Sea* by Jane Barclay (4–6 years) is the story of a brother and sister's journey by train, bus, and bicycle to reach the sea. *Animal Sneezes* by John Roy Bennett (1–5 years) takes a playful look at the sneezes of ten animals, including a porcupine and a bull.

Submissions and Payment
Guidelines available. Query with outline and first 3 chapters; or send complete ms. Accepts photocopies and simultaneous submissions if identified. SAE/IRC. Responds in 6–8 months if interested. Publication in 12–18 months. Royalty; advance.

Editor's Comments
We're particularly interested in publishing early chapter books that form a series and that feature a character children will want to follow. Stories must be well-written, well-paced, and feature a compelling plot line.

Lori Shein, Lucent Books/KidHaven
Experienced and New Science Writers

Lucent Books and its imprint, KidHaven Press, publish non-fiction library books for elementary and middle-grade readers.

"Lucent and KidHaven generate their own series and titles and maintain an ongoing list to be assigned to freelance writers," says Managing Editor Lori Shein. "We sometimes consider suggestions or proposals from authors. If a proposed title fits into an existing series, we might develop it. If a new series is suggested that meets our criteria, we might work with the author to produce that as well. The topics we choose are primarily based on school curriculum and market demands. Our books cover topics that students will be studying, writing about, and interested in."

Authors should note: "Because we are series publishers, we do not deal in unsolicited manuscripts. Book proposals are considered, but we prefer that an author be experienced with us prior to pitching them. When a first-time author approaches us, we look for a résumé, a list of publications, and a cover letter discussing the author's areas of interest or expertise. We look for writing that is clear, interesting, and well organized."

For assignments, "Once an author and our acquisitions editor decide on a title assignment, we ask the author to submit an outline for the book, including proposed chapter themes, and the first chapter of the book. This way we can evaluate the author's writing, organizational abilities, and grasp of the subject. This initial work is done on spec. We use the outline and chapter to decide whether to offer authors contracts."

All projects require "thorough research. Authors should use book, magazine, and newspaper articles, and Internet sources. Good writers who research their topics thoroughly may not use two-thirds of what they find, but they will have a deeper understanding of their topic—and that usually shows in the writing."

(Listing for Lucent Books on following page)

Lucent Books

10911 Technology Place
San Diego, CA 92127

Acquisitions Editor: Chandra Howard

Publisher's Interests

Lucent Books is an imprint of the Gale Group. Since 1988, it
has offered a list of nonfiction books produced in series for
middle and high school students. Biographies as well as
books on science, history, current events, and sports are
included in its catalogue.
Website: www.gale.com/lucent/

Freelance Potential

Published 170 titles in 2002: 5 were by agented authors. Of
the 170 titles, 30 were by unpublished writers and 50 were
by authors who were new to the publishing house. Receives
250 queries yearly.

- **Nonfiction:** Publishes middle-grade books, 8–12 years. Topics
  include political, cultural, and social history; science; current
  issues; and history. Also publishes biographies.
- **Representative Titles:** *Life in the Trenches* by Stephen Currie
  (grades 6–9) provides a gripping overview of trench warfare and
  soldiers' lives in battle during WW I; part of the American War
  Library series. *The Italian Americans* by Catherine M. Petrini
  (grades 6–9) looks at the twentieth-century influx of Italian
  immigrants to the United States; part of the Immigrants in
  America series.

Submissions and Payment

Guidelines and catalogue available. All books done on a
work-for-hire basis and by assignment only. Query with
résumé and writing samples. SASE. Response time varies.
Publication in 1 year. Flat fee, $2,500 for first book; $3,000
for subsequent books.

Editor's Comments

At this time we are particularly interested in seeing queries for
three of our series: the Overview series, the Great Medical Discoveries series, and the Way People Live series. Review some of
our titles before you consider sending a query; we have a very
specialized way of approaching subject matter. Please do not
query for single title books.

Magination Press

750 First Street NE
Washington, DC 20002

Project Editor: Cindy Gustafson

Publisher's Interests
Magination Press publishes illustrated storybooks that deal
with the psychological issues children face. While its focus is
on books that teach about feelings or emotions within a
story, its list also includes nonfiction titles for older children.
Website: www.maginationpress.com

Freelance Potential
Published 10 titles in 2002: all were developed from unsolicited
submissions. Of the 10 titles, 2 were by unpublished writers
and 3 were by authors who were new to the publishing house.
Receives 600 unsolicited mss yearly.
- **Fiction:** Published 10 story picture books, 4–10 years. Also
  publishes easy-to-read books, 4–7 years; and middle-grade
  novels, 8–12 years. Stories address family relationships, fears,
  learning, and psychological illness.
- **Nonfiction:** Publishes middle-grade books, 8–12 years; and
  young adult books, 12–18 years. Topics include grief, divorce,
  learning disabilities, and family issues. Also publishes parenting titles for adults.
- **Representative Titles:** *Mom, Dad, Come Back Soon* by Debra
  L. Pappas (3–7 years) looks at a child's feelings about being
  away from his parents for the first time. *Maybe Days* by Jennifer Wilgocki (4–8 years) looks at the issues involved with
  foster care and discusses the questions and feelings many
  foster children have.

Submissions and Payment
Guidelines and catalogue available with 10x13 SASE (2 first-
class stamps). Send complete ms. Accepts photocopies and
computer printouts. SASE. Responds in 3 months. Publication in 1 year. Royalty.

Editor's Comments
We look for books that describe an internal, psychological
process taking place in a character. Our current needs include
submissions that deal with conflict and anger management,
and books that explore issues of self-esteem in boys and girls.

Marlor Press

4304 Brigadoon Drive
St. Paul, MN 55126

Editorial Director: Marlin Bree

Publisher's Interests

Marlor Press fills its catalogue with books about boating and travel. It has a juvenile list that includes travel diaries and activity books for readers between the ages of four and twelve. It also features family travel guides focusing on the US and Europe.

Freelance Potential

Published 2 titles (1 juvenile) in 2002: both were developed from unsolicited submissions. Receives 100+ queries yearly.

- **Nonfiction:** Published 1 chapter book, 5–10 years. Also publishes activity books, 4–12 years. Topics include travel, cooking, and crafts. Also features travel diaries and journals for children, as well as boating, travel, and gardening books for adults.
- **Representative Titles:** *Grandma and Grampa's Big Book of Fun* by Jean Luttrell features 200 ideas and activities to share with grandchildren, and includes lists of materials, step-by-step illustrations, and instructions. *Kid's Squish Book* by Loris Theovin Bree & Marlin Bree (4–12 years) offers ideas for slimy, squishy, sticky things to do, from T-shirt decorating to tasty fingerpainting.

Submissions and Payment

Query with market analysis. No unsolicited mss. Accepts photocopies and computer printouts. SASE. Response time varies. Publication in 1 year. Royalty, 8–10% of net sales.

Editor's Comments

At this time, our primary need is for activity books that target children between the ages of six and twelve. Unique titles about boating and family travel are always needed as well. Queries should include a thumbnail sketch explaining what the book is about, as well as a description of some of the key selling and marketing points; tell us how your book differs from books already out there. We are willing to accept queries from both agented and unagented authors, but be sure to include some information about your credentials.

Master Books

P.O. Box 727
Green Forest, AR 72638

Acquisitions Editor: Roger Howerton

Publisher's Interests
This Christian publisher exclusively publishes biblically correct, creation-based materials that are free of references to evolution. Its juvenile list features nonfiction for toddlers through teens and includes educational, activity, novelty, and board books.
Website: www.masterbooks.net

Freelance Potential
Published 35 titles (16 juvenile) in 2002: 4 were developed from unsolicited submissions. Of the 35 titles, 1 was by an author who was new to the publishing house. Receives 600 queries, 500+ unsolicited mss yearly.
- **Nonfiction:** Published 4 concept books and 4 early picture books, 0–4 years; 4 easy-to-read books, 4–7 years; and 4 young adult books, 12–18 years. Also publishes novelty and board books, 0–4 years; activity books, 4–7 years; and educational titles, 4–18 years. Topics include religion, science, technology, and animals. Also publishes biographies.
- **Representative Titles:** *What's So Striking About Lightning?* by Roger Howerton (8–12 years) features interesting information about lightning and other weather phenomena; part of the Ask Max series. *The Big Book* by Kathleen Ruckman (pre-K–grade 2) is a picture book that emphasizes the big things in life, such as mountains, redwood trees, deserts, and oceans.

Submissions and Payment
Guidelines and catalogue available with 9x12 SASE (5 first-class stamps). Query with clips. SASE. Responds in 3 months. Publication in 1 year. Royalty.

Editor's Comments
We're interested in creation-based books; send us anything that emphasizes the power and majesty of God as Creator. We're also interested in educational books about science that emphasize and acknowledge the Bible. Books about animals are especially welcome. Don't submit fiction unless it can illustrate biblical stories allegorically.

Maval Publishing

567 Harrison Street
Denver, CO 80206

Editor: Mary Hernandez

Publisher's Interests

Founded in 1994, Maval Publishing recently launched a line of children's titles. It specializes in story picture books written for children between the ages of two and ten. All of its titles are published in both Spanish and English.
Website: www.maval.com

Freelance Potential

Published 10 titles in 2002: all were developed from unsolicited submissions. Of the 10 titles, 5 were by authors who were new to the publishing house. Receives 2,000 unsolicited mss each year.

- **Fiction:** Publishes story picture books, 2–10 years. Genres include adventure stories, fairy tales, fantasy, folklore, folktales, humor, and mystery. Also offers historical, religious, and Western fiction, multicultural and ethnic fiction, and stories about sports, nature, and the environment.
- **Nonfiction:** Publishes story picture books, 2–10 years. Topics include animals, pets, and multicultural and ethnic issues. Also features humor and biographies.
- **Representative Titles:** *Everything Is All Right Now* by Mary Hernandez (2–10 years) describes scenes of a little girl in a park who feels safe with her father. *A Nest of Birdlets* by Manny Hillman (2–10 years) is an illustrated book about how children grow and become independent.

Submissions and Payment

Guidelines available with 9x5 SASE (2 first-class stamps). Send complete ms with artwork (color prints or transparencies). Accepts simultaneous submissions if identified. SASE. Responds in 4–6 months. Publication in 18 months. Royalty.

Editor's Comments

Send us imaginative, creative, or humorous books that make a child or adult want to turn the page. Please remember that we are only interested in reviewing illustrated books for children under the age of 10. All of our titles are published in 16- to 32-page formats. Don't submit poetry books.

Mayhaven Publishing

P.O. Box 557
803 Blackburn Circle
Mahomet, IL 61853

Publisher: Doris Wenzel

Publisher's Interests
In business for more than 20 years, Mayhaven Publishing offers a range of material for children between the ages of four and twelve, as well as for adults. Its list includes nonfiction and fiction in such genres as adventure, humor, and science fiction. 30% co-op published material.
Website: www.mayhavenpublishing.com

Freelance Potential
Published 10 titles (4 juvenile) in 2002: all were developed from unsolicited submissions. Of the 10 titles, 4 were by unpublished writers and 6 were by authors who were new to the publishing house. Receives 2,000+ queries yearly.

- **Fiction:** Published 1 story picture book, 4–10 years; 2 chapter books, 5–10 years; and 2 middle-grade titles, 8–12 years. Genres include adventure, humor, and science fiction. Also publishes poetry.
- **Nonfiction:** Publishes easy-to-read titles, 4–10 years; chapter books, 5–10 years; middle-grade titles, 8–12 years; and young adult books, 12–18 years. Topics include travel, nature, cooking, history, and the West.
- **Representative Titles:** *The Monarch, The Snow Goose and The Butterfly Tree* by Gertrude Stonesifer (7–9 years) is the story of a monarch butterfly who cannot keep up with the rest of his group as they fly south, and hitches a ride on a goose. *It Happened on Alphabet Street* by Evelyn Lund (5–9 years) is a story of life in a small coastal town.

Submissions and Payment
Guidelines available. Query with 3 sample chapters. Accepts photocopies and computer printouts. SASE. Responds in 3–9 months. Publication in 12–18 months. Royalty; advance, varies.

Editor's Comments
We feature fiction and nonfiction from new and established writers and are always excited to publish new talent. Interested writers should consider entering our fiction contest.

Margaret K. McElderry Books

Simon & Schuster Children's Publishing Division
1230 Avenue of the Americas
New York, NY 10020

Vice President/Editorial Director: Emma D. Dryden

Publisher's Interests

This imprint of Simon & Schuster Children's Publishing offers a fiction list that includes early picture books through young adult novels. At this time, it is not publishing nonfiction titles.

Website: www.simonsayskids.com

Freelance Potential

Published 29 titles in 2002: 1 was developed from an unsolicited submission, 17 were by agented authors, and 10 were reprint/licensed properties. Of the 29 titles, 1 was by an unpublished writer and 8 were by authors who were new to the publishing house. Receives 4,000 queries yearly.

- **Fiction:** Published 20 early picture books, 0–4 years; 3 easy-to-read books, 4–7 years; 2 story picture books, 4–10 years; and 3 middle-grade novels, 8–12 years. Genres include adventure, fantasy, folktales, historical fiction, and humor. Also publishes poetry.
- **Representative Titles:** *Firefighters A to Z* by Chris L. Demarest is a picture book that recounts one typical day in the life of a firefighter. *Bad Dog, Dodger!* by Barbara Abercrombie (6–10 years) is the story of a boy and his mischievous dog. *You Have to Write* by Janet S. Wong (8+ years) offers tips and encouragement to students who find it difficult to attempt classroom assignments that involve writing.

Submissions and Payment

Guidelines available. Query with résumé, outline/synopsis, and first three chapters. Accepts queries by e-mail only to childrens.submissions@simonandschuster.com, with imprint clearly indicated. No unsolicited mss. Responds in 2–3 months. Publication in 2–4 years. Royalty; advance.

Editor's Comments

We're still seeking early picture books, humorous middle-grade fiction, and young adult fiction to fill our 2004–2005 lists. We're not publishing nonfiction at this time, nor will we consider science fiction.

McGraw-Hill Children's Publishing

8787 Orion Place
Columbus, OH 43240

Publisher: Tracey Dils

Publisher's Interests
This publisher is a division of McGraw-Hill Education, a leading provider of educational materials for preschools through high schools. Its catalogue is filled with reference books, picture books, and workbooks, as well as fiction and nonfiction literature for children. It also offers licensed and non-licensed coloring and activity books.
Website: www.MHKids.com

Freelance Potential
Published 500 titles in 2002. Of the 500 titles, 10 were by unpublished writers and 5 were by authors who were new to the publishing house. Receives 144 queries yearly.
- **Fiction:** Publishes toddler books, 0–4 years; easy-to-read books, 4–7 years; and story picture books, 4–10 years. Genres include fairy tales, folklore, folktales, and contemporary fiction. Also offers board books, novelty books, activity books, and books in series.
- **Nonfiction:** Publishes concept books and toddler books, 0–4 years; middle-grade books, 8–12 years; and young adult books, 12–18 years. Features reference and education titles, as well as resource materials for teachers and homeschooling materials for parents.
- **Representative Titles:** *Summer Skills for the First Grade Reader* (parents and teachers) emphasizes math and language arts skills and includes pre- and post-summer tests and guidelines for assessing a child's progress. *Bit of Everything French (Un Peu De Tout)* (teachers) teaches students French through games, activities, and cue cards.

Submissions and Payment
Query only. No unsolicited mss. SASE. Response time, publication period, and payment policy vary.

Editor's Comments
We are still interested in materials that target parents who homeschool their children. If you are qualified to write for the educational market, send us a query.

Meadowbrook Press

5451 Smetana Drive
Minnetonka, MN 55343

Submissions Editor

Publisher's Interests
Meadowbrook Press specializes in books on pregnancy, baby care, childcare, party planning, and children's activities. Humorous poetry for children also appears on its list, but it no longer considers children's fiction.
Website: www.meadowbrookpress.com

Freelance Potential
Published 16 titles (8 juvenile) in 2002: 3 were developed from unsolicited submissions and 3 were reprint/licensed properties. Receives 500 queries yearly.
- **Fiction:** Published 2 middle-grade titles, 8–12 years.
- **Nonfiction:** Published 3 easy-to-read books, 4–7 years; 1 chapter book, 5–10 years; and 2 middle-grade books, 8–12 years. Also publishes adult titles on family activities, parenting, childcare, and party planning.
- **Representative Titles:** *Discipline without Shouting or Spanking* by Jerry Wyckoff & Barbara C. Unell (parents) provides proven methods for handling common forms of childhood misbehavior, such as temper tantrums and sibling rivalry. *The Children's Busy Book* by Trish Kuffner (parents) contains 365 activities children can do to beat boredom by using things found around the house.

Submissions and Payment
Guidelines available. Query. No unsolicited mss. Accepts photocopies, computer printouts, and simultaneous submissions if identified. SASE. Responds in 4 months. Publication in 2 years. Royalty; advance.

Editor's Comments
We are no longer accepting queries or unsolicited manuscripts for children's fiction, adult fiction, or adult poetry. We will, however, consider humorous children's poetry for the Giggle Poetry section of our website. Visit our website for specific guidelines. Our needs for the coming year include parenting titles and books on child care for parents of infants through pre-teens. We do not publish picture books.

Meriwether Publishing Ltd.

885 Elkton Drive
Colorado Springs, CO 80907

Submissions Editor

Publisher's Interests

Drama students and teachers use the materials offered by
Meriwether Publishing. It publishes plays and theater-related
books and videotapes for middle school, junior high, and
high school drama classes. Church and community theater
groups also purchase its publications.
Website: www.meriwetherpublishing.com

Freelance Potential

Published 70 titles in 2002: 60 were developed from unsolicited submissions and 5 were by agented authors. Of the 70
titles, 35 were by unpublished writers and 35 were by
authors who were new to the publishing house. Receives
1,600 queries, 1,500 unsolicited mss yearly.

- **Fiction:** Publishes middle-grade titles, 8–12 years; and young
  adult books, 12–18 years. Offers one-act and full-length
  dramas, musicals, comedies, folktales, and social commen-
  taries, as well as dialogues and monologues.
- **Nonfiction:** Publishes theater reference books and how-to
  titles, 12–25 years. Topics include stage design, lighting techniques, theatrical makeup, theater games, and improvisation.
- **Representative Titles:** *Collage* by Forrest Mussleman (YA) is a
  35-minute show that includes sequences of poetry, skits, and
  comments about the joy and pain of being a teen. *Spotlight* by
  Stephanie S. Fairbanks includes short monologues that can be
  used for speech contests, acting exercises, and auditions.

Submissions and Payment

Guidelines available. Prefers query with outline, synopsis,
and sample chapter. Will accept complete ms. Accepts photocopies and simultaneous submissions if identified. SASE.
Responds in 4–6 weeks. Publication in 6 months. Royalty.
Flat fee.

Editor's Comments

Please note that we are only interested in drama materials that
are appropriate for the middle grades and up. Theater resource
materials are always welcome, as well as plays.

Milkweed Editions

Suite 300
1011 Washington Avenue South
Minneapolis, MN 55415

First Reader: Elisabeth Fitz

Publisher's Interests

This nonprofit publisher offers books that have a "humane impact on society." Under its Milkweeds for Young Readers imprint, it offers novels for readers between the ages of eight and thirteen. The novels range from fantasy, to historical fiction, to books about everyday life.
Website: www.milkweed.org

Freelance Potential

Published 15 titles (3 juvenile) in 2002: 3 were by agented authors and 2 were reprint/licensed properties. Of the 15 titles, 2 were by unpublished writers and 4 were by authors who were new to the publishing house. Receives 3,000 queries, 2,000 unsolicited mss yearly.
- **Fiction:** Publishes middle-grade novels, 8–13 years. Genres include multicultural and ethnic fiction, historical fiction, and nature stories.
- **Nonfiction:** Publishes middle-grade books, 8–13 years.
- **Representative Titles:** *The Boy with Paper Wings* by Susan Lowell (8–13 years) is the story of an 11-year-old boy, confined to bed with a viral fever, who propels himself into an exciting and fantastical adventure on a paper airplane. *The Dog with Golden Eyes* by Frances Wilbur (8–13 years) is a novel about a bored and friendless girl who adopts a full-grown arctic wolf as a pet.

Submissions and Payment

Guidelines available. Query or send complete ms. Accepts photocopies and simultaneous submissions if identified. SASE. Responds to queries in 1 month, to mss in 1–6 months. Publication in 1 year. Royalty, 7.5% of list price; advance; varies.

Editor's Comments

We are especially interested in stories with contemporary settings and fiction that explores our relationship to the natural world. Manuscripts should be of high literary quality, embody human values, and contribute to cultural understanding.

The Millbrook Press

2 Old New Milford Road
Brookfield, CT 06840

Editorial Assistant: Kristen Vibbert

Publisher's Interests

Curriculum-oriented nonfiction books appropriate for schools
and public libraries are the specialty of this publisher. Its
imprints include Millbrook Press, Twenty-First Century
Books, Roaring Book Press, and Copper Beach Books.
Website: www.millbrookpress.com

Freelance Potential

Published 160 titles in 2002: 2 were developed from unsolicited submissions, 25 were by agented authors, and 60
were reprint/licensed properties. Of the 160 titles, 1 was by
an unpublished writer and 2 were by authors who were new
to the publishing house. Receives 520 queries yearly.

- **Nonfiction:** Publishes concept books and toddler books, 0–4
  years; middle-grade books, 8–12 years; and young adult books,
  12–18 years. Topics include the arts, sports, social studies,
  math, science, and crafts. Also publishes biographies.
- **Representative Titles:** *The Hungry Hummingbird* by April Pul-
  ley Sayre (pre-K–grade 2) combines nature facts with a charm-
  ing story about a hummingbird who wants to nibble on everything red. *Insect Facts and Folklore* by L. Patricia Kite (grades
  3–6) examines the life cycles, habits, and characteristics of
  eight insects.

Submissions and Payment

Guidelines available at website. Accepts agented queries only.
No unsolicited mss. Query with résumé, outline, and sample
chapter. SASE. Responds 6–8 weeks. Publication in 12–18
months. Royalty; advance. Flat fee.

Editor's Comments

We are interested in works that have a strong, relevant tie to
the middle school curriculum, such as math, science, American history, and social studies, as well as historical and
sports biographies for grades two through eight. Material that
covers contemporary issues and multicultural topics are
especially welcome. New writers are encouraged to submit
their work through their agents.

Mitchell Lane Publishers

34 Decidedly Lane
Bear, DE 19701

President: Barbara Mitchell

Publisher's Interests
Mitchell Lane Publishers specializes in authorized biographies for children between the ages of five and eighteen. Its titles chronicle the lives of business people, politicians, actors, media personalities, musicians, and sports figures. Most of its books are published in series, and many are available in Spanish.
Website: www.angelfire.com/biz/mitchelllane/index.html

Freelance Potential
Published 43 titles in 2002: 1 was by an agented author. Of the 43 titles, 1 was by an unpublished writer and 10 were by authors who were new to the publishing house. Receives 20 queries yearly.
- **Nonfiction:** Published 15 middle-grade books, 8–12 years; and 18 young adult books, 12–18 years. Also publishes chapter books, 5–10 years. Publishes biographies written in Spanish and English about contemporary multicultural role models.
- **Representative Titles:** *Alexander Fleming and the Story of Penicillin* (grades 4–10) profiles a Scottish bacteriologist best known for his discovery of penicillin; part of the Unlocking the Secrets of Science series. *Christopher Paul Curtis* (grades 3–8) tells the story of a former factory worker who became the author of *The Watsons Go to Birmingham–1963*; part of the Real-Life Reader Biographies series.

Submissions and Payment
Work-for-hire only. Query with writing samples and résumé. Flat fee per assignment.

Editor's Comments
This year, we are looking for ideas for books about important people in science, biographies of Spanish explorers, and biographies of prominent Latinos. Peruse our catalogue and you'll see that most of the books we publish target middle-schoolers and young adults. We encourage the role models who are interviewed in our biographies to talk about social, community, and family issues.

Modern Learning Press

P.O. Box 167
Rosemont, NJ 08556

Editor: Robert Low

Publisher's Interests

Modern Learning Press is a leading educational publisher that specializes in elementary education. It features a range of material to help students, teachers, and parents with the important aspects of education and childhood.
Website: www.modlearn.com

Freelance Potential

Published 10 titles in 2002: 1 was developed from an unsolicited submission. Receives 20 queries yearly.

- **Nonfiction:** Publishes classroom materials, grades K–8. Topics include reading, language arts, spelling, literacy skills, writing, phonics, handwriting, natural science, and social studies. Also publishes parenting and professional titles about child development, school readiness, literacy, and ESL.
- **Representative Titles:** *Eagles* (grades 5–6) explains how and where this bird lives, what it eats, and how it raises its young; part of the Endangered Animals' Lives series. *Every Parent's Owner's Manual for a 5-Year-Old* by Jim Grant (parents) provides parenting information about the development and behavior of five-year-old children.

Submissions and Payment

Query with overview and short sample. Accepts photocopies and computer printouts. SASE. Response time, publication period, and payment policy vary.

Editor's Comments

Our most well-known resource is the Words I Use When I Write series, which helps students with spelling, vocabulary development, and other literacy skills. The series has grown to include a variety of classroom materials. We continue to seek submissions that help educators and parents balance children's developmental needs with the need to meet high educational standards. Send us ideas for resources that will assist students, teachers, and parents with natural science and social studies, as well as school readiness. Most of our new titles are for students in kindergarten through grade eight.

Modern Publishing

155 East 55th Street
New York, NY 10022

Editorial Director: Kathy O'Hehir

Publisher's Interests
Modern Publishing's books are marketed through chain stores,
toy stores, and bookstores. Its catalogue features licensed and
non-licensed titles for two- to ten-year-old readers, including
hardcover and paperback illustrated storybooks, coloring and
activity books, board books, educational workbooks, learning
pads, and novelty books.
Website: www.modernpublishing.com

Freelance Potential
Published 200 titles in 2002. Of the 200 titles, 4 were by
unpublished writers and 10 were by authors who were new
to the publishing house. Receives 75 queries and unsolicited
mss yearly.
- **Fiction:** Publishes activity books, workbooks, and coloring
  books, 2–10 years; licensed character books, 4–8 years; beginner novels, 6–8 years; and novelty books. Genres include fairy
  tales, nursery rhymes, adventures, and books about holidays.
- **Nonfiction:** Publishes picture books, easy-to-read books, and
  workbooks, 2–10 years. Features books based on licensed
  characters that are written to develop reading, language, and
  math skills.
- **Representative Titles:** *Lazy Lizard* is a plush, beanbag
  animal that has a fun, 14-page board book hidden inside.
  'NSYNC Sticker Book features full-color photographic stickers
  and need-to-know facts about these superstars.

Submissions and Payment
Guidelines available. Query with outline/synopsis; or send
complete ms. Accepts photocopies and simultaneous submissions if identified. Availability of artwork improves chance of
acceptance. SASE. Responds in 2 months. Publication period
varies. Royalty, by arrangement. Flat fee. Work-for-hire.

Editor's Comments
We would like to hear from writers who are familiar with our
licensed character work. At the current time, we are only
accepting projects that can be developed into series.

Mondo Publishing

980 Avenue of the Americas
New York, NY 10018

Executive Editor: Don Curry

Publisher's Interests
Mondo Publishing offers a wide variety of fiction and nonfiction for children under the age of 10. Its catalogue is filled with easy-to-read books, picture books, and chapter books, as well as biographies and sing-along audiotapes.
Website: www.mondopub.com

Freelance Potential
Published 20 titles in 2002: 4 were by agented authors and 8 were reprint/licensed properties. Of the 20 titles, 10 were by authors who were new to the publishing house. Receives 500+ queries yearly.

- **Fiction:** Published 1 early picture book, 0–4 years; 3 easy-to-read books, 4–7 years; 3 story picture books, 4–10 years; and 6 chapter books, 5–10 years. Also publishes novelty books. Genres include fantasy, mystery, folktales, adventure, humor, stories about sports and science, and contemporary and historical fiction.
- **Nonfiction:** Published 3 easy-to-read books, 4–7 years; and 4 chapter books, 5–10 years. Also publishes biographies. Topics include science, nature, animals, the environment, language arts, history, music, crafts, and hobbies.
- **Representative Titles:** *Signs of Spring* by Justine Korman Fontes (3–7 years) follows three creatures as they discover a twig with buds, a robin's feather, and bright green grass. *Where Does the Butterfly Go When It Rains?* by May Garelick (6–11 years) explores how several different animals react when it rains.

Submissions and Payment
Query. No unsolicited mss. SASE. Responds in 4–6 weeks. Publication in 1–3 years. Royalty, varies.

Editor's Comments
We continue to look for books that will appeal to children under the age of four, including toddler books, concept books, and early picture books. We need authors who can find creative ways to encourage lifelong reading.

Moody Press

Moody Bible Institute
820 North LaSalle Boulevard
Chicago, IL 60610-3284

Acquisitions Coordinator

Publisher's Interests
Moody Press seeks to edify, evangelize, and educate readers
through well-crafted works of fiction and through its nonfiction titles.
Website: www.moodypress.org

Freelance Potential
Published 100 titles (14 juvenile) in 2002: 1 was developed
from an unsolicited submission and 5 were by agented
authors. Of the 100 titles, 1 was by an unpublished writer
and 10 were by authors who were new to the publishing
house. Receives 1,000+ queries and unsolicited mss yearly.
- **Fiction:** Published 5 middle-grade books, 8–12 years; and 5
  young adult books, 12–18 years. Genres include adventure,
  Western, fantasy, mystery, suspense, and contemporary and
  historical fiction. Also publishes biblical fiction.
- **Nonfiction:** Published 2 young adult books, 12–18 years. Also
  publishes middle-grade titles, 7–12 years. Topics include religion, social issues, and sports.
- **Representative Titles:** *Treasures of the Snow* by Patricia St.
  John (YA) is a story of tragedy, anger, and repentance. *The
  Sweetest Story Ever Told* by Lysa TerKeurst (all ages) presents
  a new Christmas tradition for families.

Submissions and Payment
Guidelines available. Query with résumé, outline/synopsis
and 3 sample chapters for fiction. Accepts nonfiction proposals through agents or manuscript services. Accepts computer
printouts. SASE. Responds in 2–3 months. Publication in
12–18 months. Payment policy varies.

Editor's Comments
Send for our guidelines before submitting your work, particularly if your submission is nonfiction. We consider fiction proposals sent directly from authors, but will only consider nonfiction proposals sent through Christian manuscript services
(listed in our guidelines), literary agents, or on the recom-
mendation of a current Moody Press author.

Morehouse Publishing

4775 Linglestown Road
Harrisburg, PA 17112

Editorial Director: Debra Farrington

Publisher's Interests
Books written from a Christian point of view are the focus of
this religious publisher. Its list includes books for adults as
well as for children up to the age of eleven. Morehouse Publishing was founded in 1884.
Website: www.morehousegroup.com

Freelance Potential
Published 25 titles (4 juvenile) in 2002: 1 was developed from
an unsolicited submission. Receives 600 queries, 550 unsolicited mss yearly.
- **Fiction:** Publishes early picture books, 0–4 years; and easy-to-
  read books, 4–7 years. Genres include inspirational and religious fiction. Also publishes Bible stories.
- **Nonfiction:** Published 2 toddler books, 0–4 years; and 2 easy-
  to-read books, 4–7 years. Topics include the sacraments, religion, and Christian concepts.
- **Representative Titles:** *One Little Church Mouse* by Anne E.
  Kitch (1–3 years) is a rhyming poem about worshipping God
  together. *Stories That Jesus Told* by Patricia St. John (8–11
  years) offers a retelling of 18 parables of Jesus.

Submissions and Payment
Guidelines available. Send complete ms with résumé. Accepts
photocopies and simultaneous submissions if identified.
SASE for US returns only. Responds in 3 months. Publication in 2 years. Royalty; advance.

Editor's Comments
Our focus is on books for the mainline Christian market, and
we offer Episcopal and ecumenical titles. Each year we publish
approximately four or five picture books for children. Most of
what we produce is aimed at children up to the age of eight,
though some of our books may be appropriate for children up
to age eleven. All of our books are picture books written from a
Christian perspective. Themes of interest to us include the
Christian concepts of grace, forgiveness, and healing, and we
welcome Bible stories, illustrated prayers, and hymns.

Thomas More Publishing

200 East Bethany Drive
Allen, TX 75002

Acquisitions Director: Debra Hampton

Publisher's Interests
Thomas More publishes mostly adult-level nonfiction titles
that focus on Catholic areas of interest, Scripture, meditation, personal growth, inspiration, and prayer. Its list offers
some titles that appeal to young adults, as well as a few
books for middle-grade students.
Website: www.thomasmore.com

Freelance Potential
Published 20 titles in 2002: 2 were developed from unsolicited
submissions and 8 were by agented authors. Receives 240
queries yearly.
- **Nonfiction:** Publishes middle-grade books, 8–12 years. Also
  offers teacher guides, educational programs, and catechism
  materials, pre-K–grade 12. Topics include the sacraments,
  Christian living, family life, leadership, and lives of the saints.
- **Representative Titles:** *(My Wife Told Me) Make This World a
  Better Place for Our Grandchildren* by Tobias Jungreis (adults)
  offers suggestions for fostering understanding and patience.
  Garden of Virtues by Christina Keffler and Rebecca Donnelli
  (parents) presents a variety of ways to teach values such as
  honesty, cooperation, and respect to children.

Submissions and Payment
Query. Accepts photocopies and computer printouts. No
simultaneous submissions. SASE. Responds in 2 months.
Publication in 6 months. Payment rate varies.

Editor's Comments
Most of our titles are geared toward adults, but we also publish books that will appeal to parents and teachers working
with children. All of our books are grounded in the Catholic
faith and are based on Vatican II and the *Catechism of the
Catholic Church.* If you think you have an idea that is right for
us, send us a description of your book along with an outline
and the first chapter, if available. Include a statement of purpose and a biography that explains why you are the person to
write this particular book.

Morgan Reynolds

Suite 223
620 South Elm Street
Greensboro, NC 27406

Managing Editor: Laura Shoemaker

Publisher's Interests
This educational publisher is committed to producing nonfiction for young readers. Its titles target elementary and secondary school curricula and focus on serious history subjects. It also offers biographies of key historical figures.
Website: www.morganreynolds.com

Freelance Potential
Published 24 titles in 2002: 12 were developed from unsolicited submissions. Of the 24 titles, 2 were by unpublished writers and 10 were by authors who were new to the publishing house. Receives 400 queries, 300 unsolicited mss yearly.
- **Nonfiction:** Published 24 young adult books, 12–18 years. Topics include biography, history, music, and science.
- **Representative Titles:** *John Coltrane* by Rachel Stiffler Barron (10+ years) is a biography of one of the most influential jazz musicians of the twentieth century; part of the Masters of Music series. *Petticoat Spies* by Peggy Caravantes (10+ years) follows the lives of six women spies during the Civil War.

Submissions and Payment
Guidelines available. Query with outline and sample chapter; or send complete ms. Accepts photocopies, computer printouts, and simultaneous submissions if identified. SASE. Responds to queries in 1 month; to unsolicited mss in 1–2 months. Publication in 6–12 months. Royalty; advance.

Editor's Comments
Most of our books are published as part of a series. We prefer lively, well-written biographies of interesting figures for our biography series as well as insightful looks at key periods in history. Thorough research of your subject is a prerequisite for any submission. Your first chapter should provide the reader with the "hook" and conclude with the subject's reaching maturity. All books are 25,000 words in length, with eight to ten chapters of 2,500 to 3,000 words each. For the coming year, we would like to see queries for books on world leaders, African Americans, inventors, scientists, and writers.

National Association for the Education of Young Children

1509 16th Street NW
Washington, DC 20036-1426

Publications Editor: Carol Copple

Publisher's Interests
This non-profit publisher specializes in books for child-care professionals, parents, and teachers of children up to age eight. It features nonfiction titles and resource materials on the education of children.
Website: www.naeyc.org

Freelance Potential
Published 6 titles in 2002: 3 were developed from unsolicited submissions and 1 was a reprint/licensed property. Of the 6 titles, 3 were by authors who were new to the publishing house. Receives 50 queries yearly.
- **Nonfiction:** Publishes educational materials for adults and parents. Topics include professional development, family relationships, health, nutrition, assessment, language and literacy, social and emotional development, and violence.
- **Representative Titles:** *Advocates in Action: Making a Difference for Young Children* by A. Robinson & D. R. Stark (teachers) offers guidance on influencing policy and practice on behalf of children. *Tips and Tidbits: A Book for Family Child-Care Providers* by J. Gonzalez-Mena (parents, care givers) suggests ways to handle the important matters that arise in daily family life.

Submissions and Payment
Guidelines available. Query with outline and 3 sample chapters. Accepts photocopies and computer printouts. No simultaneous submissions. SASE. Responds in 1 month. Publication period varies. No payment.

Editor's Comments
Submissions should reflect current knowledge in the field, and should not duplicate materials already published. We look for manuscripts that establish a substantial research and theoretical base to make creative and insightful recommendations for teachers of children and adults. Manuscripts may also be directed at care givers who want basic principles that come from expert practice. We are not interested in theses, research projects, or curriculum or activity guides.

National Council of Teachers of English

1111 West Kenyon Road
Urbana, IL 61801-1096

Director of Book Publications: Zarina Hock

Publisher's Interests
Established in 1911, the National Council of Teachers of English (NCTE) publishes books of interest to English and language arts teachers working at the elementary, middle, secondary, and college levels.
Website: www.ncte.org

Freelance Potential
Published 21 titles in 2002. Receives 180 queries yearly.
- **Nonfiction:** Publishes books for English and language arts educators working with students in grades K–12 and up. Topics include teaching theory and practice; current issues in language arts education; research findings and their application in the classroom; and strategies and ideas for teaching all aspects of English.
- **Representative Titles:** *Teaching Reading in Middle School* by Laura Robb (educators, grades 6–8) offers a strategic approach to teaching reading that improves comprehension and thinking. *Math Is Language Too* by Phyllis & David Whitin (educators, grades 3–6) explores ways fourth-grade students use story, metaphor, and language to develop mathematical thinking skills and strategies.

Submissions and Payment
Guidelines available. Query with cover letter, formal proposal, chapter summaries, and table of contents. SASE. Responds in 1–2 weeks. Publication in 18 months. Royalty, varies.

Editor's Comments
While you are welcome to submit your résumé or vita with your proposal, our decision to publish depends heavily on staff assessment, recommendations from the field, and the Editorial Board's vote. We will consider your work on its merit, not on your prior publishing record, so please don't hesitate to submit a proposal or to discuss a book idea with us even if you have never published before. Don't send a complete manuscript; submit a query that includes the information we outline in our guidelines.

National Geographic Society

1145 17th Street NW
Washington, DC 20036-4688

Submissions Editor: Jo Tunstall

Publisher's Interests
The goal of the National Geographic Society is to publish books that give young readers a fresh look at the world and an appreciation for its diverse population. Its children's list offers titles on history, wildlife, and natural wonders, as well as mystery and adventure stories.
Website: www.nationalgeographic.com

Freelance Potential
Published 40 titles in 2002: 6 were by agented authors. Of the 40 titles, 1 was by an unpublished writer and 9 were by authors who were new to the publishing house. Receives 120–240 queries, 150 unsolicited mss yearly.

- **Fiction:** Published 4 story picture books, 4–10 years; and 5 middle-grade novels, 8–12 years. Genres include mystery, adventure, and books about nature and the environment.
- **Nonfiction:** Published 14 story picture books, 4–10 years; 7 chapter books, 5–10 years; and 10 middle-grade books, 8–12 years. Features books on history. Also publishes biographies; informational books, 3+ years; and reference titles, 10+ years. Topics include science, technology, animals, pets, geography, history, nature, and the environment.
- **Representative Titles:** *SuperCroc and the Origin of Crocodiles* by Christopher Sloan (10+ years) presents the latest discoveries about the lives of these animals. *Valley of Death* by Gloria Skurzynski & Alane Ferguson (8–12 years) is a fast-paced story set in Death Valley National Park; part of the Mysteries in Our National Parks series.

Submissions and Payment
Query with outline and sample chapter. Send complete ms for short works. Accepts photocopies and simultaneous submissions if identified. SASE. Responds to queries in 1 month, to mss in 3+ months. Flat fee.

Editor's Comments
We publish quality books, and we're open to submissions from authors who are experts in the field they wish to write about.

Naturegraph Publishers

P.O. Box 1047
3543 Indian Creek Road
Happy Camp, CA 96039

Managing Editor: Barbara Brown

Publisher's Interests
This publisher's catalogue is filled with books about Native American subjects, American wildlife, and natural history. While many of its books are written specifically for adults, it offers a number of titles that are appropriate for readers in middle school and high school.
Website: www.naturegraph.com

Freelance Potential
Published 2 titles in 2002: both were developed from unsolicited submissions. Of the 2 titles, 1 was by an unpublished writer and 1 was by an author who was new to the publishing house. Receives 400 queries yearly.
- **Fiction:** Publishes middle-grade novels, 8–12 years; and young adult books, 12–18 years. Genres include mythology, folktales, and Native American lore.
- **Nonfiction:** Publishes middle-grade books, 8–12 years; and young adult books, 12–18 years. Topics include Native Americans, American wildlife, animals, the environment, crafts, hiking, and backpacking. Also publishes field guides for all ages.
- **Representative Titles:** *Run to Glory* by William Sears follows a boy and his grandfather on a quest to save a red trotting colt. *Alone in the Wilderness* by Hap Gilliland provides a unique glimpse of American Indian life and culture through the eyes of a present-day Cheyenne high school student.

Submissions and Payment
Guidelines available at website. Query with outline and 1–2 sample chapters. Accepts photocopies and computer printouts. SASE. Response time and publication period vary. Royalty.

Editor's Comments
We encourage writers who are interested in submitting to us to log on to our website and review our current titles. If you have something new, original, and interesting that deals with nature or Native American subjects, we'd like to hear from you. Remember, we don't publish books for very young children.

Neal-Schuman Publishers

100 Varick Street
New York, NY 10013

Director of Publishing: Charles Harmon

Publisher's Interests
This specialty publisher targets librarians in both school and public libraries. Its list features titles that explore the topics of library management, funding, and library services.
Website: www.neal-schuman.com

Freelance Potential
Published 32 titles (2 juvenile) in 2002: 5 were developed from unsolicited submissions and 1 was a reprint/licensed property. Of the 32 titles, 26 were by unpublished writers and 26 were by authors who were new to the publishing house. Receives 300 queries, 300 unsolicited mss yearly.
- **Nonfiction:** Publishes resource materials for school media specialists and librarians. Topics include curriculum support, the Internet, technology, literary skills, reading programs, collection development, reference needs, the First Amendment, staff development, management, and communications.
- **Representative Titles:** *The 21st Century Teachers' Guide to Recommended Internet Sites* by Marvin DiGeorgio & Sylvia Lesage (librarians) offers a wealth of websites with pre-made lesson plans. *Becoming a Library Teacher* by Cheryl LaGuardia & Christine K. Oka (librarians) offers step-by-step instructions for effective preparation and teaching in today's library.

Submissions and Payment
Guidelines available. Prefers query with résumé, outline, table of contents, and sample chapter. Will accept complete ms. Accepts photocopies and computer printouts. SASE. Responds to queries in 2 weeks, to mss in 1–2 months. Publication in 10–12 months. Royalty.

Editor's Comments
If you think you have an idea that is right for our audience, we'd like to hear from you. Your submission should include a general description of your book, defining why your book is needed, how it will be written, and the audience or market to which it will be directed. Please include a table of contents, an outline, and a chapter or sample pages.

New Canaan Publishing Company

P.O. Box 752
New Canaan, CT 06840

Editor

Publisher's Interests
New Canaan Publishing specializes in educational fiction and nonfiction for children in the first through ninth grades. It also offers inspirational titles on Christian living, theology, and Bible studies for both adults and children.
Website: www.newcanaanpublishing.com

Freelance Potential
Published 4-6 titles in 2002.
- **Fiction:** Publishes chapter books, 5–10 years; and middle-grade novels, 8–12 years. Publishes educational stories, and stories with strong moral and Christian themes.
- **Nonfiction:** Publishes chapter books, 5–10 years; and middle-grade books, 8–12 years. Publishes supplementary curriculum materials, grades 1–9. Also offers devotionals.
- **Representative Titles:** *Olive, the Orphan Reindeer* by Michael Christie (5–9 years) tells the story of a young doe reindeer who is separated from her family and eventually becomes a member of Santa's sleigh team. *Stony Point—A Triangle Club Adventure* by Steven J. Givens (9–11 years) is a novel about three boys who volunteer at a retirement home and get involved in a mystery that dates back to the Civil War.

Submissions and Payment
Guidelines available. Query with synopsis; or send complete ms. Accepts photocopies and computer printouts. SASE. Responds in 10–12 months. Publication period and payment policy vary.

Editor's Comments
We're interested in supplementary education materials that build on, rather than replace, existing classroom materials. These materials should target students in the first through ninth grades. We're especially interested in submissions that help children to study on their own, to supplement their school and learning activities. Books about science and history are more likely to make it out of the slush pile. Children's books on Christian topics must be innovative.

The New England Press

P.O. Box 575
Shelburne, VT 05482

Managing Editor: Christopher Bray

Publisher's Interests

The history and heritage of New England are explored in the books from this regional publisher. Its juvenile list includes historical fiction, biographies, and history books that are appropriate for middle-grade and young adult readers. It does not accept books for beginning readers or picture books.
Website: www.nepress.com

Freelance Potential

Published 4 titles (3 juvenile) in 2002: all were developed from unsolicited submissions. Of the 4 titles, 1 was by an author who was new to the publishing house. Receives 300 queries yearly.

- **Fiction:** Publishes young adult books, 12–18 years. Genres include regional and historical fiction set in Vermont and northern New England.
- **Nonfiction:** Publishes middle-grade books, 8–12 years; and young adult books, 12–18 years. Features biographies and books about history, nature, and Vermontania.
- **Representative Titles:** *Alexander Twilight: Vermont's African-American Pioneer* by Michael T. Hahn tells the story of an African-American leader who started as an indentured laborer. *Teed Stories* by Jeff Danziger offers 12 humorous stories about the trials and tribulations of a Vermont family.

Submissions and Payment

Query with sample chapter. SASE. Responds in 3 months. Publication in 18 months. Royalty.

Editor's Comments

We were founded 25 years ago with the express purpose of publishing high-quality trade books of regional New England interest. We continue to look for young adult historical fiction set in northern New England, young adult biographies about famous northern New Englanders, and Vermont history. Send us a query that discusses the markets you would like your book to reach and how you, as an author, can contribute to the book's success.

New Harbinger Publications

5674 Shattuck Avenue
Oakland, CA 94609

Acquisitions Editor: Tesilya Hanauer

Publisher's Interests
New Harbinger publishes self-help psychology and health books. Typically, its books are based on cognitive behavioral approaches and offer step-by-step self-help for the reader. Its list includes titles for young adults and adults.
Website: www.newharbinger.com

Freelance Potential
Published 40 titles (2 juvenile) in 2002: 10 were developed from unsolicited submissions and 10 were by agented authors. Of the 40 titles, 10 were by unpublished writers and 30 were by authors who were new to the publishing house. Receives 600 queries yearly.
- **Nonfiction:** Publishes self-help psychology and health books for lay people as well as professionals.
- **Representative Titles:** *Parenting Well When You're Depressed* by Joanne Nicholson et al. (parents) offers practical tips to help parents raise their children while coping with their own depression. *Boy Talk* by Mary Polce-Lynch (parents) helps parents understand their sons' emotions and in turn help the boys express themselves.

Submissions and Payment
Guidelines and catalogue available with 9x12 SASE ($.60 postage). Query. Accepts photocopies and e-mail submissions to tesilya@newharbinger.com. SASE. Responds in 2–4 weeks. Publication in 1 year. Royalty, 10%.

Editor's Comments
We look for psychology and health self-help books that teach the average reader how to master essential life skills. Our books are also read by mental health professionals. Most of our authors are therapists or other helping professionals. While many of our books target adults, we are interested in titles for teens as well: books that talk to them directly about specific spiritual, psychological, and health conditions. If you are new to us, we strongly urge you to review some of our titles to get an idea of the kind of style we look for.

New Hope Publishers

100 Missionary Ridge
Birmingham, AL 35242-5235

Manuscript Submissions

Publisher's Interests

This publisher's mission is to offer books that motivate
women and families to share Christ's hope. Its catalogue
includes a number of parenting titles with spiritual themes,
as well as nonfiction books about Christian living for young
adults. While New Hope Publishers has published juvenile
titles in the past, it is no longer accepting manuscripts for
children's books.
Website: www.newhopepubl.com

Freelance Potential

Published 20 titles (1 juvenile) in 2002: 1 was developed from
an unsolicited submission. Receives 25 queries, 125 unsolicited mss yearly.
- **Nonfiction:** Publishes inspirational and spiritual books for
  women and young adults. Topics include prayer, spirituality,
  the Bible, and family issues.
- **Representative Titles:** *My Children, My Mission Field* by Susan
  E. Field (parents) focuses on a parent's most fundamental calling—raising children who love God, respect others, and know
  God's plan for their lives. *Growing on the Go: Devotions for
  Busy Families* by Rhonda R. Reeves (parents) includes daily
  devotions, as well as Bible thoughts, easy at-home activities,
  and brief prayers.

Submissions and Payment

Guidelines available. Prefers complete ms. Will accept query
with outline and 3 sample chapters. Accepts photocopies and
computer printouts. SASE. Response time varies. Royalty.
Flat fee.

Editor's Comments

We are experiencing unprecedented growth and are interested
in manuscripts that are relevant to Christian women, families,
and young adults. Our primary interest is in Bible studies and
nonfiction that promote spiritual development. Our mission is
to equip booksellers and readers to share the hope we profess
with families, friends, and the world.

New Leaf Press

P.O. Box 726
Green Forest, AR 72638

Acquisitions Editor: Roger Howerton

Publisher's Interests
The children's books that appear on the list of this Christian publisher range from picture books for preschool children to titles for young adults. Its books for young readers include only nonfiction books that are creation-based. New Leaf Press also offers supplementary materials for homeschooling on all grade levels.
Website: www.newleafpress.net

Freelance Potential
Published 30 titles (11 juvenile) in 2002: 6 were developed from unsolicited submissions and 2 were reprint/licensed properties. Of the 30 titles, 5 were by unpublished writers and 6 were by authors who were new to the publishing house. Receives 500 queries yearly.
- **Nonfiction:** Published 4 early picture books, 0–4 years; 4 middle-grade books, 8–12 years; and 3 young adult books, 12–18 years. Topics include current events, history, health and fitness, humor, nature and the environment, social issues, science, technology, and religion.
- **Representative Titles:** *Exploring Planet Earth* by John Hudson Tiner (10–14 years) traces the history of the earth from a Christian perspective; designed for homeschool use. *Where Do I Go From Here?* by Nicholas Comninellis (YA) includes stories of young adults who sought Bible-based guidance in making the major decisions of their lives.

Submissions and Payment
Guidelines and catalogue available with 9x12 SASE (5 first-class stamps). Query with cover letter, table of contents, synopsis, and sample chapter. Accepts photocopies and simultaneous submissions. SASE. Responds in 3 months. Publication in 12–18 months. Royalty, 10% of net.

Editor's Comments
For the coming year, we'd like to see submissions of creation-based books for children from preschool to age 12. Home-schooling materials are also needed. We publish no fiction.

Newmarket Press

15th Floor
18 East 48th Street
New York, NY 10017

Executive Editor: Keith Hollaman

Publisher's Interests

Now in its twentieth year of publishing, this company offers a list that primarily features nonfiction. Its catalogue includes books on child care and parenting, the performing arts, self-help, psychology, health, nutrition, and personal finance. It publishes only a small number of fiction titles. Its children's books target middle-grade and young adult readers.
Website: www.newmarketpress.com

Freelance Potential

Published 35 titles (5 juvenile) in 2002: most were by agented authors. Of the 35 titles, 5 were by unpublished writers and 8 were by authors who were new to the publishing house. Receives 1,200 queries yearly.

- **Fiction:** Publishes middle-grade novels, 8–12 years; and young adult novels, 12–18 years.
- **Nonfiction:** Publishes parenting books and self-help titles. Topics include child care, health, fitness, multicultural and ethnic issues, and sports.
- **Representative Titles:** *Fly Away Home* by Patricia Hermes et al. (YA) is the novelization of the film about a father and daughter who teach a gaggle of geese how to fly. *Kids and Sports* by Eric Small (parents) is a practical resource on kids and sports, written by a doctor, with advice on activities, stretching, and nutrition.

Submissions and Payment

Query with outline, clips, and detailed author biography for nonfiction. Does not accept queries or unsolicited mss for children's fiction. Accepts photocopies. SASE. Responds in 1–3 months. Publication in 1 year. Royalty; advance.

Editor's Comments

Books for parents and care givers are at the top of our current wish list. Send us something parents can use to help them in bringing up their family. While we don't expect you to reinvent the wheel, we do like ideas that offer a fresh approach. Note that we are only accepting queries for nonfiction at this time.

New Society Publishers

P.O. Box 189
Gabriola Island, British Columbia V0R 1X0
Canada

Publisher: Christopher Plant

Publisher's Interests
New Society Publishers is a progressive publishing company
that specializes in books for activists that build ecological
sustainability and a just society.
Website: www.newsociety.com

Freelance Potential
Published 22 titles in 2002: 11 were developed from unsolicited submissions, 2 were by agented authors, and 2 were
reprint/licensed properties. Of the 22 titles, 8 were by
unpublished writers and 16 were by authors who were new
to the publishing house. Receives 400 queries yearly.
- **Nonfiction:** Publishes college guides and career resources for
  young adults. Also publishes titles on education systems, family issues, child development, sustainability, business practices,
  leadership, feminism, diversity, and community issues for
  adults.
- **Representative Titles:** *The Natural Child: Parenting From the
  Heart* by Jan Hunt (parents) makes a compelling case for a
  return to attachment parenting. *Making a Difference College &
  Graduate Guide* by Miriam Weinstein (YA) profiles higher learning
  institutions that are committed to helping students learn to
  make the world a better place.

Submissions and Payment
Guidelines available. Query with proposal, table of contents,
and sample chapter. SAE/IRC. Responds in 2–3 months.
Publication in 1 year. Payment policy varies.

Editor's Comments
Our editorial goal is to publish books that help create a sus-
tainable, more peaceful and just world through nonviolent
action. We are interested in analyzing examples and situations,
and in developing theories and strategies of nonviolent social
change. Our emphasis is always inspirational, skill-oriented,
and motivational. Most of the books we publish we initiate ourselves, but we are willing to consider submissions from writers
who are familiar with our needs.

NL Associates

P.O. Box 1199
Highstown, NJ 08520

President: Nathan Levy

Publisher's Interests
NL Associates specializes in materials that develop critical thinking skills in children, and offers activities that stretch the imagination and stimulate creativity in both students and teachers. While it covers a wide range of subjects, all of its books are targeted to those involved in gifted education.
Website: www.storieswithholes.com

Freelance Potential
Published 10 titles in 2002. Receives 2 queries, 2 unsolicited mss yearly.
- **Nonfiction:** Publishes educational materials and activity books designed to develop critical thinking skills, grades 1–12. Features books on special education and titles for parents and educators.
- **Representative Titles:** *Fair Is Fair* by Sharon Creedon (5–10 years) features folktales from around the world that deal with the issue of justice. *Thirty-Three Multicultural Tales to Tell* by Pleasant DeSpain (all ages) features stories that celebrate the interconnectedness of people, nature, and cultures.

Submissions and Payment
Query or send complete ms. Response time, publication period, and payment policy vary.

Editor's Comments
Everything we publish is connected to developing critical thinking skills and gifted education. Given that, we are open to a wide range of topics. Our mission is to touch the minds of our students and teachers and to challenge their creativity and imagination. We are especially interested in ideas for activity books designed to develop logical thinking skills. Study some of the titles on our list and then, if you think your idea meets our needs, send us either a query or manuscript. We most often reject material simply because it does not meet our very specific requirements in terms of content, or because it covers a topic that we have recently addressed in a similar manner in another book.

North Country Books

311 Turner Street
Utica, NY 13501

Submissions Editor: Sheila Orlin

Publisher's Interests
Founded in 1965, this regional publisher offers quality books
about New York State. Its catalogue includes biographies,
history books, books about nature, folklore, and art and photography titles, as well as CDs, audiocassettes, video tapes,
calendars, and postcard books. It also publishes story picture
books for children.

Freelance Potential
Published 10 titles (3 juvenile) in 2002: all were developed
from unsolicited submissions. Of the 10 titles, 8 were by
unpublished writers and 8 were by authors who were new to
the publishing house. Receives 300+ queries, 200–300 unsolicited mss yearly.
- **Fiction:** Published 2 story picture books, 4–10 years. Features
  folklore about New York State.
- **Nonfiction:** Published 1 middle-grade book, 8–12 years. Topics
  include history and nature in New York State. Also publishes
  biographies, field and trail guides, and art and photography
  books for adults.
- **Representative Titles:** *Adirondack Fairy Tales* by Lettie Petrie
  features seven read-aloud stories that take children on wood-
  land adventures with animals of the Adirondack mountains.
  Abby's Search for Cooper by Paula Burns is a story about a
  golden retriever who goes on regular excursions with her family
  to Cooperstown, New York.

Submissions and Payment
Guidelines and catalogue available with 9x12 SASE ($2.18
postage). Query or send complete ms. Accepts photocopies.
SASE. Responds to queries in 1–2 months, to mss in 6–12
months. Publication in 2–5 years. Royalty.

Editor's Comments
While we are primarily a publisher of nonfiction, we do offer
some children's fiction. Remember, we're only interested in
books about New York State, including the Catskills, the
Adirondacks, the Hudson Valley, and the Finger Lakes.

North-South Books

17th Floor
11 East 26th Street
New York, NY 10010

Submissions Editor

Publisher's Interests
This well-known children's publishing house is the English-language imprint of the Swiss publisher Nord-Süd Verlag. Its list was launched in the US in 1985 and features both translations of books from around the world as well as original titles. Its books target young readers of all ages.

Freelance Potential
Published 80 titles in 2002: 5 were by agented authors.
- **Fiction:** Publishes concept books, toddler books, and early picture books, 0–4 years; easy-to-read books, 4–7 years; story picture books, 4–10 years; and chapter books, 5–10 years. Genres include adventure, drama, fairy tales, folklore, fantasy, humor, mystery, nature, the environment, and ethnic, multicultural, and contemporary fiction.
- **Nonfiction:** Publishes early picture books, 0–4 years. Topics include animals, hobbies, crafts, humor, nature, religion, science, technology, social issues, sports, and multicultural and ethnic issues.
- **Representative Titles:** *The Clown Said No* by Mischa Damjan (5–8 years) is the story of a group of circus performers who decide to rebel. *Over in the Meadow* by Olive A. Wadsworth (3–6 years) is a counting rhyme book.

Submissions and Payment
Accepts mss from agents only. Royalty; advance.

Editor's Comments
We have always been committed to bringing young children quality books that will please for years to come. All of our books are designed to delight children as well as adults. Our motto has always been quality over quantity, and we only choose the very best when it comes to new material. We strongly urge authors new to us to review several of our published titles to get a better understanding of what works for us. We are interested in building bridges between authors and illustrators from countries around the world, and our books to date have been translated into more than 30 languages.

Aimee Jackson, NorthWord Books
In the Science Field

Aimee Jackson, Executive Editor, says that the focus of NorthWord's science program is "to publish books that inspire in children a love for the natural world." It publishes fiction and nonfiction for children from birth to age 12, including board books, preschool books, picture books, and nonfiction series for trade, school, and library markets.

"We are looking for new ideas for series and stand-alone nonfiction titles," says Jackson, "primarily for 7-to-10-year-olds, and original ideas for fiction for babies, toddlers, and picture book age readers. Authors, please review our catalogue online to see which animals and themes we've already published." She is "not interested in themes outside our niche—no personal pet/animal stories, animal rehabilitation stories, or manuscripts with heavy-handed endangerment/extinction themes."

Jackson strongly recommends researching markets: "Make sure you're submitting material that fits with the publisher's program, and that the publisher hasn't already published something just like it. Find out who the current acquiring editor is and address submissions and queries to that individual. Getting published is as much about timing as it is about talent, especially in the nonfiction world."

She has no preference for series or singles, but says, "Nonfiction seems to sell better in series, though we are open to single title ideas, or even pairs. For picture books, we are looking for traditional standalone titles."

Whatever the project, says Jackson, "The author should treat their subject as any good research expert would—reading all the latest information and findings on the subject, using expert readers or interviewing experts in the field. Now, we have access to university websites, science journals, parks and museum websites (which are often geared for children and are usually quite interactive and fun). All of our science books have Web addresses included, which has become as much an expected part of the back matter as the index."

NorthWord Books for Young Readers

18705 Lake Drive East
Chanhassen, MN 55317

Acquisitions Editor

Publisher's Interests

NorthWord Books for Young Readers is an imprint of Creative Publishing International, which publishes fiction picture books and nonfiction titles for children. Its books cover such topics as nature, natural history, and wildlife. 10% co-venture published material.
Website: www.northwordpress.com

Freelance Potential

Published 20 titles in 2002. Receives 500 queries yearly.
• **Nonfiction:** Publishes story picture books, 4–10 years; and middle-grade books, 8–12 years. Topics include natural history, animals, nature, and the environment.
• **Representative Titles:** *Penguins ABC* by Kevin Schafer is a photographic concept book. *Manatees* by Kathy Feeney (grades 2–5) looks at the life of these animals; part of the Our Wild World series.

Submissions and Payment

Guidelines available at website. Query with résumé, detailed outline, sample chapters, and bibliography. Accepts photocopies and simultaneous submissions if identified. SASE. Responds in 2 months. Publication in 12–15 months. Royalty; advance. Work-for-hire.

Editor's Comments

Our goal is to give young readers an appreciation for nature, wildlife, and the natural world. While they are entertaining, all of our titles are also educational in that they strive to teach a lesson about the value of wildlife and the natural world. We welcome both new and established writers who have taken the time to study our catalogue and have a firm grip on the way we like to present material. While we accept fiction, we are not interested in anthropomorphic stories. If you are sending a nonfiction query, please make sure to include a bibliography. We are especially interested in queries for our new series, Our Wild World. These books bring readers detailed information about a particular animal and include detailed photographs.

Novalis

Saint Paul University
223 Main Street
Ottawa, Ontario K1S 1C4
Canada

Commissioning Editor: Kevin Burns

Publisher's Interests

An ecumenical publisher housed in a Catholic university, Novalis offers works designed to enlighten readers on matters of faith and spirituality. Many of its titles are published in French as well as in English. Novalis does not publish fiction, poetry, or bibliographies.

Website: www.novalis.ca

Freelance Potential

Published 60 titles (5 juvenile) in 2002: 5 were developed from unsolicited submissions and 3 were by agented authors. Of the 60 titles, 12 were by unpublished writers and 12 were by authors who were new to the publishing house. Receives 96 queries, 80 unsolicited mss yearly.

- **Nonfiction:** Publishes early picture books, 0–4 years; story picture books, 4–10 years; and young adult books, 12–18 years. Topics include biography, history, and religion. Also publishes reference titles, self-help books, and books in series.
- **Representative Titles:** *The Calming of the Storm* by Bernard Hubler & Chantall Muller van den Berghe recounts the familiar Bible story and includes a personal reflection; part of the Open Your Eyes series. *Growing Up a Friend of Jesus* by Francoise Darcy-Bérube & John Paul Bérube encourages children to live a life of prayer and integrity.

Submissions and Payment

Guidelines available. Query with clips. Accepts photocopies, disk submissions, and e-mail to kburns@ustpaul.ca. No simultaneous submissions. SAE/IRC. Responds in 6 weeks. Publication in 1 year. Royalty; advance.

Editor's Comments

For young readers, story books and activity books are among our needs for the coming year. We would also like to see submissions of parent/teacher resources that address issues concerning the spiritual lives of children. We appreciate quality writing on any topic pertaining to faith and values. Check our guidelines for specifics on preparing a proposal for us.

The Oliver Press

5707 West 36th Street
Minneapolis, MN 55416-2510

Editor: Jenna Anderson

Publisher's Interests
A publisher of nonfiction titles for young readers, The Oliver Press offers biographies of prominent leaders in the fields of politics, business, archaeology, law, science, and technology. Its catalogue also includes history and science books.
Website: www.oliverpress.com

Freelance Potential
Published 12 titles in 2002: 1 was developed from an unsolicited submission. Of the 12 titles, 1 was by an unpublished writer and 1 was by an author who was new to the publishing house. Receives 40–50 queries yearly.
- **Nonfiction:** Published 4 easy-to-read books, 4–7 years; 6 middle-grade books, 8–12 years; and 2 young adult books, 12–18 years. Topics include prominent women, business and labor, African-American leaders, archaeology, exploration, law, government, politics, religion, science, social issues, medicine, history, multicultural studies, and Jewish issues.
- **Representative Titles:** *Women of Adventure* by Jacqueline McLean (grades 5 and up) profiles women who traveled to remote and fascinating parts of the world; part of the Profiles series. *Ranchers, Homesteaders, and Traders: Frontiersmen of the South-Central States* by Kieran Doherty (grades 7 and up) discusses the people and events involved in the settlement of the central US; part of the Shaping America series.

Submissions and Payment
Guidelines available. Query with résumé, outline, and writing sample. Accepts photocopies, computer printouts, and simultaneous submissions if identified. SASE. Responds in 3–6 months. Publication in 1–2 years. Flat fee, $1,000.

Editor's Comments
We're currently looking for proposals on topics related to the history of technology for our Innovators series. Profiles of business leaders for our Business Builders series are needed as well. The writing sample you submit should be similar in reading level, style, and subject to your proposed book.

OnStage Publishing

214 East Moulton Street NE
Decatur, AL 35601

Senior Editor: Dianne Hamilton

Publisher's Interests
Founded in 1999, this publisher strives to publish books that "reach the hearts as well as the minds of children." It has a small list that includes story picture books and easy-to-read books, as well as novels for middle-grade and young adult readers.
Website: www.onstagebooks.com

Freelance Potential
Published 5 titles in 2002: all were developed from unsolicited submissions. Of the 5 titles, 4 were by authors who were new to the publishing house. Receives 1,000 unsolicited mss each year.
- **Fiction:** Published 1 story picture book, 4–10 years; 2 middle-grade novels, 8–12 years; and 1 young adult book, 12–18 years. Genres include drama; adventure; fantasy; horror; humor; mystery; suspense; romance; contemporary, historical, and science fiction; and stories about nature, the environment, and sports.
- **Nonfiction:** Published 1 easy-to-read book, 4–7 years. Topics include animals, pets, history, nature, the environment, and sports. Also publishes biographies.
- **Representative Titles:** *Write Away* by Margaret Gree & Laurel Griffith (grades 1–6) presents a series of creative writing exercises. *The Secret of Crybaby Hollow* by Darren Butler (8–12 years) is a middle-grade mystery; part of the Abbie Girl Spy Adventures series.

Submissions and Payment
Guidelines available with 9x12 SASE (3 first-class stamps). Send complete ms; include outline for nonfiction. Accepts photocopies. SASE. Responds in 2–4 weeks. Publication in 1–2 years. Royalty, varies; advance, varies.

Editor's Comments
We're looking for historical fiction, especially about World War II; all types of adventures and mysteries; mainstream and contemporary fiction; plays; and fantasies.

Orca Book Publishers

P.O. Box 468
Custer, WA 98240-0468

Publisher: Bob Tyrrell

Publisher's Interests
This children's book publisher features picture books, chapter books, middle-grade novels, and young adult titles, all written by Canadian authors.
Website: www.orcabook.com

Freelance Potential
Published 50 titles in 2002: 25 were developed from unsolicited submissions, 10 were by agented authors, and 4 were reprint/licensed properties. Of the 50 titles, 10 were by unpublished writers and 25 were by authors who were new to the publishing house. Receives 1,000 queries, 500 unsolicited mss yearly.

- **Fiction:** Published 15 story picture books, 4–10 years; 10 chapter books, 5–10 years; 10 middle-grade novels, 8–12 years; and 15 young adult novels, 12–18 years. Genres include contemporary, regional, and historical fiction.
- **Representative Titles:** *Under a Prairie Sky* by Anne Laurel Carter (4–8 years) tells the tale of a boy who rides the prairie in search of his younger brother. *Jo's Triumph* by Nikki Tate (7–11 years) is the story of a girl who disguises herself as a boy to join the Pony Express.

Submissions and Payment
Canadian authors only. Guidelines available. Query with 2–3 sample chapters for fiction. Send complete ms for picture books. Accepts photocopies and computer printouts. SASE. Responds to queries in 6 weeks, to mss in 8–12 weeks. Publication in 18–24 months. Royalty, 10% split; advance.

Editor's Comments
This year, we need teen fiction, middle-grade fiction, fiction for six- to nine-year-old children, and picture books for four- to eight-year-old children. We continue to look for contemporary stories or fantasy with a universal theme, a compelling plot, and strong, young protagonists who grow through the course of the story and who solve the central problem themselves.

Orchard Books

Scholastic Inc.
555 Broadway
New York, NY 10012-3999

Vice President/Editorial Director: Ken Geist

Publisher's Interests
Hardcover fiction for young readers is the specialty of
Orchard Books. It offers picture books and novels for
preschoolers through teens, as well as a limited number of
nonfiction titles. 10% self-, subsidy-, co-venture, or co-op
published material.
Website: www.scholastic.com

Freelance Potential
Published 30 titles in 2002: 10 were by agented authors and
12 were reprint/licensed properties. Of the 30 titles, 1 was by
an unpublished writer and 6 were by authors who were new
to the publishing house. Receives 5,000 queries yearly.
- **Fiction:** Publishes concept books, toddler books, and early picture books, 0–4 years; story picture books, 4–10 years; chapter
  books, 5–10 years; and middle-grade books, 8–12 years. Genres include multicultural, historical, and contemporary fiction;
  fairy tales; folktales; fantasy; humor; and stories about sports.
- **Nonfiction:** Publishes story picture books, 4–10 years. Topics
  include history, nature, the environment, and social issues.
- **Representative Titles:** *Flora's Blanket* by Debi Gliori (2–5
  years) is a picture book about a little bunny who can't sleep
  because her favorite blanket is missing. *The Jacob Ladder* by
  Gerald Hausman & Uton Hinds (10–13 years) is an autobio-
  graphical novel about a young Jamaican's troubled relationship with his father.

Submissions and Payment
Guidelines available. Query only. No unsolicited mss. SASE.

Editor's Comments
We receive thousands of queries yearly, so we are highly selective when choosing books for publication. Review our catalogue
and spend some time determining the kinds of books that
appeal to us. This year, we continue to seek high-quality, original picture books for children between the ages of four and
seven. Fiction for middle-grade readers is another editorial priority. Don't send titles written for parents or teachers.

Our Sunday Visitor

200 Noll Plaza
Huntington, IN 46750

Acquisitions Editor

Publisher's Interests

This Catholic publisher produces trade books and religious
educational materials, including CD-ROMs, diskettes, audios,
and videos, for adults and children. It publishes reference
books and titles relating to prayer, Catholic heritage, the
saints, and the family.
Website: www.osv.com

Freelance Potential

Published 48 titles (7 juvenile) in 2002: 1 was developed from
an unsolicited submission and 3 were reprint/licensed properties. Receives 1,300 queries yearly.

- **Nonfiction:** Publishes concept books, 0–4 years; story picture
  books, 4–10 years; chapter books, 5–10 years; middle-grade
  books, 8–12 years; and young adult books, 12–18 years.
  Topics include family issues, parish life, church heritage,
  and the lives of the saints. Also features reference titles and
  prayer books.
- **Representative Titles:** *St. Francis and His Feathered Friends*
  by Anne E. Neuberger tells the story of how Brother Francis
  encouraged the birds to praise God with their songs; part of
  the Saints for Children series. *Prove It! God* by Amy Welborn
  (YA) presents straightforward answers to questions teenagers
  have about God and the Catholic Church.

Submissions and Payment

Guidelines available. Query with résumé and sample chapters. Accepts photocopies, computer printouts, and simultaneous submissions if identified. SASE. Responds in 2–3
months. Publication in 1+ years. Royalty; advance. Flat fee.

Editor's Comments

Among the types of books we're particularly interested in publishing are those aimed at the parish and the family. For the
parish, we need books that serve the needs of religious education instructors. For the family, we'd like to see books that help
lay Catholics in their marriage vocation, and in passing their
faith on to their children. We do not accept fiction or poetry.

The Overmountain Press

P.O. Box 1261
Johnson City, TN 37605

Managing Editor: Elizabeth Wright

Publisher's Interests
Primarily a publisher of regional-interest books, The Overmountain Press publishes both children's and adult titles focusing on southern Appalachia. It specializes in picture books for children up to the age of seven and history titles for readers in third through eighth grade.
Website: www.overmountainpress.com

Freelance Potential
Published 30 titles (10 juvenile) in 2002: 3 were developed from unsolicited submissions, 3 were by agented authors, and 1 was a reprint/licensed property. Receives 500 queries each year.
- **Fiction:** Published 3 early picture books, 0–4 years; and 3 young adult books, 12–18 years. Also publishes middle-grade books, 8–12 years. Genres include folklore, folktales, mystery, and regional fiction.
- **Nonfiction:** Published 4 chapter books, 5–10 years. Also publishes story picture books, 4–10 years. Topics include Appalachia, railroad history, regional ghost lore, and science.
- **Representative Titles:** *Appalachian ABCs* by Francie Hall is an alphabet book that shows aspects of the Appalachian culture for each letter. *Apple Doll* by Kathleen Poulsen is a story that depicts the Appalachian tradition of creating a doll from an apple.

Submissions and Payment
Guidelines available with 6x9 SASE ($.85 postage). Query with résumé and sample chapters. No unsolicited mss. Accepts photocopies and computer printouts. SASE. Responds in 2–3 months. Publication in 1 year. Royalty, 15%.

Editor's Comments
Our primary interest is in southern Appalachian regional picture books for children under the age of seven. When reviewing a children's manuscript, we prefer to see copies of the illustrations at the same time we review the text. At an author's request, we can send a list of illustrators.

Richard C. Owen Publishers

P.O. Box 585
Katonah, NY 10536

Director of Children's Books: Janice Boland

Publisher's Interests
This publisher specializes in short, high-interest, easy-to-read stories for elementary and middle-school students. It offers nonfiction on a broad spectrum of subjects and fiction in a variety of genres.
Website: www.RCOwen.com

Freelance Potential
Published 15 titles in 2002: all were developed from unsolicited submissions. Of the 15 titles, 10 were by authors who were new to the publishing house. Receives 1,000 unsolicited mss yearly.

- **Fiction:** Publishes easy-to-read books, 4–7 years; story picture books, 4–10 years; and chapter books, 5–10 years. Genres include mystery; humor; folktales; stories about animals and nature; books about social, ethnic, and multicultural issues; and contemporary fiction.
- **Nonfiction:** Publishes easy-to-read books, 4–7 years; story picture books, 4–10 years; and chapter books, 5–10 years. Topics include current events, geography, music, science, nature, and the environment. Also publishes resource materials, professional development titles, and parenting books.
- **Representative Titles:** *The Fox* (grades K–2) is a story about a fox that runs, jumps, hides, swims, and ends up with a big surprise. *Jane Yolen* (grades 2–5) introduces young readers to the author of *Owl Moon* and other stories; part of the Meet the Author series.

Submissions and Payment
Guidelines available. Send complete ms. Accepts photocopies, computer printouts, and simultaneous submissions if identified. SASE. Responds in 3–6 months. Publication period varies. Payment policy varies.

Editor's Comments
This year, we are particularly interested in nonfiction books about vehicles, machines, and nature for children in kindergarten, first, and second grade.

Owl Books

Suite 200
51 Front Street East
Toronto, Ontario M5E 1B3
Canada

Submissions Editor: Anne Shone

Publisher's Interests

An imprint of Maple Tree Press, this Canadian publisher highlights the work of Canadian authors. It features both fiction and nonfiction books for children. Owl Books is also associated with the magazines *Owl*, *ChickaDEE*, and *Chirp*.

Freelance Potential

Published 10 titles in 2002. Receives 1,000+ queries yearly.

- **Fiction:** Publishes early picture books, 0–4 years; easy-to-read books, 4–7 years; and middle-grade novels, 8–12 years. Genres include contemporary fiction.
- **Nonfiction:** Publishes concept books and early picture books, 0–4 years; and middle-grade books, 8–12 years. Topics include science, nature, sports, and Canadian history. Also publishes photo essays.
- **Representative Titles:** *Wow Canada! Exploring This Land from Coast to Coast to Coast* by Vivien Bowers (8–12 years) is a portrait of Canada that takes an informative and exciting look at the splendors to see and experience across all the provinces. *What's the Matter with Albert?* by Freida Wishinsky (7–12 years) is a fascinating look at the life and accomplishments of scientist Albert Einstein.

Submissions and Payment

Send complete ms for fiction. Query with outline, sample chapters, and clips for nonfiction. Accepts photocopies, computer printouts, and simultaneous submissions if identified. SASE. Responds in 2–3 months. Publication in 2 years. Royalty.

Editor's Comments

Again this year, we are interested in receiving submissions of science activity books that show readers how their world works. Nature titles are also high on our list. Remember that we will publish only the works of Canadian authors and Canadian citizens living abroad. If you have a manuscript that will appeal to a child's innate curiosity about their world, and you are Canadian, let us look at it.

Pacific Educational Press

6365 Biological Science Road
Faculty of Education, University of British Columbia
Vancouver, British Columbia V6T 1Z4
Canada

Director: Catherine Edwards

Publisher's Interests
This educational publisher develops textbooks for teacher education programs, reference titles, and teacher resource books for educators working in kindergarten through twelfth grade. It also publishes a small number of chapter books and middle-grade novels, as well as educational nonfiction titles for readers over the age of eight.
Website: www.pep.educ.ubc.ca

Freelance Potential
Published 4 titles (2 juvenile) in 2002: 1 was a reprint/ licensed property. Of the 4 titles, 3 were by authors who were new to the publishing house. Receives 100 queries yearly.
- **Fiction:** Publishes chapter books, 5–10 years; and middle-grade novels, 8–12 years. Genres include historical and multicultural fiction.
- **Nonfiction:** Published 1 middle-grade book, 8–12 years; and 1 young adult book, 12–18 years. Also publishes books for educators about language arts, mathematics, science, social studies, multicultural education, critical thinking, fine arts, and administration.
- **Representative Titles:** *The Reluctant Deckhand* by Jan Padgett (8–11 years) is a novel about a 10-year-old girl who is fearful and resentful about having to spend the summer on a fishing boat with her mother. *The Golden Rose* by Dayle Campbell Gaetz (11+ years) is a historical novel about a girl and her family who travel to British Columbia from England in 1860.

Submissions and Payment
Guidelines available. Query with résumé, outline, and 2 sample chapters. Accepts photocopies, computer printouts, and simultaneous submissions if identified. SAE/IRC. Responds in 4–6 months. Publication in 10–18 months. Royalty.

Editor's Comments
This year, we need teacher resource books on English and language arts, mathematics, science, and social studies. We also need teacher education texts.

Pacific Press Publishing Association

1350 North Kings Road
Nampa, ID 83687

Acquisitions Editor: Tim Lale

Publisher's Interests

Books used in Seventh-day Adventist Sabbath schools are the specialty of this Christian publisher. All of its products feature biblical and inspirational topics. Its catalogue offers fiction and nonfiction for both children and adults.
Website: www.pacificpress.com

Freelance Potential

Published 29 titles in 2002. Receives 150+ queries yearly.

- **Fiction:** Publishes easy-to-read books, 4–7 years; chapter books, 5–10 years; and middle-grade novels, 8–12 years. Genres include mystery, adventure, and suspense.
- **Nonfiction:** Publishes easy-to-read books, 4–7 years; chapter books, 5–10 years; and middle-grade books, 8–12 years. Topics include animals and children. Also publishes books in series.
- **Representative Titles:** *Beautiful Bones and Butterflies* by Linda Porter Carlyle is a story of the miracle of change as seen in the transformation of a caterpillar into a butterfly; part of the Child's Steps to Jesus series. *The Boy and the Blue Balloon* by Kenneth Steven is the story of how a boy learns about the stewardship of God's creation.

Submissions and Payment

Guidelines available by mail or at website. Query. Accepts photocopies, computer printouts, disk submissions, and e-mail submissions to booksubmissions@pacificpress.com. SASE. Responds in 3 months. Publication in 6–12 months. Royalty, 6–12%; advance, to $1,500.

Editor's Comments

Our focus is on children's titles that can communicate biblical ideas unique to the Seventh-day Adventist point of view. If you are new to us, your best chance of being published is with a submission that will fit into one of our established series, such as Great Stories for Kids, or Julius and Friends, or Shoebox Kids. Study the marketplace and see how our line of books fills a unique spot, then send us a query. Picture books, true story/biographies, and historical fiction are all of interest.

Parachute Press

Suite 302
156 Fifth Avenue
New York, NY 10010

Submissions Editor

Publisher's Interests
Parachute Press is a book packager that offers novelty and
chapter books, horror stories, picture books, and easy-to-
read titles. Both fiction and nonfiction books appear in its
catalogue. Its audience includes preschoolers through young
adult readers.
Website: www.parachuteproperties.com

Freelance Potential
Published 100 titles in 2002: 1 was developed from an unsolicited submission, 50 were by agented authors, and many
were reprint/licensed properties. Of the 100 titles, 1 was by an
unpublished writer and 20 were by authors who were new to
the publishing house. Receives 240 queries, 200 unsolicited
mss yearly.

- **Fiction:** Publishes chapter books and novelty books, 5–10
  years; middle-grade novels, 8–12 years; and young adult
  books, 12–18 years. Genres include horror, mystery, romance,
  stories about sports, contemporary fiction, and humor.
- **Nonfiction:** Publishes novelty, chapter, and activity books,
  5–10 years; middle-grade titles, 8–12 years; and young adult
  books, 12–18 years. Offers humor and books about science.
- **Representative Titles:** *Turning Seventeen* (YA) is part of a new
  series published in conjunction with *Seventeen* magazine.
  Nightmare Room by R. L. Stine is a book about a place beyond
  reality, where everyday experiences meet the unexpected.

Submissions and Payment
Guidelines available for work-for-hire with SASE. Send
résumé and writing sample of no more than 5 pages. No
unsolicited mss. Accepts mss from agented authors only.
Accepts photocopies. No simultaneous submissions. SASE.
Publication in 9 months. Flat fee, $3,000–$4,000.

Editor's Comments
Most of our books are assigned on a work-for-hire basis, but
we always take a look at résumés and writing samples from
new writers.

Parenting Press, Inc.

P.O. Box 75267
Seattle, WA 98125-6100

Publisher: Carolyn Threadgill

Publisher's Interests
Parenting Press is a small house that features books that
help build confidence in children, parents, and professionals
who work with children.
Website: www.parentingpress.com

Freelance Potential
Published 6 titles (1 juvenile) in 2002: 2 were developed from
unsolicited submissions and 2 were by agented authors. Of
the 6 titles, 1 was by an unpublished writer and 4 were by
authors who were new to the publishing house. Receives
1,000+ queries yearly.
- **Nonfiction:** Published 3 story picture books, 4–10 years. Topics include self-esteem, problem-solving, conflict resolution,
  safety, values, feelings and emotions, and personal boundaries.
  Also publishes parenting titles.
- **Representative Titles:** *When You're Mad and You Know It* by
  Elizabeth Crary & Shari Steelsmith (1–3 years) helps young
  children understand strong emotions and suggests ways for
  kids to express their feelings in acceptable ways. *Bully on the
  Bus* by Carl W. Bosch (7–11 years) shows readers how to solve
  problems by evaluating choices and different options offered
  throughout the story.

Submissions and Payment
Guidelines available. Query with outline and clips or writing
samples. Accepts photocopies, computer printouts, and
simultaneous submissions if identified. SASE. Responds in 2
months. Publication in 18–24 months. Royalty, 4–8% of net.

Editor's Comments
We are interested in books that will become modern classics.
Prospective titles must have value that will endure past current popularity. We especially like material that provides
readers with problem-solving "options" rather than "shoulds."
Because we are interested in long-term titles, we field-test all
our material several times before publication. Please don't
send us children's stories or activity books.

Pauline Books & Media

50 St. Paul's Avenue
Jamaica Plain, MA 02130-3491

Children's Editor: Sr. Patricia Edward Jablonski, F.S.P.

Publisher's Interests
The children's titles that appear on this publisher's list foster
Christian values while providing wholesome, entertaining
reading for preschool children through young adults. Pauline
Books & Media does not publish fiction.
Website: www.pauline.org

Freelance Potential
Published 30 titles (11 juvenile) in 2002: 6 were developed
from unsolicited submissions and 3 were reprint/licensed
properties. Of the 30 titles, 5 were by unpublished writers
and 12 were by authors who were new to the publishing
house. Receives 500 queries yearly.

- **Nonfiction:** Published 1 early picture book, 0–4 years; 3 easy-
  to-read books, 4–7 years; 3 story picture books, 4–10 years; 3
  middle-grade books, 8–12 years; and 1 young adult book,
  12–18 years. Also publishes prayer books, coloring books, and
  activity books. Topics include religious holidays, the lives of the
  saints, and the sacraments.
- **Representative Titles:** *At the Side of David* by Eric Pakulak
  (9–13 years) is a multiple-ending Bible story about David and
  Goliath that teaches the importance of making good choices.
  The Little Lost Lamb by Geri Berger Haines (6–9 years) teaches
  trust and gratitude in this children's version of the parable of
  the Good Shepherd.

Submissions and Payment
Guidelines available. Query with synopsis and 2–3 sample
chapters. Accepts photocopies and computer printouts.
SASE. Responds in 6 months. Publication in 2–3 years.
Royalty, negotiable.

Editor's Comments
Our needs for the coming year continue to be children's Bibles
for ages four to seven; religious Christmas and Easter stories
for readers ages four to ten; books about the lives of the saints
for children from birth to age seven; and prayer books for four-
to seven-year-old readers.

Paulist Press

997 Macarthur Boulevard
Mahwah, NJ 07430

Children's Editor: Susan O'Keefe

Publisher's Interests
This Catholic publisher is offering an increasing number of children's fiction, nonfiction, and activity books. Its juvenile list includes picture books for preschoolers, prayer books, chapter books, and young adult biographies.
Website: www.paulistpress.com

Freelance Potential
Published 12 titles in 2002: 4 were developed from unsolicited submissions. Of the 12 titles, 4 were by unpublished writers and 5 were by authors who were new to the publishing house. Receives 800 queries and unsolicited mss yearly.
- **Fiction:** Publishes picture books, 2–5 years; and chapter books, 8–12 years. Features books with Christian and Catholic themes.
- **Nonfiction:** Publishes prayer books and books of blessings, 5–8 years; chapter books, 8–12 years; biographies of saints and modern heroes, 9–14 years; Catholic guidebooks, 5+ years; and gift books on saints, favorite Bible stories, and holidays, all ages. Also features books on Roman Catholic activities, traditions, and rituals.
- **Representative Titles:** *After the Funeral* by Jane Loretta Winsch (3–11 years) shows the many ways children express grief. *Amazing Grace! Lord Jesus Lives* by Carol Greene (4–7 years) is a picture book that uses rhyme to teach the Easter story.

Submissions and Payment
Guidelines available at website. Send complete ms for very short submissions; query with summary and writing sample for longer works. SASE. Responds in 4 months. Publication in 2 years. Royalty, 8%; advance, $500.

Editor's Comments
We are looking for imaginative fiction and nonfiction chapter books on Christian themes for the middle reader. We also are always looking for biographies of the saints and modern heroes. All book ideas should be religious in nature and written for the Catholic market.

Lisa Banim, Peachtree Publishers

Picture Books with Great Characters, Events

Editor Lisa Banim finds herself part of an editorial team at Peachtree, where publishing is a team business. "As individuals, we have varied interests," Banim says, "and our books reflect that, but we are also committed as a group to every project and author."

In subject matter, Peachtree projects are highly varied. Banim gives these examples: for the youngest readers, John Butler's *While You Were Sleeping*; humorous, fractured fairy tales or unusual folktales, often starring unsinkable characters, Jackie Mims Hopkins's *The Horned Toad Prince*; hilarious titles, Danny Schnitzlein's *The Monster Who Ate My Peas*; celebrations of childhood moments, Myron Uhlberg's *Flying Over Brooklyn*; and thought-provoking books for older children, *The Yellow Star*, by Carmen Agra Deedy.

The common trait? Passion. "We look for authors who demonstrate a passion for their subjects because we know that that passion will carry through to the books," says Banim. "I particularly love books that feature strong kid or animal characters who have a special outlook on a problem and unusual ways to approach it, as in *Gilbert de la Frogponde*, by Jennifer Rae," says Banim. "I also enjoy stories about characters who find joy or fantasy in everyday events, as in *Flying Over Brooklyn*. I am always intrigued by carefully researched historical picture books that offer an interesting slant on a person or event."

Most important is the power of the manuscript to draw readers in repeatedly. "We choose books that we feel are unique and *special*," says Banim, "the type of stories to which children—and the adults who read to them—will enjoy turning again and again."

(Listing for Peachtree Publishers on following page)

Peachtree Publishers

1700 Chattahoochee Avenue
Atlanta, GA 30318-2112

Submissions Editor: Helen Harriss

Publisher's Interests
Peachtree Publishers is celebrating twenty-five years in the
business. Its catalogue features picture books, chapter
books, young adult books, and parenting titles as well as
books for adults.
Website: www.peachtree-online.com

Freelance Potential
Published 20 titles in 2002: 2 were developed from unsolicited
submissions, 3 were by agented authors, and 5 were
reprint/licensed properties. Receives 20,000 queries yearly.

- **Fiction:** Publishes early picture books, 0–4 years; story picture
  books, 4–10 years; chapter books, 5–10 years; middle-grade
  novels, 8–12 years; and young adult books, 12–18 years. Genres
  include regional and multicultural fiction.
- **Nonfiction:** Publishes early picture books, 0–4 years; story
  picture books, 4–10 years; middle-grade books, 8–12 years;
  and young adult books, 12–18 years. Topics include nature
  and history. Also features parenting and educational titles,
  self-help books, and travel and recreational guides.
- **Representative Titles:** *The Three Armadillies Tuff* by Jackie
  Mims Hopkins (4–8 years) follows the adventures of three
  armadillo sisters. *Play Ball Like the Pros* by Steven Krasner
  (8–12 years) features tips from major league baseball players.

Submissions and Payment
Guidelines available. Send complete ms for works under
5,000 words. Query with résumé, outline, and 2–3 sample
chapters for longer works. Accepts photocopies and computer
printouts. No e-mail or fax queries. SASE. Responds in 4–6
months. Publication period varies. Payment policy varies.

Editor's Comments
We have been publishing books for readers of all ages since
1978. We are a small house and yet we still receive more than
20,000 queries each year. We ask new writers to review several
titles in our current catalogue before querying. We do not publish poetry, fantasy, science fiction, or short stories.

Pearson Education Canada

26 Prince Andrew Place
Don Mills, Ontario M3C 2T8
Canada

Publisher, School Division

Publisher's Interests
Educational materials on science, mathematics, and French-as-a-Second-Language are found in Pearson Education Canada's catalogue. It offers materials for kindergarten through twelfth-grade classrooms, as well as economics textbooks for college students. Computer science and general interest titles for the general public are also available from this publisher.
Website: www.pearsoned.ca

Freelance Potential
Published 36 titles in 2002. Receives 300 queries yearly.
- **Nonfiction:** Publishes mathematics, science, and French-as-a-Second-Language texts, grades K–12. Also publishes business and computer education texts, grades K–12 and up, as well as teacher guides.
- **Representative Titles:** *Relationships* by Judith Campbell (grades 9–10) is a four-color, magazine-style student book that explores issues related to family and friendship and includes a comprehensive teacher guide; part of the Life Choices series. *Canada Today* (grades 9–11) is a history text that takes an issues-based approach to examining Canada in the twentieth century and features real-life case studies, letters, and newspaper articles.

Submissions and Payment
Query with 2 sample chapters. Accepts photocopies, computer printouts, and simultaneous submissions if identified. SAE/IRC. Responds in 1 month. Publication in 3–4 years. Royalty. Flat fee.

Editor's Comments
We are committed to offering the best and most interesting writing around, to enrich the learning experiences of students at all grade levels, and to address the instruction requirements of teaching professionals. We're looking for books that will help educators get results and motivate students. Proposals should describe your book's outstanding and distinctive features.

Peartree

P.O. Box 14533
Clearwater, FL 33766

Publisher: Barbara Birenbaum

Publisher's Interests
Peartree is an educational publisher targeting elementary school and middle-grade students as well as educators, media specialists, and librarians. Its current list includes contemporary and historical fiction as well as nonfiction. 50% subsidy-published material.

Freelance Potential
Published 5 titles in 2002. Receives 100+ queries, 100 unsolicited mss yearly.
- **Fiction:** Published 2 chapter books, 5–10 years. Also publishes easy-to-read books, 4–7 years; and story picture books, 4–10 years. Genres include historical, multicultural, ethnic, religious, and humorous fiction. Also features books on nature and the environment.
- **Nonfiction:** Published 1 middle-grade book, 8–12 years.
- **Representative Titles:** *The Happy Dreidles* by Carrie Wolfberg is an early reader adventure story about two dreidles; includes directions for playing the dreidle game. *Groundhog Willie's Shadow* by Barbara Birenbaum is the story of the albino groundhog whose shadow forecasts the weather.

Submissions and Payment
Query or send complete ms. Accepts photocopies and computer printouts. Availability of artwork improves chance of acceptance. SASE. Responds in 6–8 weeks. Publication in 1 year. Payment policy varies.

Editor's Comments
We are looking for submissions from professional educators working in elementary and middle school classrooms. Original stories that blend fiction and fact are of particular interest to us. We are a small publishing house, and part of our mission is to give new writers a chance to publish their own work. Send us a manuscript that will appeal to our audience—a manuscript that is entertaining as well as educational. As always, we strongly urge writers to take the time to review several titles on our list before submitting a manuscript or query.

Pelican Publishing Company

P.O. Box 3110
Gretna, LA 70054-3110

Editorial Department

Publisher's Interests

With an emphasis on nonfiction, Pelican Publishing Company specializes in books on art, architecture, cooking, history, folklore, and social commentary. It also offers children's books, travel guides, biographies, and textbooks. Its fiction list features historical fiction only.
Website: www.pelicanpub.com

Freelance Potential

Published 91 titles (20 juvenile) in 2002: 54 were developed from unsolicited submissions, 34 were by agented authors, and 14 were reprint/licensed properties. Of the 91 titles, 18 were by unpublished writers and 54 were by authors new to the publishing house. Receives 800 queries, 1,300 unsolicited mss yearly.

- **Fiction:** Published 12 easy-to-read books, 4–7 years; and 1 middle-grade book, 8–12 years. Genres include historical, regional, and holiday-related fiction.
- **Nonfiction:** Published 6 easy-to-read books, 4–7 years; and 1 middle-grade book, 8–12 years. Topics include regional history and social commentary. Also publishes travel guides, cookbooks, biographies, and self-help titles for adults.
- **Representative Titles:** *Who's That Tripping Over My Bridge?* by Colleen Salley (5–8 years) retells the story of the three billy goats Gruff with a Louisiana setting. *L Is for Louisiana* by Cecilia Casrill Dartez (5–8 years) is an ABC book that highlights the features for which Louisiana is famous.

Submissions and Payment

Guidelines available. Query with outline and clips or writing samples. Send complete ms for easy-to-read books only. Accepts photocopies. No simultaneous submissions. SASE. Responds in 3 months. Publication in 9–18 months. Royalty.

Editor's Comments

Your query letter should discuss your book's content, anticipated length, and intended audience. Include your writing or professional background, and any promotional ideas you have.

Pembroke Publishers

538 Hood Road
Markham, Ontario L3R 3K9
Canada

Submissions Editor: Mary Macchiusi

Publisher's Interests

This Canadian publisher offers books for teachers at all grade
levels on subjects such as spelling, phonics, grammar, early
literacy, and school safety. It also offers nonfiction picture
books and chapter books for children under the age of 10, as
well as middle-grade titles.

Website: www.pembrokepublishers.com

Freelance Potential

Published 12 titles in 2002: 1 was by an agented author
and 2 were reprint/licensed properties. Receives 30 queries
each year.

- **Nonfiction:** Publishes chapter books, 5–10 years; and middle-
  grade books, 8–12 years. Topics include history, science, and
  writing. Also offers titles for educators about literacy, spelling,
  grammar, educational assessment, and school safety, as well
  as titles on home-school partnerships.
- **Representative Titles:** *Speak Up! Speak Out!* by Bob & Barbara Greenwood (5–12 years) is a kids' guide to planning,
  preparing, and presenting a speech. *Better Books! Better
  Readers!* by Linda Hart-Hewins & Jan Wells (teachers) offers
  tips on creating a classroom that fosters language learning.

Submissions and Payment

Guidelines available. Query with résumé, outline, and sample
chapters. Accepts photocopies and simultaneous submissions if identified. SAE/IRC. Responds in 1 month. Publication in 6–24 months. Royalty.

Editor's Comments

Our titles for teachers and children are all designed for practical classroom use. Books for kids should motivate them and
convince them that the skills they learn will make a difference;
they should also reflect the experiences and vocabulary of real
children. This year, we are especially interested in titles for
educators working at all grade levels. These books must provide accurate, useful information about the topics they
address, and should include concrete examples.

Sue Thies, Perfection Learning
Accurate & High-Interest Science

Perfection Learning is a 75-year-old, privately owned educational publishing company. It publishes curriculum-aligned titles to supplement science curriculum and provides content-area reading strategy teaching and practice. It also publishes high-interest, below-grade-level science titles for more recreational reading for reluctant readers. Perfection's books are geared to grades 2 to 12.

Editorial Director Sue Thies is looking for high-interest books and cutting-edge science titles, either as single titles or series. She is not interested in picture books.

Accuracy in nonfiction writing for children is important across the board, and especially in science publishing. "When I receive a fact-based manuscript from an author," says Thies, "I need to be assured that the facts have been verified by several sources because if the editors have to fact check everything, they may as well write the books themselves."

It's easier to do research today, but that makes it even more important that the work be accurate. "I know that information is more readily available, thanks to the Internet, but it's important to use reliable sources," says Thies. She prefers to see sample chapters.

(Listing for Perfection Learning Corporation
on following page)

Perfection Learning Corporation

10520 New York Avenue
Des Moines, IA 50322

Editorial Director, Books: Sue Thies

Publisher's Interests
Founded in 1926, Perfection Learning Corporation features
teacher and student curriculum materials for use in
preschools through high schools. Its specialty is high-interest
books for reluctant or below-grade-level readers.
Website: www.perfectionlearning.com

Freelance Potential
Published 100+ titles in 2002: 20 were developed from unso-
licited submissions and 10 were reprint/licensed properties.
Of the 100 titles, 15 were by unpublished writers and 20
were by authors who were new to the publishing house.
Receives 500+ queries yearly.
- **Fiction:** Publishes chapter books, 7–12 years; middle-grade
  novels, 10–14 years; and young adult books, 12–18 years.
  Genres include historical, contemporary, multicultural, ethnic,
  and science fiction; mystery; suspense; humor; folktales; and
  stories about sports.
- **Nonfiction:** Publishes chapter books, 7–12 years; and middle-
  grade books, 10–14 years. Topics include language arts, reading skills, literature, drama, history, social studies, math, science, sports, and multicultural issues.
- **Representative Titles:** *Literature and Thought* (grades 6–10)
  is a highly focused, thematic literature program that teaches
  students to be critical readers and thinkers. *A Multicultural
  Reader* (grades 6–12) is a collection of contemporary literature
  that blends the uniqueness and commonalities of all cultures.

Submissions and Payment
Guidelines available. Query with outline and 2–3 sample
chapters. Accepts photocopies, computer printouts, and
simultaneous submissions if identified. SASE. Responds in 2
months. Publication in 1 year. Payment policy varies.

Editor's Comments
We're primarily looking for books that are written at a reading
level at least two grades below the interest level. Do not submit
children's picture books.

Perigee Books

Penguin Putnam, Inc.
375 Hudson Street
New York, NY 10014

Publisher: John Duff

Publisher's Interests
Perigee Books, an imprint of Penguin Putnam, specializes in reference, self-help, and how-to titles. Its list includes parenting titles, books on family issues, and middle-grade and young adult nonfiction.
Website: www.penguinputnam.com

Freelance Potential
Published 75 titles in 2002: 1 was developed from an unsolicited submission and 74 were by agented authors. Receives 300 queries yearly.
- **Nonfiction:** Publishes middle-grade books, 8–12 years; and young adult books, 12–18 years. Topics include health, fitness, history, social issues, special education, sports, entertainment, pets, and animals. Also publishes how-to, self-help, informational, and reference books for parents
- **Representative Titles:** *The Out-of-Sync Child* by Carol Stock Kranowitz (parents) explains how sensory integration disorder can be confused with other learning disabilities, and helps parents recognize the problem. *The Perigee Visual Dictionary of Signing* by Rod R. Butterworth (parents) is an easy-to-use dictionary format to help readers improve their American sign language skills.

Submissions and Payment
Query. Accepts photocopies and computer printouts. SASE. Responds in 1-3 weeks. Publication in 18 months. Royalty; advance.

Editor's Comment
We specialize in how-to and self-help titles for youth and parents, as well as reference books. Topics include contemporary social and family issues that young people must deal with. Many new writers make the mistake of sending material that we just are not interested in. Take a look at our catalogue before you query us—make sure your topic has not been covered by us before. Please do not send us fiction, literary nonfiction, or memoirs.

Philomel Books

Penguin Putnam Books for Young Readers
345 Hudson Street
New York, NY 10014

Senior Editor: Michael Green

Publisher's Interests

This imprint of Penguin Putnam has a list that includes
picture books for early and emergent readers, middle-grade
titles, and books for adolescents. Philomel Books publishes
nonfiction in a variety of subject areas, as well as fiction of
many genres.
Website: www.penguinputnam.com

Freelance Potential

Published 30 titles in 2002: 8 were developed from unsolicited
submissions, 20 were by agented authors, and 2 were reprint/
licensed properties. Receives 1,500 queries yearly.

- **Fiction:** Publishes early picture books, 0–4 years; easy-to-read
  books, 4–7 years; story picture books, 4–10 years; chapter
  books, 5–10 years; middle-grade novels, 8–12 years; and young
  adult books, 12–18 years. Genres include contemporary, historical, and multicultural fiction and fantasy.
- **Nonfiction:** Publishes story picture books, 4–10 years; and
  young adult books, 12–18 years. Features first-person essays,
  poetry collections, and biographies.
- **Representative Titles:** *The Kingfisher's Gift* by Susan Williams
  Beckhorn (10–14 years) is a novel about a quiet girl who is
  sent to live with her grandmother after her father dies. *When
  Lightning Comes in a Jar* by Patricia Polacco (4–8 years) takes
  readers to an unforgettable family reunion.

Submissions and Payment

Guidelines available with SASE. Query with outline/synopsis
or sample chapters in sequence. Include table of contents for
nonfiction. SASE. Responds in 1–2 months. Publication in
1–2 years. Royalty.

Editor's Comments

We are dedicated to producing quality books for young people
that stretch the limits of their reality, be it culturally, imagina-
tively, historically, or artistically. We are interested in stories
that "ring true"—ones in which the author has a voice of his or
her own. This is true for both fiction and nonfiction.

Phoenix Learning Resources

12 West 31st Street
New York, NY 10001

Executive Vice President: John A. Rothermich

Publisher's Interests
This nonfiction publisher specializes in books for the school
and library markets on a wide range of topics, including
reading comprehension, science, mathematics, critical thinking, and language skills. Its materials are used by educators
working with students in preschool through high school,
older students with marginal reading skills, and students in
English-as-a-Second-Language classes.

Freelance Potential
Published 15 titles in 2002. Receives 75 queries, 30 unsolicited
mss yearly.
- **Nonfiction:** Publishes textbooks for middle-grade and young
  adult students. Also publishes biographies, books for gifted
  and special education students, and titles for use with ESL
  students. Topics include reading, writing, language arts, mathematics, science, social studies, and life and study skills.
- **Representative Titles:** *Taking the High Road* by Capriola &
  Swenson (grades 1–8) is a textbook-workbook program
  designed to make the connection between reading, listening,
  comprehending, and writing. *Sight Words* by Sharon Richard
  (grades K–4) is a developmental reading program that helps
  students master the sight words that hold our language
  together.

Submissions and Payment
Query or send complete ms with résumé. Accepts photocopies, computer printouts, and simultaneous submissions if
identified. SASE. Responds in 1–4 weeks. Publication in 1–15
months. Royalty. Flat fee.

Editor's Comments
For the coming year, we would like to see queries or manuscripts in the following subject areas: reading and math supplementary textbooks for reading age levels eight to fourteen
years, and vocabulary development supplementary textbooks
for reading levels eight to eleven years. Be sure to include your
credentials when submitting your materials to us.

The Pilgrim Press

700 Prospect Avenue East
Cleveland, OH 44115-1100

Editor: Kim M. Sadler

Publisher's Interests

Formerly known as United Church Press, this publisher
offers books for scholarly, trade, and religious audiences. Its
list includes religious curriculum materials and resources
used by clergy and laypeople who work with children.
Although it is an imprint of the United Church of Christ, its
readers include members of many denominations.
Website: www.pilgrimpress.com

Freelance Potential

Published 54 titles in 2002: 23 were developed from unsolicited submissions and 1 was by an agented author. Of the
54 titles, 1 was by an unpublished writer and 12 were by
authors who were new to the publishing house. Receives
200+ queries and unsolicited mss yearly.

- **Nonfiction:** Publishes curriculum materials for church schools;
  educational titles of interest to religious educators, clergy, parents, and care givers; and children's sermons. Also features
  informational titles on religion, social issues, and multicultural
  and ethnic topics.
- **Representative Titles:** *Daughters Arise* by Gloria Koll et al.
  is a Christian guidebook for creating retreats for girls of all
  cultures who are entering womanhood. *Jacob's Ladder* by
  Sekiya Miyoshi (4–8 years) retells the Bible story about two
  very different brothers, Jacob and Esau.

Submissions and Payment

Guidelines available. Query with table of contents and sample chapters; or send complete ms. Accepts photocopies.
SASE. Responds to queries in 6–8 weeks, to mss in 2–3
months. Publication in 9–12 months. Royalty, 8% paperback,
8% cloth; advance. Flat fee for work for hire.

Editor's Comments

Our books explore social issues, critically assess cultural
concerns, and advocate for justice and ethical excellence in
society. We are interested in clear, concise proposals that
state the significance of your work and your background.

Piñata Books

Arte Público Press
452 Cullen Performance Hall
University of Houston
Houston, TX 77204-2004

Publisher: Nicolas Kanellos, Ph.D.

Publisher's Interests
Piñata Books is the children's imprint of Arte Público Press, the oldest and largest publisher of US Hispanic literature. It is dedicated to publishing children's and young adult literature that authentically portrays the themes, characters, and customs unique to US Hispanic culture.
Website: www.arte.uh.edu

Freelance Potential
Published 30 titles in 2002: 2 were by unpublished writers and 2 were by authors who were new to the publishing house. Receives 2,000+ queries, 2,000+ unsolicited mss each year.
- **Fiction:** Published 5 story picture books, 4–10 years; 2 middle-grade books, 8–12 years; and 3 young adult novels, 12–18 years. Features contemporary fiction, anthologies, poetry, and drama.
- **Nonfiction:** Publishes young adult books, 12–18 years. Offers biographies and autobiographies.
- **Representative Titles:** *Uncle Chente's Picnic* by Diane Gonzales Bertrand (3–7 years) is a bilingual picture book about a family's preparations for a special visitor on the Fourth of July. *The Orlando Cepeda Story* by Bruce Markusen (11+ years) chronicles the highs and lows of the career of this professional baseball player who eventually made it to the Hall of Fame.

Submissions and Payment
Guidelines and catalogue available. Query with sample chapter. Will accept complete ms for easy-to-read books. Accepts photocopies and computer printouts. SASE. Responds to queries in 1 month, to mss in 3 months. Publication in 18 months. Royalty. Flat fee.

Editor's Comments
While we prefer to work with Hispanic authors, we are willing to review a proposal for any book that realistically depicts US Hispanic characters and culture. Picture books and young adult titles are particularly welcome.

Pineapple Press

P.O. Box 3899
Sarasota, FL 34230

Executive Editor: June Cussen

Publisher's Interests
This regional press features books about Florida history, events, and culture. Established in 1982, Pineapple Press offers titles for children and adults.
Website: www.pineapplepress.com

Freelance Potential
Published 24 titles (4 juvenile) in 2002: 12 were developed from unsolicited submissions and 3 were by agented authors. Of the 24 titles, 16 were by unpublished writers and 8 were by authors who were new to the publishing house. Receives 1,440 queries yearly.
- **Fiction:** Publishes young adult novels, 12–18 years. Genres include mystery, folklore, science fiction, mythology, and historical fiction relating to Florida. Also publishes adult titles.
- **Nonfiction:** Published 2 middle-grade books, 8–12 years. Topics include sports and travel relating to Florida. Also publishes adult titles.
- **Representative Titles:** *Esmeralda and the Enchanted Pond* by Susan Jane Ryan (7–10 years) follows the journey of a young girl and her dad as they visit a mysterious pond. *Giant Predators of the Ancient Seas* by Judy Cutchins & Ginny Johnston (8–12 years) explores how scientists use fossil clues to learn about the lives and habitats of sea animals.

Submissions and Payment
Guidelines available at website. Query with clips, synopsis, and 3 sample chapters for fiction. Query with table of contents and sample chapters for nonfiction. Accepts photocopies and simultaneous submissions if identified. SASE. Responds in 2 months. Publication in 12–18 months. Royalty.

Editor's Comments
Writers are encouraged to submit material that ties to the history and environment of Florida. Books that can be integrated with the school curriculum are welcome, especially adventure stories and historical fiction.

Pioneer Drama Service

P.O. Box 4267
Englewood, CO 80155-4267

Assistant Editor: Beth Somers

Publisher's Interests

Pioneer Drama Service is a full-service play publisher and drama licensing company. It offers a variety of materials for use by community and educational theaters, including many plays for children. One-act and full-length plays, musicals, and melodramas appear in its catalogue, as well as plays for holidays and special occasions.
Website: www.pioneerdrama.com

Freelance Potential

Published 20+ titles in 2002: 6 were developed from unsolicited submissions. Of the 20+ titles, 10 were by authors who were new to the publishing house. Receives 300+ queries, 300+ unsolicited mss yearly.

- **Fiction:** Publishes plays, 8+ years. Genres include comedy, mystery, fantasy, adventure, folktales, and musicals.
- **Nonfiction:** Publishes books about stage management, scene design, costumes, and acting techniques. Also offers monologue collections and scene books.
- **Representative Titles:** *The Emperor's Nightingale* by Don DiFonso (YA) is an adaption of the Hans Christian Andersen classic about an emperor saddened by the loss of his only child. *The Brementown Musicians* by Gary Peterson is an action-packed story based on the classic Grimm fairy tale about barnyard animals who want to be musicians.

Submissions and Payment

Guidelines available. Query with synopsis and clips or writing samples; or send complete ms with résumé and proof of production. Accepts photocopies, computer printouts, and simultaneous submissions if identified. SASE. Responds to queries in 1 month, to mss in 4–6 months. Publication in 3–6 months. Royalty.

Editor's Comments

We are always on the lookout for new material. We would like to see more one-acts and full-lengths, preferably with large, female-dominant casts.

Pitspopany Press

Suite 16D
40 East 78th Street
New York, NY 10021

Director of Marketing: Dorothy Tananbaum

Publisher's Interests
Fiction and nonfiction books about Judaism are the focus of
Pitspopany Press's publishing efforts. It offers titles written for
toddlers, early readers, middle-grade students, and teenagers
who are members of all branches of the Jewish faith.
Website: www.pitspopany.com

Freelance Potential
Published 11 titles in 2002: 1 was by an agented author. Of
the 11 titles, 1 was by an unpublished writer and 5 were by
authors who were new to the publishing house. Receives 40
unsolicited mss yearly.
- **Fiction:** Publishes early picture books, 0–4 years; easy-to-read
  books, 4–7 years; story picture books, 4–10 years; and middle-
  grade novels, 8–12 years. Genres include religious, historical,
  ethnic, multicultural and science fiction; mystery; adventure;
  fairy tales; and humor.
- **Nonfiction:** Publishes easy-to-read titles, 4–7 years; story picture books, 4–10 years; chapter books, 5–10 years; middle-
  grade books, 8–12 years; and young adult books, 12–18 years.
  Topics include religion, multicultural and ethnic subjects,
  health, fitness, sports, and history. Also offers self-help titles.
- **Representative Titles:** *Back of Beyond* by Dvora Waysman
  (9–13 years) is about a boy in search of a meaningful spiritual
  journey. *Best Friends* by Elisabeth Reuter (6–9 years) is a story
  that introduces children to the *Kristallnacht* and the Holocaust.

Submissions and Payment
Catalogue and guidelines available at website. Send complete
ms. Accepts photocopies and e-mail to pitspop@
netvision.net.il. Availability of artwork improves chance of
acceptance. SASE. Responds in 3 months. Publication in 4–6
months. Royalty; advance.

Editor's Comments
We continue to look for well-written books about Jewish holidays, the Sabbath, and bar and bat mitzvahs. Unpublished
writers should submit via e-mail.

Players Press

P.O. Box 1132
Studio City, CA 91614-0132

Editor: Robert W. Gordon

Publisher's Interests

This well-known theatrical publisher offers plays, dramas, and musicals for all ages, as well as nonfiction titles on subjects related to the theater. Both one-act and full-length plays are found in its catalogue.

Freelance Potential

Published 130 titles (30 juvenile) in 2002: 20 were developed from unsolicited submissions and 4 were reprint/licensed properties. Of the 130 titles, 6 were by unpublished writers and 20 were by authors who were new to the publishing house. Receives 1,200 queries yearly.

- **Fiction:** Publishes full-length and one-act plays, dramas, and musicals for all ages.
- **Nonfiction:** Published 6 middle-grade books, 8–12 years; and 20 young adult books, 12–18 years. Topics include stage management, mime, make-up, television, film, dance, costume, clowning, acting methods, and directing techniques.
- **Representative Titles:** *How to be a Goofy Juggler* features a complete course on juggling. *The Christmas Lamb* by Nellie McCaslin (grades 1–5) is a one-act play based on a European folktale about a pious woodcarver who is inspired to carve toys for children for Christmas.

Submissions and Payment

Guidelines available. Query with résumé, outline, synopsis, production flyer, program, and reviews if available. Accepts photocopies. SASE. Responds in 3–6 weeks. Publication in 3–24 months. Royalty, 10%; advance.

Editor's Comments

We're always on the lookout for new plays that have been produced. All subject matter is of interest, and plays for all venues are welcome. Our audience includes community theater groups, professional players, and amateur and school groups. Keep in mind that we will only consider submissions that include proof of a play's production. If you are submitting a musical, please include a tape of the music.

Playhouse Publishing

1566 Akron-Peninsula Road
Akron, OH 44313

Editorial Department

Publisher's Interests

Children who are beginning readers, as well as those who are
still being read to, are the target market for the books found
on this publisher's list. All of its books are board books and
all are produced on a work-for-hire basis.
Website: www.playhousepublishing.com

Freelance Potential

Published 20 titles in 2002: all were assigned.

- **Fiction:** Published 5 concept books, 5 toddler books, and 5
  early picture books, 0–4 years; and 2 easy-to-read books, 4–7
  years. Genres include adventure, fairy tales, folktales, humor,
  and religious and inspirational fiction.
- **Nonfiction:** Publishes easy-to-read titles, 4–7 years.
- **Representative Titles:** *Bow Wow Blast Off* (3–7 years) teaches
  children about outer space; part of the Little Lucy & Friends™
  series. *Peek-A-Boo Farm* (1–3 years) is a lift-the-flap book that
  teaches children about pigs, donkeys, mice, and chickens; part
  of the Picture Me™ series.

Submissions and Payment

Query with writing sample or résumé. Accepts photocopies,
e-mail submissions (no attachments) to webmaster@
playhousepublishing.com, and simultaneous submissions if
identified. SASE. Responds in 2 months. Publication in 1
year. Flat fee.

Editor's Comments

We are dedicated to finding imaginative ways to inspire young
minds to grow and learn, one book at a time. All of our books
appear under one of our three imprints: Picture Me™ Books,
Nibble Me™ Books, and Little Lucy & Friends™. All of the
books we publish are assigned. If you are interested in working
with us, send us a query that includes a writing sample and a
résumé. Then, if we like your style and feel it would work for
us, we will contact you when an appropriate project comes
along. Writers who can use language creatively and create
innovative rhyming text will get our attention.

Peg Ross, Pleasant Company
Fair Play

Pleasant Company, based in Madison, Wisconsin, is best known for its American Girl Collection of books and dolls aimed at girls ages 8 to 12. It also publishes a series: History Mysteries. "Currently, History Mysteries are the only mysteries we publish," says Acquisitions Editor Peg Ross. Pleasant Company has recently begun publishing a few single titles for their targeted audience. "If a great stand-alone mystery for girls in the 8 to 12 age range came over the transom, we'd certainly consider it."

For Pleasant Company, novels need all the essential elements: "fully realized characters that readers will care about, compelling plot, strong voice." Speaking specifically about mysteries, Ross says, "Our standalone program is still very limited, but I look for an intriguing mystery element and tight, fast-paced plotting with enough clues and red herrings to keep the reader guessing, and to create plenty of tension and suspense." She also looks for what she refers to as "fair play" in a mystery, "the solution of the mystery has to be deducible from the clues given within the story."

In the History Mysteries series specifically, Ross looks for novels where "the mystery significantly affects the protagonist's life or the lives of those she loves, so that she has a powerful personal stake in solving it." Of course, historical mysteries need to have the same "rich sense of the historical and geographical setting and impeccable historical research" she would look for in any historical fiction.

Ross will look at manuscripts or a query and first chapter. "But I certainly wouldn't advise an author to give away the solution to the mystery in her cover letter or query. Novels should feature a female protagonist of an age appropriate for the book's intended audience—which could be anywhere from 7 to 12. At this point, Pleasant Company is not looking for authors or submissions for their History Mysteries series.

(Listing for Pleasant Company Publications
on following page)

Pleasant Company Publications

8400 Fairway Place
Middleton, WI 53562-0998

Submissions Editor

Publisher's Interests

Perhaps best known for its American Girl Collection, this
publisher offers a number of other fiction series for girls ages
eight and up. It also offers craft and interactive activity titles,
as well as advice books for pre-teens that focus on relationships and social issues. It welcomes submissions from freelance writers for all of its book lines.
Website: www.americangirl.com

Freelance Potential

Published 50 titles in 2002: 2 were developed from unsolicited
submissions.

- **Fiction:** Publishes middle-grade novels, 10+ years. Genres
  include mysteries and historical and contemporary fiction.
- **Nonfiction:** Publishes middle-grade titles, 8–12 years. Features
  advice books, activity books, and interactive CD-ROMS. Topics
  include animals, crafts, hobbies, cooking, games, health, fitness, family relationships, divorce, and sports.
- **Representative Titles:** *Spring Pearl: The Last Flower* by Lau-
  rence Yep (8–12 years) features a girl living in Canton, China,
  in 1857 who must live with her father's wealthy benefactor
  after her parents die; part of the Girls of Many Lands series.
  The Feelings Book: The Care and Keeping of Your Emotions
  (8–12 years) offers girls tips on how to express their feelings,
  with advice on handling fear, anxiety, jealousy, and grief.

Submissions and Payment

Guidelines available. Prefers query with first chapter for fiction. Accepts complete ms. Accepts photocopies and simultaneous submissions if identified. SASE. Responds in 3–4
months. Publication period and payment policy vary.

Editor's Comments

This year we launched a new series, Girls of Many Lands,
which features strong 12-year-old heroines from long ago and
from lands around the globe. While this series is primarily
written by acclaimed authors, we will accept proposals from
writers with whom we have not worked in the past.

Polychrome Publishing Corporation

4509 North Francisco Avenue
Chicago, IL 60625-3808

Editorial Department

Publisher's Interests

An independent publisher, Polychrome has found a unique niche by producing books exclusively about Asian-American children. It primarily looks for books about children of Asian heritage who are growing up in the United States.
Website: www.polychromebooks.com

Freelance Potential

Published 3 titles in 2002: all were developed from unsolicited submissions. Of the 3 titles, 1 was by an unpublished writer and 1 was by an author who was new to the publishing house. Receives 3,000 queries yearly.

- **Fiction:** Publishes toddler books and early picture books, 0–4 years; chapter books, 5–10 years; and young adult titles, 12–18 years. Publishes multicultural books that promote racial, ethnic, cultural, and religious tolerance.
- **Nonfiction:** Publishes books about Asian-American culture for families and educators.
- **Representative Titles:** *One Small Girl* by Jennifer L. Chan (pre-K–grade 2) is a rhythmic, whimsical tale about a Chinese-American girl who has fun fooling grown-ups. *Chopsticks from America* by Elaine Hosozawa (grades 4–8) tells the story of two Japanese-American children who go to Japan, only to learn that the country of their forebears is not what they expected.

Submissions and Payment

Send complete ms with résumé. Accepts photocopies, computer printouts, and simultaneous submissions if identified. SASE. Responds in 3–6 months. Publication in 1–2 years. Royalty; advance.

Editor's Comments

Our philosophy is that children need a balanced multicultural education to thrive in today's world. All of the books we publish are written with that philosophy in mind. If you have an idea for a book that will validate the experiences of Asian-American children or educate readers about the Asian-American community, we urge you to contact us.

Portage & Main Press

100-318 McDermont Avenue
Winnipeg, Manitoba R3A 0A2
Canada

Marketing Director: Catherine Lennox

Publisher's Interests
This publisher's catalogue is filled with educational titles for teachers working with students in kindergarten through sixth grade. Portage & Main Press offers resource materials for teaching language arts, science, and social studies, as well as English-as-a-Second-Language materials and assessment tools. It was founded in 1967.
Website: www.portageandmainpress.com

Freelance Potential
Published 8 titles in 2002: 4 were developed from unsolicited submissions. Of the 8 titles, 4 were by unpublished writers and 4 were by authors who were new to the publishing house. Receives 60 queries, 40–50 unsolicited mss yearly.
- **Nonfiction:** Publishes educational titles and professional development resources for teachers working in grades K–6. Also publishes assessment tools and ESL materials. Topics include writing, spelling, reading, art, poetry, theater, science, and social studies.
- **Representative Titles:** *Reading Is Only the Tiger's Tail* by Robert & Marlene McCracken (teachers, grades K–4) is based on the idea that meaning is central to language learning and that children will read to learn and write to say something. *Books Alive! Using Literature in the Classroom* by Susan Hill (teachers, grades K–6) features practical ideas for using authentic literature in the classroom.

Submissions and Payment
Guidelines available with SASE (2 first-class stamps). Query with table of contents and 1 sample chapter; or send complete ms. Accepts photocopies and IBM disk submissions. SAE/IRC. Responds to queries in 1 month, to mss in 1–2 months. Publication in 6 months. Royalty, 8–12%.

Editor's Comments
We're looking for books on assessment and ESL programs, but any title that features new ideas, new activities, or novel ways of teaching elementary schoolchildren will be welcome.

Prima Publishing

3000 Lava Ridge Court
Roseville, CA 95661

Submissions Editor

Publisher's Interests

Founded in 1984, Prima Publishing was recently acquired by
the Crown Publishing Group under Random House. Books
about parenting, education, crafts, health, and travel appear
on its list.

Website: www.primapublishing.com

Freelance Potential

Published 200+ titles in 2002: 100 were developed from
unsolicited submissions, 100 were by agented authors, and
70 were by reprint/licensed properties. Of the 200+ titles, 10
were by unpublished writers. Receives 1,200 queries yearly.

- **Nonfiction:** Publishes how-to and self-help books for children,
  young adults, parents, and teachers. Also offers biographies.
  Topics include natural health, computers, cooking, sports,
  fitness, entertainment, current events, history, nature, the
  environment, science, technology, and religion.
- **Representative Titles:** *Girlwise: How to Be Confident, Capable,
  Cool, and in Control* by Julia DeVillers (YA) offers advice from
  top experts in fields from fashion to martial arts. *The Ultimate
  Book of Homeschooling Ideas* by Linda Dobson (parents)
  includes more than 1,000 learning activities for children
  between the ages of five and twelve.

Submissions and Payment

Guidelines available. Query with table of contents, outline,
and sample chapter. Accepts photocopies, computer printouts, and simultaneous submissions if identified. SASE.
Responds in 1 month. Publication in 6–12 months. Royalty;
advance.

Editor's Comments

Your query should include information about your career experience and educational credentials. Tell us what experience you
have with the subject you are addressing. Queries that generate interest among our editors usually offer information about
the book's market, target audience, and competition. Ideas for
promoting the book are also helpful.

Pro Lingua Associates

P.O. Box 1348
Brattleboro, VT 05302-1348

Senior Editor: Raymond C. Clark

Publisher's Interests
Since 1980, this educational publisher has been offering
textbooks and teacher resources for use at all grade levels of
English-as-a-Second-Language programs.
Website: www.ProLinguaAssociates.com

Freelance Potential
Published 4 titles in 2002: 2 were developed from unsolicited
submissions. Of the 4 titles, 1 was by an unpublished writer
and 1 was by an author who was new to the publishing
house. Receives 40 queries, 10 unsolicited mss yearly.
- **Fiction:** Publishes story picture books, 4–10 years; middle-
  grade books, 8–12 years; and young adult novels, 12–18 years.
  Genres include multicultural and contemporary fiction.
- **Nonfiction:** Published 4 young adult books, 12–18 years; and
  English-as-a-Second-Language materials. Topics include
  writing, comprehension, and reading. Also publishes card
  and board games to strengthen literacy skills, and teacher
  resource materials.
- **Representative Titles:** *Grandparents Are Special* by Allyson
  Rothburd (grades 5–8) is the true story of a girl who learns
  her grandmother can't read. *American Holidays* by Barbara
  Klebanow & Sara Fischer (grades 1 and up) highlights American national holidays as a way of exploring diverse cultures.

Submissions and Payment
Guidelines available. Query with résumé, table of contents,
and sample chapters; or send complete ms. Accepts photo-
copies. Availability of artwork improves chance of acceptance.
SASE. Responds to queries in 1 week, to mss in 3–4 weeks.
Publication in 1 year. Royalty.

Editor's Comments
We take teaching language very seriously. Our books and
materials stress the basics of teaching and learning writing,
reading, listening, and speaking. Many of our authors are
professional ESL teachers, but we will consider submissions
from all writers who understand the importance of literacy.

Prometheus Books

59 John Glenn Drive
Amherst, NY 14228-2197

Editor-in-Chief: Steven L. Mitchell

Publisher's Interests
Books, audio tapes, and journals for the educational, professional, scientific, library, popular, and consumer markets are the focus of Prometheus Books. Well known for its contributions in the areas of philosophy, popular science, and critical thinking, its children's list includes titles for young readers on contemporary issues.
Website: www.prometheusbooks.com

Freelance Potential
Published 2 titles in 2002: 1 was developed from an unsolicited submission. Receives 300 queries, 400 unsolicited mss each year.
- **Nonfiction:** Publishes easy-to-read books, 4–7 years. Topics include social issues, religion, health, sexuality, critical thinking, and decision making.
- **Representative Titles:** *A Birthday Present for Daniel* by Juliet C. Rothman (4+ years) shares the story of a girl whose brother died, and how she commemorates his birthday. *A Solstice Tree for Jenny* by Karen Shragg (4+ years) offers a different way to celebrate winter for a girl whose parents don't observe Christmas.

Submissions and Payment
Guidelines available. Query or send complete ms with résumé and bibliography. Accepts photocopies, computer printouts, and simultaneous submissions if identified. Availability of artwork improves chance of acceptance. SASE. Responds in 2–3 months. Publication in 12–18 months. Payment policy varies.

Editor's Comments
We continue to look for original nonfiction titles that help children age three and up learn about, and cope with, problems they face in their young lives. Interracial issues, death awareness, multicultural and religious beliefs, and decision-making skills are topics that are of interest to us. Send us titles that test the boundaries of established thought.

Publish America

P.O. Box 151
Frederick, MD 21701

Acquisitions Department

Publisher's Interests
Publish America offers a list of fiction and nonfiction books
for young adult and adult readers. Its preference is for stories
about people overcoming challenges in life.
Website: www.publishamerica.com

Freelance Potential
Published 1,000 titles (60 juvenile) in 2002: 600 were developed from unsolicited submissions and 200 were by agented
authors. Of the 1,000 titles, 200 were by unpublished writers
and 800 were by authors who were new to the publishing
house. Receives 3,000 queries, 500 unsolicited mss yearly.
- **Fiction:** Published 10 chapter books, 5–10 years; 20 middle-
  grade titles, 8–12 years; and 30 young adult books, 12–18
  years. Genres include adventure, fantasy, humor, mystery,
  romance, and contemporary, historical, multicultural, and
  Western fiction.
- **Nonfiction:** Publishes young adult books, 12–18 years. Topics
  include current events, entertainment, health, history, multicultural and ethnic issues, religion, social concerns, and special education. Also publishes self-help titles and biographies.
- **Representative Titles:** *Godfree* by Sally Guariglia is the story
  of the friendship between a Canada goose and a mallard duck.
  Adventures of the G. C. Boys: The Cure for Death by Ian Ramos
  is the story of one boy's quest to defeat death.

Submissions and Payment
Guidelines and catalogue available at website. Query or send
complete ms with biography and 9x12 SASE ($1.26 postage).
Accepts photocopies, disk submissions (Microsoft Word or
WordPerfect) and e-mail to writers@publishamerica.com.
SASE. Responds to queries in 1–2 weeks, to mss in 1–2
months. Publication in 10–12 months. Royalty, 8–12%;
advance.

Editor's Comments
We continue to look for writers who can bring us fresh stories
about individuals who overcome challenges in life.

Puffin Books

Penguin Putnam Books for Young Readers
345 Hudson Street
New York, NY 10014

Submissions Editor

Publisher's Interests

Paperback reprints of popular hardcover titles are the mainstay of this publisher, as well as some original fiction. Its list
includes picture books, mysteries, fairy tales, and biographies for young readers through young adults.
Website: www.penguinputnam.com

Freelance Potential

Published 192 titles in 2002. Receives 100+ queries yearly.
- **Fiction:** Published 8 early picture books, 0–4 years; 15 easy-
  to-read books, 4–7 years; 60 story picture books, 4–10 years;
  12 chapter books, 5–10 years; 44 middle-grade novels, 8–12
  years; and 37 young adult novels, 12–18 years. Genres
  include adventure, mystery, romance, historical fiction, and
  science fiction.
- **Nonfiction:** Published 1 story picture book, 4–10 years; and 1
  young adult book, 12–18 years. Topics include science and
  social issues.
- **Representative Titles:** *Hats Off for the Fourth of July!* by
  Harriet Ziefert (4–7 years) follows a town celebration with a
  parade and fireworks. *The Looks Book* by Esther Drill et al.
  (YA) helps young women redefine their concept of beauty while
  emphasizing self-expression, self-invention, and a healthy
  irreverence toward traditional ideals.

Submissions and Payment

Guidelines available. Query with outline/synopsis. Accepts
computer printouts. SASE. Responds in 1–3 months. Publication in 12–18 months. Royalty, 6%.

Editor's Comments

You should be aware that the majority of our titles are
paperback editions of hardcover books. We publish very few
original titles. At times, we will consider middle-grade fiction
or young adult novels. If you are determined to send us a
query about your work, take a look at our catalogue or website before you do, to see if we have already published something similar.

G. P. Putnam's Sons

345 Hudson Street
New York, NY 10014

Manuscript Editor

Publisher's Interests
This publisher creates books for children of all ages, from
birth through the teen years. An imprint of Penguin Putnam
Books for Young Readers, it offers toddler books, picture
books, chapter books, middle-grade titles, and books for
young adults.
Website: www.penguinputnam.com

Freelance Potential
Published 47 titles in 2002: 2 were developed from unsolicited
submissions. Of the 47 titles, 4 were by unpublished writers
and 10 were by authors who were new to the publishing
house. Receives 1,500 queries, 8,000 unsolicited mss yearly.
- **Fiction:** Published 3 toddler books and 13 early picture books,
  0–4 years; 13 story picture books, 4–10 years; 3 chapter books,
  5–10 years; 3 middle-grade novels, 8–12 years; and 5 young
  adult books, 12–18 years. Also publishes novelty books. Genres include contemporary and multicultural fiction.
- **Nonfiction:** Published 2 early picture books, 0–4 years; 3 story
  picture books, 4–10 years; 1 chapter book, 5–10 years; and 1
  middle-grade book, 8–12 years.
- **Representative Titles:** *Hush* by Jacqueline Woodson (12+
  years) is a novel about a girl whose family is relocated as part
  of the witness protection plan. *The Wolf Who Cried Boy* by Bob
  Hartman (4–8 years) is a spoof of the classic tale.

Submissions and Payment
Guidelines available. Send complete ms for picture books.
Query with outline/synopsis and 2 sample chapters for
chapter books. Accepts photocopies, computer printouts,
and simultaneous submissions if identified. SASE. Responds
in 2 months. Publication in 18–36 months. Royalty; advance.

Editor's Comments
We're always interested in chapter books and novels for
middle-grade and young adult readers; these books should
have unusual plotlines or settings. We don't publish books in
series; we prefer to consider individual novels only.

Rainbow Publishers

P.O. Box 261129
San Diego, CA 92196

Editorial Director: Christy Scannell

Publisher's Interests

Rainbow Publishers specializes in classroom resources for Christian educators. Its catalogue features reproducible teacher books of Bible lessons and Bible-based activities, worksheets, and games.
Website: www.rainbowpublishers.com

Freelance Potential

Published 11 titles (5 juvenile) in 2002: 4 were developed from unsolicited submissions and 7 were assigned. Of the 11 titles, 1 was by an author who was new to the publishing house. Receives 1,000 unsolicited mss yearly.

- **Fiction:** Published 3 middle-grade books, 8–12 years. Genres include inspirational and religious fiction. Also offers titles in series, 8+ years.
- **Nonfiction:** Published 2 middle-grade books, 8–12 years. Topics include crafts, hobbies, and religion. Also publishes activity books, 2–12 years.
- **Representative Titles:** *Undercover Heroes of the Bible* introduces children to God's leaders through lessons that include crafts, games, and puzzles. *God's Angels* (5–10 years) features reproducible activities for teaching lessons on angels; part of the Instant Bible Lessons series.

Submissions and Payment

Guidelines and catalogue available with 9x12 SASE (2 first-class stamps). Send complete ms with table of contents and first 3 chapters. Accepts photocopies. SASE. Responds in 3 months. Publication in 1–3 years. Royalty; advance. Flat fee.

Editor's Comments

We're interested in seeing more Bible-based puzzle series for the coming year. Submissions that cover basic topics of faith—such as the Ten Commandments, the Lord's Prayer, and communion—are also among our current needs. Our main focus is on providing educators with resources they can use to teach the Bible. Please do not submit poetry, picture books, or fiction that does not include a Bible teaching.

Raintree/Steck-Vaughn Publishers

14th Floor
15 East 26th Street
New York, NY 10010

Manager of Publishing: Susan Hoffner

Publisher's Interests
Raintree/Steck-Vaughn Publishers targets the school and
library markets with educational titles on science, technology,
health, geography, history, and social studies. Its books are
designed to promote literacy in students in kindergarten
through high school.
Website: www.raintreesteckvaughn.com

Freelance Potential
Published 184 titles in 2002: all were developed from unsolicited submissions. Receives 500 queries yearly.
- **Nonfiction:** Publishes chapter books, 5–10 years; middle-grade
  books, 8–12 years; and young adult books, 12–18 years. Topics
  include social studies, geography, health, mathematics, science, animals, technology, sports, contemporary issues, and
  arts and crafts. Also publishes reference and high-interest/low-
  readability titles and biographies.
- **Representative Titles:** *The Polar Seas* (grades 6–7) helps readers
  investigate life above and below the surface and examines the
  people, plants, and animals that live in and around the water;
  part of the Seas and Oceans series. *Why Do People Fight Wars?*
  (grades 4–6) educates readers on the complexities of war; part
  of the Exploring Tough Issues series.

Submissions and Payment
Guidelines available. Query with outline, 2 sample chapters,
and clips or writing samples. Accepts clear computer printouts and simultaneous submissions if identified. SASE.
Responds in 2–4 months. Publication in 12–18 months. Royalty; advance. Flat fee.

Editor's Comments
It is important for prospective authors to study our catalogue
before submitting a proposal. Send us something fresh and
unique that will supplement the school curricula. All of our
books are published in series, so it's usually best to send an
idea for a book that will fit into one of those existing series.
We'll need to see an outline, sample chapters, and clips.

Rayve Productions Inc.

P.O. Box 726
Windsor, CA 95492

Editor: Barbara Ray

Publisher's Interests
Established in 1989, this small publisher features storybooks
with multicultural themes for children ages four and up, as
well as business and history titles for adults.
Website: www.rayveproductions.com

Freelance Potential
Published 5 titles in 2002: 2 were developed from unsolicited
submissions. Of the 2 titles, 2 were by unpublished writers.
Receives 100+ queries and unsolicited mss yearly.// * **Fiction:** Publishes easy-to-read books, 4–7 years; story picture
  books, 4–10 years; and chapter books, 5–10 years. Genres
  include multicultural, ethnic, and historical fiction; folktales,
  and adventure stories.
* **Nonfiction:** Publishes biographies, 5 years–adult. Also publishes
  history, how-to, and business books for adults, and educational titles for parents and teachers.
* **Representative Titles:** *When Molly Was in the Hospital* by
  Debbie Duncan (3–12 years) addresses the fears and concerns
  of the siblings and families of children who need to be hospital-
  ized. *Nekane, the Lamiña & the Bear* by Frank P. Araujo (6+
  years) is a Basque folktale that pits a quick-witted heroine
  against an unusual villain.

Submissions and Payment
Guidelines available. Query with résumé for adult books.
Send complete ms for children's books. SASE. Responds in 6
weeks. Publication in 1 year. Royalty, 10%; advance, varies.

Editor's Comments
We take pride in our publications, and each project is a team
effort in which the publisher, author, and artist work together
to achieve a quality product. We are looking for unique stories and home-based business books written with energy,
accuracy, and insight. A touch of humor is always appropriate. This year, we are also looking for proposals for biographies, sports stories, ethnic folktales, and other topics suitable for young readers.

Red Deer Press

MacKimmie Library Tower, Room 813
2500 University Drive NW
Calgary, Alberta T2N 1N4
Canada

Children's Editor: Peter Carver

Publisher's Interests
Red Deer Press publishes books about Canada and on topics
of interest to Canadians. It works with Canadian authors and
illustrators only, offering children's picture books as well as
juvenile and young adult fiction.
Website: www.reddeerpress.com

Freelance Potential
Published 9 titles in 2002: 5 were by agented authors and 1
was a reprint/licensed property. Of the 9 titles, 1 was by an
author who was new to the publishing house. Receives 500
queries, 1,500 unsolicited mss yearly.
- **Fiction:** Published 3 story picture books, 4–10 years; 2 chapter
  books, 5–10 years; and 4 young adult books, 12–18 years.
  Genres include regional and contemporary fiction, adventure,
  fantasy, mystery, suspense, drama, and multicultural and
  ethnic fiction.
- **Nonfiction:** Publishes family activity books, 4+ years. Also
  offers Western titles, field guides, biographies, and anthologies
  for adults.
- **Representative Titles:** *Waiting for the Sun* by Alison Lohans
  (4–7 years) is the story of a child who is anxiously awaiting the
  birth of her new sibling. *The Saturday Appaloosa* by Thelma
  Sharp (3–6 years) tells the story of a young girl who overcomes
  her fears to help a trapped horse.

Submissions and Payment
Canadian authors only. Guidelines and catalogue available
with 9x12 SASE. Query with outline and 2 sample chapters.
Send complete ms for picture books and young adult novels.
Accepts photocopies. SASE. Responds in 4–6 months. Publi-
cation in 1–2 years. Royalty.

Editor's Comments
This year, we're specifically looking for young adult books,
picture books for ages four and up, and early-reader novels.
Tell us about your writing experience in your cover letter, and
describe books similar to yours that are now on the market.

Resource Publications, Inc.

Suite 290
160 East Virginia Street
San Jose, CA 95112

Editor: Nick Wagner

Publisher's Interests
Books about Christian ministry and education are the speciality of Resource Publications, Inc. It publishes books in four content areas: catechesis, pastoral ministry, liturgy, and service.
Website: www.rpinet.com

Freelance Potential
Published 12 titles (2 juvenile) in 2002: 2 were developed from unsolicited submissions and 1 was a reprint/licensed property. Of the 12 titles, 4 were by unpublished writers. Receives 120–180 queries yearly.
- **Fiction:** Published 1 young adult book, 12–18 years. Features activity books and educational fiction for adults.
- **Nonfiction:** Published 1 young adult book, 12–18 years. Also features educational titles and books in series. Topics include religion, liturgy, catechesis, pastoral ministry, and books on special education.
- **Representative Titles:** *The Peaceful Parenting Book* by Burt Berlowe et al. (parents) is an easy-to-use reference book designed to build confidence in parents and help them create peaceful families. *Thrills and Skills* by Steff Steinhorst (grades 6–9) is an innovative life-skills course for adolescents that teaches study skills, thinking skills, manners, goal setting and time management.

Submissions and Payment
Guidelines and catalogue available with 9x12 SASE ($1.26 postage). Query with clips. SASE. Responds in 6–8 weeks. Publication in 9–18 months. Royalty, 8% of net.

Editor's Comments
We're looking for books about liturgy that focus on one question: How can we excite people's imaginations to celebrate engaging and exciting worship? We are also interested in ideas about the future trends of catechesis in the church, pastoral ministry programs, and character-building resources for public schools.

Rising Moon

P.O. Box 1389
Flagstaff, AZ 86002

Children's Editor: Theresa Howell

Publisher's Interests
This imprint of Northland Publishing specializes in entertaining and informative picture books for young readers, as well as stories about the American Southwest, fractured fairy tales, and activity books. It no longer publishes books for middle-grade readers or young adults.
Website: www.northlandpub.com

Freelance Potential
Published 15 titles in 2002: 3 were developed from unsolicited submissions and most were by agented authors. Of the 10 titles, 1 was by an unpublished writer and 1 was by an author who was new to the publishing house. Receives 100 queries, 1,800 unsolicited mss yearly.
- **Fiction:** Published 1 concept book, 0–4 years; and 10 story picture books, 4–10 years. Also publishes activity books, novelty and board books, and bilingual Spanish/English books, 4–10 years. Genres include fairy tales, folklore, folktales, humor, and inspirational and multicultural fiction. Also publishes books about the American Southwest.
- **Representative Titles:** *Gopher Up Your Sleeve* by Tony Johnston (5–8 years) features verse about outlandish animals, including gorillas, grasshoppers, and pythons. *Clarence Goes Out West and Meets a Purple Horse* by Jean Eakman Adams (3–6 years) is a friendship story set in the American West.

Submissions and Payment
Guidelines available with 9x12 SASE ($1.72 postage). Accepts picture book manuscripts from agented and previously published authors only. Will accept unsolicited manuscripts for books with Southwest themes. SASE. Responds in 3 months. Publication in 1–2 years. Royalty, varies; advance, varies.

Editor's Comments
We're looking for picture books covering broad subjects with wide appeal and universal themes. We tend to favor books that have wry, humorous story elements. Exceptional bilingual titles (Spanish/English) are also needed.

River City Publishing

1719 Mulberry Street
Montgomery, AL 36106

Acquisitions Editor

Publisher's Interests
River City Publishing is a small press that usually only publishes one children's book a year under its River City Kids imprint. It focuses on children's picture books and young adult novels. 5% self-, subsidy-, co-venture, or co-op published material.
Website: www.rivercitypublishing.com

Freelance Potential
Published 12 titles (1 juvenile) in 2002: 6 were developed from unsolicited submissions and 4 were by agented authors. Of the 12 titles, 5 were by unpublished writers and 7 were by authors who were new to the publishing house. Receives 100 queries yearly.
- **Fiction:** Published 1 easy-to-read book, 4–7 years. Genres include adventure, humor, and multicultural fiction. Also publishes young adult novels.
- **Representative Titles:** *The Alphabet Parade* by Charles Ghigna is a rhyming book that entertains young children while helping them learn to read. *It Was Big, It Was Scary, It Was . . .* by Diana Trenda Aubut & Leslie Cannella Nordness is the story of a boy who learns that the monster under his bed is not nearly so scary when he cleans his room; part of the Elf A. Bits series.

Submissions and Payment
Guidelines available. Query with sample chapters. Accepts photocopies, computer printouts, disk submissions, and simultaneous submissions if identified. SASE. Responds in 1–6 months. Publication in 1 year. Royalty; advance, $1,000–$5,000.

Editor's Comments
We are a small press and publish few titles annually, but we feel that in limiting the number of titles we publish, we are better able to offer both our authors and our booksellers a personal touch. We are not looking for a particular kind of book; our primary concern is quality.

Simon Boughton, Roaring Brook, The Millbrook Press

Picture Books That Jump off the Shelf

Although Roaring Brook is fairly small, it publishes a wide range of picture books under three acquiring editors. Publisher Simon Boughton encourages writers to send him picture books "that tend toward the younger end—toddler, pre-K, kindergarten, and first grade." He does not want board books, but *real* picture books for this age group, an area in which opportunities have "opened up because the retail market really likes these books."

Although Boughton isn't looking for specific topics, he described his ideal books as those "that are accessible." Because chain stores don't hand-sell titles, Boughton looks "for things that sell themselves off the shelf. Parents should immediately feel the child will respond to it." Examples from Roaring Brook's list include *Get to Work, Trucks*, by Don Carter; *Night Train*, by Caroline Stutson; *My Friend Rabbit*, by Eric Rohmann; and *Tickle Tickle*, by Dakari Hru.

Boughton advises authors to submit a picture book manuscript with a brief cover letter—and places emphasis on *brief*. "I glance at the letter to see if I know the name or if they say 'my last book sold 63,000 copies.' Then I'll pay attention. There's not much more you can say in a letter that's useful."

When he reads manuscripts, Boughton looks for pieces with distinct voices. "You want to come away feeling that the author/artist sees the world in a way that speaks to you." He also encourages new writers to read, read, and read some more. "The classic beginner's mistake is telling us everything," Boughton says. "They need to know that the art tells too, that the text is subordinate in terms of detail to the art. Text is the stepping stones on which picture books travel."

Roaring Brook Press

2 Old New Milford Road
Brookfield, CT 06804

Publisher: Simon Boughton

Publisher's Interests
Established in 2001, this imprint of The Millbrook Press features picture books and fiction for children ages 4 to 18. It is interested in humorous middle-grade titles, cutting-edge young adult novels, and early picture books.
Website: www.millbrookpress.net

Freelance Potential
Published 40 titles in 2002: all were by agented authors. Of the 40 titles, 8 were by unpublished writers and 20 were by authors who were new to the publishing house.
- **Fiction:** Publishes early picture books, 0–4 years; middle-grade books, 8–12 years; and young adult books, 12–18 years. Genres include contemporary and historical fiction, mystery, suspense, adventure, drama, and humorous stories.
- **Representative Titles:** *We Wanted You* by Liz Rosenberg (5–9 years) tells the story of an adoption from the parents' point of view, from waiting to meet the baby for the first time through the growth of the family. *Shattering Glass* by Gail Giles (YA) is a suspense story that focuses on the charismatic leader of the senior class and the tragic consequences that result when he challenges the class nerd.

Submissions and Payment
Catalogue available with 8x10 SASE ($2.18 postage). Accepts material through literary agents only. All unagented queries and unsolicited mss will be returned unread. Publication in 1 year. Royalty; advance.

Editor's Comments
Agented authors who submit a middle-grade novel stand a better chance of acceptance here. Do not submit poetry or works of nonfiction. We're not interested in science fiction or fantasy, or anything of a religious or didactic nature. Curriculum-based materials are also inappropriate for our list. We are establishing an author-driven list for the upscale trade market. Since we are a small publisher, we can give each book and author with whom we work the attention they deserve.

Robins Lane Press

10726 Tucker Street
Beltsville, MD 20704

Acquisitions Editor

Publisher's Interests

Robins Lane Press publishes unique and useful books of helpful information and guidance for parents confronting complex issues of society, home, and self. While it published no new titles in 2002, it plans to resume publishing in 2003 with at least one new title a year.

Website: www.robinslane.com

Freelance Potential

Plans to resume publishing (1 or more titles) in 2003.

- **Nonfiction:** Publishes parenting titles that offer information and guidance for parents confronting complex issues of society, home, and self; easy, practical parenting ideas; and activities that engender curiosity and creative play in children.
- **Representative Titles:** *Snacktivities* by MaryAnn F. Kohl & Jean Potter (parents) is filled with edible activities that parents and kids can enjoy making together. *Around the Family Table* by Ronda Coleman (parents) brings families ideas for getting together and discussing issues important to them.

Submissions and Payment

Guidelines available. Query or send complete ms. SASE. Responds to queries in 4–6 weeks, to mss in 6–8 weeks. Publication in 9–12 months. Royalty; advance.

Editor's Comments

It takes a different kind of parent to raise children in today's world. New pressures, new technologies, new dangers, and new possibilities are changing what it means to be a kid. Our goal is to bring parents help and guidance in this new world. We are interested in writers who can offer a fresh take on topics of concern to today's mothers, fathers, and caregivers. We welcome both queries and unsolicited submissions, but we do ask that authors research their ideas thoroughly before submitting a proposal. Know your competition and have a firm grasp of the market. Tell us why we should publish your book—what makes it special and why you are the person to write it. Take the time to review our catalogue first.

Ronsdale Press

3350 West 21st Avenue
Vancouver, British Columbia V6S 1G7
Canada

Submissions Editor: Veronica Hatch

Publisher's Interests
This literary publisher offers middle-grade and young adult titles focusing on Canadian themes. Its historical fiction titles for young adults are accompanied by teachers' guides with additional historical detail, maps, and photographs. It accepts submissions from Canadian citizens and landed immigrants to Canada only.
Website: www.ronsdalepress.com

Freelance Potential
Published 10 titles (2 juvenile) in 2002: all were developed from unsolicited submissions. Of the 10 titles, 5 were by unpublished writers and all were by authors who were new to the publishing house. Receives 300 queries, 1,000 unsolicited mss yearly.

- **Fiction:** Published 1 story picture book, 4–10 years; and 1 middle-grade title, 8–12 years. Also publishes young adult books, 12–18 years. Genres include historical fiction about Canada.
- **Nonfiction:** Publishes adult titles about economics, politics, and language, as well as biographies and autobiographies.
- **Representative Titles:** *Beginnings: Stories of Canada's Past* by Ann Walsh, ed. (8–14 years) is an anthology of Canadian short stories about children who are the first to initiate important historical events. *The Tenth Pupil* by Constance Horne (8–14 years) is a story about overcoming racial prejudice in a 1930's Vancouver Island logging community.

Submissions and Payment
Canadian authors only. Guidelines available. Query with samples; or send complete ms. Accepts photocopies and computer printouts. SASE. Responds in 1–2 months. Publication in 1 year. Royalty, 10%.

Editor's Comments
We continue to look for quality historical fiction of about 120 pages for 8- to 15-year-old readers. We accept works from both new and established writers.

The Rosen Publishing Group

29 East 21st Street
New York, NY 10010

YA/Rosen Central Submissions: Iris Rosoff
PowerKids Press Submissions: Joanne Randolph

Publisher's Interests

A recognized leader in educational materials, The Rosen Publishing Group provides quality nonfiction guidance- and curriculum-based books for young adults. Its list includes titles that help teens make informed decisions about a variety of current issues.
Website: www.rosenpublishing.com

Freelance Potential

Published 500+ titles in 2002: 2 were by unpublished writers and 10 were by authors who were new to the publishing house. Receives 600+ queries yearly.

- **Nonfiction:** Publishes chapter books, 5–10 years; middle-grade books, 8–12 years; and young adult books, 12–18 years. Topics include history, science, health, the arts, animals, sports, safety, and guidance. Also publishes high-interest/low-vocabulary titles and biographies.
- **Representative Titles:** *Cheetahs* by Elizabeth Vogel (pre-K–grade 2) uses photographs to tell about the fastest animal on land. *A Christmas Holiday Cookbook* by Emily Raabe (grades K–5) teaches readers the history of this special holiday and provides recipes for Christmas treats.

Submissions and Payment

Query with outline and sample chapter. Accepts photocopies, computer printouts, and simultaneous submissions if identified. SASE. Responds in 3 months. Publication in 9 months. Royalty. Flat fee.

Editor's Comments

We are looking for material that will empower teens and give them the information they need to make smart decisions about a myriad of issues, including eating disorders, violence prevention, divorce, and self-mutilation. Our new middle school imprint, Rosen Central, is interested in books on science, economics, guidance, and substance-abuse prevention. Send us material that will capture the interest of reluctant readers who need to learn about these issues.

Running Press Book Publishers

125 South 22nd Street
Philadelphia, PA 19103-4399

Assistant to the Editorial Director: Alison Trulock

Publisher's Interests
This publisher offers a number of learning and discovery kits
for children, as well as picture books and puzzle books for
toddlers. Its adult list features books about art and architecture, craft and how-to titles, photo essays, and cookbooks.
Running Press has been in operation for more than 30 years.
Website: www.runningpress.com

Freelance Potential
Published 35 titles in 2002. Receives 800 queries yearly.
- **Nonfiction:** Publishes activity and discovery books for children,
  as well as picture and puzzle books for toddlers. Topics include
  science, technology, art, architecture, geography, and animals.
  Also offers how-to and craft books, quote books, photo essays,
  and cookbooks.
- **Representative Titles:** *The Birthday Box: A Gift of Good Wishes
  to Unlock and Treasure* by Maureen Rissik is an interactive kit
  that lets you celebrate a birthday every month and teaches
  about the zodiac and how birthdays are celebrated around the
  world; part of the Keepsakes™ series. *An Alphabet of Animals*
  by Christopher Wormell reveals a zooful of colorful animal
  images from an award-winning illustrator; part of the Miniature
  Editions™ series.

Submissions and Payment
Catalogue available. Query with outline, table of contents,
and synopsis. Accepts simultaneous submissions if identi-
fied. Availability of artwork improves chance of acceptance.
SASE. Responds in 6–8 weeks. Publication in 6–18 months.
Advance, varies.

Editor's Comments
If you peruse our website or catalogue you'll see that we publish many children's titles, most of which are innovative products designed to combine learning with fun. Our main interest
is in educational nonfiction; don't submit queries for fiction or
poetry books. Artwork is important to us, but don't send original slides, dummies, or photographs.

St. Anthony Messenger Press

28 West Liberty Street
Cincinnati, OH 45210

Managing Editor: Lisa Biedenbach

Publisher's Interests
The goal of St. Anthony Messenger Press is to educate and
inspire Catholics. It produces a list of approximately 15 to 20
books each year for readers of all ages.
Website: www.americancatholic.org

Freelance Potential
Published 25 titles (2 juvenile) in 2002: 5 were developed
from unsolicited submissions and 1 was a reprint/licensed
property. Of the 25 titles, 4 were by unpublished writers and
5 were by authors who were new to the publishing house.
Receives 300 queries yearly.
- **Nonfiction:** Published 1 story picture book, 4–10 years; and 1
  middle-grade book, 8–12 years. Topics include liturgy, the
  sacraments, prayer, spirituality, Scripture, ministry, and religious education. Also offers parenting titles.
- **Representative Titles:** *People of the Bible* by Silvia Gastaldi &
  Claire Musatti (9–12 years) looks at the life and customs of
  people in biblical times. *St. Francis in San Francisco* by Jack
  Wintz, O.F.M., (4–8 years) is a story about what it would be like
  if St. Francis visited the city named for him.

Submissions and Payment
Guidelines available. Query with outline/synopsis. Accepts
photocopies. No simultaneous submissions. SASE. Responds
in 6–8 weeks. Publication in 1–2 years. Royalty, 10%;
advance, $1,000.

Editor's Comments
Most of our books fit into one of the following categories and
we are interested in material for all of them: liturgy and sacraments; prayer and spirituality; Catholic teaching and identity;
and Scripture. Keep in mind that we look for material that is
written in a popular style with ideas that are easy to grasp,
practical, and concrete. Through our books, we endeavor to
evangelize, inspire, and inform those who search for God and
seek a richer Catholic, Christian, human life. Before you send
a query, please take the time to review some of our titles.

St. Mary's Press

702 Terrace Heights
Winona, MN 55987-1320

Middle School Editor: Steven Roe

Publisher's Interests
Saint Mary's Press is a religious publisher specializing in
fiction and nonfiction for children and young adults, ages ten
to nineteen, as well as in books for adults who minister to
youths in a variety of settings.
Website: www.smp.org

Freelance Potential
Published 20 titles (13 juvenile) in 2002: 7 were developed
from unsolicited submissions. Of the 20 titles, 5 were by
unpublished writers and 5 were by authors who were new to
the publishing house. Receives 300 queries, 250 unsolicited
mss yearly.
- **Fiction:** Publishes middle-grade novels, 8–12 years. Genres
  include drama, fantasy, and historical, contemporary, and religious fiction.
- **Nonfiction:** Published 5 middle-grade books, 8–12 years; and
  15 young adult books, 12–18 years. Topics include spirituality
  and religion.
- **Representative Titles:** *The Catholic Youth Bible* by Brian
  Singer-Towns, ed. (YA) is designed to help young people read
  the Bible regularly and make connections to Catholic beliefs
  and traditions. *The Catholic Church* by Carl Koch (YA) is
  designed for use in classes for juniors and seniors in high
  school and explores the main developments, people, and events
  that have shaped the church.

Submissions and Payment
Guidelines available. Query or send complete ms. Accepts
computer printouts, disk submissions (RTF format), and
simultaneous submissions if identified. SASE. Responds to
queries in 2 months, to mss in 2–3 months. Publication in 18
months. Royalty; 10% advance.

Editor's Comments
We are always interested in books that will fit in with the curriculum in middle and high school Catholic classrooms. Please
review our guidelines carefully before submitting a proposal.

Sandcastle Publishing

1723 Hill Drive
P.O. Box 3070
South Pasadena, CA 91031-6070

Submissions Editor

Publisher's Interests

This publisher is committed to helping those who express a desire to improve themselves through participation in the performing arts. Many of its titles include read-aloud parts for children to act out. It also publishes books that encourage post-secondary education in disadvantaged and at-risk youth. Sandcastle Publishing was founded in 1990.
Website: www.childrenactingbooks.com

Freelance Potential

Published 2 titles in 2002: both were developed from unsolicited submissions and 1 was by an unpublished writer. Receives 750–1,000 queries, 400 unsolicited mss yearly.
- **Fiction:** Publishes story picture books, 4–10 years. Features read-along stories that include parts for children to act out.
- **Nonfiction:** Publishes books about acting and the performing arts, as well as titles that promote post-secondary education.
- **Representative Titles:** *Magnificent Monologues for Kids* by Chambers Stevens features more than 100 monologues for children, including monologues specifically for boys, monologues for girls, comedic monologues, and dramatic monologues. *America's Black & Tribal Colleges* by Dr. Janet Wilson Bowman includes listings by state and city of America's tribal and black colleges and offers information about financial aid and admissions policies.

Submissions and Payment

Guidelines available. Query with résumé, synopsis, and marketing analysis for middle-grade and young adult nonfiction. Send complete ms for early reader fiction. SASE. Responds in 2–3 months. Publication period and payment policy vary.

Editor's Comments

We are not interested in reviewing book-length children's fiction this year, nor do we accept picture books for emerging readers. We are primarily interested in books for children that promote acting and the performing arts. Queries should include specific information on age ranges.

Scarecrow Press

4720 Boston Way
Lanham, MD 20706

Acquisitions Editor: Sue Easun

Publisher's Interests

Scarecrow Press offers scholarly, professional, and academic books that target educators, librarians, and school media specialists working with secondary school students. It is interested in well-researched and well-documented titles.
Website: www.scarecrowpress.com

Freelance Potential

Published 250 titles (10 juvenile) in 2002: 5 were by agented authors and 10 were reprint/licensed properties. Receives 500 queries, 250 unsolicited mss yearly.

- **Nonfiction:** Publishes resource materials and reference works for use in secondary schools. Also publishes lesson plans and project ideas, as well as books about children's and young adult literature.
- **Representative Titles:** *The World's Best Thin Books: What to Read When Your Book Report Is Due Tomorrow* by Joni Richards Bodart (grades 6–8) describes 100 readable, attention-grabbing books that have fewer than 200 pages. *Kick Butts: A Kid's Action Guide to a Tobacco-Free America* by Arlene Hirschfelder discusses the history of tobacco use in America and offers advice for remaining tobacco free.

Submissions and Payment

Guidelines available. Prefers query with résumé, table of contents, introduction, chapter summaries, and sample chapter. Accepts complete ms with curriculum vitae. Accepts photocopies, computer printouts, and simultaneous submissions if identified. SASE. Responds to queries in 2 months, to mss in 2–4 months. Publication in 6–12 months. Royalty, 8–15%.

Editor's Comments

We seek proposals that represent new treatments of traditional topics, original scholarship in developing areas, and cogent syntheses of existing research. Proposals should include descriptions of the subject matter, scope and intended purpose of the manuscript, and information about the research methods and data sources you will use.

Frank Schaffer Publications

3195 Wilson Drive NW
Grand Rapids, MI 49544

Submissions Editor

Publisher's Interests
This well-known publisher caters to teachers with supplemental educational material for readers up to the age of twelve. Most of what it publishes focuses on the topics of mathematics, writing, and reading. Frank Schaffer Publications does not publish fiction.
Website: www.mhteachers.com

Freelance Potential
Published 500 titles in 2002. Receives 1,000 queries, 500 unsolicited mss yearly.
- **Nonfiction:** Publishes concept books and toddler books, 0–4 years; and middle-grade books, 8–12 years. Topics include science, mathematics, language arts, phonics, literature, social studies, and early learning. Also offers resource materials for parents and professional educators.
- **Representative Titles:** *Skill Builders* (grades K–6) features grade-specific books with well-placed activities that help students build important skills. *Back to the Classics* (grades 3–8) features re-tellings of classic stories accompanied by dozens of activities to help readers learn the morals and key points of the stories.

Submissions and Payment
Guidelines available. Query with outline, sample pages, and market analysis; or send complete ms. Accepts photocopies and computer printouts. SASE. Responds in 6 months. Publication in 2 months. Royalty. Flat fee.

Editor's Comments
Most of the submissions we receive come from teachers and educators with extensive classroom experience. We welcome new writers with these skills. Most of the titles found on our list are workbooks for reading, math, and writing. Our primary audience includes preschool through middle school students. We do not publish books for children or parents. If you have the necessary qualifications to submit to us, please be sure to research your idea first.

Scholastic Canada Ltd.

175 Hillmount Road
Markham, Ontario L6C 1Z7
Canada

The Editors

Publisher's Interests
Scholastic Canada Ltd. publishes recreational reading for
children and young people in preschool through eighth grade.
It publishes works by Canadian authors only. Both fiction
and nonfiction appear on its list.
Website: www.scholastic.ca

Freelance Potential
Published 70 titles in 2002: 5 were by agented authors and
12 were reprint/licensed properties. Receives 3,000+ queries
each year.
- **Fiction:** Publishes story picture books, 4–10 years; chapter
  books, 5–10 years; middle-grade novels, 8–12 years; and young
  adult books, 12–18 years. Genres include adventure, mystery,
  suspense, humor, sports, drama, and contemporary and historical fiction.
- **Nonfiction:** Publishes concept books and toddler books, 0–4
  years; easy-to-read books, 4–7 years; and middle-grade books,
  8–12 years. Topics include Canadian history, regional subjects,
  animals, crafts, hobbies, technology, and sports. Also publishes
  activity books and biographies.
- **Representative Titles:** *Badger's New House* by Robin Muller
  (4–8 years) is the story of a badger who learns that he is capable of many things. *Footsteps in the Snow* by Carol Matas
  recounts the hardships the Selkirk settlers faced in building
  their homesteads in 1815; part of the Dear Canada series.

Submissions and Payment
Accepts submissions from Canadian authors only. Query
with outline and table of contents; include résumé for nonfiction. Accepts photocopies and computer printouts. No simultaneous submissions. SASE. Responds in 3 months. Publication in 2 years. Payment policy varies.

Editor's Comments
We are once again accepting unsolicited submissions, but only
from Canadian authors. We are interested in fiction and nonfiction for readers up to the age of 14.

Scholastic Inc./Trade Paperback Division

555 Broadway
New York, NY 10012

Editorial Director/Trade Paperbacks: Craig Walker

Publisher's Interests

Fiction and nonfiction for young readers are published by this well-known publisher. The list for the trade division of Scholastic includes adventure stories, mysteries, and science fiction, as well as stories about animals and sports. It currently accepts submissions through agents only.
Website: www.scholastic.com

Freelance Potential

Published 350–400 titles in 2002: all were by agented authors and 12 were reprint/licensed properties. Of the 350–400 titles, 52 were by authors who were new to the publishing house. Receives 250 queries, 150 unsolicited mss yearly.

- **Fiction:** Publishes picture books for all ages, and middle-grade novels, 8–11 years. Genres include science fiction, fantasy, adventure, mystery, and sports stories.
- **Nonfiction:** Publishes books for all ages. Topics include science, nature, and multicultural issues. Also publishes parenting titles and photoessays.
- **Representative Titles:** *How Do Apples Grow?* by Betsy Maestro (5–7 years) describes how apples mature from bud to blossom to fruit. *The House on Hackman's Hill* by Joan Lowery Nixon (9–11 years) follows the adventures of two cousins who are stranded overnight in an old mansion and terrorized by the resident evil spirit.

Submissions and Payment

Agented submissions only. Publication period and payment policy vary.

Editor's Comments

Again this year, we are looking for original middle-grade fiction that can be published in a series. Make sure your stories have strong characters and a plot suitable for eight- to ten-year-old readers. Note that you must have your work submitted through an agent; we do not accept unsolicited manuscripts.

Scholastic Professional Books

557 Broadway
New York, NY 10012-3999

Editorial/Production Coordinator: Adriane Rozier

Publisher's Interests

Language-arts specialists, teacher trainers, and curriculum specialists are the audience for the titles found on this publisher's list. A division of Scholastic Inc., its books cover educational topics for use in preschool through eighth-grade classrooms. It publishes no children's books.
Website: www.scholastic.com/professional

Freelance Potential

Published 120 titles in 2002: 8–10 were developed from unsolicited submissions. Receives 300–400 queries, 150–200 unsolicited mss yearly.

- **Nonfiction:** Publishes titles for educators working with students in pre-K–grade 8. Also offers literature-based and cross-curriculum materials for teaching reading, language arts, mathematics, science, social studies, and art, as well as books on evaluation, assessment, cooperative learning, and classroom management.
- **Representative Titles:** *Fresh & Fun: Teeth* by Jacqueline Clarke (grades K–2) features activities and other creative ideas for teaching about teeth and dental health. *Inventors & Inventions* by Lorraine Hopping Egan (grades 4–8) offers creative cross-curricular activities that teach children about the scientific method.

Submissions and Payment

Guidelines available. Query with outline and 2 sample chapters; or send complete ms. Accepts photocopies, computer printouts, and simultaneous submissions. SASE. Responds in 2 months. Publication in 12–14 months. Royalty; advance. Flat fee.

Editor's Comments

Our goal is to bring teachers the latest ideas for planning and instituting curricula. We cover all subjects and welcome submissions from those familiar with our list. We stress, however, that most of our authors are experienced educators with classroom experience.

Scorpius Digital Publishing

Box 19423
Queen Anne Station
Seattle, WA 98109

Publisher: Marti McKenna

Publisher's Interests
Established in 2000, this electronic publisher specializes in science fiction, fantasy, and horror for juvenile and young adult readers.
Website: www.scorpiusdigital.com

Freelance Potential
Published 20 titles (8 juvenile) in 2002: 2 were developed from unsolicited submissions and all were by agented authors. Of the 20 titles, 2 were by unpublished writers and 12 were by authors who were new to the publishing house. Receives 60+ queries yearly.
- **Fiction:** Published 2 story picture books, 4–10 years; 2 middle-grade novels, 8–12 years; and 4 young adult novels, 12–18 years. Genres include fantasy, folklore, folktales, horror, mystery, suspense, science fiction, historical fiction, and fairy tales. Also publishes books in series, 12–18 years.
- **Nonfiction:** Publishes multicultural and ethnic titles, regional and historical titles, self-help books, biographies, and photo essays, 4–10 years. Also publishes adult titles.
- **Representative Titles:** *The Well* by Jack Cady (YA) is a novel about the supernatural. *Hong on the Range* by William F. Wu (YA) is a rollicking cyber-Western.

Submissions and Payment
Guidelines and catalogue available at website. Query. Accepts e-mail to submissions@scorpiusdigital.com. Responds in 1 week. Publication in 6 months. Royalty.

Editor's Comments
We believe that e-books, the newest form of books with their own functionality, are here to stay. Our mission is to publish the very best science fiction, fantasy, and horror titles in electronic form. New writers have the best chance of success with us by presenting a well-written, engaging book in a professional manner. We continue to need more interactive, hyperlinked titles for all ages. Please do not send us queries for romance, inspirational, or religious books.

Scott Foresman

1900 East Lake Avenue
Glenview, IL 60025

Administrative Assistant: Maria Sandoval

Publisher's Interests
A publisher of curriculum materials, Scott Foresman offers titles for teaching language arts, reading, mathematics, social studies, science, and music to kindergarten through sixth-grade students. Its imprints include Scott Foresman-Addison Wesley and Silver Burdett Ginn. Software, audio-video materials, and online resources are also found in its catalogue.
Website: www.scottforesman.com

Freelance Potential
Published 1,000 titles in 2002. Of the 1,000 titles, 50 were by authors who were new to the publishing house. Receives 350 queries yearly.

- **Nonfiction:** Publishes textbook-based curriculum programs and teacher resources for grades K–6. Subjects include reading, language arts, science, social studies, mathematics, music, spelling, handwriting, technology, early learning, and bilingual education. Also offers educational software, audio and visual materials, and online resources.
- **Representative Titles:** *Mathematics Interactive Big Book* (grade K) is designed for teachers to use in small groups to teach and reinforce math skills. *Penguins on Parade* (grades 1–2) is an easy-to-read mini book that improves phonics and language skills.

Submissions and Payment
Query with résumé, outline, and sample chapters. Accepts photocopies and computer printouts. SASE. Responds in 2 months. Publication in 1–3 years. Royalty. Flat fee.

Editor's Comments
As a leading elementary education publisher, we're interested in seeing queries for new materials for all curriculum areas. We value writing that conveys information in a clear, easy-to-grasp style, and we're open to works that would contribute to our high-quality programs. Ideas for incorporating Spanish with reading, mathematics, science, and social studies programs continue to be an important need.

SeaStar Books

North-South Books
17th Floor
11 East 26th Street
New York, NY 10010

Editor-in-Chief: Andrea Spooner

Publisher's Interests
A division of North-South Books, SeaStar Books features a list of hardcover picture books for young readers, as well as middle-grade novels and chapter books. A limited number of nonfiction titles are also found in its catalogue.

Freelance Potential
Published 25 titles in 2002: 12 were by agented authors and 2 were reprint/licensed properties. Of the 25 titles, 1 was by an author who was new to the publishing house. Receives 50 queries, 1,200 unsolicited mss yearly.

- **Fiction:** Published 2 easy-to-read books, 4–7 years; 12 story picture books, 4–10 years; 2 chapter books, 5–10 years; and 4 middle-grade books, 8–12 years. Genres include contemporary and historical fiction, fairy tales, folktales, adventure, fantasy, and humor.
- **Nonfiction:** Publishes easy-to-read books, 4–7 years; story picture books, 4–10 years; and middle-grade titles, 8–12 years. Topics include animals, pets, history, nature, the environment, religion, and social issues.
- **Representative Titles:** *Good Night, Fairies* by Kathleen Hague (4–7 years) is a bedtime story about the lives of fairies. *Oh Lord, I Wish I Was a Buzzard* by Polly Greenberg (5–8 years) is the story of a little girl who harvests cotton from dawn to dusk with her family.

Submissions and Payment
Send complete ms for short fiction. Query with 3 sample chapters for novels. Query for nonfiction. Accepts photocopies. SASE. Responds in 3 months. Publication in 2–3 years. Royalty, 5–10%; advance, varies.

Editor's Comments
In the coming season, we are especially interested in reviewing submissions of books of Jewish, Hispanic, and other ethnic interests. Manuscripts that will appeal to boys are also a continuing interest, as are middle-grade historical novels and contemporary novels.

Seedling Publications

4522 Indianola Avenue
Columbus, OH 43214-2246

Submissions Editor: Lynn Salem

Publisher's Interests
Founded in 1991 by reading specialists, Seedling Publications offers high-quality books that support and encourage
beginning readers. Some of its titles are also available in
Spanish editions. Assessment tools and training materials for
parents and literacy volunteers are included in its catalogue
as well.
Website: www.seedlingpub.com

Freelance Potential
Published 25 titles in 2002: 5 were developed from unsolicited
submissions. Of the 25 titles, 2 were by unpublished writers
and 2 were by authors who were new to the publishing house.
Receives 200 unsolicited mss yearly.

- **Fiction:** Published 10 easy-to-read books, 4–7 years. Genres
  include adventure, fairy tales, stories about sports, and humor.
- **Nonfiction:** Published 15 easy-to-read books, 4–7 years. Topics
  include science, nature, animals, multicultural events, mathematics, and technology.
- **Representative Titles:** *Where Does the Teacher Sleep?* (4–7
  years) is a humorous story that questions whether the teacher
  sleeps in various locations of the school. *Bridges* by Lynn
  Salem & Josie Stewart (4–7 years) explores a variety of struc-
  tures while connecting the concept of bridges to a child's world.

Submissions and Payment
Send complete ms. Accepts photocopies, computer printouts,
and simultaneous submissions if identified. SASE. Responds
in 6 months. Publication in 1 year. Payment policy varies.

Editor's Comments
We will not review your manuscript unless it appears in an 8-,
12-, or 16-page format (including the title page). Please note
that our maximum length is between 150 and 200 words. We
will only consider reading materials that will assure the success of young, emergent readers. Use natural language, but do
not submit rhyming stories, full-length picture books, poetry
books, or chapter books.

Silver Dolphin Books

5880 Oberlin Drive
San Diego, CA 92121

Submissions Editor

Publisher's Interests

Silver Dolphin Books is a publisher of children's nonfiction.
An imprint of the Advantage Publishers Group, it offers
innovative, interactive novelty books for children under the
age of six, as well as educational nonfiction titles for middle-
grade readers.
Website: www.advantagebooksonline.com

Freelance Potential

Published 55 titles in 2002: all were reprint/licensed properties. Receives 50+ unsolicited mss yearly.
- **Nonfiction:** Published 5 concept books, 5 toddler books, and 5
  early picture books, 0–4 years; 5 easy-to-read books, 4–7
  years; 5 story picture books, 4–10 years; and 10 middle-grade
  books, 8–12 years. Topics include the alphabet, animals, numbers, magic, science, and history.
- **Representative Titles:** *Ancient Greece* by Stewart Ross (8–12
  years) includes a timeline, glossary, and index for reference, as
  well as a fully illustrated display board and a miniature replica
  to build; part of the History in Stone Series. *Desmond Discovers
  Shapes and Colors* (3–5 years) is an oversized laminated board
  book that provides young children with an interactive introduction to shapes and colors.

Submissions and Payment

Guidelines available. Send complete ms. Availability of artwork improves chance of acceptance. SASE. Responds in 1
month. Publication period and payment policy vary.

Editor's Comments

At this time we are only accepting juvenile submissions that
are accompanied by artwork; no submissions of stories without
illustrations will be considered. We use our knowledge of
market trends to publish books that are bold, colorful, and
striking, with broad appeal. All of our books are educational
and developmental in an innovative, creative way. Children not
only read and learn, but interact and play with our books. We
suggest that you read our guidelines before you submit.

Silver Moon Press

Suite 622
160 Fifth Avenue
New York, NY 10010

Managing Editor: Hope Killcoyne

Publisher's Interests

Silver Moon Press publishes fiction and nonfiction titles for middle-grade readers, all marketed to schools and libraries. Its focus is on history and curriculum materials that cover science, social studies, and language arts. Stand-alone titles as well as books in series appear on its list.
Website: www.silvermoonpress.com

Freelance Potential

Published 6 titles in 2002: 4 were developed from unsolicited submissions. Of the 6 titles, 4 were by unpublished writers and 4 were by authors who were new to the publishing house. Receives 100 queries, 80 unsolicited mss yearly.

- **Fiction:** Publishes middle-grade novels, 8–12 years. Genres include historical, multicultural, and ethnic fiction; adventure; mystery; folktales; and books about family issues.
- **Nonfiction:** Publishes chapter books, 8–12 years. Topics include history, politics, geography, civil rights, ecology, nature, the environment, science, and technology. Also publishes biographies and test preparation material for language arts.
- **Representative Titles:** *Ride for Freedom: The Story of Sybil Ludington* (8–12 years) commemorates the vital role a 16-year-old girl played during the American Revolution. *Thunder on the Sierra* by Kathy Balmes (8–12 years) is the story of an orphaned boy and the dangers he faces during the California Gold Rush.

Submissions and Payment

Guidelines available. Query with sample chapters for stand-alone titles. Query with outline, synopsis of each book, and sample chapter of first book for series titles. Accepts computer printouts and simultaneous submissions if identified. SASE. Responds in 2 months. Publication period and payment policy vary.

Editor's Comments

For our historical fiction titles, we have a particular interest in the American Revolution, Colonial times, and New York State history.

Silver Whistle

Harcourt, Inc.
15 East 26th Street
New York, NY 10010

Submissions Editor

Publisher's Interests
Harcourt's Silver Whistle imprint publishes picture books for early readers, longer fiction for middle-grade and young adult readers, and biographies for all ages.
Website: www.harcourtbooks.com

Freelance Potential
Published 14 titles in 2002: 1 was developed from an unsolicited submission and 10 were by agented authors. Of the 14 titles, 1 was by an unpublished writer. Receives 500 queries, 1,500 unsolicited mss yearly.
- **Fiction:** Publishes concept books, toddler books, and early picture books, 0–4 years; easy-to-read books, 4–7 years; story picture books, 4–10 years; chapter books, 5–10 years; middle-grade books, 8–12 years; and young adult books, 12–18 years. Genres include inspirational and contemporary fiction and adventure stories.
- **Nonfiction:** Publishes early picture books, 0–4 years; and story picture books, 4–10 years. Also publishes biographies and books about history.
- **Representative Titles:** *Beverly Billingsly Borrows a Book* by Alexander Stadler (3–7 years) introduces young readers to the world of the local public library. *A Story for Bear* by Dennis Haseley (5–8 years) is a story about a bear who becomes mesmerized by a young woman's stories of far-off lands.

Submissions and Payment
Guidelines available with SASE. Send complete ms for picture books. Send synopsis and sample chapter for longer fiction. Query for nonfiction, biographies, and collections. Accepts photocopies and simultaneous submissions. SASE. Responds to queries in 1 month, to mss in 3 months. Payment policy varies.

Editor's Comments
In longer fiction, we are looking for strong voices and characters in storylines that are involving and that touch the heart. We're also interested in picture books and biographies.

Simon & Schuster Books for Young Readers

1230 Avenue of the Americas
New York, NY 10020

Submissions Editor

Publisher's Interests

Simon & Schuster is now home to many of the most well-known children's imprints, including Simon & Schuster Books for Young Readers, Atheneum Books, Margaret K. McElderry, Aladdin Paperbacks, Simon Pulse, Little Simon, and Simon Spotlight. Fiction and nonfiction for children of all ages are found in its catalogue.
Website: www.simonsayskids.com

Freelance Potential

Published 75 titles in 2002: 60 were by agented authors and 2 were reprint/licensed properties. Receives 2,500 queries each year.

- **Fiction:** Publishes toddler books and early picture books, 0–4 years; easy-to-read books, 4–7 years; story picture books, 4–10 years; chapter books, 5–10 years; middle-grade novels, 8–12 years; and young adult novels, 12–18 years.
- **Nonfiction:** Publishes story picture books, 4–10 years; and middle-grade titles, 8–12 years. Topics include mathematics, science, nature, history, and social issues. Also offers anthologies and biographies.
- **Representative Titles:** *Giggle, Giggle, Quack* by Doreen Cronin (3–7 years) is a story of a duck who outsmarts the farmer's brother. *The Voyage of Patience Goodspeed* by Heather Vogel Frederick (8–12 years) is the story of a nineteenth-century girl whose father takes her on a three-year ocean voyage.

Submissions and Payment

Guidelines available. Query via e-mail only with outline/synopsis and sample chapters to childrens.submissions@simonandschuster.com. Include imprint name in subject line. No unsolicited mss. Responds in 2 months. Publication in 2–4 years. Royalty; advance.

Editor's Comments

Due to recent events, we are no longer accepting query letters or unsolicited manuscripts through the mail. We will consider query letters sent via e-mail only.

Small Horizons

P.O. Box 669
Far Hills, NJ 07931

Publisher: Dr. Joan S. Dunphy

Publisher's Interests
Small Horizons is an imprint of New Horizon Press. It targets
mental health professionals and teachers. Its list features
self-help books that help children learn how to deal with
crises. Topics covered include family issues, adoption, tolerance, self-esteem, peer pressure, and divorce.
Website: www.newhorizonpressbooks.com

Freelance Potential
Published 3 titles in 2002: 1 was developed from an unsolicited submission. Of the 3 titles, all were by unpublished
writers. Receives 100 queries yearly.
- **Fiction:** Publishes story picture books, 4–10 years. Features
  books about psychological and social concerns, coping skills,
  tolerance, and service.
- **Nonfiction:** Publishes self-help titles for children and adults.
  Topics include parenting, family issues, women's rights, minority concerns, politics, multicultural and ethnic issues, relationships, careers, and teaching children.
- **Representative Titles:** *I Am So Angry I Could Scream* by Laura
  Fox (educators) helps teach children how to channel and release
  anger in positive ways. *The Special Raccoon* by Kim Carlisle (4–9
  years) helps children learn about handicaps and love.

Submissions and Payment
Guidelines available. Query with résumé, outline, 2 sample
chapters, and market comparison. Accepts photocopies and
computer printouts. Availability of artwork improves chance
of acceptance. SASE. Responds in 3 months. Publication
period varies. Royalty, 75% net; advance.

Editor's Comments
Our self-help books are written for adults who work with children, as well as for children themselves. All of our titles are
geared toward helping children learn to cope with difficult situations in their lives in ways that are positive instead of self-
destructive. Writers who have professional skills in working
with children are invited to send queries.

Smith and Kraus

P.O. Box 127
Lyme, NH 03768

Submissions

Publisher's Interests
The books found in the catalogue of Smith and Kraus target teachers, directors, and actors who work in amateur and professional theater. Included on its list are monologues, plays, and other resource materials related to drama. It offers a line of books specifically written for performers ages seven to twenty-two, entitled Young Actors.
Website: www.smithkraus.com

Freelance Potential
Published 15 titles in 2002: 1 was developed from an unsolicited submission and 20 were reprint/licensed properties. Receives 240 queries yearly.
- **Nonfiction:** Publishes plays, scenes, and monologues; grades K–12. Topics include dramatic literature from around the world, folklore, and classic tales. Also offers instructional books for teachers; anthologies and collections of work by contemporary playwrights; translations; books on career development; and period and special-interest monologues.
- **Representative Titles:** *Dramatizing Aesop's Fables: Creative Scripts for the Classroom* by Louise Thistle (grades K–8) is a classroom-tested resource that presents the narrative mime approach. *Anyone Can Produce Plays with Kids* by L. E. McCullough gives readers all the basic information they need to stage plays in their community or classroom.

Submissions and Payment
Catalogue available. Query with résumé. Accepts photocopies, computer printouts, and simultaneous submissions if identified. SASE. Responds in 1 month. Publication in 1 year. Royalty; advance. Flat fee.

Editor's Comments
If you are interested in submitting your work to us, please send a query that includes a letter of introduction, a synopsis, and a sample of your writing, as well as any published reviews. Keep in mind that we only publish plays that have been produced. Monologues must also come from produced plays.

Soundprints

353 Main Avenue
Norwalk, CT 06851-1552

Assistant Editor: Chelsea Shriver

Publisher's Interests

A publisher of nature and wildlife books for children from
birth to age ten, Soundprints offers fictional titles that are
based on fact. Its books appear as parts of series, each
adhering to strict specifications. Many of its titles are packaged with a companion toy or audiotape.
Website: www.soundprints.com

Freelance Potential

Published 26 titles in 2002: 2 were developed from unsolicited
submissions and 10 were reprint/licensed properties. Of the
26 titles, 2 were by unpublished writers and 3 were by authors
who were new to the publishing house. Receives 200 queries
each year.

- **Fiction:** Published 10 toddler books, 0–4 years; 8 story picture
  books, 4–10 years; and 8 chapter books, 5–10 years. Publishes
  stories about animals, nature, and the environment. Also offers
  multicultural and adventure stories.
- **Representative Titles:** *Mallard Duck at Meadow View Pond* by
  Wendy Pfeffer (pre-K–grade 2) follows the life of a duck from his
  hatchling days until he flies away to start a family of his own;
  part of the Smithsonian's Backyard series. *Hedgehog Haven* by
  Deborah Dennard (grades 1–4) describes life in an English
  hedgerow community from the viewpoint of a young hedgehog;
  part of the Soundprints' Wild Habitats series.

Submissions and Payment

Guidelines available. Query with clips or writing samples.
Accepts photocopies and computer printouts. SASE.
Responds in 1 month. Publication period varies. Flat fee.

Editor's Comments

As a publisher with strict guidelines and well-defined series,
we are not often able to accept unsolicited manuscripts. Our
authors are most often contracted on a work-for-hire basis,
and they create manuscripts that adhere to our specifications.
Please submit writing samples or published clips if you would
like to be considered for future projects.

Sourcebooks

Suite 139
1935 Brookdale Road
Naperville, IL 60532

Submissions: Peter Lynch

Publisher's Interests
Sourcebooks is primarily a nonfiction publisher with a list of titles that covers such topics as entertainment, history, sports, self-help, business, and parenting. It accepts fiction from agents only, and it is not publishing children's books at this time.
Website: www.sourcebooks.com

Freelance Potential
Published 160 titles in 2002: 5 were developed from unsolicited submissions,155 were by agented authors, and 5 were reprint/licensed properties. Receives 500 queries, 1,500 unsolicited mss yearly.
- **Nonfiction:** Publishes self-help titles. Topics include parenting, single parenting, family issues, childbirth, multicultural issues, and lifestyle issues.
- **Representative Titles:** *Teen Beauty Secrets* by Diane Irons (YA) offers fashion tips and techniques. *The Parenting Bible* by Robin Goldstein & Janet Gallant brings parents answers to the questions they wouldn't ask the pediatrician.

Submissions and Payment
Guidelines and catalogue available. Query with résumé, synopsis, table of contents, 2 sample chapters, and market analysis. Accepts photocopies, computer printouts, and simultaneous submissions if identified. SASE. Responds in 4–6 weeks. Publication in 1 year. Royalty, 6–15%.

Editor's Comments
We are interested in books that will establish a unique standard in their subject area. We look for books with a well-defined, strong target market. We follow a somewhat out-of-date model for book publishing that makes our passion for books central. In short, we believe in authorship. We work with our authors to develop great books that find and inspire a wide audience. We believe in helping develop our authors' careers, and recognize that a well-published, successful book is often a cornerstone.

The Speech Bin

1965 25th Avenue
Vero Beach, FL 32960

Senior Editor: Jan J. Binney

Publisher's Interests
This publisher specializes in books that can be used by
children and adults with communication disorders. Many
of the books from The Speech Bin are used as resource
materials by rehabilitation professionals, such as speech-
language pathologists, audiologists, and occupational and
physical therapists.
Website: www.speechbin.com

Freelance Potential
Published 10 titles in 2002: 5 were developed from unsolicited
submissions. Receives 500+ queries yearly.
- **Fiction:** Publishes picture books, 4–10 years. Features stories
  that deal with stuttering, conversation, phonology, articulation,
  communication, and language skills.
- **Nonfiction:** Publishes concept books and early picture books,
  0–4 years; story picture books, 4–10 years; and middle-grade
  books, 8–12 years. Topics include stuttering, phonology, articulation, and language skills. Also features textbooks and how-
  to titles for parents, speech pathologists, and occupational
  therapists.
- **Representative Titles:** *The Many Voices of Paws* by Julie Dze-
  waltowski Reville shows young stuttering children how to modify their speaking rates and vocal behaviors in a way that's
  easy for them to understand. *RULES: Remediating Unintelligible
  Linguistic Expressions of Speech* by Jane C. Webb & Barbara
  Duckett is a remedial speech program for preschool and elementary children.

Submissions and Payment
Guidelines available with #10 SASE ($.37 postage); catalogue
available with 9x12 SASE ($1.49 postage). Query with
résumé and outline/synopsis. Accepts photocopies. SASE.
Responds in 1–2 months. Publication in 1 year. Royalty.

Editor's Comments
We're always interested in reviewing proposals for well-
researched titles on communications disorders. Tell us your
book's goals and describe the setting it will be used in.

Sports Publishing Inc.

804 North Neil
Champaign, IL 61820

Acquisitions Editor: Mike Pearson

Publisher's Interests
Established in 1989, Sports Publishing features a range of
titles that cover a variety of sports and athletes. It offers
biographies, histories, encyclopedias, and a series for children in grades three to five entitled Kids Superstars.
Website: www.sportspublishinginc.com

Freelance Potential
Published 150 titles (5 juvenile) in 2002. Receives 50 queries
each year.
- **Fiction:** Publishes middle-grade novels, 8–14 years. Features
  stories about sports and athletes.
- **Nonfiction:** Publishes middle-grade titles, 8–14 years. Topics
  include auto racing, baseball, basketball, football, golf, and
  hockey. Also publishes biographies.
- **Representative Titles:** *Mark McGwire: Mac Attack!* by Rob
  Rains (9–14 years) describes how baseball player McGwire
  overcame poor eyesight and various injuries to become one of
  today's most legendary players. *Drew Bledsoe: Patriot Rifle* by
  Mike Shalin (9–14 years) follows the career of this football
  superstar who holds the NFL record for most pass completions
  in a single game.

Submissions and Payment
Guidelines available. Query with outline, synopsis, 2–3
sample chapters, competition analysis, and résumé. Accepts
photocopies, computer printouts, and e-mail queries to
mpearson@sagamore.com. SASE. Response time varies.
Publication period and payment policy vary.

Editor's Comments
We continue to look for authors who can write accurately and
enthusiastically about sports figures and personalities. If you
choose to submit your work to us, be sure to tell us what
makes your book different from all the other sports books
available. Compare your work to others, and highlight the
strengths and weaknesses. You are encouraged to visit our
website to see other titles we have published.

Standard Publishing

8121 Hamilton Avenue
Cincinnati, OH 45231

Managing Director, Consumer Products: Diane Stortz
Managing Director, Church Resources: Paul Leonard

Publisher's Interests
This publisher offers books for children ages ten to twelve, as
well as Bible curriculum materials and resource books for
adults working with Christian children. Picture books, board
books, early reader chapter books, and devotions are all
found in its current catalogue.
Website: www.standardpub.com

Freelance Potential
Published 63 titles (43 juvenile) in 2002: 8 were reprint/
licensed properties. Of the 63 titles, 1 was by an unpublished
writer and 3 were by authors who were new to the publishing
house. Receives 500 queries, 1,500 unsolicited mss yearly.
- **Fiction:** Publishes concept books, 0–4 years; and story picture
  books, 4–10 years. Genres include religious fiction.
- **Nonfiction:** Publishes early picture, concept, and toddler
  books, 0–4 years; story picture books, 4–10 years; and young
  adult books, 12–18 years. Features activity books, coloring
  books, religious education titles, devotionals, and reference
  books, as well as Bible study guides.
- **Representative Titles:** *A Basket Bed for Baby Moses* (2+ years)
  is a lift-the-flap board book about a baby in a basket, a caring
  princess, and a clever sister, which is designed to encourage the
  development of language skills. *One Tiny Baby* by Mark Taylor
  (3–7 years) is a Christmas story that is also a counting book.

Submissions and Payment
Guidelines available. Query with outline/synopsis and 1–2
sample chapters. Send complete ms for picture books only.
Accepts photocopies, computer printouts, and simultaneous
submissions if identified. SASE. Responds in 2–3 months.
Publication in 18 months. Royalty. Flat fee.

Editor's Comments
Many of our children's books are written on assignment or
developed by packagers; only a small portion of our list comes
from freelance submissions. If you are interested in submitting
material, please follow our guidelines carefully.

Starseed Press

P.O. Box 1082
Tiburon, CA 94920

Managing Editor: Jan Phillips

Publisher's Interests

Starseed Press is the children's imprint of HJ Kramer. Its editorial focus is on books that encourage positive values in young readers, as well as those that build self-esteem and promote nonviolence. The titles published by HJ Kramer and Starseed Press appear in the catalogue of New World Library, a publisher of adult titles on inspirational, metaphysical, and New Age topics.

Website: www.nwlib.com

Freelance Potential

Published 2 titles in 2002. Of the 2 titles, 1 was by an unpublished writer and 1 was by an author who was new to the publishing house. Receives 1,500 queries yearly.

- **Fiction:** Published 1 toddler book and 1 early picture book, 0–4 years. Also publishes story picture books, 4–10 years. Genres include inspirational fiction. Also publishes nature stories, and books about personal growth and self-esteem.
- **Representative Titles:** *Positively Mother Goose* by Diane Loomans et al. (4–10 years) is a collection of the classic nursery rhymes rewritten to promote self-esteem, lifelong learning, and innovative thinking. *Bless Your Heart* by Holly Bea is a story of two children exploring the seaside and discovering that all of life is a blessing and a gift from the Creator.

Submissions and Payment

Query. No unsolicited mss. No submissions via fax or e-mail. SASE. Responds in 8–10 weeks. Publication in 6–18 months.

Editor's Comments

We publish titles of an inspirational or spiritual nature, but we do not stress any particular religion or religious beliefs. Books with strong Christian themes are not appropriate for us. Queries for books that encourage self-esteem in children continue to remain among our needs for the coming year. Consult a copy of the New World Library catalogue for an overview of the types of books we publish. You will see that our titles share a common goal—to awaken personal potential.

Stemmer House Publishers

2627 Caves Road
Owings Mills, MD 21117

President: Barbara Holdridge

Publisher's Interests
Focusing on nonfiction, Stemmer House publishes books for young readers up to the age of twelve, as well as adult titles. It does not publish books for young adults.
Website: www.stemmer.com

Freelance Potential
Published 4 titles in 2002: 3 were developed from unsolicited submissions. Of the 4 titles, 1 was by an unpublished writer and 2 were by authors who were new to the publishing house. Receives 1,000–1,500 queries, 900 unsolicited mss each year.

- **Nonfiction:** Published 1 easy-to-read book, 4–7 years; 1 story picture book, 4–10 years; 1 chapter book, 5–10 years; and 1 middle-grade book, 8–12 years. Topics include natural history, art, music, and geography. Also publishes biographies and adult titles.
- **Representative Titles:** *Will You Sting Me? Will You Bite?* by Sara Swan Miller (5–12 years) explores the world of insects and explains how to tell the difference between the harmful and harmless varieties. *The Rainforest Encyclopedia* by Julia Pinkham introduces readers to the animals and plants found in the world's great rainforests.

Submissions and Payment
Guidelines and catalogue available with 9x12 SASE ($1.26 postage). Send complete ms for nonfiction picture books. Query with outline/synopsis and 2 sample chapters for longer works. Accepts photocopies, computer printouts, and simultaneous submissions. SASE. Responds in 2 weeks. Publication in 1–3 years. Royalty; advance.

Editor's Comments
We're declaring a moratorium on fiction picture books at this time. We believe the market is glutted with them, and we're not interested in adding to it. Nonfiction is welcome, but we want only excellence. Send us something original and universal, not something that springs from a current event or fills a vacuum.

Sterling Publishing Company

387 Park Avenue South
New York, NY 10016-8810

Acquisitions Editor: Frances Gilbert

Publisher's Interests

This publisher's juvenile list consists primarily of nonfiction titles. Sterling Publishing Company offers how-to, craft, and activity titles; joke and riddle books; and reference works. It also has a new line of preschool and picture books. It publishes very little fiction.
Website: www.sterlingpub.com

Freelance Potential

Published 200 titles in 2002: 25 were developed from unsolicited submissions, 10 were by agented authors, and 50 were reprint/licensed properties. Of the 200 titles, 20 were by unpublished writers. Receives 500 queries yearly.

- **Nonfiction:** Publishes how-to, activity, craft, and reference books, 0–18 years. Topics include science, math, games, optical illusions, origami, mazes, and magic.
- **Representative Titles:** *Baby Hang On: Hang on Elephant!* by Harry Alexander is a board book for very young readers that tells of a baby elephant's quest to find out why he has a trunk. *Six-Minute Nature Experiments* by Faith Brynie features 40 imaginative science experiments that use household items to demonstrate concepts of nature such as gravity, evaporation, friction, density, and absorption.

Submissions and Payment

Guidelines available. Query with outline. Accepts photocopies, computer printouts, and simultaneous submissions if identified. SASE. Response time varies. Publication in 1 year. Royalty; advance.

Editor's Comments

Innovative books that teach young readers a craft, skill, or activity will capture our attention. If you review our catalogue or log on to our website, you'll find that most of the material we publish takes a very "hands-on" approach. Please note that our primary interests are in the areas of science, math, puzzles, and games. We will also consider ideas for our newer preschool line.

Stoddart Kids Books

895 Don Mills Road
400-2 Park Center
Toronto, Ontario M3B 2T6
Canada

Publisher: Kathryn Cole

Publisher's Interests

Toddlers through teens read the titles developed by Stoddart
Kids Books. Along with picture books and easy-to-read titles,
it offers novels for middle-grade readers and young adults.
Nonfiction about history and science also appears in its cata-
logue. It accepts submissions from Canadian authors only.
Website: www.stoddartkids.com

Freelance Potential

Published 19 titles in 2002: 6 were developed from unsolicited
submissions, 4 were by agented authors, and 1 was a
reprint/licensed property. Of the 19 titles, 6 were by unpublished writers and 10 were by authors who were new to the
publishing house. Receives 600 queries yearly.

- **Fiction:** Published 1 early picture book, 0–4 years; 4 easy-to-
  read books, 4–7 years; 6 story picture books, 4–10 years; 1
  chapter book, 5–10 years; 3 middle-grade books, 8–12 years;
  and 1 young adult book, 12–18 years. Genres include historical and contemporary fiction and suspense.
- **Nonfiction:** Published 3 middle-grade books, 8–12 years. Features books about science and history.
- **Representative Titles:** *I'm a Hop Hop Hoppity Frog* by
  Lawrence Northey (3–7 years) is a rhyming picture book about
  a frog who can't sit still. *A Taste of Perfection* by Laura
  Langston (10+ years) is a novel about a girl who must spend
  the summer at her grandmother's house when her father loses
  his job.

Submissions and Payment

Canadian authors only. Query. No unsolicited mss. SASE.
Responds in 2–3 months. Publication in 12–18 months. Payment policy varies.

Editor's Comments

For beginning readers, we're interested in picture books that
deal with historical or multicultural topics. Most of the young
adult fiction we publish addresses contemporary themes.
Please note that we only accept queries from Canadian writers.

Storytellers Ink Publishing Co.

P.O. Box 33398
Seattle, WA 98133-0398

Editor-in-Chief: Quinn Currie

Publisher's Interests

Storytellers Ink specializes in books that deal with nature, the environment, wildlife, and animals. Its mission is to cultivate compassion and a sense of responsibility toward all living creatures in readers between the ages of two and twelve. All of its titles are distributed free of charge as part of a national literacy program. Approximately ten percent of its titles are no longer under copyright protection.
Website: www.storytellers-ink.com

Freelance Potential

Published 6–8 titles in 2002. Receives 120 queries yearly.
- **Fiction:** Publishes adventure, folktales, fantasy, and multicultural and ethnic fiction, 2–12 years. Features stories about the environment, nature, and animals.
- **Nonfiction:** Publishes biographies and books about the environment, nature, animals, and social issues. Publishes bilingual, multicultural, and ethnic titles.
- **Representative Titles:** *Animal U* by Robertson Davies (grade 6) is a fable about a group of animals who take over a university and assume human roles. *Bishop the Cat and Mrs. Lin* by Amy Reichert (grade 2) tells the story of an abandoned cat who is befriended by a lonely woman and illustrates how acts of kindness can have far-reaching effects.

Submissions and Payment

Send complete ms. Accepts photocopies and simultaneous submissions if identified. SASE. Response time, publication period, and payment policy vary.

Editor's Comments

The mission of our publishing house is to instill in young readers a lifelong passion for reading. We also want them to learn to care about the creatures who share the earth with us, the environment, and the world around us. If you have a story that will help us accomplish that goal and that will both educate and delight our audience, we encourage you send us your manuscript.

Teacher Created Materials

6421 Industry Way
Westminster, CA 92683

Editor-in-Chief: Sharon Coan

Publisher's Interests
This publisher offers classroom-tested educational materials
for use in preschools, elementary schools, and middle
schools. Workbooks, resource materials, and activity titles
dealing with math, writing, geography, social studies, and art
are found in its catalogue.
Website: www.teachercreated.com

Freelance Potential
Published 200 titles in 2002. Receives 360 queries yearly.
- **Nonfiction:** Publishes workbooks and activity books, pre-
  K–grade 12. Topics include art, geography, history, social studies, science, mathematics, reading, phonics, spelling, writing,
  language arts, and technology. Also publishes teacher resource
  materials on student testing, gifted education, multiple intelligences, reading plans, assessment techniques, classroom management, and professional development.
- **Representative Titles:** *Ellis Island Immigration* by Dr. Andi Stix
  & Frank Hrbek (grades 5 and up) simulates a voyage on a ship
  from Europe, investigates the conditions that motivated immigration, and compares the lives of different ethnic groups after
  they settled in America. *My Body* (grades 1–4) describes body
  parts and their functions and includes a life-size human-body
  replica.

Submissions and Payment
Guidelines available. Query with outline or table of contents,
summary, and 10–12 sample pages. Accepts photocopies,
computer printouts, and simultaneous submissions if identified. SASE. Responds in 6 months. Publication in 6–12
months. Flat fee.

Editor's Comments
We seek quality educational materials that have been successfully used in classrooms. We're interested in developing
resources in all subject areas that have practical use in
preschools, elementary schools, and middle schools. Virtually
all of our authors are educators.

Teacher Ideas Press/Libraries Unlimited

Suite A-200, 7730 East Belleview Avenue
Greenwood Village, CO 80111

Acquisitions Editor: Barbara Ittner

Publisher's Interests

Books that offer innovative teaching ideas, practical lessons, and classroom-tested activities are available from this publisher. Its titles cover whole language, literature, and library connections, as well as math, science, and social studies. Most of its titles are written by educators working in kindergarten through high school.
Website: www.lu.com

Freelance Potential

Published 12 titles in 2002: few were developed from unsolicited submissions. Receives 400 queries yearly.

• **Nonfiction:** Publishes curriculum titles. Features bilingual books, grades K–6; and activity books, grades K–12. Also features biographies, professional reference titles, gifted education titles, and regional books. Topics include science, mathematics, social studies, whole language, literature, and library connections.

• **Representative Titles:** *Character Education* by Sharron L. McElmeel (teachers, grades K–5) includes information about picture books, novels, biographies, and nonfiction titles that illustrate character traits. *Literature Lures* by Nancy J. Polette & Joan Ebbesmeyer (teachers, grades 6–8) explains how to use picture books and novels to motivate middle school readers.

Submissions and Payment

Guidelines available. Query with sample chapters, table of contents, and résumé; or send complete ms with résumé. Accepts photocopies, computer printouts, and simultaneous submissions if identified. SASE. Responds in 2–3 months. Publication in 10–12 months. Royalty.

Editor's Comments

We're looking for books by educators, for educators. In your manuscript proposal, you must include information on the scope and purpose of the book, your methodology and presentation, and a sample chapter. Explain the need for your book and how it offers a special approach to its subject.

Teaching & Learning Company

P.O. Box 10
1204 Buchanan Street
Carthage, IL 62321-0010

Vice President of Production: Jill Day

Publisher's Interests

Teachers and parents working with children in preschool through middle school use the supplementary educational materials offered by this publisher. Social studies, science, arts and crafts, mathematics, and responsibility education are among the subjects covered by its resource titles. Its catalogue also includes classroom decorations and banners.
Website: www.TeachingLearning.Com

Freelance Potential

Published 50 titles in 2002: 5 were developed from unsolicited submissions. Of the 50 titles, 2 were by unpublished writers and 3 were by authors who were new to the publishing house. Receives 350 unsolicited mss yearly.

- **Nonfiction:** Publishes educational resource materials for use in pre-K–grade 8. Topics include language arts, social studies, current events, biography, mathematics, computers, science, nature, the environment, animals, pets, holidays, arts and crafts, hobbies, multicultural and ethnic issues, and responsibility education. Also offers materials for gifted and special education classrooms.
- **Representative Titles:** *Character Building* (pre-K–grade 3) is a literature-based theme unit designed to teach honesty, respect, responsibility, and compassion. *Kid Contraptions* (grades K–3) features cross-curriculum science projects that turn everyday items into original contraptions.

Submissions and Payment

Guidelines available. Send complete ms. Accepts photocopies and computer printouts. SASE. Responds in 6–9 months. Publication in 1–3 years. Payment policy varies.

Editor's Comments

We realize that creating a book that we are proud of is truly a team effort. That's why our editorial and production departments work closely with our authors. Our titles enjoy a culturally diverse readership; this diversity should be reflected in the material you send us.

TEACH Services, Inc.

254 Donovan Road
Brushton, NY 12916

Editor: Wayne Reid

Publisher's Interests
This publisher develops nonfiction books for both children and adults on topics such as health, fitness, religion, and history. It also offers biographies and vegetarian cookbooks for adults. TEACH Services, Inc. is a privately owned, Seventh-day Adventist organization established in 1984. 25% self-, subsidy-, co-venture, or co-op published material.
Website: www.teachservicesinc.com

Freelance Potential
Published 45 titles in 2002: 10 were developed from unsolicited submissions and 35 were reprint/licensed properties. Of the 45 titles, 7 were by unpublished writers and 8 were by authors who were new to the publishing house. Receives 200 queries, 40 unsolicited mss yearly.
- **Nonfiction:** Published 3 easy-to-read books, 4–7 years; 4 story picture books, 4–10 years; 6 chapter books, 5–10 years; 8 middle-grade titles, 8–12 years; and 4 young adult books, 12–18 years. Topics include history, health, fitness, nature, and religion. Also offers self-help titles, biographies, and poetry books.
- **Representative Titles:** *Pioneer Stories of the Second Advent Message* by A. W. Spalding tells children about the pioneers of the second advent movement and explains the beginnings of the movement. *Young Eleanor Roosevelt* by Francene Sabin chronicles the young life of this ground-breaking First Lady; part of the Easy Biographies series.

Submissions and Payment
Guidelines and catalogue available at website or with 9x12 SASE ($2.18 postage). Query. Accepts photocopies, IBM disk submissions, and simultaneous submissions if identified. SASE. Responds in 1 week. Publication in 6 months. Royalty, 10%.

Editor's Comments
We look for material that is timely, well written, and has appeal to a clearly defined market. Please note that we do not publish fiction or fantasy.

Texas Tech University Press

P.O. Box 41037
Lubbock, TX 79409-1037

Submissions Editor: Judith Keeling

Publisher's Interests
Books for young adults and adults relating to the American
West are featured by this publisher, as well as titles on a
variety of subjects.
Website: www.ttup.ttu.edu

Freelance Potential
Published 20 titles (2 juvenile) in 2002: 18 were developed
from unsolicited submissions and 2 were by agented authors.
Of the 20 titles, 16 were by unpublished writers and 19 were
by authors who were new to the publishing house. Receives
180–240 queries yearly.
- **Fiction:** Published 2 middle-grade novels, 8–12 years.
  Genres include contemporary fiction, mystery, and suspense.
  Also publishes stories about nature and the environment,
  and poetry.
- **Nonfiction:** Publishes books for children and adults. Topics
  include regional history, Texana, sports, Southwest literature,
  American history, Vietnam studies, science, and nature. Also
  publishes literary criticism.
- **Representative Titles:** *An Ancient Hole* by Eileen Johnson &
  Patricia Martin is an activity book about the history of Lubbock
  Lake. *The Great Storm* by Lisa Waller Rogers (8–12 years) is a
  fictional diary that recounts the Galveston hurricane of 1900.

Submissions and Payment
Guidelines available at website. Query with clips. Accepts
photocopies. Responds in 1–2 months. Publication in 1 year.
Royalty; 10%.

Editor's Comments
At this time, we are interested in books about the American
West, especially biographies, history, natural history, memoirs, and travel. We would also like to see titles on the natural
sciences, classical studies, literature of conflict, and costume
and textile history. All material that merits further consideration is reviewed by outside readers and must be approved by
our editorial committee.

Third World Press

P.O. Box 19730
7822 South Dobson
Chicago, IL 60619

Assistant to the Publisher

Publisher's Interests
For more than 30 years, Third World Press has dedicated itself
to publishing progressive black and African-centered material
that is both life-giving and life-saving to the African-American
community and other African communities in the Diaspora. It
features fiction and nonfiction for children of all ages.

Freelance Potential
Published 6 titles (2 juvenile) in 2002: 2 were developed from
unsolicited submissions and 2 were by agented authors. Of
the 6 titles, 4 were by unpublished writers and 5 were by
authors who were new to the publishing house. Receives 200
queries, 400 unsolicited mss yearly.
- **Fiction:** Publishes concept, toddler, and early picture books,
  0–4 years; easy-to-read books, 4–7 years; story picture books,
  4–10 years; chapter books, 5–10 years; middle-grade novels,
  8–12 years; and young adult books, 12–18 years. Features
  books about African, African-American, and Caribbean life.
- **Nonfiction:** Publishes easy-to-read books, 4–7 years; story picture books, 4–10 years; chapter books, 5–10 years; middle-
  grade books, 8–12 years; and young adult books, 12–18 years.
  Topics include ethnic and multicultural issues.
- **Representative Titles:** *Very Young Poets* by Gwendolyn Brooks
  is an inspiring instructional book for young and beginning
  writers. *The Future and Other Stories* by Ralph Cheo Thurmon
  presents 15 short stories that portray a variety of themes from
  black culture, from jazz to religion.

Submissions and Payment
Guidelines available. Prefers query with synopsis. Accepts
unsolicited mss in July only. Accepts photocopies, computer
printouts, and simultaneous submissions. SASE. Response
time varies. Publication in 1 year. Royalty.

Editor's Comments
We look for the maximum effect of creative expression and cultural enlightenment in all genres, including children's and
young adult titles that may otherwise not have an outlet.

Charles C. Thomas Publishers Ltd.

2600 South First Street
Springfield, IL 62704

Editor: Michael P. Thomas

Publisher's Interests

Books about early childhood, elementary, and high school education are available from Charles C. Thomas. Its catalogue also includes titles on special education, physical education, school psychology, and educational administration. It has been publishing since 1928.
Website: www.ccthomas.com

Freelance Potential

Published 800 titles in 2002: 600 were developed from unsolicited submissions. Receives 600 queries and unsolicited mss yearly.

- **Nonfiction:** Publishes titles for educators, pre-K–grade 12. Topics include early childhood, elementary, secondary, and higher education; reading; research and statistics; physical education and sports; special education; the learning disabled; teaching the blind and visually impaired; gifted and talented education; and speech and language pathology. Also offers some parenting titles.
- **Representative Titles:** *A Human Development View of Learning Disabilities: From Theory to Practice* by Corrine E. Kass & Cleborne D. Maddux presents a strategy for designing day-to-day, individualized lessons for learning disabled students from kindergarten through adulthood. *Improving Leadership in Student Affairs Administration: A Case Approach* by Arthur Sandeen presents case studies that offer insight for those who aspire to become student affairs leaders.

Submissions and Payment

Guidelines and catalogue available at website. Query or send complete ms. Accepts disk submissions. SASE. Responds in 1 week. Publication in 6–8 months. Royalty.

Editor's Comments

Our goal is to publish original, significant titles that will accommodate current educational needs and become standard texts and classics in their fields. We always give prompt and careful consideration to manuscripts submitted to us.

Thompson Educational Publishing

Suite 200
6 Ripley Avenue
Toronto, Ontario M6S 3N9
Canada

Submissions Editor: Keith Thompson

Publisher's Interests

Based in Canada, this educational publisher specializes in books to be used in colleges and universities. Its audience includes both Canadian and US students, and most of the titles that appear in its catalogue concentrate on topics that relate to the social sciences and the humanities.
Website: www.thompsonbooks.com

Freelance Potential

Published 6 titles in 2002: all were developed from unsolicited submissions. Of the 6 titles, 4 were by unpublished writers and 4 were by authors who were new to the publishing house. Receives 20 queries yearly.

- **Nonfiction:** Publishes undergraduate textbooks and single-author monographs for use in undergraduate education. Topics include social studies, sociology, social work, economics, communications, native studies, labor studies, and sports.
- **Representative Titles:** *Testifying on Behalf of Children* by Robin Vogl & Nick Bala (professionals) is designed to be used by those who must testify in court proceedings on behalf of a child or children. *Juvenile Justice Systems* by Nicholas Bala et al. (professionals) looks at how different countries deal with issues related to juvenile crime and violence.

Submissions and Payment

Guidelines available. Query with curriculum vitae and market analysis. Accepts e-mail submissions to publisher@ thompsonbooks.com. SAE/IRC. Response time, publication period, and payment policy vary.

Editor's Comments

Both new and established authors are welcome here. If you have a submission you wish us to consider, please query with your curriculum vitae after studying our guidelines. These guidelines are now available at our website and will give you a good idea of the kinds of material that interest us at this time. Keep in mind that we publish only textbooks related to the social sciences and the humanities.

Tilbury House, Publishers

2 Mechanic Street
Gardiner, ME 04345

Publisher: Jennifer Elliott

Publisher's Interests

This New England publisher features a catalogue that includes children's picture books, teacher guides, and books on subjects related to Maine, New England, and maritime topics. Its children's list targets readers between seven and twelve years of age.

Website: www.tilburyhouse.com

Freelance Potential

Published 9 titles (3 juvenile) in 2002: 5 were developed from unsolicited submissions and 1 was a reprint/licensed property. Of the 9 titles, 1 was by an unpublished writer and 6 were by authors who were new to the publishing house. Receives 300–400 queries and unsolicited mss yearly.

- **Fiction:** Published 1 story picture book, 4–10 years. Genres include multicultural and ethnic fiction. Also features stories about nature.
- **Nonfiction:** Published 1 story picture book, 4–10 years. Topics include multicultural subjects, animals, nature, the environment, history, and social studies.
- **Representative Titles:** *Lucy's Family Tree* by Karen Halvorsen Schreck (grades 3–6) is the story of an adopted girl who learns the true meaning of family—that it comes in many different forms. *Sea Soup: Phytoplankton* by Mary M. Cerullo (grades 3–7) looks at the science of phytoplankton.

Submissions and Payment

Guidelines available. Prefers query with outline/synopsis and sample chapters. Accepts partial ms with outline, or complete ms. Accepts photocopies and computer printouts. SASE. Responds in 1 month. Publication in 1 year. Royalty; advance, negotiable.

Editor's Comments

We continue to seek picture books for children ages seven to twelve that deal with issues of cultural diversity, nature, or the environment. We want books that will appeal to children as well as parents, and to the educational market.

Megan Tingley Books

Little, Brown and Company
Time and Life Building
1271 Avenue of the Americas
New York, NY 10020

Assistant Editor: Alvina Ling

Publisher's Interests

This Little, Brown and Company imprint features story
picture books for young readers, concept and early picture
books for the very young, and nonfiction for middle-grade
readers.
Website: www.twbookmark.com

Freelance Potential

Published 23 titles in 2002: 17 were by agented authors and
1 was a reprint/licensed property. Receives 600+ queries
each year.

- **Fiction:** Published 2 concept books, 3 toddler books, and 1
  early picture book, 0–4 years; and 12 story picture books, 4–10
  years. Also published 2 lift-the-flap books. Genres include contemporary and multicultural fiction and stories about music
  and holidays.
- **Nonfiction:** Published 3 middle-grade books, 8–12 years. Also
  publishes story picture books, 4–10 years; and self-help titles.
  Topics include crafts, hobbies, and multicultural and ethnic
  issues.
- **Representative Titles:** *Bill Grogan's Goat* by Mary Ann Hoberman (4–8 years) is a story about a goat whose appetite for
  clothes gets him in all sorts of trouble. *FEG: Ridiculous Poems
  for Intelligent Children* by Robin Hirsch (10+ years) includes 23
  poems that introduce children to literary and historical figures.

Submissions and Payment

Guidelines available. Reviews materials submitted by literary
agents or sent at the direct solicitation of the editors only. No
unsolicited mss or queries. Accepts photocopies. SASE.
Responds in 2 months. Royalty; advance.

Editor's Comments

Do not send proposals for "genre" novels, such as romance,
mystery, or science fiction stories. We're primarily interested in
books that will appeal to very young children. Picture books
should have fewer than 1,000 words. We also continue to seek
stories that have strong female characters.

Torah Aura Productions

4423 Fruitland Avenue
Los Angeles, CA 90058

Submissions Editor: Jane Golub

Publisher's Interests
This religious publisher specializes in textbooks for Jewish
schools. Its mission is to foster a love of learning and a foundation for learning, while teaching students about Judaism.
Website: www.torahaura.com

Freelance Potential
Published 15 titles (3 juvenile) in 2002. Of the 15 titles, 1
was by an author who was new to the publishing house.
Receives 30 unsolicited mss yearly.
- **Fiction:** Publishes chapter books, 5–10 years; middle-grade
  novels, 8–12 years; and young adult books, 12–18 years.
  Genres include religious and inspirational fiction with Jewish
  themes.
- **Nonfiction:** Publishes story picture books, 4–10 years; chapter
  books, 5–10 years; middle-grade books, 8–12 years; and young
  adult books, 12–18 years. Topics include religion, history, current events, and family issues—all as they relate to Judaism.
  Also publishes books on Jewish law, prayer, and the Bible.
- **Representative Titles:** *Dear Hope . . . Love, Grandma* by Hilda
  A. Hurwitz & Hope R. Wasburn (8–11 years) is a story about a
  grandmother who teaches her granddaughter about the past.
  Sofer, The Story of a Torah Scroll by Dr. Eric Ray (5–12 years) is
  the story of how a Torah is made.

Submissions and Payment
Send complete ms. Accepts photocopies. SASE. Responds in
6 months. Publication in 18 months. Royalty, 10%.

Editor's Comments
Our goal is to get Jewish kids reading about Judaism and
Jewish life. We welcome authors who understand our mission
and are familiar with our books. Keep in mind that our books
are used in the classroom and should be appropriate for such
settings, but that does not preclude them from also being
entertaining and fulfilling. We feel the best way to get children
to want to know about their faith and the history of Judaism is
to bring them to a love of the written word.

Tor Books

175 Fifth Avenue
New York, NY 10010

Children's/Young Adult Editor: Jonathan Schmidt

Publisher's Interests

Founded in 1980, this imprint of Tom Doherty Associates
publishes hardcover and softcover science fiction and fantasy
books for middle-grade, young adult, and adult readers. Its
list also includes some general interest and how-to titles
about science and crafts.
Website: www.tor.com

Freelance Potential

Published 25 titles in 2002: 22 were by agented authors. Of
the 25 titles, 3 were by unpublished writers. Receives 1,200
unsolicited mss yearly.

- **Fiction:** Publishes middle-grade books, 8–12 years; and young
  adult novels, 12–18 years. Genres include fantasy and science
  fiction.
- **Nonfiction:** Publishes middle-grade books, 8–12 years; and
  young adult books, 12–18 years. Features general interest and
  how-to titles, as well as books about science and crafts.
- **Representative Titles:** *The Wood Wife* by Terri Windling is an
  adventure about a woman who changes her life when she
  starts a journey of self-discovery. *Briar Rose* by Jane Yolen is a
  story about a woman who travels to Poland to discover the
  truth about her family and its mysterious beginnings.

Submissions and Payment

Send synopsis and first 3 chapters. Accepts photocopies,
computer printouts, and simultaneous submissions if identified. Availability of artwork improves chance of acceptance.
SASE. Responds in 4–6 months. Publication in 18–24
months. Royalty; advance.

Editor's Comments

Many people ask us: "What are the odds of getting published
by Tor?" The answer is, for very good books, the odds are
excellent. Please be sure to send the first three chapters of
your book. No matter how good your synopsis is, it's difficult
for us to get a good sense of the book if you send us chapters
4, 17, and 32.

Toy Box Productions

7532 Hickory Hills Court
Whites Creek, TN 37189

Submissions Editor

Publisher's Interests
Toy Box Productions is committed to creating quality read-along and audio-interactive storybooks for children, with original illustrations, songs, music, and sound effects.
Website: www.crttoybox.com

Freelance Potential
Published 6 titles in 2002: all were assigned. Of the 2 titles, 1 was by an unpublished writer.
- **Fiction:** Published 2 story picture books, 4–10 years; and 2 chapter books, 5–10 years. Also publishes middle-grade books, 8–12 years; and educational titles, 4–8 years. Genres include Western, historical, and religious fiction.
- **Nonfiction:** Publishes story picture books, 4–10 years; and chapter books, 5–10 years. Also publishes biographies, and history-related audio sets for adults. Topics include history and religion.
- **Representative Titles:** *Holy Moses* (4–10 years) features original sing-along songs that explore the parting of the Red Sea, the Ten Commandments, and the delivery of God's people to the land of milk and honey. *Tombstone: The Town Too Tough To Die* is an audio book that features the stories of the OK Corral, the Crystal Palace, the Earps, and Doc Holliday.

Submissions and Payment
Query with résumé and clips. All work is done on assignment only. Accepts photocopies. Response time and publication period vary. Payment policy varies.

Editor's Comments
We publish books and soundtracks that children can read and listen to. We need books for both parents and children that help strengthen reading skills and memorization, while encouraging quality time together. Our Bible Stories for Kids features character voices and music that make the stories come alive, and our Back Yard Adventure series offers readers an opportunity to meet interesting people as they learn about social and historical events.

Tricycle Press

P.O. Box 7123
Berkeley, CA 94707

Assistant Editor: Abigail Samoun

Publisher's Interests

Tricycle Press features activity books, chapter books, and picture books that help readers ages 2 through 18 understand themselves and the world around them.
Website: www.tenspeed.com

Freelance Potential

Published 20 titles in 2002: 2 were developed from unsolicited submissions, 8 were by agented authors, and 1 was a reprint/licensed property. Of the 20 titles, 5 were by unpublished writers and 10 were by authors who were new to the publishing house. Receives 15,000 unsolicited mss yearly.

- **Fiction:** Publishes concept books, toddler books, and early picture books, 0–4 years; easy-to-read books, 4–7 years; story picture books, 4–10 years; chapter books, 5–10 years; and middle-grade titles, 8–14 years. Also publishes activity books. Topics include nature, the environment, and contemporary issues.
- **Nonfiction:** Published 3 concept books, 0–4 years; 8 story picture books, 4–10 years; and 2 middle-grade books, 8–12 years. Topics include real-life issues, gardening, and cooking.
- **Representative Titles:** *Storm Boy* by Paul Owen Lewis (5–7 years) is a compelling tale about a Haida prince's adventures on the American Northwest coast. *First Book of Sushi* by Amy Wilson Sanger (1–3 years) is a board book that introduces the favorite Japanese finger food.

Submissions and Payment

Guidelines and catalogue available with 9x12 SASE ($1.26 postage). Send complete ms for picture books. Send 2–3 sample chapters for chapter books, or one-half of the manuscript for activity books. No queries. Accepts photocopies, computer printouts, and simultaneous submissions if identified. SASE. Responds in 2–6 months. Publication period varies. Royalty.

Editor's Comments

We suggest that you find a niche or a new angle on a familiar subject and let us know how your book is different from all the others out there.

Turtle Press

P.O. Box 290206
Wethersfield, CT 06129-0206

Editor: Cynthia Kim

Publisher's Interests
Children who are actively involved in, or interested in, the martial arts read the juvenile titles published by Turtle Press. Its catalogue includes books on martial arts fitness, combat arts, self-defense, taekwando, and competitions. It also publishes books about teaching martial arts to children.
Website: www.turtlepress.com

Freelance Potential
Published 6 titles in 2002: 5 were developed from unsolicited submissions. Of the 6 titles, 2 were by authors who were new to the publishing house. Receives 400–500 queries yearly.
- **Fiction:** Publishes chapter books, 5–10 years. Features stories about the martial arts, including adventure stories.
- **Nonfiction:** Publishes chapter books, 5–10 years. Topics include martial arts, self-improvement, fitness, health, sports, and Eastern philosophy.
- **Representative Titles:** *Parents' Guide to Martial Arts* by Ruth Hunter & Debra Fritsch helps parents navigate through the confusing world of martial arts and offers advice on finding the right art, choosing the right school, and evaluating an instructor's teaching methods. *Everyday Warriors* by Ruth Hunter is written to help children understand and apply the values they learn through martial arts.

Submissions and Payment
Guidelines available. Query. SASE. Responds in 2–3 weeks. Publication period and payment policy vary.

Editor's Comments
We will consider submissions for all types of books dealing with the martial arts, including titles on fitness, self-improvement, and Eastern philosophy—but you must send us a tightly focused query that includes specific details about the book's subject matter. Include information about your qualifications for writing the book. If your query appeals to us, we'll ask for an outline, a table of contents, some sample chapters, sample artwork, and a market analysis.

Twenty-First Century Books

2 Old New Milford Road
Brookfield, CT 06804

Submissions Editor: Kristen Vibbert

Publisher's Interests
Supplementary, curriculum-oriented nonfiction books for
teen readers and libraries are offered by this imprint of Millbrook Press. Its catalogue features single titles as well as
series books.
Website: www.millbrookpress.com

Freelance Potential
Published 45 titles in 2002: 10 were by agented authors.
Receives 100 queries yearly.
- **Nonfiction:** Publishes young adult novels, 12–18 years. Topics
  include science, technology, health, medicine, history, social
  studies, contemporary issues, language arts, government,
  politics, and sports. Also publishes biographies and multicultural titles.
- **Representative Titles:** *Alternative Medicine* by Thomas J. Billi-
  teri (grades 7 and up) discusses various treatments and thera-
  pies and explores how alternative medicine differs from Western medicine. *Teen Fathers Today* by Ted Gottfried (grades 7
  and up) looks at the complex and emotional issues of teen
  fatherhood, including attitudes, responsibility, finances, and
  family problems.

Submissions and Payment
Agented submissions only. Query with outline, sample chapter, and publishing history. Accepts simultaneous submissions if identified. SASE. Responds in 2 months. Publication
in 1–2 years. Royalty; advance.

Editor's Comments
We continue to seek material that can be tied to the middle
school and high school curricula, especially in the areas of
math, science, American history, and social studies, as well
as age-appropriate biographies. Research our backlist and be
sure your material is relevant to our publishing program.
Material aimed at teachers and parents are not appropriate
for us. Please note that we do not accept fiction, picture
books, or novelty submissions.

Tyndale House Publishers

351 Executive Drive
Carol Stream, IL 60188

Manuscript Review Committee

Publisher's Interests
Tyndale House is a Christian publisher that offers "resources
that minister to your spiritual needs." Its children's imprint,
Tyndale Kids, offers Bibles, Bible storybooks, and devotional
books, as well as music, videos and games.
Website: www.tyndale.com

Freelance Potential
Published 250 titles (35 juvenile) in 2002: 2 were developed
from unsolicited submissions and 75 were by agented
authors. Receives 500 queries yearly.
- **Nonfiction:** Publishes concept books and toddler books, 0–4
  years; easy-to-read titles, 4–7 years; story picture books, 4–10
  years; middle-grade titles, 8–12 years; and young adult titles,
  12–18 years. Features books about Christian faith. Also publishes parenting books.
- **Representative Titles:** *The Spell* by Bill Myers is a novel about
  a girl who begins a scare campaign complete with spells and
  curses; part of the Forbidden Doors series. *Just Plain Me* (8–12
  years) is a devotional journal for girls that offers an authentic
  and humorous look at the life issues faced by a typical 11-
  year-old girl.

Submissions and Payment
Guidelines available. Accepts work from agented authors,
Tyndale authors, or authors introduced through other publishers only. E-mail submissions to manuscripts@
tyndale.com. SASE. Responds in 3 months. Publication period varies. Royalty; advance. Flat fee.

Editor's Comments
Our mission is to take the truth of Scripture and bring it home
in such a way that kids can understand and get excited about.
We are no longer reviewing unsolicited manuscripts by authors
we are unfamiliar with. You must submit through a literary
agent, have published with us before, or be known to us
through other publishers to have your work considered for
publication.

UAHC Press

633 Third Avenue
New York, NY 10017

Editorial Director: Rabbi Hara Person

Publisher's Interests
As the publishing division of the Union of American Hebrew
Congregations, UAHC Press brings its audience books for "a
lifetime of Jewish learning." Its catalogue offers religious edu-
cational titles for all ages, from preschool to adult students.
Website: www.uahcpress.com

Freelance Potential
Published 22 titles (14 juvenile) in 2002: 10 were developed
from unsolicited submissions, 1 was by an agented author,
and 1 was a reprint/licensed property. Of the 22 titles, 2
were by unpublished writers and 7 were by authors new to
the publishing house. Receives 200 queries, 600 mss yearly.
- **Fiction:** Published 2 story picture books, 4–10 years. Also publishes early picture books, 0–4 years. Genres include Judaism,
  Bible stories, and religious and historical fiction.
- **Nonfiction:** Published 1 toddler book and 1 early picture book,
  0–4 years; 1 chapter book, 5–10 years; and 3 young adult
  books, 12–18 years. Topics include Jewish history, holidays,
  the Holocaust, and Hebrew. Also publishes bar and bat mitz-
  vah study guides.
- **Representative Titles:** *The High Holy Days* by Camille Kress
  introduces early learners and young readers to the symbols
  and themes of the High Holidays and Jewish autumn festivals.
  Jewish U by Scott Aaron (YA) is a hands-on guide to "living
  Jewish" on a college campus.

Submissions and Payment
Guidelines available. Query with résumé, outline, and 2 sample chapters. Send complete ms for picture books. Accepts
photocopies, computer printouts, and simultaneous submissions if identified. SASE. Response time and publication
period vary. Royalty; advance.

Editor's Comments
For the coming year, we'd like to see more in the way of text-
book material, as well as nonfiction and picture books on Jewish topics. Please don't send young adult fiction at this time.

Upstart Books

P.O. Box 800
Fort Atkinson, WI 53538-0800

Publications Director: Matt Mulder

Publisher's Interests

Formerly known as Highsmith Press, this publisher offers
resources for teachers, librarians, media specialists, and others
who work with children in classroom or library settings. Its
titles reinforce library, Internet, and reading skills in elemen-
tary-grade through high school students.
Website: www.highsmith.com

Freelance Potential

Published 12 titles in 2002: 3 were developed from unsolicited
submissions. Of the 12 titles, 3 were by unpublished writers
and 3 were by authors who were new to the publishing house.
Receives 150 queries, 75 unsolicited mss yearly.

- **Nonfiction:** Publishes elementary and middle-grade titles, 6–12
  years. Also features educational resource materials for teachers
  and librarians, pre-K–grade 12. Topics include storytelling,
  study skills, and literature activities.
- **Representative Titles:** *A Travel Guide Through Children's Literature* by Hope Blecher-Sass et al. (pre-K–grade 6) is a bibliography of children's books that provides websites and contact
  information for the real places that are the settings of each
  book. *Crash, Bang, Boom* by Karen Gibson (grades K–6) uses
  popular children's books to introduce and reinforce such literary devices as alliteration, characterization, cause and effect,
  simile, and metaphor.

Submissions and Payment

Prefers query with outline or sample chapters for manuscripts longer than 100 pages. Prefers complete ms for
shorter works. Accepts photocopies and computer printouts.
SASE. Responds in 2 months. Publication period varies.
Royalty, 10–12%; advance.

Editor's Comments

Many of our titles are written by teachers, librarians, and
media specialists. We continue to seek resource books that
teach and reinforce library and Internet skills, as well as reading enrichment titles and books on the skill of storytelling.

UXL

27500 Drake Road
Farmington Hills, MI 48331-3535

Publisher: Thomas Romig

Publisher's Interests
This imprint of the Gale Group features illustrated, easy-to-read reference titles for students in middle school. It offers titles both online and in print on subjects such as history, social studies, literature, science, technology, the arts, sports, and careers.
Website: www.gale.com/uxl/index.htm

Freelance Potential
Published 20 titles in 2002. Of the 20 titles, 10 were by authors who were new to the publishing house.
- **Nonfiction:** Publishes middle-grade titles, 8–12 years. Topics include science, health, nutrition, history, social studies, current events, multicultural subjects, and careers. Features curriculum-based reference books and encyclopedias.
- **Representative Titles:** *Constitutional Amendments: From Freedom of Speech to Prohibition* (grades 6–8) is a three-volume resource that covers each of the 27 amendments and the unratified amendments and provides the history and social context of the amendment process. *African Biography* (grades 6–8) is a biographical resource that profiles 75 current and historical African figures, including writers, artists, politicians, and religious leaders.

Submissions and Payment
Catalogue available at website. Query with résumé and writing samples. Accepts photocopies and computer printouts. No simultaneous submissions. Response time varies. Publication period varies. Flat fee.

Editor's Comments
Log on to our website; you'll see that we look for ideas for easy-to-read reference materials that make learning fun. If you have experience with educational writing, contact us. Send a résumé and a description of your credentials; if we have a project that's appropriate for you, we will contact you. Because we are primarily interested in titles for our existing series, we discourage submissions of complete manuscripts.

J. Weston Walch, Publisher

P.O. Box 658
321 Valley Street
Portland, ME 04104-0658

Editor-in-Chief: Susan Blair

Publisher's Interests
This publisher specializes in supplemental educational materials for middle school, high school, and adult education classrooms. J. Weston Walch's titles cover language arts, social studies, mathematics, and science, as well as school-to-career transitions.
Website: www.walch.com

Freelance Potential
Published 55 titles in 2002. Receives 400 queries yearly.
- **Nonfiction:** Publishes young adult books, 12–18 years. Features curriculum materials on reading, language arts, mathematics, science, social studies, and art. Also offers books about careers, special education titles, and books for teachers and guidance counselors.
- **Representative Titles:** *Understanding and Using Good Grammar* by Genevieve Walberg Schaefer (grades 8 and up) includes 150 reproducible lessons, exercises, and tests to assist students with the more complicated points of grammar. *Multicultural Science and Math Connections* by Beatrice Lumpkin et al. (grades 5–9) features readings and activities that help students explore discoveries, scientists, and mathematicians from underrepresented cultures.

Submissions and Payment
Guidelines available. Query with résumé, outline, table of contents, and sample chapter. Accepts photocopies and simultaneous submissions if identified. SASE. Responds in 2–4 months. Publication period varies. Royalty. Flat fee.

Editor's Comments
Please remember that we are not a fiction publisher; don't send children's storybooks or novels. We are interested in practical teaching tools that have been successfully used in classrooms. This year, we are mainly interested in English and language arts resource materials, but we also will consider titles that relate to the mathematics, science, and social studies middle school and high school curricula.

Walker and Company

435 Hudson Street
New York, NY 10014

Submissions Editor

Publisher's Interests
Established in 1961, Walker and Company publishes both
fiction and nonfiction children's books, including picture
books and middle-grade and young adult titles.
Website: www.walkerbooks.com

Freelance Potential
Published 32 titles in 2002: 1 was developed from an unsolicited submission, 10 were by agented authors, and 3 were
reprint/licensed properties. Of the 32 titles, 1 was by an
unpublished writer and 10 were by authors who were new to
the publishing house. Receives 600 queries, 1,900 unsolicited
mss yearly.

- **Fiction:** Published 1 early picture book, 0–4 years; 9 story picture books, 4–10 years; 2 middle-grade novels, 8–12 years; and
  3 young adult books, 12–18 years. Genres include historical
  and contemporary fiction.
- **Nonfiction:** Published 1 concept book, 0–4 years; 8 story picture books, 4–10 years; 6 middle-grade books, 8–12 years; and
  1 young adult book, 12–18 years. Topics include social issues
  and history. Also publishes biographies.
- **Representative Titles:** *Are Trees Alive?* by Debbie S. Miller
  (3–7 years) tells young readers how trees live and grow, and
  how they get their food. *Champion: The Story of Muhammad Ali*
  by Jim Haskins (6–10 years) follows the athlete from childhood
  through his professional career.

Submissions and Payment
Guidelines available. Query with outline and 3–5 sample
chapters. Send complete ms for picture books. Accepts photocopies, computer printouts, and simultaneous submissions
if identified. SASE. Responds in 3–4 months. Publication in
18–24 months. Royalty; advance.

Editor's Comments
We take pride in finding and fostering new voices in children's
literature. Our strongest needs are for middle-grade and young
adult novels. We'll also consider well-paced picture books.

Warner Press

P.O. Box 2499
1200 East Fifth Street
Anderson, IN 46018-9988

Product Marketing Editor: Karen Rhodes

Publisher's Interests

Warner Press is a Christian publishing house whose catalogue includes a variety of children's products, such as puzzles, coloring books, and activity books for church and educational use. Its target audience includes children ages three to twelve.

Website: www.warnerpress.com

Freelance Potential

Published 12 titles in 2002: 4 were developed from unsolicited submissions. Receives 30 queries, 25 mss yearly.

- **Fiction:** Publishes story picture books, 4–10 years. Also publishes novelty and board books. Features religious fiction.
- **Nonfiction:** Publishes resource materials for religious educators, 3–12 years. Offers workbooks, classroom resources, devotionals, and activity and coloring books.
- **Representative Titles:** *The Princess and the Kiss* is a story of God's gift of purity. *Egermeier's Bible Story Book* by Elsie Egermeier (4+ years) features more than 300 Bible stories accompanied by questions and answers related to each story.

Submissions and Payment

Guidelines available. Query or send complete ms. Accepts photocopies. SASE. Responds in 10–12 weeks. Publication in 12–18 months. Flat fee.

Editor's Comments

Since its foundation in the early 1800's the mission of our ministry has been to inspire and educate. Our catalogue includes products for Christians everywhere. Our goal is to proclaim the Gospel of Jesus Christ. We have recently begun to include a number of storybooks for three- to twelve-year-old children. All our books are designed to instill Christian values in our readers. Nonfiction for this age range is also welcome, but please remember that we only publish material with Christian themes. All too often we receive submissions that simply do not fit our very specific needs. You may send us a query with a sample chapter or a completed manuscript.

Wayne State University Press

The Leonard N. Simons Building
4809 Woodward Avenue
Detroit, MI 48201-1309

Acquisitions Editor: Jane Hoehner

Publisher's Interests
This publisher is an established university press that offers informative books about metropolitan Detroit and the Great Lakes region, as well as titles that reflect the interests of scholars, libraries, and the general public.
Website: http://wsupress.wayne.edu/

Freelance Potential
Published 50 titles (2 juvenile) in 2002: 10 were developed from unsolicited submissions, 1 was by an agented author, and 10 were reprint/licensed properties. Receives 180 queries, 100 unsolicited mss yearly.

- **Nonfiction:** Publishes middle-grade books, 8–12 years. Topics include Michigan history, the Upper Peninsula, and the Great Lakes. Also publishes titles on Jewish folklore and anthropology, Renaissance studies, labor history, urban studies, German theory, speech and language pathology, and contemporary film and television.
- **Representative Titles:** *Albert Kahn: Builder of Detroit* by Roger Matuz (10+ years) is a biography of the architect who designed some of the most significant buildings in the greater Detroit area. *Escape to Freedom: The Story of Elizabeth Denison Forth* by Mark F. McPherson (10+ years) traces the experiences of a woman from a family of slaves who managed to fund the building of the St. James Chapel.

Submissions and Payment
Guidelines available. Query with résumé, clips, table of contents, and chapter-by-chapter outline; or send complete ms. Accepts photocopies, computer printouts, and e-mail submissions to jane.hoehner@wayne.edu. SASE. Responds in 2–3 weeks. Publication in 15 months. Royalty, 7.5–10%.

Editor's Comments
We have recently added children's books to our list of regional titles, and we continue to seek submissions for material that reflects the interests of our readers and contributes to the advancement of teaching and research.

Weigl Educational Publishers

6325 10th Street
Calgary, Alberta T2H 2Z9
Canada

Managing Editor: Kara Turner

Publisher's Interests
This Canadian educational publisher specializes in materials
for use in elementary and secondary school classrooms in
both Canada and the US. Distance learning materials also
appear in its catalogue. Weigl does not publish fiction.
Website: www.weigl.com

Freelance Potential
Published 100+ titles in 2002: 10 were developed from unsolicited submissions. Of the 100+ titles, 1 was by an unpublished writer and 10 were by authors who were new to the
publishing house. Receives 100 queries yearly.
* **Nonfiction:** Published 26 easy-to-read books, 4–7 years; 60
  middle-grade books, 8–12 years; and 8 young adult books,
  12–18 years. Topics include social studies, history, science,
  nature, art, career guidance, and multicultural, ethnic, and
  global issues.
* **Representative Titles:** *Albertans Past, Present, Future* by
  Kathryn G. Dueck & Kathryn E. Galvin (grades 4–6) looks at all
  aspects of Albertan history. *Canadian Families* by Emily Ody-
  nak, ed. (grades 1–3) helps students learn about their roots.

Submissions and Payment
Send résumé only. No unsolicited mss or queries. Accepts
photocopies, computer printouts, and e-mail to kara@
weigl.com. SAE/IRC. Responds in 6 months. Publication in 2
years. Work-for-hire fee paid on acceptance of ms.

Editor's Comments
While Canadian classroom resources continue to be the focus
of our work, we have doubled our list of classroom and library
resources in the last year. We strive to bring our readers the
very best in teaching and library resources. Given that, we are
interested in hearing from writers with a background in education who can write for both the US and Canadian markets.
Keep in mind that all of our titles and textbooks conform to
national curricula. Please send a résumé only. All work is done
on a work-for-hire basis.

What's Inside Press

P.O. Box 16965
Beverly Hills, CA 90209

Submissions Editor: Shalen Williams

Publisher's Interests
What's Inside Press is a children's publisher that offers books
for toddlers through teenagers. It publishes a line of fiction
that includes picture books, novelty books, and books in
series. This publisher sponsors an annual literary award, the
Brant Point Prize, which recognizes excellence in unpublished
writing for children and young adults.
Website: www.whatsinsidepress.com

Freelance Potential
Published 10 titles in 2002. Of the 10 titles, 5 were by
authors who were new to the publishing house. Receives
2,500 queries yearly.
- **Fiction:** Publishes story picture books, 4–10 years; and young
  adult novels, 12–18 years. Also publishes novelty and board
  books, books in series, and educational and informational
  books.
- **Representative Titles:** *Mind Your Manners, S'il Vous Plait* by
  Kingsley Foster (3–7 years) is an illustrated guide to polite
  behavior and proper social etiquette; part of the Kitty in the
  City series. *A Warm Place in the Shade* by Laura Gwen Owens
  (11–17 years) is a coming-of-age story that spans two Christ-
  mases about a girl who learns her father is not the man she
  thought he was.

Submissions and Payment
Query only. No unsolicited mss. E-mail queries to
submit@whatsinsidepress.com. SASE. Responds in 6–8
weeks. Publication in 18–30 months. Royalty; 8–10%.

Editor's Comments
We believe that books can give wings to a child's imagination
and that positive themes and messages in literature will
empower a young mind for a lifetime. That makes being a publisher of children's books both a great privilege and a great
responsibility. Because we are a small publisher, every book
we publish is an important part of our identity. We nurture
each and every project we undertake.

Whitecap Books Ltd.

351 Lynn Avenue
North Vancouver, British Columbia V7J 2C4
Canada

Rights and Acquisitions Associate: Leanne McDonald

Publisher's Interests
This publishing house offers books covering a wide range of
fiction and nonfiction topics for children between the ages of
three and twelve, and for adult readers. 10% self-, subsidy-,
co-venture, or co-op published material.
Website: www.whitecap.ca

Freelance Potential
Published 63 titles (10 juvenile) in 2002: 6 were developed
from unsolicited submissions, 4 were by agented authors,
and 17 were reprint/licensed properties. Of the 63 titles, 8
were by unpublished writers and 17 were by authors new to
the publishing house. Receives 1,000 queries yearly.
- **Fiction:** Published 2 story picture books, 4–10 years; and 4
  chapter books, 5–10 years. Genres include adventure, fantasy,
  sports, nature, and contemporary fiction.
- **Nonfiction:** Published 4 easy-to-read books, 4–7 years. Topics
  include regional subjects, Canadian history, family issues,
  nature, the environment, natural history, and science. Also
  publishes parenting, history, and nature books for adults.
- **Representative Titles:** *The Disappearing Dinosaur* by Andrea
  & David Spalding (8–12 years) follows two techno-savvy adven-
  turers; part of the Adventure Net series. *Welcome to the World
  of Wild Horses* by Diane Swanson (4–7 years) traces the history
  of the wild horses of the North American West; part of the Welcome to the World of . . . series.

Submissions and Payment
Guidelines available. Query with outline/synopsis, table of
contents, and sample chapter. Accepts photocopies, computer
printouts, and simultaneous submissions if identified.
SAE/IRC. Responds in 2–3 months. Publication in 1 year.
Royalty, negotiable; advance.

Editor's Comments
We continue to look for queries for nonfiction for four- to
twelve-year-old readers. Topics related to natural history
are at the top of our list.

White Mane Publishing Company

P. O. Box 708
63 West Burd Street
Shippensburg, PA 17257

Acquisitions Department

Publisher's Interests
This specialty house features a children's imprint, White
Mane Kids, that offers books on history and historical fiction
for middle-grade and young adult readers. Most of its titles
relate to the Civil War period of American history. 10% self-,
subsidy-, or co-op published material.

Freelance Potential
Published 14 titles in 2002: all were developed from unsolicit-
ed submissions. Receives 360 queries yearly.
- **Fiction:** Publishes middle-grade books, 8–12 years; and young
  adult books, 12–18 years. Genres include historical fiction.
  Features books about the American Civil War.
- **Nonfiction:** Publishes young adult books, 12–18 years. Topics
  include history and the American Civil War.
- **Representative Titles:** *The Whispering Rod* by Nancy Kelley
  follows the story of 14-year-old Hannah, a young girl living in
  Puritan New England. *Off to Fight* is the story of a 13-year-old
  boy who decides to fight with the Army of Virginia after John
  Brown's raid.

Submissions and Payment
Guidelines available. Query. Accepts photocopies. SASE.
Responds in 2–3 months. Publication in 12–18 months. Pay-
ment policy varies.

Editor's Comments
We take pride in providing children's titles that are both entertaining and educational. All our books are historically accurate
and target readers age nine and up. We welcome queries from
new writers familiar with our list. We require that you first
send for a copy of our proposal guidelines. Materials submitted
without this form will not be evaluated. We ask for a statement
of purpose, marketing ideas, a sample paragraph that would
appear on your book's dust jacket, and a basic outline of your
book—including proposed number of photos, maps, pages, and
words. Let us know if you plan to include a bibliography
and/or an index.

Kathy Tucker, Albert Whitman
On Novels & Unexpected Endings

Albert Whitman & Company, based near Chicago, Illinois, publishes books for children up to 12 years old. "We publish two novels every year," says Editor-in-Chief Kathy Tucker, "and we could consider a good mystery as one of those." Tucker likes mysteries in which the ending is unexpected, "yet when you look back at the story, it's inevitable." In fact, Tucker thinks this kind of ending applies to many books "so that the plot resolves in some way." She makes up an example to illustrate her meaning: "When you look back at the story you think, 'Well, of course. She was a good artist, therefore she solved her problem by drawing a picture for her grandmother.'"

Tucker looks for character-driven novels. "They are going to be judged by librarians and critics. If the plot is more character-driven, then you're going to identify with what the character is doing. The more you identify with the character, the more you're going to care about what happens—not just in children's books but in adult books, too."

Albert Whitman publishes the well-known Boxcar Children series, and they are not looking for writers for that series. "We have a set of writers who are doing it—that's working out pretty well for us."

For single title novels, writers should submit an outline or a summary plus three sample chapters. Should a writer 'give away' the ending when submitting a mystery proposal? Tucker says, "You're telling the editor about this, so I think you could give it all away. I think it's important to show you've thought the whole thing through. It's easier to write three chapters. It's harder to write the whole book. You can set up the whole thing but this doesn't mean you can resolve it."

Albert Whitman & Company

6340 Oakton Street
Morton Grove, IL 60053-2723

Editor-in-Chief: Kathleen Tucker

Publisher's Interests

Picture books, chapter books, and novels for children up to
the age of 12 appear in this publisher's catalogue. It offers
fiction as well as nonfiction titles, many of which deal with
feelings and emotions, multicultural issues, and sensitive
topics such as divorce and bullying.
Website: www.albertwhitman.com

Freelance Potential

Published 30 titles in 2002: 3 were by agented authors and 2
were reprint/licensed properties. Of the 30 titles, 2 were by
unpublished writers and 8 were by authors who were new to
the publishing house. Receives 300 queries, 4,500 unsolicited
mss yearly.
- **Fiction:** Published 10 early picture books, 0–4 years; 1 chapter
  book, 5–10 years; and 1 middle-grade novel, 8–12 years. Genres include mystery, humor, and historical fiction.
- **Nonfiction:** Published 8 early picture books, 0–4 years. Topics
  include family life, social issues, and ethnic and multicultural
  issues. Also publishes biographies.
- **Representative Titles:** *Birthday Zoo* by Deborah Lee Rose is a
  humorous rhyming story about a group of zoo animals who
  celebrate a boy's birthday. *Apples Here* by Will Hubbell is a
  read-aloud picture book that describes the way apples grow
  throughout the year.

Submissions and Payment

Guidelines available. Send complete ms for picture books.
Query with 3 sample chapters for novels and nonfiction. Indicate if package is a query or ms. Accepts simultaneous submissions. SASE. Responds to queries in 6 weeks, to mss in
3–4 months. Publication in 18–24 months. Royalty; advance.

Editor's Comments

Please keep in mind that we publish very few novels, so the
competition here is particularly fierce. We will consider biographies, but we prefer those that have not been fictionalized. If
you're submitting a picture book, do not include illustrations.

Wiley Children's Books

John Wiley
111 River Street
Hoboken, NJ 07030

Editor: Kate Bradford

Publisher's Interests
This children's imprint of a well-known nonfiction publisher targets readers in the middle grades and in their teenage years. Its list includes books about science, mathematics, and history, as well as biographies. Parenting titles are also available from this publisher.
Website: www.wiley.com/children

Freelance Potential
Published 20 titles (19 juvenile) in 2002: 2 were developed from unsolicited submissions and 3 were by agented authors. Receives 300 queries yearly.
- **Nonfiction:** Publishes middle-grade books, 8–12 years; and young adult books, 12–18 years. Topics include history, mathematics, science, nature, arts and crafts, multicultural issues, and sports. Also offers biographies, activity books, and books about parenting.
- **Representative Titles:** *Take Action! A Guide to Active Citizenship* by Marc Kielburger & Craig Kielburger (10–15 years) is written to equip young people with the tools they need to make a difference on local, national, and global levels. *Build a Better Mousetrap* by Ruth Kassinger (8–12 years) features fun, hands-on projects that teach kids history and science while developing their inventive instincts.

Submissions and Payment
Guidelines available. Query with résumé, outline, sample chapter, artwork if applicable, and summary of primary market and competition. Accepts photocopies, computer printouts, and simultaneous submissions if identified. SASE. Responds in 1–3 months. Publication in 18 months. Royalty; advance.

Editor's Comments
We always need innovative educational titles for 8- to 18-year-old readers. Biographies are welcome, as are books about science, mathematics, and history. Queries should provide a detailed description of the target audience.

Williamson Publishing

P.O. Box 185
Charlotte, VT 05445

Editorial Director: Susan Williamson

Publisher's Interests

Williamson Publishing is known for four series: Little Hands, Kids Can, Quick Start for Kids, and Kaleidoscope Kids. Its list is comprised of nonfiction titles for children between the ages of five and fourteen that are designed for use with their parents and teachers.

Website: www.williamsonbooks.com

Freelance Potential

Published 25 titles in 2002: 10 were developed from unsolicited submissions and 2 were by agented authors. Of the 25 titles, 5 were by unpublished writers and 5 were by authors who were new to the publishing house. Receives 1,000 queries yearly.

- **Nonfiction:** Publishes easy-to-read books, 4–7 years. Also publishes active learning titles, pre-K and up. Topics include arts and crafts, history, science, math, and multicultural subjects.
- **Representative Titles:** *Paper-Folding Fun!* by Ginger Johnson (8+ years) features fifty craft projects; part of the Kids Can series. *Ancient Rome!* by Avery Hart & Sandra Gallagher (8–14 years) explores the culture and ideas of ancient Rome; part of the Kaleidoscope Kids series.

Submissions and Payment

Query with outline and sample chapters. Accepts photocopies and computer printouts. SASE. Responds in 3–4 months. Publication in 12–18 months. Royalty; advance. Flat fee.

Editor's Comments

We have very specific needs for the coming year for our award-winning Kaleidoscope Kids series, and while we will consider other material, queries that fall into one of these categories will get our attention. In the field of science, we would like queries about insects, human genomes, or global warming for readers between eight and fourteen. In the area of history, we want to see queries for books on colonial times, the Civil War, the Revolutionary War, and the Vietnam War. Please do not send unsolicited manuscripts.

Windward Publishing

3943 Meadowbrook Road
Minneapolis, MN 55426

President: Alan E. Krysan

Publisher's Interests
Windward Publishing develops nonfiction paperback books
for early readers through young adults. A division of Finney
Company, an independent publisher of educational materials,
it specializes in books about science, natural history, and
outdoor recreation.
Website: www.finney-hobar.com

Freelance Potential
Published 12 titles (10 juvenile) in 2002: 10 were developed
from unsolicited submissions and 2 were reprint/licensed
properties. Of the 12 titles, 2 were by unpublished writers
and 4 were by authors who were new to the publishing
house. Receives 60 queries, 30 unsolicited mss yearly.
- **Nonfiction:** Published 1 easy-to-read book, 4–7 years; 2 story
  picture books, 4–10 years; 2 chapter books, 5–10 years; 4
  middle-grade titles, 8–12 years; and 2 young adult books,
  12–18 years. Topics include animals, nature, gardening, horti-
  culture, agriculture, recreation, science, and sports.
- **Representative Titles:** *Maybe I'll Grow Up to Be a Bullfrog!* by
  Wilma Clark Erwin tells the story of the metamorphosis of a
  tadpole into a frog. *Dolphins & Whales* by Larry N. Brown discusses the adaptations, ecology, identification, and life histories of mammals that live in the waters off the coasts of the
  southeastern United States and the West Indies.

Submissions and Payment
Send complete ms with artwork. Accepts photocopies, computer printouts, and simultaneous submissions. Availability
of artwork improves chance of acceptance. Accepts 8x10 or
35mm B/W or color prints or transparencies, line art, and
drawings. SASE. Responds in 4–6 weeks. Publication in 6–8
months. Royalty, 10% of net.

Editor's Comments
We continue to look for high-quality titles of educational value
for children over the age of three. Most of our titles deal with
natural history, science, and outdoor recreation.

Wizards of the Coast

P.O. Box 707
Renton, WA 98057-0707

Submissions Editor

Publisher's Interests
This popular publisher specializes in "shared-world" series titles. Its books include sword and sorcery, epic high fantasy, Asian fantasy, and high fantasy for young adult readers. All writing is done on a for-hire basis.
Website: www.wizards.com

Freelance Potential
Published 50+ titles in 2002. Receives 1,200 queries yearly.
- **Fiction:** Publishes young adult novels, 12–18 years. Genres include adventure and science fiction, and medieval, heroic, and epic fantasy.
- **Representative Titles:** *Dragons of a Vanished Moon* by Margaret Weis & Tracy Hickman (YA) follows the conquests of the warrior Mina and the small band of heroes who dare to defy her; part of the War of Souls series. *Crown of Fire* by Ed Greenwood (YA) is a heroic tale of the wielder of spellfire from the Forgotten Realm; part of the Forgotten Realm trilogy.

Submissions and Payment
Guidelines available. Query with 10-page writing sample. All work is assigned. Accepts photocopies and simultaneous submissions if identified. SASE. Responds in 4 months. Publication in 1 year. Payment policy varies.

Editor's Comments
Consult our website for current information on our books—this is the best way for you to become familiar with the type of novels we publish. At this time, we are considering authors for our Magic: The Gathering and Legend of the Five Rings series. Our needs change from year to year, and our Forgotten Realms and Dragonlance lines fill quickly with the works of established authors. We do not, and will not, publish novels not strictly tied to one of these properties, even if our editors agree that the book is wonderful. We will not break this rule for anyone. Once you understand our needs, we invite you to send us a writing sample in the appropriate genre. We evaluate your writing at this point, not your story line.

Wolfhound Press

Merlin Publishing
16 Upper Pembroke Street
Dublin 2
Ireland

Editorial Department

Publisher's Interests
This imprint of the Irish press, Merlin Publishing, features
nonfiction titles and fiction for 4- to 18-year-old readers. Its
list includes books based on the history, literature, and culture of Ireland.
Website: www.wolfhound.ie

Freelance Potential
Published 45 titles (15 juvenile) in 2002: 2 were developed
from unsolicited submissions and 1 was a reprint/licensed
property. Receives 300 queries, 300 unsolicited mss yearly.
- **Fiction:** Publishes story picture books, 4–10 years; middle-
  grade novels, 8–12 years; and young adult novels, 12–18 years.
  Genres include historical, multicultural, adventure, and contemporary fiction; mystery; and romance.
- **Nonfiction:** Publishes middle-grade books, 8–12 years.
  Topics include nature and the environment. Also publishes
  biographies.
- **Representative Titles:** *Murder at Drushee* by Cora Harrison is
  a historical mystery from the time of Saint Patrick and the Bre-
  hon Laws. *Who's There?* by Dominick Tobin is a chilling tale of
  murder and evil in which two teenagers must save a tortured
  spirit from the past.

Submissions and Payment
Guidelines and submissions form available at website.
Prefers complete ms with synopsis and author biography.
Will accept résumé and chapter outline for nonfiction only.
Accepts photocopies and computer printouts. SAE/IRC.
Responds in 3–12 months. Publication in 2 years. Royalty;
advance. Flat fee.

Editor's Comments
We welcome submissions from new writers and encourage
you to send us a synopsis of your work. This year, we are
especially interested in picture books for young children and
biographies of historical figures. Note that we do not accept
poetry or short stories.

Woodbine House

6510 Bells Mill Road
Bethesda, MD 20817

Acquisitions Editor: Nancy Gray Paul

Publisher's Interests
Parents and teachers of children with special needs are the target audience for this publisher. Woodbine House offers both fiction and nonfiction titles as well as some children's literature on the subject of children with disabilities.
Website: www.woodbinehouse.com

Freelance Potential
Published 10 titles (2 juvenile) in 2002: 6 were developed from unsolicited submissions and 4 were by agented authors. Of the 10 titles, 5 were by unpublished writers and 4 were by authors who were new to the publishing house. Receives 1,000 queries, 600 unsolicited mss yearly.
- **Fiction:** Published 1 story picture book, 4–10 years; and 1 middle-grade book, 8–12 years. All stories feature children with disabilities.
- **Nonfiction:** Publishes educational titles and parent guides. Topics include autism, cerebral palsy, Down Syndrome, epilepsy, and others. Also publishes some titles for children ages 4–12.
- **Representative Titles:** *Incredible Edible Gluten-Free Food for Kids* by Sheri L. Sanderson (adults) features more than 150 recipes as well as guidelines for selecting and preparing foods for children in need of gluten-free diets. *Children with Traumatic Brain Injury* by Lisa Schoenbrodt, ed. (parents) offers parents the hope and support needed to help children recover.

Submissions and Payment
Guidelines available. Query with outline, 3 sample chapters, and clips. Accepts ms for picture books only. Accepts photocopies, computer printouts, and simultaneous submissions if identified. SASE. Responds to queries in 1 month, to mss in 3 months. Publication in 1–2 years. Royalty.

Editor's Comments
We will consider books on autism, Down Syndrome, and spina bifida. We will also look at submissions related to non-developmental disabilities as well.

Workman Publishing Company

708 Broadway
New York, NY 10003-9555

Submissions Editor: Margot Herrera

Publisher's Interests
This well-known publisher offers books for all ages, as well as novelty items, catalogues, games, reference materials, and calendars. It publishes no fiction. Many of its books are published in board-book format.
Website: www.workman.com

Freelance Potential
Published 40 titles (12 juvenile) in 2002: most were by agented authors. Of the 40 titles, 3 were by unpublished writers and 6 were by authors who were new to the publishing house.
Receives 1,000 queries, 2,000 unsolicited mss yearly.
- **Fiction:** Published 1 toddler book, 0–4 years; and 1 story picture book, 4–10 years. Also publishes board and novelty books. Features humor and books about nature.
- **Nonfiction:** Published 1 concept book and 2 early picture books, 0–4 years; 3 story picture books, 4–10 years; 2 middle-grade books, 8–12 years; and 2 young adult books, 12–18 years. Topics include nature, the environment, science, sports, cooking, and games. Also offers activity books and calendars.
- **Representative Titles:** *The Squiggly Wigglys* by Elizabeth Koda-Callan (4–8 years) is a storybook in which each page includes an illustration with a jiggly chain that enables the reader to change the character's outline. *Bathtime* (3–5 years) features ten original poems and stories with more than 100 questions and answers that will keep kids entertained while splashing in the tub.

Submissions and Payment
Guidelines available. Query with clips or send ms with illustrations for fiction. Query with table of contents, outline/synopsis, sample chapters, and clips for nonfiction. Accepts photocopies and computer printouts. SASE. Responds in 6 weeks. Publication period varies. Royalty; advance.

Editor's Comments
Send us a unique idea for a board book, game, or gift book. We are interested in submissions for all age groups.

World Book

Suite 2000
233 North Michigan Avenue
Chicago, IL 60601

Product Development Director: Paul A. Kobasa

Publisher's Interests

Established in 1917, this educational publisher offers accurate, objective, and reliable research materials for both children and adults. It features encyclopedias, reference sources, and multi-media products.
Website: www.worldbook.com

Freelance Potential

Published 15 titles in 2002.

- **Nonfiction:** Publishes easy-to-read books, 4–7 years; middle-grade books, 8–12 years; and young adult books, 12–18 years. Topics include social studies, cultural studies, science, nature, history, geography, Spanish, arts and crafts, hobbies, careers, and the environment. Also publishes biographies, activity books, how-to titles, and reference materials.
- **Representative Titles:** *My Body* (grades K–3) is a reference book that examines this topic from a child's point of view; part of the World Book Ladders series. *Life in the Deserts* (grades 3–8) helps students understand the complexities of this ecosystem and the environmental issues that affect its delicate balance; part of the World Book Ecology series.

Submissions and Payment

Catalogue available with 9x12 SASE. Query with outline or synopsis. No unsolicited mss. Accepts simultaneous submissions if identified. SASE. Responds in 1–2 months. Publication in 18 months. Payment rate and policy vary.

Editor's Comments

We are committed to publishing encyclopedias and references that meet the highest standards of editorial excellence, while keeping pace with the technological developments that define our computer age. To get an idea of our publishing program, prospective writers are encouraged to look at our award-winning *Student Discovery Encyclopedia*, as well as our new *Myths and Legends* titles. At this time, we are interested in ideas that complement TutorLink, our innovative peer-tutoring program.

Wright Group/McGraw-Hill

Suite 100
19201 120th Avenue NE
Bothell, WA 98011

Submissions Editor

Publisher's Interests

Wright Group/McGraw-Hill is an educational publisher
featuring curriculum materials and supplementary resource
materials for use in preschool through sixth-grade classrooms. Its language arts materials include literacy programs
and titles for shared and guided reading, as well as high-
interest/low-reading-level books. It also offers materials for
teaching mathematics.
Website: www.wrightgroup.com

Freelance Potential

Published 225 titles in 2002: 30 were developed from unsolicited submissions, 30 were by agented authors, and 16
were reprint/licensed properties. Of the 225 titles, 35 were by
authors who were new to the publishing house. Receives 300
queries, 200 unsolicited mss yearly.

- **Fiction:** Publishes easy-to-read books, 4–7 years; story picture
  books, 4–10 years; chapter books, 5–10 years; and middle-
  grade books, 8–12 years. Genres include Western, contemporary, ethnic, and multicultural fiction; adventure; fantasy; folklore; mystery; and science fiction.
- **Nonfiction:** Publishes easy-to-read titles, 4–7 years. Topics
  include animals, crafts, history, and multicultural and ethnic
  subjects. Also offers biographies.
- **Representative Titles:** *My Wonderful Aunt* (6–12 years) is a
  collection of rhyming adventure stories that offer shared reading experiences to older students. *Pattern Blocks* (grades K–12)
  features 20 challenging, instant math investigations and open-
  ended questions designed to motivate students; part of the 20
  Thinking Questions series.

Submissions and Payment

Guidelines available at website.

Editor's Comments

We're looking for captivating materials, strategies, and proven
ideas to make teaching more effective and engaging. Send us
ideas for innovative literacy and math products.

XC Publishing

16006 19th Avenue CT E
Tacoma, WA 98445

Editor: Cheryl Dyson

Publisher's Interests

This small publishing house specializes in science fiction,
horror, mystery, and romance titles. Its list includes books
for readers of all ages. Future plans call for producing electronic books, audio books, and a line of paperbacks. It no
longer publishes nonfiction.
Website: www.xcpublishing.com

Freelance Potential

Published 10 titles in 2002: all were developed from unsolicited
submissions. Of the 10 titles, 8 were by unpublished writers
and all were by authors who were new to the publishing
house. Receives 250 queries yearly.
- **Fiction:** Published 1 young adult book, 12–18 years. Genres
  include fantasy, horror, mystery, suspense, romance, and science fiction. Also publishes adult titles.
- **Representative Titles:** *Queen of Diamonds* by Richard L.
  Graves (YA–Adult) is a mystery that involves the sale of diamonds. *The Gauntlet Thrown* by Cheryl Dyson (YA–Adult) follows the fantastic adventures of Brydon Redwing and his quest
  for an ancient item of potent magic.

Submissions and Payment

Guidelines available. Query with clips or writing samples.
Accepts photocopies, disk submissions, and e-mail submissions to editor@xcpublishing.com. Availability of artwork
improves chance of acceptance. SASE. Responds in 1 week.
Publication in 4–6 months. Royalty, 40%.

Editor's Comments

We are now seeking submissions of manuscripts for children
of all ages, along with young adult books. However, we will only
look at submissions of science fiction, romance, horror, and
mysteries. With new publishers cropping up seemingly daily,
we plan to stand apart from the pack by limiting our list to
only those titles of the highest quality and by offering many
novel-related extras on our website, such as maps, screen-
savers, artwork, puzzles, and games.

Zephyr Press

P.O. Box 66006
Tucson, AZ 85728-6006

Acquisitions Editor: Veronica Durie

Publisher's Interests

This publisher creates materials for use in special education and gifted classrooms. Assessment materials and professional development titles for educators are also found in its catalogue. Zephyr Press designs its products to be used in kindergarten through twelfth-grade classrooms.
Website: www.zephyrpress.com

Freelance Potential

Published 8 titles in 2002: 4 were developed from unsolicited submissions. Of the 8 titles, 4 were by unpublished writers and 6 were by authors who were new to the publishing house. Receives 250 queries yearly.

- **Nonfiction:** Published 8 middle-grade books, 8–12 years. Features educational titles, grades K–12. Topics include multiple intelligences, brain-based learning, thinking skills, science, technology, mathematics, history, and character education.
- **Representative Titles:** *Inside Brian's Brain* by Nancy Margulies (grades 6–12) is a comic book that teaches kids about the basic neurobiology of the brain and how to improve the brain's ability to function well. *Passport to Learn* by Jacque Melin (grades 4–8) features projects that challenge high-potential learners, while teaching them language arts, social studies, math, science, and leadership skills.

Submissions and Payment

Guidelines and submission packet available. Send completed submission packet, detailed outline, and sample chapter. Accepts photocopies and computer printouts. Availability of artwork improves chance of acceptance. SASE. Responds in 3–6 months. Publication in 1–2 years. Royalty, varies.

Editor's Comments

We cater to highly motivated educators. Their busy schedules mean that they need to access and apply information quickly, and they need to know very concretely "how to do it." That's why we look for practical, concise, well-crafted books. Please don't send us anything too wordy or overly theoretical.

Zonderkidz

Zondervan Publishing House
5300 Patterson Avenue SE
Grand Rapids, MI 49530

Editor: Barbara Scott

Publisher's Interests
Zonderkidz, the children's group of Zondervan, focuses on publishing and promoting developmentally-appropriate, biblically based books, as well as Bibles, gifts, and videos. Its audience includes children age 12 and younger.
Website: www.zonderkidz.com

Freelance Potential
Published 70–80 titles in 2002. Of the 70–80 titles, 6 were by authors who were new to the publishing house. Receives 5,000 queries yearly.
- **Fiction:** Publishes concept books, toddler books, and early picture books, 0–4 years; easy-to-read books, 4–7 years; story picture books, 4–10 years; chapter books, 5–10 years; and middle-grade novels, 8–12 years. Genres include humor, romance, mystery, and inspirational fiction.
- **Nonfiction:** Publishes concept books, toddler books, and early picture books, 0–4 years; easy-to-read titles, 4–7 years; story picture books, 4–10 years; chapter books, 5–10 years; and middle-grade books, 8–12 years. Also features Bibles, biographies, and devotionals. Topics include religion and social issues.
- **Representative Titles:** *The Legend of the Valentine* by Katherine Grace Bond (4–8 years) is the story of a boy who learns the meaning of forgiveness. *Snug as a Bug?* by Amy E. Imbody (4–6 years) is a rhyming picture book about children who think they would rather sleep under a tree than in their own beds.

Submissions and Payment
Guidelines available at www.zondervan.com. Query with sample chapter. Accepts faxes to 616-698-3454 and e-mail submissions to www.EPCA.org. No unsolicited submissions accepted via regular mail. SASE. Responds in 6 weeks. Publication in 18 months. Royalty, varies.

Editor's Comments
We continue to welcome unsolicited submissions of Bible-based fiction and nonfiction, but note that we will no longer consider submissions sent through the mail.

Additional Listings

We have selected the following publishers to offer you additional marketing opportunities. Most of these publishers have special submissions requirements or they purchase a limited number of juvenile titles each year.

For published authors, we include information about houses that produce reprints of previously published works. For writers who are proficient in foreign languages, we list publishers of foreign-language material. You will also find publishers who accept résumés only; who work with agented authors; or who usually accept unsolicited submissions, but due to a backlog, are not accepting material at this time.

As you survey these listings, you may find that a small regional press is a more appropriate market for your submission than a larger publisher. Also, if you are involved in education or are a specialist in a certain field, consider sending your résumé to one of the educational publishers—you may have the qualifications they are looking for.

Publishers who usually accept unsolicited submissions but were not accepting unsolicited material at our press time are designated with an ⊗. *Be sure to contact the publisher before submitting material to determine the current submissions policy.*

As you review the listings that follow, use the Publisher's Interests section as your guide to the particular focus of each house.

A & B Publishers Group

100 Atlantic Avenue
Brooklyn, NY 11238

Managing Editor: Maxwell Taylor

Publisher's Interests
Books that encourage cultural diversity and inspire self-esteem
are the specialty of this small publishing house. A & B
Publishers Group also offers a line of fiction and nonfiction titles
for children and young adults.
Website: www.anbonline.com

Freelance Potential
Published 26 titles (15 juvenile) in 2002: 18 were developed
from unsolicited submissions and 8 were by agented authors.
Receives 800 queries yearly.
Submissions and Payment: Query with sample chapters and
table of contents. Accepts photocopies, computer printouts, and
simultaneous submissions. SASE. Responds in 2–3 months.
Publication period varies. Royalty, 4–5%; advance, $500.

Abbeville Kids

Suite 500
116 West 23rd Street
New York, NY 10011

Editor: Susan Costello

Publisher's Interests
Fiction and nonfiction books for young readers up to twelve
years of age are the mainstay of this publisher. It will consider
picture books and illustrated story books. 50% self-, subsidy-,
co-venture, or co-op published material.
Website: www.abbeville.com

Freelance Potential
Published 10 titles (1 juvenile) in 2002. Receives 120 unsolicited mss yearly.
Submissions and Payment: Send complete ms with illustrations.
Prefers agented authors. Accepts photocopies and computer
printouts. SASE. Responds in 5 weeks. Publication in 18–24
months. Royalty; advance. Flat fee.

Abingdon Press

201 Eighth Avenue South
Nashville, TN 37203

Editor: Peg Augustine

Publisher's Interests
Abingdon Press publishes toddler books, easy-to-read books, and story picture books for children between the ages of two and twelve. Many of its titles feature multicultural and religious themes. Bilingual, novelty, and board books also appear on its list. 50% co-op published material.

Freelance Potential
Published 20 titles in 2002: 3 were developed from unsolicited submissions and 4 were by agented authors. Receives 600 queries yearly.
Submissions and Payment: Guidelines available. Query. Accepts photocopies and e-mail submissions to paugustine@ umpublishing.org. SASE. Responds in 3 months. Publication in 2 years. Royalty, 5–10%. Flat fee, $1,000+.

Activity Resources Company

20655 Hathaway Avenue
Hayward, CA 94541

Editor: Mary Laycock

Publisher's Interests
This company targets the education market with books and materials related to the teaching of mathematics in kindergarten through grade nine. Committed to filling the needs of math teachers, it offers books, manipulatives, and games about geometry, algebra, probability, statistics, logic, measurement, functions, mental math, and discrete math.
Website: www.activityresources.com

Freelance Potential
Published 4 titles in 2002. Receives 25–30 queries yearly.
Submissions and Payment: Query with résumé, sample chapter, and bibliography. Accepts photocopies, computer printouts, and simultaneous submissions if identified. SASE. Responds in 2–4 weeks. Publication in 1 year. Royalty, varies.

Alyson Wonderland

Suite 1000
6922 Hollywood Boulevard
Los Angeles, CA 90028

Editor

Publisher's Interests
Alyson Wonderland books explore the political, legal, financial, medial, spiritual, social, and sexual aspects of gay, lesbian, and bisexual life. It also features a line of books for children living in gay, lesbian, or bisexual households.
Website: www.alyson.com

Freelance Potential
Published 52 titles (1 juvenile) in 2002: 39 were developed from unsolicited submissions and 7 were by agented authors. Receives 1,000+ queries yearly.
Submissions and Payment: Guidelines available. Query with 1-page synopsis and available artwork. No unsolicited mss. Accepts photocopies and computer printouts. SASE. Responds in 10–12 weeks. Publication in 2 years. Payment policy varies.

Amirah Publishing

P.O. Box 54146
Flushing, NY 11354

President: Yahiya Emerick

Publisher's Interests
This small specialty publisher features titles for children ages five and up, as well as for adults, that focus on the Muslim experience in the West. Educational textbooks on religious themes, and religious, multicultural, and ethnic fiction for young readers and teens are needed at this time. New writers are encouraged to submit a query for material that relates to the publisher's editorial focus.

Freelance Potential
Published 10 titles (9 juvenile) in 2002: all were assigned. Receives 25 queries yearly.
Submissions and Payment: Query. Accepts e-mail submissions to amirahpbco@aol.com and simultaneous submissions. SASE. Responds in 4–6 weeks. Publication in 4–6 months. Flat fee.

Aquila Communications Ltd.

2642 Diab Street
St. Laurent, Quebec H4S 1E8
Canada

President: Sami Kelada

Publisher's Interests
This publisher specializes in books and other reading-related materials for French-as-a-Second-Language programs for students ages eight to eighteen. Genres include adventure, mystery, humor, horror, and fantasy. All material submitted must be written in French, or easily translatable into French.
Website: www.aquilacommunications.com

Freelance Potential
Published 300 titles in 2002: 1 was by an unpublished writer. Receives 500 queries yearly.
Submissions and Payment: Guidelines available. Query with synopsis. Accepts photocopies. SAE/IRC. Responds in 1 month. Publication in 2–6 months. Royalty, 5%. Flat fee, $50–$500+.

Association for Childhood Education International

Suite 215, 17904 Georgia Avenue
Olney, MD 20832-2277

Director, Editorial Department: Anne Bauer

Publisher's Interests
This educational publisher offers resource books, reference books, videotapes, and audio tapes for teachers, parents, and child-development professionals at all levels. Topics cover early education, classroom intervention, curriculum development, classroom activities, and standardized testing.
Website: www.acei.org

Freelance Potential
Published 3 titles in 2002. Receives 120 unsolicited mss yearly.
Submissions and Payment: Guidelines available. Send complete ms. Accepts photocopies, computer printouts, and disk submissions (ASCII or Microsoft Word 5.0). SASE. Responds in 2 weeks. Publication in 1–3 years. Provides contributor's copies in lieu of payment.

ATL Press

P.O. Box 4563 T Station
Shrewsbury, MA 01545

Submissions Editor

Publisher's Interests
ATL Press publishes books related to science, including astronomy, biochemistry, and earth science. They also welcome fiction.
Website: www.atlpress.com

Freelance Potential
Published 12 titles in 2002: 2 were developed from unsolicited submissions and 1 was by an agented author. Of the 12 titles, 2 were by authors who were new to the publishing house. Receives 100–150 queries yearly.
Submissions and Payment: Guidelines available at website. Query with sample chapters and résumé; or send complete ms with résumé. Accepts photocopies, computer printouts, and IBM disk submissions. SASE. Responds in 3–4 weeks. Publication in 2–4 months. Royalty.

Avocet Press

19 Paul Court
Pearl River, NY 10965

Editor: Cynthia Webb

Publisher's Interests
A small, independent publisher, Avocet Press specializes in quality literature that ranges from poetry, to mysteries, to historical fiction. It is particularly interested in submissions of work that will awaken readers to angles of the world they may not have noticed before. Avocet Press publishes books for young adult and adult readers.
Website: www.avocetpress.com

Freelance Potential
Published 8 titles in 2002: 4 were developed from unsolicited submissions. Receives 2,400 queries yearly.
Submissions and Payment: Guidelines available at website. Query. SASE. Response time varies. Publication period varies. Royalty; advance.

Azro Press

PMB 342
1704 Llano St B
Santa Fe, NM 87505

Submissions Editor

Publisher's Interests
Dedicated to publishing the works of authors and illustrators who live in the American Southwest, Azro Press offers picture books for children between the ages of two and six; easy-to-read titles for ages five to eight; and fiction for children between eight and ten. It recently launched a new imprint, Green Knees, which features books written and illustrated by children.
Website: www.azropress.com

Freelance Potential
Plans to resume publishing (1 or more titles) in 2003.
Submissions and Payment: Guidelines available with #10 SASE (1 first-class stamp). Not accepting queries or unsolicited mss until late 2003.

Baker Book House Company

6030 East Fulton
Ada, MI 49301

Submissions Editor

Publisher's Interests
Established more than 60 years ago, Baker Book House Company features children's picture books, storybooks, and middle-grade titles that show the presence of God in the lives of readers. It seeks true-to-the-Bible stories with age-appropriate concepts, language, and illustrations.
Website: www.bakerbooks.com

Freelance Potential
Published 30 titles (24 juvenile) in 2002: all were by agented authors. Of the 30 titles, 1 was by an unpublished writer. Receives 100 queries yearly.
Submissions and Payment: Catalogue available at website. Agented submissions only. No unsolicited mss. Response time varies. Publication in 1–2 years. Royalty.

Ballyhoo Books

P.O. Box 534
Shoreham, NY 11786

Executive Editor: Liam Gerrity

Publisher's Interests
This publisher's list features craft books, how-to titles, and activity books on nature, the environment, science, and history for middle-grade children. It does not publish fiction.

Freelance Potential
Published 2 titles in 2002: both were developed from unsolicited submissions. Receives 300 queries, 100 unsolicited mss each year.

Submissions and Payment: Guidelines available. Query with outline and 3 sample chapters for long works. Send complete ms for shorter works. Accepts photocopies, computer printouts, and simultaneous submissions if identified. SASE. Responds to queries in 2 weeks, to mss in 1–2 months. Publication in 6–12 months. Royalty; advance. Flat fee.

Barefoot Books Ltd.

124 Walcot Street
Bath BA1 5BG
United Kingdom

Submissions Editor

Publisher's Interests
Barefoot Books celebrates art and story with books that inspire children to read deeper, search further, and explore their own creative gifts. It is looking for children's picture books and anthologies for readers up to 12 years of age, as well as original material with themes of personal independence, enthusiasm for learning, and acceptance of other traditions.
Website: www.barefootbooks.com

Freelance Potential
Published 25 titles in 2002.
Submissions and Payment: Guidelines available at website. Send complete ms with artwork. Accepts photocopies and computer printouts. SAE/IRC. Response time, publication period, and payment policy vary.

Barron's Educational Series

250 Wireless Boulevard
Hauppauge, NY 11788

Acquisitions Editor: Wayne Barr

Publisher's Interests
This publisher develops titles for the school and library markets.
It features fiction and nonfiction for children of all ages. 50%
self-, subsidy-, co-venture, or co-op published.
Website: www.barronseduc.com

Freelance Potential
Published 100 titles (80 juvenile) in 2002. Of the 100 titles, 5
were by unpublished writers and 5 were by new authors.
Receives 1,000 queries, 600 mss yearly.
Submissions and Payment: Guidelines available. Send complete
ms with résumé for fiction. Query with résumé, table of contents,
outline/synopsis, 2 sample chapters and description of audience
for nonfiction. SASE. Responds to queries in 1–3 months, to mss
in 6–8 months. Publication in 2 years. Royalty; advance. Flat fee.

Bay Light Publishing

P.O. Box 3032
Mooresville, NC 28117

Publisher: Charlotte Soutullo

Publisher's Interests
Founded in 1998, this Christian publisher features books for children ages four to twelve, including religious and inspirational fiction, story picture books, and series titles. Bay Light Publishing
seeks original works with Christian themes.
Website: www.baylightpub.com

Freelance Potential
Published 3 titles in 2002: each was developed from unsolicited submissions. Receives 25 queries, 25 unsolicited mss
each year.
Submissions and Payment: Query with clips or send complete
ms for fiction. Query with résumé for nonfiction. Accepts photocopies and simultaneous submissions. SASE. Responds in 3–6
weeks. Publication in 1 year. Flat fee.

Alexander Graham Bell Association for the Deaf and Hard of Hearing

3417 Volta Place NW
Washington, DC 20007-2778

Director of Publications: Elizabeth Quigley

Publisher's Interests
The Alexander Graham Bell Association for the Deaf and Hard of Hearing is the largest organization and information center on pediatric hearing loss. It offers nonfiction books that address a variety of issues related to children and deafness, as well as fiction titles and inspirational biographies for children with hearing loss. At this time, it seeks books in Spanish that address cochlear implants and the use of hearing aids to promote speech.
Website: www.agbell.org

Freelance Potential
Published 3 titles in 2002. Receives 5 unsolicited mss yearly.
Submissions and Payment: Guidelines available. Send up to 15 ms pages. Accepts computer printouts. SASE. Responds in 3 months. Publication in 9–16 months. Royalty, to 10%.

BePuzzled

University Games Corporation
2030 Harrison Street
San Francisco, CA 94110

General Manager: Steve Peek

Publisher's Interests
BePuzzled offers mystery stories paired with jigsaw puzzles that provide literal and visual clues to solving the mystery. Its children's list features thrillers aimed at seven- to nine-year-old readers. It will not consider stories that include violence, terrorists, profanity, or any references to drugs or sex.
Website: www.areyougame.com

Freelance Potential
Published 16 titles (10 juvenile) in 2002: all were developed from unsolicited submissions. Receives 500 queries yearly.
Submissions and Payment: Guidelines available. Query with short mystery story sample. Accepts computer printouts. SASE. Responds in 2 weeks. Publication in 1 year. Buys world rights. Flat fee.

Bick Publishing House

307 Neck Road
Madison, CT 06443

President: Dale Carlson

Publisher's Interests
Bick Publishing House was founded to bring professional information to adult and young adult readers. Its list includes titles
on psychology, science, meditation, special needs, disabilities,
and wildlife rehabilitation. It does not accept submissions for
fiction or picture books.
Website: www.bickpubhouse.com

Freelance Potential
Published 2 titles in 2002: 1 was by an agented author.
Receives 100 queries yearly.
Submissions and Payment: Guidelines and catalogue available
with 9x12 SASE ($1.26 postage). Query. Accepts photocopies.
SASE. Responds in 2 weeks. Publication in 1 year. Royalty,
10% net; advance.

A & C Black

37 Soho Square
London W1D 3QZ
United Kingdom

Submissions Editor: Claire Weatherhead

Publisher's Interests
A & C Black publishes high-quality educational titles for the
school and educational market. Nonfiction topics include
literacy, numeracy, and other cross-curriculum subjects.
Contemporary fiction for readers ages eight and up is offered,
as well as many fiction titles for reluctant readers.
Website: www.acblack.com

Freelance Potential
Published 85 titles (52 juvenile) in 2002: 40 were by agented
authors. Receives 600 queries yearly.
Submissions and Payment: Guidelines available. Query with
résumé. Accepts photocopies and e-mail queries to childrens@
acblack.com. SASE. Responds in 1 week. Publication period and
payment rates vary.

Blushing Rose Publishing

123 Bolinas Road
Fairfax, CA 94930

Publisher: Nancy Cogan Akmon

Publisher's Interests
This specialty publisher offers gift books for all ages, as well as other gift items, including diaries, travel journals, angel books, wedding photograph albums, baby albums, guest books, Christmas albums, and flower books. Children's books compose a small section of each year's list. New writers familiar with the company's work are welcome to query, but it is no longer reviewing unsolicited manuscripts. 10% self-, subsidy, co-venture, or co-op published material.
Website: www.blushingrose.com

Freelance Potential
Published 5 titles in 2002.
Submissions and Payment: Query. No unsolicited mss. SASE. Response time, publication period, and payment policy vary.

Books of Wonder

Room 806
216 West 18th Street
New York, NY 10011

Editor: Peter Glassman

Publisher's Interests
Founded in 1980, Books of Wonder specializes in original Oz stories by L. Frank Baum, as well as original Oz novels in the tradition of Baum's Oz books. It also features a line of gift editions of classic stories and tales. At this time, Books of Wonder is accepting submissions for Oz stories only.
Website: www.booksofwonder.com

Freelance Potential
Published 4 titles in 2002: all were developed from unsolicited submissions. Receives 40 unsolicited mss yearly.
Submissions and Payment: Guidelines available. Send complete ms. Accepts photocopies and computer printouts. SASE. Responds in 6 months. Publication in 6 months. Publication period varies. Royalty; advance.

The Boxwood Press

138 Ocean View Boulevard
Pacific Grove, CA 93950

Editorial Assistant: Patricia Kelly

Publisher's Interests
This publisher is known for its nonfiction and practical guides
on science, nature, and history, as well as autobiographies and
biographies. Its list also features novels and poetry books for all
ages. Boxwood Press has recently reorganized, and it is currently
seeking submissions for its children's division. New writers are
especially welcome.
Website: www.boxwoodpress.com

Freelance Potential
Published 10 titles in 2002: 2 were assigned.
Submissions and Payment: Guidelines and catalogue available
at website. Query with clips or send complete ms. Accepts photocopies and simultaneous submissions. SASE. Response time and
publication period vary. Payment policy varies.

Camex Books

535 Fifth Avenue
New York, NY 10017

Submissions Editor: Victor Benedetto

Publisher's Interests
This publisher offers books for preschool children through
young adults. Its list includes novelty books, picture books,
fairy tales, mysteries, folktales, romance fiction, and adventure
stories. Its nonfiction selections include self-help titles, books
on special-interest subjects, and celebrity biographies. While
query letters and unsolicited submissions are not accepted, the
editors will take phone calls from prospective authors who wish
to discuss their project.

Freelance Potential
Published 20 titles in 2002: 10 were by agented authors.
Submissions and Payment: No queries or unsolicited mss.
Editors prefer writers to call 212-682-8400 before submitting
work. Publication in 6 months. Royalty; advance. Flat fee.

Candlewick Press

2067 Massachusetts Avenue
Cambridge, MA 02140

Submissions Editor

Publisher's Interests
Candlewick Press publishes high-quality, unique books for children. Its list includes picture books, early chapter books, middle-grade novels, nonfiction for all ages, and poetry.
Website: www.candlewick.com

Freelance Potential
Published 180 titles in 2002: 70 were developed from unsolicited submissions, 130 were by agented authors, and 10 were reprint/licensed properties. Of the 180 titles, 4 were by unpublished writers and 25 were by authors who were new to the publishing house. Receives 4,000 queries, 10,000 unsolicited mss yearly.
Submissions and Payment: Not accepting queries or unsolicited mss at this time.

Carousel Press

P.O. Box 6038
Berkeley, CA 94706-0038

Publisher: Carole T. Myers

Publisher's Interests
Books on regional travel and travel-related topics are the specialty of this small publisher. Although many of its titles target adult readers, several are intended for young travelers and families. Its catalogue also includes books on national family attractions, travel games and activities, and weekend getaways. It is interested in receiving ideas for unique travel opportunities.
Website: www.carousel-press.com

Freelance Potential
Published 1 title in 2002. Receives 100 queries yearly.
Submissions and Payment: Query with table of contents and sample chapter. Accepts photocopies and computer printouts. SASE. Responds in 1 month. Publication in 1 year. Royalty; advance.

Cavendish Children's Books

99 White Plains Road
Tarrytown, NY 10591

Editor-at-Large: Margery Cuyler

Publisher's Interests
Cavendish Children's Books is an imprint of Marshall
Cavendish. It offers picture books, fiction, and nonfiction titles
for young readers at all levels. Its catalogue includes mystery,
humor, folklore, and historical and contemporary fiction.
Marshall Cavendish also features another imprint, Benchmark
Books, which publishes curriculum-related, nonfiction titles on
various subjects.
Website: www.marshallcavendish.com

Freelance Potential
Published 40 titles in 2002: 2 were developed from unsolicited submissions and 10 were by agented authors.
Submissions and Payment: Cavendish Children's Books is not
accepting manuscripts at this time.

Challenger Publishing

P.O. Box 428
Flagstaff Hill SA 5159
Australia

Acquisitions Editor

Publisher's Interests
Established in 2000, this new e-book publisher is seeking original children's fiction and young adult novels, as well as biographies and parenting titles.
Website: www.challengerbooks.com

Freelance Potential
Published many titles in 2002: all were developed from unsolicited submissions. Of the titles published, most were by
unpublished writers and all were by authors new to the publishing house. Receives 1,200 queries yearly.
Submissions and Payment: Guidelines and catalogue available
at website. Query with synopsis and clips; or send complete
ms. Accepts IBM disk submissions and e-mail submissions to
submissions@challengerbooks.com. SAE/IRC. Royalty; advance.

Chaosium

Suite 5
900 Murmansk Street
Oakland, CA 94607

Editor-in-Chief: Lynn Willis

Publisher's Interests
The fiction titles that appear on this publisher's list include
fantasy, horror, Arthurian legends, and tales of the occult.
Chaosium also produces resource books related to these genres
and role-playing games for young adults.
Website: www.chaosium.com

Freelance Potential
Published 18 titles in 2002: 4 were by agented authors. Of the
18 titles, 2 were by unpublished writers and 3 were by authors
new to the publishing house. Receives 20 queries yearly.
Submissions and Payment: Guidelines available. Query with
summary and writing samples. Accepts photocopies and
Macintosh disk submissions. SASE. Responds in 1–2 weeks.
Publication in 1–2 years. Flat fee, $.03–$.05 per word.

The Children's Nature Institute

1440 Harvard Street
Santa Monica, CA 90404

Submissions Editor

Publisher's Interests
Founded in 1985, this non-profit organization strives to improve
the quality and scope of education for young children through
interactive experiences with nature. Its goal is to inspire a sense
of respect and responsibility for the environment in children,
their families, and teachers. The list for this company includes
activity books about science and nature for five- to eight-year-
old children.
Website: www.childrensnatureinstitute.org

Freelance Potential
Published 2 titles in 2002. Receives 4 queries yearly.
Submissions and Payment: Send complete ms with résumé.
Accepts photocopies and computer printouts. SASE. Response
time varies. Publication period and payment policy vary.

China Books & Periodicals

2929 24th Street
San Francisco, CA 94110-4126

Editorial Director: Greg Jones

Publisher's Interests
Books and periodicals on Chinese language and culture are the specialty of this publisher. Its children's list features books for 6- to 15-year-old readers. Other Chinese cultural products, such as music, videos, and software, also appear in its catalogue.
Website: www.chinabooks.com

Freelance Potential
Plans to resume publishing (1 or more titles) in 2003. Receives 300 queries yearly.
Submissions and Payment: Catalogue available at website. Query with sample chapter or clips. Accepts photocopies, computer printouts, e-mail queries to greg@chinabooks.com, and simultaneous submissions if identified. SASE. Responds in 3 months. Publication in 1 year. Royalty, 8–12%.

Chrysalis Children's Books

64 Brewery Road
London N7 9NT
England

Submissions: Chester Fisher

Publisher's Interests
Chrysalis Children's Books publishes a wide range of fiction and nonfiction for readers up to the age of 14. Its list includes educational titles, novelty and board books, activity books, and bilingual titles. It is not interested in submissions of teen fiction. Submissions of nonfiction books are preferred at this time.
Website: www.chrysalisbooks.co.uk

Freelance Potential
Published 200 titles in 2002. Receives 80 unsolicited mss each year.
Submissions and Payment: Catalogue available at website. Send complete ms. Availability of artwork improves chance of acceptance. Accepts photocopies. SAE/IRC. Responds in 1 month. Publication period and payment policy vary.

C.I.S. Publishers and Distributors

180 Park Avenue
Lakewood, NJ 08701

Editorial Director: Mr. Ellinson

Publisher's Interests
Parenting books, self-help titles, and biographies appear on
this publisher's list, along with fiction for readers of all ages.
The primary focus of C.I.S. Publishers is on material that
reflects traditional Jewish values. Fiction with Jewish themes,
and stories written from an Orthodox Jewish perspective, are
among its current needs. C.I.S. Publishers and Distributors
was founded in 1984.

Freelance Potential
Published 50 titles in 2002: 1 was developed from an unsolicited
submission. Receives 250 queries yearly.
Submissions and Payment: Query with résumé and sample
chapters. Accepts computer printouts. SASE. Responds in 1
month. Publication in 1–2 years. Royalty. Flat fee.

The Colonial Williamsburg Foundation

Publications Department, P.O. Box 1776
Williamsburg, VA 23187-1776

Senior Editor/Writer: Donna Sheppard

Publisher's Interests
Historical fiction, picture books, and activity books for young
readers that relate to colonial Virginia or eighteenth-century
Williamsburg are found on this publisher's list. Writers who
wish to query must be familiar with the titles in its catalogue.
Website: www.history.org

Freelance Potential
Published 3 titles in 2002: all were developed from unsolicited
submissions and all were by agented authors. Of the 3 titles, 1
was by an author who was new to the publishing house.
Receives 25 queries yearly.
Submissions and Payment: Query with sample chapters.
Accepts photocopies and computer printouts. SASE. Responds
in 3 months. Publication period varies. Royalty. Flat fee.

Conari Press

Suite 101
2550 9th Street
Berkeley, CA 94710

Editorial Associate: Julie Kessler

Publisher's Interests
Relationships, personal growth, and spirituality are among the topics covered by the books Conari Press produces each year. It also offers parenting titles and titles related to women's issues. 20% self- and co-op published material.
Website: www.conari.com

Freelance Potential
Published 35 titles in 2002: 1 was developed from an unsolicited submission, 10 were by agented authors, and 1 was a reprint/licensed property. Receives 500 queries yearly.
Submissions and Payment: Guidelines available. Query with outline and sample chapters. Accepts photocopies and simultaneous submissions if identified. SASE. Responds in 3 months. Publication in 1–3 years. Royalty; advance.

Consortium Publishing

640 Weaver Hill Road
West Greenwich, RI 02817-2261

Chief of Publications: John M. Carlevale

Publisher's Interests
Established in 1990, this publisher offers teacher resources and student textbooks on childhood development, early education, counseling, self-help, and child abuse. 5% self-, subsidy-, co-venture, or co-op published material.

Freelance Potential
Published 20 titles in 2002: 2 were developed from unsolicited submissions and 1 was by an agented author. Of the 20 titles, 2 were by unpublished writers and 1 was by an author new to the publishing house. Receives 150 queries yearly.
Submissions and Payment: Guidelines available. Query or send complete ms with résumé. Accepts photocopies, computer printouts, and Macintosh disk submissions (Microsoft Word). SASE. Responds in 1–2 months. Publication in 3 months. Royalty.

Contemporary Books

Suite 900
130 E. Randolph Street
Chicago, IL 60601

Submissions Editor: Betsy Lane

Publisher's Interests
A division of McGraw-Hill, Contemporary Books publishes books for adult education classes, including GED and English-as-a-Second-Language programs. Prospective authors must consult our guidelines, available by mail and at our website, for our detailed submissions requirements.
Website: www.contemporarybooks.com

Freelance Potential
Published several titles in 2002. Receives 480 queries yearly.
Submissions and Payment: Guidelines available. Query with résumé, prospectus, table of contents, sample chapters, and market analysis. Accepts photocopies and disk submissions. SASE. Response time varies. Publication period and payment policy vary.

Continental Press

520 East Bainbridge Street
Elizabethtown, PA 17022

Vice President, Publications: Beth Spencer

Publisher's Interests
Continental Press publishes educational textbooks, early readers, and instructional materials for students in kindergarten through adult education, as well as teacher and classroom resource materials. It welcomes manuscripts for single titles and series, and proposals for programs that have been classroom tested.
Website: www.continentalpress.com

Freelance Potential
Published 50 titles in 2002. Of the 50 titles, 2 were by authors who were new to the publishing house. Receives 50 unsolicited mss yearly.
Submissions and Payment: Guidelines available. Query or send complete ms. Accepts computer printouts. SASE. Responds in 2 months. Publication period and payment policy vary.

Cornell Maritime Press

P.O Box 456
Centreville, MD 21617

Managing Editor: Charlotte Kurst

Publisher's Interests
A small house located in Maryland, Cornell Maritime Press specializes in books for the merchant marine, practical books for serious boaters, and regional works related to the Chesapeake Bay, Maryland, or the Delmarva Peninsula. It publishes two children's books each year under its Tidewater imprint. All of its children's books have regional themes.

Freelance Potential
Published 12 titles (3 juvenile) in 2002. Receives 600 queries each year.
Submissions and Payment: Guidelines available. Query with synopsis and sample chapters. Accepts photocopies and computer printouts. SASE. Responds in 1 month. Publication in 7 months. Royalty.

Cottonwood Press

Suite 398
107 Cameron Drive
Fort Collins, CO 80525

Editor: Cheryl Thurston

Publisher's Interests
Creative and practical classroom materials for English and language arts teachers of grades five through high school are featured by this publisher.
Website: www.cottonwoodpress.com

Freelance Potential
Published 4 titles in 2002: 1 was developed from an unsolicited submission. Of the 4 titles, 1 was by an unpublished writer and 1 was by an author who was new to the publishing house. Receives 60 queries, 120 unsolicited mss yearly.
Submissions and Payment: Guidelines available. Query with sample pages or send complete ms. Accepts computer printouts and simultaneous submissions. SASE. Responds in 1–4 weeks. Publication in 6–12 months. Royalty, 10%.

Course Crafters

44 Merrimac Street
Newburyport, MA 01950

Editorial Director: Sherry Litwack

Publisher's Interests
A book packager and developer, Course Crafters works with many educational publishers, including Scholastic, SRA/McGraw Hill, and Berlitz Publishing. In addition, it plans to publish some of its own titles in the future. Its editors encourage freelance writers of fiction, nonfiction, and educational materials to contact them to discuss some of the many writing opportunities they provide.
Website: www.coursecrafters.com

Freelance Potential
Published 50 titles in 2002.
Submissions and Payment: Guidelines available. Query with clips. Accepts photocopies and disk submissions. SASE. Responds in 1 month. Publication in 1–2 years. Flat fee.

The Creative Company

123 South Broad Street
Mankato, MN 56001

Editor: Aaron Frisch

Publisher's Interests
This publisher offers nonfiction titles organized in series for children in kindergarten through grade six. Its books cover the topics of science, sports, and geography. While it primarily targets school and library markets, it does sell a select number of picture books to the trade market.

Freelance Potential
Published 100 titles in 2002: 8 were developed from unsolicited submissions and 4 were by agented authors. Of the 100 titles, 1 was by an unpublished writer and 4 were by authors new to the publishing house. Receives 25 unsolicited mss yearly.
Submissions and Payment: Guidelines available. Send complete ms. Accepts photocopies. SASE. Responds in 10–12 weeks. Publication in 2 years. Flat fee.

Delmar Learning

Executive Woods
5 Maxwell Drive
Clifton Park, NY 12065

Acquisitions Editor: Erin O'Connor

Publisher's Interests
Books and software for education professionals and early childhood education students appear in this publisher's catalogue.
Website: www.delmarlearning.com

Freelance Potential
Published 25 titles in 2002: 3 were developed from unsolicited submissions and 1 was a reprint/licensed property. Of the 25 titles, 4 were by unpublished writers. Receives 120 queries each year.
Submissions and Payment: Guidelines available. Query with résumé, description of project, detailed outline, and sample chapters. Accepts photocopies, computer printouts, and simultaneous submissions if identified. SASE. Responds in 1 month. Publication in 2 years. Royalty; advance; grant.

Different Books

3900 Glenwood Avenue
Golden Valley, MN 55422

Editor: Roger Hammer

Publisher's Interests
With titles for middle-grade and young adult readers, Different Books is seeking original works with positive characters who overcome adversities despite their disabilities.

Freelance Potential
Published 3 titles in 2002: each was developed from an unsolicited submission. Of the 3 titles, each was by an unpublished writer new to the publishing house. Receives 1,000 queries, 300 unsolicited mss yearly.
Submissions and Payment: Guidelines available. Query or send complete ms. Accepts photocopies and computer printouts. No simultaneous submissions. SASE. Responds to queries in 1 week, to mss in 2 months. Publication in 1 year. Royalty. Flat fee for each new printing.

Dog-Eared Publications

P.O. Box 620863
Middleton, WI 53562-0863

Publisher: Nancy Field

Publisher's Interests
Dog-Eared Publications aims to turn young children into environmentally aware earth citizens and foster a love of science and nature. It offers middle-grade readers nonfiction titles, interactive materials, activity books, and mysteries about science and nature.
Website: www.dog-eared.com

Freelance Potential
Published 3 titles (2 juvenile) in 2002: 1 was a reprint/licensed property. Receives 120 queries yearly.
Submissions and Payment: Query with outline/synopsis. No unsolicited mss. Prefers e-mail queries to field@dog-eared.com. Accepts photocopies, computer printouts, and disk submissions. SASE. Response time varies. Publication period varies. Royalty; advance.

Doral Publishing

Suite 225 West
10451 Palmeras Drive SW
Sun City, AZ 85373

Publisher: Alvin Grossman

Publisher's Interests
This specialty publisher features books on dog handling, breeding, nutrition, training, hunting, and search and rescue, as well as titles on specific breeds of dogs.
Website: www.doralpub.com

Freelance Potential
Published 9 titles (1 juvenile) in 2002: 3 were developed from unsolicited submissions and 3 were by agented authors. Of the 9 titles, 1 was by an unpublished writer and 4 were by new authors. Receives 50 queries yearly.
Submissions and Payment: Guidelines available. Query with sample chapter and table of contents. Availability of artwork improves chance of acceptance. SASE. Responds in 2 weeks. Publication in 10 months. Royalty, 10% of net.

Eastgate Systems

134 Main Street
Watertown, MA 02472

Acquisitions Editor: Diane Greco

Publisher's Interests
Publishing books for all ages, including juvenile fiction and
nonfiction, Eastgate Systems seeks work in hypertext form—
linked texts, pictures, sound, and video. E-books and downloadable manuscripts, however, are not accepted.
Website: www.eastgate.com

Freelance Potential
Published 3 titles in 2002: all were developed from unsolicited
submissions. Receives 25 unsolicited mss yearly.
Submissions and Payment: Guidelines available at website.
Send complete ms. Accepts disk submissions, CD-ROMS, URL
submissions to dgreco@eastgate.com, and simultaneous sub-
missions if identified. SASE. Responds in 4–6 weeks.
Publication in 1 year. Royalty, 15%; advance.

ESP Publishers, Inc.

Suite 444
1212 North 39th Street
Tampa, FL 33605

Editor: Dan Brooks

Publisher's Interests
This educational publisher offers textbooks and workbooks for
use in kindergarten through twelfth-grade classrooms. All of its
books are curriculum-based. Subjects covered include geography, health and fitness, history, mathematics, social issues,
science, technology, and the environment.
Website: www.espbooks.com

Freelance Potential
Published 100–150 titles in 2002: all were by agented authors.
Receives 24 queries, 4 unsolicited mss yearly.
Submissions and Payment: Query or send complete ms.
Accepts photocopies, computer printouts, and simultaneous
submissions if identified. SASE. Responds in 1 week.
Publication period and payment policy vary.

Excelsior Cee Publishing

P.O. Box 5861
Norman, OK 73070

Publisher: J. C. Marshall

Publisher's Interests
How-to, self-help, and inspirational titles appear on this publisher's list, along with biographies, humor, books on family-related issues, and personal philosophies. Excelsior Cee does not publish fiction.
Website: www.excelsiorcee.com

Freelance Potential
Published 10 titles in 2002: 6 were developed from unsolicited submissions. Receives 700–1,000 queries yearly.
Submissions and Payment: Query with synopsis; include sample chapter for longer works. Accepts photocopies, computer printouts, and simultaneous submissions if identified. SASE. Responds in 6 weeks. Publication in 6 months. Payment policy varies.

Fearon Teacher Aids

3195 Wilson Drive NW
Grand Rapids, MI 49544

Publisher: George Bratton

Publisher's Interests
Teacher references and resources for preschool through eighth-grade classrooms are the specialty of this educational publisher. Its list includes books, workbooks, and reproducibles for a variety of curriculum areas including language arts, critical thinking, early learning, and social studies.

Freelance Potential
Published several titles in 2002: most were developed from unsolicited submissions. Receives 500+ queries yearly.
Submissions and Payment: Query with résumé. Accepts photocopies, computer printouts, disk submissions, and simultaneous submissions if identified. SASE. Response time varies.
Publication period and payment policy vary.

Fiesta City Publishers

P.O. Box 5861
Santa Barbara, CA 93150-5861

President: Frank E. Cooke

Publisher's Interests
Books on singing, songwriting, music, musical instruments, and cooking for middle-grade and young adult students are offered in this publisher's list. It is interested in original musical plays and how-to books for musical instruction, as well as educational material about music and the theater. New writers are invited to submit queries for their work. 50% self-, subsidy, co-venture, or co-op published material.

Freelance Potential
Published 2 titles in 2002. Receives 60 queries yearly.
Submissions and Payment: Query with clips or writing samples. Accepts photocopies and simultaneous submissions if identified. SASE. Responds in 1–2 months. Publication period varies. Royalty.

Focus Publishing

502 Third Street NW
Bemidji, MN 56601

President: Jan Haley

Publisher's Interests
This Christian publisher produces books that promote the lordship of Jesus Christ in the lives of readers. It seeks real-life problem-solving titles using Christian values for young adults.
Website: www.focuspublishing.com

Freelance Potential
Published 5 titles in 2002: all were developed from unsolicited submissions. Of the 5 titles, 4 were by authors new to the publishing house. Receives 800 queries yearly.
Submissions and Payment: Guidelines available. Query with synopsis; include market description for fiction. Availability of artwork improves chance of acceptance. Accepts photocopies and computer printouts. SASE. Responds in 1 week. Publication in 6 months. Royalty, 7.5–10%.

Fondo de Cultura Economica USA

2293 Verus Street
San Diego, CA 92154

Submissions Editor: B. Mireles

Publisher's Interests
This publisher offers books written in Spanish for Latin American residents of all ages who live in the US. Its juvenile list includes picture books, middle-grade books, and young adult titles, fiction as well as nonfiction.
Website: www.fceusa.com

Freelance Potential
Published 40 titles in 2002: 3–5 were developed from unsolicited submissions and 35 were by agented authors. Receives 300 queries yearly.
Submissions and Payment: Query with résumé. Accepts photocopies, computer printouts, and disk submissions. Availability of artwork improves chance of acceptance. SASE. Responds in 6 months. Publication in 6 months. Royalty; advance. Flat fee.

Franklin Watts

Scholastic Inc.
90 Sherman Turnpike
Danbury, CT 06816

Editor-in-Chief: Kate Nunn

Publisher's Interests
This library imprint of Scholastic features nonfiction, curriculum-based titles and biographies for schools and libraries. Its list targets middle-grade and young adult readers.
Website: www.scholastic.com

Freelance Potential
Published 250 titles in 2002: 5 were developed from unsolicited submissions, 20 were by agented authors, and 25–30 were reprint/licensed properties. Of the 250 titles, 8 were by unpublished writers and 13 were by authors new to the publishing house. Receives 1,000+ queries yearly.
Submissions and Payment: Query with résumé, proposal, outline, and sample chapters. No unsolicited mss. SASE. Responds in 3–5 weeks. Publication period and payment policy vary.

Gallopade International

P.O. Box 2779
Peachtree City, GA 30269

Editorial Department

Publisher's Interests
Gallopade International publishes educational products for students ages seven through seventeen. Its product line covers topics related to each of the 50 states, foreign languages, science, mathematics, and writing. It also offers books on black heritage, character-building, and sex education.
Website: www.gallopade.com

Freelance Potential
Published 600 titles (505 juvenile) in 2002: 6 were by unpublished writers and 6 were by authors who were new to the publishing house. Receives 25 queries yearly.
Submissions and Payment: Query with résumé. No unsolicited manuscripts. SASE. Responds in 2 days. Publication period varies. Flat fee.

Gefen Publishing House

12 New Street
Hewlett, NY 11557-2012

Editor: Ilan Greenfield, Jr.

Publisher's Interests
Headquartered in Jerusalem, this publisher distributes its own titles as well as those of other Israeli publishers. Its list, which focuses on Jewish culture, includes a selection of children's books.
Website: www.israelbooks.com

Freelance Potential
Published 30 titles (5 juvenile) in 2002: most were developed from unsolicited submissions. Of the 30 titles, 20 were by authors who were new to the publishing house. Receives 240 queries, 100+ unsolicited mss yearly.
Submissions and Payment: Guidelines available. Query or send complete ms. Accepts photocopies, computer printouts, and simultaneous submissions if identified. SASE. Response time, publication period, and payment policy vary.

David R. Godine, Publisher

9 Hamilton Place
Boston, MA 02108

Editorial Department

Publisher's Interests
This small publisher has a list that features children's fiction
for preschool through young adult readers. It is interested in
unique, original picture books and middle-grade novels.
Website: www.godine.com

Freelance Potential
Published 25 titles (12 juvenile) in 2002: 10 were developed
from unsolicited submissions and 10 were reprint/licensed
properties. Of the 25 titles, 4 were by unpublished writers
and 10 were by authors who were new to the publishing
house. Receives 1,000+ queries yearly.
Submissions and Payment: Catalogue available at website.
Query. No unsolicited mss. Publication period and payment
policy vary.

Good Year Books

294 Jefferson Road
Parsippany, NJ 07054

Editorial Director

Publisher's Interests
Good Year Books offers professional resource books for teachers
working with students in preschool through high school. It also
produces a wide range of materials for parents that supplement
the school and homeschool curricula.
Website: www.goodyearbooks.com

Freelance Potential
Published 10–15 titles in 2002. Receives 200 unsolicited mss
each year.
Submissions and Payment: Guidelines available. Prefers
complete ms; will accept query with 1–2 sample chapters and
outline/synopsis. Accepts photocopies, computer printouts,
disk submissions, and simultaneous submissions. SASE.
Responds in 3 months. Publication in 18 months. Flat fee.

Greenwillow Books

HarperCollins Children's Books
1350 Avenue of the Americas
New York, NY 10019

Editorial Department

Publisher's Interests
Greenwillow Books, a well-known imprint of HarperCollins, publishes concept books, toddler books, and picture books for young children; contemporary middle-grade and young adult fiction; and nonfiction on nature, animals, and the environment for children under seven years of age. It is not accepting queries or unsolicited manuscripts at this time.
Website: www.harperchildrens.com

Freelance Potential
Published 45 titles in 2002: 2 were developed from unsolicited submissions and 5 were by agented authors. Receives 5,500 queries, 8,000+ unsolicited mss yearly.
Submissions and Payment: Not accepting queries or unsolicited mss at this time.

GT Publications

P.O. Box 34
New Ipswich, NH 03071

Editor: Mike Hills

Publisher's Interests
This publisher features nonfiction and fiction books by and about gay youth. It seeks original material that is both intellectual and entertaining.
Website: www.gtpublications.com

Freelance Potential
Published 5 titles in 2002: all were developed from unsolicited submissions. Of the 5 titles, 3 were by unpublished writers and all were by authors new to the publishing house. Receives 60 queries, 35 unsolicited mss yearly.
Submissions and Payment: Guidelines available with 4x9 SASE ($.74 postage). Query with clips for fiction. Send complete ms for nonfiction. Accepts photocopies. SASE. Responds in 1–6 months. Publication in 3–6 months. Royalty, 10%; advance, $450.

Harcourt Canada Ltd.

55 Horner Avenue
Toronto, Ontario M8Z 4X6
Canada

Director of Research & Development: Nancy Reilly

Publisher's Interests
Textbooks and classroom materials for students in kindergarten through grade 12 are featured in the catalogue of this imprint of Harcourt Company. Its titles cover science, social studies, music, language arts, mathematics, and media education.
Website: www.harcourtcanada.com

Freelance Potential
Published 50 titles (30 juvenile) in 2002: all were by agented authors and 10 were reprint/licensed properties. Of the 50 titles, 6 were by authors who were new to the publishing house. Receives 200 queries yearly.
Submissions and Payment: Query. No unsolicited mss. SAE/IRC. Responds in 6–12 months. Publication period and payment policy vary.

Harvard Common Press

535 Albany Street
Boston, MA 02118

Publisher: Bruce Shaw

Publisher's Interests
The Harvard Common Press is a small, independent publisher of trade books. It specializes in parenting and child-care books, cookbooks, and health and beauty titles. Topics covered by some of its current titles include childbirth, parenting, child care, pregnancy, and discipline.
Website: www.harvardcommonpress.com

Freelance Potential
Published 15 titles in 2002. Receives 1,200 queries yearly.
Submissions and Payment: Guidelines available. Query with résumé, outline, 1–2 sample chapters, and market analysis. Accepts photocopies, computer printouts, and simultaneous submissions if identified. SASE. Responds in 1–3 months. Publication period varies. Royalty, 5%; advance, $1,500+.

Hodder Children's Books

338 Euston Road
London NW1 3BH
United Kingdom

Editorial Assistant, Nonfiction: Katie Sergeant

Publisher's Interests
This British publisher features picture books, beginning readers, storybooks, and chapter books for children, as well as nonfiction titles for young readers.
Website: www.hodderheadline.co.uk

Freelance Potential
Published 500 titles in 2002: 10 were developed from unsolicited submissions, 200 were by agented authors, and 20 were reprint/licensed properties. Receives 3,000 queries, 2,000 unsolicited mss yearly.
Submissions and Payment: Query with synopsis or send complete ms. Accepts photocopies and computer printouts. SAE/IRC. Responds in 3–6 months. Publication in 12–18 months. Royalty; advance. Flat fee.

Holloway House Publishing Group

8060 Melrose Avenue
Los Angeles, CA 90046

Submissions Editor: Raymond Locke

Publisher's Interests
Biographies of role models for young adults appear on the list of this publishing company, which targets an African-American audience. While most of its titles are assigned, it will consider queries or submissions for its Black American series.
Website: www.hollowayhousebooks.com

Freelance Potential
Published 14 titles in 2002: Receives 500 queries, 600 unsolicited mss yearly.
Submissions and Payment: Guidelines available. Query with résumé; or send complete ms. Accepts photocopies, computer printouts, and disk submissions. SASE. Responds to queries in 3 weeks, to mss in 3 months. Publication period and payment policy vary.

Horizon Publishers

P.O. Box 490
50 South 500 West
Bountiful, UT 84011-0490

Submissions Editor: Doug Cox

Publisher's Interests
General trade books appear on the list of Horizon Publishers, along with titles for members of the Mormon religion. It does not publish secular or educational books for children or teens.
Website: www.horizonpublishers.com

Freelance Potential
Published 20 titles in 2002: 18 were developed from unsolicited submissions and 2 were by agented authors. Receives 100 queries, 200 unsolicited mss yearly.
Submissions and Payment: Guidelines available. Query or send complete ms. Accepts photocopies and computer printouts. SASE. Responds to queries in 1–3 months, to mss in 4–5 months. Publication period varies. Royalty, 8%; advance, $100–$500. Flat fee.

Huntington House Publishers

P.O. Box 53788
Lafayette, LA 70505

Publisher: Mark Anthony

Publisher's Interests
Huntington House Publishers offers adult nonfiction titles as well as some inspirational fiction for young adults. It is actively seeking manuscripts on such topics as education, current events, women's issues, and family issues. Authors must be ready for an aggressive marketing and publicity schedule.
Website: www.huntingtonhousebooks.com

Freelance Potential
Published 10–20 titles in 2002. Receives 2,000 queries yearly.
Submissions and Payment: Guidelines available. Query with 200- to 300-word proposal. No unsolicited mss. Accepts photocopies, computer printouts, and simultaneous submissions if identified. SASE. Responds in 3–4 months. Publication in 6–8 months. Royalty.

Hyperion Books for Children

114 Fifth Avenue
New York, NY 10011

Editor-in-Chief: Andrea Pinkney

Publisher's Interests
An imprint of The Walt Disney Company, this well-known publisher features board books, picture books, chapter books, and novels for preschool, elementary, middle-grade, and young adult readers. It is not currently accepting unsolicited submissions. Hyperion Books suggests that new writers contact the Children's Book Council or the Society of Children's Book Writers and Illustrators for information on publishing opportunities currently available.
Website: www.disney.com

Freelance Potential
Published 197 titles (183 juvenile) in 2002.
Submissions and Payment: Not accepting queries or unsolicited manuscripts at this time.

Illumination Arts

P.O. Box 1865
Bellevue, WA 98009

Editorial Director: Ruth Thompson

Publisher's Interests
Enlightening fiction and nonfiction picture books with inspirational and spiritual themes for four- to ten-year-old children are offered by this small publishing house.
Website: www.illumin.com

Freelance Potential
Published 5 titles in 2002: all were developed from unsolicited submissions. Of the 5 titles, 1 was by an unpublished writer and 4 were by authors who were new to the publishing house. Receives 2,000 queries yearly.
Submissions and Payment: Guidelines available. Query or send complete ms with sample illustrations. Accepts simultaneous submissions if identified. SASE. Response time, publication period, and payment policy vary.

ImaJinn Books

P.O. Box 162
Hickory Corners, MI 49060-0162

Senior Editor: Linda Kichline

Publisher's Interests
Established in 1998, this publisher features children's and
young adult fantasy and science fiction titles. It seeks fast-paced,
action-packed stories with strong sci-fi or fantasy elements.
Website: www.imajinnbooks.com

Freelance Potential
Published 30 titles (2 juvenile) in 2002: all were developed
from unsolicited submissions. Of the 30 titles, 1 was by an
author who was new to the publishing house. Receives 180–
240 queries yearly.
Submissions and Payment: Guidelines and catalogue available
with #10 SASE ($.60 postage). Query. No unsolicited mss.
SASE. Responds in 2–3 months. Publication in 18 months.
Royalty, 8%.

InQ Publishing Co.

P.O. Box 10
North Aurora, IL 60542

Publisher: Jana Fitting

Publisher's Interests
InQ Publishing offers books and products related to child
care, health and safety, and education. Game books, activity
books, how-to titles, and a line of books and products specifically for babysitters and day-care providers appear on its list. It
is not interested in reviewing submissions of poetry, children's
fiction, or novels. 5% self-, subsidy-, co-venture, or co-op published material.
Website: www.inqpub.com

Freelance Potential
Published 4 titles in 2002. Receives 50 queries yearly.
Submissions and Payment: Query with writing samples. No
unsolicited mss. Accepts photocopies. SASE. Responds in 6
weeks. Publication in 18 months. Payment policy varies.

Iron Crown Enterprises

112 Goodman Street
Charlottesville, VA 22902

Managing Editor

Publisher's Interests
Iron Crown Enterprises is a publisher of adventure games, board games, role-playing games, puzzles, and card games for adults and young adults. Writers who would like to submit an idea for consideration should first consult the company's detailed guidelines, available at the website or by mail.
Website: www.ironcrown.com

Freelance Potential
Published 6 titles in 2002. Receives 10–20 queries yearly.
Submissions and Payment: Guidelines available. Query with outline/synopsis and writing sample. Accepts computer print-outs, disk submissions, and e-mail queries to ozmar_ice@yahoo.com. SASE. Responds in 6 months. Publication in 6–12 months. Royalty, 2–6%; advance, $100. Flat fee, $500–$1,500.

January Productions

116 Washington Avenue
Hawthorne, NJ 07507

Creative Director: Barbara Peller

Publisher's Interests
January Productions features high-interest/low-reading-level books, videos, sound filmstrips, and early learning cassettes for schools and libraries. Topics include language arts, study skills, consumerism, and computers. It is interested in original material that enhances traditional classroom lessons and helps preschool through high school students develop social and cognitive skills.
Website: www.awpeller.com

Freelance Potential
Receives 100 queries, 50 unsolicited mss yearly.
Submissions and Payment: Catalogue available at website. Prefers query with outline/synopsis. Accepts complete ms with résumé. Accepts photocopies. SASE. Response time and publication period vary. Flat fee, $325–$375.

KIDSZIP LTD

43 Rue Barbés, Peht Ivry
Ivry-sur-Seine, 94200
France

Editor

Publisher's Interests
This French e-publishing house offers fiction and nonfiction
titles for young readers between three and thirteen years of
age. All of its titles are translated into five languages.
Website: www.kidszip.com

Freelance Potential
Published 100 titles (90 juvenile) in 2002: most were developed
from unsolicited submissions. Of the 100 titles, 50 were by
authors new to the publishing house. Receives 4,800 queries
each year.
Submissions and Payment: Guidelines and catalogue available at website. Send complete ms. Accepts e-mail submissions
through website. SASE. Responds in 2 months. Publication in
3 months. Royalty, to 8%.

Kingfisher

215 Park Avenue South
New York, NY 10003

Submissions Editor

Publisher's Interests
With a focus on nonfiction books for children ages two and up,
Kingfisher offers picture books, anthologies, foreign language
materials, and series titles. An imprint of Houghton Mifflin
Company, it also publishes fiction titles and books on science,
nature, the environment, animals, geography, myths and legends, holidays, and food. Kingfisher is not accepting unsolicited
manuscripts at this time; all work is done by assignment only.
Website: www.houghtonmifflinbooks.com/kingfisher

Freelance Potential
Published 60 titles in 2002: all were by agented authors.
Submissions and Payment: Catalogue available with 9x12
SASE (5 first-class stamps). All work is assigned by publisher.
No unsolicited mss.

Kodiak Media Group

P.O. Box 1029-A
Wilsonville, OR 97070

Marketing Director: Rhonda Grabenhorst-Pachl

Publisher's Interests
A special interest publisher, Kodiak Media Group focuses on topics related to raising and educating hearing-impaired and deaf children. Its audience includes teachers, parents, administrators, and others involved in special education. While it will accept queries, most of its books are done in-house.

Freelance Potential
Published 2 titles in 2002. Receives 10 queries, 10 unsolicited mss yearly.
Submissions and Payment: Query or send complete ms. Accepts photocopies, computer printouts, and simultaneous submissions if identified. Accepts camera-ready artwork and B/W prints. SASE. Responds in 1 month. Publication period varies. Royalty, negotiable.

LangMarc Publishing

P.O. Box 90488
Austin, TX 78709

Submissions Editor

Publisher's Interests
LangMarc Publishing is a small press that specializes in inspirational fiction and nonfiction books for young adults. Its list includes science and technology titles, as well as humor, and inspirational and religious fiction. At this time, it will consider well-written, practical nonfiction that speaks to today's young adults, thought-provoking stories for teens, and titles that focus on positive feelings and attitudes toward difficult issues in adolescent years.
Website: www.langmarc.com

Freelance Potential
Published 4 titles (1 juvenile) in 2002.
Submissions and Payment: Query. Response time varies. Publication in 9 months. Payment policy varies.

Leadership Publishers Inc.

P.O. Box 8358
Des Moines, IA 50301-8358

Editor: Dr. Lois F. Roets

Publisher's Interests
Teacher and administrator reference materials, and acceleration and enrichment programs for kindergarten through grade 12, are offered by this educational publisher.

Freelance Potential
Published 2 titles in 2002. Of the 2 titles, 1 was by an unpublished writer and 1 was by an author who was new to the publishing house. Receives 15 queries yearly.
Submissions and Payment: Send for guidelines and catalogue before submitting (SASE with 2 first-class stamps). Then query with table of contents, outline, and 2 sample chapters. Accepts photocopies and computer printouts. No simultaneous submissions. SASE. Responds in 2 months. Publication in 6–12 months. Royalty, 10%. Flat fee.

Lion Books

Suite B
210 Nelson Road
Scarsdale, NY 10583

Editor: Harriet Ross

Publisher's Interests
Lion Books specializes in young adult nonfiction with a specific interest in easy-to-read political histories and biographies of minority personalities. Its list also includes fiction for younger children, and juvenile titles on sports and crafts. It would like to see submissions by new writers who are familiar with ethnic nonfiction. Lion Books does not accept unsolicited manuscripts.

Freelance Potential
Published 11 titles (9 juvenile) in 2002: 5 were developed from unsolicited submissions. Of the 11 titles, 2 were by unpublished writers. Receives 50–70 queries yearly.
Submissions and Payment: Query with outline. No unsolicited mss. Accepts photocopies. SASE. Responds in 1 month. Publication in 6 months. Royalty; advance. Flat fee.

Little Blue Works

7419 Ebbert Drive SE
Port Orchard, WA 98367

Editor: Cris Newport

Publisher's Interests
This publisher offers books that show the world through the eyes
of children and teens. It seeks titles for its My Adventure series.
Website: www.windstormcreative.com

Freelance Potential
Published 60 titles (20 juvenile) in 2002: most were developed
from unsolicited submissions and 2 were reprint/licensed
properties. Of the 60 titles, 48 were by unpublished writers
and 48 were by authors new to the publishing house.
Receives 10,000+ queries yearly.
Submissions and Payment: Guidelines available at website.
Submissions that do not indicate a website visit will not be
opened. Query with 1-page synopsis. SASE. Response time and
publication period vary. Royalty, 10–15%.

Living the Good News

Suite 400
600 Grant Street
Denver, CO 80203

Editorial Management Team

Publisher's Interests
Living the Good News publishes books with a spiritual emphasis,
including children's books, family-building books, and religious
education books. For the coming year, it is looking for children's
fiction, poetry, and nonfiction titles.

Freelance Potential
Published 12 titles in 2002: 1 was developed from an unsolicited submission and 2 were by agented authors. Of the 12
titles, 1 was by an unpublished writer. Receives 150 queries
each year.
Submissions and Payment: Query with sample chapter. Accepts
photocopies, computer printouts, Macintosh disk submissions,
and simultaneous submissions. SASE. Responds in 2 months.
Publication in 2 years. Royalty.

James Lorimer & Company

35 Britain Street
Toronto, Ontario M5A 1R7
Canada

Acquisitions Editor

Publisher's Interests
This publisher features contemporary stories that reflect Canada's
multicultural society. It seeks realistic story lines dealing with
social issues in Canadian settings. James Lorimer considers submissions from Canadian authors only.
Website: www.lorimer.ca

Freelance Potential
Published 20 titles (8 juvenile) in 2002: 2 were developed
from unsolicited submissions and 2 were reprint/licensed
properties. Of the 20 titles, 2 were by unpublished writers.
Receives 96 queries yearly.
Submissions and Payment: Canadian authors only. Query with
outline/synopsis and 2 sample chapters. SASE. Responds in 4–6
months. Publication period varies. Royalty; advance.

The Love and Logic Press

2207 Jackson Street
Golden, CO 80401-2300

Publisher

Publisher's Interests
This publisher's catalogue features books, videos, and audio
tapes for parents, teachers, and professionals who work with
children. The material it offers focuses on issues related to
child development, education, and psychology. Its philosophy is
that love allows children to grow through their mistakes, and
logic helps them live with the consequences of their choices.
Website: www.loveandlogic.com

Freelance Potential
Published 2 titles in 2002. Receives 300 queries yearly.
Submissions and Payment: Query with proposal or outline.
Accepts photocopies, computer printouts, and simultaneous
submissions. SASE. Responds in 1 month. Publication in 18
months. Royalty, 5–7%.

LTDBooks

200 North Service Road West, Unit 1, Suite 301
Oakville, Ontario L6M 2Y1
Canada

Editors: Dee Lloyd & T. K. Sheils

Publisher's Interests
Electronic books and a limited number of paperbacks for readers
age 12 and up are the specialty of this Canadian publisher. It
seeks historical and contemporary romance, mystery, horror,
fantasy, mainstream fiction, and science fiction.
Website: www.ltdbooks.com

Freelance Potential
Published 40 titles (4 juvenile) in 2002: most were developed
from unsolicited submissions. Receives 50 queries, 50 unsolicited mss each year.
Submissions and Payment: Guidelines available at website.
Query with 3–5 page synopsis and first 3 chapters. Accepts
queries on disk (RTF format) and e-mail queries to editor@
ltdbooks.com. Royalty, 30%.

The Lutterworth Press

P.O. Box 60
Cambridge CB1 2NT
United Kingdom

Managing Editor: Adrian Brink

Publisher's Interests
Originally founded as the Religious Tract Society in London
more than 200 years ago, this publisher is now dedicated to providing literature with an emphasis on moral values for young
readers and adults. Its list includes picture books and nature
stories for toddlers; fiction for five- and six-year-old children;
middle-grade novels and mysteries; and humor, fairy tales, and
fantasy for four- to ten-year-old readers.
Website: www.lutterworth.com

Freelance Potential
Published 12 titles in 2002.
Submissions and Payment: Query with outline/synopsis and
1 or 2 sample chapters. Artwork improves chance of acceptance.
SAE/IRC. Responds in 2 months. Royalty.

Mage Publishers

1032 29th Street NW
Washington, DC 20007

Submissions Editor: Amin Sepehri

Publisher's Interests
Mage Publishers features high-quality English language books
about Persian culture, including history, biographies, poetry,
and children's tales and legends.
Website: www.mage.com

Freelance Potential
Published 3 titles in 2002: 1 was developed from an unso-
licited submission and 2 were reprint/licensed properties.
Receives 50 queries, 25 unsolicited mss yearly.
Submissions and Payment: Guidelines available at website.
Query or send complete ms. Accepts photocopies and computer
printouts. Availability of artwork improves chance of acceptance.
SASE. Responds in 1–3 months. Publication in 9–15 months.
Royalty; advance.

Majestic Books

P.O. Box 19097
Johnston, RI 02919

Publisher: Cindy MacDonald

Publisher's Interests
This publisher specializes in softcover collections of short
stories and poems written by children under 18 years of age. It
will consider original material on all subjects suitable for young
adult readers.

Freelance Potential
Published 2 titles in 2002: both were developed from unsolicited submissions. Receives 600 unsolicited mss yearly.
Submissions and Payment: Guidelines available. Catalogue,
$3.50. Send complete ms to 2,000 words. All submissions must
include age of author. Accepts photocopies, computer printouts,
disk submissions (WordPerfect), and simultaneous submissions
if identified. SASE. Responds in 2 weeks. Publication in 6
months. Royalty, 10%.

Marsh Media

8025 Ward Parkway Plaza
Kansas City, MO 64112

Submissions Editor: Joan K. Marsh

Publisher's Interests
Established in 1969, this publisher specializes in multi-media
kits for children in kindergarten through grade four. Its storybooks with accompanying videos and teaching guides offer programs for character education. Topics covered include personal
development, friendship, honesty, self-control, respect, courtesy,
trust, creative thinking, responsibility, ecology, personal power,
and risk-taking.
Website: www.marshmedia.com

Freelance Potential
Published 1 title in 2002: it was assigned. Receives 12
queries yearly.
Submissions and Payment: Query with résumé. SASE.
Response time, publication period, and payment policy vary.

McGraw-Hill School Division

21st Floor
2 Penn Plaza
New York, NY 10121

Editor: Andre Mattis

Publisher's Interests
This publishing unit of The McGraw-Hill Companies is dedicated
to educating children and to helping educational professionals
by providing high-quality material and services. It offers classroom materials, activity books, series titles, and educational
titles for students in kindergarten through grade six. Subjects
covered include bilingual education, language arts, science,
math, reading, and social studies.
Website: www.mhschool.com

Freelance Potential
Published 50 titles in 2002.
Submissions and Payment: Query with résumé. SASE. All
materials are written on assignment. No unsolicited mss.
Response time and publication period vary. Flat fee.

Midwest Traditions

3710 North Morris Boulevard
Shorewood, WI 53211

Director: Philip Martin

Publisher's Interests
The books published by Midwest Traditions focus on American
heritage, Native American legends, and regional topics related
to life in the American Midwest. It offers historical fiction, ghost
stories, and folklore for readers ages eight and up, and nonfiction for readers of all ages. Prospective authors should have
first hand knowledge of the subject they are writing about.

Freelance Potential
Published 3 titles in 2002: all were developed from unsolicited
submissions. Of the 3 titles, 2 were by unpublished writers.
Receives 36 queries yearly.
Submissions and Payment: Guidelines available. Query with
sample chapters. Accepts photocopies and computer printouts.
SASE. Responds in 4–5 weeks. Publication in 1 year. Royalty.

Miles Kelly Publishing

Bardfield Centre, Great Bardfield
Braintree CM6 4SL
United Kingdom

Submissions Editor

Publisher's Interests
This independent British publisher features a list of children's
illustrated books. It offers children's encyclopedias, atlases, quiz
books, and posters, as well as novelty books, poetry, and fiction.
At this time, Miles Kelly Publishing is interested in reference
books and quiz books for young readers. Topics include animals,
geography, history, mathematics, nature, the environment, science, and technology.
Website: www.mileskelly.net

Freelance Potential
Published 90+ titles in 2002.
Submissions and Payment: Guidelines available at website.
Query with clips. SASE. Response time varies. Publication period
varies. Flat fee.

Morning Glory Press

6595 San Haroldo Way
Buena Park, CA 90620-3748

President: Jeanne Lindsay

Publisher's Interests
Fiction and nonfiction titles on contemporary topics that concern teen parents are the specialty of Morning Glory Press. Its list also includes titles for adults who work with teens. This publisher seeks books that deal with teen pregnancy, teen fathers, abuse, parenting, child development, life skills, and relationships.
Website: www.morningglorypress.com

Freelance Potential
Published 6 titles in 2002: 1 was developed from an unsolicited submission. Of the 6 titles, 1 was by an author who was new to the publishing house. Receives 20 queries yearly.
Submissions and Payment: Query. Accepts photocopies. SASE. Responds in 1–3 months. Publication in 6–8 months. Royalty; advance, $500.

Mountain Meadow Press

P.O. Box 447
Kooskia, ID 83539

Submissions Editor

Publisher's Interests
Established in 1983, this regional publisher specializes in titles on Pacific Northwest history and travel for adults. It also offers several homeschooling texts and materials based on the Pacific Northwest. Mountain Meadow Press is not currently accepting unsolicited manuscripts.
Website: www.mountainmeadowpressonline.com

Freelance Potential
Published 3 titles in 2002. Receives 6 queries and unsolicited mss yearly.
Submissions and Payment: Catalogue available at website. Query only. No unsolicited mss. Accepts photocopies and computer printouts. SASE. Responds in 3 months. Publication period varies. Royalty.

Mount Olive College Press

634 Henderson Street
Mount Olive, NC 28365

Acquisitions Editor: Pepper Worthington

Publisher's Interests
Established in 1990 by Mount Olive College, this press seeks to
encourage and advance the experiences, scholarship, and
thoughts of North Carolina authors. For middle-grade readers, it
seeks stories about animals and humorous fiction. For middle-
grade nonfiction, it would like to see self-help books, as well as
books on nature and religion. These titles should be about 3,000
words in length.

Freelance Potential
Published 2 titles in 2002.
Submissions and Payment: Catalogue available. Query with
outline/synopsis and 3 sample chapters; or send complete ms.
Accepts photocopies and computer printouts. SASE. Responds in
6–12 months. Publication in 1 year. Payment rates negotiable.

Munchweiler Press

P.O. Box 2529
Victorville, CA 92393-2529

Publisher: Ted Lish

Publisher's Interests
This small house specializes in picture books for readers
between the ages of four and eight. It looks for silly stories that
also have a moral.
Website: www.munchweilerpress.com

Freelance Potential
Published 4 titles in 2002: all were developed from unsolicited
submissions. Of the 4 titles, 1 was by an unpublished writer
and 3 were by new authors. Receives 50–60 mss yearly.
Submissions and Payment: Guidelines available. Send complete ms. Accepts photocopies, computer printouts, disk submissions, e-mail to publisher@munchweilerpress.com, and
simultaneous submissions if identified. SASE. Responds in 2
months. Publication in 1 year. Royalty, 5%. Flat fee.

National Resource Center for Youth Services

College of Continuing Education, University of Oklahoma, Tulsa
4502 East 41st Street
Tulsa, OK 74135
Marketing Manager: Rhoda Baker

Publisher's Interests
This publisher features inspirational and motivational books for at-risk teens and the adults who work with them. Topics cover substance abuse, suicide, sexual behavior, and communication.
Website: www.nrcys.ou.edu

Freelance Potential
Published 15 titles in 2002: 1 was developed from an unsolicited submission. Of the 15 titles, 1 was by an unpublished writer and 1 was by an author new to the publishing house. Receives 50 unsolicited mss yearly.
Submissions and Payment: Guidelines available. Query with outline and 1–3 sample chapters. Accepts computer printouts and disk submissions. SASE. Responds in 1–3 months. Publication in 8–18 months. Royalty.

Natural Heritage Books

P.O. Box 95, Station O
Toronto, Ontario M4A 2M8
Canada

Submissions Editor: Jane Gibson

Publisher's Interests
Canadian history, heritage, and culture are the focus of the books published by this specialty house. It features fiction and nonfiction for middle-grade readers, as well as titles on Canada's natural heritage for adults.
Website: www.naturalheritagebooks.com

Freelance Potential
Published 15 titles (2 juvenile) in 2002: 5 were developed from unsolicited submissions. Of the 15 titles, 4 were by unpublished writers and 12 were by authors who were new to the publishing house. Receives 160 queries yearly.
Submissions and Payment: Query with clips or writing samples. Accepts photocopies. SAE/IRC. Responds in 8–12 weeks. Publication in 1–2 years. Royalty; advance.

Tommy Nelson

P.O. Box 141000
Nashville, TN 37214-1000

Vice President of Children's Publishing: Dee Ann Grand

Publisher's Interests
Established in 1996, this religious publisher features products that awaken a child's imagination, and offers products that show the wonder of the world, the adventure of living, the mystery of imagination, and the fun of childhood. Publisher Tommy Nelson offers board books, picture books for children, and middle-grade and young adult fiction. It also offers devotionals, audio cassettes, compact disks, videos, games, and toys. It is not accepting new material at this time.
Website: www.tommynelson.com

Freelance Potential
Published 50 titles in 2002. Receives 3,000 queries, 4,000 unsolicited mss yearly.
Submissions and Payment: No queries or unsolicited mss.

Nomad Press

P.O. Box 875
Route 5 South
Norwich, VT 05055

Acquisitions Editor: Lauri Berkenkamp

Publisher's Interests
Nomad Press is a small, independent publisher that features a series of parenting guides that offer advice with a sense of humor. It appreciates submissions from authors who have been published, but will consider the works of all writers.
Website: www.nomadpress.net

Freelance Potential
Published 6 titles in 2002: 3 were developed from unsolicited submissions. Of the 6 titles, 1 was by an unpublished writer. Receives 120 queries yearly.
Submissions and Payment: Guidelines available at website. Send complete ms. Accepts photocopies and disk submissions. SASE. Responds in 1–3 months. Publication in 6–18 months. Royalty. Flat fee.

Our Child Press

79 Woodbine Avenue
Paoli, PA 19301

President: Carol Hallenbeck

Publisher's Interests
Books on adoption, parenting, and interracial families are the specialty of this small publishing house. 50% self-, subsidy-, co-venture, or co-op published material.
Website: www.ourchildpress.com

Freelance Potential
Published 2 titles in 2002: 1 was developed from an unsolicited submission and 1 was a reprint/licensed property. Of the 2 titles, 1 was by an unpublished writer. Receives 50 queries, 35 unsolicited mss yearly.
Submissions and Payment: Guidelines available. Query with outline/synopsis; or send complete ms. Accepts photocopies and computer printouts. SASE. Responds to queries in 1 month, to mss in 3 months. Publication in 1 year. Royalty.

Pacific View Press

P.O. Box 2657
Berkeley, CA 94702

Acquisitions Editor: Pam Zumwalt

Publisher's Interests
The children's book imprint of Pacific View Press is Dragon House, which publishes nonfiction for readers ages 8 to 12. It is interested in titles on the history and culture of the Pacific Rim.
Website: www.pacificviewpress.com

Freelance Potential
Published 2 titles in 2002: 1 was developed from an unsolicited submission. Of the 2 titles, 1 was by an unpublished writer and 1 was by an author who was new to the publishing house. Receives 200 queries yearly.
Submissions and Payment: Guidelines available. Query with outline and sample chapter. Accepts photocopies. SASE. Responds in 1 month. Publication period varies. Royalty, 8–10%; advance, $500–$1,000.

Parkway Publishers

P.O. Box 3678
Boone, NC 28607

President: Rao Aluri

Publisher's Interests
Nonfiction books for children and adults that highlight the history, nature, and culture of western North Carolina are the specialty of this regional publisher.

Freelance Potential
Published 10 titles (3 juvenile) in 2002: all were developed from unsolicited submissions and 1 was a reprint/licensed property. Of the 10 titles, 2 were by unpublished writers and 8 were by authors who were new to the publishing house. Receives 10–15 unsolicited mss yearly.
Submissions and Payment: Send complete ms. Accepts photocopies, computer printouts, and IBM disk submissions (Microsoft Word or WordPerfect). SASE. Responds in 2–6 weeks. Publication in 6–12 months. Royalty, 10%.

Paws IV Books

Suite 260
615 Second Avenue
Seattle, WA 98104

Senior Editor: Kate Rogers

Publisher's Interests
Fiction and nonfiction books on the culture, history, and lifestyle of the West Coast for 4- to 10-year-old children are the speciality of this regional publisher. It is interested in original material on the Alaskan wilderness, Alaskan nature, and multicultural issues. Paws IV Books is not currently accepting unsolicited manuscripts for children's books.
Website: www.SasquatchBooks.com

Freelance Potential
Published 2 titles in 2002: both were developed from unsolicited submissions. Receives 200 unsolicited mss yearly.
Submissions and Payment: Send complete ms with résumé and clips. SASE. Responds in 4 months. Publication period varies. Royalty; advance.

Pearson Learning Group

299 Jefferson Road
Parsippany, NJ 07054

V. P. Publisher: Celia Argiriou

Publisher's Interests
The Pearson Learning Group publishes educational materials for use with students in kindergarten through high school. Its books cover all curriculum areas, and most are published as parts of series. Adult education materials and books for English-as-a-Second Language programs also appear in its catalogue.
Website: www.pearsonlearning.com

Freelance Potential
Published 50 titles in 2002: 1 was developed from an unsolicited submission and 1 was a reprint/licensed property. Of the 50 titles, 1 was by an unpublished writer. Receives 30 queries yearly.
Submissions and Payment: Query with résumé and writing sample. SASE. Response time, publication period, and payment policy vary.

Pebble Beach Press Ltd.

P.O. Box 1171
Pebble Beach, CA 93953

Submissions Editor: C. R. Wojciechawski

Publisher's Interests
Informational titles, poetry, romance, and fantasy for young adults and adults are featured on the list from this publisher. It is interested in material about contemporary issues, sexual preferences, the divinity of the God and Goddess in heaven, and controlling one's life.

Freelance Potential
Published 4 titles in 2002 (2 juvenile): 1 was developed from an unsolicited submission. Of the 4 titles, 4 were by unpublished writers and 3 were by authors who were new to the publishing house. Receives 120 queries yearly.
Submissions and Payment: Guidelines available. Query with clips. Accepts photocopies. SASE. Responds in 2 months. Publication in 1 year. Royalty.

Peel Productions

P.O. Box 546
Columbus, NC 28722-0546

Editor: Susan DuBosque

Publisher's Interests
This small, tightly focused publisher concentrates on how-to-draw books for children between the ages of eight and fourteen. It also offers a series entitled ABC Riddles for beginning readers. All of its books are published as part of a series; it does not consider single titles.
Website: www.peelbooks.com

Freelance Potential
Published 6 titles in 2002. Of the 6 titles, 1 was by an unpublished writer and 1 was by an author who was new to the publishing house. Receives 1,400 queries yearly.
Submissions and Payment: Query or send complete ms. SASE. Response time varies. Publication period varies. Payment policy varies.

Penguin Books Canada Limited

Suite 300, 10 Alcorn Avenue
Toronto, Ontario M4V 3B2
Canada

Submissions Editor

Publisher's Interests
This company will consider the works of Canadian authors only. Penguin Books Canada Limited is a division of the Pearson Group. Most of its titles target young adult readers, but it also offers non-illustrated children's books for readers ages eight and up. Many of the books in its catalogue are fiction, but it does offer a select number of nonfiction historical books.
Website: www.penguin.ca

Freelance Potential
Published 80 titles in 2002.
Submissions and Payment: Canadian authors only. No unsolicited submissions. Accepts submissions from literary agents only. SASE. Responds in 1 month. Publication in 1–2 years.

Perspectives Press, Inc.

P.O. Box 90318
Indianapolis, IN 46290-0318

Editor: Pat Johnston

Publisher's Interests
Now in its twentieth year of publishing, this small house specializes in titles on topics related to infertility and adoption. Its
titles target parents and families.
Website: www.perspectivespress.com

Freelance Potential
Published 3 titles in 2002: all were developed from unsolicited
submissions and all were by agented authors. Of the 3 titles,
all were by unpublished writers and all were by authors new to
the publishing house. Receives 300 queries yearly.
Submissions and Payment: Guidelines available at website.
Query with résumé and outline. No unsolicited mss. Accepts
photocopies and computer printouts. SASE. Responds in 2
weeks. Publication in 9–18 months. Royalty, 5–15%.

Piano Press

P.O. Box 85
Delmar, CA 92014-0085

Editor: Elizabeth C. Axford

Publisher's Interests
Entertaining and educational materials for teaching music to
elementary school children are the focus of this publisher. It also
features music-related poetry.
Website: www.pianopress.com

Freelance Potential
Published 23 titles in 2002: 10 were developed from unsolicited submissions. Of the 23 titles, 2 were by unpublished
writers and 9 were by authors who were new to the publishing house. Receives 30 queries yearly.
Submissions and Payment: Guidelines available. Query for fiction and nonfiction. Send complete ms for poetry. Accepts photocopies, computer printouts, and disk submissions (Microsoft
Word). SASE. Responds in 2–4 months. Publication in 1 year.

Pippin Press

Gracie Station, Box 1347
229 East 85th Street
New York, NY 10028

Publisher: Barbara Francis

Publisher's Interests

This publisher's list includes fiction and nonfiction books for
seven- to ten-year-old readers, memoirs and autobiographies,
and innovative picture books. It is interested in queries for material written by minority authors, and humorous titles for children ages four through ten.

Freelance Potential

Published 4 titles in 2002: all were developed from unsolicited
submissions. Of the 4 titles, 2 were by unpublished writers
and 2 were by authors who were new to the publishing house.
Receives 1,500 queries yearly.
Submissions and Payment: Guidelines available. Query. No
unsolicited mss. SASE. Responds in 3 months. Publication in
1–2 years. Royalty; advance.

The Place in the Woods

3900 Glenwood Avenue
Golden Valley, MN 55422-5302

Editor & Publisher: Roger Hammer

Publisher's Interests

Books that promote awareness of all American cultures appear on
this publisher's list, along with books that demonstrate triumph
over adversity and those that feature main characters with disabilities. Its titles target teachers and librarians, as well as children.
10% self-, subsidy, co-venture, or co-op published material.

Freelance Potential

Published 3 titles in 2002: each was developed from an unsolicited submission. Of the 3 titles, each was by an unpublished
writer. Receives 1,000 queries, 300 unsolicited mss yearly.
Submissions and Payment: Guidelines available. Query or
send complete ms. Accepts computer printouts. No simultaneous submissions. SASE. Responds in 1–4 weeks. Publication in
18 months. Royalty. Flat fee.

Playwrights Canada Press

17 Wolseley Street
Toronto, Ontario M5T 1A5
Canada

Publisher: Angela Rebeiro

Publisher's Interests
With a list that features Canadian writers only, Playwrights
Canada Press specializes in plays for all ages, including contemporary drama and mysteries. Its list also offers monologues
and texts on drama. Writers must include proof of production
of their work by an Equity theater company.
Website: www.playwrightscanada.com

Freelance Potential
Published 20 titles (4 juvenile) in 2002: 2 were developed from
unsolicited submissions. Receives 10–15 queries yearly.
Submissions and Payment: Canadian authors only. Query
with synopsis. Accepts computer printouts and simultaneous
submissions. SASE. Responds in 6–12 months. Publication in
5 months. Royalty.

Polar Bear & Company

P.O. Box 311
Brook Street
Solon, ME 04979

Director: Ramona duHoux

Publisher's Interests
Polar Bear & Company publishes fiction, including multicultural
fiction and folktales, for children and young adults. Nonfiction
titles about nature and the environment also appear on its list.
50% self-, subsidy-, co-venture, or co-op published material.
Website: www.polarbearandco.com

Freelance Potential
Published 6 titles (3 juvenile) in 2002: 5 were developed from
unsolicited submissions. Receives 50 queries yearly.
Submissions and Payment: Guidelines available. Query;
include outline/synopsis and sample chapter for fiction.
Accepts photocopies, computer printouts, and simultaneous
submissions if identified. SASE. Responds in 2–4 weeks.
Publication in 1 year. Royalty.

Prep Publishing

1110½ Hay Street
Fayetteville, NC 28305

Submissions Editor: Anne McKinney

Publisher's Interests
Judeo-Christian titles and Christian fiction and nonfiction are
the mainstay of this publisher. It is interested in children's titles
that stress Christian morality, values, and ethics.
Website: www.prep-pub.com

Freelance Potential
Published 10 titles in 2002: all were developed from unsolicited
submissions. Of the 10 titles, 2 were by unpublished writers
and 2 were by authors who were new to the publishing house.
Receives 5,000 queries, 1,000 unsolicited mss yearly.
Submissions and Payment: Guidelines and catalogue available.
Query with synopsis or send complete ms with $225 reading fee.
Accepts photocopies. SASE. Responds in 3 months. Publication
in 18 months. Royalty; 15%.

Pruett Publishing Company

Suite A-9
7464 Arapahoe Road
Boulder, CO 80303-1500

Editor: Jim Pruett

Publisher's Interests
This nonfiction publisher specializes in books about the natural
beauty and history of the American West. Its children's list targets students in grades four through twelve. Pruett Publishing
welcomes the work of first-time authors.
Website: www.pruettpublishing.com

Freelance Potential
Published 8 titles in 2002. Receives 300 queries, 300 unsolicited
mss yearly.
Submissions and Payment: Guidelines available. Query or
send complete ms. Accepts photocopies, computer printouts,
and simultaneous submissions if identified. SASE. Responds to
queries in 2 weeks, to mss in 1–2 months. Publication period
varies. Royalty, 10–12%; advance, to $1,000.

Quixote Press

1854 345th Avenue
Wever, IA 52658

President: Bruce Carlson

Publisher's Interests
In addition to titles for a general adult audience, Quixote Press offers a list of books for children up to the age of 10. Its children's nonfiction covers topics such as crafts, hobbies, and gardening, while its fiction features humorous and regional themes. 50% self-, subsidy-, co-venture, or co-op published material.

Freelance Potential
Published 35 titles in 2002: 9 were developed from unsolicited submissions. Of the 35 titles, 21 were by unpublished writers. Receives 50 unsolicited mss yearly.
Submissions and Payment: Guidelines available. Send complete ms. Accepts photocopies, computer printouts, and simultaneous submissions if identified. SASE. Responds in 1 week. Publication in 6 months. Royalty.

Rainbow Books, Inc.

P.O. Box 430
Highland City, FL 33846-0430

Editorial Director: Betsy Lampe

Publisher's Interests
Rainbow Books, a nonfiction publisher, offers self-help books for middle-grade readers on topics of particular interest to them, such as bullies, cheating, and other behaviorial problems.

Freelance Potential
Published 20 titles in 2002: 16 were developed from unsolicited submissions and 2 were by agented authors. Of the 20 titles, 13 were by unpublished writers. Receives 20 mss yearly.
Submissions and Payment: Guidelines available. Prefers complete ms with author biography. Accepts query with word count, table of contents, and author biography. Accepts photocopies, computer printouts, and simultaneous submissions if identified. SASE. Responds in 6 weeks. Publication in 1 year. Royalty, 6%+; advance.

Ranch Works

P.O. Box 23565
Columbia, SC 29224

Publisher: J. Ranch

Publisher's Interests
This specialty publisher features a list of children's science books as well as science resource books for adults working with children. All the books found on Ranch Works' list are educational in nature and target children in kindergarten through grade eight. It does not offer writers' guidelines; prospective authors should send for a catalogue or visit the publisher's website.
Website: www.sciencespiders.com

Freelance Potential
Published 2 titles in 2002: both were assigned.
Submissions and Payment: Catalogue available with #10 SASE (2 first-class stamps). Send complete ms. Accepts B/W prints or transparencies. SASE. Response time, publication period, and payment policy vary.

Rand McNally

8255 North Central Park
Skokie, IL 60076

Editorial Director: Laurie Borman

Publisher's Interests
Rand McNally, the well-known mapmaker, features a line of children's titles targeted to boys and girls ages three to twelve. Their list includes activity books, maps for home and school, travel games, atlases, and reference books. All writing for Rand McNally is done on a work-for-hire basis, and interested writers are invited to submit a résumé. Unsolicited manuscripts and queries are not considered.
Website: www.randmcnally.com

Freelance Potential
Published 4 titles in 2002: all were assigned. Of the 4 titles, 2 were by authors who were new to the publishing house.
Submissions and Payment: Send résumé only. All work is done on assignment.

Random House Children's Books

61-63 Uxbridge Road
Ealing, London W5 5SA
United Kingdom

Editorial Assistant: Kelly Cauldwell

Publisher's Interests
Formerly known as Transworld Children's Books, this book publisher is the juvenile division of Random House UK. It features fiction for readers of all ages, including early picture books, chapter books, middle-grade novels, and young adult books. Adventure, fantasy, mystery, and animal stories are found on its list. It is currently accepting submissions from literary agents only.
Website: ww.kidsatrandomhouse.co.uk

Freelance Potential
Published 200 titles in 2002. Receives 2,000–3,000 queries each year.
Submissions and Payment: Accepts submissions from agented authors only. Publication in 1–2 years. Royalty; advance.

Random House Children's Publishing

1540 Broadway
New York, NY 10036

Submissions Editor

Publisher's Interests
Adventure, fantasy, humor, and mystery, as well as biographies and books about current events, history, animals, science, and sports are the mainstay of this well-known publisher. Because of the high volume of submissions it receives, Random House Children's Publishing will consider submissions through literary agents only. Random House recommends that you consult *The Literary MarketPlace* for a listing of agencies.
Website: www.randomhouse.com

Freelance Potential
Published 300 titles in 2002.
Submissions and Payment: Accepts submissions through literary agents only. No queries or unsolicited mss. Response time, publication period, and payment policy vary.

Redbird Press

P.O. Box 11441
Memphis, TN 38111

Editor: Virginia McLean

Publisher's Interests
Books about various cultures, written for children between the ages of six and twelve, appear in the catalogue of Redbird Press. Each title is produced with an accompanying audio CD that introduces children to the sounds of a foreign land by including a sampling of the country's language, music, and folktales. Children's drawings illustrate each title.

Freelance Potential
Plans to resume publishing (1 or more titles) in 2004. Receives 30 queries yearly.
Submissions and Payment: Query with outline/synopsis and writing samples or clips. Accepts photocopies, computer print-outs, and simultaneous submissions if identified. SASE. Response time, publication period, and payment policy vary.

Rocky River Publishers

P.O. Box 1679
Shepherdstown, WV 25443

Acquisitions Editor

Publisher's Interests
This publisher offers books that provide innovative approaches to help parents, teachers, counselors, and child-care workers assist children as they grow to adulthood. It is interested in creative, educational material on substance abuse, self-esteem, and safety.
Website: www.rockyriver.com

Freelance Potential
Published 10 titles in 2002. Receives 240 queries, 720 unsolicited mss yearly.
Submissions and Payment: Guidelines available. Query or send complete ms. Accepts photocopies. Availability of artwork improves chance of acceptance. SASE. Response time varies. Publication in 9–18 months. Royalty; 8–12% of net (softcover), 10–15% of net (hardcover); advance, $500.

Salina Bookshelf

624½ North Beaver Street
Flagstaff, AZ 86004

Publisher: Eric Lockard

Publisher's Interests
Established in 1994, this publisher specializes in bilingual
English/Navajo picture books for four- to seven-year-old
readers, as well as nonfiction titles on the Navajo language.
Its current interests include multicultural stories and bilingual
folktales.
Website: www.salinabookshelf.com

Freelance Potential
Published 5 titles in 2002. Receives 150–200 unsolicited mss
each year.
Submissions and Payment: Send complete ms. Accepts photocopies, computer printouts, disk submissions (Adobe Acrobat),
and e-mail submissions to lockard@primenet.com. SASE.
Responds in 3 weeks. Publication in 4–6 months. Royalty,

Sandlapper Publishing

1281 Amelia Street
Orangeburg, SC 29115

Managing Editor: Amanda Gallman

Publisher's Interests
Works of nonfiction about South Carolina, including history,
biography, travel, nature, culture, literature, cooking, and
photography are the specialty of this regional publisher. It
seeks material that provides insight into the lifestyle or history of
South Carolina. It is especially interested in submissions of
educational mysteries for children, and historical biographies
for young readers.

Freelance Potential
Published 3 titles in 2002. Receives 150 queries yearly.
Submissions and Payment: Guidelines available. Query with
résumé, outline/synopsis, 3 sample chapters, and bibliography.
Accepts photocopies and computer printouts. SASE. Responds
in 2 months. Publication in 2 years. Royalty.

Sandpiper Paperbacks

222 Berkeley Street
Boston, MA 02116

Editor: Eden Edwards

Publisher's Interests
Although this imprint of Houghton Mifflin publishes primarily
fiction and nonfiction reprints for early and middle-grade readers,
its catalogue also includes innovative young adult fiction about
contemporary issues.
Website: www.hmco.com

Freelance Potential
Published 35 titles in 2002: all were reprint/licensed proper-
ties. Receives 100 queries, 200 unsolicited mss yearly.
Submissions and Payment: Guidelines available with SASE.
Query with sample chapter or send complete ms. Accepts photo-
copies, computer printouts, and simultaneous submissions.
SASE. Responds to queries in 3–8 weeks, to mss in 3–5 months.
Publication period and payment policy vary.

Sasquatch Books

Suite 260
615 Second Avenue
Seattle, WA 98104

Senior Editor: Kate Rogers

Publisher's Interests
Sasquatch Books, a division of Pacific Northwest Press, publishes
regional adult nonfiction and fiction, and children's books with a
national appeal. Its list includes titles on travel, the environment, gardening, literature, and parenting. It is not accepting
unsolicited manuscripts for children's books at this time.
Website: www.SasquatchBooks.com

Freelance Potential
Published 40 titles (3 juvenile) in 2002. Receives 200 unsolicited mss yearly.
Submissions and Payment: Guidelines available. Send complete
ms. Accepts photocopies and computer printouts. SASE.
Response time varies. Publication period and payment policy
varies.

Scholastic Book Group

Scholastic Inc.
555 Broadway
New York, NY 10012

Publisher: Jean Feiwel

Publisher's Interests
The Scholastic Book Group is composed of eight imprints:
Scholastic Press, Orchard Books, Scholastic Reference,
Scholastic Inc., Arthur A. Levine Books, Cartwheel Books,
The Blue Sky Press, and Scholastic Paperbacks. Long a leader
in children's publishing, Scholastic is perhaps best known at
this time as the American publisher of J. K. Rowling's Harry
Potter books. At this time, the group is not accepting unso-
licited manuscripts.
Website: www.scholastic.com

Freelance Potential
Published 500 titles in 2002.
Submissions and Payment: Query only; no unsolicited manu-
scripts at this time.

School Zone Publishing

P.O. Box 777
1819 Industrial Drive
Grand Haven, MI 49417

Editor: Lisa Carmona

Publisher's Interests
Supplementary educational materials for students ages three to
twelve are the specialty of this publisher. It offers a full line of
workbooks, flashcards, game cards, software, and resources for
parents, teachers, and children. Although it does not accept
unsolicited manuscripts, it will consider the résumés and writing
samples of educational professionals.
Website: www.schoolzone.com

Freelance Potential
Published 20 titles in 2002: 4 were by agented authors.
Receives 100 queries yearly.
Submissions and Payment: Query with résumé and writing
samples. No unsolicited mss. Response time and publication
period vary. Flat fee.

Seaburn Publishing

P.O. Box 2085
Astoria, NY 11103

President: Tyra Mason

Publisher's Interests
Seaburn Publishing features a line of children's books in addition to its general trade titles for an adult readership. These include concept books for toddlers, easy-to-read books for older children, and young adult fiction and nonfiction. Seaburn also offers inspirational literature designed to enlighten readers.
Website: www.seaburn.com

Freelance Potential
Published 23 titles (8 juvenile) in 2002: 2 were developed from unsolicited submissions and 1 was by an agented author. Receives 120 queries yearly.
Submissions and Payment: Guidelines available. Query. Accepts photocopies and computer printouts. SASE. Responds in 1 month. Publication in 4 months. Royalty.

Seal Press

Suite 375
300 Queen Anne Avenue North
Seattle, WA 98109

Editorial Department

Publisher's Interests
Owned and operated by women, Seal Press is an independent publisher that focuses on diverse nonfiction from a feminist perspective. It seeks original material on parenting and family life, but will consider submissions sent through literary agents only.
Website: www.sealpress.com

Freelance Potential
Published 16 titles in 2002: 4 were developed from unsolicited submissions, 6 were by agented authors, and 4 were reprint/licensed properties. Of the 16 titles, 2 were by unpublished writers. Receives 1,000 queries yearly.
Submissions and Payment: Accepts submissions from agented authors only. Responds in 6 weeks. Publication period and payment policy vary.

Serendipity Systems

P.O. Box 140
San Simeon, CA 93452

Publisher: John Galuszka

Publisher's Interests
This e-book publisher specializes in material that can take advantage of computer-enhanced features. It is interested in hypertext novels, mixed-media work, interactive fiction, experimental work, and reference material on literature and writing.
Website: www.s-e-r-e-n-d-i-p-i-t-y.com.

Freelance Potential
Published 4 titles in 2002: 2 were developed from unsolicited submissions. Of the 4 titles, 2 were by unpublished writers. Receives 480 queries yearly.
Submissions and Payment: Guidelines available at website. Query. Accepts e-mail queries to bookware@thegrid.net. No hard copy submissions. Responds in 2 weeks. Publication in 2 months. Royalty.

17th Street Productions

11th Floor
151 West 26th Street
New York, NY 10001

Editorial Assistant: Jennifer Klein

Publisher's Interests
Owned by Alloy Online, creators of the successful teen website, this publisher specializes in books for teens. Its list offers fiction and nonfiction topics of interest to teens of both sexes.
Website: www.alloy.com

Freelance Potential
Published 100 titles in 2002: 5 were developed from unsolicited submissions and 20 were by agented authors. Of the 100 titles, 10 were by unpublished writers and 15 were by authors new to the publishing house. Receives 600 queries yearly.
Submissions and Payment: Query with résumé, detailed plot outline, and 2 sample chapters. Accepts photocopies and computer printouts. SASE. Responds in 1–2 months. Publication in 9–15 months. Royalty, to 4%; advance, $3,000.

Shen's Books

40951 Fremont Boulevard
Fremont, CA 94538

Owner: Renee Ting

Publisher's Interests
Children's books relating to the culture, history, folklore, and traditions of Asia, Eastern Europe, and Latin America are the specialty of this publisher.
Website: www.shens.com

Freelance Potential
Published 2 titles in 2002: 1 was developed from an unsolicited submission. Of the 2 titles, 1 was by an unpublished writer and both were by authors who were new to the publishing house. Receives 50 unsolicited mss yearly.
Submissions and Payment: Send complete ms. Accepts computer printouts, disk submissions (Microsoft Word), and simultaneous submissions if identified. SASE. Responds in 6–12 months. Publication in 18 months. Payment rate varies.

Shining Star Publications

3195 Wilson Drive NW
Grand Rapids, MI 49544

Publisher: Carol Marcotte

Publisher's Interests
Shining Star Publications, a division of McGraw-Hill Children's Books, produces materials designed to be used by teachers and children in religious education programs. In addition to teacher resource materials, its list includes Bible activity books, workbooks, plays, puzzles, and posters. All of its products are geared toward children in preschool through eighth grade.
Website: www.mhkids.com

Freelance Potential
Plans to resume publishing (35 or more titles) in 2003. Receives 50 queries yearly.
Submissions and Payment: Guidelines available. Query with clips and sample pages. SASE. Responds in 2–6 weeks. Publication in 1 year. Flat fee.

Simon Pulse

Simon & Schuster
1230 Avenue of the Americas
New York, NY 10020

Submissions Editor

Publisher's Interests
Contemporary fiction novels, nonfiction titles, and biographies of pop culture personalities for teens are the specialty of this imprint, formerly known as Pocket Pulse.
Website: www.simonsays.com

Freelance Potential
Published 200 titles in 2002: 190 were by agented authors and 150 were reprint/licensed properties. Of the 200 titles, 1 was by an unpublished writer and 3 were by authors who were new to the publishing house. Receives 1,000+ queries and unsolicited mss yearly.
Submissions and Payment: Guidelines available. Accepts agented submissions only. SASE. Response time varies. Publication in 6–24 months. Payment policy varies.

Siphano Picture Books

Regent's Place, 338 Euston Road
London NW1 3BT
England

Editor

Publisher's Interests
Siphano Picture Books publishes high-quality picture books for three- to seven-year-old children. It prefers material with likeable characters, humor, and imagination.
Website: www.siphano.com

Freelance Potential
Published 8 titles in 2002: 1 was developed from an unsolicited submission. Of the 8 titles, 1 was by an unpublished writer and 1 was by an author who was new to the publishing house. Receives 120 queries yearly.
Submissions and Payment: Guidelines available at website. Query with clips. Accepts e-mail to info@siphano.com and simultaneous submissions. SASE. Responds in 2–3 months. Publication in 6 months. Payment policy varies.

Smith and Kraus Books for Kids

177 Lyme Road
Hanover, NH 03755

Publisher: Marisa Smith

Publisher's Interests
This leading publisher of theater books also offers a list of children's titles. Smith and Kraus for Kids offers picture books for four- to eight-year-old readers and chapter books for 10- to 14-year-old readers. It also features a range of plays, acting guides, monologues, anthologies, and theater arts books for students through grade 12.
Website: www.SmithKraus.com

Freelance Potential
Published 2 titles in 2002.
Submissions and Payment: Query with résumé for fiction. Query with outline for nonfiction. Accepts photocopies, computer printouts, and simultaneous submissions. SASE. Responds in 2 months. Publication in 1 year. Royalty; advance. Flat fee.

Soho Press

853 Broadway
New York, NY 10003

Submissions Editor: Laura Hruska

Publisher's Interests
A wide range of literary fiction is offered by this publisher. Although Soho Press is not interested in juvenile literature, it will consider parenting guides for adults.
Website: www.sohopress.com

Freelance Potential
Published 45 titles in 2002: 6 were developed from unsolicited submissions, 6 were by agented authors, and 19 were reprint/licensed properties. Of the 38 titles, 5 were by unpublished writers and 12 were by authors who were new to the publishing house. Receives 2,400 queries yearly.
Submissions and Payment: Guidelines available. Query with 3 sample chapters. Accepts photocopies. SASE. Responds in 6 weeks. Publication in 12–15 months. Royalty; advance.

Southern Early Childhood Association

P.O. Box 55930
Little Rock, AR 72215-5930

Director of Research & Development: Brenda Hancock

Publisher's Interests
Covering topics of interest to early childhood professionals and parents, this publisher is currently seeking submissions on literacy development, arts and movement, and teacher instruction. 50% self-, subsidy-, co-venture, or co-op published material.
Website: www.southernearlychildhood.org

Freelance Potential
Published 2 titles in 2002: 1 was developed from an unsolicited submission and both were by unpublished writers. Receives 4 unsolicited mss yearly.
Submissions and Payment: Guidelines available. Send 4 copies of complete ms. Accepts disk submissions (WordPerfect or Microsoft Word). SASE. Responds in 4 months. Publication in 9–12 months. No payment.

Starry Puddle Publishing

1923 North Gramercy Place
Los Angeles, CA 90068

Publisher: Anthony Boyd

Publisher's Interests
This publisher offers humorous picture books and easy-to-read fiction for children between the ages of four and eight. Starry Puddle Publishing donates 10% of all of its proceeds to children's arts and education programs.
Website: www.starrypuddle.com

Freelance Potential
Published 2 titles in 2002: 1 was by an agented author and 1 was a reprint/licensed property.
Submissions and Payment: Guidelines available at website or with SASE ($1.72 postage). Send complete ms with artwork if applicable. Accepts simultaneous submissions and e-mail submissions to publisher@starrypuddle.com. SASE. Responds in 2–3 months. Publication in 6–12 months. Royalty; advance.

Stiles-Bishop Productions Inc.

12652 Killion
Valley Village, CA 91607

Editor: Kathryn Bishop

Publisher's Interests
This highly specialized publisher offers 36-page, full-color stories for readers between four and ten years of age. All of its books are based on stories from a radio series, and most of its stories are based on traditional fairy tales. Authors are invited to submit age-appropriate stories, and submissions that include artwork, especially color artwork, are of special interest and will get a careful look.

Freelance Potential
Published 1 title in 2002. Receives 5 queries yearly.
Submissions and Payment: Query. Availability of artwork improves chance of acceptance. Accepts photocopies and computer printouts. SASE. Responds in 2 weeks. Publication in 6 months. Royalty. Flat fee.

The Story Place

#1611
1735 Brantley Road
Fort Myers, FL 33907-3920

Submissions Editor

Publisher's Interests
The Story Place publishes quality fiction and nonfiction books geared toward children ages four to eleven—titles with timeless humor that bring important lessons to life. Its list includes fairy tales, science fiction, sports stories, Westerns, and adventure stories. Topics include animals, religion, science, and humor. Submissions are currently closed, but the publisher plans to reopen its acquisitions department in the near future.
Website: www.thestoryplace.com

Freelance Potential
Published 2 titles in 2002: both were developed from unsolicited submissions. Receives 30 unsolicited mss yearly.
Submissions and Payment: Guidelines available. Not currently accepting queries, manuscripts, or illustrations.

Story Time Stories That Rhyme

P.O. Box 416
Denver, CO 80201

Customer Service

Publisher's Interests
Story Time Stories That Rhyme publishes easy-to-read stories for children that educate, entertain, inform, and rhyme. It also offers workbooks, coloring books, reproducibles, audiotapes, and art from story characters. It is specifically interested in proposals for educational and reader's theater titles.
Website: www.storytimestoriesthatrhyme.com

Freelance Potential
Published 3 titles in 2002. Of the 3 titles, 2 were by authors who were new to the publishing house. Receives 3 queries each year.
Submissions and Payment: Guidelines available. Query. No unsolicited mss. SASE. Response time varies. Publication and payment policies vary.

Success Publications

3419 Dunham Road
Warsaw, NY 14599

Publisher: Allan Smith

Publisher's Interests
Success Publications accepts freelance submissions for informational and how-to books for the middle-grade and young adult markets. The books that appear on its list cover topics such as crafts, hobbies, and the entertainment industry. Success Publications also offers parenting titles.

Freelance Potential
Published 3 titles (1 juvenile) in 2002: 2 were developed from unsolicited submissions. Receives 200 unsolicited mss yearly.
Submissions and Payment: Guidelines available. Send complete ms. Accepts photocopies. Availability of artwork improves chance of acceptance. B/W or color prints or transparencies. SASE. Responds in 2 weeks. Publication in 3 months. Payment policy varies.

Sunburst Technology

101 Castleton Street
Pleasantville, NY 10507

Submissions: Joan Jacobsen

Publisher's Interests
This educational publisher features multimedia products on
guidance and health for use in kindergarten through twelfth-
grade classrooms, as well as material on language arts, math,
science, the Internet, social studies, and creativity.
Website: www.sunburst.com

Freelance Potential
Published 75 titles in 2002: 1 was developed from an unsolicited submission. Receives 150 queries, 20 unsolicited
mss yearly.
Submissions and Payment: Query with résumé and writing
sample. Accepts product concept proposals with accompanying
graphics. SASE. Responds in 3–6 weeks. Publication period and
payment policy vary.

Teachers & Writers Collaborative

5 Union Square West
New York, NY 10003-3306

Editor: Christina Davis

Publisher's Interests
This non-profit organization was founded to provide teachers
and writers with a forum to explore the connection between writing and reading. It features books for children and adults on
teaching writing, oral history, creative nonfiction, and fiction
writing. It seeks original material for all age levels.
Website: www.twc.org

Freelance Potential
Published 5 titles in 2002: 1 was a reprint/licensed property.
Receives 100–200 queries yearly.
Submissions and Payment: Query with résumé, outline, market
analysis, and sample chapter. Accepts photocopies and computer
printouts. SASE. Responds in 3 months. Publication in 18
months. Royalty; advance.

Teachers College Press

1234 Amsterdam Avenue
New York, NY 10027

Acquisitions

Publisher's Interests
This publisher specializes in textbooks, professional titles, and
materials for students, faculty, practioners, and researchers. Its
list includes titles on child development, special education, and
curriculum trends, 5% co-venture published material.
Website: www.teacherscollegepress.com

Freelance Potential
Published 50+ titles in 2002: 7 were developed from unsolicited submissions, 1 was by an agented author, and 3 were
reprint/licensed properties. Receives 2,400 queries yearly.
Submissions and Payment: Guidelines available. Query with 2
copies of prospectus, outline, introduction, and 2 sample chapters. Accepts photocopies and computer printouts. SASE.
Responds in 1 month. Publication period varies. Royalty.

Thistledown Press

633 Main Street
Saskatoon, Saskatchewan S7H 0J8
Canada

Submissions Editor: Jesse Stothers

Publisher's Interests
This Canadian publisher features short fiction collections, novels,
and poetry with appropriate themes for young adults. It considers
submissions from Canadian authors only.
Website: www.thistledown.sk.ca

Freelance Potential
Published 14 titles (4 juvenile) in 2002: 2 were developed from
unsolicited submissions and 4 were by agented authors. Of the
14 titles, 3 were by unpublished writers and 5 were by authors
new to the publishing house. Receives 600 queries yearly.
Submissions and Payment: Canadian authors only. Guidelines
and catalogue available with #14 SASE ($.98 Canadian postage)
and at website. Query with outline and sample chapter. SASE.
Responds in 1 week. Publication in 3 months. Royalty.

J. N. Townsend Publishing

4 Franklin Street
Exeter, NH 03833

Submissions Editor: Jeremy Townsend

Publisher's Interests
Since 1986, this small publisher has specialized in fiction and nonfiction nature and animal books for children and young adults. It doesn't plan to sign any children's titles in 2002–2003.
Website: www.jntownsendpublishing.com

Freelance Potential
Published 7 titles in 2002: 1 was developed from an unsolicited submission, and 2 were by agented authors. Of the 7 titles, 2 were by unpublished writers and 2 were by new authors. Receives 150 queries, 75 unsolicited mss yearly.
Submissions and Payment: Guidelines and catalogue available with 5x8 SASE. Query for nonfiction; send complete ms for fiction. Accepts photocopies. SASE. Responds in 1–3 months. Publication in 1 year. Royalty.

Tradewind Books Ltd.

2216 Stephens Street
Vancouver, British Columbia V6K 3W6
Canada

Publisher: Michael Katz

Publisher's Interests
This Canadian publisher specializes in storybooks and nonfiction nature titles for four- to eight-year-old readers.
Website: www.tradewindbooks.com

Freelance Potential
Published 4 titles in 2002: 1 was developed from an unsolicited submission. Of the 4 titles, 2 were by unpublished writers and 3 were by authors who were new to the publishing house. Receives 1,500 queries yearly.
Submissions and Payment: Query with résumé and sample chapter for fiction. Send complete ms with résumé for nonfiction. All submissions must indicate that writers have read a selection of the publisher's works. Accepts photocopies. SAE/IRC. Responds in 1 month. Publication in 3 years. Royalty; advance.

Turtle Books

Suite 525
866 United Nations Plaza
New York, NY 10017

Publisher: John R. Whitman

Publisher's Interests
Since 1996, this publisher has offered a small list of English
and Spanish illustrated children's books for readers between
two and ten years of age. The company is located in the heart
of Manhattan, in the Turtle Bay district.
Website: www.turtlebooks.com

Freelance Potential
Published 6 titles in 2002: 2 were developed from unsolicited
submissions and 3 were by agented authors. Of the 6 titles, 2
were by unpublished writers and 2 were by authors new to the
publishing house. Receives 1,000+ unsolicited mss yearly.
Submissions and Payment: Send complete ms. Accepts photocopies and computer printouts. SASE. Response time varies.
Publication in 1 year. Royalty; advance.

Two Bytes Publishing

P.O. Box 633
Stratford, CT 06615-0633

President: Elizabeth F. Clark

Publisher's Interests
Nonfiction picture books and activity books for children age 10
and up are featured by this publisher. Its list includes titles on
art and history for young readers, as well as nonfiction books for
adults. It is currently interested in books on historical figures
suitable for children.

Freelance Potential
Published 2 titles in 2002: both were developed from unsolicited submissions by unpublished writers. Receives 24
queries, 24 unsolicited mss yearly.
Submissions and Payment: Query with sample chapters or
send complete ms. Accepts photocopies and Macintosh disk submissions. SASE. Responds to queries in 1 week, to mss in 4–6
months. Publication in 4-10 months. Royalty, 8–15%.

Two Lives Publishing

P.O. Box 736
Ridley Park, PA 19078

Editor: Bobbi Combs

Publisher's Interests
Books for children living in lesbian, gay, bisexual, and transgender families are the focus of this publisher. It seeks books of integrity that depict children, friends, and family in positive ways.
Website: www.twolives.com

Freelance Potential
Published 3 titles in 2002: all were developed from unsolicited submissions. Of the 3 titles, all were by unpublished writers new to the publishing house. Receives 20 queries, 60 unsolicited mss yearly.
Submissions and Payment: Guidelines available. Send complete ms. Accepts photocopies, disk submissions, and e-mail submissions to bcombs@twolives.com. SASE. Responds in 2 months. Publication in 3 years. Royalty, 5%; advance, $500–$1,000.

Unity House

Unity School of Christianity
1901 NW Blue Parkway
Unity Village, MO 64065-0001

Associate Editor: Raymond Teague

Publisher's Interests
Unity House is the publishing imprint of Unity School of Christianity, a nondenominational religious organization. Its list includes nonfiction for young adults and fiction for children between the ages of five and twelve.
Website: www.unityworldhq.org

Freelance Potential
Published 5 titles (1 juvenile) in 2002: 3 were developed from unsolicited submissions. Of the 5 titles, 1 was by an unpublished writer and 3 were by authors new to the publishing house. Receives 400 queries and unsolicited mss yearly.
Submissions and Payment: Guidelines available by mail and at website. Query. SASE. Responds in 6–8 weeks. Publication in 11 months. Royalty.

VGM Career Books

Suite 900
130 East Randolph Street
Chicago, IL 60601

Editor: Denise Betts

Publisher's Interests
Books on careers and educational success for middle-grade students, young adults, and college-level students are the mainstay of this publisher. It is interested in nonfiction titles that can appear as part of a series.

Freelance Potential
Published 40 titles in 2002: 36 were developed from unsolicited submissions and 4 were by agented authors. Of the 40 titles, 39 were by unpublished writers and 1 was by a new author. Receives 200 queries yearly.
Submissions and Payment: Guidelines available. Query with résumé and clips or writing samples. Accepts photocopies and computer printouts. SASE. Response time, publication period, and payment rate vary.

Viking Children's Books

Penguin Putnam Books for Young Readers
345 Hudson Street
New York, NY 10014

Editorial Department

Publisher's Interests
This well-known children's publisher is a division of Penguin Putnam. Its list includes fiction and nonfiction titles for toddlers to young adults. Due to an overwhelming number of submissions, Viking Children's Books is not able to consider queries or unsolicited manuscripts at this time. Check our website often for changes in our submissions policy.
Website: www.penguinputnam.com

Freelance Potential
Published 75 titles in 2002. Receives 3,000 queries and unsolicited mss yearly.
Submissions and Payment: Catalogue available online or with an SASE. Not accepting queries or unsolicited manuscripts at this time.

Visual Education Corporation

P.O. Box 2321
14 Washington Road
Princeton, NJ 08540

Acquisitions Editor: Jewel Moulthrop

Publisher's Interests
Textbooks, ancillary books, and reference titles for kindergarten
through grade 12 educators are the focus of this specialty publisher. Visual Education Corporation features custom-tailored
publishing services for nonfiction titles for use in school
libraries, including concept development, text research, and
writing and editing. All work is assigned. Do not submit unsolicited manuscripts.

Freelance Potential
Published 12–15 titles in 2002: all were assigned. Of the
12–15 titles, 5 were by new authors.
Submissions and Payment: All work is assigned. Guidelines
available. Query with résumé and clips. SASE. Response time
varies. Publication period varies. Flat fee.

WaterBrook Press

Suite 160
2375 Telstar Drive
Colorado Springs, CO 80920

Senior Editor: Ron Lee

Publisher's Interests
WaterBrook Press, a division of Random House, Inc., specializes in books with spiritual themes. It is no longer accepting
manuscripts and will only review queries from agents.

Freelance Potential
Published 60 titles (8 juvenile) in 2002: 1 was developed from
an unsolicited submission, 37 were by agented authors, and 5
were reprint/licensed properties. Of the 60 titles, 1 was by an
unpublished writer and 19 were by authors new to the publishing house. Receives 1,000+ queries yearly.
Submissions and Payment: Catalogue available with 9x12
SASE. Accepts queries submitted through literary agents only.
No unsolicited mss. Responds in 4–6 weeks. Publication in 1
year. Payment policy varies.

Windswept House Publishers

P.O. Box 159
Mt. Desert, ME 04660

Manuscript Editor

Publisher's Interests
This regional publisher is devoted to producing high-quality children's picture books, young adult novels, and adult fiction and nonfiction. Established in 1983, it specializes in books about the environment, history, people, culture, nature, and wildlife of Maine, as well as general New England and environmental topics. New and established writers are invited to submit a proposal for titles that suit its editorial focus.
Website: www.booknotes.com/windswept

Freelance Potential
Published 2+ titles in 2002.
Submissions and Payment: Guidelines available with SASE. Query. No unsolicited mss. SASE. Response time varies. Publication and payment policy vary.

Winslow Press

10th Floor
115 East 23rd Street
New York, NY 10010

Submissions Editor

Publisher's Interests
Winslow Press has created a partnership of the printed word and the World Wide Web. Each of its books has its own interactive website to further explore the book's theme. It seeks material for children that combines creative thought with technology.
Website: www.winslowpress.com

Freelance Potential
Published several titles in 2002: 2 were developed from unsolicited submissions. Receives 100 queries, 1,200 unsolicited mss yearly.
Submissions and Payment: Guidelines available with SASE (1 first-class stamp). Query with or send complete ms. Accepts photocopies. SASE. Responds to queries in 1 month, to mss in 3–4 months. Publication period varies. Royalty; advance.

Winslow Publishing

P.O. Box 38012
550 Eglinton Avenue West
Toronto, Ontario M5N 3A8 Canada

President & Publisher: Michelle West

Publisher's Interests
Books on crafts, how-to titles, and craft supplies are featured in the catalogue of this small publisher. While it commissions many of its titles, its editors are especially interested in queries for craft books for children between the ages of five and ten. All of its products are marketed through direct mail. Books that include art will get a closer look.
Website: www.winslowpublishing.com

Freelance Potential
Published 2 titles in 2002. Receives 20–30 queries yearly.
Submissions and Payment: Query with sample illustrations. Availability of artwork improves chance of acceptance. Accepts simultaneous submissions if identified. SAE/IRC. Responds in 2 weeks. Publication in 2–3 months. Flat fee.

Wordware Publishing

Suite 200
2320 Los Rios Boulevard
Plano, TX 75074

Acquisitions Editor: Ginnie Bivona

Publisher's Interests
Software, workbooks, and educational materials that prepare students for Texas state and district exams are offered by this publisher, as well as curriculum-related nonfiction titles for grades three through twelve.
Website: www.republicoftexaspress.com

Freelance Potential
Published 36 titles (6 juvenile) in 2002: 1 was by an agented author. Of the 36 titles, 4 were by unpublished writers. Receives 100+ queries yearly.
Submissions and Payment: Guidelines available. Query with biography. Accepts photocopies, computer printouts, disk submissions, and simultaneous submissions if identified. SASE. Responds in 6 weeks. Publication in 1 year. Royalty.

Zigzag Children's Books

8 Blenheim Court
Brewery Road
London N7 9NT, England

Editor: Steve Evans

Publisher's Interests
This publisher creates books and novelties to inform and educate young readers. Its nonfiction titles range from early learning
concepts for very young readers to reference titles and encyclopedias for older children.
Website: www.chrysalisbooks.co.uk/zigzag.htm

Freelance Potential
Published 30 titles in 2002: 7 were developed from unsolicited
submissions. Of the 30 titles, 1 was by an unpublished
writer and 1 was by an author new to the publishing house.
Receives 50 unsolicited mss yearly.
Submissions and Payment: Send complete ms with résumé.
Accepts photocopies and Macintosh disk submissions. SAE/IRC.
Responds in 2 months. Publication period varies. Flat fee.

Zino Press Children's Books

2348 Pinehurst Drive
Middleton, WI 53562

Editor: David Schreiner

Publisher's Interests
This children's publisher features titles that teach positive values
of kindness and tolerance to readers ages five to eight. It seeks
original fiction with an unusual story, and nonfiction or multicultural literature that covers unique topics.
Website: www.zinopress.com

Freelance Potential
Published 2–3 titles in 2002: 1 was by an unpublished writer
and 1 was by an author who was new to the publishing
house. Receives 800 unsolicited mss yearly.
Submissions and Payment: Guidelines and catalogue available
at website. Send complete ms. Accepts photocopies, computer
printouts, and simultaneous submissions. SASE. Responds in 4
months. Publication period varies. Payment policy varies.

Contests and
Awards

Selected Contests & Awards

Whether you enter a contest for unpublished writers or submit your published book for an award, you will have an opportunity to have your book read by established writers and qualified editors. Participating in a competition can increase recognition of your writing and possibly open more doors for selling your work. If you don't win and the winning entry is published, try to read it to see how your work compares with its competition.

To be considered for the contests and awards that follow, your entry must fulfill all of the requirements mentioned. Most are looking for unpublished article or story manuscripts, while a few require published works. Note special entry requirements, such as whether or not you can submit the material yourself, need to be a member of an organization, or are limited in the number of entries you can send. Also, be sure to submit your article or story in the standard manuscript submission format.

For each listing, we've included the address, the contact, a description, the entry requirements, the deadline, and the prize. In some cases, the 2003 deadlines were not available at press time. We recommend that you write to the addresses provided and ask for an entry form and the contest guidelines, which usually specify the current deadline.

AML Awards

Association of Mormon Letters
125 Hobble Creek Canyon
Springville, UT 84663

Description
The Association of Mormon Letters presents awards annually in several categories including children's literature, middle-grade literature, young adult literature, humor, and personal essay. It accepts previously unpublished submissions only.
Website: www.aml-online.org
Length: Varies for each category.
Requirements: No entry fee. Accepts photocopies and computer printouts. Author's name should not appear on manuscript. Include a separate cover letter including author's name, address, phone number. Visit the website or send an SASE for guidelines prior to submitting your work.
Prizes: Cash prizes in varying amounts are presented in each category.
Deadline: July 1.

Atlantic Writing Competition

Writers' Federation of Nova Scotia
1113 Marginal Road
Halifax, Nova Scotia B3H 4P7
Canada

Description
Open to all writers living in the Atlantic Canadian provinces, this annual contest accepts books, plays, short stories, and short non-fiction. Each entry is returned at the end of the competition with written comments to help writers become ready for publication.
Website: www.writers.ns.ca
Length: Length varies for each category.
Requirements: Entry fee, $10 (members), $15 (non-members). Writers who have had a book published may not enter in the genre in which they have previously been published. Author's name must not appear on manuscript. Manuscripts are not returned. Send an SASE or visit the website for complete guidelines.
Prizes: Cash prizes ranging from $50 to $150 are awarded.
Deadline: August.

AWP/Thomas Dunne Books
Novel Award

Mail Stop 1E3
George Mason University
Fairfax, VA 22030

Description
Open to all writers, this annual competition accepts previously
unpublished original works in English. The competition is presented by Associated Writing Programs.
Website: www.awpwriter.org
Length: From 60,000 words.
Requirements: Entry fee, $10 for members; $20 for non-members. Manuscripts must include a cover page with author's
name, address, phone number, and manuscript title. All
entrants are required to read the guidelines before entering;
visit the website or send an SASE. Manuscripts will not be
returned.
Prizes: Winner receives an offer to enter into a contract with
Thomas Dunne Books, providing a $10,000 advance.
Deadline: Between January 1 and February 28.

The Boston Globe-Horn Book **Awards**

The Horn Book
Suite 200
56 Roland Street
Boston, MA 02129

Description
These annual book awards honor excellence in literature for children and young adults. They are considered among the most
prestigious in the nation. A committee of three judges evaluates
books submitted by United States publishers and selects winners on the basis of their overall creative excellence.
Website: www.hbook.com/bghb.html
Length: No length requirements.
Requirements: No entry fee. Publishers may submit up to eight
books from each of their juvenile imprints in the following categories: fiction or poetry, nonfiction, and picture books. Visit the
website for complete guidelines, or send an SASE.
Prizes: $500 and an engraved silver bowl. Honor books may also
be named.
Deadline: May 15 of each year.

CNW/FFWA Florida State Writing Competition

CNW/FFWA
P.O. Box A
North Stratford, NH 03590

Description
Open to all writers, this annual competition presents awards in 11 categories including children's literature short story, children's nonfiction, nonfiction book chapter, and poetry.
Website: www.writers-editors.com
Length: No length limitations.
Requirements: Entry fee, $5 for members of CNW/FFWA; $10 for nonmembers. Multiple entries are accepted, as long as each entry is accompanied by an entry fee. Use paper clips only. Author's name must not appear on manuscript. Send an SASE for complete contest guidelines and official entry form, or visit the website.
Prizes: First through third prizes will be awarded in each category. Winners receive cash awards ranging from $50 to $100.
Deadline: March 15.

The Dana Awards

Mary Elizabeth Parker
7207 Townsend Forest Court
Browns Summit, NC 27214-9634

Description
Encouraging emerging writers, the Dana Awards honor quality writing in the categories of novel, short fiction, and poetry. All entries must be previously unpublished original work that contains clear, developed themes.
Website: www.danaawards.com
Length: Lengths vary for each category.
Requirements: Entry fees, one short story or five poems, $10; novel entries, $20. Multiple submissions are accepted. E-mail danaawards@pipeline.com for questions regarding the contest.
Prizes: Winners in each category receive a cash prize of $1,000.
Deadline: October 31. Send an SASE for complete contest guidelines and official entry form, or visit the website.

Marguerite de Angeli Contest

Marguerite de Angeli Contest
Delacorte Press/Random House, Inc.
1540 Broadway
New York, NY 10036

Description

This annual contest, named for the famous children's book author and illustrator, seeks submissions of contemporary or historical middle-grade fiction set in North America. This contest is open to all writers who have not published a middle-grade novel.
Length: From 80 to 144 typewritten pages.
Requirements: No entry fee. Limit 2 entries per competition. No simultaneous submissions or foreign-language translations. Accepts photocopies. Include a brief plot summary and cover letter. Send an SASE for return of manuscript. For complete guidelines, send an SASE.
Prizes: Winner receives a book contract for a hardcover and paperback edition, including an advance and royalties. The award consists of $1,500 cash and $3,500 in royalties.
Deadline: Manuscripts must be postmarked by June 30.

Delacorte Press Contest for a First Young Adult Novel

Random House, Inc.
1540 Broadway
New York, NY 10036

Description

This contest is held annually to encourage the writing of contemporary young adult fiction. It is open to all US and Canadian writers who have not previously published a young adult novel. Manuscripts must have a contemporary setting, and should be suitable for young adults from ages 12 to 18.
Length: From 100 to 224 typewritten pages.
Requirements: No entry fee. Limit two manuscripts per competition. Accepts photocopies, if legible. Manuscripts under consideration for this contest may not be submitted to other publishers. Author's name should appear only on cover letter. Title of manuscript should appear on each page of the manuscript. Send an SASE for return of manuscript.
Prizes: $1,500 in cash and a $6,000 advance on royalties.
Deadline: December 31.

Gardenia Press First Novel Writing Competition

P.O. Box 18601
Milwaukee, WI 53218-0601

Description
Sponsored by Gardenia Press, this competition accepts submissions of fiction. It is open to authors who have not had work of any nature published for $500 or more within the last five years.
Website: www.gardeniapress.com
Length: From 45,000 to 175,000 words.
Requirements: Entry fee, $40 per piece. Multiple entries are accepted. Accepts photocopies and computer printouts. Manuscripts will not be returned. Entries should include a cover letter including author's name, address, telephone number, e-mail address, word count, and suggested genre.
Prizes: Grand-prize winner is guaranteed publication by Gardenia Press. First-place winner receives a late model Desktop PC, and second-place winner receives a $200 gift certificate.
Deadline: August 16.

Golden Kite Awards

Society of Children's Book Writers and Illustrators
8271 Beverly Blvd.
Los Angeles, CA 90048

Description
Held annually, these awards honor the most outstanding children's books written by members of SCBWI and published during the preceding year. Awards are presented in four categories: fiction, nonfiction, picture book text, and picture book illustration.
Website: www.scbwi.org
Length: No length requirements.
Requirements: No entry fee. No anthologies or translations. Submit 3 copies of each book per entry category. Books must be submitted during the calendar year of original publication.
Prizes: Winners in each category receive a Golden Kite statuette. Honor plaques are also awarded. Winners are announced at the SCBWI summer national conference.
Deadline: December 15. Request contest guidelines and addresses for the three judges in each category.

The Barbara Karlin Grant

SCBWI
8271 Beverly Blvd.
Los Angeles, CA 90048

Description
The Society of Children's Book Writers and Illustrators (SCBWI)
sponsors this grant to encourage excellence in children's picture
books. These grants provide assistance to both full and associate
SCBWI members who have never had a picture book published.
Website: www.scbwi.org
Length: 8 typed, double-spaced pages.
Requirements: No entry fee. One picture book manuscript per
applicant. Requests for applications may be made beginning
October 1 of each year. Instructions for mailing and written
material are sent with application forms.
Prizes: $1,500 grant; $500 runner-up grant, to be used on items
to encourage further writing.
Deadline: Postmarked between April 1 and May 15 of each year.
Request contest application for additional information.

The Vicky Metcalf Awards
Canadian Authors Association Awards
P.O. Box 419
320 South Shores Road
Campbelford, Ontario K0L 1L0
Canada

Description
Established in 1963, these annual awards were created by the
Toronto librarian whose name they bear. Awards are presented in
different categories including "Body of Work," which accepts
entries of fiction, nonfiction, and picture books.
Website: www.canauthors.org/awards/metcalf.html
Length: Length varies with each category.
Requirements: No entry fee. Authors must be Canadian.
Requirements vary for each category. A writer may only win "A
Body of Work" or "Short Story Award" once. Send an SASE or
visit the website for contest guidelines for additional information.
Prizes: Cash awards ranging between $1,000 and $10,000 are
presented to the winners. Winners announced in May.
Deadline: December 31 of each year.

Milkweed Prize for Children's Literature

Milkweed Editions
1011 Washington Ave. South, Suite 300
Minneapolis, MN 55415-1246

Description
This annual award is presented to the best manuscript accepted for publication by Milkweed Editions during the current year for the 8–13 age group. It looks to encourage writers to turn their attention to this important age group.
Website: www.milkweed.org
Length: From 90 to 200 typewritten pages.
Requirements: No entry fee. Entries must have been accepted for publication by Milkweed during the calendar year by a writer not previously published by Milkweed. Picture books and collections of stories are not eligible. All entries must follow Milkweed's usual children's manuscript guidelines. Send an SASE for complete information.
Prizes: Winners receive a $10,000 cash advance on royalties.
Deadline: Ongoing.

National Children's Theatre Festival

Actors' Playhouse at the Miracle Theatre
280 Miracle Mile
Coral Gables, FL 33134

Description
This competition invites the submission of original scripts for musicals targeting the 5-to-12 age group. It accepts previously unpublished entries and prefers plays that are appealing to children and adults.
Website: www.actorsplayhouse.org
Length: Running time, 50 minutes.
Requirements: Entry fee, $10 per piece. Accepts photocopies and computer printouts. Multiple submissions are accepted. Include an SASE for return of manuscript. Complete guidelines are available online or with an SASE.
Prizes: Winner receives a cash prize of $500 and a full production of their play.
Deadline: August 1. Winners will be announced in October.

Newbery Medal Award

American Library Association
50 East Huron
Chicago, IL 60611

Description

Recognized as the most prestigious award in the US in the field of children's literature, the Newbery Medal has been presented annually since 1922 by the American Library Association. It honors the authors of the most distinguished original contributions to children's literature during the preceding calendar year.

Website: www.ala.org/alsc/newbery.html

Length: No length requirements.

Requirements: No entry fee. Multiple submissions are accepted. All entries must have been published during the preceding calendar year; restricted to citizens or residents of the US. Send an SASE for guidelines and additional information.

Prizes: Newbery Medal. Honor books may also be named.

Deadline: December 31 of each year.

New Voices New Worlds
First Novel Award

Hyperion Books for Children
114 Fifth Avenue
New York, NY 10011

Description

Sponsored by Hyperion Books for Children, this annual award is presented to the best work of contemporary or historical fiction for ages 8 to 12, set in the US, that reflects the diverse ethnic and cultural heritage of our country. It is open to all US writers.

Website: www.hyperionbooksforchildren.com.

Length: 100 to 240 pages.

Requirements: No entry fee. Entries must include an entry form to be eligible. Accepts photocopies, if legible. Send an SASE for return of manuscript. No simultaneous submissions. Send an SASE or visit the website for contest guidelines and entry form.

Prizes: Prizes include a standard book contract with a $7,500 advance, and a $1,500 cash prize.

Deadline: Entries are accepted between April 1 and August 31.

NWA Novel Contest

National Writers Association
3140 S. Peoria Street #295
Aurora, CO 80014

Description
The purpose of this contest is to encourage the development
of creative skills, and to recognize and reward outstanding
ability in the area of novel writing. It accepts unpublished
entries only.
Website: www.nationalwriters.com
Length: To 90,000 words.
Requirements: Entry fee, $35 per piece. Multiple submissions
are accepted. Accepts computer printouts and photocopies.
Include an SASE for return of manuscript. Send an SASE or visit
the website for complete guidelines.
Prizes: First-prize, $500; second-prize, $250; third-prize, $150.
Fourth- through tenth-place winners receive a book and an
honor certificate.
Deadline: April 1. Winners are announced in June.

Once Upon a World Book Award

Museum of Tolerance
9786 West Pico Boulevard
Los Angeles, CA 90035

Description
Sponsored by The Museum of Tolerance, this award recognizes
children's literature with themes of tolerance and diversity. Submissions should reinforce mutual understanding and illustrate the
effects of stereotyping and intolerance. Books should allow children to root for the underdog.
Length: No length requirements.
Requirements: No entry fee. All submissions must have been
published in the year prior to the award. Submissions should
be for children ages 6 to 10 and may be fiction, nonfiction, or
poetry. A nomination form must accompany each submission.
Send an SASE for complete contest guidelines and nomination
form.
Prizes: Winners receive a cash prize of $1,000.
Deadline: To be announced.

Pacific Northwest Writers Association Literary Contests

PNWA
P.O. Box 2016
Edmonds, WA 98020-9516

Description
PNWA presents several contests annually in categories including juvenile/young adult novel, nonfiction book or memoir, juvenile memoir short story, and adult short story. Only original, previously unpublished work will be accepted.
Website: www.pnwa.org
Length: Varies for each category.
Requirements: Entry fee, $35 for members; $45 for non-members. Multiple entries are accepted. Accepts photocopies and computer printouts. All entries must include an official entry form; available with an SASE or on the website. Submit two copies of each entry. Send an SASE or visit the website for complete information.
Prizes: Winners receive cash prizes ranging from $150 to $600.
Deadline: February 16.

PEN/Norma Klein Award for Children's Fiction

PEN American Center
568 Broadway
New York, NY 10012

Description
This triennial prize recognizes an emerging voice of literary merit among American writers of children's fiction. Candidates for this award are new authors whose books demonstrate the adventuresome and innovative spirit that characterizes children's literature.
Length: From 64 to 200 typewritten pages.
Requirements: No entry fee. Accepts photocopies and computer printouts. Candidates may not nominate themselves. The judges welcome nominations from authors and editors of children's books. Nominating letters should describe the author's work in some detail. Send an SASE for complete contest guidelines and further information.
Prizes: A cash award of $3,000 will be presented to the winner. Winners will be announced in the spring.
Deadline: December 15.

Edgar Allan Poe Awards

Mystery Writers of America
17 East 47th Street, 6th Floor
New York, NY 10017

Description
Mystery Writers of America sponsors this competition, which offers awards in several categories including children's mystery and young adult mystery. It honors the best mysteries published in the year preceding the contest and looks to enhance the visibility of the mystery genre.
Website: www.mysterynet.com/mwa
Length: Length requirement varies for each category.
Requirements: No entry fee. Entries may only be submitted in one category. Submit a copy of the entry to each member of the appropriate judging committee. Official entry form is required. Send an SASE for contest guidelines and official entry form.
Prizes: $1,500 in cash and a $6,000 advance on royalties.
Deadline: Deadlines vary for each category. Winners are announced in late April.

Skipping Stones Awards

Skipping Stones Awards
P.O. Box 3939
Eugene, OR 97403

Description
Focusing on multicultural awareness, these annual awards honor exceptional contributions to ecological and multicultural education. Books, magazines, and educational videos are considered in each of the four categories: Ecology & Nature, Educational Videos, Multicultural & International, and Teaching Resources.
Website: www.efn.org/~skipping
Length: No length requirements.
Requirements: Entry fee, $50 per piece. Multiple entries are acceptable. Send 4 copies of each book and magazine entry; 2 copies of each video. Only entries produced in the preceding calendar year are eligible.
Prizes: Cash prizes are awarded to first- through fourth-place winners. Winning entries are reviewed in *Skipping Stones*.
Deadline: January 15.

Kay Snow Writing Contest

Willamette Writers
Suite 5A
9045 SW Barbour Blvd
Portland, OR 97219-4027

Description
This annual contest looks to promote new writers in memory of
the group's founder, Kay Snow. Awards are presented in several
categories including juvenile fiction, juvenile nonfiction, adult fiction, and student writing.
Website: www.willamettewriters.com
Length: Length varies for each category.
Requirements: Entry fee, $10 for members; $15 for nonmembers. Submit three copies of each entry. Author's name must not
appear on manuscript. Request complete contest guidelines or
visit website for additional information.
Prizes: Cash prizes ranging from $50 to $300 are awarded in
each category. A Liam Callen award will also be presented to the
best overall entry with a cash prize of $500.
Deadline: May 15th.

Southwest Writers Contests

Southwest Writers Workshop
1338-B Wyoming Blvd. NE
Albuquerque, NM 87112

Description
Sponsored by the Southwest Writers Workshop, this annual contest offers awards in several categories including middle-grade
novel, young adult novel, children's picture book, and nonfiction
book. It offers writers an opportunity to have their work read and
judged by professional editors and agents.
Website: www.southwestwriters.org
Length: Lengths vary for each category.
Requirements: Submit two copies of each entry. Each entry
must be accompanied by an official entry form. Author's name
should appear on the entry form only. Multiple entries are
accepted. All entries must be typed.
Prizes: Winners receive cash prizes ranging from $75–$100.
Deadline: May 1. Send an SASE for complete contest guidelines
and official entry form, or visit the website.

Peter Taylor Prize for the Novel

Knoxville Writers Guild
P.O. Box 2565
Knoxville, TN 37901-2565

Description
Open to both published and unpublished writers living in the US, this annual competition looks to identify and publish novels of high literary quality.
Website: www.knoxvillewritersguild.org
Length: 40,000 words minimum.
Requirements: Entry fee, $20. Multiple submissions are accepted provided that each is accompanied by an entry fee. Entries must be on standard white paper. Manuscripts will not be returned. Include an SASE for contest results.
Prizes: The prize includes a $1,000 cash award, publication of the novel by the University of Tennessee Press, and a standard royalty contract.
Deadline: Entries must be postmarked between February 1 and April 30.

Jackie White Memorial National Children's Playwriting Contest

Columbia Entertainment Company
309 Parkade Blvd.
Columbia, MO 65202

Description
This contest looks to encourage the development of large cast plays for production. All entries must be suitable and entertaining for all ages. It accepts plays in many genres including comedy, musical, fantasy, and drama.
Length: 90 minutes running time.
Requirements: Entry fee, $10 per piece. Multiple entries are accepted. Accepts photocopies and computer printouts. Include résumé, character descriptions, and act/scene synopses. Send an SASE for return of script.
Prizes: Winner receives $250 cash award.
Deadline: June 1 of each year. Request complete contest guidelines for further information.
Submissions Received: Receives 45 submissions each competition; 20% by unpublished writers.

Work-In-Progress Grants

Society of Children's Book Writers and Illustrators
8271 Beverly Boulevard
Los Angeles, CA 90048

Description
SCBWI presents 4 grants annually in the categories of General
Work-In-Progress Grant; Grant for Contemporary Novel for
Young People; Nonfiction Research Grant; and a Grant for a
work whose author has never had a book published. The grants
were established to assist children's book writers in the completion of a specific project.
Website: www.scbwi.org
Length: 750-word synopsis and writing sample from the entry
that is no more than 2,500 words.
Requirements: No entry fee. Requests for applications may be
made beginning October 1 of each year. Instructions and guidelines are sent with application forms.
Prizes: Cash awards of $1,500 and $500 are awarded in each
category.

Writers Union of Canada Writing for Children Competition

24 Ryerson Avenue
Toronto, ON M5T 2P3
Canada

Description
Open to Canadian citizens who have not yet been published in
book format, this competition is held annually. It accepts fiction or
nonfiction prose for children.
Website: www.writersunion.ca
Length: To 1,500 words.
Requirements: Entry fee, $15 per entry. Accepts computer
printouts and photocopies. Include a separate cover sheet with
name, address, phone number, and whether the entry is fiction
or nonfiction. Author's name should not appear on manuscript
itself. Visit the website or send an SASE for guidelines.
Prizes: A cash award of $1,500 is presented to the winner. The
winning entry and 11 finalists will be submitted to a Canadian
publisher of children's books.
Deadline: April 23.

Indexes

2003 Market News

New Listings ☆

Advocacy Press
AML Awards
Annick Press
AWP/Thomas Dunne
  Books
Baker Book House
  Company
A & C Black Publishers
Chrysalis Children's Books
Contemporary Books
Cook Communications
The Creative Company
Exclamation! Publishers
Faith Kids
Focus on the Family
  Publishing
Gardenia Press First Novel
  Writing Contest
GT Publications
Imajinn Books
LangMarc Publishing
Legacy Press
Lightwave Publishing, Inc.
Marsh Media
Master Books
Miles Kelly Publishing
Mountain Meadow Press
Mount Olive College Press
Munchweiler Press
National Children's Theatre
  Festival

National Council of
  Teachers of English
New Harbinger Publications
Nomad Press
North Country Books
Novalis Publishing
NWA Novel Contest
OnStage Publishing
Pacific Northwest Writers
  Association Literary
  Contests
Pebble Beach Press Ltd.
Portage & Main Press
Ranchworks
River City Publishing
Roaring Brook Press
Shen's Books
Simon Pulse
Siphano Picture Books
Success Publications
Thistledown Press

2003 Market News

Deletions/Name Changes

Archives Press/Homemade Books: Unable to locate
Jason Aronson Inc.: Removed at editor's request
Blessing Our World: Listed as BOW Books
Bookmice.com Inc.: Unable to locate
Centering Corporation: Not publishing at this time
Collins Children's Books: Did not respond
Court Wayne Press: Unable to locate
Editorial Concepts: Unable to locate
eNovel.com: Unable to locate
ERIC/EDINFO Press: Listed as Family Learning Association/ ERIC/REC Press
Laura Geringer Books: Not currently accepting submissions
Glencoe/McGraw-Hill: Did not respond
Good Apple: Ceased publication
Heian International: Did not respond
Highsmith Press: Listed as Upstart Books
Hi-Time*Pflaum: Removed at editor's request
Human Kinetics: Removed at editor's request
Ideals Children's Books: Listed as Eager Minds Press
Interstate Publishers, Inc.: Ceased publication
Michael Kesend Publishing: Did not respond
KidtoonProductions: Ceased publication
Kudlicka Publishing: Did not respond
Learning Triangle Press: Will be gradually phasing out
Loyola Press: Removed at editor's request
MapleInk Publishing: Unable to locate
Moon Mountain Publishing: Not accepting material
Ottenheimer Publishers: Going out of business
Piccadilly Books: Removed at editor's request
Pink Tree Press: Ceased publication
Ragged Bears Publishing: Did not respond
Ragweed Press: Unable to locate
Sierra Club Books for Children: Removed at editor's request
Social Science Education Consortium: Removed at editor's request
SpanPress Inc.: Unable to locate
Starlight Writer Publications: Did not respond
Transworld Children's Books: Listed as Random House Children's Books
Twayne Publishers: Company sold, unable to locate
United Church Press: Listed as The Pilgrim Press
Welcome Enterprises, Inc.: Unable to locate
Whispering Coyote Press: See Charlesbridge

Category Index

To help you find the appropriate market for your query or manuscript, we have compiled a selective index of publishers according to the types of books they currently publish.

If you don't find a category that exactly fits your material, try a broader term that covers your topic. For example, if you have written a middle-grade biography, look through the list of publishers for both Middle-Grade (Nonfiction) *and* Biography. If you've written a young adult mystery, look under Mystery/Suspense *and* Young Adult (Fiction). Always check the publisher's listing for explanations of specific needs.

For your convenience, we have listed all of the categories that are included in this Index.

Activity Books
Adventure
Animals/Pets
Bilingual (Fiction)
Bilingual
  (Nonfiction)
Biography
Board Books
Canadian
  Publishers
Chapter Books
  (Fiction)
Chapter Books
  (Nonfiction)
Concept Books
Contemporary
  Fiction
Crafts/Hobbies
Current Events
Drama
Early Picture Books
  (Fiction)
Early Picture Books
  (Nonfiction)
Easy-to-Read
  (Fiction)
Easy-to-Read
  (Nonfiction)
Education/Resource
  Material
Fairy Tales

Fantasy
Folklore/Folktales
Geography
Gifted Education
Health/Fitness
High-Interest/
  Low-Vocabulary
Historical Fiction
History (Nonfiction)
Horror
How-to
Humor
Inspirational Fiction
Language Arts
Mathematics
Middle-Grade
  (Fiction)
Middle-Grade
  (Nonfiction)
Multicultural/
  Ethnic (Fiction)
Multicultural/Ethnic
  (Nonfiction)
Mystery/Suspense
Nature/Environment
Parenting
Photo Essays
Picture Books
  (Fiction)
Picture Books
  (Nonfiction)

Plays
Reference Books
Regional (Fiction)
Regional
  (Nonfiction)
Religious (Fiction)
Religious
  (Nonfiction)
Romance
Science Fiction
Science/Technology
Self-Help
Series
Social Issues
Social Sciences
Special Education
Sports (Fiction)
Sports (Nonfiction)
Story Picture Books
  (Fiction)
Story Picture Books
  (Nonfiction)
Toddler Books
  (Fiction)
Toddler Books
  (Nonfiction)
Travel
Western
Young Adult (Fiction)
Young Adult
  (Nonfiction)

Activity Books

Absey and Company 79
Augsburg Books 91
Ballyhoo Books 445
The Benefactory 100
Carson-Dellosa Publishing Company 118
Chicago Review Press 123
The Children's Nature Institute 453
Childswork/Childsplay 127
Christian Ed. Publishers 129
Chrysalis Children's Books 454
The Colonial Williamsburg Foundation 455
Cottonwood Press 458
Creative Learning Press 144
Dandy Lion Publications 154
May Davenport, Publishers 155
Didax 161
Dog-Eared Publications 461
Dover Publications 167
Edupress 178
Evan-Moor Educational Publishers 186
Forest House Publishing Company 197
Fulcrum Publishing 204
Gibbs Smith, Publisher 205
Greene Bark Press 211
Group Publishing 214
Heritage House 231
Honor Books 235
Humanics 237
Hunter House Publishers 238
Iron Crown Enterprises 474
Kar-Ben Publishing 256
Leadership Publishers Inc. 477
Learning Horizons 261
Learning Resources 262
Legacy Press 264
Marlor Press 277
Master Books 278
Modern Publishing 289
NL Associates 307
Pauline Books & Media 325
Paulist Press 326
Pleasant Company Publications 346
Rainbow Publishers 355
Rand McNally 497
Resource Publications, Inc. 359
Rising Moon 360
Robins Lane Press 364
Running Press Book Publishers 367
Shining Star Publications 505
Sterling Publishing Company 393
Story Time Stories That Rhyme 510
Teacher Created Materials 396
Teacher Ideas Press/Libraries Unlimited 397
Tricycle Press 409
Two Bytes Publishing 514
Warner Press 418

Adventure

All About Kids Publishing 85
Anchorage Press Plays 87
Aquila Communications Ltd. 442
Atheneum Books for Young Readers 90
A/V Concepts Corporation 92
Avon Books 94
Bethany House Publishers 102
BOW Books 108
Breakwater Books 112
The Brookfield Reader 114
Camex Books 450
Clarion Books 133
Coteau Books 139
Covenant Communications 140
Crocodile Books, USA 149
Crossway Books 151
May Davenport, Publishers 155
Dover Publications 167
Down East Books 169
Dutton Children's Books 172
E. M. Press 181
Focus on the Family Publishing 196
Formac Publishing Company Ltd. 198
Frances Foster Books 200
Gibbs Smith, Publisher 205
Gulliver Books 217
Hachai Publishing 218
Innovative Kids 243
Just Us Books 254
Little, Brown and Company 271
Lobster Press 273
Margaret K. McElderry Books 281
Modern Publishing 289
Moody Press 291
Pioneer Drama Service 341
Playhouse Publishing 344

Random House Children's Books 498
Random House Children's
  Publishing 498
Rayve Productions Inc. 357
Red Deer Press 358
River City Publishing 361
Scholastic Book Group 502
Scholastic Canada Ltd. 373
Seedling Publications 379
Silver Moon Press 381
Soundprints 386
The Story Place 509
Storytellers Ink Publishing Co. 395
Turtle Press 410
Viking Children's Books 516
Whitecap Books Ltd. 422

Animals/Pets

Abdo Publishing Company 78
All About Kids Publishing 85
Benchmark Books 99
The Benefactory 100
Charlesbridge Publishing 120
Creative Editions 142
Creative Education 143
Creative With Words
  Publications 146
Crocodile Books, USA 149
Doral Publishing 461
Dover Publications 167
E. M. Press 181
Falcon Publishing 190
Gibbs Smith, Publisher 205
Graphic Arts Center
  Publishing Co. 210
Gulliver Books 217
Hendrick-Long Publishing
  Company 230
Henry Holt and Company 234
iPicturebooks, Inc. 247
Bob Jones University Press 252
Kingfisher 475
Learning Horizons 261
Master Books 278
Maval Publishing 279
Miles Kelly Publishing 483
Mount Olive College Press 485
National Geographic Society 297
North-South Books 309
NorthWord Books for Young
  Readers 311

OnStage Publishing 314
Pleasant Company Publications 346
Random House Children's
  Publishing 498
The Rosen Publishing Group 366
Running Press Book Publishers 367
SeaStar Books 378
Seedling Publications 379
Silver Dolphin Books 380
Soundprints 386
The Story Place 509
Storytellers Ink Publishing Co. 395
Tilbury House, Publishers 404
J.N. Townsend Publishing 513
Windward Publishing 428

Bilingual (F)

Children's Book Press 124
I. E. Clark Publications 134
Cricket Books 147
Fondo de Cultura
  Economica USA 465
Rising Moon 360
Salina Bookshelf 500
Turtle Books 514

Bilingual (NF)

Abingdon Press 440
Aquila Communications Ltd. 442
Chrysalis Children's Books 454
Encore Performance Publishing 182
Family Learning Assoc/ERIC/
  REC Press 191
Fondo de Cultura
  Economica USA 465
Forest House Publishing
  Company 197
Gallopade International 466
Gryphon House 215
Hampton-Brown Books 219
Heinemann 229
Incentive Publications 242
Kingfisher 475
McGraw-Hill School Division 482
Mitchell Lane Publishers 287
Pearson Learning Group 490
Portage & Main Press 348
Salina Bookshelf 500
Scott Foresman 377
Storytellers Ink Publishing Co. 395

Teacher Ideas Press/Libraries
Unlimited 397

Biography

Absey and Company 79
Aladdin Paperbacks 82
Avisson Press 93
Alexander Graham Bell Assn.
for the Deaf 447
Blue Marlin Publications 105
The Boxwood Press 450
Camex Books 450
Challenger Publishing 452
Chicago Review Press 123
C.I.S. Publishers and
Distributors 455
Crossquarter Publishing Group 150
Eerdmans Books for Young
Readers 179
Enslow Publishers 184
Excelsior Cee Publishing 463
The Feminist Press 194
Franklin Watts 465
Greenhaven Press 212
HarperTrophy Paperbacks 225
Hendrick-Long Publishing
Company 230
Holloway House Publishing
Group 470
Houghton Mifflin Children's
Books 236
Bob Jones University Press 252
Just Us Books 254
Lerner Publishing Group 265
Linnet Books 269
Lion Books 477
Lucent Books 275
Mage Publishers 481
The Millbrook Press 286
Mitchell Lane Publishers 287
Mondo Publishing 290
Morgan Reynolds 294
North Country Books 308
Novalis Publishing 312
The Oliver Press 313
OnStage Publishing 314
Paulist Press 326
Piñata Books 339
Prima Publishing 349
Random House Children's
Publishing 498

Rayve Productions Inc. 357
Ronsdale Press 365
Sandlapper Publishing 500
Simon Pulse 506
Sports Publishing Inc. 389
Stemmer House Publishers 392
Storytellers Ink Publishing Co. 395
Teacher Ideas Press/Libraries
Unlimited 397
Teaching & Learning Company 398
TEACH Services, Inc. 399
Toy Box Productions 408
Twenty-First Century Books 411
Two Lives Publishing 515

Board Books

Abingdon Press 440
Bess Press 101
Chrysalis Children's Books 454
Honor Books 235
John Hunt Publishing 239
Hyperion Books for Children 472
Innovative Kids 243
Kar-Ben Publishing 256
Alfred A. Knopf Books for Young
Readers 259
Little Simon 272
Master Books 278
McGraw-Hill Children's
Publishing 282
Tommy Nelson 487
Playhouse Publishing 344
Rising Moon 360
Silver Dolphin Books 380
Standard Publishing 390
Warner Press 418
What's Inside Press 421
Workman Publishing Company 432

Canadian Publishers

Annick Press 88
Arnold Publishing 89
Beach Holme Publishing 97
Borealis Press Limited 107
Breakwater Books 112
Coteau Books 139
Creative Bound 141
Formac Publishing
Company Ltd. 198
Harcourt Canada Ltd. 469

Heritage House	231	Holiday House	233
Key Porter Books	258	Henry Holt and Company	234
James Lorimer & Company	479	Hyperion Books for Children	472
LTDBooks	480	Imperial International	241
Natural Heritage Books	486	Bob Jones University Press	252
Orca Book Publishers	315	KIDSZIP LTD	475
Owl Books	320	Alfred A. Knopf Books for Young	
Pearson Education Canada	329	Readers	259
Pembroke Publishers	332	Mayhaven Publishing	280
Penguin Books Canada Limited	491	Mondo Publishing	290
Playwrights Canada Press	494	New Canaan Publishing	
Red Deer Press	358	Company	300
Ronsdale Press	365	North-South Books	309
Scholastic Canada Ltd.	373	Orca Book Publishers	315
Stoddart Kids Books	394	Orchard Books	316
Thistledown Press	512	The Overmountain Press	318
Thompson Educational		Richard C. Owen Publishers	319
Publishing	403	Pacific Educational Press	321
Tradewind Books Ltd.	513	Pacific Press Publishing	
		Association	322

Chapter Books (F)

Absey and Company	79	Parachute Press	323
Alef Design Group	84	Paulist Press	326
All About Kids Publishing	85	Peartree	330
Avon Books	94	Philomel Books	336
Bantam Doubleday Dell Books for		Polychrome Publishing	
Young Readers	96	Corporation	347
Bethany House Publishers	102	Publish America	352
BOW Books	108	Puffin Books	353
Candlewick Press	451	G. P. Putnam's Sons	354
Clarion Books	133	Random House Children's	
Coteau Books	139	Books	498
Cricket Books	147	Rayve Productions Inc.	357
Dial Books for Young Readers	160	Red Deer Press	358
Dorling Kindersley	166	Scholastic Book Group	502
Eakin Press	174	Scholastic Canada Ltd.	373
Educators Publishing Service	177	SeaStar Books	378
E. M. Press	181	Shen's Books	505
Faith Kids	189	Silver Whistle	382
Farrar, Straus & Giroux	192	Simon & Schuster Books for	
The Feminist Press	194	Young Readers	383
Formac Publishing		Smith and Kraus Books for Kids	507
Company Ltd.	198	Soundprints	386
Frances Foster Books	200	Stoddart Kids Books	394
Graphic Arts Center		Third World Press	401
Publishing Co.	210	Torah Aura Productions	406
Hachai Publishing	218	Tricycle Press	409
Hampton-Brown Books	219	Turtle Press	410
HarperCollins Children's Books	224	Whitecap Books Ltd.	422
HarperTrophy Paperbacks	225	Albert Whitman & Company	425
Hodder Children's Books	470	The Wright Group/	
		McGraw Hill	434

Zonderkidz 437

Chapter Books (NF)

Abdo Publishing Company 78
Alef Design Group 84
Behrman House 98
Benchmark Books 99
Blackbirch Press 104
Breakwater Books 112
Candlewick Press 451
Carolrhoda Books 117
Children's Press 125
Chronicle Books 132
Critical Thinking Books &
 Software 148
Crown Books for Young
 Readers 152
Discovery Enterprises 162
Facts On File 188
Faith Kids 189
Falcon Publishing 190
Falcon Publishing 190
Family Learning Assoc/ERIC/
 REC Press 191
The Feminist Press 194
Ferguson Publishing Company 195
Forest House Publishing
 Company 197
Fulcrum Publishing 204
Harcourt Religion Publishers 223
HarperTrophy Paperbacks 225
Hodder Children's Books 470
John Hunt Publishing 239
Hyperion Books for Children 472
Imperial International 241
Incentive Publications 242
KIDSZIP LTD 475
Lerner Publishing Group 265
Lobster Press 273
Marlor Press 277
Meadowbrook Press 283
Mitchell Lane Publishers 287
Mondo Publishing 290
National Geographic Society 297
New Canaan Publishing
 Company 300
Our Sunday Visitor 317
Pacific Press Publishing
 Association 322
Paulist Press 326
Pembroke Publishers 332

Perfection Learning
 Corporation 334
Pitspopany Press 342
Raintree Steck-Vaughn
 Publishers 356
The Rosen Publishing Group 366
Silver Moon Press 381
Smith and Kraus Books for Kids 507
Standard Publishing 390
Stemmer House Publishers 392
TEACH Services, Inc. 399
Torah Aura Productions 406
Toy Box Productions 408
Tricycle Press 409
Turtle Press 410
UAHC Press 413
Windward Publishing 428

Concept Books

Atheneum Books for Young
 Readers 90
Augsburg Books 91
Boyds Mills Press 109
Broadman & Holman Publishers 113
Cartwheel Books 119
Charlesbridge Publishing 120
Children's Press 125
Chronicle Books 132
Cook Communications
 Ministries 138
Covenant Communications 140
Crown Books for Young Readers 152
Dial Books for Young Readers 160
DiskUs Publishing 163
Dorling Kindersley 166
Dutton Children's Books 172
Gifted Education Press 206
Greenwillow Books 468
Hachai Publishing 218
Harcourt Children's Books 222
HarperCollins Children's Books 224
Harvest House Publishers 226
Honor Books 235
Houghton Mifflin Children's
 Books 236
Humanics 237
Just Us Books 254
Kar-Ben Publishing 256
Little, Brown and Company 271
Little Simon 272
Master Books 278

McGraw-Hill Children's Publishing	282
The Millbrook Press	286
North-South Books	309
Orchard Books	316
Our Sunday Visitor	317
Philomel Books	336
Playhouse Publishing	344
Rising Moon	360
Frank Schaffer Publications	372
Seaburn Publishing	503
Silver Dolphin Books	380
The Speech Bin	388
Standard Publishing	390
Third World Press	401
Megan Tingley Books	405
Tricycle Press	409
Two Lives Publishing	515
Tyndale House Publishers	412
Viking Children's Books	516
Walker and Company	417
Workman Publishing Company	432
Zonderkidz	437

Arthur A. Levine Books	266
Moody Press	291
Morning Glory Press	484
Orca Book Publishers	315
Orchard Books	316
Richard C. Owen Publishers	319
Owl Books	320
Parachute Press	323
Perfection Learning Corporation	334
Piñata Books	339
Pleasant Company Publications	346
Pro Lingua Associates	350
Publish America	352
G. P. Putnam's Sons	354
Red Deer Press	358
Roaring Brook Press	363
Saint Mary's Press	369
Sandpiper Paperbacks	501
Silver Whistle	382
Simon Pulse	506
Stoddart Kids Books	394
Texas Tech University Press	400
Megan Tingley Books	405
Turtle Books	514
Two Lives Publishing	515
Whitecap Books Ltd.	422
Wolfhound Press	430

Contemporary Fiction

Aladdin Paperbacks	82
Annick Press	88
Barron's Educational Series	446
Beach Holme Publishing	97
Bethany House Publishers	102
A & C Black Publishers	448
The Brookfield Reader	114
Carolrhoda Books	117
Cavendish Children's Books	452
Chronicle Books	132
Coteau Books	139
Cricket Books	147
Crossway Books	151
E. M. Press	181
Farrar, Straus & Giroux	192
Forward Movement Publications	199
Girl Press	207
Greenwillow Books	468
Harcourt Children's Books	222
Bob Jones University Press	252
Just Us Books	254
Alfred A. Knopf Books for Young Readers	259
Lee & Low Books	263

Crafts/Hobbies

Ballyhoo Books	445
Creative Teaching Press	145
Evan-Moor Educational Publishers	186
Focus on the Family Publishing	196
Forest House Publishing Company	197
Group Publishing	214
Humanics	237
Lark Books	260
Legacy Press	264
Lion Books	477
The Millbrook Press	286
Naturegraph Publishers	298
Pleasant Company Publications	346
Quixote Press	496
Rainbow Publishers	355
Scholastic Book Group	502
Sterling Publishing Company	393
Success Publications	510
Teaching & Learning Company	398

Tor Books   **407**
Wiley Children's Books   **426**
Williamson Publishing   **427**
Winslow Publishing   **519**
World Book   **433**

Current Events

Facts On File   **188**
Focus on the Family Publishing   **196**
Huntington House Publishers   **471**
Lerner Publishing Group   **265**
New Leaf Press   **304**
Pebble Beach Press Ltd.   **490**
Publish America   **352**
Random House Children's
  Publishing   **498**
Sandpiper Paperbacks   **501**
Teaching & Learning Company   **398**
UXL   **415**

Drama

Anchorage Press Plays   **87**
Baker's Plays   **95**
Borealis Press Limited   **107**
Boynton/Cook Publishers   **110**
Children's Story Scripts   **126**
I. E. Clark Publications   **134**
Contemporary Drama Service   **137**
Dramatic Publishing   **170**
Encore Performance Publishing   **182**
Samuel French, Inc.   **202**
Heuer Publishing Company   **232**
Hunter House Publishers   **238**
Lillenas Publishing Company   **268**
Meriwether Publishing Ltd.   **284**
North-South Books   **309**
OnStage Publishing   **314**
Piñata Books   **339**
Pioneer Drama Service   **341**
Players Press   **343**
Playwrights Canada Press   **494**
Saint Mary's Press   **369**
Sandcastle Publishing   **370**
Smith and Kraus   **385**
Smith and Kraus Books for Kids   **507**

Early Picture Books (F)

Atheneum Books for Young
  Readers   **90**
Augsburg Books   **91**

Bantam Doubleday Dell Books for
  Young Readers   **96**
Bess Press   **101**
Beyond Words Publishing   **103**
Blue Marlin Publications   **105**
Blue Sky Press   **106**
Boyds Mills Press   **109**
Breakwater Books   **112**
Cartwheel Books   **119**
Charlesbridge Publishing   **120**
Chronicle Books   **132**
Cook Communications
  Ministries   **138**
Covenant Communications   **140**
Dial Books for Young Readers   **160**
Dorling Kindersley   **166**
Down East Books   **169**
Eakin Press   **174**
Frances Foster Books   **200**
Guardian Press   **216**
Gulliver Books   **217**
Hachai Publishing   **218**
Hampton-Brown Books   **219**
Harcourt Children's Books   **222**
HarperCollins Children's Books   **224**
Holiday House   **233**
Houghton Mifflin Children's
  Books   **236**
Incentive Publications   **242**
The Judaica Press   **253**
Kar-Ben Publishing   **256**
Lee & Low Books   **263**
Little, Brown and Company   **271**
Lobster Press   **273**
The Lutterworth Press   **480**
Margaret K. McElderry Books   **281**
Mondo Publishing   **290**
Morehouse Publishing   **292**
Orchard Books   **316**
The Overmountain Press   **318**
Owl Books   **320**
Philomel Books   **336**
Playhouse Publishing   **344**
Polychrome Publishing
  Corporation   **347**
Puffin Books   **353**
G. P. Putnam's Sons   **354**
Random House Children's
  Books   **498**
Roaring Brook Press   **363**
Sandpiper Paperbacks   **501**

Silver Whistle	382
Simon & Schuster Books for Young Readers	383
Siphano Picture Books	506
Starseed Press	391
Stoddart Kids Books	394
Megan Tingley Books	405
Two Lives Publishing	515
Walker and Company	417
Albert Whitman & Company	425
Zonderkidz	437

Early Picture Books (NF)

Abdo Publishing Company	78
Aladdin Paperbacks	82
Blue Marlin Publications	105
Cartwheel Books	119
The Children's Nature Institute	453
Concordia Publishing House	136
Continental Press	457
Cook Communications Ministries	138
Covenant Communications	140
Dial Books for Young Readers	160
Didax	161
Down East Books	169
Free Spirit Publishing	201
Gulliver Books	217
Hampton-Brown Books	219
Honor Books	235
John Hunt Publishing	239
Kar-Ben Publishing	256
Learning Horizons	261
Little Blue Works	478
Master Books	278
North-South Books	309
Novalis Publishing	312
Owl Books	320
Pauline Books & Media	325
Peachtree Publishers	328
G. P. Putnam's Sons	354
Sandpiper Paperbacks	501
Silver Dolphin Books	380
Silver Whistle	382
Siphano Picture Books	506
The Speech Bin	388
UAHC Press	413
Albert Whitman & Company	425
Workman Publishing Company	432
Zonderkidz	437

Easy-to-Read (F)

Abbeville Kids	439
Abingdon Press	440
Augsburg Books	91
Azro Press	444
Bantam Doubleday Dell Books for Young Readers	96
Bay Light Publishing	446
Alexander Graham Bell Assn. for the Deaf	447
BePuzzled	447
Bethany House Publishers	102
BOW Books	108
Boyds Mills Press	109
The Brookfield Reader	114
Cavendish Children's Books	452
Challenger Publishing	452
Chronicle Books	132
Clear Light Publishers	135
The Colonial Williamsburg Foundation	455
Cook Communications Ministries	138
Creative Teaching Press	145
Critical Thinking Books & Software	148
Jonathan David Publishers	156
Dial Books for Young Readers	160
DiskUs Publishing	163
Dutton Children's Books	172
Eager Minds Press	173
Eakin Press	174
Educators Publishing Service	177
Eerdmans Books for Young Readers	179
Faith Kids	189
Family Learning Assoc/ERIC/ REC Press	191
Farrar, Straus & Giroux	192
Formac Publishing Company Ltd.	198
Guardian Press	216
Hampton-Brown Books	219
Hampton Roads Publishing	220
HarperCollins Children's Books	224
HarperTrophy Paperbacks	225
Hodder Children's Books	470
ImaJinn Books	473
Bob Jones University Press	252
The Judaica Press	253

Kaeden Books   255
Kar-Ben Publishing   256
Lion Books   477
Little Blue Works   478
Little, Brown and Company   271
Living the Good News   478
Lobster Press   273
The Lutterworth Press   480
Magination Press   276
Margaret K. McElderry Books   281
McGraw-Hill Children's
  Publishing   282
Mondo Publishing   290
Morehouse Publishing   292
North-South Books   309
Richard C. Owen Publishers   319
Owl Books   320
Pacific Press Publishing
  Association   322
Paws IV Books   489
Peartree   330
Pelican Publishing Company   331
Philomel Books   336
Playhouse Publishing   344
Polar Bear & Company   494
Puffin Books   353
Quixote Press   496
Rayve Productions Inc.   357
River City Publishing   361
Roaring Brook Press   363
Scholastic Book Group   502
SeaStar Books   378
Seedling Publications   379
Simon & Schuster Books for
  Young Readers   383
Starry Puddle Publishing   508
Stoddart Kids Books   394
Story Time Stories That Rhyme   510
Tradewind Books Ltd.   513
Tricycle Press   409
Viking Children's Books   516
Whitecap Books Ltd.   422
Winslow Press   518
The Wright Group/McGraw Hill   434
Zonderkidz   437

Easy-to-Read (NF)

Abbeville Kids   439
Abingdon Press   440
Azro Press   444
Blackbirch Press   104

Boyds Mills Press   109
Broadman & Holman Publishers   113
Carolrhoda Books   117
Cartwheel Books   119
Cavendish Children's Books   452
Children's Press   125
Chrysalis Children's Books   454
Concordia Publishing House   136
Creative Teaching Press   145
Jonathan David Publishers   156
Dial Books for Young Readers   160
Discovery Enterprises   162
Dorling Kindersley   166
Eerdmans Books for Young
  Readers   179
Faith Kids   189
Family Learning Assoc/ERIC/
  REC Press   191
Forest House Publishing
  Company   197
Free Spirit Publishing   201
Harcourt Religion Publishers   223
HarperCollins Children's Books   224
Hodder Children's Books   470
Honor Books   235
Jewish Lights Publishing   250
Kaeden Books   255
Lerner Publishing Group   265
Living the Good News   478
Master Books   278
Mayhaven Publishing   280
Meadowbrook Press   283
Modern Publishing   289
Mondo Publishing   290
The Oliver Press   313
OnStage Publishing   314
Pacific Press Publishing
  Association   322
Pauline Books & Media   325
Paws IV Books   489
Pitspopany Press   342
Prometheus Books   351
Redbird Press   499
Seaburn Publishing   503
SeaStar Books   378
Seedling Publications   379
Silver Dolphin Books   380
Stemmer House Publishers   392
Story Time Stories That Rhyme   510
TEACH Services, Inc.   399
Third World Press   401

Tradewind Books Ltd.	513
Tricycle Press	409
Tyndale House Publishers	412
UXL	415
Weigl Educational Publishers	420
Whitecap Books Ltd.	422
Williamson Publishing	427
Windward Publishing	428
Winslow Press	518
World Book	433

Education/Resource Material

Absey and Company	79
Activity Resources Company	440
Advocacy Press	80
Africa World Press	81
ALA Editions	83
Alef Design Group	84
Amirah Publishing	441
Amsco School Publications	86
Arnold Publishing	89
Association for Childhood Education Int'l	442
A/V Concepts Corporation	92
Barron's Educational Series	446
Behrman House	98
Alexander Graham Bell Assn. for the Deaf	447
The Benefactory	100
Bess Press	101
Blackbirch Press	104
A & C Black Publishers	448
Boynton/Cook Publishers	110
Breakwater Books	112
The Bureau for At-Risk Youth	115
Butte Publications	116
Carson-Dellosa Publishing Company	118
Childswork/Childsplay	127
Child Welfare League of America	128
Christian Ed. Publishers	129
Christopher-Gordon Publishers, Inc.	131
Concordia Publishing House	136
Consortium Publishing	456
Contemporary Books	457
Continental Press	457
Cottonwood Press	458
Course Crafters, Inc.	459
Creative Education	143
Creative Learning Press	144
Creative Teaching Press	145
Critical Thinking Books & Software	148
CSS Publishing Company	153
Dandy Lion Publications	154
Dawn Publications	158
Delmar Learning	460
Didax	161
Discovery Enterprises	162
Displays for Schools	164
Dover Publications	167
Dramatic Publishing	170
Educational Ministries	176
Educators Publishing Service	177
Edupress	178
Encore Performance Publishing	182
Enslow Publishers	184
ESP Publishers, Inc.	462
ETC Publications	185
Evan-Moor Educational Publishers	186
Exclamation! Publishers	187
Family Learning Assoc/ERIC/ REC Press	191
Fearon Teacher Aids	463
Ferguson Publishing Company	195
Franklin Watts	465
Free Spirit Publishing	201
Samuel French, Inc.	202
Front Street Books	203
Fulcrum Publishing	204
Gallopade International	466
Gifted Education Press	206
Goodheart-Willcox	209
Good Year Books	467
Group Publishing	214
Gryphon House	215
Hampton-Brown Books	219
Harcourt Canada Ltd.	469
Harcourt Religion Publishers	223
Hayes School Publishing Company	227
Hazelden Foundation	228
Heinemann	229
Heuer Publishing Company	232
Humanics	237
Hunter House Publishers	238
Huntington House Publishers	471
Imperial International	241
Incentive Publications	242

Innovative Kids 243
International Reading Association 245
InterVarsity Press 246
Jalmar Press/Innerchoice Publishing 248
January Productions 474
JIST Works 251
Kaeden Books 255
Key Curriculum Press 257
Kodiak Media Group 476
Leadership Publishers Inc. 477
Learning Horizons 261
Learning Resources 262
Linnet Books 269
Linworth Publishing 270
The Love and Logic Press 479
Marsh Media 482
Master Books 278
McGraw-Hill Children's Publishing 282
McGraw-Hill School Division 482
Modern Learning Press 288
Modern Publishing 289
Thomas More Publishing 293
Morgan Reynolds 294
Mountain Meadow Press 484
National Assn. for the Educ. of Young People 295
National Council of Teachers of English 296
Neal-Schuman Publishers 299
New Canaan Publishing Company 300
New Society Publishers 306
NL Associates 307
Pacific Educational Press 321
Pearson Education Canada 329
Pearson Learning Group 490
Peartree 330
Pembroke Publishers 332
Phoenix Learning Resources 337
Piano Press 492
Pilgrim Press 338
Pioneer Drama Service 341
The Place in the Woods 493
Portage & Main Press 348
Pro Lingua Associates 350
Prometheus Books 351
Raintree Steck-Vaughn Publishers 356

Ranchworks 497
Resource Publications, Inc. 359
Rocky River Publishers 499
St. Anthony Messenger Press 368
Sandcastle Publishing 370
Scarecrow Press 371
Frank Schaffer Publications 372
Scholastic Professional Books 375
School Zone Publishing 502
Scott Foresman 377
Shining Star Publications 505
Silver Dolphin Books 380
Small Horizons 384
Smith and Kraus 385
Southern Early Childhood Association (SECA) 508
The Speech Bin 388
Story Time Stories That Rhyme 510
Sunburst Technology 511
Teacher Created Materials 396
Teacher Ideas Press/Libraries Unlimited 397
Teachers & Writers 0
Teachers & Writers Collaborative 511
Teachers College Press 512
Teaching & Learning Company 398
Charles C. Thomas, Publisher 402
Thompson Educational Publishing 403
Toy Box Productions 408
UAHC Press 413
Upstart Books 414
VGM Career Books 516
Visual Education Corporation 517
J. Weston Walch, Publisher 416
Warner Press 418
Weigl Educational Publishers 420
What's Inside Press 421
Williamson Publishing 427
Woodbine House 431
Wordware Publishing 519
The Wright Group/McGraw Hill 434
Zephyr Press 436
Zig Zag Children's Books 520

Fairy Tales

Baker's Plays 95
Beyond Words Publishing 103
Blue Sky Press 106
Books of Wonder 449
Camex Books 450

Charlesbridge Publishing 120
Creative Editions 142
Creative With Words
  Publications 146
Dover Publications 167
Eager Minds Press 173
Guardian Press 216
Henry Holt and Company 234
Innovative Kids 243
iPicturebooks, Inc. 247
Key Porter Books 258
The Lutterworth Press 480
Mage Publishers 481
Modern Publishing 289
North-South Books 309
Orchard Books 316
Playhouse Publishing 344
Rising Moon 360
Seedling Publications 379
Stiles-Bishop Productions Inc. 509
The Story Place 509

iPicturebooks, Inc. 247
Arthur A. Levine Books 266
LTDBooks 480
Margaret K. McElderry Books 281
Milkweed Editions 285
Moody Press 291
Pebble Beach Press Ltd. 490
Pioneer Drama Service 341
Random House Children's Books 498
Random House Children's
  Publishing 498
Red Deer Press 358
Saint Mary's Press 369
Scholastic Inc./Trade Paperback
  Division 374
Scorpius Digital Publishing 376
Storytellers Ink Publishing Co. 395
Tor Books 407
Whitecap Books Ltd. 422
Wizards of the Coast 429
XC Publishing 435

Fantasy

All About Kids Publishing 85
Anchorage Press Plays 87
Aquila Communications Ltd. 442
Atheneum Books for Young
  Readers 90
A/V Concepts Corporation 92
Avon Books 94
Books of Wonder 449
Chaosium 453
Contemporary Drama Service 137
Creative Teaching Press 145
Cricket Books 147
Crocodile Books, USA 149
DAW Books 157
Domhan Books 165
Dover Publications 167
Dutton Children's Books 172
Farrar, Straus & Giroux 192
Formac Publishing
  Company Ltd. 198
Frances Foster Books 200
Gibbs Smith, Publisher 205
Greene Bark Press 211
Guardian Press 216
Harcourt Children's Books 222
Henry Holt and Company 234
Holiday House 233
ImaJinn Books 473

Folklore/Folktales

Advocacy Press 80
Africa World Press 81
Baker's Plays 95
Blue Marlin Publications 105
Blue Sky Press 106
Books of Wonder 449
The Brookfield Reader 114
Camex Books 450
Chronicle Books 132
Clarion Books 133
Contemporary Drama Service 137
Creative Editions 142
Creative Teaching Press 145
Creative With Words
  Publications 146
Crocodile Books, USA 149
Jonathan David Publishers 156
Dover Publications 167
Eager Minds Press 173
Eldridge Publishing Company 180
Fulcrum Publishing 204
Gibbs Smith, Publisher 205
Graphic Arts Center
  Publishing Co. 210
Guardian Press 216
Henry Holt and Company 234
Innovative Kids 243
Interlink Publishing Group 244

Kar-Ben Publishing	**256**
Key Porter Books	**258**
Margaret K. McElderry Books	**281**
Meriwether Publishing Ltd.	**284**
Midwest Traditions	**483**
Naturegraph Publishers	**298**
North-South Books	**309**
The Overmountain Press	**318**
Richard C. Owen Publishers	**319**
Pineapple Press	**340**
Pioneer Drama Service	**341**
Playhouse Publishing	**344**
Polar Bear & Company	**494**
Rayve Productions Inc.	**357**
Redbird Press	**499**
Rising Moon	**360**
Salina Bookshelf	**500**
Scorpius Digital Publishing	**376**
Shen's Books	**505**
Smith and Kraus	**385**
Storytellers Ink Publishing Co.	**395**
Turtle Books	**514**

Geography

Abdo Publishing Company	**78**
Amsco School Publications	**86**
Arnold Publishing	**89**
Children's Press	**125**
The Creative Company	**459**
Creative Learning Press	**144**
Didax	**161**
Eakin Press	**174**
ESP Publishers, Inc.	**462**
Hendrick-Long Publishing Company	**230**
Innovative Kids	**243**
Kingfisher	**475**
Learning Resources	**262**
Miles Kelly Publishing	**483**
National Geographic Society	**297**
Raintree Steck-Vaughn Publishers	**356**
Running Press Book Publishers	**367**
Teacher Created Materials	**396**
World Book	**433**

Gifted Education

Continental Press	**457**
Creative Learning Press	**144**
Dandy Lion Publications	**154**
Free Spirit Publishing	**2??**
Gifted Education Press	**206**
Heinemann	**229**
Leadership Publishers Inc.	**477**
National Council of Teachers of English	**296**
NL Associates	**307**
Phoenix Learning Resources	**337**
Teacher Created Materials	**396**
Teacher Ideas Press/Libraries Unlimited	**397**
Teaching & Learning Company	**398**
Charles C. Thomas, Publisher	**402**
Zephyr Press	**436**

Health/Fitness

Bick Publishing House	**448**
Branden Publishing Company	**111**
The Bureau for At-Risk Youth	**115**
Chelsea House Publishers	**122**
Creative Bound	**141**
Crossquarter Publishing Group	**150**
ESP Publishers, Inc.	**462**
Frederick Fell Publishers	**193**
Gallopade International	**466**
Greenwood Publishing Group	**213**
Harvard Common Press	**469**
Hunter House Publishers	**238**
InQ Publishing Co.	**473**
New Harbinger Publications	**302**
New Leaf Press	**304**
Newmarket Press	**305**
Perigee Books	**335**
Pitspopany Press	**342**
Pleasant Company Publications	**346**
Prima Publishing	**349**
Prometheus Books	**351**
Raintree Steck-Vaughn Publishers	**356**
The Rosen Publishing Group	**366**
Sunburst Technology	**511**
TEACH Services, Inc.	**399**
Charles C. Thomas, Publisher	**402**
Turtle Press	**410**
Twenty-First Century Books	**411**
UXL	**415**

High-Interest/ Low-Vocabulary

Abdo Publishing Company	**78**

A/V Concepts Corporation **92**
A & C Black Publishers **448**
Children's Press **125**
Enslow Publishers **184**
Hampton-Brown Books **219**
Imperial International **241**
January Productions **474**
Richard C. Owen Publishers **319**
Perfection Learning Corporation **334**
Raintree Steck-Vaughn
  Publishers **356**
The Rosen Publishing Group **366**
The Wright Group/McGraw Hill **434**

Historical Fiction

Aladdin Paperbacks **82**
Anchorage Press Plays **87**
Atheneum Books for Young
  Readers **90**
Avocet Press **443**
Avon Books **94**
Barron's Educational Series **446**
Beach Holme Publishing **97**
Bethany House Publishers **102**
Blue Marlin Publications **105**
Blue Sky Press **106**
Branden Publishing Company **111**
Breakwater Books **112**
The Brookfield Reader **114**
Carolrhoda Books **117**
Cavendish Children's Books **452**
Clear Light Publishers **135**
The Colonial Williamsburg
  Foundation **455**
Coteau Books **139**
Cricket Books **147**
Crossway Books **151**
May Davenport, Publishers **155**
Discovery Enterprises **162**
Eager Minds Press **173**
Ebooksonthe.net **175**
E. M. Press **181**
Exclamation! Publishers **187**
Focus on the Family
  Publishing **196**
Frances Foster Books **200**
Front Street Books **203**
Graphic Arts Center
  Publishing Co. **210**
Gulliver Books **217**
Hachai Publishing **218**

Harcourt Children's Books **222**
Holiday House **233**
Bob Jones University Press **252**
Lee & Low Books **263**
LTDBooks **480**
Maval Publishing **279**
Margaret K. McElderry Books **281**
Midwest Traditions **483**
Milkweed Editions **285**
Moody Press **291**
The New England Press **301**
Orca Book Publishers **315**
Orchard Books **316**
Pacific Educational Press **321**
Peartree **330**
Pelican Publishing Company **331**
Perfection Learning Corporation **334**
Philomel Books **336**
Pineapple Press **340**
Pleasant Company Publications **346**
Publish America **352**
Puffin Books **353**
Rayve Productions Inc. **357**
Ronsdale Press **365**
Saint Mary's Press **369**
Scholastic Book Group **502**
Shen's Books **505**
Silver Moon Press **381**
Stoddart Kids Books **394**
Toy Box Productions **408**
Turtle Books **514**
UAHC Press **413**
White Mane Publishing
  Company **423**
Albert Whitman & Company **425**
Wolfhound Press **430**

History (NF)

Absey and Company **79**
Advocacy Press **80**
Amsco School Publications **86**
Arnold Publishing **89**
Avisson Press **93**
Ballyhoo Books **445**
Behrman House **98**
Benchmark Books **99**
The Boxwood Press **450**
Charlesbridge Publishing **120**
Chelsea House Publishers **122**
Creative Education **143**
Creative Learning Press **144**

Creative Teaching Press 145
Crown Books for Young Readers 152
Jonathan David Publishers 156
Discovery Enterprises 162
Displays for Schools 164
Dover Publications 167
Eager Minds Press 173
Eakin Press 174
Enslow Publishers 184
ESP Publishers, Inc. 462
ETC Publications 185
Facts On File 188
Falcon Publishing 190
Forest House Publishing
  Company 197
Fulcrum Publishing 204
Greenhaven Press 212
Greenwood Publishing Group 213
Gulliver Books 217
Hendrick-Long Publishing
  Company 230
Heritage House 231
Holiday House 233
Henry Holt and Company 234
Houghton Mifflin Children's
  Books 236
Interlink Publishing Group 244
Kaeden Books 255
Lerner Publishing Group 265
Linnet Books 269
Lion Books 477
Lucent Books 275
Mage Publishers 481
Miles Kelly Publishing 483
Morgan Reynolds 294
National Geographic Society 297
Natural Heritage Books 486
The New England Press 301
New Leaf Press 304
North Country Books 308
Novalis Publishing 312
The Oliver Press 313
OnStage Publishing 314
Pacific View Press 488
Parkway Publishers 489
Paws IV Books 489
Pembroke Publishers 332
Penguin Books Canada
  Limited 491
Pitspopany Press 342
Prima Publishing 349

Pruett Publishing Company 495
Raintree Steck-Vaughn
  Publishers 356
Random House Children's
  Publishing 498
Rayve Productions Inc. 357
The Rosen Publishing Group 366
Sandlapper Publishing 500
Silver Moon Press 381
Sourcebooks 387
Texas Tech University Press 400
Tilbury House, Publishers 404
Twenty-First Century Books 411
Two Bytes Publishing 514
UXL 415
Viking Children's Books 516
Weigl Educational Publishers 420
White Mane Publishing
  Company 423
Wiley Children's Books 426
Williamson Publishing 427
Windswept House Publishers 518
Windward Publishing 428
World Book 433
Zephyr Press 436

Horror

A/V Concepts Corporation 92
Chaosium 453
LTDBooks 480
Parachute Press 323
XC Publishing 435

How-to

Ballyhoo Books 445
Charles River Media 121
Chicago Review Press 123
Creative Learning Press 144
Dramatic Publishing 170
E. M. Press 181
Excelsior Cee Publishing 463
Frederick Fell Publishers 193
Fiesta City Publishers 464
Goodheart-Willcox 209
Group Publishing 214
InQ Publishing Co. 473
InterVarsity Press 246
Legacy Press 264
Meriwether Publishing Ltd. 284
Peel Productions 491

Perigee Books 335
Players Press 343
Prima Publishing 349
Running Press Book Publishers 367
Scholastic Book Group 502
Smith and Kraus Books for Kids 507
Sterling Publishing Company 393
Success Publications 510
Tor Books 407
Winslow Publishing 519
World Book 433

Humor

All About Kids Publishing 85
Annick Press 88
Aquila Communications Ltd. 442
Blue Marlin Publications 105
Breakwater Books 112
Cavendish Children's Books 452
Creative With Words
  Publications 146
May Davenport, Publishers 155
Eldridge Publishing Company 180
Encore Performance Publishing 182
Excelsior Cee Publishing 463
Formac Publishing
  Company Ltd. 198
Front Street Books 203
Gibbs Smith, Publisher 205
Girl Press 207
Innovative Kids 243
LangMarc Publishing 476
Little, Brown and Company 271
The Lutterworth Press 480
Maval Publishing 279
Mayhaven Publishing 280
Nomad Press 487
Parachute Press 323
Pippin Press 493
Quixote Press 496
Random House Children's
  Publishing 498
River City Publishing 361
Roaring Brook Press 363
Scholastic Canada Ltd. 373
Starry Puddle Publishing 508
The Story Place 509
Albert Whitman & Company 425
Workman Publishing Company 432
Zonderkidz 437

Inspirational Fiction

Bay Light Publishing 446
Bethany House Publishers 102
Beyond Words Publishing 103
BOW Books 108
Ebooksonthe.net 175
Eerdmans Books for Young
  Readers 179
Faith Kids 189
Frederick Fell Publishers 193
Focus on the Family Publishing 196
Hampton Roads Publishing 220
Huntington House Publishers 471
Illumination Arts 472
The Judaica Press 253
LangMarc Publishing 476
Lightwave Publishing , Inc. 267
Morehouse Publishing 292
National Resource Center for
  Youth Services 486
Tommy Nelson 487
Pacific Press Publishing
  Association 322
Rainbow Publishers 355
Rising Moon 360
Seaburn Publishing 503
Starseed Press 391
Torah Aura Productions 406
WaterBrook Press 517

Language Arts

Amsco School Publications 86
Boynton/Cook Publishers 110
Butte Publications 116
Carson-Dellosa Publishing
  Company 118
Christopher-Gordon
  Publishers, Inc. 131
Cottonwood Press 458
Creative Learning Press 144
Critical Thinking Books &
  Software 148
Edupress 178
Evan-Moor Educational
  Publishers 186
Fearon Teacher Aids 463
Gryphon House 215
Hampton-Brown Books 219
Harcourt Canada Ltd. 469

Hayes School Publishing
Company 227
Imperial International 241
Incentive Publications 242
International Reading
Association 245
January Productions 474
Learning Resources 262
Linworth Publishing 270
McGraw-Hill School Division 482
Modern Learning Press 288
Modern Publishing 289
National Council of Teachers of
English 296
Pacific Educational Press 321
Pembroke Publishers 332
Phoenix Learning Resources 337
Portage & Main Press 348
Pro Lingua Associates 350
Frank Schaffer Publications 372
Scholastic Professional Books 375
Scott Foresman 377
Silver Moon Press 381
Southern Early Childhood
Association (SECA) 508
Teacher Created Materials 396
J. Weston Walch, Publisher 416
The Wright Group/McGraw Hill 434

Mathematics

Activity Resources Company 440
Amsco School Publications 86
Benchmark Books 99
Carson-Dellosa Publishing
Company 118
Cartwheel Books 119
Christopher-Gordon
Publishers, Inc. 131
Creative Learning Press 144
Creative Teaching Press 145
Critical Thinking Books &
Software 148
Dandy Lion Publications 154
Didax 161
Edupress 178
Evan-Moor Educational
Publishers 186
Gallopade International 466
Greenwood Publishing Group 213
Gryphon House 215
Harcourt Canada Ltd. 469

Hayes School Publishing
Company 227
Heinemann 229
Imperial International 241
Kaeden Books 255
Key Curriculum Press 257
Learning Horizons 261
Learning Resources 262
McGraw-Hill School Division 482
Miles Kelly Publishing 483
The Millbrook Press 286
Modern Publishing 289
Mount Olive College Press 485
Pacific Educational Press 321
Pearson Education Canada 329
Phoenix Learning Resources 337
Frank Schaffer Publications 372
Scholastic Professional Books 375
Scott Foresman 377
Simon & Schuster Books for
Young Readers 383
Sterling Publishing Company 393
Sunburst Technology 511
Teacher Created Materials 396
Teacher Ideas Press/Libraries
Unlimited 397
Teaching & Learning Company 398
Twenty-First Century Books 411
J. Weston Walch, Publisher 416
Wiley Children's Books 426
Williamson Publishing 427
The Wright Group/McGraw Hill 434
Zephyr Press 436

Middle-Grade (F)

Abbeville Kids 439
Aladdin Paperbacks 82
Annick Press 88
Atheneum Books for Young
Readers 90
Augsburg Books 91
Avon Books 94
Azro Press 444
Baker Book House Company 444
Bantam Doubleday Dell Books
for Young Readers 96
Barefoot Books Ltd. 445
Bay Light Publishing 446
Beach Holme Publishing 97
Bethany House Publishers 102
Blue Sky Press 106

Boyds Mills Press 109
Branden Publishing Company 111
Candlewick Press 451
Carolrhoda Books 117
Cavendish Children's Books 452
Child Welfare League of America 128
C.I.S. Publishers and
 Distributors 455
Clarion Books 133
I. E. Clark Publications 134
Contemporary Drama Service 137
Cook Communications
 Ministries 138
Coteau Books 139
Cricket Books 147
Crossway Books 151
Different Books 460
Discovery Enterprises 162
Domhan Books 165
Dorling Kindersley 166
Down East Books 169
Dutton Children's Books 172
Eakin Press 174
Eastgate Systems 462
Educators Publishing Service 177
Eerdmans Books for Young
 Readers 179
E. M. Press 181
Faith Kids 189
Farrar, Straus & Giroux 192
The Feminist Press 194
Fondo de Cultura
 Economica USA 465
Formac Publishing
 Company Ltd. 198
Forward Movement Publications 199
Frances Foster Books 200
Front Street Books 203
David R. Godine, Publisher 467
Greenwillow Books 468
Gulliver Books 217
Hampton-Brown Books 219
Hampton Roads Publishing 220
Harcourt Children's Books 222
HarperCollins Children's Books 224
Hyperion Books for Children 472
ImaJinn Books 473
Imperial International 241
Just Us Books 254
Key Porter Books 258
KIDSZIP LTD 475

Alfred A. Knopf Books for
 Young Readers 259
Arthur A. Levine Books 266
Living the Good News 478
Lobster Press 273
The Lutterworth Press 480
Magination Press 276
Mayhaven Publishing 280
Margaret K. McElderry Books 281
Meadowbrook Press 283
Meriwether Publishing Ltd. 284
Milkweed Editions 285
Moody Press 291
National Geographic Society 297
Natural Heritage Books 486
Naturegraph Publishers 298
Tommy Nelson 487
New Canaan Publishing
 Company 300
The New England Press 301
Newmarket Press 305
OnStage Publishing 314
Orca Book Publishers 315
Orchard Books 316
The Overmountain Press 318
Richard C. Owen Publishers 319
Owl Books 320
Pacific Educational Press 321
Pacific Press Publishing
 Association 322
Pacific View Press 488
Parachute Press 323
Peachtree Publishers 328
Pelican Publishing Company 331
Penguin Books Canada Limited 491
Perfection Learning Corporation 334
Philomel Books 336
Piñata Books 339
Pippin Press 493
Pleasant Company Publications 346
Polar Bear & Company 494
Pro Lingua Associates 350
Publish America 352
Puffin Books 353
G. P. Putnam's Sons 354
Rainbow Publishers 355
Random House Children's Books 498
Roaring Brook Press 363
Ronsdale Press 365
Saint Mary's Press 369
Sandpiper Paperbacks 501

Scholastic Canada Ltd.	373
Scholastic Inc./Trade Paperback Division	374
Scorpius Digital Publishing	376
SeaStar Books	378
Silver Moon Press	381
Silver Whistle	382
Sports Publishing Inc.	389
Stoddart Kids Books	394
Texas Tech University Press	400
Torah Aura Productions	406
Tor Books	407
Toy Box Productions	408
Unity House	515
Viking Children's Books	516
Walker and Company	417
White Mane Publishing Company	423
Albert Whitman & Company	425
Winslow Press	518
Wolfhound Press	430
Woodbine House	431
The Wright Group/McGraw Hill	434
Zonderkidz	437

Middle-Grade (NF)

Abbeville Kids	439
Abdo Publishing Company	78
Advocacy Press	80
Alef Design Group	84
Arnold Publishing	89
A/V Concepts Corporation	92
Baker Book House Company	444
Ballyhoo Books	445
Behrman House	98
Benchmark Books	99
Bess Press	101
Beyond Words Publishing	103
Blackbirch Press	104
Blue Marlin Publications	105
Blue Sky Press	106
Boyds Mills Press	109
Breakwater Books	112
Candlewick Press	451
Cavendish Children's Books	452
Chelsea House Publishers	122
Chicago Review Press	123
Children's Press	125
China Books & Periodicals	454
Chronicle Books	132
Chrysalis Children's Books	454

Clear Light Publishers	135
Creative Education	143
Critical Thinking Books & Software	148
Crown Books for Young Readers	152
May Davenport, Publishers	155
Jonathan David Publishers	156
Didax	161
Different Books	460
Discovery Enterprises	162
Dog-Eared Publications	461
Dorling Kindersley	166
Dutton Children's Books	172
Eastgate Systems	462
Ebooksonthe.net	175
Eerdmans Books for Young Readers	179
Enslow Publishers	184
ETC Publications	185
Facts On File	188
Faith Kids	189
Falcon Publishing	190
Family Learning Assoc/ERIC/ REC Press	191
Farrar, Straus & Giroux	192
The Feminist Press	194
Ferguson Publishing Company	195
Fiesta City Publishers	464
Fondo de Cultura Economica USA	465
Forward Movement Publications	199
Franklin Watts	465
Free Spirit Publishing	201
Front Street Books	203
Fulcrum Publishing	204
Hampton Roads Publishing	220
Harcourt Religion Publishers	223
HarperTrophy Paperbacks	225
Hazelden Foundation	228
Hendrick-Long Publishing Company	230
Heritage House	231
Honor Books	235
Houghton Mifflin Children's Books	236
Hunter House Publishers	238
John Hunt Publishing	239
Hyperion Books for Children	472
Impact Publishers	240
Incentive Publications	242
Bob Jones University Press	252

Just Us Books 254
Key Curriculum Press 257
Key Porter Books 258
KIDSZIP LTD 475
Lark Books 260
Legacy Press 264
Lerner Publishing Group 265
Arthur A. Levine Books 266
Lightwave Publishing, Inc. 267
Little, Brown and Company 271
Living the Good News 478
Lobster Press 273
Lucent Books 275
Magination Press 276
McGraw-Hill Children's
  Publishing 282
Meadowbrook Press 283
Mitchell Lane Publishers 287
Morehouse Publishing 292
Thomas More Publishing 293
National Geographic Society 297
Natural Heritage Books 486
Naturegraph Publishers 298
New Canaan Publishing
  Company 300
The New England Press 301
New Leaf Press 304
North Country Books 308
NorthWord Books for Young
  Readers 311
The Oliver Press 313
Our Sunday Visitor 317
Owl Books 320
Pacific Educational Press 321
Pacific Press Publishing
  Association 322
Pacific View Press 488
Parkway Publishers 489
Pauline Books & Media 325
Peartree 330
Pelican Publishing Company 331
Pembroke Publishers 332
Perigee Books 335
Pineapple Press 340
Pippin Press 493
Pitspopany Press 342
Players Press 343
Pleasant Company Publications 346
Polar Bear & Company 494
Pruett Publishing Company 495
Rainbow Books, Inc. 496

Rainbow Publishers 355
Raintree Steck-Vaughn
  Publishers 356
The Rosen Publishing Group 366
St. Anthony Messenger Press 368
Saint Mary's Press 369
Sandpiper Paperbacks 501
Frank Schaffer Publications 372
SeaStar Books 378
Silver Dolphin Books 380
Silver Moon Press 381
Simon & Schuster Books for
  Young Readers 383
The Speech Bin 388
Sports Publishing Inc. 389
Stemmer House Publishers 392
Success Publications 510
TEACH Services, Inc. 399
Texas Tech University Press 400
Third World Press 401
Megan Tingley Books 405
Torah Aura Productions 406
Tyndale House Publishers 412
Upstart Books 414
UXL 415
VGM Career Books 516
Walker and Company 417
Weigl Educational Publishers 420
White Mane Publishing
  Company 423
Wiley Children's Books 426
Williamson Publishing 427
Windward Publishing 428
Winslow Press 518
Wolfhound Press 430
World Book 433
Zephyr Press 436

Multicultural/Ethnic (F)

A&B Publishers Group 439
Abingdon Press 440
All About Kids Publishing 85
Amirah Publishing 441
Beach Holme Publishing 97
Beyond Words Publishing 103
Borealis Press Limited 107
Carolrhoda Books 117
Children's Book Press 124
Chronicle Books 132
I. E. Clark Publications 134
Clear Light Publishers 135

Cricket Books 147
Crocodile Books, USA 149
Jonathan David Publishers 156
Domhan Books 165
Educators Publishing Service 177
Encore Performance Publishing 182
The Feminist Press 194
Fondo de Cultura
  Economica USA 465
Frances Foster Books 200
Gefen Publishing House 466
Guardian Press 216
Hachai Publishing 218
Imperial International 241
iPicturebooks, Inc. 247
Just Us Books 254
Alfred A. Knopf Books for Young
  Readers 259
Lee & Low Books 263
James Lorimer & Company 479
Maval Publishing 279
Milkweed Editions 285
Orchard Books 316
Richard C. Owen Publishers 319
Pacific Educational Press 321
Peartree 330
Perfection Learning Corporation 334
Philomel Books 336
Piñata Books 339
The Place in the Woods 493
Polar Bear & Company 494
Polychrome Publishing
  Corporation 347
Pro Lingua Associates 350
G. P. Putnam's Sons 354
Rayve Productions Inc. 357
Rising Moon 360
River City Publishing 361
Salina Bookshelf 500
Shen's Books 505
Silver Moon Press 381
Soundprints 386
Storytellers Ink Publishing Co. 395
Third World Press 401
Tilbury House, Publishers 404
Megan Tingley Books 405
Turtle Books 514
Two Lives Publishing 515
Wolfhound Press 430
Zino Press Children's Books 520

Multicultural/Ethnic (NF)

A&B Publishers Group 439
Advocacy Press 80
Amirah Publishing 441
Avisson Press 93
Benchmark Books 99
Borealis Press Limited 107
Branden Publishing Company 111
The Bureau for At-Risk Youth 115
Carson-Dellosa Publishing
  Company 118
Chelsea House Publishers 122
Children's Book Press 124
Clear Light Publishers 135
Jonathan David Publishers 156
Dawn Publications 158
Domhan Books 165
Eakin Press 174
Enslow Publishers 184
Facts On File 188
The Feminist Press 194
Forest House Publishing
  Company 197
Gallopade International 466
Gefen Publishing House 466
Greenwood Publishing Group 213
Holloway House Publishing
  Group 470
iPicturebooks, Inc. 247
Lee & Low Books 263
Arthur A. Levine Books 266
Linnet Books 269
Lion Books 477
James Lorimer & Company 479
Lucent Books 275
Natural Heritage Books 486
Newmarket Press 305
The Oliver Press 313
Pilgrim Press 338
Pitspopany Press 342
The Place in the Woods 493
Polychrome Publishing
  Corporation 347
Redbird Press 499
Seedling Publications 379
Small Horizons 384
Sourcebooks 387
Storytellers Ink Publishing Co. 395
Tilbury House, Publishers 404
Turtle Press 410

Twenty-First Century Books	411	Scholastic Canada Ltd.	373
Weigl Educational Publishers	420	Scholastic Inc./Trade Paperback	
Albert Whitman & Company	425	Division	374
Wiley Children's Books	426	Texas Tech University Press	400
Williamson Publishing	427	Two Lives Publishing	515
Windswept House Publishers	518	Albert Whitman & Company	425
		Wolfhound Press	430
		XC Publishing	435

Mystery/Suspense

Aladdin Paperbacks	82	Zonderkidz	437
Aquila Communications Ltd.	442		

Nature/Environment

Atheneum Books for Young			
Readers	90	Aladdin Paperbacks	82
Avocet Press	443	Ballyhoo Books	445
Avon Books	94	The Benefactory	100
Baker's Plays	95	Bick Publishing House	448
Beach Holme Publishing	97	Blackbirch Press	104
BePuzzled	447	The Boxwood Press	450
Branden Publishing Company	111	Boyds Mills Press	109
The Brookfield Reader	114	The Children's Nature Institute	453
Camex Books	450	Creative Editions	142
Carolrhoda Books	117	Creative Education	143
Cavendish Children's Books	452	Creative With Words	
Coteau Books	139	Publications	146
Covenant Communications	140	Crocodile Books, USA	149
May Davenport, Publishers	155	Crossquarter Publishing Group	150
Domhan Books	165	Dawn Publications	158
Down East Books	169	Dog-Eared Publications	461
Formac Publishing		ESP Publishers, Inc.	462
Company Ltd.	198	Falcon Publishing	190
Greene Bark Press	211	Forest House Publishing	
Harcourt Children's Books	222	Company	197
Heuer Publishing Company	232	Gibbs Smith, Publisher	205
Holiday House	233	The Globe Pequot Press	208
The Judaica Press	253	Graphic Arts Center	
Just Us Books	254	Publishing Co.	210
LTDBooks	480	Greenwillow Books	468
The Lutterworth Press	480	Greenwood Publishing Group	213
Maval Publishing	279	Gulliver Books	217
Moody Press	291	Hendrick-Long Publishing	
The Overmountain Press	318	Company	230
Richard C. Owen Publishers	319	Heritage House	231
Parachute Press	323	Henry Holt and Company	234
Perfection Learning Corporation	334	iPicturebooks, Inc.	247
Pineapple Press	340	Kingfisher	475
Pioneer Drama Service	341	Learning Horizons	261
Pleasant Company Publications	346	Lerner Publishing Group	265
Puffin Books	353	Arthur A. Levine Books	266
Random House Children's Books	498	The Lutterworth Press	480
Random House Children's		Maval Publishing	279
Publishing	498	Miles Kelly Publishing	483
Sandlapper Publishing	500	Milkweed Editions	285

Naturegraph Publishers 298
The New England Press 301
New Leaf Press 304
North Country Books 308
NorthWord Books for Young
 Readers 311
Owl Books 320
Peartree 330
Polar Bear & Company 494
Prima Publishing 349
Sandlapper Publishing 500
Sasquatch Books 501
Scholastic Inc./Trade Paperback
 Division 374
Seedling Publications 379
Soundprints 386
Starseed Press 391
Stemmer House Publishers 392
TEACH Services, Inc. 399
Texas Tech University Press 400
Tilbury House, Publishers 404
J.N. Townsend Publishing 513
Tradewind Books Ltd. 513
Weigl Educational Publishers 420
Whitecap Books Ltd. 422
Wiley Children's Books 426
Windswept House Publishers 518
Windward Publishing 428
Workman Publishing Company 432

Frederick Fell Publishers 193
Free Spirit Publishing 201
Gifted Education Press 206
Goodheart-Willcox 209
Good Year Books 467
Gryphon House 215
Harvard Common Press 469
Hazelden Foundation 228
Horizon Publishers 471
Humanics 237
Huntington House Publishers 471
John Hunt Publishing 239
InQ Publishing Co. 473
InterVarsity Press 246
Jalmar Press/Innerchoice
 Publishing 248
Living the Good News 478
The Love and Logic Press 479
Magination Press 276
Meadowbrook Press 283
Modern Learning Press 288
Thomas More Publishing 293
Morning Glory Press 484
New Hope Publishers 303
Newmarket Press 305
New Society Publishers 306
Nomad Press 487
Our Child Press 488
Parenting Press, Inc. 324
Peachtree Publishers 328
Perigee Books 335
Perspective Press 492
Prima Publishing 349
Resource Publications, Inc. 359
Robins Lane Press 364
Sasquatch Books 501
School Zone Publishing 502
Seal Press 503
Small Horizons 384
Soho Press 507
Sourcebooks 387
The Speech Bin 388
Success Publications 510
Teaching & Learning Company 398
Charles C. Thomas, Publisher 402
WaterBrook Press 517
Woodbine House 431

Parenting

Advocacy Press 80
Africa World Press 81
Alef Design Group 84
Alyson Wonderland 441
Association for Childhood
 Education Int'l 442
Behrman House 98
Butte Publications 116
Carousel Press 451
Challenger Publishing 452
Chicago Review Press 123
Childswork/Childsplay 127
Christian Publications 130
C.I.S. Publishers and
 Distributors 455
Conari Press 456
Creative Bound 141
Crossway Books 151
Dawn Publications 158
Excelsior Cee Publishing 463

Photo Essays

Owl Books 320
Running Press Book Publishers 367

Scholastic Book Group 502
Scholastic Inc./Trade Paperback
  Division 374
Scorpius Digital Publishing 376

Picture Books (F)

Abbeville Kids 439
Absey and Company 79
Azro Press 444
Baker Book House Company 444
Barefoot Books Ltd. 445
Beyond Words Publishing 103
Blushing Rose Publishing 449
Camex Books 450
Candlewick Press 451
Cavendish Children's Books 452
Clarion Books 133
Clear Light Publishers 135
The Colonial Williamsburg
  Foundation 455
Creative Editions 142
Cricket Books 147
Dutton Children's Books 172
Fondo de Cultura
  Economica USA 465
Front Street Books 203
David R. Godine, Publisher 467
Greenwillow Books 468
Harvest House Publishers 226
Hodder Children's Books 470
Hyperion Books for Children 472
Illumination Arts 472
Alfred A. Knopf Books for
  Young Readers 259
Little Blue Works 478
Mondo Publishing 290
Munchweiler Press 485
Tommy Nelson 487
NorthWord Books for Young
  Readers 311
Paulist Press 326
Peachtree Publishers 328
Pippin Press 493
Puffin Books 353
River City Publishing 361
Roaring Brook Press 363
Salina Bookshelf 500
Scholastic Inc./Trade Paperback
  Division 374
Shen's Books 505
Siphano Picture Books 506

Smith and Kraus Books for Kids 507
The Speech Bin 388
Standard Publishing 390
Starry Puddle Publishing 508
Tricycle Press 409
Albert Whitman & Company 425
Windswept House Publishers 518
Zino Press Children's Books 520

Picture Books (NF)

Abbeville Kids 439
Azro Press 444
Baker Book House Company 444
Barefoot Books Ltd. 445
Beyond Words Publishing 103
Blushing Rose Publishing 449
Candlewick Press 451
The Creative Company 459
Dawn Publications 158
Dutton Children's Books 172
Fondo de Cultura
  Economica USA 465
Greenwillow Books 468
Hampton Roads Publishing 220
Henry Holt and Company 234
Houghton Mifflin Children's
  Books 236
Illumination Arts 472
Kingfisher 475
Little Blue Works 478
The Lutterworth Press 480
Modern Publishing 289
Mondo Publishing 290
New Leaf Press 304
Peachtree Publishers 328
Pembroke Publishers 332
Roaring Brook Press 363
Salina Bookshelf 500
Smith and Kraus Books for Kids 507
Standard Publishing 390
Tricycle Press 409
Two Bytes Publishing 514
Viking Children's Books 516
Zino Press Children's Books 520

Plays

Anchorage Press Plays 87
Children's Story Scripts 126
I. E. Clark Publications 134
Discovery Enterprises 162

Dramatic Publishing 170
Eldridge Publishing Company 180
Encore Performance Publishing 182
Fiesta City Publishers 464
Samuel French, Inc. 202
Heuer Publishing Company 232
Lillenas Publishing Company 268
Meriwether Publishing Ltd. 284
Pioneer Drama Service 341
Players Press 343
Playwrights Canada Press 494
Shining Star Publications 505
Smith and Kraus 385
Smith and Kraus Books for Kids 507

Reference Books

ALA Editions 83
Amsco School Publications 86
Arnold Publishing 89
Association for Childhood
  Education Int'l 442
Barron's Educational Series 446
Borealis Press Limited 107
The Bureau for At-Risk Youth 115
Displays for Schools 164
Dramatic Publishing 170
Family Learning Assoc/ERIC/
  REC Press 191
Ferguson Publishing Company 195
Greenhaven Press 212
Greenwood Publishing Group 213
International Reading
  Association 245
InterVarsity Press 246
JIST Works 251
Leadership Publishers Inc. 477
Lillenas Publishing Company 268
Linnet Books 269
McGraw-Hill Children's
  Publishing 282
Meriwether Publishing Ltd. 284
Miles Kelly Publishing 483
Mountain Meadow Press 484
National Geographic Society 297
Neal-Schuman Publishers 299
New Society Publishers 306
Novalis Publishing 312
Our Sunday Visitor 317
Perigee Books 335
Serendipity Systems 504
Sterling Publishing Company 393

Teacher Ideas Press/Libraries
  Unlimited 397
UXL 415
Visual Education Corporation 517
Workman Publishing Company 432
Zig Zag Children's Books 520

Regional (F)

Bess Press 101
Chicago Review Press 123
Cornell Maritime Press 458
Coteau Books 139
Down East Books 169
Graphic Arts Center
  Publishing Co. 210
James Lorimer & Company 479
The New England Press 301
Orca Book Publishers 315
The Overmountain Press 318
Paws IV Books 489
Peachtree Publishers 328
Pelican Publishing Company 331
Pineapple Press 340
Red Deer Press 358
Sasquatch Books 501
Turtle Books 514
Windswept House Publishers 518

Regional (NF)

Azro Press 444
Bess Press 101
Cornell Maritime Press 458
Down East Books 169
E. M. Press 181
Falcon Publishing 190
The Globe Pequot Press 208
Graphic Arts Center
  Publishing Co. 210
Hendrick-Long Publishing
  Company 230
Heritage House 231
James Lorimer & Company 479
Midwest Traditions 483
Mountain Meadow Press 484
Mount Olive College Press 485
Natural Heritage Books 486
The New England Press 301
The Overmountain Press 318
Pacific View Press 488
Parkway Publishers 489

Paws IV Books	489
Pelican Publishing Company	331
Pineapple Press	340
Pruett Publishing Company	495
Redbird Press	499
Red Deer Press	358
Sandlapper Publishing	500
Sasquatch Books	501
Scholastic Canada Ltd.	373
Teacher Ideas Press/Libraries Unlimited	397
Texas Tech University Press	400
Tilbury House, Publishers	404
Wayne State University Press	419
Windswept House Publishers	518

Religious (F)

Alef Design Group	84
Amirah Publishing	441
Augsburg Books	91
Baker Book House Company	444
Bay Light Publishing	446
Broadman & Holman Publishers	113
Christian Ed. Publishers	129
C.I.S. Publishers and Distributors	455
Cook Communications Ministries	138
Crossway Books	151
Educational Ministries	176
Eerdmans Books for Young Readers	179
Eldridge Publishing Company	180
Encore Performance Publishing	182
Faith Kids	189
Frederick Fell Publishers	193
Focus on the Family Publishing	196
Forward Movement Publications	199
Samuel French, Inc.	202
Gefen Publishing House	466
Hachai Publishing	218
Harvest House Publishers	226
Innovative Kids	243
The Judaica Press	253
LangMarc Publishing	476
Legacy Press	264
Lightwave Publishing, Inc.	267
Living the Good News	478
Maval Publishing	279
Moody Press	291

Morehouse Publishing	292
Tommy Nelson	487
New Canaan Publishing Company	300
Pacific Press Publishing Association	322
Paulist Press	326
Peartree	330
Pebble Beach Press Ltd.	490
Playhouse Publishing	344
Prep Publishing	495
Quixote Press	496
Rainbow Publishers	355
Saint Mary's Press	369
Torah Aura Productions	406
Toy Box Productions	408
UAHC Press	413
Warner Press	418
WaterBrook Press	517

Religious (NF)

Absey and Company	79
Alef Design Group	84
Amirah Publishing	441
Baker Book House Company	444
Behrman House	98
Broadman & Holman Publishers	113
Christian Ed. Publishers	129
Christian Publications	130
Concordia Publishing House	136
Cook Communications Ministries	138
Crossway Books	151
CSS Publishing Company	153
Jonathan David Publishers	156
DiskUs Publishing	163
Displays for Schools	164
Eager Minds Press	173
Eerdmans Books for Young Readers	179
E. M. Press	181
Focus on the Family Publishing	196
Focus Publishing	464
Forward Movement Publications	199
Gefen Publishing House	466
Group Publishing	214
Hachai Publishing	218
Harcourt Religion Publishers	223
Harvest House Publishers	226
Horizon Publishers	471
John Hunt Publishing	239
InterVarsity Press	246

Jewish Lights Publishing 250
The Judaica Press 253
Legacy Press 264
Lightwave Publishing, Inc. 267
Living the Good News 478
Master Books 278
Morehouse Publishing 292
Thomas More Publishing 293
Mount Olive College Press 485
New Hope Publishers 303
New Leaf Press 304
Novalis Publishing 312
The Oliver Press 313
Our Sunday Visitor 317
Pacific Press Publishing
  Association 322
Pauline Books & Media 325
Pebble Beach Press Ltd. 490
Pilgrim Press 338
Prep Publishing 495
Prometheus Books 351
Publish America 352
Rainbow Publishers 355
Resource Publications, Inc. 359
St. Anthony Messenger Press 368
Saint Mary's Press 369
SeaStar Books 378
Shining Star Publications 505
Standard Publishing 390
The Story Place 509
TEACH Services, Inc. 399
Torah Aura Productions 406
Toy Box Productions 408
Tyndale House Publishers 412
WaterBrook Press 517

Romance

Camex Books 450
Creative With Words
  Publications 146
Domhan Books 165
LTDBooks 480
Parachute Press 323
Pebble Beach Press Ltd. 490
Wolfhound Press 430
XC Publishing 435

Science Fiction

Atheneum Books for Young
  Readers 90

A/V Concepts Corporation 92
Crossquarter Publishing Group 150
DAW Books 157
Ebooksonthe.net 175
ImaJinn Books 473
LTDBooks 480
Mayhaven Publishing 280
Perfection Learning Corporation 334
Pineapple Press 340
Scholastic Inc./Trade Paperback
  Division 374
Scorpius Digital Publishing 376
The Story Place 509
Tor Books 407
Wizards of the Coast 429
XC Publishing 435

Science/Technology

Abdo Publishing Company 78
ALA Editions 83
Amsco School Publications 86
ATL Press 443
Ballyhoo Books 445
Benchmark Books 99
Bick Publishing House 448
Blackbirch Press 104
The Boxwood Press 450
Boyds Mills Press 109
Carson-Dellosa Publishing
  Company 118
Cartwheel Books 119
Charles River Media 121
Chelsea House Publishers 122
The Children's Nature Institute 453
Children's Press 125
Christopher-Gordon
  Publishers, Inc. 131
The Creative Company 459
Creative Education 143
Creative Learning Press 144
Critical Thinking Books &
  Software 148
Dandy Lion Publications 154
Dog-Eared Publications 461
Dover Publications 167
Edupress 178
ESP Publishers, Inc. 462
Evan-Moor Educational
  Publishers 186
Facts On File 188
Frederick Fell Publishers 193

Gallopade International 466
Greenwood Publishing Group 213
Gryphon House 215
Hampton Roads Publishing 220
Harcourt Canada Ltd. 469
HarperTrophy Paperbacks 225
Hayes School Publishing
  Company 227
Heinemann 229
Houghton Mifflin Children's
  Books 236
Imperial International 241
Incentive Publications 242
iPicturebooks, Inc. 247
Kaeden Books 255
Kingfisher 475
LangMarc Publishing 476
Learning Resources 262
Linworth Publishing 270
Lobster Press 273
Master Books 278
McGraw-Hill School Division 482
Miles Kelly Publishing 483
The Millbrook Press 286
Morgan Reynolds 294
Neal-Schuman Publishers 299
The Oliver Press 313
Owl Books 320
Pearson Education Canada 329
Pembroke Publishers 332
Phoenix Learning Resources 337
Portage & Main Press 348
Raintree Steck-Vaughn
  Publishers 356
Ranchworks 497
Random House Children's
  Publishing 498
The Rosen Publishing Group 366
Running Press Book Publishers 367
Frank Schaffer Publications 372
Scholastic Inc./Trade Paperback
  Division 374
Scholastic Professional Books 375
Scott Foresman 377
Seedling Publications 379
Silver Dolphin Books 380
Simon & Schuster Books for
  Young Readers 383
The Speech Bin 388
Sterling Publishing Company 393
Sunburst Technology 511

Teacher Created Materials 396
Teacher Ideas Press/Libraries
  Unlimited 397
Teaching & Learning Company 398
Texas Tech University Press 400
Tor Books 407
Twenty-First Century Books 411
UXL 415
Viking Children's Books 516
J. Weston Walch, Publisher 416
Weigl Educational Publishers 420
Wiley Children's Books 426
Williamson Publishing 427
Windward Publishing 428
World Book 433
Zephyr Press 436

Self-Help

A&B Publishers Group 439
The Bureau for At-Risk Youth 115
Camex Books 450
C.I.S. Publishers and
  Distributors 455
Conari Press 456
Consortium Publishing 456
Creative Bound 141
DiskUs Publishing 163
Ebooksonthe.net 175
Excelsior Cee Publishing 463
Frederick Fell Publishers 193
Free Spirit Publishing 201
Hazelden Foundation 228
Hunter House Publishers 238
Jalmar Press/Innerchoice
  Publishing 248
Jewish Lights Publishing 250
Magination Press 276
Marsh Media 482
Thomas More Publishing 293
Mount Olive College Press 485
National Resource Center for Youth
  Services 486
New Harbinger Publications 302
Newmarket Press 305
Parenting Press, Inc. 324
Perigee Books 335
Prima Publishing 349
Rainbow Books, Inc. 496
Robins Lane Press 364
Scorpius Digital Publishing 376
Small Horizons 384

568

Sourcebooks 387
Starseed Press 391
Megan Tingley Books 405
Turtle Press 410
Unity House 515

Series

Abdo Publishing Company 78
Bay Light Publishing 446
Books of Wonder 449
Charles River Media 121
Chelsea House Publishers 122
Children's Press 125
Cook Communications Ministries 138
DAW Books 157
The Feminist Press 194
Greenhaven Press 212
Holloway House Publishing
 Group 470
Honor Books 235
Innovative Kids 243
Kingfisher 475
Legacy Press 264
Lucent Books 275
McGraw-Hill School Division 482
Mitchell Lane Publishers 287
Novalis Publishing 312
Pearson Learning Group 490
Peel Productions 491
Rainbow Publishers 355
Resource Publications, Inc. 359
Soundprints 386
Unity House 515
VGM Career Books 516
What's Inside Press 421

Social Issues

Alyson Wonderland 441
Avon Books 94
Alexander Graham Bell Assn.
 for the Deaf 447
A & C Black Publishers 448
Branden Publishing Company 111
Broadman & Holman Publishers 113
Charlesbridge Publishing 120
Children's Book Press 124
Childswork/Childsplay 127
Conari Press 456
Consortium Publishing 456
Creative Teaching Press 145

Crown Books for Young Readers 152
Different Books 460
Ebooksonthe.net 175
Enslow Publishers 184
Facts On File 188
Focus Publishing 464
Forward Movement Publications 199
Free Spirit Publishing 201
Front Street Books 203
Girl Press 207
Greenhaven Press 212
Greenwood Publishing Group 213
GT Publications 468
Hazelden Foundation 228
Hunter House Publishers 238
Jalmar Press/Innerchoice
 Publishing 248
Jewish Lights Publishing 250
LangMarc Publishing 476
Lerner Publishing Group 265
James Lorimer & Company 479
Lucent Books 275
The Lutterworth Press 480
National Resource Center for
 Youth Services 486
New Harbinger Publications 302
New Leaf Press 304
The Oliver Press 313
Our Child Press 488
Parenting Press, Inc. 324
Perigee Books 335
Pilgrim Press 338
The Place in the Woods 493
Prometheus Books 351
Rainbow Books, Inc. 496
Robins Lane Press 364
Scott Foresman 377
Small Horizons 384
Thompson Educational
 Publishing 403
UXL 415
Walker and Company 417
Woodbine House 431

Social Sciences

Africa World Press 81
Arnold Publishing 89
Barefoot Books Ltd. 445
Benchmark Books 99
The Bureau for At-Risk
 Youth 115

Chicago Review Press 123
Critical Thinking Books &
  Software 148
Edupress 178
ESP Publishers, Inc. 462
Evan-Moor Educational
  Publishers 186
Facts On File 188
Fearon Teacher Aids 463
Harcourt Canada Ltd. 469
Hayes School Publishing
  Company 227
Heinemann 229
John Hunt Publishing 239
Impact Publishers 240
Incentive Publications 242
Linnet Books 269
The Love and Logic Press 479
Magination Press 276
McGraw-Hill School Division 482
The Millbrook Press 286
Modern Learning Press 288
New Society Publishers 306
Phoenix Learning Resources 337
Portage & Main Press 348
Raintree Steck-Vaughn
  Publishers 356
Frank Schaffer Publications 372
Scholastic Professional Books 375
Storytellers Ink Publishing Co. 395
Sunburst Technology 511
Teachers College Press 512
Thompson Educational
  Publishing 403
Tilbury House, Publishers 404
Twenty-First Century Books 411
J. Weston Walch, Publisher 416
Weigl Educational Publishers 420
World Book 433

Special Education

Alexander Graham Bell Assn.
  for the Deaf 447
Bick Publishing House 448
The Bureau for At-Risk Youth 115
Butte Publications 116
Childswork/Childsplay 127
Continental Press 457
Dandy Lion Publications 154
Displays for Schools 164
Educators Publishing Service 177

Forest House Publishing
  Company 197
Free Spirit Publishing 201
Group Publishing 214
Heinemann 229
Incentive Publications 242
International Reading
  Association 245
JayJo Books 249
Kaeden Books 255
Kodiak Media Group 476
Leadership Publishers Inc. 477
National Council of Teachers of
  English 296
NL Associates 307
Perigee Books 335
Phoenix Learning Resources 337
Publish America 352
Resource Publications, Inc. 359
The Speech Bin 388
Teachers College Press 512
Teaching & Learning Company 398
Charles C. Thomas, Publisher 402
J. Weston Walch, Publisher 416
Woodbine House 431
The Wright Group/McGraw Hill 434
Zephyr Press 436

Sports (F)

Avocet Press 443
The Brookfield Reader 114
Formac Publishing
  Company Ltd. 198
Harcourt Children's Books 222
Mayhaven Publishing 280
Mondo Publishing 290
Parachute Press 323
Perfection Learning
  Corporation 334
Orca Book Publishers 315
Scholastic Inc./Trade Paperback
  Division 374
Seedling Publications 379
Sports Publishing Inc. 389
Turtle Press 410
Whitecap Books Ltd. 422

Sports (NF)

Avon Books 94
Branden Publishing Company 111

Chelsea House Publishers 122
Children's Press 125
The Creative Company 459
Creative Editions 142
Creative With Words
  Publications 146
Crown Books for Young Readers 152
Gulliver Books 217
Lion Books 477
Lucent Books 275
The Millbrook Press 286
Newmarket Press 305
OnStage Publishing 314
Pineapple Press 340
Pitspopany Press 342
Prima Publishing 349
The Rosen Publishing Group 366
Scholastic Book Group 502
Sourcebooks 387
Sports Publishing Inc. 389
Texas Tech University Press 400
Charles C. Thomas, Publisher 402
Thompson Educational
  Publishing 403
Turtle Press 410
Twenty-First Century Books 411
UXL 415
Wiley Children's Books 426

Story Picture Books (F)

Abbeville Kids 439
Abingdon Press 440
Absey and Company 79
Advocacy Press 80
Aladdin Paperbacks 82
Alef Design Group 84
All About Kids Publishing 85
Augsburg Books 91
Baker Book House Company 444
Bantam Doubleday Dell Books
  for Young Readers 96
Bay Light Publishing 446
Bess Press 101
Bethany House Publishers 102
Blue Marlin Publications 105
Blue Sky Press 106
Borealis Press Limited 107
BOW Books 108
Branden Publishing Company 111
Broadman & Holman Publishers 113
The Brookfield Reader 114

Carolrhoda Books 117
Charlesbridge Publishing 120
Children's Book Press 124
Child Welfare League of
  America 128
Clarion Books 133
Clear Light Publishers 135
Covenant Communications 140
Creative Editions 142
Creative Education 143
Crocodile Books, USA 149
Crossway Books 151
May Davenport, Publishers 155
Jonathan David Publishers 156
Dial Books for Young Readers 160
Eager Minds Press 173
Eerdmans Books for Young
  Readers 179
Frances Foster Books 200
Fulcrum Publishing 204
Gibbs Smith, Publisher 205
Graphic Arts Center
  Publishing Co. 210
Greene Bark Press 211
Guardian Press 216
Hampton-Brown Books 219
Hampton Roads Publishing 220
Harcourt Children's Books 222
HarperCollins Children's Books 224
HarperTrophy Paperbacks 225
Hodder Children's Books 470
Holiday House 233
Henry Holt and Company 234
Interlink Publishing Group 244
The Judaica Press 253
Just Us Books 254
Key Porter Books 258
Lee & Low Books 263
Arthur A. Levine Books 266
Lobster Press 273
Magination Press 276
Maval Publishing 279
Mayhaven Publishing 280
Margaret K. McElderry Books 281
McGraw-Hill Children's
  Publishing 282
Mondo Publishing 290
National Geographic Society 297
North Country Books 308
North-South Books 309
OnStage Publishing 314

Orca Book Publishers 315
Peartree 330
Philomel Books 336
Piñata Books 339
Pro Lingua Associates 350
Puffin Books 353
G. P. Putnam's Sons 354
Rayve Productions Inc. 357
Red Deer Press 358
Rising Moon 360
Ronsdale Press 365
Sandcastle Publishing 370
Scholastic Book Group 502
Scholastic Canada Ltd. 373
Scorpius Digital Publishing 376
SeaStar Books 378
Silver Whistle 382
Simon & Schuster Books for
  Young Readers 383
Siphano Picture Books 506
Small Horizons 384
Soundprints 386
Stiles-Bishop Productions Inc. 509
Stoddart Kids Books 394
Third World Press 401
Tilbury House, Publishers 404
Megan Tingley Books 405
Toy Box Productions 408
Viking Children's Books 516
Walker and Company 417
Warner Press 418
What's Inside Press 421
Wolfhound Press 430
Woodbine House 431
Workman Publishing Company 432
The Wright Group/McGraw Hill 434
Zonderkidz 437

Story Picture Books (NF)

Abbeville Kids 439
Abingdon Press 440
All About Kids Publishing 85
Augsburg Books 91
Baker Book House Company 444
The Benefactory 100
Bess Press 101
Beyond Words Publishing 103
Blackbirch Press 104
Blue Marlin Publications 105

Broadman & Holman Publishers 113
Cartwheel Books 119
Charlesbridge Publishing 120
Children's Book Press 124
Children's Press 125
Concordia Publishing House 136
Covenant Communications 140
Creative Education 143
Crocodile Books, USA 149
Crown Books for Young
  Readers 152
CSS Publishing Company 153
Dawn Publications 158
Dial Books for Young Readers 160
Down East Books 169
Eager Minds Press 173
Eakin Press 174
Family Learning Assoc/ERIC/
  REC Press 191
Fulcrum Publishing 204
Hachai Publishing 218
Holiday House 233
Honor Books 235
Interlink Publishing Group 244
The Judaica Press 253
Key Porter Books 258
Learning Horizons 261
Lee & Low Books 263
Arthur A. Levine Books 266
Lightwave Publishing, Inc. 267
Little, Brown and Company 271
Maval Publishing 279
National Geographic Society 297
NorthWord Books for Young
  Readers 311
Novalis Publishing 312
Our Sunday Visitor 317
The Overmountain Press 318
Richard C. Owen Publishers 319
Parenting Press, Inc. 324
Pauline Books & Media 325
Peachtree Publishers 328
Pitspopany Press 342
St. Anthony Messenger Press 368
Scholastic Book Group 502
SeaStar Books 378
Simon & Schuster Books for Young
  Readers 383
The Speech Bin 388

Standard Publishing 390
Stemmer House Publishers 392
Sterling Publishing Company 393
TEACH Services, Inc. 399
Tilbury House, Publishers 404
Megan Tingley Books 405
Torah Aura Productions 406
Toy Box Productions 408
Tricycle Press 409
Tyndale House Publishers 412
Walker and Company 417
Windward Publishing 428
Workman Publishing Company 432

Toddler Books (F)

Abingdon Press 440
All About Kids Publishing 85
Blue Sky Press 106
Cartwheel Books 119
Chronicle Books 132
Crossway Books 151
Dial Books for Young Readers 160
DiskUs Publishing 163
Dorling Kindersley 166
Educational Ministries 176
Farrar, Straus & Giroux 192
Greenwillow Books 468
Guardian Press 216
Harcourt Children's Books 222
HarperCollins Children's Books 224
Houghton Mifflin Children's
  Books 236
Kar-Ben Publishing 256
Lee & Low Books 263
Lightwave Publishing, Inc. 267
Little, Brown and Company 271
Little Simon 272
McGraw-Hill Children's
  Publishing 282
Playhouse Publishing 344
Polychrome Publishing
  Corporation 347
G. P. Putnam's Sons 354
Simon & Schuster Books for
  Young Readers 383
Soundprints 386
Starseed Press 391
Third World Press 401
Megan Tingley Books 405
Workman Publishing Company 432
Zonderkidz 437

Toddler Books (NF)

Abingdon Press 440
Augsburg Books 91
Broadman & Holman Publishers 113
Cartwheel Books 119
Charlesbridge Publishing 120
Chicago Review Press 123
Cook Communications Ministries 138
Crown Books for Young Readers 152
DiskUs Publishing 163
Dorling Kindersley 166
Greenwillow Books 468
Harvest House Publishers 226
Honor Books 235
Humanics 237
John Hunt Publishing 239
Jewish Lights Publishing 250
Kar-Ben Publishing 256
Learning Horizons 261
McGraw-Hill Children's
  Publishing 282
The Millbrook Press 286
Morehouse Publishing 292
Orchard Books 316
Running Press Book Publishers 367
Frank Schaffer Publications 372
Seaburn Publishing 503
Silver Dolphin Books 380
Standard Publishing 390
Tyndale House Publishers 412
UAHC Press 413

Travel

Abdo Publishing Company 78
Carousel Press 451
Chelsea House Publishers 122
Fulcrum Publishing 204
The Globe Pequot Press 208
Interlink Publishing Group 244
Leadership Publishers Inc. 477
Marlor Press 277
Rand McNally 497
Sasquatch Books 501

Western

Domhan Books 165
Ebooksonthe.net 175
Gibbs Smith, Publisher 205
Moody Press 291
The Story Place 509

573

Turtle Books — 514

Young Adult (F)

A&B Publishers Group — 439
Absey and Company — 79
Advocacy Press — 80
Africa World Press — 81
Aladdin Paperbacks — 82
Amirah Publishing — 441
Annick Press — 88
Atheneum Books for Young Readers — 90
ATL Press — 443
A/V Concepts Corporation — 92
Avocet Press — 443
Avon Books — 94
Bantam Doubleday Dell Books for Young Readers — 96
Beach Holme Publishing — 97
Bethany House Publishers — 102
Blue Sky Press — 106
Borealis Press Limited — 107
Boyds Mills Press — 109
Breakwater Books — 112
The Brookfield Reader — 114
Camex Books — 450
Carolrhoda Books — 117
Challenger Publishing — 452
Chaosium — 453
C.I.S. Publishers and Distributors — 455
Clarion Books — 133
I. E. Clark Publications — 134
Clear Light Publishers — 135
Contemporary Drama Service — 137
Coteau Books — 139
Course Crafters, Inc. — 459
Covenant Communications — 140
Creative Editions — 142
Cricket Books — 147
Crossquarter Publishing Group — 150
May Davenport, Publishers — 155
DAW Books — 157
Discovery Enterprises — 162
DiskUs Publishing — 163
Domhan Books — 165
Down East Books — 169
Dutton Children's Books — 172
Eastgate Systems — 462
Ebooksonthe.net — 175
Farrar, Straus & Giroux — 192

Frederick Fell Publishers — 193
Focus on the Family Publishing — 196
Fondo de Cultura Economica USA — 465
Formac Publishing Company Ltd. — 198
Frances Foster Books — 200
Front Street Books — 203
Girl Press — 207
David R. Godine, Publisher — 467
Graphic Arts Center Publishing Co. — 210
Greenwillow Books — 468
Hampton Roads Publishing — 220
HarperCollins Children's Books — 224
HarperTrophy Paperbacks — 225
Henry Holt and Company — 234
Huntington House Publishers — 471
ImaJinn Books — 473
Bob Jones University Press — 252
The Judaica Press — 253
Key Porter Books — 258
LangMarc Publishing — 476
Arthur A. Levine Books — 266
Little Blue Works — 478
Lobster Press — 273
Majestic Books — 481
Margaret K. McElderry Books — 281
Meriwether Publishing Ltd. — 284
Moody Press — 291
Naturegraph Publishers — 298
Tommy Nelson — 487
The New England Press — 301
Newmarket Press — 305
OnStage Publishing — 314
Orca Book Publishers — 315
The Overmountain Press — 318
Parachute Press — 323
Peachtree Publishers — 328
Pebble Beach Press Ltd. — 490
Penguin Books Canada Limited — 491
Philomel Books — 336
Piñata Books — 339
Pineapple Press — 340
Polar Bear & Company — 494
Polychrome Publishing Corporation — 347
Pro Lingua Associates — 350
Publish America — 352
Puffin Books — 353
G. P. Putnam's Sons — 354

Random House Children's Books 498
Red Deer Press 358
Resource Publications, Inc. 359
River City Publishing 361
Roaring Brook Press 363
Ronsdale Press 365
Sandpiper Paperbacks 501
Scholastic Canada Ltd. 373
Scorpius Digital Publishing 376
Seaburn Publishing 503
Serendipity Systems 504
17th Street Productions 504
Silver Whistle 382
Simon Pulse 506
Stoddart Kids Books 394
Third World Press 401
Thistledown Press 512
Torah Aura Productions 406
Tor Books 407
Viking Children's Books 516
Walker and Company 417
WaterBrook Press 517
What's Inside Press 421
White Mane Publishing Company 423
Windswept House Publishers 518
Wizards of the Coast 429
Wolfhound Press 430
XC Publishing 435

Young Adult (NF)

A&B Publishers Group 439
Alef Design Group 84
Amirah Publishing 441
Annick Press 88
Arnold Publishing 89
ATL Press 443
Avisson Press 93
Bantam Doubleday Dell Books
for Young Readers 96
Behrman House 98
Bess Press 101
Beyond Words Publishing 103
Bick Publishing House 448
Blackbirch Press 104
Branden Publishing Company 111
Charles River Media 121
Chelsea House Publishers 122
Chicago Review Press 123
China Books & Periodicals 454
Christian Publications 130
Clear Light Publishers 135

Contemporary Drama Service 137
Course Crafters, Inc. 459
Creative Editions 142
Creative Education 143
Critical Thinking Books &
Software 148
Crossquarter Publishing Group 150
Crown Books for Young Readers 152
CSS Publishing Company 153
Didax 161
Different Books 460
Domhan Books 165
Dorling Kindersley 166
Dutton Children's Books 172
Eastgate Systems 462
Ebooksonthe.net 175
Enslow Publishers 184
ETC Publications 185
Facts On File 188
Falcon Publishing 190
Farrar, Straus & Giroux 192
Frederick Fell Publishers 193
Ferguson Publishing Company 195
Fiesta City Publishers 464
Focus on the Family Publishing 196
Focus Publishing 464
Fondo de Cultura
Economica USA 465
Forward Movement Publications 199
Franklin Watts 465
Front Street Books 203
Girl Press 207
Greenhaven Press 212
GT Publications 468
Hampton Roads Publishing 220
HarperTrophy Paperbacks 225
Harvest House Publishers 226
Hazelden Foundation 228
Hendrick-Long Publishing
Company 230
Holiday House 233
Holloway House Publishing
Group 470
Houghton Mifflin Children's
Books 236
John Hunt Publishing 239
Hyperion Books for Children 472
Impact Publishers 240
Imperial International 241
Iron Crown Enterprises 474
Jewish Lights Publishing 250

Bob Jones University Press 252
Key Curriculum Press 257
Key Porter Books 258
LangMarc Publishing 476
Lark Books 260
Lerner Publishing Group 265
Arthur A. Levine Books 266
Lightwave Publishing, Inc. 267
Lion Books 477
Little Blue Works 478
Little, Brown and Company 271
Lucent Books 275
Magination Press 276
Majestic Books 481
Mayhaven Publishing 280
McGraw-Hill Children's
  Publishing 282
The Millbrook Press 286
Mitchell Lane Publishers 287
Morgan Reynolds 294
National Resource Center for
  Youth Services 486
Naturegraph Publishers 298
The New England Press 301
New Harbinger Publications 302
New Leaf Press 304
Novalis Publishing 312
The Oliver Press 313
Our Sunday Visitor 317
Pacific Educational Press 321
Parkway Publishers 489
Pauline Books & Media 325
Peachtree Publishers 328
Perfection Learning
  Corporation 334
Perigee Books 335
Piñata Books 339
Pitspopany Press 342
Players Press 343
Polar Bear & Company 494
Prima Publishing 349
Pruett Publishing Company 495
Publish America 352
Raintree Steck-Vaughn
  Publishers 356
Resource Publications, Inc. 359
The Rosen Publishing Group 366
Saint Mary's Press 369
Seaburn Publishing 503
17th Street Productions 504
Simon Pulse 506

Standard Publishing 390
Success Publications 510
TEACH Services, Inc. 399
Third World Press 401
J.N. Townsend Publishing 513
Twenty-First Century Books 411
Two Bytes Publishing 514
Tyndale House Publishers 412
UAHC Press 413
Unity House 515
VGM Career Books 516
Walker and Company 417
Weigl Educational Publishers 420
White Mane Publishing Company 423
Wiley Children's Books 426
Windward Publishing 428
World Book 433

Publisher and Contest Index

If you do not find a particular publisher, turn to page 539 for a list of deletions and name changes.

★ indicates a newly listed publisher or contest

A

A&B Publishers Group	439
Abbeville Kids	439
Abdo Publishing Company	78
Abingdon Press	440
Absey and Company	79
Activity Resources Company	440
★ Advocacy Press	80
Africa World Press	81
Aladdin Paperbacks	82
(See Simon & Schuster)	
ALA Editions	83
Alef Design Group	84
All About Kids Publishing	85
Alyson Wonderland	441
Amirah Publishing	441
★ AML Awards	523
Amsco School Publications	86
Anchorage Press Plays	87
★ Annick Press	88
Aquila Communications Ltd.	442
Arnold Publishing	89
Association for Childhood Education Int'l	442
Atheneum Books for Young Readers	90
(See Simon & Schuster)	
Atlantic Writing Competition	523
ATL Press	443
Augsburg Books	91
A/V Concepts Corporation	92
Avisson Press	93
Avocet Press	443
Avon Books	94
★ AWP/Thomas Dunne Books Novel Award	524
Azro Press	444

B

★ Baker Book House Company	444
Baker's Plays	95
Ballyhoo Books	445
Bantam Doubleday Dell Books for Young Readers	96
(See Random House)	
Barefoot Books Ltd.	445
Barron's Educational Series	446
Bay Light Publishing	446
Beach Holme Publishing	97
Behrman House	98
Alexander Graham Bell Assn. for the Deaf	447
Benchmark Books	99
The Benefactory	100
BePuzzled	447
Bess Press	101
Bethany House Publishers	102
Beyond Words Publishing	103
Bick Publishing House	448
Blackbirch Press	104
★ A & C Black Publishers	448
Blue Marlin Publications	105
Blue Sky Press	106
(See Scholastic Inc.)	
Blushing Rose Publishing	449
Books of Wonder	449
Borealis Press Limited	107
The Boston Globe-Horn Book Awards	524
BOW Books	108
The Boxwood Press	450
Boyds Mills Press	109
Boynton/Cook Publishers	110
Branden Publishing Company	111
Breakwater Books	112

Broadman & Holman
Publishers 113
The Brookfield Reader 114
The Bureau for At-Risk
Youth 115
Butte Publications 116

C

Camex Books 450
Candlewick Press 451
Carolrhoda Books 117
Carousel Press 451
Carson-Dellosa
Publishing Company 118
Cartwheel Books 119
(See Scholastic Inc.)
Cavendish Children's
Books 452
Challenger Publishing 452
Chaosium 453
Charlesbridge Publishing 120
Charles River Media 121
Chelsea House
Publishers 122
Chicago Review Press 123
Children's Book Press 124
The Children's Nature
Institute 453
Children's Press 125
(See Scholastic Inc.)
Children's Story Scripts 126
Childswork/Childsplay 127
Child Welfare League of
America 128
China Books &
Periodicals 454
Christian Ed. Publishers 129
Christian Publications 130
Christopher-Gordon
Publishers, Inc. 131
Chronicle Books 132
★ Chrysalis Children's
Books 454
C.I.S. Publishers and
Distributors 455
Clarion Books 133
I. E. Clark Publications 134
Clear Light Publishers 135
CNW/FFWA Florida
State Writing
Competition 525
The Colonial Williamsburg
Foundation 455

Conari Press 456
Concordia Publishing
House 136
Consortium Publishing 456
★ Contemporary Books 457
Contemporary Drama
Service 137
Continental Press 457
★ Cook Communications
Ministries 138
Cornell Maritime Press 458
Coteau Books 139
Cottonwood Press 458
Course Crafters, Inc. 459
Covenant
Communications 140
Creative Bound 141
★ The Creative Company 459
Creative Editions 142
Creative Education 143
Creative Learning Press 144
Creative Teaching Press 145
Creative With Words
Publications 146
Cricket Books 147
Critical Thinking Books
& Software 148
Crocodile Books, USA 149
Crossquarter Publishing
Group 150
Crossway Books 151
Crown Books for Young
Readers 152
(See Random House)
CSS Publishing
Company 153

D

The Dana Awards 525
Dandy Lion
Publications 154
May Davenport,
Publishers 155
Jonathan David
Publishers 156
DAW Books 157
Dawn Publications 158
Marguerite de Angeli
Contest 526
Delacorte Press Contest
for a First Young
Adult Novel 526
Delmar Learning 460

Dial Books for Young
   Readers   160
Didax   161
Different Books   460
Discovery Enterprises   162
DiskUs Publishing   163
Displays for Schools   164
Dog-Eared Publications 461
Domhan Books   165
Doral Publishing   461
Dorling Kindersley   166
Dover Publications   167
Down East Books   169
Dramatic Publishing   170
Dutton Children's Books 172

E

Eager Minds Press   173
Eakin Press   174
Eastgate Systems   462
Ebooksonthe.net   175
Educational Ministries 176
Educators Publishing
   Service   177
Edupress   178
Eerdmans Books for
   Young Readers   179
Eldridge Publishing
   Company   180
E. M. Press   181
Encore Performance
   Publishing   182
Enslow Publishers   184
ESP Publishers, Inc. 462
ETC Publications   185
Evan-Moor Educational
   Publishers   186
Excelsior Cee Publishing 463
★ Exclamation! Publishers 187

F

Facts On File   188
★ Faith Kids   189
Falcon Publishing   190
Family Learning Assoc/
   ERIC/REC Press 191
Farrar, Straus & Giroux 192
Fearon Teacher Aids 463
Frederick Fell
   Publishers   193
The Feminist Press 194
Ferguson Publishing
   Company   195

Fiesta City Publishers 464
★ Focus on the Family
   Publishing   196
Focus Publishing   464
Fondo de Cultura
   Economica USA 465
Forest House Publishing
   Company   197
Formac Publishing
   Company Ltd.   198
Forward Movement
   Publications   199
Frances Foster Books 200
Franklin Watts   465
   (See Scholastic Inc.)
Free Spirit Publishing 201
Samuel French, Inc. 202
Front Street Books 203
Fulcrum Publishing 204

G

Gallopade International 466
★ Gardenia Press First
   Novel Writing
   Competition   527
Gefen Publishing House 466
Gibbs Smith, Publisher 205
Gifted Education Press 206
Girl Press   207
The Globe Pequot Press 208
David R. Godine,
   Publisher   467
Golden Kite Awards 527
Goodheart-Willcox 209
Good Year Books   467
Graphic Arts Center
   Publishing Co. 210
Greene Bark Press 211
Greenhaven Press 212
Greenwillow Books 468
Greenwood Publishing
   Group   213
Group Publishing   214
Gryphon House   215
★ GT Publications   468
Guardian Press   216
Gulliver Books   217

H

Hachai Publishing 218
Hampton-Brown Books 219
Hampton Roads
   Publishing   220

Harcourt Canada Ltd. **469**
Harcourt Children's
  Books **222**
Harcourt Religion
  Publishers **223**
HarperCollins Children's
  Books **224**
  (See also Avon Books,
  Greenwillow Books, and
  Harpertrophy Paperbacks)
HarperTrophy Paperbacks **225**
Harvard Common Press **469**
Harvest House
  Publishers **226**
Hayes School Publishing
  Company **227**
Hazelden Foundation **228**
Heinemann **229**
Hendrick-Long Publishing
  Company **230**
Heritage House **231**
Heuer Publishing
  Company **232**
Hodder Children's Books **470**
Holiday House **233**
Holloway House Publishing
  Group **470**
Henry Holt and Company **234**
Honor Books **235**
Horizon Publishers **471**
Houghton Mifflin
  Children's Books **236**
Humanics **237**
Hunter House Publishers **238**
Huntington House
  Publishers **471**
John Hunt Publishing **239**
Hyperion Books for
  Children **472**

I

Illumination Arts **472**
★ ImaJinn Books **473**
Impact Publishers **240**
Imperial International **241**
Incentive Publications **242**
Innovative Kids **243**
InQ Publishing Co. **473**
Interlink Publishing
  Group **244**
International Reading
  Association **245**

InterVarsity Press **246**
iPicturebooks, Inc. **247**
Iron Crown Enterprises **474**

J

Jalmar Press/Innerchoice
  Publishing **248**
January Productions **474**
JayJo Books **249**
Jewish Lights Publishing **250**
JIST Works **251**
Bob Jones University
  Press **252**
The Judaica Press **253**
Just Us Books **254**

K

Kaeden Books **255**
Kar-Ben Publishing **256**
The Barbara Karlin Grant **528**
Key Curriculum Press **257**
Key Porter Books **258**
KIDSZIP LTD **475**
Kingfisher **475**
Alfred A. Knopf Books
  for Young Readers **259**
  (See Random House)
Kodiak Media Group **476**

L

★ LangMarc Publishing **476**
Lark Books **260**
Leadership Publishers Inc. **477**
Learning Horizons **261**
Learning Resources **262**
Lee & Low Books **263**
★ Legacy Press **264**
Lerner Publishing Group **265**
Arthur A. Levine Books **266**
  (See Scholastic Inc.)
★ Lightwave Publishing, Inc. **267**
Lillenas Publishing
  Company **268**
Linnet Books **269**
Linworth Publishing **270**
Lion Books **477**
Little Blue Works **478**
Little, Brown and
  Company **271**
Little Simon **272**
  (See Simon & Schuster)
Living the Good News **478**
Lobster Press **273**

James Lorimer &
Company 479
The Love and Logic Press 479
LTDBooks 480
Lucent Books 275
The Lutterworth Press 480

M

Mage Publishers 481
Magination Press 276
Majestic Books 481
Marlor Press 277
★ Marsh Media 482
★ Master Books 278
Maval Publishing 279
Mayhaven Publishing 280
Margaret K. McElderry
Books 281
(See Simon & Schuster)
McGraw-Hill Children's
Publishing 282
McGraw-Hill Publishing
(See Fearon Teacher Aids,
McGraw-Hill Children's
Publishing, McGraw Hill
School Division, Frank
Schaffer Publications,
Shining Star Publications,
The Wright Group/McGraw
Hill)
McGraw-Hill School
Division 482
Meadowbrook Press 283
Meriwether Publishing
Ltd. 284
The Vicky Metcalf Awards 528
Midwest Traditions 483
★ Miles Kelly Publishing 483
Milkweed Editions 285
Milkweed Prize for
Children's Literature 529
The Millbrook Press 286
Mitchell Lane Publishers 287
Modern Learning Press 288
Modern Publishing 289
Mondo Publishing 290
Moody Press 291
Morehouse Publishing 292
Thomas More
Publishing 293
Morgan Reynolds 294
Morning Glory Press 484
★ Mountain Meadow Press 484

★ Mount Olive College
Press 485
★ Munchweiler Press 485

N

National Assn. for the Educ.
of Young People 295
★ National Children's
Theatre Festival 529
★ National Council of
Teachers of English 296
National Geographic
Society 297
National Resource Center
for Youth Services 486
Natural Heritage Books 486
Naturegraph Publishers 298
Neal-Schuman
Publishers 299
Tommy Nelson 487
Newbery Medal Award 530
New Canaan Publishing
Company 300
The New England Press 301
★ New Harbinger
Publications 302
New Hope Publishers 303
New Leaf Press 304
Newmarket Press 305
New Society Publishers 306
New Voices New Worlds
First Novel Award 530
NL Associates 307
★ Nomad Press 487
★ North Country Books 308
North-South Books 309
NorthWord Books for
Young Readers 311
★ Novalis Publishing 312
★ NWA Novel Contest 531

O

The Oliver Press 313
Once Upon a World Book
Award 531
★ OnStage Publishing 314
Orca Book Publishers 315
Orchard Books 316
(See Scholastic Inc.)
Our Child Press 488
Our Sunday Visitor 317
The Overmountain Press 318

Richard C. Owen
Publishers 319
Owl Books 320

P

Pacific Educational Press 321
★ Pacific Northwest Writers
Association Literary
Contests 532
Pacific Press Publishing
Association 322
Pacific View Press 488
Parachute Press 323
Parenting Press, Inc. 324
Parkway Publishers 489
Pauline Books & Media 325
Paulist Press 326
Paws IV Books 489
Peachtree Publishers 328
Pearson Education
Canada 329
Pearson Learning Group 490
Peartree 330
★ Pebble Beach Press Ltd. 490
Peel Productions 491
Pelican Publishing
Company 331
Pembroke Publishers 332
Penguin Books Canada
Limited 491
Penguin Putnam
(See Dial Books for
Young Readers, Dutton
Children's Books, Perigee
Books, Philomel Books,
Puffin Books, G. P.
Putnam's Sons, and
Viking Children's Books)
PEN/Norma Klein Award
for Children's Fiction 532
Perfection Learning
Corporation 334
Perigee Books 335
Perspective Press 492
Philomel Books 336
Phoenix Learning
Resources 337
Piano Press 492
Pilgrim Press 338
Piñata Books 339
Pineapple Press 340
Pioneer Drama Service 341
Pippin Press 493

Pitspopany Press 342
The Place in the Woods 493
Players Press 343
Playhouse Publishing 344
Playwrights Canada
Press 494
Pleasant Company
Publications 346
Edgar Allan Poe Awards 533
Polar Bear & Company 494
Polychrome Publishing
Corporation 347
★ Portage & Main Press 348
Prep Publishing 495
Prima Publishing 349
Pro Lingua Associates 350
Prometheus Books 351
Pruett Publishing
Company 495
Publish America 352
Puffin Books 353
G. P. Putnam's Sons 354

Q

Quixote Press 496

R

Rainbow Books, Inc. 496
Rainbow Publishers 355
Raintree Steck-Vaughn
Publishers 356
★ Ranchworks 497
Rand McNally 497
Random House
(See Bantam Doubleday
Dell BFYR, Crown BFYR,
Alfred A. Knopf BFYR,
Random House Children's
Books, and Random
House Children's
Publishing)
Random House Children's
Books 498
Random House Children's
Publishing 498
Rayve Productions Inc. 357
Redbird Press 499
Red Deer Press 358
Resource Publications,
Inc. 359
Rising Moon 360
★ River City Publishing 361
★ Roaring Brook Press 363

582

Robins Lane Press 364
Rocky River Publishers 499
Ronsdale Press 365
The Rosen Publishing Group 366
Running Press Book Publishers 367

S

St. Anthony Messenger Press 368
Saint Mary's Press 369
Salina Bookshelf 500
Sandcastle Publishing 370
Sandlapper Publishing 500
Sandpiper Paperbacks 501
Sasquatch Books 501
Scarecrow Press 371
Frank Schaffer Publications 372
Scholastic Inc.
(See Blue Sky Press, Cartwheel Books, Children's Press, Franklin Watts, Arthur A. Levine Books, Orchard Books, Scholastic Book Group, Scholastic Canada Ltd., Scholastic Inc./ Trade Paperback Division, Scholastic Professional Books)
Scholastic Book Group 502
Scholastic Canada Ltd. 373
Scholastic Inc./Trade Paperback Division 374
Scholastic Professional Books 375
School Zone Publishing 502
Scorpius Digital Publishing 376
Scott Foresman 377
Seaburn Publishing 503
Seal Press 503
SeaStar Books 378
Seedling Publications 379
Serendipity Systems 504
17th Street Productions 504
★ Shen's Books 505
Shining Star Publications 505
Silver Dolphin Books 380
Silver Moon Press 381
Silver Whistle 382

Simon & Schuster Books for Young Readers 383
Simon & Schuster Children's Publishing Division
(See Aladdin Paperbacks, Atheneum BFYR, Little Simon, Margaret K. McElderry Books, Simon Pulse, Simon & Schuster BFYR)
★ Simon Pulse 506
(See Simon & Schuster)
★ Siphano Picture Books 506
Skipping Stones Awards 533
Small Horizons 384
Smith and Kraus 385
Smith and Kraus Books for Kids 507
Kay Snow Writing Contest 534
Soho Press 391
Soundprints 386
Sourcebooks 387
Southern Early Childhood Association (SECA) 508
Southwest Writers Contests 534
The Speech Bin 388
Sports Publishing Inc. 389
Standard Publishing 390
Starry Puddle Publishing 508
Starseed Press 391
Stemmer House Publishers 392
Sterling Publishing Company 393
Stiles-Bishop Productions Inc. 509
Stoddart Kids Books 394
The Story Place 509
Storytellers Ink Publishing Co. 395
Story Time Stories That Rhyme 510
★ Success Publications 510
Sunburst Technology 511

T

Peter Taylor Prize for the Novel 535
Teacher Created Materials 396

Teacher Ideas Press/
  Libraries Unlimited **397**
Teachers & Writers
  Collaborative **511**
Teachers College Press **512**
Teaching & Learning
  Company **398**
TEACH Services, Inc. **399**
Texas Tech University
  Press **400**
Third World Press **401**
★ Thistledown Press **512**
Charles C. Thomas,
  Publisher **402**
Thompson Educational
  Publishing **403**
Tilbury House,
  Publishers **404**
Megan Tingley Books **405**
Torah Aura Productions **406**
Tor Books **407**
J.N. Townsend
  Publishing **513**
Toy Box Productions **408**
Tradewind Books Ltd. **513**
Tricycle Press **409**
Turtle Books **514**
Turtle Press **410**
Twenty-First Century
  Books **411**
Two Bytes Publishing **514**
Two Lives Publishing **515**
Tyndale House
  Publishers **412**

U

UAHC Press **413**
Unity House **515**
Upstart Books **414**
UXL **415**

V

VGM Career Books **516**
Viking Children's Books **516**
Visual Education
  Corporation **517**

W

J. Weston Walch,
  Publisher **416**
Walker and Company **417**
Warner Press **418**
WaterBrook Press **517**

Wayne State University
  Press **419**
Weigl Educational
  Publishers **420**
What's Inside Press **421**
Whitecap Books Ltd. **422**
White Mane Publishing
  Company **423**
Jackie White Memorial
  National Children's
  Playwriting Contest **349**
Albert Whitman &
  Company **425**
Wiley Children's Books **426**
Williamson Publishing **427**
Windswept House
  Publishers **518**
Windward Publishing **428**
Winslow Press **518**
Winslow Publishing **519**
Wizards of the Coast **429**
Wolfhound Press **430**
Woodbine House **431**
Wordware Publishing **519**
★ Work-In-Progress **536**
Workman Publishing
  Company **432**
World Book **433**
The Wright Group/
  McGraw Hill **434**
★ Writers Union of Canada
  Writing for Children
  Competition **536**

XYZ

XC Publishing **435**
Zephyr Press **436**
Zig Zag Children's Books **520**
Zino Press Children's
  Books **520**
Zonderkidz **437**